Myanmar (Burma)

Northern Myanmar
p271

Mandalay & Around
p234

Western Myanmar
p307

Bagan & Central Myanmar
p141

Eastern Myanmar
p196

Southwestern Myanmar
p86

Yangon
p34

Southeastern Myanmar

D1025573

Simon Richmond,
David Eimer, Adam Karlin, Nick Ray, Regis St Louis

Contents

STREET FOOD AT BOGYOKE AUNG SAN MARKET P54, YANGON

2P2PLAY / SHUTTERSTOCK ©

SHWE YAUNGHWE KYAUNG P197, NYAUNGSHWE

CHANTAL DE BRUIJNE / SHUTTERSTOCK ©

Contents

UNDERSTAND

SURVIVAL GUIDE

SPECIAL FEATURES

Welcome to Myanmar

It's the dawn of a more democratic era in this extraordinary land, where the landscape is scattered with gilded pagodas and the traditional ways of Asia endure.

Golden Wonders

'This is Burma', wrote Rudyard Kipling. 'It will be quite unlike any land you know about.' Amazingly, more than a century later, Myanmar retains the power to surprise and delight even the most jaded of travellers. Be dazzled by the 'winking wonder' of Shwedagon Paya. Contemplate the 4000 sacred stupas scattered across the plains of Bagan. Stare in disbelief at the Golden Rock at Mt Kyaiktiyo, teetering impossibly on the edge of a chasm. These are all important Buddhist sights in a country where pious monks are more revered than rock stars.

The New Myanmar

In 2015, Myanmar voted in its first democratically elected government in more than half a century. Sanctions have been dropped and the world is rushing to do business here. Relaxing of censorship has led to an explosion of new media and an astonishing openness in public discussions of once-taboo topics. Swathes of the country, off-limits for years, can now be freely visited. Modern travel conveniences, such as mobile phone coverage and internet access, are now common, but largely confined to the big cities and towns, where the recent economic and social improvements are most obvious.

Traditional Life

In a nation with more than 100 ethnic groups, exploring Myanmar can often feel like you've stumbled into a living edition of the *National Geographic*, c 1910! For all the momentous recent changes, Myanmar remains at heart a rural nation of traditional values. Everywhere, you'll encounter men wearing skirt-like *longyi*, both genders smothered in *thanakha* (traditional make-up) and betel-chewing grannies. People still get around in trishaws and, in rural areas, horse and cart. Drinking tea – a British colonial affectation – is enthusiastically embraced in thousands of traditional teahouses.

Simple Pleasures

Thankfully, the pace of change is not overwhelming, leaving the simple pleasures of travel in Myanmar intact. Drift down the Ayeyarwady (Irrawaddy) River in an old river steamer or luxury cruiser. Stake out a slice of beach on the blissful Bay of Bengal. Trek through pine forests to minority villages in the Shan Hills without jostling with scores of fellow travellers. Best of all, you'll encounter locals who are gentle, humorous, engaging, considerate, inquisitive and passionate – they want to play a part in the world, and to know what you make of their world. Now is the time to make that connection.

Why I Love Myanmar

By Simon Richmond, Writer

It doesn't matter whether this is your first or 51st visit to Myanmar: you won't fail to notice the energy, hope and possibilities for the future that hang in the air. Exiles are returning, joining others in rising to the challenge of bringing their country into the 21st century at the same time as preserving the best of the past. Myanmar has many problems to fix but its people remain as stoic and charming as ever. Slow down, sit, listen and connect with them – it's the best way to appreciate what's truly golden about this land.

For more about our writers, see p448

Above: Mahamuni Paya (p241), Mandalay

Myanmar (Burma)

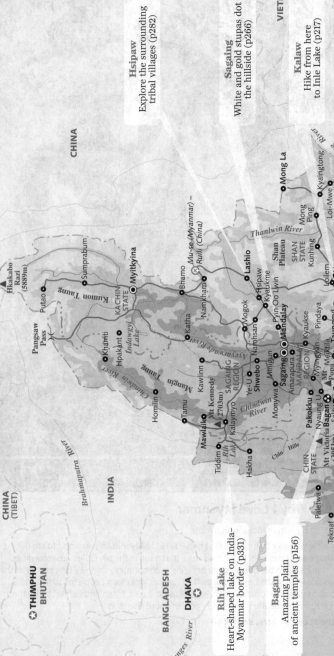

200 km
120 miles

Rih Lake
Heart-shaped lake on India–Myanmar border (p331)

Bagan
Amazing plain of ancient temples (p156)

Hsipaw
Explore the surrounding tribal villages (p282)

Sagaing
White and gold stupas dot the hillside (p266)

Kalaw
Hike from here to Inle Lake (p217)

Inle Lake
Fishers, ruined stupas and floating markets (p206)

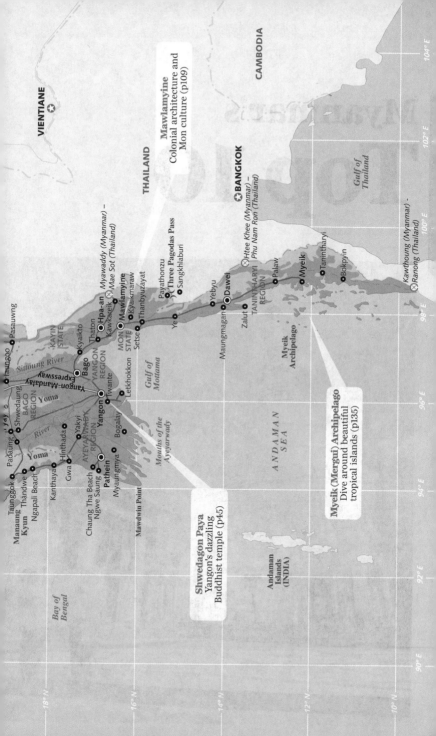

VIENTIANE

CAMBODIA

THAILAND

Mawlamyine
Colonial architecture and
Mon culture (p109)

BANGKOK

Gulf of
Thailand

Htee Khee (Myanmar) –
Phu Nam Ron (Thailand)

Myawaddy (Myanmar) –
Mae Sot (Thailand)

Three Pagodas Pass
Sangkhlaburi

Payathonzu

Kawthoung (Myanmar) –
Ranong (Thailand)

Pasauwng

Taunggok

Sittoung River

Toungoo

Shwedaung

Padaung

Pyay

Yoma

Manaung
Kyun

Thandwe

Ngapali Beach

BAGO
REGION

Yoma

Bago

YANGON
REGION

Yangon–Mandalay
Expressway

Letkhokkon

Thaton

Kyaikto

KAYIN
STATE

Hpa-an

Kawkareik

Mawlamyine

Kyaikmaraw

MON
STATE

Setse

Thanbyuzayat

Ye

Yebyu

Maungmagan

Dawei

Zalut

Palaw

Myeik

Bokpyin

Taninthayi

TANINTHARYI
REGION

Myeik
Archipelago

River

Yakyi

Hinthada

AYEYARWADY
REGION

Bogalay

Myaungmya

Pathein

Gwa

Kanthaya

Chaung Tha Beach

Ngwe Saung

Mawtin Point

Twante

Mouths of the
Ayeyarwady

Gulf of
Mottama

ANDAMAN
SEA

Bay of
Bengal

Andaman
Islands
(INDIA)

Shwedagon Paya
Yangon's dazzling
Buddhist temple (p45)

Myeik (Mergui) Archipelago
Dive around beautiful
tropical islands (p135)

Myanmar's
Top 10

1

Shwedagon Paya

1 Is there a more stunning monument to religion in Southeast Asia? We don't think so. In fact, the sheer size and mystical aura of Yangon's (Rangoon's) gilded masterpiece may even cause you to question your inner atheist. But it's not all about quiet contemplation: Shwedagon Paya (p45) is equal parts religious pilgrimage and amusement park, and your visit may coincide with a noisy ordination ceremony or fortune-telling session. If you're looking for a reason to linger in Yangon before heading elsewhere in the country, this is it.

Inle Lake

2 Almost every visitor to Myanmar makes it to Inle Lake (p197) and for good reason: vast and serene, the lake is large enough for everyone to come away with their own, unique experience of life here. If you're counting days, hit the hot-spots: the temples, markets and floating gardens. With more time, you can explore the remote corners of the lake, visit the fishing villages around it, or hike in the nearby hills. Whatever you do, the memories of gliding across Inle's placid waters will stay with you forever.

PATRICK FOTO / SHUTTERSTOCK ©

OCTOBERSONATA / SHUTTERSTOCK ©

CHINNAPHONG MUNGSIRI / GETTY IMAGES ©

Bagan

3 Despite damage wrought by the 2016 earthquake, the 3000-plus temples scattered across the plains of Bagan (p156) remain an awesome sight. Most of the 11th- to 13th-century vintage temples have been renovated, as Bagan is an active religious site and place of pilgrimage. Yes, there are tour buses and crowds at the top sunset-viewing spots, but they can be avoided. Pedal off on a bike and have your own adventure amid the not-so-ruined temples, or float over the incredible scene in a hot-air balloon.

Sagaing

4 A place of pilgrimage for Myanmar Buddhists, Sagaing (p266) is an easy day trip from Mandalay. Its stint as a royal capital may have been brief (just four years) but it established itself and endures as an intellectual centre of gravity for Buddhist traditions. The town is dominated by low hills covered by numerous white and gold stupas – a spectacular sight in themselves. But also take time to visited the cave monastery Tilawkaguru (pictured left), filled with some of the most impressive preserved cave paintings in the country.

Mawlamyine

5 A virtual time capsule of the Raj, Mawlamyine (p109) has changed little since the colonial era. The former capital of British Burma, Mawlamyine's mix of historic architecture, imposing churches, hilltop temples and a busy harbour remains so timeless that you can still see why writers George Orwell and Rudyard Kipling drew on the city for inspiration. Surrounding Mawlamyine are tropical islands and deep caves, as well as villages where the area's unique Mon culture remains strong, yet visitor numbers remain mysteriously low, allowing all the more space for you. Win Sein Taw Ya (p116)

Myeik Archipelago

6 About 800 barely populated islands with white-sand beaches sitting in a turquoise sea, some of the best diving in the region, roving sea gypsies and barely a hotel or tourist to be seen. It's hard to believe that a place like the Myeik Archipelago (p135) still exists in Southeast Asia. Accessing these gorgeous islands takes time and is not cheap, but those who make the investment will get to live out every beach junkie's fantasy in one of the last unknown areas of Asia.

Mrauk U

7 The temples, monasteries, ruined palace and crumbling city walls of the former Rakhine capital of Mrauk U (p318) stand as a permanent reminder of what a remarkable place it must have been at its zenith in the 16th century. Back then, wide-eyed Western visitors compared the city to London or Venice. But Mrauk U is no museum piece; its temples are surrounded by working villages and emerald-green rice fields. Best of all, Mrauk U sees no more than 5000 foreigners a year, so you're likely to have this ruined splendour to yourself.
Kothaung Paya (p322)

Hsipaw

8 Attractive, laid-back Hsipaw (p282) is ideally placed for quick, easy hikes into fascinating Shan and Palaung villages, as well as more strenuous ones to barely visited hamlets. The surrounding area feels far less discovered than the treks available around Kalaw, or much of Southeast Asia. Hsipaw itself is a historic town with a royal past – it has its very own Shan palace – and an area known as 'Little Bagan', full of ancient stupas. There's also a great morning market by the Dokhtawady River.

Kalaw

9 With its cooler temperatures, higher elevations and many locals descended from Nepali Gurkha soldiers, Kalaw (p217) boasts an almost Himalayan atmosphere. Unsurprisingly, this is one of the best places in Myanmar for upcountry treks, with the authorities relaxed about foreign visitors getting off the beaten track. As you hike through the Danu, Pa-O and Taung Yo villages that dot the forests, fields, trails and roads that link Kalaw with Inle Lake, you'll get a real insight into the lives of the hill peoples who populate the area.

Rih Lake

10 Stranded in splendid isolation on the Myanmar–India border, Rih Lake (p331) is small but perfectly formed: a heart-shaped, mystical body of water surrounded by lushly forested hills. As spectacular as the lake is, the rugged journey here through the little-seen mountains, valleys and villages of northern Chin State is also memorable. Only a handful of foreign travellers visit each year, so you are guaranteed attention from the friendly locals. Don't expect much in the way of comfort, or tourist facilities. Instead, revel in being way off the beaten track.

Need to Know

For more information, see Survival Guide (p403)

Currency
Burmese kyat (K)

Language
Burmese

Visas
Everyone requires a visa. Single-entry tourist visas last 28 days.

Money
Cash mainly. ATMs accepting international cards are available in major cities and tourist areas. Bring pristine US bills for exchange.

Mobile Phones
Mobile phone numbers begin with 09. Prepaid SIM cards are widely available and can be used in unlocked phones. If your handset is locked, it's possible to buy a smartphone in Myanmar for as little as US$80.

Time
Myanmar Standard Time (GMT/UTC plus 6½ hours)

When to Go

Mandalay
GO Nov-Feb

Pyin Oo Lwin
GO Nov-Feb

Mrauk U
GO Oct-Mar

Bagan
GO Nov-Feb

Yangon
GO Nov-Jan

Warm to hot summers, mild winters

Tropical climate, wet & dry seasons

High Season
(Dec–Feb)

➡ Rains least (if at all, in some places) and is not so hot.

➡ Book accommodation and transport well ahead for this busy travel season.

Shoulder
(Oct & Nov, Mar & Apr)

➡ March to May, Yangon often reaches 104°F (40°C). Areas around Bagan and Mandalay are hotter.

➡ Cooler in the hill towns of Shan State.

➡ All forms of transport booked solid during Thingyan in April.

Low Season
(May–Sep)

➡ The southwest monsoon starts mid-May and peaks from July to September.

➡ The dry zone between Mandalay and Pyay gets the least rain. Rain can make roads impassable anywhere (especially in the delta region).

Useful Websites

Go-Myanmar.com (www.go-myanmar.com) Plenty of up-to-date travel-related information and advice.

Myanmar Tourism Federation (http://myanmar.travel) Inspirational pictures, good background info and travel tips.

Online Burma/Myanmar Library (www.burmalibrary.org) Database of books and past articles on Myanmar.

Ministry of Hotels & Tourism (www.myanmartourism.org) Government department with some useful information.

Myanmar Now (www.myanmar-now.org) News and features.

Lonely Planet (www.lonely planet.com/myanmar) Destination information, hotel bookings, traveller forum and more.

Important Numbers

Myanmar's country code	☏95
International access code	☏00
Ambulance (Yangon)	☏192
Fire (Yangon)	☏191
Police (Yangon)	☏199

Exchange Rates

The US dollar is the only foreign currency that's readily exchanged and/or accepted as payment for goods and services.

Australia	A$1	K1050
Canada	C$1	K1038
Europe	€1	K1450
Japan	¥100	K1214
New Zealand	NZ$1	K983
UK	UK£1	K1702
US	US$1	K1369

For current exchange rates, see www.xe.com.

Daily Costs

Budget: Less than US$50

➡ Hostel or guesthouse: US$10–30

➡ Local restaurant or street-stall meal: US$2–5

➡ Travel on buses: US$1–5

Midrange: US$50–150

➡ Double room in a midrange hotel: US$50–100

➡ Two-course meal in midrange restaurant: US$5–10

➡ Hiring a guide: US$10 per person per day

➡ Pathein parasol: US$1–20

Top End: More than US$150

➡ Double room in top-end hotel: US$150–500

➡ Two-course restaurant meal plus bottle of wine: US$40–70

➡ Driver and guide: US$100 per day

➡ Fine lacquerware bowl: US$200

Opening Hours

Cafes and teashops 6am to 6pm

Banks 9am to 5pm Monday to Friday

Government offices and post offices 9.30am to 4.30pm Monday to Friday

Restaurants 11am to 9pm

Shops 9am to 6pm

Arriving in Myanmar

Yangon International Airport If you haven't pre-arranged a transfer with your hotel or travel agent, a taxi from the airport to the city centre will be K8000 to K12,000; it takes 45 minutes to one hour.

Mandalay International Airport A whole/shared taxi into Mandalay costs K12,000/4000 (one hour).

Overland arrival Walk across borders with Thailand at Tachileik–Mae Sai, Myawaddy–Mae Sot, Kawthoung–Ranong and Htee Khee–Phu Nam Ron.

Getting Around

A few remote destinations are accessible only by flight or boat, but many others, including key tourist sites, can be reached by road or rail. Poor and over-stretched infrastructure means patience and a tolerance for discomfort are part and parcel of your journey.

Air Fast; reasonably reliable schedules, but there have been safety issues with some airlines.

Bus Frequent; reliable services, speed depends on state of road; overnight trips save on accommodation.

Car Total flexibility but can be expensive; some destinations require a government-approved guide and driver.

Boat Chance to interact with locals and pleasant sightseeing, but slow and only covers a few destinations.

Train Interaction with locals and countryside views. Can be uncomfortable, slow and suffer long delays.

For much more on **getting around**, see p418

What's New

E-Visas
E-visas can be used to enter Myanmar not only at international airports in Yangon (Rangoon), Mandalay and Nay Pyi Taw, but also at three land border checkpoints, between Myanmar and Thailand: Tachileik, Myawaddy and Kawthaung.

Southern Myanmar Towns
Visit places that have only recently become accessible to overland travellers, such as the charming town of Ye (p119), or Dawei (p127), from where you can access the deserted beaches at Maungmagan (p127).

National Museum
If you're passing through Myanmar's surreal capital Nay Pyi Taw, the enormous National Museum has some beautifully displayed works, particularly from the Bagan period. (p147)

Than Daung Gyi
Interact with Kayin locals, stay in a B&B and explore vestiges of old colonial days in the newly accessible hillside village of Than Daung Gyi. (p145)

U Thant House
The beautifully restored former home of U Thant in Yangon is a fitting memorial to the UN Secretary-General from 1961 to 1971. (p53)

Travel in Chin State
The need for permission to visit much of Chin State has been lifted, allowing access to remote locations, such as heart-shaped Rih Lake. (p326)

Death Railway Museum
WWII buffs will want to visit the Death Railway Museum located where the railway, immortalised in the film *The Bridge on the River Kwai*, ended in Thanbyuzayat. (p117)

Buses to Mrauk U
Bus services running from Bagan and Mandalay save considerable time and money for travellers wanting to visit this archaeological treasure in Rakhine State. (p164)

Werawsana Jade Pagoda
Looking like a giant piece of Burmese kryptonite, the Werawsana Jade Pagoda in Amarapura is built entirely out of this semi-precious stone. (p262)

Sailing to Loikaw
Either taking the public ferry or chartering a private boat is a great way to connect Inle Lake and little-visited Loikaw in Kayah State. (p229)

Whitewater Rafting in Putao
As the snow-capped Himalayas are more plugged in to the rest of Myanmar with several daily flights to Putao, newcomer Icy Myanmar is offering exhilarating whitewater-rafting trips in the remote north. (p305)

For more recommendations and reviews, see **lonelyplanet.com/myanmar-burma**

If You Like...

Buddhas & Temples

Shwesandaw Paya Ride the ferry across the Yangon River to visit Twante and this 2500-year-old pagoda. (p88)

Win Sein Taw Ya Gawp at the 560ft-long buddha reclining on the lush hillsides of Yadana Taung, accessible from Mawlamyine. (p116)

Mrauk U Fall under the spell of the old Rakhine capital, dotted with ruined and restored temples and monasteries. (p318)

Sagaing Leafy paths shade the routes to 500 hilltop and riverside stupas and a community of some 6000 monks and nuns. (p266)

Bodhi Tataung The glimmering 424ft standing Buddha here is the second tallest in the world, dominating the landscape for miles around. (p179)

Food & Drink

Street eats Street vendors serve great, cheap snacks and meals throughout Myanmar, but the best are in Yangon. (p70)

Myanmar teahouse Having breakfast or an afternoon snack at a teahouse is a unique experience that provides more than a caffeinated kick. (p383)

Toddy Sample this alcoholic drink made from jaggery (palm sugar) on the way to or from Mt Popa. (p173)

Red Mountain Estate Pedal to this winery outside Nyaungshwe to sample wine produced from Shan Hills grapes. (p201)

Markets & Shopping

Bogyoke Aung San Market Drop by this historic Yangon market for handicrafts from around the country. (p54)

Art Gallery of Bagan Watch artisans craft lacquerware bowls and other ornaments at workshops in Myinkaba and nearby New Bagan. (p167)

Shwe Sar Umbrella Workshop Visit here to buy the graceful, painted paper umbrellas that are a speciality of Pathein. (p96)

Puppets If you enjoyed the classic marionette shows in Mandalay, why not adopt a puppet character of your own? (p256)

Gems markets Mogok's morning and afternoon gems markets make for fascinating people-watching and there's no pressure to buy. (p289)

Activities & Adventures

Kalaw Along with Pindaya and Hsipaw, Kalaw is one of the best locations in Myanmar for short, easily arranged hill-tribe village treks. (p218)

Balloon rides Marvel at Bagan's temples, bathed in the beautiful light of dawn, from the basket of a hot-air balloon. (p156)

Monywa Embarkation point for travellers seeking to boat-hop the Chindwin River to newly permit-free towns to the north. (p176)

Whitewater rafting Contact Icy Myanmar in Putao to arrange rafting trips down the far north's beautiful rivers with rapids mostly of Grades 3 or 4. (p305)

Indawgyi Wetland Wildlife Sanctuary There are thrilling bird- and wildlife-spotting opportunities at this northern Myanmar lake. (p296)

Mt Victoria Climb this 10,016ft peak in Chin State, Myanmar's second-tallest mountain. (p326)

Myeik Archipelago Spectacular diving awaits those adventurous enough to seek out these southern Myanmar islands. (p137)

Green Hill Valley Interact gently with retired elephants at this ethically run camp and reforestation project near Kalaw. (p219)

Beautiful Landscapes

Inle Lake The hype is justified for this serene lake fringed by floating gardens, stilt-houses and Buddhist temples. (p206)

Shwesandaw Paya A 10-storey tall buddha watches over Pyay, its hilltop location providing sweeping views across town. (p151)

Mt Zwegabin Get a bird's-eye view from the summit of the tallest of the limestone mountains that ring Hpa-an. (p125)

Than Daung Gyi Peaceful hillside village with vistas over the surrounding lush forests. (p145)

National Landmark Gardens Survey the spectacle of the surreal capital Nay Pyi Taw at these gardens showcasing Myanmar's grand sites in miniature. (p146)

Gokteik Viaduct Peer down on a densely forested ravine as your train rattles over Myanmar's longest and highest railway bridge. (p280)

Ethnic Diversity

Kyaingtong Mingle with Shan and tribal people from the surrounding hills at the central and twice-weekly water-buffalo markets. (p223)

Hsipaw Trek from this low-key country town to meet Shan and Palaung tribal villagers. (p282)

Mawlamyine Soak up the laid-back atmosphere of this tropical town that's the heart of Mon culture. (p109)

Myitkyina Proud of its Kachin culture and host to two huge tribal festivals. (p291)

Loikaw Arrange visits to Kayan villages from the capital of Kayah State, only recently opened to visitors. (p229)

Myeik In this southern Myanmar port, encounter descendants of Chinese and Indian traders as well as Bamar, Mon and Moken people. (p131)

Chin State Here the largely Christian Chin people spend Sundays in the region's many churches. (p326)

Top: Train crossing the Gokteik Viaduct (p280)
Bottom: Traditional bracelets worn by Akha women (p226), near Kyaingtong

Month by Month

January

Peak season and, if Chinese New Year falls within the month, even busier with local tourists and those from the region. Note New Year's Day is not a public holiday in Myanmar.

☆ Independence Day

Celebrating the end of colonial rule in Burma, this major public holiday on 4 January is marked by nationwide fairs, including a week-long one at Kandawgyi Lake in Yangon.

☆ Manao Festival

Costumed dancing, copious drinking of rice beer and 29 cows or buffalo sacrificed to propitiate *nat* (traditional spirits) are part of this Kachin State Day event, held in Myitkyina on 10 January.

☆ Ananda Pahto Festival

Stretching over a couple of weeks in January (but sometimes in December, depending on the Myanmar lunar calendar), this is one of the biggest religious festivals in Bagan.

February

A busy travel season, with the weather beginning to get warmer. If Chinese New Year happens to fall in this month, watch out for a boost in travel activity.

☆ Shwedagon Festival

The lunar month of Tabaung (which can also fall in March) signals the start of the Shwedagon Festival, the largest *paya pwe* (pagoda festival) in Myanmar.

March

A great month for travelling around Myanmar, with generally fair weather in most locations and only a low chance of rain.

☆ Yangon Photo Festival

This celebration of photography (www.yangonphoto.com) is held at Yangon's Institut Française and other venues across the city, and includes exhibitions, a conference and workshops.

April

It's steaming hot and with many locals off work and on the move during the New Year celebrations, securing transport, booking hotels and even finding a restaurant open for a meal can be tricky.

☆ Buddha's Birthday

The full-moon day of Kason (falling in April or May) is celebrated as Buddha's birthday, the day of his enlightenment and the day he entered *nibbana* (nirvana). Watering ceremonies are conducted at banyan trees within temple and monastery grounds.

☆ Water Festival (Thingyan)

Lasting from three days to a week, depending on whether the holiday falls over a weekend, this celebration welcomes in Myanmar's New Year.

PAYA PWE

Nearly every active paya (Buddhist temple) or *kyaung* (Burmese Buddhist monastery) community hosts occasional celebrations of their own, often called *paya pwe* (pagoda festivals). Many occur on full-moon days and nights from January to March, following the main rice harvest, but the build-up can last for a while. All such festivals follow the 12-month lunar calendar and so their celebration can shift between two months from year to year.

To check dates of these and other festivals, go to the festival calendar of the Britain-Myanmar Society (www.shwepla.net/Calendar/ThinkCal.mv).

🎎 Dawei Thingyan

The male residents of the tropical seaside town of Dawei (Tavoy) don huge, 13ft bamboo-frame effigies and dance down the streets to the beat of the *kalakodaun*, an Indian drum.

June

Pack your raincoat and sturdy umbrella, as Myanmar gets doused by monsoon rains. Roads can be flooded and flights to coastal destinations are sharply reduced.

🎎 Start of the Buddhist Rains Retreat

The full moon of Waso is the start of the three-month Buddhist Rains Retreat (aka Buddhist Lent), when young men enter monasteries and no marriages take place. Prior to the full-moon day, a robe-offering ceremony to monks is performed.

August

The monsoon is still in full swing so be prepared for damp days and transport hitches.

🎎 Taungbyone Nat Pwe

Myanmar's most famous animist celebration is held at Taungbyone, 13 miles north of Mandalay, and attracts thousands of revellers, many of them homosexual or transgender.

October

Rain is still a possibility but that means everything is very green – making this a great time to visit Bagan, for example.

🎎 Thadingyut

Marking the end of Buddhist Lent, this festival of lights celebrates the descent of Buddha from heaven. People place candles in their windows and it's a popular time for weddings and monk pilgrimages.

🎎 Tazaungdaing

The full-moon night of Tazaungmon (which can also fall in November), known as Tazaungdaing, is a second 'festival of lights', particularly famous for the fire-balloon competitions in Taunggyi.

November

The start of the main tourist season sees cooler weather and still-lush landscapes.

🎎 National Day

Held on the waning of Tazaungmon (usually in late November), this public holiday celebrates student protests back in 1920, seen as a crucial step on the road to independence.

🎎 Irrawaddy Literary Festival

Launched in Yangon in 2013, since 2014 this festival (www.irrawaddylitfest.com) has been held in Mandalay. Local writers are joined by celebrated international literary and media figures, including the likes of Jung Chang, Fergal Keane and Tan Twan Eng.

December

Peak travel season with many visitors heading to the country over the Christmas–New Year break. Christmas itself is celebrated by many Christian Kayin, Kachin and Chin people.

🎎 Kayin New Year

On the first waxing moon of Pyatho (which can also happen in January), the Kayin New Year is considered a national holiday, with Kayin communities (clustered in Insein near Yangon and Hpa-An) wearing traditional dress.

Itineraries

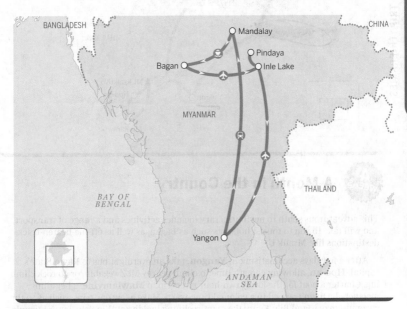

2 WEEKS Myanmar's Highlights

Myanmar's top locations form the bedrock of this travel plan that includes a train and boat ride as well as downtime beside lovely Inle Lake.

Fly into **Yangon** where you'll spend your first couple of days acclimatising. Take a walking tour around the historic downtown area, chill out beside Kandawgyi Lake and visit Shwedagon Paya at sunset. Nip across the Yangon River to Dalah, a slice of rural Myanmar.

Board the overnight sleeper train to **Mandalay**. In three or four days you can see the old capital's sights as well as make day trips to places such as Mingun, home to a giant earthquake-cracked stupa; U Bein's Bridge at Amarapura; and Monywa, where you can climb halfway up inside the world's tallest standing buddha.

Catch the fast boat from Mandalay to **Bagan**; set aside three days to explore the thousands of ancient temples scattered across the countryside. For amazing views, sign up for a hot-air balloon ride or climb sacred Mt Popa.

Fly to beautiful **Inle Lake**, where motor-powered dugout canoes take you to floating markets. Make a day trip to the Shwe Oo Min Cave near **Pindaya** to see 8000 buddha images or arrange some light trekking.

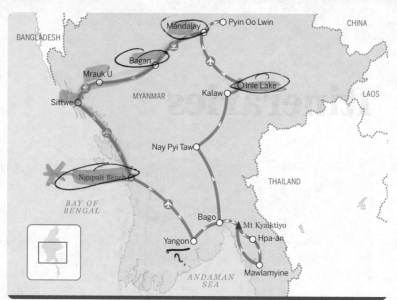

4 WEEKS A Month in the Country

This adventurous south to north itinerary includes activities and a range of transport, and will take to you to tourist hotspots such as Bagan, as well as off-the-beaten-track destinations like Mrauk U.

After a few days acclimatising in **Yangon**, take an overnight bus to Kayin State's capital, **Hpa-an**, allowing enough time to climb nearby Mt Zwegabin, or go rock climbing. Charter a boat for the lovely two-hour river trip to **Mawlamyine**, a beguiling, melancholic town trapped in a colonial time-warp. Make a few day trips, such as to the coconut-crazy island Bilu Kyun, the giant reclining buddha at Win Sein Taw Ya temple, or Thanbyuzayat War Cemetery.

On your way north, pause at the fabulous, golden boulder stupa balanced atop **Mt Kyaiktiyo** and the old royal capital of **Bago**, stacked with impressive temples. Follow the highway north to Myanmar's contemporary capital **Nay Pyi Taw**, a visit that plunges you into the deepest depths of the bizarre. Hop on the slow train from here to **Kalaw**, from where you can organise a two-night trek to magical **Inle Lake**.

Save time by flying from Heho, Inle Lake's airport, to **Mandalay**. The former royal capital is a great base for visiting several ancient sites. If the heat is getting you down, drive two hours and breathe fresh cool air in the colonial-era getaway of **Pyin Oo Lwin**.

Take a boat or bus ride west of Mandalay to the remarkable temple-strewn plains of **Bagan**. A new bus service makes it possible to go directly from here to **Mrauk U**. Once a powerful, cosmopolitan city, it's now one of Myanmar's most atmospheric backwaters, an idyllic location dotted with hundreds of ancient stupas and monasteries. Reserve a day for another river trip to visit nearby Chin villages.

Take a ferry from Mrauk U to Rakhine State's capital of **Sittwe**, from where you can fly south for some R&R on beautiful **Ngapali Beach**. Tan topped up, fly to **Yangon** where you can do some last-minute sightseeing and shopping, perhaps making a day trip to the Delta town of Twante, or learning how to cook Burmese food.

Plan Your Trip
Before You Go

Although travel here is a breeze compared to the past, Myanmar still isn't a spontaneous destination to visit. Careful pretrip planning, from getting your visa and travel money sorted, to weighing up transport options and arranging any necessary permits and guides, will make your visit here all the smoother.

Getting Your Visa

Getting a visa is straightforward. The key things to know include the following:

➡ Everyone requires a visa to visit Myanmar.

➡ Start the process no later than three weeks before your trip: a month before to be safe.

➡ If there is no Myanmar embassy or consulate near where you live, it may be possible to apply for a visa online (an e-visa) and pick up the stamp at the airport on arrival.

➡ Currently e-visas can also be used at three borders between Myanmar and Thailand: Tachileik, Myawaddy and Kawthaung.

Travel Restrictions & Arranging Permits

Much of Myanmar needs no prior permission to visit, but some areas are completely off-limits and others require permits. When securing such permission consider the following:

➡ It takes time – plan on a minimum of at least two weeks. Permission may come more quickly but sometimes takes longer.

➡ Applications should be made via specialist travel agencies who will arrange the permit as part of a package tour, which will generally include accommodation, a licensed tourist guide, a car and driver (with their meal and accommodation covered, too).

Predeparture Checklist

☐ Apply for a visa.
☐ Book hotels, flights and river cruises.
☐ Sort out any necessary permits for travel to restricted areas.
☐ Stock up on brand-new US dollar bills.
☐ Arrange any necessary vaccinations.

Don't Forget

☐ all-purpose electrical-plug adapter
☐ torch (flashlight) for power blackouts
☐ warm jacket for chilly overnight bus rides
☐ flip-flops or sandals
☐ bug spray
☐ prescription medicines

WOJTEK CHMIELEWSKI / SHUTTERSTOCK ©

Top: Woman in a Chin village (p327)

Bottom: Red Mountain Estate (p201), Nyaungshwe

BURMA OR MYANMAR?

When in 1989 the military junta ditched Burma (along with all other colonial-era place names, such as Rangoon, Pagan, Bassein and Arakan) in favour of Myanmar, the reasoning was that this name was more inclusive of the nation's diverse ethnic population. That was a spurious argument since both Burma and Myanmar have the same etymological roots in the Burmese language: the former is the spoken name, the latter is how the name is written in Bamar.

During the years of military dictatorship, what to call the country was highly politicised, democracy supporters favouring Burma. However, today, that polarisation is fading into the past. Aung San Suu Kyi, addressing some of the nation's diplomats in her role as Foreign Minister in April 2016, said they could call the country either Burma or Myanmar. Although accustomed to calling it Burma herself, she vowed to sometimes use Myanmar – all in the spirit of diplomacy!

We use Myanmar as the default name for the country, with Burma used for periods before 1989 and when it's the name of an organisation, eg Burma Campaign UK. 'Burmese' is used for the Bamar people (not for all of the country's population, which we term 'the people of Myanmar'), the food and the language.

➡ You will need to pay fees that are part of the tour package; these can cost anything from US$200 to US$1000 per day depending on what you plan to do.

Check with your country's government travel advice (p412) and also double-check with local travel agencies.

Restricted Areas

In January 2013, government bans on travel to restricted areas of Myanmar, including places in Chin, Kayah, Kayin, Shan and Kachin states, were partially lifted. For a map of where you can travel freely and where you need government permission, see www.tourismtransparency.org/no-go-zones-changes.

Confusion over the rules has led to some travellers being turned back from some areas, so make thorough inquiries before you set out and, if possible, travel in the company of a Burmese speaker.

Some restrictions still apply, including to the following destinations, which are of interest to travellers and for which you will need a permit:

Chin State Paletwa and Matupi

Kachin State Bhamo

Mandalay Region Mogok

Shan State Taunggyi to Kyaingtong overland

Choosing Accommodation

Bookings for most accommodation in Myanmar can be made directly online with the establishment or via local travel agents. Advance bookings are strongly advised for the busiest holiday season from December through to February.

Staying in a monastery is usually only possible at those that run meditation courses for foreign students.

Online accommodation rental operations, such as Airbnb, do have some listings for Myanmar, but note it's currently illegal to stay in a private home.

Family-Run Guesthouses

Often with just five or so rooms and a lounge, which are shared with three or four generations of a family, these budget-level guesthouses can be a highlight of your trip, offering connections with local life and inexpensive deals (under US$20 for a double). Most rooms come with a fan or some sort of air-conditioning unit, though electricity frequently cuts out after midnight. Some guesthouses are better than others, however, and like budget hotels, you'll find some with squashed mosquitoes left on the walls.

Budget Hotels

In many towns, your only options will be a couple of four-storey, modern hotels. In some hotels you will find dark cell-like rooms with a shared bathroom on the ground floor (usually for locals only), and two types of nicer rooms on upper floors. Some have lifts. Some keep their generators on 24 hours; others just for a few hours at night and in the morning. Most cost US$20 to US$50 for a double.

Have a look before taking the higher-priced 'deluxe' rooms; they often cost an extra US$10 for a refrigerator and writing desk that you may not use. Other deluxe rooms offer more space, nicer flooring and maybe satellite TV.

Midrange & Top-End

Upper-midrange and top-end hotels vary widely in terms of quality and value for money. There are few genuine boutique hotels, for example. When making your choice, ask about the hotel's commitment to local and sustainable issues, such as its employment practices and whether funds are provided for community projects and local charities.

Transport Options

For some destinations in Myanmar you'll have no option but to fly. For others, depending on the time you have available, there's the choice also of rail, road and – in a few cases – boat. Using a mix of transport types is a great way to get the most out of your time in Myanmar, with trains and government-run ferries being best for interaction with locals.

Bookings are fairly straightforward. All domestic airlines provide online booking and it's also possible to book online for bus and train tickets via travel agencies.

Government-run ferries are becoming less common as a way to get around, although there are some private boat services in certain locations. For anything approaching comfortable travel on Myanmar's rivers, the only option is a luxury cruise.

If time is limited but you want to cover plenty of ground, consider hiring a car and driver. Self-drive isn't really an option, although in a few locations, such as Mandalay, you can hire motorbikes.

Train travel is not a good option if you are on a tight schedule – they are notorious for long delays.

TRANSPORT COMPARISON TABLE

ROUTE	AIR	BUS	TRAIN	BOAT
Yangon–Mandalay	1hr 25min; from US$85	9hr; ordinary/VIP bus K11,000/20,500	15½hr; ordinary/upper class/sleeper K4650/9300/12,750	n/a
Yangon–Bagan	70min; US$100-110	10hr; K15,500	16hr; ordinary/upper class/sleeper K4500/6000/16,500	n/a
Yangon–Inle Lake	70min; from US$130 (to Heho)	12hr; ordinary/VIP bus K15,000/18,500 (to Taunggyi)	n/a	n/a
Yangon–Ngapali	50min; from US$101	14hr; K15,000	n/a	n/a
Mandalay–Inle Lake	30min; from US$56	6-8hr; from K12,000	n/a	n/a
Mandalay–Bagan	30min; from US$56	6hr; from K8000	8hr; ordinary/upper class K4000/10,000	11hr; US$35
Bagan–Inle Lake	40min; from US$70	10hr; from K11,000 (to Taunggyi)	n/a	n/a

Sunset cruise on the Ayeyarwady (Irrawaddy) River in Bagan (p165)

Boat

A cruise along Myanmar's major rivers is the stuff of many travellers' dreams, a chance to soak up Myanmar's largely unsullied landscape and lifestyle in all its lush glory. The main drawback of this mode of travel is speed – or lack thereof. Boat trips for many routes are loosely scheduled in terms of days, not hours. Make sure you bring plenty of diversions and/or a willingness to make conversation with fellow passengers.

The level of comfort on the boats depends on your budget. IWT ferries and private boats may be relatively inexpensive but you get what you pay for – they are very low on frills and highly uncomfortable for lengthy journeys. You certainly won't go hungry, though, as all long-distance ferries have an on-board cook and are visited at most stops by a variety of locals selling food and drink.

For comforts, such as a bed with a mattress and fully plumbed bathroom, your only option will be to join a cruise on a luxury boat (p422). Rates will usually include all meals and excursions from the boat. The starting point for most trips is either Bagan or Mandalay, but occasionally itineraries originate in Yangon.

Routes

There are 5000 miles of navigable river in Myanmar, with the most important river being the Ayeyarwady (Irrawaddy). Even in the dry season, boats can travel from the delta region (dodging exposed sandbars) all the way north to Bhamo, and in the wet they can reach Myitkyina.

The ability of you being able to make such a journey, though, is another matter, as foreigners are barred from certain routes – at the time of research, for example, it was not possible for foreign visitors to travel on any boats heading into or out of Myitkyina. This situation may change in the future.

One other key thing to keep in mind is the direction in which to travel. Journeys heading north (ie against the flow of the river) take days longer than those going south with the river – this is especially the case on the lumbering IWT ferries.

The key riverboat routes that *can* be built into a travel itinerary include the following:

Yangon–Mandalay Rarely offered route on luxury cruises.

Mandalay–Bagan On the IWT ferry or private boats.

Mandalay–Bhamo–Katha A few private fast-boat services, but mostly done on the IWT.

Mawlamyine–Hpa-an By private boat.

Sittwe–Mrauk U By private boats or IWT ferry.

Khamti–Monywa Chindwin River route on IWT ferries and private boats. A few luxury boats also sail along the Chindwin.

Organised Tours

There are hundreds of businesses across Myanmar calling themselves travel agencies, but only a handful can be considered full-service, experienced tour agencies, with a track record of arranging visits to all corners of the country.

Joining an organised tour is seldom necessary, nor ideally the best way to see Myanmar. If your travel plans are straightforward, it's very easy to make your own arrangements.

However, for certain parts of the country that require permits or for off-the-beaten track travel plans, specific interests and adventure activities, the services of a reputable agency come into their own.

See travel agencies (p415) and specific destinations for listings.

Arranging Private Guides

If you're used to having a car at the airport waiting for you, and guides showing you where to go, either contact a Myanmar-based travel agent before a trip, or give yourself a couple of days to do so once you arrive. Travel agencies (p415) and often hotels can help set up private guides and transport.

Ask to pay as you go to ensure that your money is spread out and to use different guides at each destination rather than one guide for the whole trip. Talk with more

Reclining Buddha near Kyaikthanlan Paya (p1...

than one agent, telling them what you want, to gauge offers.

Some agents are keen to ensure you have adequate travel insurance covering medical emergencies for your trip. Their concerns are well founded, as quality medical care in Myanmar isn't readily available. An insurance policy that covers medi-vac is wise.

Activities

If you're planning a trekking or diving trip to Myanmar, it's best to check well in advance with operators about your preferred dates and how this fits into local weather patterns and the possibility of joining an organised tour or not. For example, diving is restricted to the dry season, ie between November and April.

Likewise, most river cruises are not scheduled during the wet season from April to the end of September, and you won't be able to go hot-air ballooning during this season either.

Money Tips

In the vast majority of cases you'll be paying for everything in cash – typically Myanmar's local currency, kyat, but sometimes US dollars. If you're dealing with a travel agent, you can usually pay in advance for some of your expenses (hotels, transport), on top of which a processing fee of around 5% may be charged.

Although banks and moneychangers have been instructed by the government to accept all dollars whatever their age and condition, you'll run into far fewer problems if you bring brand-new greenbacks for exchange to kyat: this means bills from 2006 or later that are in mint condition, ie no folds, stamps, stains, writing or tears. Keep them in a flat wallet as you travel.

TRAVEL LITERATURE

The Trouser People (Andrew Marshall; 2012) The new edition includes Marshall's eyewitness account of the 2007 Saffron Revolution.

Golden Earth (Norman Lewis; 1952) What's amazing about Lewis' vivid account of travelling in the turbulent Burma of 1951 is how little some things have changed.

Finding George Orwell in Burma (Emma Larkin; 2004) Perceptive account contrasting Orwell's time in Burma as a colonial policeman with Larkin's own travels in the modern era.

ATMs accepting international cards are common in cities and major towns (but not elsewhere). A few places such as hotels, tourist restaurants and shops also take credit cards. But with dodgy power supplies and telecommunications, such electronic means of payment cannot be guaranteed – so come prepared with plenty of cash.

What to Wear

Unless you are planning a luxury cruise along one of the country's rivers, it's unlikely you'll need anything formal or fancy to wear. The key things to remember are that you will be taking your shoes on and off quite a lot to visit temples, enter homes etc, so flip-flops or sandals are recommended. Also, both men and women should respectfully keep their legs and upper bodies fully clothed when visiting religious buildings – a *longyi* (sarong) or shawl can work for a quick cover-up in such cases.

If you're visiting any of Myanmar's higher-altitude areas, bring warm clothes to counter cooler temperatures and chilly nights.

Regions at a Glance

Yangon

Temples
Shopping
Food

Paya Pilgrimages

Yangon's unmissable Shwedagon Paya, Bago's plethora of temples, the water-bound Yele Paya at Kyauktan and Pathein's Shwemokhtaw Paya make the entire region perfect for those with a passion for *paya*.

Arts, Crafts & Markets

Yangon offers a growing range of shops stocked with quality handicrafts, quirky cultural items and genuine antiques. In particular, look out for interesting and affordable contemporary art and crafts from socially responsible businesses. The city's fresh-produce markets are also vibrant and great for browsing and photo ops.

Diverse Cuisines

Offering the country's best selection of Burmese and international food, Yangon's dynamic restaurant scene covers an ever-expanding range of cuisines – everything from Indian nibbles to Shan noodles to Mexican and Japanese. The more adventurous will want to sample the city's multiple street-food offerings.

p34

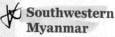

Southwestern Myanmar

Temples
Beaches
Crafts

Temples Galore

Bago (Pegu) alone could probably win the temple stakes for just about any city in Myanmar, but the water-bound Yele Paya at Kyauktan and the Shwemokhtaw Paya in Pathein make the entire region an area worth investigating for temple freaks.

Easy-Access Beaches

Chaung Tha Beach and Ngwe Saung Beach probably won't fit everybody's notion of a picture-postcard desert beach, but they're clean, sunny and the easiest beaches to reach in Myanmar.

Myanmar Handicrafts

View Myanmar's famed silk and cotton parasols being created at workshops in Pathein. Twante's Oh-Bo Pottery Sheds turn out clay containers of varying shapes and sizes.

p86

Southeastern Myanmar

Beaches
Temples
Culture

Myeik Archipelago

Southern Myanmar's Myeik Archipelago covers more than 800 largely uninhabited islands, making it the country's, if not mainland Southeast Asia's, ultimate beach destination.

Mt Kyaiktiyo (Golden Rock)

There are enough temples in and around Mawlamyine alone to keep you busy for a lifetime, but the indisputable highlight of the region is Mt Kyaiktiyo (Golden Rock) – a must-do religious pilgrimage for everyone in Myanmar.

Mon People

You will probably never have heard of the Mon people before, so let one of the excellent Mawlamyine-based guides introduce you to the culture via the area's tidy sugar-palm-lined towns, seaside temples and island-bound villages.

p105

Bagan & Central Myanmar

Temples
Shopping
Scenery

Paya Beyond Bagan

You'll find thousands of temples in Bagan, but also worth seeking out are the Nat shrine at Mt Popa and the pilgrimage temples of Shwesandaw Paya in Taungoo, Shwesandaw Paya in Pyay and Shwemyetman Paya in Shwedaung.

Lacquerware & Blankets

Bagan is also famous for its exquisitely decorated lacquerware; watch artisans create it in workshops in Myinkaba and New Bagan. Across the Ayeyarwady River, Pakokku is famous for its patterned blankets.

Panoramic Views

Get an eyeful of the countryside from atop the temple at Mt Popa's summit or from one of the hot-air balloons flying over Bagan at dawn.

p141

Eastern Myanmar

Outdoors
Culture
Food

Boat Rides & Hiking

Tramping between tea plantations in Pindaya; buzzing around in a boat on Inle Lake; scaling mountains outside Kalaw; visiting a Loi longhouse outside Kyaingtong...just a few of the outdoor pursuits possible in eastern Myanmar.

Shan & Pa-O People

The country's far east boasts exceptional cultural diversity – even by Myanmar standards. Learn about Pa-O culture around Inle Lake, or about Shan culture and language and their similarities with those of neighbouring Thailand in Kyaingtong.

Authentic Shan Food

From *shàn k'auq·s'wèh,* Shan-style noodle soup, to *ngà t'ămìn jin,* a turmeric-tinged rice dish, a stay in eastern Myanmar is your chance to try authentic Shan food at the source.

p196

Mandalay & Around

Temples
Culture
Food

Ancient Stupas & Temples

Arguably more interesting than Mandalay's fine monastic buildings are the older stupas and temples on the sites of several older former capitals, including what would have been the world's biggest stupa (Mingun) had it been finished.

Performing Arts

Myanmar's cultural capital offers intimate traditional dance performances, marionette shows and the famed Moustache Brothers' vaudevillian rants.

Upper Burmese Cuisine

Mandalay is a great destination for cheap Upper Burmese cuisine, which fans say is heartier than Yangon food. A high population of expat Chinese has blessed the city with a slew of excellent Chinese eateries.

p234

Northern Myanmar

Outdoors
Culture
Boating

Himalayan Hiking

Hike to unspoilt hill-tribe villages that are easily accessible on short hikes from Hsipaw and Kyaukme. Given permits and a bigger budget, intrepid travellers can trek deep into Myanmar's Himalayan foothills from Putao.

Meet Myanmar's Minority People

Immerse yourself in the region's fascinating cultural mix, including Chinese-influenced Lashio, Shan and Palaung villages around Hsipaw, and the Kachin capital Myitkyina, home to two of Myanmar's biggest and most colourful 'minority' festivals.

River Trips

You'll hardly see another foreigner on the no-frills public boats chugging down the Ayeyarwady River. Or for more of a rush, consider a whitewater-rafting trip on the dramatic Malikha River near Putao.

p271

Western Myanmar

Temples
Beaches
Mountains

Ancient Palaces & Teak Monasteries

Temples and a ruined palace are scattered across the lush hillsides of the old Rakhine capital of Mrauk U. Sittwe's giant Lokananda Paya and the teak buildings of the Shwezedi Kyaung monastic complex are also worth searching out.

Ngapali Beach

Idyllic stretches of palm-fringed sand hardly come more perfectly formed than those of Ngapali Beach.

Mountain Hikes

Brave the rough roads of Chin State as they wind up to 8000ft or more and hike to the summits of Mt Victoria and Mt Kennedy, passing through Chin villages where the way of life has barely changed in centuries.

p307

On the Road

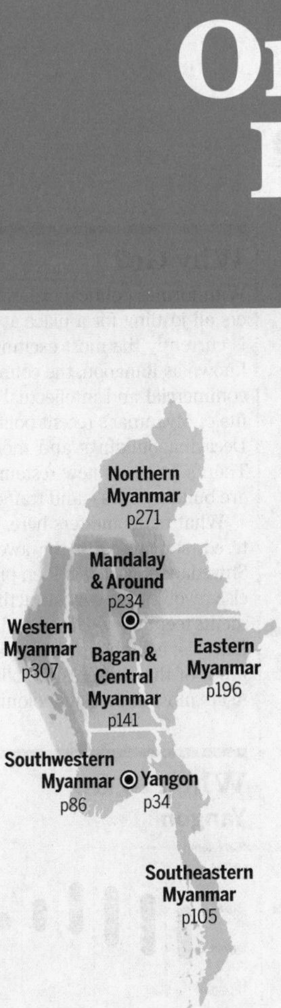

Northern
Myanmar
p271

Mandalay
& Around
p234

Western
Myanmar
p307

Bagan &
Central
Myanmar
p141

Eastern
Myanmar
p196

Southwestern
Myanmar
p86

Yangon
p34

Southeastern
Myanmar
p105

Yangon

POP 5,160,510 / 01

Best Places to Eat

➡ Rangoon Tea House (p69)

➡ Pansuriya (p69)

➡ Feel Myanmar Food (p68)

➡ Green Gallery (p70)

➡ Rau Ram (p71)

➡ Le Planteur (p74)

Best Places to Sleep

➡ Loft Hotel (p63)

➡ Alamanda Inn (p66)

➡ Belmond Governor's Residence (p64)

➡ Yama Dormitory (p62)

➡ Pickled Tea Hostel (p65)

➡ Sule Shangri-la (p65)

Why Go?

With former political exiles, big-time investors and adventurers all jostling for a place at the city's table, Yangon (ရန်ကုန်) is currently the most exciting place to be in Myanmar. Once known as Rangoon, the country's largest metropolis is also its commercial and intellectual hub. And it's reaping the benefits of Myanmar's recent political and economic liberalisation. Decaying buildings and monuments are being spruced up. There's a rash of new restaurants, bars and shops. And there are building sites – and traffic jams – everywhere.

What really matters here, though, is what has always mattered, starting with the awe-inspiring Buddhist monument Shwedagon Paya, a golden pinnacle around which everything else revolves. Equally attractive is downtown Yangon, its pavements teeming with food and book vendors; colourful open-air markets; neighbouring temples, mosques and churches (living proof of the city's cosmopolitanism); and some of Southeast Asia's most impressive colonial architecture.

When to Go
Yangon

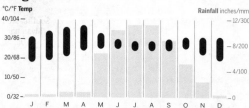

Oct–Feb Daytime heat is tolerable and evenings are often cool.	Mar–May Hottest time of year. April's Water Festival (Thingyan) can cause disruption to travel.	Jun–Sep Wet season, but showers are often short and shouldn't inconvenience; hotels are cheaper.

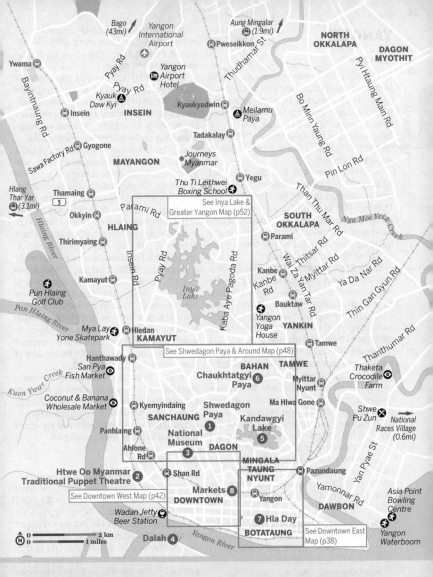

Yangon Highlights

1 **Shwedagon Paya** (p45) Offering a prayer of wonder at the pyramid of gold.

2 **Htwe Oo Myanmar Traditional Puppet Theatre** (p78) Being charmed by a puppet performance.

3 **National Museum** (p39) Witnessing the treasures of Myanmar's past.

4 **Dalah** (p51) Riding the ferry across the Yangon River to the rural neighbourhood of Dalah, best explored on a bicycle or photography tour.

5 **Kandawgyi Lake** (p51) Taking an early-morning or evening stroll on the boardwalk around the lake.

6 **Chaukhtatgyi Paya** (p51) Admiring the giant reclining Buddha.

7 **Hla Day** (p79) Shopping for souvenirs at social-enterprise shops.

8 **Markets** (p54) Getting off the beaten track at Yangon's sensory-stimulating fish, coconut and banana markets.

YANGON ရန်ကုန်

History

In 1755 King Alaungpaya conquered central Myanmar and built a new city at Dagon, a village that had existed for centuries around the Shwedagon Paya. He renamed the place Yangon, meaning 'end of strife', and, a year later, following the destruction of Thanlyin (Syriam) across the river, built it up into an important seaport.

In 1841 the city was virtually destroyed by fire; the rebuilt town again suffered extensive damage during the Second Anglo-Burmese War in 1852. The British, the new masters, renamed the city Rangoon (a corruption of Yangon) and mapped out a grand building plan for what would become the capital of their imperial colony.

By the 1920s Rangoon was thriving as a port and key stopover point for steamships in the region; notable international visitors included Rudyard Kipling, W Somerset Maugham, Aldous Huxley and HG Wells. In 1937 Amelia Earhart dropped in during the second of her attempts to fly around the world.

The city was also the spawning ground for Burmese independence. When that independence came in 1948, Rangoon continued as the nation's capital. However, its fortunes took a turn for the worse when military rule was imposed in 1962. The Burmese road to socialism as promulgated by General Ne Win and his cohorts drove Rangoon, like the rest of the country, to the brink of ruin.

In 1989 the junta decreed the city would once again be known as Yangon. Six years later the military announced that the newly constructed city of Nay Pyi Taw in central Myanmar was to be the nation's capital. Yangon again suffered as government ministries departed from the downtown area, leaving behind empty and uncared for state buildings.

In late 2007 Yangon was the centre of huge nationwide fuel protests, which were led by Buddhist monks. The protests quickly escalated into antigovernment demonstrations, which resulted in the deaths of many protestors and worldwide condemnation.

In May 2008 the worst natural disaster in Myanmar's recent history, Cyclone Nargis, hit the south of the country. Yangon was declared a disaster area by the government. However, when reconstruction work began, it was found that most of the city had escaped major structural damage. By mid-June 2008, electricity and telecommunications were back to normal, and shops and restaurants had reopened with brand-new, corrugated-tin roofs.

Since the 2010 elections, Yangon's fortunes have skyrocketed along with its land prices, as both local and foreign investors scramble to grab a foothold here. A game-changer will be the Yangon–Dalah bridge connecting the city's downtown to rural areas across the Yangon River: ground was broken on this in 2016 with the aim of completing the crossing by 2020.

In the meantime, decades of economic stagnation and under-investment are only too apparent in the city's slums and creaking, frequently overwhelmed infrastructure – something you'll quickly realise as you crawl into town in a taxi from the airport.

YANGON STREET NAMES

The English terms 'street' and 'road' are often used interchangeably in Yangon for the single Burmese word *làn*. Hence, some local maps may read Shwegondine Rd, while others will say Shwe Gone Daing Rd or Shwe Gone Daing St; in Burmese, it's simply Shwe Gone Daing Làn. We use the most common English version that travellers encounter.

And as the previous examples demonstrate, different maps may also present the actual names of streets differently; eg Shwegondine Rd is Shwegondaing Rd on some local maps.

Sights

Yangon is divided into 33 townships and addresses are usually suffixed with these (eg 3 Win Gabar Lane, Bahan). Back in the mists of time, Yangon was a village centred on Shwedagon Paya, but the British shifted its centre south towards Yangon River. This is Downtown Yangon. Shwedagon and nearby Kandawgyi Lake are covered mainly by Dagon and Bahan townships; in the latter is the area referred to as Golden Valley, a choice address for the city's moneyed elite. Further north are more leafy areas surrounding Inya Lake and stretching up to Yangon International Airport. The city's townships also spill south across the Yangon River to Dalah.

Downtown Yangon

★ **Botataung Paya** BUDDHIST TEMPLE
(ဗိုလ်တထောင်ဘုရား; Map p38; Strand Rd, Botataung; US$5 or K6000; 6am-9.30pm)

YANGON IN ...

Two Days

Take a **walking tour** (p56) of downtown Yangon and drop by the gorgeous **Musmeah Yeshua Synagogue** (p40). Tour the **National Museum** (p39), followed by lunch at **Feel Myanmar Food** (p68). Take an afternoon stroll in **People's Park** (p51) before ascending to **Shwedagon Paya** (p45) in time for sunset.

Start day two at the riverside **Botataung Paya** (p36). Browse the traditional market **Theingyi Zei** (p54) and the more tourist-oriented **Bogyoke Aung San Market** (p54). Lunch at **Rangoon Tea House** (p69). Admire the giant reclining Buddha at the **Chaukhtatgyi Paya** (p51) and the gorgeous sitting Buddha at nearby **Ngahtatgyi Paya** (p51). An amble around part of **Kandawgyi Lake** (p51) can be followed by a performance by **Htwe Oo Myanmar Traditional Puppet Theatre** (p78).

Four Days

Hop on the ferry to **Dalah** (p51) to view the city from the Yangon River. Return to Yangon to visit the incense-clouded temple **Kheng Hock Keong** (p43) and then head to **19th St** (p70) for a grilled-food feast.

On day four, board the **Yangon Circle Line** (p59). Break your journey at Kyemyindaing to explore the **Coconut & Banana Wholesale Market** (p54) and Tadakalay for the kitsch, fun **Meilamu Paya** (p55). Eat at **Taing Yin Thar** (p74) or **Minn Lane Rakhaing Monte & Fresh Seafood** (p74), both at the north end of **Inya Lake** (p55). Head back downtown to live it up at **Blind Tiger** (p75) or **Yangon Yangon** (p75).

YANGON SIGHTS

Botataung's spacious riverfront location and lack of crowds give it a more down-to-earth spiritual feeling than Shwedagon or Sule Paya. Its most original feature is the dazzling zig-zag corridor, gilded from floor to ceiling, that snakes its way around the hollow interior of the 131ft golden *zedi* (stupa). Look out for a bronze Buddha that once resided in the royal palace in Mandalay, and a large pond full of hundreds of terrapin turtles.

The temple is named after the 1000 military leaders who escorted hair relics of the Buddha from India to Myanmar more than 2000 years ago. For one six-month period, this paya (religious monument) is said to have harboured eight strands of the Buddha's hair before they were distributed elsewhere.

A bomb from an Allied air raid in November 1943 scored a direct hit on the unfortunate paya. After the war the Botataung was rebuilt in a very similar style to its predecessor, but with one important and unusual difference: unlike most *zedi,* which are solid, the Botataung is hollow, and you can walk through it.

There's a gold leaf–coated maze inside the *zedi,* with glass showcases containing many of the ancient relics and artefacts, including small silver-and-gold Buddha images, which were sealed inside the earlier stupa.

Reconstruction also revealed a small gold cylinder holding two small body relics and a strand of hair, said to belong to the Buddha, which is reputedly still in the stupa.

On the northern side of the stupa is a hall containing a large **gilded bronze Buddha**, cast during the reign of King Mindon Min. At the time of the British annexation, it was kept in King Thibaw Min's glass palace, but after King Thibaw was exiled to India, the British shipped the image to London. In 1951 the image was returned to Myanmar and placed in the Botataung Paya.

In the southwest corner of the temple is a *nat* (spirit being) **pavilion** containing images of Thurathadi (the Hindu deity Saraswati, goddess of learning and music) and Thagyamin (Indra, king of the *nat*) flanking the thoroughly Myanmar *nat* Bobogyi.

The terrapin turtle pool is in the southeast corner. Most of the turtles are fairly small, but every now and again a truly monstrous one sticks its head out of the water.

Sule Paya

BUDDHIST STUPA

(ဆူးလေဘုရား; Map p42; cnr Sule Paya Rd & Mahabandoola Rd, Pabedan; K3000; ☺5am-9pm) It's not every city where the primary traffic circle is occupied by a 2000-year-old golden temple. This 46m *zedi,* said to be older than

Downtown East

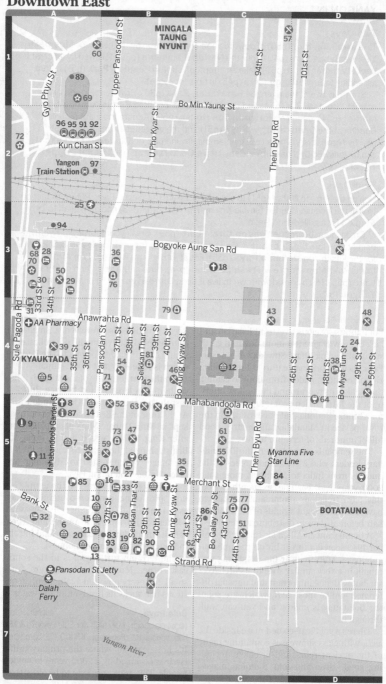

Shwedagon Paya, is an example of modern Asian business life melding with ancient Burmese tradition.

Just after the sun has gone down is the most atmospheric time to visit the temple.

The central stupa's name, Kyaik Athok, translates in the Mon language as 'the stupa where a Sacred Hair Relic is enshrined'. As with many other ancient Myanmar shrines, it has been rebuilt and repaired many times over the centuries.

The gilded *zedi* is unusual in that its octagonal shape continues right up to the bell and inverted bowl. Near the north entrance look for the small golden *karaweik* (royal barge designed in the shape of a mythical bird), which you can load with a prayer card, then winch up a chain to deposit the card in a shrine higher up the stupa (K1000).

The exterior base of the temple is surrounded by small shops and all the familiar nonreligious activities that seem to be a part of every *zedi* in Myanmar.

Besides its significance as a landmark and meeting place, maybe its most mundane function is as a milestone from which all addresses to the north are measured.

National Museum (Yangon) MUSEUM
(အမျိုးသားပြတိုက်; Map p42; ☏01-371 540; 66/74 Pyay Rd, Dagon; K5000; ☻9.30am-4.30pm Tue-Sun) Even though the museum's collection is appallingly labelled and often badly lit, the treasures that lie within this cavernous building deserve a viewing. The highlight is the spectacular 26ft-high, jewel-encrusted Sihasana (Lion Throne), which belonged to King Thibaw Min, the last king of Myanmar. It's actually more of an entrance doorway than a throne but let's not quibble – it's more impressive than your front door.

Further signs that the kings of old didn't understand the meaning of the word 'subtlety' are the ornate beds, silver and gold rugs, flashy palanquins (one of which is palatial in size and splendour), ivory kitchen chairs, some breathtaking ceremonial dresses and a collection of betel-nut holders and spittoons.

The upper-floor galleries, several of which were under renovation during our last visit, take you on an amble through natural history, prehistory, art and the cultures of Myanmar's national races. The Buddha Images gallery on the 4th floor is well worth searching out.

On the ground floor there's a model of the colonial-era State House demolished in 1978; the chandeliers that hang on each floor of the museum are all that remain of it.

Downtown East

Mahabandoola Garden PARK

(မဟာဗန္ဓုလပန်းခြံ; Map p38; Mahabandoola Garden St, Kyauktada; ⊙6am-6pm) **FREE** This park offers pleasant strolling in the heart of the downtown area and views of surrounding heritage buildings including City Hall, the High Court and the old Rowe & Co department store, now a bank.

The most notable feature in the Mahabandoola Garden is the **Independence Monument** (လွတ်လပ်ရေးကျောက်တိုင်), a 165ft white obelisk surrounded by two concentric circles of *chinthe* (half-lion, half-dragon deity). There's also a children's playground.

When laid out by the British in 1868, the park was called Fytche Sq after Sir Albert Fytche, chief commissioner at the time. Later it was renamed Victoria Park to commemorate the queen whose statue used to stand where the Independence Monument is today. After Independence, the park was renamed to honour General Thado Mahabandoola, a Burmese hero who conquered Assam and died in the First Anglo-Burmese War in 1824.

For a year or two following the 1988–90 prodemocracy uprisings, the park was occupied by soldiers; many of the more violent events of the time took place nearby.

Musmeah Yeshua Synagogue SYNAGOGUE

(Map p42; ☑01-252 814; 85 26th St, Pabedan; ⊙10am-1pm Mon-Sat) The lovingly maintained interior of this 1896 building contains a *bimah* (platform holding the reading table for the Torah) in the centre of the main sanctuary and a women's balcony upstairs. The wooden ceiling features the original blue-and-white Star of David motif. It's best to contact Sammy Samuels at info@myanmarshalom.com to be sure of gaining access to the synagogue.

The synagogue was once the focal point of an influential community of Sephardic Jews from India and Baghdad that at its height in the early 20th century numbered 2500.

Very occasionally (usually on Jewish high holidays) services are held in the synagogue, which has one of the Yangon Heritage Trust's blue plaques.

Ministers Office HISTORIC BUILDING

(Secretariat; Map p38; 300 Thein Byu Rd, Kyauktada) Although currently closed to the public, it's worth making a circuit of this spectacular red-brick complex, which takes up a 16-acre block. Built in stages between 1889 and 1905, the Secretariat was the British seat of government for Burma. General Aung San and six of his colleagues were assassinated here in 1947. The complex also housed independent Burma's first National Assembly.

When the capital moved to Nay Pyi Taw in 2005, the building, renamed the Ministers Office, was mostly abandoned and its roof suffered damaged during Cyclone Nargis.

A reprieve came in 2011 when the Ministry of Construction selected it as one of five key Yangon heritage buildings to undergo renovations. A private group has since taken over the lease and plans include a cultural centre and historical museum, which will include Aung San's old office and the room where he was gunned down. This section is open to the public once a year on Martyrs' Day.

It's likely to be years before the barbed wire comes down and the public can once again enter the grounds and view the building from the flame tree–shaded lawns surrounding it. A technical study has put the cost of full restoration of the 400,000-sq-ft building at at least US$100 million.

Strand Hotel HISTORIC BUILDING

(Map p38; www.hotelthestrand.com; 92 Strand Rd, Kyauktada) Opened in 1901, and run by the famed Sarkies brothers (they also owned Raffles in Singapore and the Eastern and Oriental in Penang), this historic hotel in its early years hosted the likes of Rudyard Kipling, George Orwell and W Somerset Maugham.

The hotel was built by Turkish-Armenian contractor Tigran Nierces Joseph Catchatoor, who is buried around the corner in the cemetery next to the Armenian Church of St John the Baptist (p45).

In 1913 an annex was built next door; this now houses the Australian Embassy. During WWII, the Japanese took over the

Downtown West

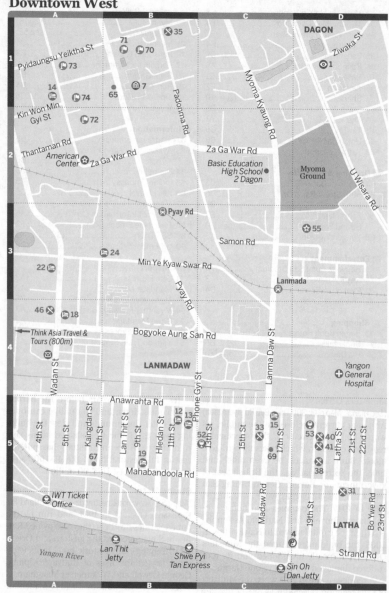

running of the Strand, which they renamed the Yamato Hotel.

Burmese nationals were allegedly not allowed to stay in the hotel until 1945. From 1962 to 1989, in what was quite possibly its darkest period, the Strand was owned and managed by the Burmese government. In 1979 when Tony Wheeler reviewed the Strand for the first edition of this guidebook, he found a 'tatty and dilapidated' colonial relic where you were more likely to encounter rats than a soft bed and a hot shower.

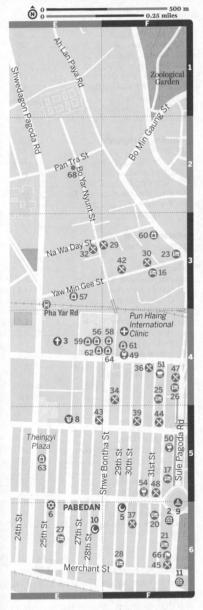

Yangon Heritage Trust
HISTORIC BUILDING

(YHT; Map p38; ☏01-240 544; www.yangon heritagetrust.org; 22/4 Pansodan St, Kyauktada; ⏱9am-5pm Mon-Fri) FREE The small gallery of historic photographs here gives an idea of how downtown Yangon used to look. There's a great view of lower Pansodan St's grand facades from the open balcony, particularly of the bomb-damaged Yangon Region Court and the art-deco Myanmar Economic Bank 2 opposite.

It also organises heritage walking tours (US$30 per person, minimum of five people) covering three different circuits around downtown.

Kheng Hock Keong
TAOIST TEMPLE

(Map p42; 426-432 Strand Rd, Latha; ⏱5am-9pm) FREE Supported by a Hokkien association, Yangon's largest Chinese (Taoist) temple is most lively from around 6am to 9am when it's thronged with worshippers offering candles, flowers and incense to the Buddhist and Taoist altars within.

The temple is dedicated to the sea goddess Mazu, who occupies the central altar and is flanked to the right by Guan Gong, the embodiment of loyalty and bravery, and on the left by Bao Sheng Da Di, the god of medicine.

St Mary's Cathedral
CHURCH

(Map p38; ☏01-245 647; www.yangonarchdiocese. org; 372 Bo Aung Kyaw St, Botataung; ⏱Mass 6am & 5pm, plus 8am & 10am Sun) Myanmar's largest Catholic cathedral is an impressive red-brick building dating to 1909. The neo-Gothic design is mainly down to Dutch architect Jos Cuypers, who modified a more Byzantine structure created by Henry Hoyne-Fox.

The floridly decorated interior with its red-, white- and green-brick patterns and painted statues is quite an eye-opener.

Holy Trinity Cathedral
CHURCH

(Map p42; 446 Bogyoke Aung San Rd, Dagon) Yangon's principal Anglican church was designed by India-based architect Robert Fellowes Chisholm. The red-brick-painted neo-Gothic structure took nine years to construct, opening in 1895. It has minimal concessions to its tropical location such as the roofed entrance to provide some protection from rain.

Those interested in WWII should look for the Forces Chapel dedicated to Allied forces who perished during the conflict in Burma. Regimental crests decorate its walls. There's also a Regiments Memorial to the Chindits (an Allied Special Forces) at the southeastern edge of the cathedral compound.

In 1993, the Strand was brought back to something of its former glory under the supervision of Adrian Zecha, founder of the Aman Resorts. In 2016 it was closed again for several months for a head-to-toe refurbishment that will eventually see an entirely new section added to the hotel's rear.

Downtown West

◎ Sights

1 Dargah of Bahadur Shah Zafar............D1
2 Former Ministry of Hotels & Tourism ...F6
3 Holy Trinity Cathedral........................E4
4 Kheng Hock Keong............................D6
5 Mogul Shia Mosque...........................F6
6 Musmeah Yeshua Synagogue.............E6
7 National Museum (Yangon)................B1
8 Sri Kali..E5
9 Sule Paya.......................................F6
10 Surti Sunni Jamah Mosque E6
11 Yangon Stock Exchange F6

⊜ Sleeping

12 4 Rivers Youth Hostel........................B5
13 Agga Youth Hotel.............................B5
14 Belmond Governor's Residence...........A1
15 Best Western Chinatown Hotel C5
16 Loft Hotel......................................F3
17 May Shan Hotel F5
18 MGM Hotel A4
19 New Yangon Hotel............................B5
20 Okinawa (2) Guest House...................F6
21 Okinawa Guest House........................F6
22 Panda Hotel....................................A3
23 Parkroyal Yangon.............................F3
24 RGN City Lodge................................B3
25 Scott...F4
26 Sule Shangri-la................................F4
27 White House Hotel............................E6
28 Willow Inn......................................F6

⊗ Eating

29 Aung Mingalar Shan Noodle
    Restaurant F3
30 Bijin...F3
    Burmese Sweets Vendors ....(see 61)
31 Cherry Mann...................................D5
32 Craft...E3
33 Cyclo..C5
34 Danuphyu Daw Saw Yee Myanma
    Restaurant..................................F4
35 Feel Myanmar Food...........................B1
36 Golden Bell....................................F4
37 Golden Tea.....................................F6
38 Grilled Snack Stalls D5
39 Ingyin New South India Food Centre F5

40 Kaung Myat.....................................D5
41 Kosan Cafe.....................................D5
42 Le Petit Comptoir F3
43 New Delhi.......................................E5
44 Nilar Biryani & Cold Drink..................F5
45 Samusa Thoke Vendor F6
46 Shan Yoe Yar A4
47 Summer Palace F4
48 Thone Pan Hla.................................F5

⊝ Drinking & Nightlife

49 Bar Boon..F4
50 Black Hat..F5
51 Cafe Genius F4
52 Hummingbird...................................C5
53 Kosan Double Happiness Bar D5
    Press Office ....(see 32)
54 Shwe Bali F5

⊚ Entertainment

55 National Theatre D3

⊜ Shopping

56 Bogyoke Aung San Market...................E4
57 Gallery Sixty Five.............................E3
    Globe Tailoring ....(see 36)
58 Heritage Gallery F4
59 Myanmar Yanant Textile E4
60 New Zero Art Space F3
61 Parkson Mall...................................F4
62 Shinon Myanmar...............................E4
63 Theingyi Zei....................................E5
    Turquoise Mountain
    Jewellery ....(see 14)
64 Yo Ya May F4

ⓘ Information

65 Asian Trails B1
66 Canadian Embassy F6
67 Columbus Travels & Tours..................A5
68 Discovery DMC.................................E2
69 Flymya..C5
70 French Embassy...............................B1
71 Indonesian Embassy.........................B1
72 Lao Embassy...................................A2
73 Malaysian Embassy...........................A1
74 Sri Lankan Embassy A1

Sri Varada Raja Perumal Temple

HINDU TEMPLE

(Map p38; 135-137 51st St, Botataung; ⊘6.30-11.30am & 6-8.30pm) Dedicated to Vishnu, this lavishly decorated Hindu temple dates from 1928 and was built by the Indian businessman Dr S Ramanatha Reddiar. It has the classic South Indian *gopuram* style of entrance tower covered with Hindu deities.

The temple's main festival is a 10-day event in May or June and includes a flower procession.

Sri Kali

HINDU TEMPLE

(Map p42; 295 Konezdan Rd, Pabedan; ⊘5-11am & 3-9pm) Devoted to the Hindu goddess Kali, this temple was built in 1871 before the flood of Indian migrants came to the city during British colonial rule. It features a highly decorative *gopuram*. Also look for the flocks of pigeons resting on overhead power lines, evoking Hitchcock's *The Birds*! This is one of the locations for Thaipusam (p62), the festival famous for colourful street processions featuring acts of ritual self-mutilation.

Armenian Apostolic
Church of St John the Baptist   CHURCH
(Map p38; ☑ 01-242 318; www.yangonarmenian church.org; 66 Bo Aung Kyaw St, Kyauktada) Yangon's oldest church, built in 1862 and consecrated a year later, served Yangon's Armenian trading community, who have been in Myanmar since the 17th century. It's a modest, sparsely decorated yet handsome building.

Surti Sunni Jamah Mosque   MOSQUE
(Map p42; 149 Shwe Bontha St, Pabedan) Built in the 1860s, this is thought to be Yangon's oldest surviving Muslim place of worship. Its pair of large minarets flanks an equally imposing arched entrance tower.

◉ Shwedagon Paya & Around

★ Shwedagon Paya   BUDDHIST TEMPLE
(ရွှေတိဂုံဘုရား; Map p48; www.shwedagon pagoda.com; Singuttara Hill, Dagon; K8000; ⊙4am-10pm) One of Buddhism's most sacred sites, the 325ft *zedi* here is adorned with 27 metric tons of gold leaf, along with thousands of diamonds and other gems, and is believed to enshrine eight hairs of the Gautama Buddha as well as relics of three former buddhas.

Four entrance stairways lead to the main terrace. Visit in the cool of dawn if you want tranquillity. Otherwise, pay your respects when the golden stupa flames crimson and burnt orange in the setting sun.

The following covers the history and layout of Shwedagon Paya. Guides (they'll locate you before you can find them) can provide more details. Tour agencies can also arrange guides; a good, regularly scheduled tour, including the surrounding area, is offered by **Khiri Travel** (Map p38; ☑ 01-375 577; http://khiri. com; 1st fl, 5/9 Bo Galay Zay St, Botataung).

➡ History
Legend has it that there's been a stupa on Singuttara Hill for 2600 years, ever since two merchant brothers, Tapussa and Ballika, met the Buddha. He gave them eight of his hairs to take back to Myanmar, a land ruled by King Okkalapa. Okkalapa enshrined the hairs in a temple of gold, together with relics of three former buddhas, which was then enclosed in a temple of silver, then one of tin, then copper, then lead, then marble and, finally, one of plain iron-brick.

Archaeologists suggest that the original stupa was built by the Mon people some time between the 6th and 10th centuries. In common with many other ancient *zedi* in earthquake-prone Myanmar, it has been rebuilt many times. During the Bagan (Pagan) period of Myanmar's history (10th to 14th centuries), the story of the stupa emerged

MAUSOLEUMS AROUND SHWEDAGON PAYA

Several prominent Myanmar citizens are buried near Shwedagon Paya. Near the north entrance to the stupa is the **Martyrs' Mausoleum** (အာဇာနည်ဗိမာန်; Map p48; Arzani St, Bahan; K3000; ⊙8am-5pm Tue-Sun), housing the remains of General Aung San and the six comrades who were assassinated on 19 July 1947. The Soviet-style, red-painted concrete complex, surrounded by beautifully manicured grounds, was fully renovated in 2016 in time for Martyrs' Day, the first to be celebrated by a government led by Aung San's daughter.

The original timber mausoleum was destroyed after a North Korean terrorist strike in 1983, which killed 20 people (but not the target, visiting South Korean general Chun Doo-Hwan). To the right of the entrance to the mausoleum look for the smaller, free **Korean Martyrs Memorial** commemorating those who died in the attack.

South of the stupa along Shwedagon Paya Rd are four mausoleums. The one closest to the stupa is that of former UN secretary-general **U Thant** (ဦးသန့်ဂူဗိမာန်; Map p48). A chapter in *The River of Lost Footsteps* by his grandson Thant Myint-U recounts the horrific details of U Thant's burial in 1969 when students fought with the military and riots resulted in hundreds of dead, many more imprisoned and martial law being imposed.

Next along is **Suphayalat's Mausoleum** (စုဘုရားလတ်ဂူဗိမာန်; Map p48). Having been exiled to India with her husband and daughters in 1885, Burma's last queen was allowed to return to Rangoon in 1919, three years after King Thibaw's death, but was kept under house arrest by the British colonial authorities until her death in 1925.

Bringing up the rear are the tombs of Aung San's widow, **Daw Khin Kyi** (ဒေါ်ခင်ကြည်ဂူဗိမာန်; Map p48), and the famous poet and intellectual **Thakin Kodaw Hmaing** (သခင်ကိုယ်တော်မှိုင်းဂူဗိမာန်; Map p48; Shwedagon Paya Rd, Dagon).

Shwedagon Paya

WHAT TO LOOK FOR

A pair of giant ❶ **Chinthe** guard the southern covered entrance, from Shwedagon Pagoda Rd; of the four covered arcades leading up Singuttara Hill this is considered the main entrance.

Halfway up, branch off in either direction for a peaceful stroll along the lower terrace of Shwedagon. Flanking this concrete footpath that encircles the hill are monasteries and resting houses for pilgrims.

Continue around to the northern covered entrance, climb the final flights of steps and emerge onto the main terrace to a dazzling explosion of decoration. Ahead rises the golden ❷ **central stupa** surrounded by ❸ **planetary posts**, as well as many other shrines, *tazaung* (small pavilions) and religious statuary.

In the terrace's northeast corner an open-sided pavilion covering the ❹ **Shwedagon inscription** stones stands in the shadow of the ❺ **Naungdawgyi Paya**.

For a close-up detail of the jewel-encrusted ❻ **hti** at the top of the central stupa view the gorgeous photos in the ❼ **photo gallery** or use one of several telescopes dotted around the main terrace – there's one outside Shwedagon's small museum.

TOP TIPS

➡ Arrive early morning or late afternoon towards sunset Monday to Friday.

➡ Dress respectfully and remove your shoes before entering the temple precincts. Walk clockwise around the stupa.

➡ The north gate and northwest corner between the Friday and *Rahu* planetary posts are prime photo spots.

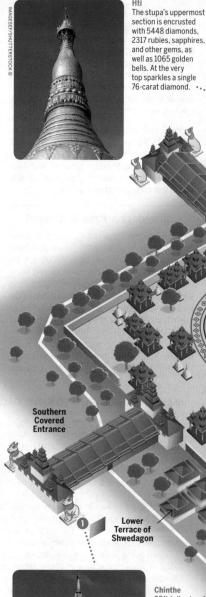

Hti
The stupa's uppermost section is encrusted with 5448 diamonds, 2317 rubies, sapphires, and other gems, as well as 1065 golden bells. At the very top sparkles a single 76-carat diamond.

IMAGESEF/SHUTTERSTOCK ©

Southern Covered Entrance

Lower Terrace of Shwedagon

Chinthe
30ft-tall pairs of these legendary half-lion, half-dragon beasts guard each of the four covered walkways up Singuttara Hill to the paya's central platform.

PAUL D SMITH/SHUTTERSTOCK ©

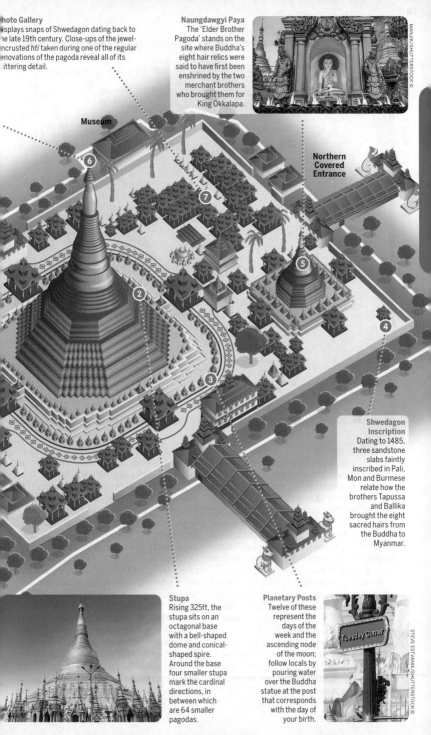

Photo Gallery
Displays snaps of Shwedagon dating back to the late 19th century. Close-ups of the jewel-encrusted *hti* taken during one of the regular renovations of the pagoda reveal all of its glittering detail.

Museum

Naungdawgyi Paya
The 'Elder Brother Pagoda' stands on the site where Buddha's eight hair relics were said to have first been enshrined by the two merchant brothers who brought them for King Okkalapa.

MANJIK/SHUTTERSTOCK ©

Northern Covered Entrance

Shwedagon Inscription
Dating to 1485, three sandstone slabs faintly inscribed in Pali, Mon and Burmese relate how the brothers Tapussa and Ballika brought the eight sacred hairs from the Buddha to Myanmar.

Stupa
Rising 325ft, the stupa sits on an octagonal base with a bell-shaped dome and conical-shaped spire. Around the base four smaller stupa mark the cardinal directions, in between which are 64 smaller pagodas.

Planetary Posts
Twelve of these represent the days of the week and the ascending node of the moon; follow locals by pouring water over the Buddha statue at the post that corresponds with the day of your birth.

STEVE ESTVANIK/SHUTTERSTOCK ©

Tuesday Corner

Shwedagon Paya & Around

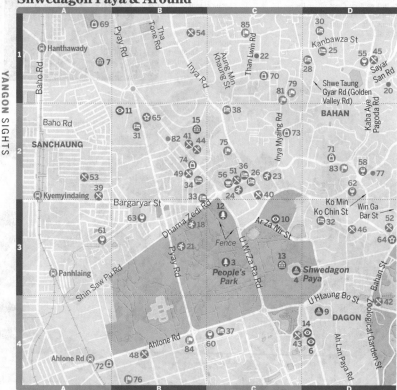

from the mists of legend to become hard fact. Near the top of the eastern stairway is a brick inscribed with the date 1485.

In the 15th century, the tradition of gilding the stupa began. Queen Shinsawbu, who was responsible for many improvements to the stupa, provided her own weight (88lb) in gold, which was beaten into gold leaf and used to cover the structure. Her son-in-law, Dhammazedi, went several better, offering four times his weight and that of his wife in gold.

In 1612 Portuguese renegade adventurer Filipe de Brito e Nicote raided the stupa from his base in Thanlyin and carried away Dhammazedi's 300-ton bell, with the intention of melting it for cannons. As the British were to do later with another bell, he accidentally dropped it into the river where it remains.

During the 17th century, the monument suffered earthquake damage on eight occasions. Worse was to follow in 1768, when a quake brought down the whole top of the

zedi. King Hsinbyushin had it rebuilt to virtually its present height, and its current configuration dates from that renovation.

British troops occupied the compound for two years immediately after the First Anglo-Burmese War in 1824. In 1852, during the Second Anglo-Burmese War, the British again took the paya, the soldiers pillaged it once more and it remained under military control for 77 years, until 1929. Prior to the British takeover of southern Myanmar there had been defensive earthworks around the paya, but these were considerably extended by the British. The emplacements for their cannons can still be seen outside the outer wall.

In 1871 the provision of a new *hti* (the umbrella-like decorative top of a stupa) by King Mindon Min from Mandalay caused considerable head-scratching for the British, who were not at all keen for such an association to be made with the still-independent part of Myanmar.

The huge earthquake of 1930, which totally destroyed the Shwemawdaw in Bago, caused only minor damage to Shwedagon. The following year it wasn't so lucky, when the paya suffered from a serious fire.

After another minor earthquake in 1970, the *zedi* was clad in bamboo scaffolding, which extended beyond King Mindon's 100-year-old *hti,* and was refurbished. The stupa also had to be repaired following the 2008 Cyclone Nargis.

During recent centuries, the Shwedagon Paya was the scene for much political activity during the Myanmar independence movement – Aung San Suu Kyi spoke to massive crowds here in 1988 and the temple was also at the centre of the monks' protests in 2007.

➡ **Temple Layout**
The hill on which the stupa stands is 167ft above sea level with the entire complex

covering 114 acres. As is common with all temples in Myanmar, the main terrace is approached by four **zaungdan** (covered walkways), each of which is flanked at its entrance by a pair of 30ft-tall *chinthe.* If you don't want to climb the steps, there are lifts at the southern, eastern and northern entrances, while the western *zaungdan* has sets of escalators.

All but the western *zaungdan* are lined with stalls selling flowers – both real and beautifully made paper ones – for offerings, buddha images, ceremonial umbrellas, books, antiques, incense sticks and much more. There are also fortune tellers and money-exchange booths.

You emerge from the shade of the *zaungdan* into a visual cacophony of technicoloured glitter at the marble-floored **main terrace**, littered with pavilions and worship halls containing buddha images and two giant cast-iron bells.

At the centre of the terrace **Shwedagon Paya** sits on a square plinth, which stands 21ft above the clutter of the main platform and immediately sets the stupa above the lesser structures. Smaller stupas sit on this raised platform level – four large ones mark the four cardinal directions, four medium-sized ones mark the four corners of the plinth and 60 small ones run around the perimeter.

From this base, the *zedi* rises first in three terraces, then in 'octagonal' terraces and then in five circular bands. The shoulder of the bell is decorated with 16 'flowers'. The bell is topped by the 'inverted bowl', another traditional element of stupa architecture, and above this stand the mouldings, then the 'lotus petals'. These consist of a band of downturned petals, followed by a band of upturned petals. The banana bud is the final element of the *zedi* before the jewel-encrusted *hti* tops it.

Around the stupa's base, **12 planetary posts** conform to the days of the week; locals pray at the station that represents the day they were born. If you want to join them, and don't know the day of your birth, the fortune tellers at the temple have almanacs that will provide the answer. Note that Wednesday is divided into births in the morning and births in afternoon – for the latter you worship at the Rahu post at the northwest corner of the stupa base.

Before leaving the main terrace pop into the small **museum** (ရွှေတိဂုံဘုရားပြတိုက်;

Shwedagon Paya & Around

⏱9am-4pm Tue-Sun) **FREE**, which is chock full of buddha statues and religious ornaments. Look for the scale model of the stupa and the beautiful painting of the temple by MT Hla. The **photo gallery** is also well worth a look, particularly for the close-up snaps it displays of the top of the stupa.

★ **Ngahtatgyi Paya** BUDDHIST TEMPLE

(ငါးထပ်ကြီးဘုရား; Map p48; Shwegondine Rd, Tamwe; US$2 or K2000; ⏱6am-8pm) One of Yangon's, if not Myanmar's, most gorgeous Buddha images is this 46ft-tall seated one at the Ngahtatgyi Paya, sitting in calm gold and white repose with a healthy splash of precious stones to boot. In fact, it's worth seeing for its carved wooden backdrop alone.

A lovely approach to the temple is to walk up via the monasteries scattered along Bogyoke Aung San Museum Lane.

★ **Chaukhtatgyi Paya** BUDDHIST TEMPLE

(ခြောက်ထပ်ကြီးဘုရား; Map p48; Shwegondine Rd, Tamwe; ⏱6am-8pm) Housed in a large metal-roofed shed, this beautiful 213ft-long reclining Buddha is hardly publicised at all even though it's larger than a similar well-known image in Bago. The statue's placid face, with glass eyes, is topped by a crown encrusted with diamonds and other precious stones.

Close to the Buddha's feet is the small shrine to Ma Thay, a holy man who has the power to stop rain and grant sailors a safe journey.

Attached to the temple complex is the **Shweminwon Sasana Yeiktha Meditation Centre**, where large numbers of locals gather to meditate. It's not hard to find someone to show you around the adjoining monasteries.

★ **People's Park** PARK

(ပြည်သူ့ဉယျာဉ်; Map p48; U Wi Za Ra Rd, Dagon; K300; ⏱7am-7pm) Notable for its splendid views of the west side of Shwedagon Paya, this well-tended park offers plenty of pleasant features such as flower gardens and ponds; fountains, including one made of concentric rings of white elephants; and treetop observation platforms linked by fun swinging bridges.

More quirky aspects include a decommissioned Myanmar Airways Fokker you can climb inside, a fighter jet, an old steam train and a planetarium.

At the park's northwest corner is the **Natural World Amusement Park** (☏09 862 2249; www.naturalworldamusementpark.com; Ahlone Rd, Dagon; incl with People's Park; ⏱7am-7pm) with rides such as bumper cars and a log-flume roller coaster. Facing onto Dhammazedi Rd is the kid's amusement park **Happy Zone** (⏱9am-9pm).

Also with an entrance on Dhammazedi Rd is **Resistance Park** (တော်လှန်ရေးပန်းခြံ; U Wi Za Ra Rd, Dagon; ⏱7am-7pm) **FREE**; walls separate this area from People's Park.

Kandawgyi Lake LAKE

(ကန်တော်ကြီး; Map p48; Kan Yeik Thar Rd, Dagon; K3000) Also known as Royal Lake, this artificial lake, built by the British as a reservoir, is most attractive at sunset, when the glittering Shwedagon is reflected

---

DON'T MISS

DALAH

Until the bridge is completed in 2020, the quickest way to access Dalah is to make the 10-minute **ferry** (Map p38; 1-way/return K2000/4000; ⏱5.30am-9.30pm, every 15min) journey across the river from downtown Yangon. The contrast between the city's grand colonial edifices and urban buzz, and Dalah's sleepy, rural Myanmar atmosphere couldn't be more acute, and is a large part of the attraction of a visit. Travellers often go straight from Dalah to the pleasant town of Twante (p88), a 30- to 45-minute drive west into the delta. However, there's plenty to see in Dalah including a lively daily market, a shipbuilding yard and the great social enterprise **Chuchu** (☏09 79258 2795; www.facebook.com/kyutkyutmm; 507 Khaye Rd, Kamaksit; ⏱9am-5pm).

The fun starts on the ferry. Along with city and river views, there's a lively scene on board as hawkers sell everything from sun hats and *paan* (areca nut and/or tobacco wrapped in a betel leaf and chewed as a mild stimulant) to bags of speckled eggs and sweet snacks. Almost certainly you'll be approached by touts for the trishaw and motorbike taxis in Dalah – even in the terminal before boarding the ferry. Beware as these touts have a reputation for scamming unsuspecting travellers when negotiating hourly rates for rides. The going rate is K5000 per hour for either a trishaw or a motorbike taxi.

To avoid such problems sign up for a tour: an excellent cycling tour is offered by Unchartered Horizons (p58) that includes nearby Seikgyi island, which is even more rural than Dalah; or you could improve your photography immensely with Myanmar Photography Tours (p79), led by expat snapper Don Wright.

Inya Lake & Greater Yangon

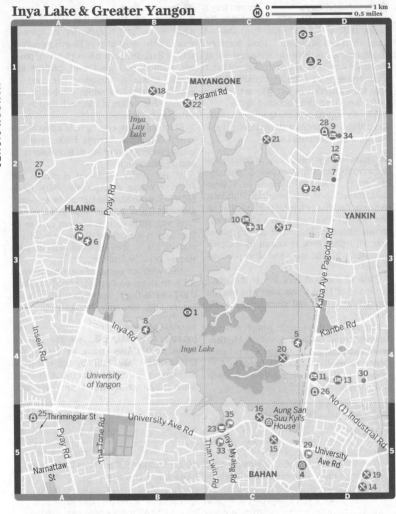

in its calm waters. The boardwalk, which runs mainly along the southern and western sides of the lake (and which is free to wander), is also an ideal place for an early-morning jog or stroll.

Just east of the Kandawgyi Palace Hotel, on the southern side of the lake, floats a **Shin Upagot** shrine. Upagot is a Bodhisattva (Buddhist saint) who is said to protect human beings in moments of mortal danger.

The eastern side of the lake, for which you'll have to pay the admission charge, is dominated by a small park, a kids' playground

and Karaweik Palace (p78), a reinforced concrete reproduction of a royal barge. There are plenty of lakeside cafes here, good spots for a drink at sunset.

On the lake's north side, the quirky **Utopia Tower** (Kandawgyi Lake, off Nat Maukt Rd, Tamwe; viewing deck K200; ⊙10am-10pm) is a giant pile of artificial rocks housing bars, karaoke, a massage parlour and, on the 5th floor, a viewing deck. On the ground floor, **Summit Art** (☑09 500 5849; ⊙9am-5.30pm) showcases the impasto canvases of owner-painter Myint Soe and other local artists.

Inya Lake & Greater Yangon

YANGON SIGHTS

Maha Wizaya Zedi — BUDDHIST TEMPLE
(Map p48; U Htaung Bo St, Dagon; K200; ⊙5am-9pm) This well-proportioned *zedi*, built on General Ne Win's orders in the early 1980s to commemorate the unification of Theravada Buddhism in Myanmar, is connected by a pedestrian bridge to the southern gateway to Shwedagon Paya. The *zedi* is hollow, its inside decorated with a forest of fake trees and a beautiful blue dome showing star constellations. The king of Nepal contributed sacred relics for the *zedi* relic chamber and General Ne Win had it topped with an 11-level *hti* – two more levels than the *hti* at Shwedagon.

U Thant House — HISTORIC BUILDING
(ဦးသန့်နေအိမ်; Map p48; www.yangonheritage trust.org/u-thant-house; 31 Panwa St, Bahan; donation K5000; ⊙10am-5pm Fri-Sun) When his grandson Thant Myint-U discovered his grandfather's house in the old Windermere estate area in 2012, the place was a wreck. It has since been beautifully restored by Yangon Heritage Trust and stands as a fitting memorial to U Thant, the United Nation secretary-general from 1961 to 1971 and one of Myanmar's most respected international politicians.

Fascinating archival photographs hang in the house, showing U Thant with the great and good of the era – everyone from Khruschev to John Lennon and Yoko Ono. There's also some video footage of him giving speeches. The house and its gardens are also used for lectures and events.

Bogyoke Aung San Museum — MUSEUM
(ဗိုလ်ချုပ်အောင်ဆန်းပြတိုက်; Map p48; 15 Bogyoke Aung San Museum St, Bahan; K300; ⊙9.30am-4.40pm Tue-Sun) The home in which Aung San lived with his family for just over two years before he was assassinated in July 1947 was given a spring clean in time for Martyrs' Day 2016. Newly on display is a car driven by the general, but you'll have to work hard to imagine what life was like inside the house, which is sparsely furnished and has old family photos and a few personal possessions.

Daw Kin Kyi, Aung San's widow, and three children, including Aung San Suu Kyi, stayed on living here until 1953 when their second son Lin drowned in the pond in the colonial mansion's grounds.

Drug Elimination Museum — MUSEUM
(မူးယစ်ဆေးဝါးတိုက်ဖျက်ရေးပြတိုက်; Map p48; ☏01-505 016; cnr Hanthawaddy & Kyun Taw Rds, Kamaryut; K5000; ⊙9am-4pm Tue-Sun) This gigantic time capsule of junta-era propaganda is a mind-bending experience. It vilifies the effects of class A drugs on Myanmar's

LOCAL KNOWLEDGE

YANGON'S MARKETS

Every Yangon township has its own *zei* (market, often spelt *zay*) – exploring them can be fun, educational and a chance to interact with locals.

The most tourist-friendly market is **Bogyoke Aung San Market** (Map p42; Bogyoke Aung San Rd, Dagon; ⊙10am-5pm Tue-Sun). Half a day could easily be spent wandering around this sprawling covered market, sometimes called by its old British name, Scott Market. It has more than 2000 shops and the largest selection of Myanmar handicrafts and souvenirs you'll find under several roofs, from lacquerware, Shan shoulder bags and velvet slippers, to puppets and jewellery. It's also a good place to find tailors. Pick up some nice slippers here, convenient for all the on-and-off demanded by paya protocol, and a *longyi* (sarong-style lower garment); **U Maung Maung** in the main hall has a good selection ranging from cotton ones from K5500 to silk-mix ones from K9500.

Covering several blocks of downtown Yangon, **Theingyi Zei** (Map p42; Shwedagon Pagoda Rd, Pabedan; ⊙9am-7pm) is popular with locals for household goods and textiles, but it's also renowned for its large selection of traditional herbs, cosmetics and medicines, which can be found on the ground floor of the easternmost building. Traditional herbal shampoo, made by boiling the bark of the Tayaw shrub with big black *kin pun* (acacia pods), is sold in small plastic bags; this is the secret of Myanmar women's smooth, glossy hair. Fresh produce in attractive, colourful piles is sold along 26th St, adjacent to Theingyi Zei.

You'll need to get up very early (or not bother going to bed) to catch the **San Pya Fish Market** (စံပြငါးဈေး; Kye Myin Daing Kannar Rd, Kye Myin Daing; ⊙24hr) at full throttle. Far from pretty but compulsively fascinating, Yangon's wholesale fish market is a heady assault on the senses and best experienced between 2am and 8am when boats unload their catches and deals are done with market traders and buyers for restaurants and hotels.

Far less smelly and a great daytime attraction is the nearby **Coconut & Banana Wholesale Market** (အုန်းသီးငှက်ပျောသီးလက်ကားဈေး; Kyemyindaing Jetty, Kyemyindaing Strand Rd, Kyemyindaing; ⊙24hr). Whole branches of bananas, towering piles of coconuts, bales of sugar cane and, in season, mammoth amounts of mangoes, make an eye-catching display beside the Hlaing River.

---

society while also glorifying the role of the military in supposedly stamping out their production and trade. Cue, dioramas of the opium wars, a huge life-sized poppy field, and ghastly depictions of addiction set against the triumphant efforts of the Tatmadaw. Keep in mind as you wander the vast, three-floored building (with pigeons flying around through gaps in the roof) that Myanmar remains the world's second-largest producer of opium.

Dargah of Bahadur Shah Zafar MAUSOLEUM
(Map p42; Ziwaca St, Dagon; ⊙8am-8pm) FREE
Covered in silks and strewn with sweet-smelling petals, the mausoleum of India's last Mughal emperor is place of pilgrimage for Indians, Muslims and others interested in the history of the Raj. Bahadur Shah Zafar II, who had a reputation as a talented Urdu poet, was exiled to Rangoon along with his wife (who is also buried here) and family in 1858 following the failed Sepoy Rebellion in Delhi. He died four years later in November 1862.

At that time the ex-emperor's shrouded corpse was hastily buried in an anonymous grave in his prison enclosure. A mausoleum was later built on the location of the prison, but the grave itself remained a mystery until 1991 when workmen discovered it 3.5ft underground during excavations for a new structure at the site.

The mausoleum is part of a functioning mosque. You can read more about Bahadur Shah Zafar's life and death in William Dalrymple's *The Last Mughal*.

State Fine Arts School HISTORIC BUILDING
(Map p52; 131 Kaba Aya Pagoda Rd, Bahan; ⊙9am-4.30pm Mon-Sat) Built in the early 20th century as the grand home of shipping and rubber magnate Lim Chin Tsong, this is another decaying but highly evocative slice of Yangon's architectural heritage. On the ground floor, beneath the pagoda-like tower, is a gallery of student art.

Explore upstairs to find murals painted by Ernest and Dod Proctor, who later in their careers had their works hung in London's Tate Gallery and National Portrait Gallery.

Rangoon War Cemetery
CEMETERY

(ရန်ကုန်စစ်သချိုင်း; Map p48; www.cwgc.org; off Pyay Rd, Sanchaung; ⊘7am-5pm) The smaller of Yangon's two cemeteries dedicated to the fallen servicemen of WWII in Burma is located down a quiet lane near the Jasmine Palace Hotel. This was the first burial ground set up after the liberation of Yangon from the Japanese in 1945. It contains 1381 graves – 86 are unidentified.

⊙ Inya Lake & Greater Yangon

★ Meilamu Paya
BUDDHIST TEMPLE

(မယ်လမုဘုရား; Thudhamar Rd, North Okkalapa; ⊘6am-8pm) Situated next to the Nga Moe Yeik creek, this Disneyland-ish pagoda is a hoot. Larger-than-life 3D stucco depictions of the Buddha's life and practice litter the compound. A giant crocodile houses a gallery displaying the legend of Mei La Mu, the girl born from a mangrove fruit, after whom the temple is named.

There are teahouses in the complex overlooking the creek and you can take a boat across the water to another cluster of stupas.

The temple is a short walk from Tadakalay Station on the Yangon Circle Line.

Inya Lake
LAKE

(အင်းယားကန်; Map p52) Inya Lake, created by the British as a reservoir in 1883, is roughly five times larger than Kandawgyi. The best spots from which to view the lake are the parks running along part of Pyay Rd and Kaba Aye Pagoda Rd. The paths are open to the sun so bring an umbrella for shade.

The lake's perimeter is one of the most exclusive areas of the city to live; University Ave Rd, on the lake's southern side, is the location of Aung San Suu Kyi's home, where she spent her years of house arrest, as well as the US Embassy.

If you're into sailing, drop by the Yangon Sailing Club (p58), which is open to nonmembers on Friday nights for drinks and has a lovely lakeside setting.

Kaba Aye Paya
BUDDHIST TEMPLE

(ကမ္ဘာအေးဘုရား; Map p52; 68 Kaba Aye Pagoda Rd, Mayagone; K3000; ⊘5am-9pm) This overly glitzy 'world peace' zedi, about 5 miles north of the city centre, was built for the 1954–56 Sixth Buddhist Synod. The centrepiece is a 118ft-high hollow paya with five gateways, each guarded by an image of Buddha. In the centre is a statue that has claimed to be the largest Buddha cast from silver in Myanmar.

Mahapasana
CAVE

(မဟာပါသာဏလိုဏ်ဂူ; Map p52; Kaba Aye Pagoda Rd, Mayagone; ⊘24hr) FREE Totally artificial, this 'great cave' is where the Sixth Buddhist Synod was held in 1954–56 to coincide with the 2500th anniversary of the Buddha's enlightenment. Measuring 456ft by 371ft, the cave, which can accommodate up to 10,000 people, took only 14 months to build. It helped that there were 63,000 volunteer labourers. Grand religious ceremonies are still held here.

National Races Village
PARK

(Yandar Rd, Thaketa; K5000; ⊘7.30am-5.30pm) Traditional houses of the Kachin, Kayah, Kayin, Chin, Bamar, Mon, Rakhine and Shan are dotted around this lush, landscaped compound hugging the Bago River, just north of the Yangon side of the Thanlyin Bridge. The best thing to do here is go for a cycle – the park is large and you can rent a bicycle (K500 per hour, K1000 deposit) to get around.

Beside each house, handicrafts and souvenirs are sold but they're all jumbled up and not particularly great quality.

Thaketa Crocodile Farm
FARM

(သာကေတမိကျောင်းမွေးမြူရေးစခန်း; Thaketa Industrial Estate, Tharkyta; K1000; ⊘6am-6pm) Off the main road from Yangon to Thanlyin, at the end of a bumpy road leading into the Thaketa Industrial Estate, is this government-run farm that breeds rare crocodiles to maintain their population. Some of the saltwater crocs are monsters, growing up to 15ft long. Watching their fanged mouths snap around tossed pieces of fish will send a chill down your spine.

Boardwalks keep you at a safe distance and lead over concrete pools and the mangroves next to Pazundaung Creek. There's also a dubious circus-style 'show' where you may learn some more about the lives of these frightening creatures.

Taukkyan War Cemetery
CEMETERY

(ထောက်ကြန့်စစ်သချိုင်း; www.cwgc.org; Pyay Rd, Taukkyan; ⊘7am-5pm) Eleven miles north of Yangon's airport is this huge, immensely sad but beautifully maintained cemetery. It contains the graves of 6374 Allied soldiers who died in the Burma and Assam campaigns of WWII. There is also a memorial bearing the names of the almost 27,000 soldiers who died with no known grave. Bago-bound buses from the Aung Mingalar Bus Terminal all pass Taukkyan.

The cemetery was opened in 1951. As you walk around reading the names of those who died and the epitaphs commemorating them, the heat of the sun seems to fade and the noise of the road recedes, leaving you alone in the silence of your own thoughts.

Kyauk Daw Kyi BUDDHIST TEMPLE
(Mindhama Hill, Mingalardon; ⊙6am-6pm) **FREE**
Not far from the airport, this immense seated Buddha was carved from a single piece of marble found outside Mandalay in 1999. The partially finished statue was painstakingly transported to Yangon by boat and train (on a specially built track) a year later, events that are depicted in the complex's modern murals.

🏃 Activities

★**Kokine Swimming Club** SWIMMING
(Map p48; 23 Sayar San Rd, Bahan; K10,000; ⊙6am-8pm, closed 10am-3pm Mon) Offering two well-maintained 100ft outdoor pools, this club for serious swimmers has been going since 1904. There are also small gyms attached to the changing rooms.

Pun Hlaing Golf Club GOLF
(http://punhlaingestate.com; Pun Hlaing Golf Estate Ave, Hlaing Tharya; green fees Mon-Thu US$65, Fri US$33, Sat & Sun US$90; ⊙6am-5pm Mon, to 9pm Tue-Sun) Take a glimpse at Yangon's elite at this course, designed by Gary Player. Maintained by a staff of 300, it's the verdant centrepiece of a private housing estate across the Hlaing River. Hiring a caddy is an extra US$10 and buggy rental K30,000.

Royal Green River CRUISE
(Map p38; Botataung Jetty, Botataung; regular/dinner cruise US$20/30) The largest of the private boats offering sunset cruises (Tuesday and Wednesday at 5pm) and dinner cruises (Friday to Sunday) on the Yangon River.

Yangon Rhythm CRUISE
(Map p38; ☑01-206 266; Botataung Jetty, Botataung; cruise US$10) One of the cheaper private operators running hour-long sunset cruises from Botataung Jetty (departs 5pm).

Aqua Inya Golf Driving Range GOLF
(Map p52; ☑01-657 758; Mya Kyun Thar Amusement Park, Kabar Aya Pagoda Rd, Mayangone; ⊙6am-8pm) Practise your golf swing by aiming at targets floating in Inya Lake. This wacky concept includes staff rowing out in the lake to recover the balls. Even if you're

---

🏃 City Walk
Downtown Yangon

START THONE PAN HLA
FINISH GOLDEN TEA
LENGTH APPROX 1.4 MILES; TWO TO THREE HOURS

Start in the cool hours of the morning, with a caffeine boost and Burmese-style breakfast at ❶ **Thone Pan Hla** (p76), a typical Myanmar teahouse.

Near the teahouse is the 2200-year-old ❷ **Sule Paya** (p37), the geographic and commercial heart of the city, and where the British-designed grid street pattern was centred. Make a circle or two around the temple to get just the right angle for your photograph; good views can be had from the pedestrian bridge that rises from the west side of Mahabandoola St to the terrace level of the pagoda.

To the east of Sule Paya is ❸ **City Hall**, a colossal lilac- and purple-painted colonial building adorned with traditional Myanmar decorative detail such as peacocks, *nagas* (serpents) and three-tiered *pyatthat* turrets. Nip around the back of the building to see the Municipal Corporation of Rangoon insignia still on the iron gates.

On the next corner further east on Mahabandoola Rd is the ❹ **Ayeyarwady Bank**, once Rowe & Co department store, dubbed the 'Harrods of the East'. Across the street is the ❺ **Immanuel Baptist Church**, originally built in 1830, though the present structure dates from 1885.

Continuing south you'll pass the Queen Anne–style ❻ **High Court** with its bell clock tower and rooftop lion statues. Pop into the neatly tended Mahabandoola Garden to enjoy the greenery and take a closer look at the ❼ **Independence Monument** (p40). Exit on Sule Pagoda Rd and head towards Yangon River past the monumental neoclassical ❽ **Yangon Stock Exchange**, originally built in 1937 to house the Reserve Bank of India.

Turning left, a colonnade of iconic columns stretches along the Strand facade of the former Yangon Region Office Complex; at the time of research this was being restored as the luxury ❾ **Kempinski Yangon Hotel**. Next door is the red-brick ❿ **Customs House**, built in 1915, and still

functioning for its original purpose as is the nearly century-old, two-faced bracketed clock hanging from building's white tower.

On the corner with Pansodan St stands the pastel-coloured **11 Yangon Divisional Court**, one of the city's oldest masonry structures dating from around 1900. The bomb damage the building suffered during WWII is still visible on the Bank St side of the complex. The opposite corner is taken up with the grand **12 Myanma Port Authority** building with its striking square corner tower and bas-relief sculptures of ships on the facade.

Two blocks further along is the **13 Strand Hotel** (p41). The air-conditioned lobby, cafe and bar make a good rest stop. Consider writing a postcard and then posting it at the **14 Central Post Office** (p82), dating from 1908; note the lovely beaux-arts portico.

Return to turn right on lower Pansodan St. Monumental buildings line what was considered Yangon's prime business address a century ago. Several, such as the **15 Myanmar Agricultural Development Bank** and the graceful **16 Inland Waterways Department**, have weathered the passage of time well, while others, such as **17 Sofaer's Building**, are in desperate need of attention. This crumbling

Italianate-style building, constructed by the Jewish-Baghdadi trader Isaac A Sofaer, still has original features such as Manchester floor tiles.

At the corner with Merchant St and north along 37th St are many streetside **18 bookstalls** (p80); the area is known as Yangon's open-air library for obvious reasons. Turn right at the junction of Mahabandoola Rd and head west until you reach the corner of the block occupied by the **19 Ministers Office** (p41), a giant red-brick pile also known as the Secretariat from the times when it was the nucleus of British power in the country.

Return to Sule Paya along Mahabandoola Rd, noting **20 Myanma Post & Telecommunications**; during the 1950s almost 200,000 international cables a year came in and out of this building. West of Sule Paya, continue down Mahabandoola Rd through the chaotic Indian and Chinese quarters. Several mosques are here, including the 1918 **21 Mogul Shia Mosque** and the **22 Surti Sunni Jamah Mosque** (p45), Yangon's oldest Muslim place of worship dating to the 1860s. End the walking tour with a well-earned cuppa at **23 Golden Tea** (p76).

not playing, we recommend coming here for cheap beers at sunset overlooking the lake.

Yangon Yoga House
YOGA

(www.yangonyogahouse.com; Rm 4, Yankin Lan Thwe (1), off Yankin Rd, Yankin; classes US$12) Go online to book a place at the drop-in classes at this high-quality yoga studio, a short drive east of Inya Lake.

Bike World Explores Myanmar
CYCLING

(Map p52; 01-527 636; www.cyclingmyanmar. com; 10F Khapaung Rd, Hlaing; bike rental & guide from K15,000) Contact Aussie expat Jeff Parry about his guided bike rides. Explore downtown Yangon on Friday nights (9.30pm to around midnight) or on Sundays take a half-day ride (from 6.30am) into the countryside.

Thu Ti Leithwei Boxing School
HEALTH & FITNESS

(09 25586 3344; www.facebook.com/thutti lethwei; 893 Wun Tharet Khitta Lan, off Kaba Aye Rd, Mayangone; 1hr session K5000) Lone Chaw, former national champion, runs this school where you can get fit learning the moves of *let-hwei* (Burmese kickboxing). Be warned – it's a high-intensity workout.

Yangon Sailing Club
BOATING

(Map p52; 01-535 298; www.yangonsailing.com; 132 Inya Rd, Kamaryut; 9am-8pm) Established in 1924, this sailing club opens its doors to nonmembers on Friday nights when it's a very pleasant lakeside spot for drinks. Temporary membership, which will allow you to do some sailing, is K10,000 per day or, with boat hire, K5000 per hour.

LOCAL KNOWLEDGE

HOTEL SWIMMING POOLS

Nonguests can use the pools at the following hotels.

Belmond Governor's Residence (p64) Free as long as you eat at the restaurant.

Chatrium Hotel (p66) US$25.

Hotel Parami (p67) US$10.

Jasmine Palace Hotel (p67) US$10, including the gym.

Parkroyal Yangon (p65) US$30, including the gym.

Sule Shangri-la (p65) US$12, 9am to 5pm Monday to Friday only.

Dora
CRUISE

(Map p38; 01-531 313; www.cruiseinmyanmar. com; Botataung Jetty, Botataung; cruise US$45) Enjoy the scenery along Yangon's river and harbour on this one-hour cruise (morning or sunset; minimum 10 people). Drinks and snacks are included and the 63ft teak-decked boat is handsomely appointed. Day trips to Twante can also be arranged.

For a fraction of the cost, you could do a return trip on the Dalah ferry (p51).

Nemita by Lilawadee Spa
SPA

(Map p48; 01-544 500; www.chatrium.com; Chatrium Hotel, Pho Sein Rd, Tamwe; 1hr massage US$30; 10am-midnight) International-standard spa that offers a full range of treatments including reasonably priced massage and reflexology.

Seri Beauty & Health
MASSAGE

(Map p48; 01-534 396; 118 Dhama Zedi Rd, Bahan; massage per hr K10,000; 9am-6pm) Not Yangon's most upmarket beauty parlour, but conveniently located. It offers reasonably priced massages and a full range of beautification services. There's another **branch** (Map p48; 01-534 205; 144 Dhama Zedi Rd; 9am-6pm) a few doors down.

Tours

★ Uncharted Horizons
CYCLING

(Map p38; 09 97117 6085; www.uncharted -horizons-myanmar.com; 109 49th St, Botataung; half-/full-day tour from K42,000/65,000) This adventure-tours operation is run by enthusiastic and knowledgeable Austrian Jochen Meissner. It offers four biking itineraries around Yangon, including a fantastic trip to Dalah and nearby Seikgyi island, where you'll pedal around idyllic rural villages.

Other half-day tours cover lesser-known parts of Yangon, while the full day is a 43 mile marathon to Twante. The company also runs biking and trekking tours across Myanmar, particularly in Chin State.

Yangon Walking Tours
WALKING

(http://opening-up-burma-travel.info; tours per person from US$30, min 2 people) Knowledgeable expat editor and writer Bob Percival and other local guides lead a variety of walking tours, usually lasting three hours, around downtown Yangon. Themes include heritage buildings, religious buildings and George Orwell. Longer tours around the city and further afield into the Ayeyarwady Delta region are also available.

DON'T MISS

YANGON CIRCLE LINE

Although it can feel like travelling in a washing machine on spin cycle, the **Yangon Circle Line** (Map p38; non air-con/air-con carriage K100/200; ☺6.10am, 8.20am, 8.35am, 10.10am, 10.45am, 11.30am, 11.50am, 1.05pm, 1.40pm, 2.25pm, 4.40pm & 5.10pm) is a fun way to circumnavigate the city. It's a chance to interact with passengers and vendors on commuter trains and see off-the-beaten-track areas of Yangon. The train is least crowded after 10am and before 4pm, and at weekends.

You're not locked into the full three-hour, 30-mile circuit: disembark at any of the 38 stations and taxi back to the centre once you've had enough. You can use the train to avoid congested roads and get close to northern attractions, such as Meilamu Paya (p55).

Trains leave from platform 6/7 at Yangon train station, accessed off Pandsodan St; tickets are bought on the platform. Trains go in either direction and some don't make the full circuit. A long ride on the Circle Line is not advisable if you suffer from travel sickness.

Changes are on the way: Japan has provided Myanmar Railways with US$200 million to buy 11 new six-carriage trains and upgrade tracks so that a circuit can be completed in less than two hours.

 Courses

Several monasteries and meditation centres in Yangon welcome foreigners, although stays of 10 days are generally preferred.

Dhamma Joti
Vipassana Centre HEALTH & WELLBEING
(Map p48; ☎01-549 290; www.vridhamma.org; Ngahtatgyi Paya Rd, Bahan) Following the Vipassana teachings of SN Goenka, this simple, peaceful retreat is just a short walk from Shwedagon Paya and Kandawgyi Lake. Meditators must sign up for the introductory 10-day course and share accommodation.

Panditarama
Meditation Centre HEALTH & WELLBEING
(Map p48; ☎01-535 448; www.panditarama.net; 80A Than Lwin Rd, Bahan) Established in 1990 by Sayadaw U Pandita, formerly a chief meditation teacher at the Mahasi centre, this respected facility also runs the Panditarama Forest Meditation Centre at Hse Main Gon, 40 miles northeast of Yangon off the highway to Bago. It has courses in English for visitors prepared to stay for one week or longer.

Chanmyay Yeiktha
Meditation Centre HEALTH & WELLBEING
(Map p52; ☎01-661 479; www.facebook.com/chanmyaymeditation.centreyangon; 55A Kaba Aye Pagoda Rd, Mayangone) Meaning 'peaceful retreat', Chanmyay Yeiktha was founded by a Mahasi disciple, Sawadaw U Janaka. There is also a countryside branch at Hmawbi, around a one-hour drive north of Yangon. One-month stays are preferred.

Mahasi
Meditation Centre HEALTH & WELLBEING
(Map p48; ☎01-541 971; www.mahasi.org.mm; 16 Thathana Yeiktha Rd, Bahan) An English *dhamma* (Buddhist teachings) talk (3pm to 5pm) is open to anyone at Yangon's most famous meditation centre, founded in 1947 by the late Mahasi Sayadaw, perhaps Myanmar's greatest meditation teacher. For courses, it only accepts foreigners who can stay for at least one week.

✯ Festivals & Events

Yangon Photo Festival ART
(www.yangonphoto.com; ☺Mar) With Aung San Suu Kyi as its patron, this celebration of photography is held in March at Yangon's Institut Française (p75) and other venues across the city, and includes exhibitions, a conference and workshops.

Yoma Yangon Marathon SPORTS
(www.yomayangonmarathon.com; ☺Jan) This international marathon around the city has been held since 2013. It includes options for a half-marathon, 10km run and 3km fun run.

Shwedagon Paya Festival RELIGIOUS
(☺Feb/Mar) Crowds of pilgrims descend on Shwedagon for the country's largest *paya pwe* (pagoda festival), which takes place over the last full moon before the Myanmar New Year.

Botatuang Paya Festival RELIGIOUS
(☺early Jan) This temple festival features market stalls and fairground rides, including human-powered Ferris wheels.

Temples of Myanmar

Yangon's Shwedagon Paya, Mandalay's Mahamuni Paya and Bagan's plain of temples shouldn't be missed, but there are also many other lesser known Buddhist religious sites that will impress you with their beauty and spiritual power.

SEAN PAVONE / SHUTTERSTOCK ©

1. Mt Kyaiktiyo (Golden Rock; p107)
This gravity-defying gilded rock, set atop a remote hill, is one of Myanmar's most important pilgrimage sites.

2. Bagan (p156)
With more than 3000 temples spread across Bagan, the sheer size of this ancient complex is astonishing.

3. Buddha statue (p361)
Gilded statues are found all over Myanmar, decorated with layers of gold leaf applied by devotees.

4. Bronze bells (p191)
Pick up a souvenir from the hawkers that line the entrances to the active places of worship in Bagan.

5. Novice monks (p361)
The bright red robes of the Buddhist monks are usually reserved for novices under 15.

LIGHTRECORDS / SHUTTERSTOCK ©

PHUONG D. NGUYEN / GETTY IMAGES ©

FILM FESTIVALS

There's no better city for Myanmar cinephiles than Yangon with several historic cinemas such as **Nay Pyi Daw Cinema** (Map p38; 242-248 Sule Paya Rd, Kyauktada; tickets from K1000) and **Thamada Cinema** (Map p38; 5 Ah Lan Pagoda Rd, Dagon; tickets from K1000) clustered downtown and modern multiplexes located in major shopping malls. Tickets start at about K1000 per seat and you can see Myanmar romantic dramas and action features, Bollywood musicals, kung-fu smash-ups and Hollywood blockbusters.

For more independent movies and documentaries, both local and international, coincide your visit with one of Yangon's film festivals – tickets are often free. Held at the end of January, **&Proud** (www.andproud.net; ⊙ Jan) focuses on LGBT themes. The **Human Rights Human Dignity International Film Festival** (www.hrhdiff.org; ⊙ Jun) is a chance to see long- and short-form cinema on human-rights issues. The **Wathann Film Festival** (www.wathannfilmfestival.com; ⊙ Sep/Oct) highlights short movies in three categories: short fiction, documentary and new vision. And lastly, **Memory! International Film Heritage Festival** (www.memoryfilmfestival.org; ⊙ Nov) dedicated to preserving Asia's fragile cinematic legacy.

Thaipusam RELIGIOUS
(⊙ Jan or Feb) Held at Yangon's Hindu temples, Thaipusam involves colourful processions and ritual piercings of the flesh. The date depends on the lunar calendar.

Martyrs' Day CULTURAL
(⊙ 19 Jul) Commemorates the assassination of Bogyoke (General) Aung San and his comrades. Events are held at the Martyrs' Mausoleum (p45) and Ministers Office (p41).

Water Festival (Thingyan) CULTURAL
(⊙ Apr) The Myanmar New Year is celebrated in wet pandemonium.

Buddha's Birthday RELIGIOUS
(⊙ Apr/May) Celebrate the Buddha's enlightenment at temples across Yangon.

Independence Day CULTURAL
(⊙ 4 Jan) Includes a seven-day fair at Kandawgyi Lake.

🛏 Sleeping

Many new hotels and hostels have opened in Yangon and more are on the way. There are options to suit all budgets, but quality places with individual character and style remain rare. The widest choice is in downtown Yangon, but Bahan or Sanchaung is a generally quieter base, convenient for walking to Shwedagon Paya and Kandawgyi Lake.

Downtown Yangon

★**Yama Dormitory** HOSTEL $
(Map p38; ☎ 01-203 712; www.yamadormitory-yangon.com; 195 Bo Myat Tun Rd, Botataung; dm/

s/d/tw K25,000/65,000/78,000/91,000; ❄ @ 🛜) This hostel has high-quality, bunk-bed dorms with privacy curtains and spacious, simply designed private rooms. There are good facilities too, including a DIY laundry and panoramic rooftop bar, which give Yama the edge in the budget stakes.

Scott HOSTEL $
(Map p42; ☎ 01-246 802; www.scottmyanmar. com; 198 31st St, Pabedan; dm/tr US$12/15; ❄ @ 🛜) You'll need the thighs of a mountain climber to negotiate the stairs up to the dorms *and* the upper-level bunks in this appealing hostel opened in 2015. It's just steps from the old Scott Market after which it's named. The conversion of the old warehouse has bags of charm, including a flock of wooden birds presiding over the ground-floor cafe.

Chan Myaye Guest House GUESTHOUSE $
(Map p38; ☎ 01-382 022; www.chanmyayeyangon. com; 256/276 Mahabandoola Garden St, Kyauktada; s/d/tr/q US$22/32/42/60; ❄ 🛜) Encouraging signs greet you on each landing as you climb the stairs to the 4th floor to this spick and span guesthouse. Most rooms don't have windows, but a lovely big family room sleeps four at the front. It has a communal balcony with classic downtown Yangon views and friendly staff.

May Fair Inn GUESTHOUSE $
(Map p38; ☎ 01-253 454; maytinmg@gmail.com; 57 38th St, Kyauktada; s/d/tr K25,000/40,000/45,000; ❄ 🛜) Family-run, and ever reliable, this old-fashioned place is best for the traveller looking for tranquillity rather than a party.

Agga Youth Hotel
HOSTEL $

(Map p42; ☎01-225 460; www.aggayouthhotel.com; 86 12th St, Landmadaw; dm/s/d with shared bathroom from US$8/16/26, s/d/tr with private bathroom US$20/30/40) Of the several backpacker hostels that have sprung up in the Chinatown area, this one offers the most spacious and well-kept dorms. Rooms have balconies, it's professionally run and the rooftop restaurant is a plus. The group runs a couple of other nearby properties.

Okinawa (2) Guest House
HOSTEL $

(Map p42; ☎01-385 728; 89 32nd St, Pabedan; d US$28, dm/s with shared bathroom US$10/20; ❋⑤) The second branch of Okinawa offers simple, cramped but clean rooms and a key location steps from Sule Paya.

Three Seasons Hotel
GUESTHOUSE $

(Map p38; ☎01-901 0066; threeseasonshotel7@gmail.com; 83-85 52nd St, Pazundaung; s/d/tr US$25/30/40; ❋@⑤) The nine rooms in this homey guesthouse are old-fashioned but spacious and spotless and come with big bathrooms. The outdoor terrace, with tree shade, is a decent place to sit and watch the world cruise by. Staff are very friendly and helpful. It is located on a block that is quiet at night, so you should be able to sleep undisturbed.

Mother Land Inn 2
HOTEL $

(Map p38; ☎01-291 343; www.myanmarmotherlandinn.com; 433 Lower Pazundaung Rd, Pazundaung; s/d US$30/35, dm/s/d with shared bathroom US$12/27/30; ❋@⑤) Rooms are clean and reasonably sized, although a little old-fashioned, and it's a long walk or a short taxi ride from the heart of downtown, but staff are helpful and pleasant and offer sound travel advice and services. The free airport transfer and a solid breakfast are other pluses.

MGM Hotel
HOTEL $

(Map p42; ☎01-212 455; www.hotel-mgm.com; 160 Wadan St, Lanmadaw; s/d/tr US$35/40/45; ❋⑤) Solid digs on the western edge of downtown. Rooms vary in size, from the very large to the less spacious, but all are well maintained and come with windows and reasonable bathrooms. Staff can book bus tickets and the wi-fi connection is reliable.

4 Rivers Youth Hostel
HOSTEL $

(Map p42; ☎09 79988 7215; www.fourrivershostels.com; 79 12th St, Lanmadaw; 3-/8-bed dm US$10/9; ❋⑤) Dorms only at this hostel in a two-storey house in the heart of downtown.

Don't expect windows, but the dorms are clean, if compact, with comfortable beds. There's a small communal area and kitchen, and the staff are eager to please.

New Yangon Hotel
HOTEL $

(Map p42; ☎01-210 157; www.newyangonhotel.com; 830 Mahabandoola Rd, Lanmadaw; r from US$40; ❋⑤) Not many of the rooms in this modern hotel, close by Lan Thit Jetty, offer views of the river. Never mind; the rooftop breakfast room and bar does, and that's the main reason to stay here.

Beautyland Hotel II
HOTEL $

(Map p38; ☎01-240 054; www.goldenlandpages.com/beauty; 188-192 33rd St, Kyauktada; s/d US$30/40; ❋⑤) Tidy and decent-sized, if old-school, rooms, and efficient staff make this a reliable budget choice. The cheapest rooms don't have windows, while the more expensive ones boast heaps of natural light.

Okinawa Guest House
GUESTHOUSE $

(Map p42; ☎01-374 318; 64 32nd St, Pabedan; d US$28, dm/s with shared bathroom US$10/20; ❋⑤) The interior of this bougainvillea-fronted guesthouse is a bizarre hotchpotch of decorations and building styles that blend wood, bamboo and red brick. The rooms are small and dark but very clean. Noise can be an issue. If full, its second branch, Okinawa (2), is nearby.

Willow Inn
HOSTEL $

(Map p42; ☎09 77386 6383; www.thewillowinnmyanmar.com; 1st fl, 644 Merchant Rd, Pabedan; dm/s/d with shared bathroom from US$15/25/49, d with private bathroom US$59; ❋⑤) Noise from the busy street is an issue and there's no sign outside, but otherwise this small hostel in a heritage building offers a modicum of style and is well maintained. A simple breakfast is served on the building's spacious balcony.

White House Hotel
HOTEL $

(Map p42; ☎01-240 780; www.whitehousehotelyangon.blogspot.com; 69/71 Kon Zay Dan St, Pabedan; s/d with air-con US$18/24, with fan & shared bathroom from US$7/11; ❋⑤) Pluses are the generous breakfasts, rooftop terrace and useful travel desk. The negatives are a thigh-burning number of stairs, small and (at the cheapest rates) windowless rooms and basic bathrooms. There's also a curfew from midnight to 5am, so it's not for late-night revellers.

★ Loft Hotel
HOTEL $$

(Map p42; ☎01-393 112; www.theloftyangon.com; 33 Yaw Min Gee St, Dagon; s/d/ste from

US$160/180/280; ❄ @ 🛜) Designer fairy dust has been cast over a 1960s warehouse transforming it into this appealing boutique hotel in a very handy location. New York City–style loft rooms and split-level suites sport exposed-brick walls, floor-to-ceiling windows, arty black-and-white prints and contemporary furnishings. The garden area to the rear is a small oasis.

Hotel @ Yangon Heritage   HOTEL $$
(Map p38; ☎ 01-398 262; www.hotelyangon heritage.com; 184/186 Sule Pagoda Rd, Kyaukta-da; s/d/tr US$55/60/80; ❄ 🛜) Some design thought has been put into the conversion of this grand old building into a small hotel. Walls are painted a tasteful grey, setting off a sprinkling of colourful local crafts, and some original features such as pillars feature in rooms. It has stairs only (and they're steep) and the front rooms suffer from street noise.

The 4th-floor bar with a view is a plus.

RGN City Lodge   HOTEL $$
(Map p42; ☎ 01-230 0150; www.rgncitylodge. com; 142C Min Ye Kyaw Swar Rd, Lanmadaw; r from US$60; ❄ 🛜) This appealing hotel with a modern look and friendly staff is in a quiet downtown location. Colour-tinted old photos of Rangoon contrast nicely with the gold and white colour schemes of the rooms; the deluxe ones sport nice wicker furniture, too. The buffet breakfast has a choice of European, Burmese and Chinese dishes.

May Shan Hotel   HOTEL $$
(Map p42; ☎ 09 79969 9430; www.may shan.com; 115 Sule Paya Rd, Kyauktada; s/d/tr US$45/55/79; ❄ @ 🛜) The single rooms are pretty tight and lack windows, but the combination of convenient location, gracious service and ample amenities make the May Shan a top option in this area. The triple rooms (ask for room 601) are spacious and overlook Sule Paya. There's a great rooftop terrace to hang out and enjoy the view.

Best Western Chinatown Hotel   HOTEL $$
(Map p42; ☎ 01-251 080; www.bestwesternasia. com; 127-137 Anawrahta Rd, Latha; r from US$80; ❄ @ 🛜) Swathes of dove-grey marble and some contemporary furniture give a good first impression of this appealing hotel, opened in 2015. It's in a handy location too. The furnishings in the compact room are not top quality but some effort has been made with the design, placing it a cut above the run-of-the-mill competitors. Front-facing rooms offer direct views towards Shwedagon.

Panda Hotel   HOTEL $$
(Map p42; ☎ 01-212 850; www.myanmarpanda hotel.com; 205 Wadan St, Lanmadaw; r from US$75; ❄ @ 🛜) This 13-storey high-rise west of the city centre offers bright, old-fashioned yet enticing rooms with decent bathrooms. It's in a peaceful residential area and is popular with tour groups.

East Hotel   HOTEL $$
(Map p38; ☎ 01-7313 5311; www.east.com.mm; 234-240 Sule Pagoda Rd, Kyaukada; r US$90; ❄ @ 🛜) A dash of contemporary style helps this hotel stand out from the downtown midrange crowd. Take note, though, if you prefer your ablutions to be private from your room buddy: the bathrooms are not sealed off from the rest of the bedroom.

Panorama Hotel   HOTEL $$
(Map p38; ☎ 01-253 077; www.panoramaygn. com; 294-300 Pansodan St, Kyauktada; s/d from US$80/90; ❄ @ 🛜) Old-fashioned it may be, but the centrally located, 10-storey Panorama lives up to its name with rooms offering distant views towards Shwedagon Paya. Rooms are vast and generally well appointed.

New Aye Yar Hotel   HOTEL $$
(Map p38; ☎ 01-256 938; www.newayeyarhotel. com; 170-176 Bo Aung Kyaw St, Botataung; s/d from US$70/75; ❄ @ 🛜) This high-rise midrange has avoided the tropical rot that has struck down so many of its cousins. Rooms are a decent size, bathrooms have baths as well as showers, and there are views at the higher levels.

Aung Tha Pyay Hotel   HOTEL $$
(Map p38; ☎ 01-378 663; www.aungthapyay hotel.com; 74-80 38th St, Kyauktada; r/ste US$65/75; ❄ @ 🛜) This appealing place offers simply decorated, spruce rooms that are functional and spacious. The attached bathrooms have shower only. It's not worth paying extra for the suites, which offer little more than the standard rooms.

★ Belmond
Governor's Residence   LUXURY HOTEL $$$
(Map p42; ☎ 01-229 860; www.belmond.com/govern ors-residence-yangon; 35 Taw Win St, Dagon; r/ste from US$600/900; ❄ @ 🛜 🛁) The epitome of colonial luxury, the Governor's Residence in the 1920s was a guesthouse for important nationals of the Kayah ethnic group. The handsome rooms have ever-so-lightly-perfumed air, teak floors, cloudy soft beds and stone baths with rose-petal water. The pool merges

gently into the lawns and sparkles in reflected beauty. A major plus is the excellent range of free daily activities including bike rides and cooking classes.

★ Sule Shangri-la   HOTEL $$$

(Map p42; ☑01-242 828; www.shangri-la.com; 223 Sule Pagoda Rd, Pabedan; s/d/ste from US$236/253/347; ❄@☎☲) Still commonly known by its former name Traders, this well-established and professionally run hotel has been upgraded to the luxe Shangri-la brand. The rooms sport decor in gold and burgundy, it has excellent in-house dining and drinking options, as well as a decent-sized outdoor pool.

Strand Hotel   HOTEL $$$

(Map p38; ☑01-243 377; www.hotelthestrand. com; 92 Strand Rd, Kyauktada; r from US$488; ❄@☎☲) Yangon's most storied hotel was undergoing a major head-to-toe renovation during our latest visit. The original building's 31 suites will be upgraded with new air-conditioning, sound and communications systems, as well as a dash of contemporary styling in the decor.

The new wing, to the rear, will include more suites, a pool and spa. If you can't afford

to stay, visit for a drink in the bar, high tea in the lounge or a splurge lunch at the cafe.

Parkroyal Yangon   HOTEL $$$

(Map p42; ☑01-250 388; www.parkroyalhotels. com; 33 Ah Lan Pya Paya Rd, Dagon; r from US$220; ❄@☎☲) This well-run, centrally located business hotel offers rooms featuring all the amenities you'd expect at this price. It also has a good pool, tennis courts and gym including aerobics and yoga classes (US$30 for nonguests). Breakfast is not included.

Shwedagon Paya & Around

★ Pickled Tea Hostel   HOSTEL $

(Map p48; ☑09 25090 3363; www.pickledtea hostel.com; 11 Myaynigone Zay St, Sanchaung; dm/s/tw with shared bathroom from US$20/38/54; ❄☎) On the edge of happening Sanchaung and a 15-minute walk from Shwedagon Paya, this appealing hostel has large and posh dorms, with proper beds and lockers. There's also an attractive outside terrace and small communal area inside.

Business Alliance Hotel   BUSINESS HOTEL $

(Map p48; ☑01-524 844; www.businessalliance hotelygn.com; 126A Dhama Zedi Rd, Bahan; dm/d

---

RESTORING OLD YANGON

Set up in April 2012, the Yangon Heritage Trust (p43) is the chief guardian of the city's architectural legacy, under threat from a double whammy of decades of neglect combined with landowners eager to take advantage of the booming property market and sell to developers who have little to no interest in heritage preservation. Only 189 properties – all publicly owned – are currently listed as historically significant by the Yangon City Development Committee (YCDC). Listing provides no legal protection, so YHT is pushing for laws and public policy to sensitively develop the city. It's working with both the Yangon Region government and YCDC to ensure best-practice conservation methods are adopted – and having small measures of success.

One inspiring example is **491–501 Merchant St** (Map p38; http://turquoisemoun tain.org/project-entries/turquoise-mountain-myanmar; 491-501 Merchant St, Kyauktada), a collaboration between YHT and the nonprofit Turquoise Mountain on the restoration of a two-storey colonial building occupied by around 80 residents from 12 families spanning the city's multiethnic and religious population. The residents and their businesses, which include traditional tea shops, a barber and paper recycling, stayed in place during the restoration, which took 10 months from the start of construction in 2015. Around 250 workers were trained in restoration skills – some are now employed on other projects across the city such as the historic Yangon General Hospital. *Under One Roof,* a video about the project, can be viewed at www.vimeo.com/171511836.

Merchant St is among the growing number of buildings around Yangon affixed with a YHT 'blue plaque' listing its history and significance in Bamar and English. The next collaboration with the city and Turquoise Mountain is set to be the former **Ministry of Hotels & Tourism building** (Map p42; 77-91 Sule Pagoda Rd, Pabedan). The plan is to turn this stately, but dilapidated, 1905-vintage construction, which has been empty for a decade, into a centre for tourism businesses and workshop space for traditional crafts.

US$20/60; ❋@🛜) You wouldn't expect to find dorm rooms (four beds in each) in this business-oriented hotel, and they're not advertised on the website. The dorms have no windows, but otherwise they're fine and the location is a short walk from Shwedagon.

★ **Alamanda Inn** BOUTIQUE HOTEL **$$**
(Map p48; ☑ 01-534 513; http://hotel-alamanda. com; 60B Shwe Taung Gyar Rd/Golden Valley Rd, Bahan; s/d from US$110/120; ❋@🛜) Set in a blissfully quiet compound, the Alamanda combines 10 spacious and attractively decorated rooms. The most expensive room is the suite in the old servants' quarters, with its own private garden. There's an excellent attached French restaurant and bar.

Savoy Hotel BOUTIQUE HOTEL **$$**
(Map p48; ☑ 01-526 289; www.savoy-myanmar. com; 129 Dhama Zedi Rd, Bahan; s/d US$190/260, ste s/d US$280/390; ❋@🛜🏊) Everything inside the Savoy is done well. Hallways, rooms and even the lavish bathrooms are stocked with photographs, antiques, handicrafts and sculptures, and it takes little imagination to feel as if you are some Raj-era royal. The restaurant and bar are popular with expats.

Winner Inn HOTEL **$$**
(Map p48; ☑ 01-535 205; www.winnerinnmyan mar.com; 42 Than Lwin Rd, Bahan; s/tw/d from US$50/60/70; ❋@🛜) This low-slung building is in a quiet, leafy suburb and has spotless rooms with old-fashioned desks and pictures on the walls. The communal areas have plenty of well-positioned chairs waiting for you to collapse into them with a book.

Merchant Hotel HOTEL **$$**
(Map p48; ☑ 01-544 426; www.merchantyangon. com; 67/71 New Yaytershay Rd, Bahan; r from US$65; ❋@🛜) While there are plenty of colourful canvases decorating the corridors and rooms of this self-styled 'contemporary art boutique' hotel, the overall feel is tacky, reinforced by walls of fake greenery in the restaurant area. Still, it's a great location and offers an expansive astro-turfed roof with close-up Shwedagon views. The cheapest rooms are windowless.

Rose Garden Hotel HOTEL **$$**
(Map p48; ☑ 01-371 992; www.theroseyangon. com; 171 Upper Pansodan Rd, Dagon; r/ste from US$160/250; ❋@🛜🏊) After standing half-built for years, the mammoth Rose Garden is up and running and offering decent standard rooms and facilities on a rather grand scale. Rooms offer big walk-in showers and teak floors with tasteful black-and-white photos for decoration.

My Hotel HOTEL **$$**
(Map p48; ☑ 01-230 4445; www.myhotelmyanmar. com; 275 Bargayar Rd, Sanchaung; r from US$90; ❋@🛜) Traditional woven fabrics add a nice touch to pillows and bed runners in the spacious rooms at this pleasant hotel on the fringe of Sanchaung. Many rooms and the top-floor restaurant have superb views of Shwedagon across nearby People's Park.

Hotel Esperado BUSINESS HOTEL **$$**
(Map p48; ☑ 01-861 9486; www.hotelesperado. com; 23 Kan Yeik Thar Rd, Mingalar Taung Nyunt; r/ste from US$130/280; ❋@🛜) It's worth paying a little extra for the front-facing rooms at this modern business hotel as they offer spectacular views across Kandawgyi Lake towards Shwedagon. Everyone gets to see this beguiling panorama from the rooftop restaurant and bar where breakfast is served. If you like the art displayed in the hotel corridors, it's all for sale.

Hotel M HOTEL **$$**
(Map p48; ☑ 01-230 6227; www.hotelminmyan mar.com; 29 Kanbawza St, Bahan; r from US$170; ❋@🛜🏊) With all the images of Marilyn Monroe plastered around this new, reasonably chic property, you'd be forgiven for thinking the owners had named it after the Hollywood actress. Rooms are a decent size and there's a nice pool set in a leafy garden, plus a small gym.

Classique Inn HOTEL **$$**
(Map p48; ☑ 01-525 557; www.classique-inn.com; 53B Shwe Taung Gyar Rd/Golden Valley Rd, Bahan; r from US$70; ❋@🛜) Located in a secluded villa in the posh Golden Valley neighbourhood, this leafy, family-run place offers 11 cosy, attractive rooms, which vary greatly in size. Deluxe rooms have teak and bamboo furnishings. Warm service (including travel arrangements), good breakfast and a homey atmosphere are all pluses.

Chatrium Hotel HOTEL **$$$**
(Map p48; ☑ 01-544 500; www.chatrium.com; 40 Natmauk Rd, Tamwe; r/ste US$299/500; ❋@🛜🏊) Since Hilary Clinton stayed here there's been a steady stream of VIPs checking in. It's easy to see why. It might not be Yangon's most historic or charming hotel, but it's professionally run and offers more style than most at this price point. The large pool, gym and excellent spa are other pluses.

ⓘ YANGON FOR CHILDREN

While you might think twice at pushing a pram along downtown's crowded and cracked pavements, Yangon isn't such a bad place for a family vacation. You're likely to find baby-changing facilities at major shopping malls and top hotels. Kids of all ages will need some ground rules about hygiene, and should avoid approaching any of the many stray dogs you're likely to encounter.

There are good free outdoor playgrounds in Mahabandoola Garden (p40), People's Park (p51), where you'll also find the amusement park Natural World (p51), and at the Nat Mauk Rd end of Kandawgyi Lake (p51). A short taxi ride east of downtown there's a chance to splash around at **Yangon Waterboom** (☑ 09 190 616; www.yangonwaterboom. com; Shu Khin Thar Park, Yamone Nar Rd, Dowpone; adult/child Tue-Fri K20,000/15,000, Sat & Sun K25,000/20,000; ☉ 9am-7pm Tue-Sun) and go tenpin bowling at **Asia Point Bowling Centre** (☑ 09 79855 9233; View Point Amusement Park, Thaketa Shukhintha, Dawbon; K2500; ☉ noon-11pm). If you have a skateboard handy, then head over to the international-standard **Mya Lay Yone Skatepark** (www.facebook.com/pushingmyanmar; off Ba Yint Naung Rd, Kamayut) FREE where your kids can join local children and teens learning to skateboard.

Families recommend **Parami Pizza** (Map p52; ☑ 01-860 4809; www.paramipizza.com; 56 Sayar San Rd, Bahan; pizza K8000-17,000; ☉ 11am-11pm; ☎ 🅿 👪) not only for its food but also for its supervised indoor fun gym; the Ottoman Room in the nearby Acacia Tea Salon (p74) is covered with cushions, doubling as a romper room for energetic kids.

Summit Parkview
HOTEL $$$

(Map p48; ☑ 01-211 888; www.summityangon. com; 350 Ahlone Rd, Dagon; s/d from US$127/130; ✳ @ 🛜 🏊) Some of the ageing Summit's rooms have been refurbished; the best ones, for which you'll pay a small premium, overlook nearby Shwedagon Paya. The beds are big and the rooms sizeable by Yangon standards. The pool area was out of commission on our most recent visit. The upgrade is expected to be ready by the end of 2017.

🛏 Inya Lake & Greater Yangon

Thanlwin Guesthouse
GUESTHOUSE $

(Map p52; ☑ 01-542 677; www.thanlwinguesthouse. com; Y25 Pyinnyawaddy Estate, Yankin; dm/r with shared bathroom from US$17/40, r with private bathroom US$50; ✳ 🛜) Hidden away in a private housing estate behind the Sedona Hotel is this small, relaxed guesthouse with a good range of quality rooms. Parquet floors and ethnic photos on the two-storey house's walls add character, as does the bamboo-covered dining area in the garden where breakfast is served.

Yangon Airport Hotel
HOTEL $

(☑ 01-533 354; www.yangonairporthotel.com; 45-55 Airport Rd, Insein; r US$50; ✳ 🛜) If you need to be close by the airport, this no-frills but perfectly pleasant and clean hotel will serve your needs. It also provides free transfers to the airport around half a mile away.

Hotel Parami
HOTEL $$

(Map p52; ☑ 01-658 118; www.hotelparamiyangon. com; 2 Parami Rd, Mayangone; r/ste US$150/260; ✳ @ 🛜 🏊) It's a shame that a new condo rising beside Inya Lake now blocks this stylish hotel's view towards Shwedagon. However, the surroundings are very leafy and there's a pleasant rooftop pool and bar to compensate. Rooms are nicely designed and spacious.

Jasmine Palace Hotel
BUSINESS HOTEL $$

(Map p48; ☑ 01-230 4402; www.jasminepalace hotel.com; 341 Pyay Rd, Sanchaung; r from US$95; ✳ @ 🛜 🏊) You can't miss this golden tower looming over Pyay Rd and housing 255 spacious rooms, the best with views towards Shwedagon. Aimed at the business traveller, it's handily located midway between the airport and downtown. It offers good facilities including a partly covered pool, spa and gym.

Inya Lake Hotel
HOTEL $$

(Map p52; ☑ 01-966 2866; www.inyalakehotel. com; 37 Kaba Aye Pagoda Rd, Yankin; r/ste from US$140/260; ✳ @ 🛜 🏊) If you'd prefer chilling out in a serene lakeside location, this mammoth property, designed by a Russian in the 1950s, offers big, light-filled rooms with wooden floors and balconies with elegant minimalism. There's a good-sized pool and tennis courts.

Super Hotel
BUSINESS HOTEL $$

(Map p52; ☑ 09 79720 9000; www.superhotel.co.jp; 51D Kaba Aye Pagoda Rd, Mayangone; r from US$110;

✳ @ 🛜) This is super indeed and geared to Japanese businesspeople, with Japanese breakfast and rooftop communal bathing pools, both indoor and out. There's a choice of pillows and pyjamas for guests and many rooms have good views over Inya Lake.

Sedona Hotel
HOTEL **$$**

(Map p52; 📞 01-860 5377; www.sedonahotels. com.sg; r/ste from US$150/260; ✳ @ 🛜 ▣) You know exactly what you'll be getting at the Sedona: peace, quiet and professional service. The new Inya wing offers the spiffiest rooms, some with great views across to Inya Lake.

Bike World
Explores Myanmar Inn
GUESTHOUSE **$$**

(Map p52; 📞 01-527 636; www.bwemtravel.com; 10F Khapaung Rd, Hlaing; s/d US$50/70; ✳ @ 🛜) In a secluded location, and run by an Australian-Burmese couple as an extension of their bicycle-tour company, this inn offers functional private rooms. The singles are a little cramped, but the overall ambience is pleasant. There is a common room for hanging out in. A plus is the on-site pizza-delivery service.

🍴 Eating

Yangon's dining scene is the best in the country for quality and diversity. You'll find all the regional Myanmar cooking styles, such as Shan and Rakhine, plus an ever-expanding selection of international restaurants, including Thai, Japanese, Chinese, Korean, Italian and Indian. Eat early – by 10pm all but a handful of places will be closed.

Few of Yangon's top-end restaurants can justify their high prices when it comes to value for money. If a restaurant's menu quotes prices in US dollars, the bill will still be payable in kyat.

🍴 Downtown Yangon

★ Feel Myanmar Food
BURMESE **$**

(Map p42; 📞 01-511 6872; www.feelrestaurant. com; 124 Pyidaungsu Yeiktha St, Dagon; dishes from K1500, curries from K3800; ⊘ 6am-11pm; 🛜) This long-running operation is a fine place to start discovering Burmese cuisine. There's a big choice of freshly made dishes on display – just go up to the counter and point out what you'd like. All meals come with soup, a plate of salad veggies and a small dessert. Outside, more stalls sells sweets and other takeaways.

It's very popular at lunchtime with locals and foreign-embassy staff.

★ Nilar Biryani & Cold Drink
INDIAN **$**

(Map p42; 216 Anawrahta Rd, Pabedan; biryani from K2600; ⊘ 4am-11pm; 🗍) Giant cauldrons full of spices, broths and rice bubble away at the front of this Indian joint. It's always packed and with good reason: for this price, these biryanis are probably among the best your lips will meet. There are plenty of other delicious options on the picture menu at the counter – your meal will be brought to you.

Danuphyu Daw Saw
Yee Myanma Restaurant
BURMESE **$**

(Map p42; 📞 01-248 977; 175-177 29th St, Pabedan; dishes from K3500; ⊘ 9am-9pm; 🗍) This traditional shophouse restaurant is the local's choice for decent Burmese food downtown. It's a little more expensive than similar places, but the various curries are tasty and all dishes are served with sides of soup (the sour vegetable soup is particularly good) and *ngapi ye*, a pungent dip served with parboiled veggies and fresh herbs.

There's a brief English-language menu, but your best bet is to choose directly from the selection of dishes behind the counter.

999 Shan Noodle Shop
NOODLES **$**

(Map p38; 130/B 34th St, Kyauktada; noodle dishes from K1500; ⊘ 6am-7pm; 🗍) A handful of tables are crammed into this tiny, brightly coloured eatery behind City Hall. The menu includes noodles such as *Shàn k'auq swèh* (thin rice noodles in a slightly spicy chicken broth) and *myi shay* (Mandalay-style noodle soup), and tasty non-noodle dishes such as Shan tofu (actually made from chickpea flour) and delicious Shan yellow rice with tomato.

Myaung Mya Daw Cho
BURMESE **$**

(Map p38; 149 51st St, Pazundaung; noodles K700; ⊘ 6-9.30am) There are indoor seats but patrons here usually sit outside where the delicious *mohinga* – thin rice noodles in a spicy fish broth, topped with fresh coriander – is prepared and dished up every morning.

There's another branch near Shwedagon Paya.

Myaung Mya Daw Cho
BURMESE **$**

(Map p48; 📞 01-559 663; 118A Yay Tar Shay Old St, Bahan; noodles K700; ⊘ 5-11am) This famous place is a great breakfast stop before or after visiting Shwedagon Paya, specialising in *mohinga*. You can eat the fish-soup noodles inside or get them as takeaway outside for K300.

Aung Mingalar
Shan Noodle Restaurant
NOODLES $

(Map p42; Bo Yar Nyunt St, Dagon; mains K2000; ⊘7am-9pm; 📶) Open to the street on two sides, this is an excellent spot to indulge simultaneously in people-watching and noodle-slurping. It's a simple and easygoing restaurant with a cafe-like feel.

Nam Kham Family
Shan Restaurant
SHAN $

(Map p38; ☑ 09 3035 9584; 134 37th St, Kyauktada; noodles from K1000; ⊘6am-6.30pm Mon-Sat) This tiny restaurant split across two neighbouring units serves the usual Shan noodle dishes plus a variety of point-and-choose curries, soups, stir-fries and other dishes served over rice.

Cyclo
VIETNAMESE $

(Map p42; ☑ 01-251 062; www.cycloresto-yangon. com; 133 Lanmadaw St, Lanmadaw; pho from K3200; ⊘7am-10pm; 📶📶) One of the best places in town for a nourishing bowl of *pho* (noodle soup). The many options have a rich broth and you can choose from a variety of noodles. The menu also features spring rolls, salads and a number of more expensive grilled meat and hotpot dishes. This is also a fine spot for real Vietnamese coffee (K2000).

Cherry Mann
BURMESE $

(Map p42; 80 Latha St, Latha; mains from K3000; ⊘10.30am-11pm; 📶) Excellent and friendly Muslim restaurant; a fine spot for kebabs, curries and biryanis, with *paratha* (Indian-style bread) to accompany them. The kebabs are especially fine, but all the food is clean and tasty. You may have to wait for a table at busy times. No alcohol is served.

New Delhi
INDIAN $

(Map p42; ☑ 09 7320 1518; 274 Anawrahta Rd, Pabedan; curries from K2500; ⊘5.30am-9.30pm; 📶) It looks unprepossessing, but the Muslim-influenced South Indian dishes, such as a rich mutton curry, taste great. There are also meat-free options including *puris* (puffy breads), *idli* (rice ball), various *dosai* (savoury pancakes) and banana-leaf *thalis* (meals; K1500).

Craft
SINGAPOREAN $

(Map p42; ☑ 09 96060 8333; www.facebook.com/ craftmm; 33 Nawaday St, Dagon; mains K1500-4000; ⊘7am-11pm; 📶📶) Of the several new cafes and eateries that have sprung up around this busy corner in the Yawmingyi district, this is the largest and slickest – as you might expect from a Singaporean coffee-shop chain. The laksa noodles are perfectly fine, if not amazing, and you can also enjoy light bites such as *kaya* (coconut jam) on toast.

Kosan Cafe
INTERNATIONAL $

(Map p42; ☑ 09 42803 8032; www.kosanmyanmar. com; 108 19th St, Latha; ⊘1-11pm; 📶) The original Kosan has restyled itself into an all-day cafe serving snacks such as banana and honey toast and pancakes, since it's opened its Kosan Double Happiness Bar (p76) up the street. However, you can still just get a reasonably decent mojito here for K1000 and draught beer is K800.

Ingyin New South
India Food Centre
SOUTH INDIAN $

(Map p42; 232 Anawrahta Rd, Pabedan; mains from K800; ⊘5am-10pm; 📶) The cheery staff here do the crispiest and tastiest *dosai* (savoury pancakes) in central Yangon. It's a good place for a *thali* as well, and it has tea and Indian sweets if you require dessert.

Bharat Restaurant
SOUTH INDIAN $

(Map p38; ☑ 01-382 253; 356 Mahabandoola Rd, Kyauktada; mains from K800; ⊘6am-8.30pm; 📶) Specialising in southern Indian dishes, Bharat's tidy interior and marble-topped tables make a nice change from the long cafeteria-style tables at the Indian places on Anawrahta Rd.

★Rangoon Tea House
BURMESE $$

(Map p38; ☑ 01-122 4534; www.facebook.com/ rangoonteahouse; 1/F 77-79 Pansodan Rd, Kyauktada; mains from K4500; ⊘8am-10pm; 📶📶) This stylishly designed hipster teahouse is as popular with locals as it is with travellers. It serves traditional Burmese cuisine, locally inspired cocktails, and curries and biryanis. All the usual teahouse snacks are available – tea-leaf salads, samosas, *paratha* (Indian-style bread) and *bao* – but in bigger portions (hence the higher prices). And they're less oily than you'll get elsewhere.

The drinks are equally good, with the Mandalay rum sour especially potent. Cocktails start at K6500, but are half-price during daily happy hour from 4pm to 7pm. If you just want a cup of tea, you can get that too, although it will set you back K1500.

★Pansuriya
BURMESE $$

(Map p38; ☑ 09 77894 9170; www.facebook.com /pansuriyamyanmar; 102 Bo Galay Say St, Botataung; ⊘7am-10pm; 📶) An inspired addition to Yangon's modern Burmese restaurants, Pansuriya

LOCAL KNOWLEDGE

YANGON'S STREET EATS

Yangon's street-food options can be both overwhelming and challenging (pork offal on a skewer, anyone?). Here are the best places to sample some of our favourite street eats.

Samusa Thoke Vendor (Map p42; Merchant St, Pabedan; K500; ☺7am-6pm) Get *samusa thoke* – tasty samosas chopped up and served with fresh herbs and a thin lentil gravy – from this vendor near Mahabandoola Park.

Bein Mont Vendor (Map p38; cnr Bogyoke Aung San & Yay Kyaw Rds, Pazundaung; pancakes K200; ☺6.30-10.30am) Head to this vendor for *bein mont* – delicious sweet pancakes topped with nuts and seeds. They are served fresh off the grill by an *amay* (mother) who reputedly makes the best ones in Yangon. Ideal for breakfast on the go.

Mote Lin Ma Yar Vendor (Map p38; cnr Anawrahta Rd & 37th St, Kyauktada; K300; ☺8am-9pm) Come here for *mote lin ma yar*, nicknamed the 'couple's snack' because the two small mounds of the sticky rice flour, ginger, salt, onion and sugar mixture are grilled separately then combined into a single piece.

Grilled Snack Stalls (Map p42; 19th St, Latha; BBQ skewer from K400; ☺5-11pm) Every night, the strip of 19th St between Mahabandoola and Anawrahta Rds hosts dozens of stalls and open-air restaurants serving delicious grilled snacks.

Shwe Bali (Map p42; 112 Bo Sun Pat Rd, Pabedan; lassi from 600K per glass; ☺10am-10.30pm) Deliciously curdy glasses of the Indian yoghurt drink, lassi, are served here.

Buthi Kyaw Vendor (Map p38; cnr Anawratha & Thein Byu Rds, Pazuntaung; K1000; ☺4-9pm) For some of Yangon's crispiest battered and deep-fried chunks of gourd, head to this vendor. The snack is served with a spicy/sour tamarind dipping sauce.

Burmese Sweets Vendors (Map p42; Bogyoke Aung San Rd, Dagon; from K50; ☺9am-5pm Tue-Sun) In front of FMI Centre, a handful of streetside vendors sell delicious Burmese sweets ranging from *shwe-t'aumi'n* ('golden' sticky rice) to *mou'n-se'in-ba'un* (a type of steamed cake topped with shredded coconut).

trades on its evocative building's heritage and is plastered with memorabilia and art, some of it for sale. The curries and salads (try the tamarind-leaf one) are excellent.

⭐**Green Gallery** THAI **$$**
(Map p38; ☎09 3131 5131; www.facebook.com/yangongreengallery; 58 52nd St, Botataung; ☺noon-3pm & 6-9pm Tue-Fri, 1-3pm & 6-9pm Sat & Sun; ☎🖥) So popular it's a good idea to book ahead, this hole-in-the-wall place has bags of atmosphere and is run by Bo, a friendly young Myanmar woman who used to live in Thailand. The food, including curries, soups and salads, is superfresh, authentically spicy and comes in generous portions.

⭐**Shan Yoe Yar** SHAN **$$**
(Map p42; ☎09 25056 6695; www.facebook.com/shanyoeyar; 169 Wadan St, Lanmadaw; mains K2500-13,000; ☺7am-10.30pm; ☎🖥) A century-old wooden mansion has been expertly renovated into Yangon's most upmarket Shan restaurant. Among the delicious dishes on the menu are a luscious Mine Tauk aubergine curry and Inlay-style pork curry. Set menus start at K7000.

⭐**Gekko** JAPANESE **$$**
(Map p38; ☎01-386 986; www.gekkoyangon.com; 535 Merchant St, Kyauktada; mains US$8-12; ☺11am-11pm; ☎🖥) This justly popular and stylish restaurant and lounge bar is on the ground floor of the historic Sofaer building. Japanese dishes, such as sushi and grilled skewers of meat and veg, prepared in the open kitchen, are the mainstay. There are some Korean and Vietnamese foods on the menu, too. The best vibe is in the evenings, with live jazz every Friday from 7pm until 10pm.

Menya Koi Nobori JAPANESE **$$**
(Map p38; ☎09 79527 4691; 285 Mahanbandoola Garden St, Kyauktada; mains K3900-6500; ☺11am-midnight; 🖥) Although it doesn't look too promising, this humble *izakaya* (Japanese gastropub) serves some great food, including sashimi and sushi. Try the *tsukemen* – ramen (wheat noodles) served dry to be dipped in broth and finished with all kinds of toppings.

Gringos Chalingos MEXICAN **$$**
(Map p38; ☎01-245 631; www.facebook.com/gringos chilangos; 257 Bo Aung Kyaw St, Kyauktada; mains

K3000-5000; ⊙11am-11pm; 🛜📶) There has been a rash of Mexican restaurants breaking out across Yangon recently. This is our favourite, serving delicious, freshly made tacos, salads, tortas (sandwiches) and the like from an open kitchen. It's a stylish, two-level place with a long bar where you can enjoy beer cocktails and other drinks. Happy hour runs from 5.30pm to 7.30pm Monday to Friday.

Bijin
JAPANESE $$

(Map p42; ☑ 09 97065 3966; 26B Yaw Min Gyi St, Dagon; mains K3000-6000; ⊙5.30-11pm; 🛜📶) Look for the low white door to enter this convivial *izakaya* (Japanese gastropub), popular with Japanese expats. Sake and Kirin draught beer go nicely with the range of tasty small plates, including grilled aubergine with miso paste and minced chicken patties. Also try the *oden,* various foods simmered in a light stock.

Rasa Lasa
MALAYSIAN $$

(Map p38; ☑ 09 79884 4191; www.facebook.com/rasalasa.mm; 462 Thein Phyu Rd, Mingalar Taung Nyunt; mains K4500; ⊙8am-11pm; 🛜📶) This two-level, brightly decorated joint is the place to come for authentic and tasty Malaysian hawker food. On the menu are dishes such as the rice meal nasi goreng, curry laksa, stir-fried carrot cake and the dessert *cendol.*

The Taj
INDIAN $$

(Map p38; ☑ 09 97266 2518; www.facebook.com/the-taj-777003445715431; B9 Aung San Stadium North Stand, Upper Pansodan Rd, Mingalar Taung; mains K5000-12,000; ⊙11.30am-10pm; 📶) Some Indian expats swear the Taj's biryanis are the best in town: the chicken one we ordered was certainly packed with meat and flavourful spices and nicely presented. Another great dish was the *ma ki dal,* a creamy and moreish cup of stewed red lentils.

Kaung Myat
BURMESE $$

(Map p42; ☑ 09 3000 2687; 110 19th St, Latha; mains from K4000, barbecue from K400; ⊙noon-11.30pm; 📶) One of the most popular of the many barbecue restaurants on busy 19th St: this is where Anthony Bourdain dined when he passed through Yangon. Pick from the skewers on display, which include meat, seafood and veggie options, or order dishes from the menu. Draught beers for K750 and bottles for K2000 also pull in the traveller crowd.

Padonmar
BURMESE $$

(Map p48; ☑ 01-122 0616; www.myanmar-restaurantpadonmar.com; 105-107 Kha Yae Bin Rd, Dagon; mains K7000-15,000; ⊙11am-11pm; 🛜📶) Padonmar (meaning 'lotus flower') may be geared to the coach-tour crowd, but still serves high-quality, value-for-money food with set menus from K9000. In good weather you can dine in the garden, but the interior, painted with traditional scenic and figurative murals, is also lovely.

Be Le
CHINESE $$

(Junior Duck; Map p38; ☑ 01-249 421; Pansodan St Jetty, Kyauktada; mains from K2000; ⊙11am-10.30pm; 📶) Occupying one of the old ferry terminals, this pleasant Chinese restaurant is one the best places in town to soak up a river view (not that it has much competition!) and some breezes. The food is decent; most go for the roast duck (K8300 for a small portion).

It's part of the Golden Duck chain of restaurants, which also has a **branch** (Map p48; ☑ 01-240 216; Kan Taw Mingalar Garden, Shwedagon Pagoda Rd, Dagon; mains K2000-10,000; ⊙10am-10pm; 🛜📶) with a great view of the south of Shwedagon Paya.

Monsoon
SOUTHEAST ASIAN $$

(Map p38; ☑ 01-295 224; 85-87 Thein Byu Rd, Botataung; mains from K3000; ⊙10am-11pm; ✴❄🛜📶) Located in an airy colonial townhouse, Monsoon is perfect for those intimidated by Yangon's more authentic options. The menu also spans the rest of mainland Southeast Asia, with sections from Thailand, Vietnam, Cambodia and Laos.

Fat Ox Bar
PUB FOOD $$

(Map p38; ☑ 09 97580 0552; www.facebook.com/the-fat-ox-bar-yangon-507435879416989; 81 50th St, Botataung; mains K11,000; ⊙10am-1am; 🛜📶) Run by a British expat, this gastropub is roomy and has a convivial feel. It's likely the only place in Yangon you'll find a Cornish pasty and it also makes its own pies and sausages. You can even get an all-day English breakfast. Head here Sunday for a full-on roast lunch with pud. Note it's one of the few bars in the town that stays open after 11pm.

★Rau Ram
FUSION $$$

(Map p38; ☑ 09 45516 0657; www.rauram.com; 64B Yay Kaw St, Pazundaung; mains K12,000-25,000; ⊙5-11pm Tue-Sun; 🛜📶) Effortlessly channelling Southeast-Asian chic, this place east of downtown hits the mark with its Vietnamese-inspired menu made for sharing. The Hokkaido scallop crudo is a refreshing starter, the root-vegetable rendang and *bo kho* (beef brisket and oxtail stew with garlic bread) both satisfying mains.

Summer Palace
CHINESE $$$

(Map p42; 01-242 828; www.shangri-la.com/yangon/suleshangrila/dining/restaurants/summer-palace; Sule Shangri-la, Sule Pagoda Rd; mains US$5-15, dim sum buffet US$25; 11am-2.30pm & 5-10pm;) This high-quality lunchtime dim-sum buffet is an absolute steal. It has an extensive and delicious range of traditional Chinese dumplings and sweet and savoury snacks. And the deal also covers the full menu, which includes soups and main dishes. Even better is that the price drops to US$19 from June to September during rainy season.

Union Bar & Grill
INTERNATIONAL $$$

(Map p38; 09 42010 1854; www.unionyangon.com; 42 Strand Rd, Botataung; mains K9000-33,000; restaurant 10am-11pm, bar to 2am;) Occupying a corner of the Red Cross Building, this restaurant and bar oozes urban sophistication with nods to its dockside location in the artwork. The brasserie-style menu of appealing pizzas, burgers, smoked meats, and salads is high-quality comfort food.

Tin Tin
MEXICAN $$$

(Map p38; 09 97559 9856; www.facebook.com/tintinyangon; 116-118 Bo Galay Za St, Botataung; mains K7000-19,500; 11am-11pm;) Mexican food is the flavour of the moment for the moneyed and expats of Yangon. The team behind Union Bar & Grill and Gekko (p70) have been quick to pick up on the trend. They bring their sophisticated style to this narrow, two-level space where they serve decent renditions of tacos, burritos etc.

Le Petit Comptoir
FRENCH $$$

(Map p42; 09 97472 5870; http://lepetitcomptoir.strikingly.com; 42 Yaw Min Gee St, Dagon; mains K7000-16,000; 11am-10pm Tue-Sun;) A little rough around the edges, but that suits the relaxed style of this bistro specialising in simple home-style French cooking (several menu items hail from other parts of Europe, such as gazpacho and Greek salad). If you want to go traditional, stick with the beef bourguignon and luscious lemon tart.

Shwedagon Paya & Around

Xi Yang Yang
TAIWANESE $

(Map p48; 01-502 582; 4 Nyaung Tong Rd, Sanchaung; dumplings from K2000; 8am-10pm;) You can see the top-quality Taiwanese-style soup dumplings (*xiao long bao*) being made on the ground-floor kitchen of this superpopular Sanchaung eatery.

Agape
BURMESE $

(Map p48; 01-518 239; 18 Shwe Pyi Aye St, Sanchaung; mains K1000; 9am-8.30pm Mon-Sat;) The Sanchaung area is home to many Kachin people and this no-frills restaurant, near the Kachin church, serves the hearty, mildly spicy dishes typical of the northern Myanmar state. The minced chicken, noodles and dumplings are recommended.

Aung Thukha
BURMESE $

(Map p48; 01-525 194; 17A 1st St, Bahin; curries from K3000; 10am-9pm) This long-standing institution is an ideal place to sample a wide range of Myanmar food – everything from rich, meaty curries to light, freshly made salads. It's almost constantly busy, but manages to maintain gentle, friendly service and a palpable old-school atmosphere, making the experience akin to eating at someone's home.

Sharky's
INTERNATIONAL $$

(Map p48; 01-524 677; 117 Dhama Zedi Rd, Bahan; pizza from K11,000; 8am-10pm;) Ye Htut Win (aka Sharky) worked in catering for 20 years in Switzerland before returning to Yangon with the dream of making cheese and other quality eats. The result is this gourmet heaven – part deli, part restaurant serving excellent thin-crust pizza and other dishes with Sharky's own fine ingredients.

The tempting selection of gelato is reason enough to make a beeline here. There's also a **branch** (Map p38; 01-252 702; 81 Pansodan St, Kyauktada; pizza from K11,000; 8am-10pm;) on Pansodan St.

House of Memories
BURMESE, INTERNATIONAL $$

(Map p48; 01-525 195; www.houseofmemoriesmyanmar.com; 290 U Wi Za Ra Rd, Bahan; mains K6500-12,000; 11am-11pm;) Located off U Wi Za Ra Rd, in a mock-Tudor colonial villa stuffed with antiques and old photos (and including an office where General Aung San once worked), this is an interesting place to dine on dishes such as hearty beef curry and an authentically smoky-tasting grilled-eggplant salad. There's live music in the piano bar downstairs on Friday and Saturday evenings.

Rih Lake
BURMESE $$

(Map p48; 01-502 761; www.facebook.com/pages/therihlake; 67B Dhama Yone St, Sanchaung; mains K3000; 9am-8pm;) Named after a heart-shaped body of water in Chin State, the Rih Lake serves the tasty cuisine of the Chin, and also sells Chin costumes and fabrics. The excellent and nicely presented

SOCIAL ENTERPRISE RESTAURANTS & CAFES

Yangon has several restaurants and cafes set up as social enterprises or self-sustaining charitable businesses to help those in need.

LinkAge (Map p38; ☑ 09 4958 3618; 1st fl, 141 Seikkan Tha St, Kyauktada; meals K1000-3000; ⊙ 10am-10pm; ❀ 🖬) This colourful restaurant and art gallery is run by the social-development project Forever that helps train street kids and generates income for a shelter as well as other projects. Multicourse set Myanmar meals are a good deal at K6000 to K8000.

Yangon Bakehouse (Map p48; www.yangonbakehouse.com; Pearl Condo, Kaba Aye Pagoda Rd, Bahan; sandwiches & salads K2500-5000; ⊙ 7am-5pm Mon-Fri, 8am-5pm Sat; 🛜 🖬) A model enterprise of its kind, the Bakehouse works with disadvantaged women who have fallen on hard times because of debt or family problems. It pays its trainees twice the going monthly wage as well as providing counselling and work skills. The newer **branch** (Map p48; ☑ 09 97711 7932; 30 Inya Rd, Kamayut; mains from K4000-8250; ⊙ 7am-7.30pm; 🛜 🖬), tucked off Inya Rd (look for the sign near the Inya Hotel), is a chilled spot, perfect for a lazy breakfast, lunch or light bite of sandwiches, cakes and snacks.

Shwe Sa Bwe (Map p52; ☑ 09 42100 5085; www.facebook.com/shwesabwe; 20 Malikha St, Mayangone; lunch/dinner from K19,000/32,000; ⊙ noon-2pm & 6.30-9.30pm Tue-Sun, closed Jul & Aug; 🛜 🖬) Based in a beautifully decorated mansion, this restaurant and catering training school is the best fine-dining in Yangon for the price. No wonder the graduates go on to work at the city's best hotels and restaurants. You can choose from set meals of two or three courses. There's an intake of 22 students per year chosen from across Myanmar and coming from disadvantaged (but not destitute) backgrounds. Training is provided in both front-of-house and kitchen skills under the supervision of French chefs. As a prelude to a meal you can tour the premises and learn about the aims of the venture.

Cafe Genius (Map p42; www.cafe-genius.com; 220 31st St, Pabedan; ⊙ 10am-7pm; 🛜) This cute cubbyhole of a cafe offers decent Fair Trade coffee, tea, smoothies and sandwiches. Its coffee is sourced from the highlands of Shan State. Beans can be bought by the bag with 10% of sale proceeds donated to schools in the villages of farming families.

platter (K6500) is the way to go and features *sa buti* (corn soup) and millet plus rice.

Garden Bistro   INTERNATIONAL **$$**

(Map p48; ☑ 01-546 488; www.edenhotelsand resorts.com; Kandawgyi Relaxation Zone, cnr Bahan & Kan Yeik Thar Sts, Bahan; mains K4000-11,000; ⊙ 7am-10.30pm; 🛜 🖬) Popular for breakfast meetings with the embassy and business crowd (it does excellent dim sum until 2pm), the Garden Bistro is also a pleasant spot for a light meal or afternoon tea overlooking Kandawgyi Lake. There's direct access to the lakeside boardwalk here without having to pay the K300 entry fee applicable at the eastern end of the lake.

Edo Zushi   JAPANESE **$$**

(Map p48; ☑ 09 25904 0853; http://sagittarius-myanmar.com; 290B U Wi Za Ra Rd, Kamaryut; mains US$6-15; ⊙ 11am-11pm Mon-Sat, 5-9pm Sun; 🖬) This is one of Yangon's better Japanese restaurants and it's a stylish and relaxed place to sample good sushi, noodles, rice bowls and

tempura. Sit at the counter and watch the chefs at work, or get some privacy in one of the whitewashed mansion's several rooms.

Onyx Wine Tree Restaurant   STEAK **$$**

(Map p48; ☑ 01-542 543; www.facebook.com/ onyxmyanmar; 12B Bogyoke Museum Rd, Bahan; mains K8500-20,000; ⊙ 11am-11pm; 🛜 🖬) Good quality, value-for-money steak and other meat dishes are the order of the day at Onyx, housed in a stark, contemporary premises opposite the German embassy. Korean management means there are some Korean dishes (*bulgogi* and steamed ribs) on the menu, too. There's live music from 7.30pm to 10.30pm on Sunday.

Mañana   MEXICAN **$$**

(Map p48; ☑ 09 77739 3316; www.facebook. com/mañana-407737416082072; GA-15 Pearl Condo D, Kaba Aye Pagoda Rd, Bahan; mains K2000-7000; ⊙ 9am-10pm; 🛜 🖬) Mexican owner Nidia Amaya brings an authentic touch to Mañana's food and decor. All the usual south-of-the-border favourites are on the menu including tacos, tostadas and burritos. Some recipes veer less successfully into fusion territory. Happy hour for both food and drinks runs 3pm to 6pm.

Acacia Tea Salon PASTRIES $$

(Map p52; www.acaciateasalon.com; 52 Sayasan St, Bahan; mains from K8000; ◯bakery 7.30am-9pm, cafe 8.30am-10pm; 🛜🗷) This colonial-style tea salon, patisserie and restaurant occupies a chic whitewashed mansion. There's a takeaway section stocking all the lovely cakes, biscuits and savouries made here. For an indulgent time, treat yourself to one of its afternoon teas (K15,000 or K25,000). Its Moroccan room, covered in warm-coloured soft cushions, is a lovely chill-out space.

SK Hot Pot CHINESE $$

(Golden Happy Hot Pot; Map p48; ☑01-559 339; 18 Ko Min Ko Chin St, Dagon; mains K900-2300; ◯10.30am-11pm; 🗷) This vast hall is Yangon's most famous and most popular hotpot joint. Join hundreds of other diners in choosing the raw ingredients (on platters that are colour coded for their price, starting at K800 for vegetables) from the bank of freezers then cooking them in vats of a spicy Sichuan-style broth (K3800). A meal should be less than K6000.

Although it's open during the day, it's most fun to come at night when the main dining hall is packed.

Inya Lake & Greater Yangon

★ Le Planteur INTERNATIONAL $$

(Map p52; ☑01-514 230; http://leplanteur.net; 80 University Ave Rd, Bahan; mains bistro/restaurant from K10,000/39,000; ◯11am-2pm & 6-11pm; 🛜🗷) Le Planteur offers stylish dining in a serene location beside Inya Lake. There's a choice between the affordable bistro and the fancier, higher-priced restaurant, as well as a wine bar. The quick lunch deal (two/three courses US$12/18) is a great way to sample the food, or come for afternoon tea (2pm to 5.30pm, from noon Sunday). There's also a branch of souvenir shop Yangoods (p81) here.

★ Taing Yin Thar BURMESE $$

(Map p52; ☑01-966 0792; www.taingyinthar.com.mm; cnr May Kha & Parami Rds, Mayangone; mains K3000-6000; ◯10am-midnight; 🛜🗷) An airy wood-beamed dining hall with verandahs for outdoor dining is the setting for this pan-Myanmar restaurant. On the menu is a wide range of ethnic dishes that you're unlikely to find elsewhere, including plenty of vegetarian options.

It also claims to not use MSG, and to cook with pure peanut oil.

Minn Lane Rakhaing
Monte & Fresh Seafood SEAFOOD $$

(Map p52; ☑01-656 941; 16 Parami Rd, Mayangone; mains from K4500; ◯11am-10pm) Spice lovers should skip Thai and head directly to this boisterous Rakhine-themed grilled-seafood hall, popular with local families on a night out. The eponymous *monte* (actually *moún-di*) is a noodle soup (K600) featuring rice noodles and an intensely peppery broth. There's all manner of grilled fish and seafood, too, for reasonable prices. If you prefer your pepper on the side, order Rakhine salad, a spicy noodle salad.

Green Elephant BURMESE $$

(Map p52; ☑01-537 751; www.greenelephant-restaurants.com; 37 University Ave Rd, Bahan; mains K9000-15,000; ◯11am-11pm; 🛜🗷) Popular with tour groups, the Green Elephant is a safe but tasty-enough introduction to Myanmar cuisine. Four-course set menus start at K12,000 and it also does Thai and Chinese food. You'll also find a small crafts shop here.

Sabai@DMZ THAI $$

(Map p52; ☑01-860 5178; Mya Kyun Tha Park, Kaba Aye Pagoda Rd, Yankin; mains from K3500; ◯11.30am-2.30pm & 5-9.30pm; 🗷) The serene lakeside location of this Thai-owned place is the main draw, with dining on an open terrace in good weather. The menu is extensive and appetising. The range of salads is particularly impressive if you're craving a light lunch in the heat of the day.

There's a second **branch** (Map p48; ☑01-525 078; 30 Kaba Aye Pagoda Rd, Bahan; mains from K3500; ◯11am-2.30pm & 5.30-9.30pm; 🗷) tucked away in a leafy valley further south along Kaba Aye Pagoda Rd.

Alamanda Inn FRENCH $$$

(Map p48; ☑01-534 513; http://hotel-alamanda.com; 60B Shwe Taung Gyar Rd/Golden Valley Rd, Bahan; meals K9000-16,000; ◯7am-11pm; 🛜🗷) In a quiet residential neighbourhood, this breezy open-air restaurant and bar under a covered patio is a relaxing place to put the cares of Yangon behind you. The house specialities are tagines and couscous, but it also does good steaks and sandwiches, and killer cocktails.

L'Opera Restaurant
ITALIAN $$$

(Map p52; ☑01-665 516; www.operayangon.com; 62D U Tun Nyein St, Mayangone; mains K16,000-85,000; ⊙restaurant 11am-2pm & 6-10pm, cafe 8am-5pm; ✳🖢📶) One of Yangon's most elegant restaurants, L'Opera is staffed by well-trained and smartly dressed waiters, but more important is the Italian owner and chef's meticulous preparation. The outdoor garden seating is a bonus in good weather. Next to the bakery at the front of the property is the small cafe Il Fornaio.

🍷 Drinking & Nightlife

As with its restaurant scene, Yangon is experiencing a boom in drinking and nightlife options with some highly stylish places coming online. However, the vast majority of bars close by 11pm. Locals prefer hanging out in a teahouse, air-conditioned cafe, or a ubiquitous beer station, the favourite place to catch satellite-TV broadcasts of soccer matches.

There are several social events that, should you be in town at the right time, provide an opportunity to mingle with the local and expat population. There's a free drinks party every Tuesday night from 7pm at Pansodan Gallery (p80). It's a friendly scene with gallery owner Aung Soe Min and his expat wife helping the crowd connect with local culture and art. The couple also run **Pansodan Scene** (Map p38; www.pansodan.com; 144 Pansodan St, Kyauktada; ⊙10am-6pm), a community art space further down Pansodan St where larger events and various launches happen. Cultural centres are also big on the events scene with both **Institut Française** (Map p48; ☑01-536 900; http://institutfrancais-birmanie.com; 340 Pyay Rd, Sanchaung; ⊙library 9am-12.30pm & 2-6pm Tue-Sat; 🖢) and **Goethe Villa** (Map p48; www.goethe.de/ins/mm/en/index.html; 8 Komin Kochin Rd, Bahan) hosting lectures, movies, exhibitions and concerts; the latter's 'Berlin Berlin' club nights shouldn't be missed.

For more information on Yangon's nightlife and entertainment scene check out **Myanmore** (www.myanmore.com), which publishes a free, weekly pamphlet guide, available in several bars, cafes and restaurants around town, and the monthly magazine *In Depth*.

🍷 Downtown Yangon

★ Blind Tiger
COCKTAIL BAR

(Map p38; ☑09 78683 3847; www.blindtiger-yangon.com; 93/95 Seikkan Thar Rd, Kyauktada; cocktails from K6000; ⊙4-11pm; 🖢) Giant paintings of Myanmar girls, faces daubed in *thanakha*, dominate the walls of Blind Tiger's new, roomier digs. The onetime speakeasy has emerged from the shadows to lead the way as one of Yangon's top cocktail bars. All drinks are half-price during daily happy hour from 5pm to 7pm. It has great burgers and tapas too.

★ 7th Joint Bar & Grill
BAR

(Map p38; ☑09 20060 0552; www.facebook.com/7thjoint; 47th St, off Mahabandoola Rd, Botataung; ⊙5pm-1am) Did someone say reggae? Guess so, from all the posters of Bob Marley and reggae-inspired graffiti on the walls of this hopping bar. It's become infamous as one of the handful of downtown watering holes to keep late hours. Check its Facebook page for details of live gigs and open-mic nights.

Look for the scrum of taxi drivers on Mahabandoola Rd and you'll know you're at the right place.

★ Yangon Yangon
BAR

(Map p38; ☑01-255 131; www.facebook.com/yangonyangonrooftop; Sakura Tower, 339 Bogyoke Aung San Rd, Kyauktada; ⊙4-11pm; 🖢) Its tag line is '250ft in the sky' and you'll certainly know it when you step out on to the Sakura's Tower's open rooftop with powerhouse views across downtown Yangon. A great spot to catch sunset and party on into the night.

★ Fahrenheit
GAY & LESBIAN

(Map p38; ☑09 78063 5844; www.facebook.com/fahrenheitygn; Bogyoke Aung San Rd, Pazundaung; ⊙5-11pm, from 4pm Fri; 🖢) Fahrenheit has created a buzz as a LGBT-friendly bar with Queer Tuesday earmarked as an informal meet-up. It's a slickly designed space in which to sample Tex-Mex food and sip quirky cocktails such as the Beer-Rita, a beer combined with a frozen margarita. During Friday happy hour you can get cocktails for K3000.

The owners also run the popular **FAB club nights** (www.facebook.com/eventsyg) for the LGBT community, currently hosted at J-One Music Bar (p77).

Black Hat
BAR

(Map p42; ☑09 97027 0079; 143-149 Sule Pagoda Rd, Kyauktada; ⊙11am-11pm; 🖢) Burmese and Hollywood stars from the golden age of movies gaze down on customers at this quirky retro-styled 'wine bar and Burmese tapas restaurant' that is actually best visited for its reasonably priced cocktails, mocktails or juices.

LOCAL KNOWLEDGE

YANGON'S TOP TEAHOUSES

The following is our shortlist of Yangon's traditional teahouses – more than just places to sample a reviving brew, they're also great for breakfast, a snack or a light meal.

Lucky Seven (Map p38; 49th St, Pazundaung; snacks from K500; ☺6am-5.30pm Mon-Sat, to noon Sun; ☝) The most central of this small chain of high-class traditional tea shops, Lucky Seven is more than a cuppa pit stop. Its streetside tables are fringed by greenery and an ornamental pond. The *mohinga* (K600) is outstanding – order it with a side of crispy gourd or flaky-pastry savoury buns.

Thone Pan Hla (Map p42; 454 Mahabandoola Rd, Pabedan; snacks K400-600; ☺6am-7.30pm; ☝) Close to Sule Paya Thone, this is a good place to stop as you wander the downtown area. There's an English-language menu of teahouse staples including fried rice for breakfast.

Shwe We Htun (Map p38; 81 37th St, Kyauktada; snacks K300; ☺6am-6pm, to 1pm Sun) This buzzing old-school teahouse on the bookstall street serves better-quality food than most.

Man Myo Taw Café (Map p38; 347 Mahabandoola Rd, Kyauktada; snacks K500; ☺5am-8pm) Representing the Chinese end of the teahouse spectrum, this tidy place offers good steamed buns (both barbecued pork and bean), coffee and the usual range of Burmese teas.

Golden Tea (Map p42; ☎09 514 3197; 99 Bo Sun Pat Rd, Pabedan; snacks from K300; ☺6am-9pm; ☝) This centrally located Muslim-run place is a good choice for breakfast; later in the day it serves tasty *s'uanwi'n-mauk'in* (semolina cakes).

Yatha Teashop (Map p38; 353 Mahabandoola Rd, Kyauktada; snacks from K200; ☺5.30am-8.30pm Mon-Sat, to 12.30pm Sun) This classic Muslim-style teahouse provides fresh samosas and *paratha* (fried flatbread).

Golden Bell (Shwe Khaung Laung; Map p42; 365 Bogyoke Aung San Rd, Pabedan; snacks K450) You can get decent steamed buns, noodles, baked cakes and pastries, as well as the usual range of teas here. It's a handy rest spot when visiting Bogyoke Aung San Market.

See p383 for more about ordering food and drinks in teahouses.

Hummingbird COCKTAIL BAR
(Map p42; ☎09 96365 1501; www.facebook.com/hummingbirdyangon; 76 Pongyi St, Lanmadaw; ☺11am-11pm) Hands down the coolest bar in Chinatown, Hummingbird occupies a whitewashed three-storey colonial building. It was closed for renovations when we dropped by but should be back in business now, serving up cocktails and South American–inspired food, and hosting the occasional club night.

50th Street Bar & Grill BAR
(Map p38; ☎01-397 060; www.50thstreetyangon.com; 9-13 50th St, Botataung; ☺11am-midnight; ☝) One of Yangon's longest-established Western-style bars, in a handsomely restored colonial building, 50th Street continues to draw in a largely expat crowd with its mix of event nights, free pool table and sport on the TVs. Happy hour is 8pm to 10pm Monday to Friday and all day Sunday.

Kosan Double Happiness Bar BAR
(Map p42; ☎09 42803 8032; www.kosanmyanmar.com; 19th St, Latha; ☺11am-1am) At the quieter northern end of 19th St, this second branch of Kosan is more a traditional cocktail bar than its original nearby venue (p69). Cheap beers and cocktails draws in locals and travellers to create a double-happy atmosphere.

Wadan Jetty Beer Station BAR
(Wadan Jetty, Lanmadaw; ☺6am-9pm) Entering the docks from the main road, turn right at the waterfront to find this small beer station with a cluster of outdoor seating. It's a great spot for sunset drinks when you can also watch (or join in) with locals playing football or the local sport of *chinlon*.

Bar Boon BAR
(Map p42; www.facebook.com/barboonmyanmar; FMI Centre, 380 Bogyoke Aung San Rd, Pabedan; ☺7.30am-9pm; ☝) Recharge at this contemporary-styled cafe serving up great

coffee, iced tea and Dutch beer along with tasty but pricey snacks and pastries. The outdoor terrace offers decent people-watching near Bogyoke Aung San Market.

Press Office
CAFE

(Map p42; ☑ 09 26178 0491; www.thepressofficecafe.com; 31-4 Plaza 31, Bo Yar Nyunt St, Dagon; ⊙ 8am-8pm Mon-Fri, 9am-8pm Sat & Sun; 🛜) There's stiff competition for the top indie coffeehouse in the Yaw Min Gee area. This unpretentious place, favoured by expats and hipster Yangonites, gets our vote with its good selection of drinks, scrummy cakes and bakes, and support for local artists. There's plenty of table space upstairs to perch your laptop too.

Strand Bar
BAR

(Map p38; www.hotelthestrand.com; Strand Hotel, 92 Strand Rd, Kyauktada; ⊙ 10am-11pm; ☎) Primarily an expat scene, this classic bar inside the Strand Hotel (p41) offers an impressive range of foreign liquors behind its polished wooden counter.

Shwedagon Paya & Around

★ Rough Cut
BAR

(Map p48; ☑ 09 42116 7423; www.facebook.com/theroughcut.ygn; 19 Min St, Saunchaung; ⊙ 10am-10pm; ☎) Cafe by day, bar by night and art space throughout, this compact, comfy space is a home-from-home for Yangon's hipsters. Regular evening events that draw in a mixed local and expat crowd are Thursday's openmic night and Sunday's indie movies screenings. Arty photography hangs on the wall and it sells local indie-music CDs.

★ Penthouse
COCKTAIL BAR

(Map p48; ☑ 09 77123 9924; www.facebook.com/the-penthouse-201548120201732; 271-273 Bargaryar St, Sanchaung; ⊙ 11am-1am; ☎) At the time of research, this sophisticated rooftop space was one of the coolest spots to see and be seen in Yangon. You'll have to cram into one small corner of its spacious outdoor area to get a view of Shwedagon but otherwise the soft-cushioned horseshoe seating around low tables creates a mellow vibe for cocktail sipping and Myanmar star-spotting.

Lab Wine & Tapas Bar
WINE BAR

(Map p48; ☑ 09 25067 5289; www.facebook.com/thelabyangon; 70A Shwegondaine Rd, Bahan; tapas from K6000; ⊙ 5.30pm-midnight) The Lab has Tunisian owners so you'll find some Tunisian wines on the menu alongside the usual European suspects. It serves a decent range of

strong cocktails, too, with happy hour running 5.30pm to 7pm daily. The tapas dishes, including chorizo and potatoes, tortilla and garlic prawns etc, are also worth sampling.

Roof Alchemy
COCKTAIL BAR

(Map p48; ☑ 09 25427 2460; www.facebook.com/roofalchemy; Yangon International Hotel Compound, 330 Ahlone Rd, Dagon; ⊙ 5pm-2am) If you'd rather photograph your drinks than actually drink them, then this is place for you. A 'cocktail professor from Amsterdam' designed these crazy concoctions, involving smoke, homemade infusions and syrups, ice baking and other molecular monkey business. However, few live up to their visual promise on the menu – the lurid green-hued, rum-based 'Lonely Planet' included.

Still, it's a fun place and popular with a local crowd keen to have a good night out.

Vista Bar
COCKTAIL BAR

(Map p48; www.facebook.com/vistabaryangon; 168 Shwegondine Rd, Bahan; ⊙ 4.30pm-12.30am; ☎) The knockout view of glowing golden Shwedagon Paya by night is the big draw of this rooftop bar which has recently expanded its floor space. The cocktails, which start at K4000, are pretty decent, too.

Cask 81
BAR

(Map p48; ☑ 09 79981 8181; www.facebook.com/cask81; 81 Kaba Aye Pagoda Rd, Bahan; ⊙ 8am-midnight; ☎) Cafe by day, this two-level place, tucked off the main road, morphs into a sophisticated bar specialising in whiskey by night. Its comfy leather sofas will help cushion the impact of the hefty bill. Happy hour is 6pm to 8pm daily.

J-One Music Bar
CLUB

(Map p48; ☑ 01-546 954; http://jonemusicbar.com; 11F Bocho St, Bahan) This venue is currently used by **YG Events** (www.facebook.com/eventsyg) to host its FAB LGBT-friendly parties, usually on the last Saturday of the month from 10pm to 2am. Entry is K5000. Follow the signs pointing behind the Union Business Centre.

Winstar
BEER STATION

(Map p48; ☑ 09 862 2100; 17-20 Sanchaung St, Sanchaung; ⊙ 10am-11pm) Very much a local party scene, this street of beer stations and small restaurants is a short walk north of People's Park. Winstar is the biggest beer station along the strip. It has an English menu and a relaxed vibe popular with all ages. It's a great place to watch a soccer match.

Nervin Cafe & Bistro CAFE
(Map p48; www.nervincafe.com; Karaweik Oo-Yin Kabar, Kandawgyi Nature Park, Mingalar Taung Nyunt; mains K5000; ☺10am-10pm; ☏) The most contemporary of the cluster of cafes and restaurants at the east end of Kandawgyi Lake – an area you have to pay K300 to enter. Nervin offers caffeinated drinks and smoothies along with light meals such as club sandwiches with fries and fresh salads.

Coffee Circles CAFE
(Map p48; www.thecoffeecircles.com; 107 Dhama Zedi Rd, Bahan; mains K3650-5000; ☺7am-midnight; ☏) Located in front of Guest Care Hotel, this chic cafe-bar serves real coffee and has a menu ranging from Thai to burgers. There's an outdoor section on the roof from where you might just glimpse the tip of Shwedagon Paya.

🍷 Inya Lake & Greater Yangon

GTR Club CLUB
(Map p52; ☎09 513 5061; www.facebook.com/gtr club; 37 Kaba Aye Pagoda Rd, Mayangone; ☺9pm-3am) If you fancy mingling and dancing with Yangon's elite youth, this is the place to do it. There's a good sound system, drink prices are reasonable and there's usually no cover charge.

Fuji Coffee House CAFE
(Map p52; ☎01-535 371; 116 University Ave Rd, Kamaryut; ☺7.30am-10.30pm; ☏) Next to the US Embassy, this classy lounge-cafe has the atmosphere of an upmarket-hotel lobby.

☆ Entertainment

Decades of political repression have taken their toll on Yangon's rock and alternative live-music scene. The movement **Jam It!** (www.facebook.com/jamitmyanmar) aims to give young Burmese musicians and artists a voice and platform at acoustic gigs around the city – see their Facebook page for details. A compilation CD of Jam It! artists is for sale at the Rough Cut (p77), which is one of a handful of venues to hold regular open-mic nights; others include 7th Joint Bar & Grill (p75) and 50th Street Bar & Grill (p76).

★ Htwe Oo Myanmar

Traditional Puppet Theatre PUPPET THEATRE
(☎01-211 942; www.htweoomyanmar.com; 1st fl, 12 Yama St, Ahlone; adult/child K10,000/5000, minimum 2 people) Book ahead for this utterly charming cultural experience by Htwe and his family who stage traditional puppet shows in their front living room. They've travelled the world and won awards for their shows, which last around an hour. The shows include English explanations and you can inspect and play with the beautiful puppets.

If you'd like to buy one of the puppets – far superior in quality to those found in Yangon's tourist markets and shops – Htwe can arrange this with the master puppet maker for around US$60.

★ Thein Byu

Indoor Stadium SPECTATOR SPORT
(Map p48; Thein Byu Rd, Mingala Taung Nyunt) Venue for fast, and sometimes furious, *myanma let-hwei* (traditional kickboxing) matches – which are well worth attending. Depending on the contest, admission can range from free to K15,000 for general seating and up to K50,000 for VIP seating.

Bogyoke
Aung San Stadium SPECTATOR SPORT
(Map p38; ☎09 97207 6383; Gyo Phyu St, Dagon) This ageing 40,000-seat stadium, opposite Yangon Train Station, is the home ground for Yangon United FC and used for soccer matches in the Myanmar National League (www.themnl.com).

Karaweik Palace DANCE
(Map p48; ☎01-295 744; www.karaweikpalace. com; Kandawgyi Park Compound, Mingalar Taung Nyunt; dinner & show advance booking/at the door K33,000/37,000; ☺6-9pm) Although the buffet meal served is universally slated, the stage inside this concrete replica of a Burmese royal barge is the only place in Yangon where you can watch a cultural show of traditional dance and music.

National Theatre THEATRE
(Map p42; Myoma Kyaung Rd, Dagon) Opened in 1991, the National Theatre is a boxy modern structure, which little reflects traditional Burmese architecture. That said, the venue is increasingly being put to good use for a variety of shows, including international dance, drama and music, so it's worth inquiring what's on while you're in Yangon.

🛍 Shopping

Yangon has plenty of interesting art, furniture and antiques for sale, but much of it's too bulky for travellers and there are few bargains to be had. Prices for tailor-made clothes, however, are among the lowest in Southeast Asia and there's a growing number of outlets for quality traditional and contemporary crafts.

🔒 Downtown Yangon

⭐ Hla Day
ARTS & CRAFTS

(Map p38; ☏ 09 45052 1184; www.hladay myanmar.org; 1st fl, 81 Pansodan St, Kyauktada; ⊙10am-10pm) Meaning 'beautiful' in Burmese, Hla Day is a welcome addition to Yangon's growing band of social-enterprise shops. It offers quality contemporary and traditional handicrafts sourced from local producers often struggling to overcome disability, exclusion and poverty. You'll find colourful women's and kids' clothing, soft toys, stationery, jewellery, homewares and more here.

⭐ Pomelo for Myanmar
ARTS & CRAFTS

(Map p38; www.facebook.com/pomeloformyan mar; 89 Thein Pyu Rd, Botataung; ⊙10am-9.30pm) One of the best selection of contemporary handicrafts in Yangon – and all produced by projects supporting disadvantaged groups in Myanmar. Fall in love with the colourful papier-mâché dogs and bags featuring bold graphic images, as well as the exquisite Chin weavings and jewellery made from recycled materials.

⭐ Myanhouse
ARTS & CRAFTS

(Map p38; ☏ 09 7316 9056; www.facebook.com/ myanhouse-1568180660136840; 56-60 Pansodan St, Kyauktada; ⊙9am-7pm) Like a compact Bogyoke Aung San Market, this downtown emporium offers a wide range of handicrafts including puppets, rosewood boxes, woven baskets and an excellent range of local fabrics and *longyi* from across Myanmar.

⭐ Yo Ya May
ARTS & CRAFTS

(Map p42; 1st fl, front block, Bogyoke Aung San Market, Bogyoke Aung San Rd, Dagon; ⊙10am-5pm Tue-Sun) There's a wonderful array of hill-tribe textiles at this long-running stall in Bogyoke Aung San Market (p54). As well as weavings produced by the Karen and Kachin, you'll find colourful works of Chin State, such as blankets and shawls embroidered with scenes of village life.

It also has more stock in its **Chin Chili** stall further along the hall.

Myanmar Yanant Textile
CLOTHING

(Map p42; www.facebook.com/myanmaryanant; 24 West B Bogyoke Aung San Market, Bogyoke Aung San Rd, Dagon; ⊙9am-5pm Tue-Sun) Hand-woven and naturally dyed cotton from Meikhtila is the base for these traditional clothes and accessories such as scarves, caps and bags. The colour palette is a range of organic blues and browns derived from herbs, tree bark and other botanicals.

Shinon Myanmar
ARTS & CRAFTS

(Map p42; ☏ 09 42026 3133; 5/6 East A-block, Bogyoke Aung San Market, Bogyoke Aung San Rd, Dagon; ⊙9am-5pm Tue-Sun) Prettily packaged small souvenirs such as soaps, local teas, incense sticks and traditional cloth pouches are sold at this stall in the front block of the market.

Heritage Gallery
ANTIQUES

(Map p42; 1st fl, front block, Bogyoke Aung San Market, Bogyoke Aung San Rd, Dagon; ⊙10am-5pm Tue-Sun) Offers a good selection of authentic and reproduction antiques and retro items with an emphasis on lacquerware. Some local interest books, too.

Run YGN
FASHION & ACCESSORIES

(Map p38; ☏ 01-245 527; www.facebook.com/ run-ygn-clothing-offical-page-319873458182074; 335 Bo Aung Kyaw St, Kyauktada; ⊙10am-8pm) Local hip-hop star SZ is the owner of this hip streetwear brand. It offers high-quality T-shirts, tank tops, caps and backpacks emblazoned with bold and colourful Myanmar-themed designs.

Bagan Book House
BOOKS

(Map p38; ☏ 01-377 227; 100 37th St, Kyauktada; ⊙8.30am-6.30pm) This Yangon institution has one of the most extensive selections of English-language books on Myanmar and Southeast Asia. Genial owner U Htay Aung really knows his stock, which includes tomes dating to the 19th century.

Wired on 39
PHOTOGRAPHY

(Map p38; ☏ 09 25437 7278; www.donwright images.com; 200 39th St, Kyauktada; ⊙10am-6pm) Photographer Don Wright sells his appealing images of Myanmar people and places here along with his wire sculptures. Also here are locally tailored dresses and skirts made from fabrics sourced from various regions of Myanmar.

Don runs his photography courses and **tours** (1/2/3 or more people K50,000/45,000/ 40,000) from the gallery.

Turquoise Mountain Jewellery
JEWELLERY

(Map p42; http://turquoisemountain.org/project -entries/turquoise-mountain-myanmar; Belmond Governor's Residence, 35 Taw Win St, Dagon) A nonprofit NGO, Turquoise Mountain aims to help revive traditional crafts. Its first venture has been in jewellery, where local

DON'T MISS

CONTEMPORARY ART GALLERIES

Even if you're not in the market for a new piece of art, Yangon's galleries are great places to browse a varied range of exhibitions.

Lokanat Gallery (Map p38; ☎ 01-382 269; www.lokanatgalleries.com; 1st fl, 58-62 Pansodan St, Kyauktada; ⊙ 9am-5pm) **FREE** The grand dame of the art scene has been hosting shows, which change weekly, since 1971. It's worth visiting for a chance to peek inside the historic Sofaer's Building.

Pansodan Gallery (Map p38; ☎ 09 513 0846; www.pansodan.com; 1st fl, 286 Pansodan St; ⊙ 10am-6pm) Owner-artist Aung Soe Min stocks a huge variety of Myanmar contemporary and antique art, the latter including some truly unique antique prints, advertisements and photos that make wonderful souvenirs.

Myanmar Deitta (Map p38; ☎ 0-93173 6154; www.deitta.org; 3rd fl, 49 44th St, Botataung; ⊙ noon-5pm Tue-Sun) Named for the pali word for 'in front of one's eyes', Deitta is a non-profit working with local and international documentary photographers, filmmakers and multimedia artists. There's some fascinating work shown here that illuminates daily life in contemporary Myanmar in all its grit and glory.

Myanm/art (Map p38; https://myanmartevolution.com; 3rd fl, 98 Bo Galay Za St, Botataung; ⊙ 11am-5pm) This cutting-edge gallery, reading room and exhibition space also stocks some great reproductions of vintage tourism posters for Burma.

River Gallery (Map p38; ☎ 01-378 617; www.rivergallerymyanmar.com; Chindwin Chambers, 33/35 37th St, Kyauktada; ⊙ 10am-6pm) Started by New Zealander Gill Pattison in 2005, this classy gallery, with entrances both on 37th and 38th St, features the works of some 50 leading and emerging artists. Works, priced in US dollars, range from postcard sets to major sculptural installations.

New Zero Art Space (Map p42; www.newzeroartspace.net; 1st fl, 202 United Condo, Ah Lan Pya Pagoda Rd, Dagon; ⊙ 10am-5pm Tue-Fri) **FREE** Aiming to empower a new generation of artists, New Zero promotes edgier works in a variety of forms including sculptures, video, performance art and photography.

Gallery Sixty Five (Map p42; ☎ 01-246 317; www.gallerysixtyfive.com; 65 Yaw Min Gee St, Dagon; ⊙ 10am-6pm) On the ground floor of a colonial-era mansion, this private gallery is dedicated to revolving exhibits of contemporary creations.

KZL Art Studio & Gallery (Map p48; ☎ 01-230 4105; http://kzlartgallerymyanmar.com; 184/84A Shwe Tuang Gone/Golden Hill Rd, Bahan; ⊙ 10am-6pm) The home of artist Khin Zaw Latt, who has an international reputation, has a gallery of his and other artists' works, plus his studio space.

artisans are trained to produce pieces designed by ethical jeweller Pippa Small using gold and semiprecious stones.

You can observe the artisans at work in their small workshop next to the Loft Hotel (p63). The beautiful pieces are sold at a stall within the hotel.

Bookstalls BOOKS
(Map p38; 37th St, Kyauktada; ⊙ 9am-8pm) Old hardbacks, paperbacks and textbooks are jumbled on the ground and at stalls along this street near the junction with Merchant St and around the corner to Pansodan St. Several stalls have novels and nonfiction books in English and a few other European languages.

Globe Tailoring FASHION & ACCESSORIES
(Map p42; ☎ 01-253 924; 367 Bogyoke Aung San Rd, Pabedan; ⊙ 9.30am-5.30pm) Well regarded by local expats for women's and men's tailoring, this tailor is run by U Aung Soe. A shirt without/with fabric costs K10,000/15,000, trousers with fabric K30,000 and a suit around US$120.

Tip-Top Tailors FASHION & ACCESSORIES
(Map p38; ☎ 01-245 428; 287 Mahabandoola Rd, Botataung; ⊙ 9.30am-6pm Mon-Sat) Three generations of the same family have run this reliable tailor shop. Bring them your own fabric and they can craft a shirt from as little as K6000. Trousers cost K13,000.

Shwedagon Paya & Around

★ FXB Showroom   ARTS & CRAFTS
(Map p48; ☑ 01-556 324; www.fxb.org/programs/
myanmar; 294/3 Shwe Gon Daing Rd, Bahan;
☺ 9am-5.30pm) The showroom of this international NGO, dedicated to fighting poverty and
AIDS, has products made from locally woven
cotton in myriad colours, including adorable
soft toys, cushions, rugs and other crafts. It
also sells furniture. Profits are used for training, education and community programs.

Yangoods   FASHION & ACCESSORIES
(Map p48; ☑ 09 26107 6370; www.yangoods.com;
62 Shan Gone St, Sanchaung; ☺ 11am-8pm) This
accessories and souvenirs brand is known
for its sepia portraits and images of old Burma jazzed up with pop-art colours. It offers
high-quality bags, pouches, cushions and
stationery among other things.

This is its main branch but it also has outlets in Bogyoke Aung San Market (p54) and
Le Planteur (p74).

Nandawun   GIFTS & SOUVENIRS
(Map p48; ☑ 01-221 271; www.myanmarhandi
crafts.com; 55 Baho Rd, Ahlone; ☺ 9am-6pm) This
house-bound shop spans two storeys and just
about every Myanmar souvenir, from lacquer
vessels to replicas of antique scale weights.
The upstairs bookshop has a good selection
of titles on obscure Myanmar topics.

Monument Books   BOOKS, TOYS
(Map p48; ☑ 01-536 306; www.monument-books.
com; 150 Dhama Zedi Rd, Bahan; ☺ 8.30am-
8.30pm) A modern and well-stocked bookshop. In addition to a good selection of books
on local and international topics, there's a
reasonable selection of Western toys on the
2nd floor.

Patrick Robert   HOMEWARES
(Map p48; ☑ 01-513 709; Mangosteen Mansion, 24
Inya Myaing Rd, Bahan; ☺ 10am-5pm Mon-Sat) The
former home of the French designer who restored the Governor's Residence in the 1990s
has a large showroom offering many attractive gifts and decorative home items. Most of
the pieces are locally made and use materials
such as mother-of-pearl, lacquer and teak.

Marketplace by CityMart   FOOD & DRINKS
(Map p48; Dhama Zedi Rd, Bahan; ☺ 9am-9pm)
One of the best-stocked outlets of Yangon's
top supermarket chain offers a complex that
also sports the **Popular** bookstore (with a
reasonable selection of English-language

titles), and **Ananda Coffee & Cocoa**, selling
locally produced coffee.

Inya Lake & Greater Yangon

Augustine's Souvenir Shop   ANTIQUES
(Map p52; ☑ 01-524 052; www.augustinesouvenir.
com; 25 Thirimingalar St, Kamayut; ☺ 11.30am-7pm
Mon-Fri, 2-7.30pm Sat & Sun) One of Yangon's
most captivating shopping destinations is
split between the narrow tall white house
and the store room opposite. A virtual museum of Myanmar antiques, there's a particular emphasis on wooden items, including
carved figures, chests and wall hangings.

Elephant House   ARTS & CRAFTS
(Map p52; www.elephant-house.com; 37 University Ave Rd, Bahan; ☺ 10am-9pm) Alongside the
Green Elephant (p74) restaurant, this shop
sells a small selection of Burmese housewares,
primarily high-quality and attractive lacquerware and rattan baskets, bowls and the like.

Myanmar Plaza   MALL
(Map p52; 92 Kaba Aye Pagoda Rd, Yankin; ☺ 9am-
9pm) Anchoring a new business tower and
hotel complex, this five-floor shopping mall
is the place to head if you're in search of
bland international brand-name anonymity
and a bunch of eating and cafe options.

Fashion and souvenir brand Vestige has
an outlet with a so-so cafe here.

Vestige   FASHION & ACCESSORIES
(Map p52; ☑ 09 25107 7462; www.vestigemyan
mar.com; 12 Parami Rd, Mayangone; ☺ 9am-5pm)
Vestige stocks Myanmar-themed T-shirts,
bags, stationery, tea and other souvenir
goods that mix contemporary and traditional styles. It also sells Portuguese wines.

Nagar Glass Factory   GLASS
(Map p52; ☑ 01-526 053; 152 Yaw Gi Kaung Rd,
Hlaing; ☺ 8am-4pm) In operation from 1957
until 2008, when Cyclone Nargis destroyed
its production facilities, the factory still
has an enormous stock of glass in shades
of green, blue, white and red (the most expensive) scattered in heaps throughout its
jungly grounds. It's an extraordinary place
to explore but do douse yourself in mosquito
repellent before entering.

Junction Square   MALL
(Map p48; http://junctioncentregroup.com/junction-
square.html; Kyun Taw Rd, Hlaing; ☺ 9am-10.30pm;
🛜) One of Yangon's fanciest shopping malls
is worth a mooch for fashions and other
items, plus its onsite multiplex cinema.

ℹ Information

DANGERS & ANNOYANCES

You are far less likely to be robbed here than in almost any other big city in Southeast Asia. Having said that, rich foreigners and badly lit side streets at night don't mix, and you should be careful at such times.

A far bigger danger is getting hit by a motorist, stumbling on the uneven paving slabs or even disappearing completely into a sewage-filled pothole. Keep your eyes peeled for such obstacles and carry a torch at night.

Treat taxi touts and guides on the Dalah ferry with caution – some, in conjunction with the trishaw and motorbike-taxi drivers, have been known to rip off the unsuspecting.

EMERGENCIES

Your home embassy may be able to assist with advice during emergencies or serious problems.

There isn't always an English-speaking operator on the following numbers; you might need the help of a Burmese speaker.

Ambulance	☑ 192
Fire	☑ 191
Police	☑ 199

GAY & LESBIAN TRAVELLERS

Same-sex sexual activity remains illegal in Myanmar. The Buddhist faith also takes a dim view of homosexuality. Even so, the ongoing political reforms and associated freedoms in media and civil rights have allowed the previously superdiscrete LGBT community to be become more visible. Yangon celebrated its first gay pride in 2012 and the &Proud (p62) LGBT film festival is a fixed point on the city's calendar.

Social enterprise YG organises the monthly **Fab Party** (www.facebook.com/eventsyg) for the LGBT community and friends, and Tuesday is queer night at Fahrenheit (p75). For more information on LGBT issues in Myanmar, see the website of local human-rights project **Colours Rainbow** (www.colorsrainbow.com).

INTERNET ACCESS

Nearly all hotels and many restaurants, cafes and bars offer free wi-fi; there's even free wi-fi at Shwedagon Paya. There are also plenty of internet shops around town. It's inexpensive to pick up a SIM card and data package for your smartphone.

Server speeds have improved, but still tend to be frustratingly slow in comparison to almost any other country – this is not the place to download movies.

MEDICAL SERVICES

There are several private and public hospitals in Yangon, but the fees, service and quality may vary. There are also some useful pharmacies in town including ones in CityMart supermarkets – you'll find these at the **Parkson Mall** (Map p42; FMI Centre, 380 Bogyoke Aung San Rd, Dagon; ⊗8am-5pm) and Marketplace by CityMart (p81).

AA Pharmacy (Map p38; ☑ 01-253 231; 142-146 Sule Paya Rd, Kyauktada; ⊗8am-9pm) Just north of Sule Paya.

International SOS Clinic (Map p52; ☑01-657 922; www.internationalsos.com; Inya Lake Hotel, 37 Kaba Aye Pagoda Rd, Mayangone) Your best bet in Yangon for emergencies, this clinic claims to be able to work with just about any international health insurance and has a 24-hour emergency centre.

Pun Hlaing International Clinic (Map p42; ☑ 01-243 010; http://punhlaingsiloamhospitals.com; 4th fl, FMI Centre, Bogyoke Aung San Rd, Dagon; ⊗9am-7pm Mon-Sat, 10am-7pm Sun) Reliable, centrally located healthcare.

Yangon General Hospital (Map p42; ☑01-256 112; Bogyoke Aung San Rd, Pabedan) The biggest hospital in Myanmar.

MONEY

You'll get the best rates for changing money at the airport and at official bank exchange counters in places such as Bogyoke Aung San Market and Shwedagon Paya.

There are many ATMs dotted around Yangon that accept international Visa and MasterCards; there's a K5000 charge for using these ATMs.

POST

Central Post Office (Map p38; 39-41 Bo Aung Kyaw St, cnr Strand Rd, Kyauktada; ⊗7.30am-6pm Mon-Fri) Stamps are for sale on the ground floor, but go to the 1st floor to send mail.

DHL (Map p42; ☑ 01-215 516; www.dhl.com; 58 Wadan St, Lanmadaw; ⊗8am-6pm Mon-Fri, to 2pm Sat) Courier and logistics company that sends parcels and mail worldwide.

TOURIST INFORMATION

Ministry of Hotels & Tourism Tourist Information Centre (MTT; Map p38; ☑01-252 859; www.myanmartourism.org; 118 Mahabandoola Garden St, Kyauktada; ⊗9am-4.30pm) Can answer some of your questions about Yangon and travel around Myanmar and has some official leaflets and free maps. It no longer offers its own tourism products and will refer you to other travel agents for specific assistance.

USEFUL WEBSITES

Coconuts Yangon (http://yangon.coconuts.co) Weekly news snippets from Yangon and across Myanmar.

Myanmore Yangon (www.myanmore.com/yangon) Best source for discovering what's going on in the city. Also publishes a free weekly printed leaflet and the monthly *In Depth* magazine.

Yangon Life (www.yangonlife.com.mm) Packed with plenty of useful info.

Yangonite (www.yangonite.com) Expat-authored site with plenty of listings and other features.

ℹ Getting There & Away

AIR

Yangon International Airport (☎ 01-533 031; Mingalardon; ☎) is Myanmar's main international gateway and hub for domestic flights.

Airlines here include **Air Bagan** (☎ 01-504 888; www.airbagan.com), **Air KBZ** (☎ 01-372 977; www.airkbz.com), **Air Mandalay** (☎ 01-525 488; www.airmandalay.com), **Asian Wings** (☎ 01-516 654; www.asianwingsairways.com), **Golden Myanmar Airlines** (☎ 09 97799 3000; www.gmairlines.com), **Mann Yadanarpon Airlines** (☎ in Yangon 01-656 969; www.airmyp.com), **Myanmar National Airlines** (Map p38; ☎ 01-378 603; www.flymna.com; 104 Strand Rd, Kyauktada) and **Yangon Airways** (☎ 01-383 100; www.yangonair.com).

BOAT

There are several jetties along the Yangon River, but those interested in travelling by boat only need to be familiar with three – all other departure points are for cargo or routes that don't allow foreign passengers.

Lan Thit Jetty (Map p42) From here, **IWT** (Inland Water Transport; Map p42; Wadan jetty) runs ferries to the Delta towns of Labutta, Myaungmya and Hpayapon. Check here for the schedule and to buy tickets.

Pansodan St Jetty (Map p38; Strand Rd, Kyauktada) The jumping-off base for ferries to **Dalah** (p51).

Sin Oh Dan Jetty (Map p42; off Strand Rd, Latha) Used by private ferry boats to delta towns including Bogalay.

A few privately owned companies operate luxury cruises (p422) between Yangon, Bagan and Mandalay.

Myanma Five Star Line (Map p38; ☎ 09 5129 5279; www.fasa.org.sg; 132-136 Thein Byu Rd, Botataung) Check with this company about whether it's possible to hop on one of their cargo ships heading to other ports around Myanmar.

Shwe Pyi Tan Express (Map p42; ☎ 01-230 3003; www.shwepyitan.com; Phone Gyi St) Runs daily express boats to Bogalay from Yangon's Phone Gyi Jetty.

BUS

There are two major bus terminals that service Yangon:

Aung Mingalar Bus Terminal (Aung Mingalar St, Mingaladon) In the city's northeast and for bus lines leaving for the northern part of Myanmar, as well as for Kyaiktiyo (Golden Rock), Mawlamyine (Moulmein) and destinations to the south. A taxi here from downtown Yangon costs K7000 and takes around 45 minutes to one hour.

Hlaing Thar Yar Bus Terminal (Pathein Rd, Haing Thar Yar) For travel to Ayeyarwady Division and destinations west of Yangon including Chaung Tha Beach, Ngwe Saung Beach and Pathein. By taxi (K7000) the terminal is 45 minutes to one hour west of the city centre across the Hlaing River.

Most signs at the bus terminals are in Burmese; however, English-speaking touts anxious to steer you in the right direction are in abundance. To avoid the hassle and attention, make sure your taxi driver knows where you want to go and, even better, the name of the specific bus company. Showing the driver your ticket will do; if you don't have a ticket, ask a Burmese speaker to write the information on a slip of paper.

Keep in mind that journey times can differ immensely from the estimates we've given, and depend on road conditions and the health of your bus.

Many hotels and travel agencies can book tickets for you and several agents and bus companies have offices alongside Bogyoke Aung San Stadium (p78); expect to pay a couple thousand kyat more here than if you buy tickets at the stations – a few bus companies offer transfers from the stadium to the bus stations, which can be handy.

Bus companies with offices at the Bogyoke Aung San Stadium:

Elite Express (Map p38; ☎ 09 97783 8644; Aung San Stadium, Dagon) Runs high-quality air-con buses to Bagan, Mandalay, Monywa, Nay Pyi Taw and Taunggyi.

Mandalar Minn (Map p38; ☎ 09 7323 1000; Aung San Stadium, Dagon) Departures for Bagan, Mandalay and Pyin Oo Lwin.

Shwe Mandalar (Map p38; ☎ 01-706 071; Aung San Stadium, Dagon) Departures for Bagan, Mandalay and Pyin Oo Lwin.

Teht Lann Express (Map p38; ☎ 01-375 939) Departures for Lashio, Mandalay and Pyin Oo Lwin.

TRAIN

Yangon train station (Map p38; 📱 01-251 181; Khun Chan St, Mingalar Tuang Nyunt; ⊘ 6am-4pm) is a short walk north of Sule Paya; advance tickets should be purchased at the adjacent **Myanmar Railways Booking Office** (Map p38; Bogyoke Aung San Rd; ⊘7am-3pm), where you can also check the latest timetables.

Major destinations that can be reached by daily departures from Yangon include Bagan, Bago, Kyaikto, Mandalay, Mawlamyine, Nay Pyi Taw, Pyay, Taungoo and Thazi.

YANGON TRANSPORT CONNECTIONS

The following shows travel times and costs between Yangon and Myanmar's main destinations.

DESTINATION	BUS	TRAIN	AIR
Bago	K4000; 2½hr	2hr; ordinary/upper class K600/1200	
Chaung Tha Beach	K10,000; 7hr		
Dawei	K15,300; 16hr		40min; US$100
Heho (for Inle Lake & Kalaw)			1hr 10min; US$84
Hpa-an	ordinary/VIP bus K7000/15,000; 7-8hr		
Hsipaw	ordinary/VIP K15,000/20,300; 15hr		
Kalaw	ordinary/VIP K15,000/18,500; 10-12hr		
Kyaikto	5hr; K8000	4-5hr; ordinary/upper class K1200/2400	
Lashio	ordinary/VIP K15,000/20,300; 15hr		1hr 45min; US$136
Loikaw	19hr; K13,300		1hr; $100
Mandalay	ordinary/VIP K11,000/20,500; 9hr	15½hr; ordinary/upper class/sleeper K4650/9300/12,750	1hr 25min; US$85
Mawlamyine	ordinary/VIP K6000-10,000; 7hr	9-11hr; K2150/4300	
Myitkyina	ordinary/VIP K38,000/48,000; 22hr		1hr 40min; US$120
Nay Pyi Taw	ordinary/VIP K7200/9000; 5-6hr	9hr; ordinary/upper class/sleeper K2800/5600/7700	1hr; US$111
Ngwe Saung Beach	K10,000; 6-7hr		
Nyaung U (for Bagan)	K15,500; 10hr	16hr; ordinary/upper class/sleeper K4500/6000/16,500	70min; US$100-110
Pathein	K7000; 4hr		
Pyay	K5500; 6hr	7-8hr; ordinary K1950	
Sittwe	K21,000; 24hr		1hr 50min; US$106
Taunggyi (for Inle Lake)	ordinary/VIP K15,000/18,500; 12hr		70min; US$130 (to Heho)
Taungoo	K4500; 6hr	7hr; ordinary/upper class/sleeper K2000/4000/12,750	
Thandwe (for Ngapali)	K15,000; 14hr		50min; US$101

Though inexpensive, trains are slow, uncomfortable and tend to be plagued by delays.

ⓘ Getting Around

TO/FROM THE AIRPORT

Taxi drivers will approach you before you exit the airport terminal. The fare for a ride from the airport to downtown Yangon (12 miles) is around K8000 and can take up to an hour or more, if traffic is heavy.

BUS

Yangon has scores of competing private buses. They tend to be old and packed to the rafters. Routes are confusing and there's virtually no English, spoken or written. If you're determined, the typical fare within central Yangon is K100 (use small bills – bus conductors don't tend to have change). Prices often double at night, but they're still cheap and still crowded.

A positive development, however, is the quasi-public Bus Rapid Transit (BRT) system that started in February 2016. These modern, yellow, air-conditioned buses run along two routes through downtown Yangon and to the north of the city. Pay the driver, either with the exact K300 fare or with a prepaid card (K1500 before you add credit; can be bought from ticket centres including at Botahtaung, Myangigon and Hledan). Unlike private buses, BRT buses should be boarded at the front and exited through the middle doors.

TAXI

Yangon taxis are one of the best deals in Asia, despite not using a meter. Most drivers speak at least some English (although it's advisable to have someone write out your destination in Burmese) and they are almost universally honest and courteous.

All licensed taxis have a visible taxi sign on the roof, but many other drivers will let you negotiate a fare.

The following should give you an idea of what to pay: a short hop (such as from the Strand to Bogyoke Market) will be K1500; double this distance will be K2000; from downtown to Shwedagon Paya and the southern half of Bahan township will be K3000 depending on the state of traffic; from downtown to the Inya Lake area costs K4000.

From downtown to either bus terminal, drivers ask for K7000 and the trip takes from 45 minutes to an hour. You can also hire a taxi for about K5000 an hour. For the entire day, you should expect to pay around K40,000 depending on the quality of the vehicle and your negotiating skills. Be sure to work out all details before you agree to a price and itinerary.

For all types of taxi, the asking fares usually leap by 30% or so after sunset and on weekends. Late-night taxis – after 11pm or so – often cost double the day rate, mainly because the supply of taxis is considerably lower than in the day, so the drivers are able to charge more.

CAR

Rates for hiring a car and driver and including petrol can be as low as US$19.50 (four hours) or US$32.50 (eight hours) around Yangon with an online agency such as **Flymya** (Map p42; ☑ 09 79797 8881; https://flymya.com; Lanmadaw Plaza, Latha) or **Oway** (Map p48; ☑ 09 45045 0601; www.oway.com.mm; 9th fl Grand Myay Nu Tower, 6/38 Myay Nu St, Sanchaung). Cars and drivers can also be arranged through a travel agent or hotel front desk.

TRAIN

Yangon Circle Line (p59) loops out north from Yangon to Insein, Mingaladon and North Okkalapa townships and then back into the city, taking around three hours for the full circuit.

TRISHAW

In Myanmar, trishaw passengers ride with the driver, but back-to-back (one facing forward, one backward). These contraptions are called *saiqka* (as in sidecar) and to ride one costs about K1000 for short journeys. Given the heaviness of downtown Yangon's traffic during the day, you may find trishaw drivers reluctant to make long journeys across town at this time.

Southwestern Myanmar

Best Places to Eat

➡ Shwe Ya Min Restaurant (p101)

➡ Ume Restaurant & Bar (p103)

➡ Shwe Ayar (p97)

Best Places to Sleep

➡ Akariz Resort (p100)

➡ Amazing Chaung Tha Resort (p101)

➡ Hill Garden Hotel (p100)

➡ Bay of Bengal Resort (p103)

➡ Emerald Sea Resort (p103)

Why Go?

South and west of Yangon is the Ayeyarwady Delta (ဧရာဝတီ), a stunning patchwork of greenery floating on rivers, tributaries and lakes that stretches to the Bay of Bengal. A key rice-growing area, the delta is also home to historic towns such as Pathein, which makes the best base for exploring the region, and Thanlyin. In the far west of the delta are the beach resorts of Chaung Tha and Ngwe Saung, long-time favourite sea and sand escapes for Yangonites.

A couple of hours east of Yangon is Bago (ပဲခူး), once capital of southern Myanmar and home to many historic pagodas, monasteries and palaces that date back over a thousand years. Bago can be visited as a day trip from Yangon, or it makes an easy first stop as you set out on your tour of the country.

When to Go

Southwestern Myanmar

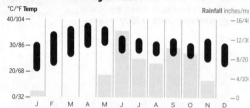

Mar–May Temperatures can reach scorching.

Nov–Jan The days are comfortable during the winter with an average high of 32°C.

Jun–Oct Rainy season rice planting makes the Delta region the greenest part of Myanmar.

Thanlyin & Kyauktan
သန်လျင်/ကျောက်တန်း

POP 268,063 / 📞 056

An easy escape from Yangon is a visit to the historic town of Thanlyin and nearby Kyauktan, east of the city across the Bago River – both towns house important pagodas.

The notorious Portuguese adventurer Filipe de Brito e Nicote ran his own little kingdom from Thanlyin in the late 16th and 17th centuries. He sided with the Mon in their struggle against the Bamar, before being impaled by his enemies in 1613.

Thanlyin was a major port, until it was eclipsed by Yangon in the late 18th century. It was briefly the base of the French East India Company and the first place in Myanmar to receive Christian missionaries and have its own church. The ruins of a **Portuguese-built church**, dating to 1750, can be found not far from the Thanlyin Bridge.

Under British rule, Thanlyin was known as 'Syriam' and was the site of a major oil refinery.

◉ Sights

Kyaik-Khauk Paya　BUDDHIST STUPA
(ကျိုက်ခေါက်ဘုရား; Kyaik-Khauk Pagoda Rd, Thanlyin; K2000; ⊙daylight) A couple of miles south of Thanlyin's centre is this gilded Mon-style stupa, similar in design to Shwedagon and said to contain two Buddha hairs delivered to the site by the great sage himself. There are stupendous views from its hilltop location.

Yele Paya　BUDDHIST TEMPLE
(ရေလယ်ဘုရား; Kyauktan; K2000; ⊙1st/last boat 6am/6pm) At Kyauktan, 7.5 miles southeast of Thanlyin, is a sparkling floating temple adrift on a chocolate river. You can feed the massive catfish splashing about at the temple complex's edge. To reach the islet,

SOUTHWESTERN MYANMAR THANLYIN & KYAUKTAN

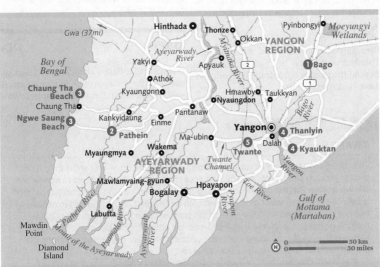

Southwestern Myanmar Highlights

❶ Bago (p88) Cycling around the ancient temples, palaces, monasteries and giant Buddhas that dominate this historic former capital.

❷ Pathein (p94) Basing yourself in this bustling delta city, where you can admire the artistry and skill needed

to make its famed silk and cotton parasols.

❸ Chaung Tha Beach (p99) and **Ngwe Saung Beach** (p102) Riding a motorbike taxi along deserted beaches and jungle tracks between these two beach resorts, or just lazing in the sand and surf.

❹ Thanlyin & Kyauktan Exploring the ancient pagodas dotted around these delta towns.

❺ Shwesandaw Paya (p88) Joining the locals on their daily commute by riding the ferry across the Yangon River to visit Twante and this 2500-year-old pagoda.

catch one of the launch ferries (K5000 return) from the riverbank.

In the town is a small pagoda perched on top of a hill beside the river, plus a hectic, flyblown and rather fishy market, which reaches its climax in the morning.

🏃 Activities

Flavours of Myanmar Cooking School
COOKING

 (📞09 863 5066; www.myanmargoodnewstravel. com; 4/50 Kyaik Khauk Pagoda Rd, Thanlyin; per person US$85, min 2 people) This expertly taught, hands-on Burmese cooking class is held in a pleasant garden setting just across the Bago River from Yangon. The six-hour program covering 10 dishes (various diets can be catered for, including vegetarian) includes a shopping trip to Thanlyin market and a visit to a local monastery to make a donation.

Because the classes are outdoors, the courses generally run only between October and March in dry season. You will have to arrange your own transport to Thanlyin.

🍴 Eating

Beer gardens line the main road through Thanlyin on the way to Kyaik-Khuak Paya. Beyond the pagoda is 'central' Thanlyin, and more basic restaurants.

If you've hired a driver, stop at **Shwe Pu Zun** (Golden Prawn; 📞01-553 062; www. shwepuzuncake.com; 14A Minnandar Rd, Dawbon; desserts from K1100; ⊙8am-8pm; ❄ 📶), a huge modern bakery-cafe, located between Yangon and Thanlyin, specialising in sweets; the *faluda* (mixture of custard, ice cream and jelly; K1200) is famous.

Near the Kyauktan ferry landing are several simple restaurants and food stalls.

ℹ Getting There & Around

The most convenient way to visit both Thanlyin and Kyauktan is to hire a taxi in Yangon (K40,000 for a half-day). By taxi, it takes an hour to get to Thanlyin. Kyauktan is another 15 minutes' drive southeast of Thanlyin.

If you're passionate about Myanmar's uncomfortable local transport or are counting kyat, buses to Thanlyin (K300, two hours, 16 miles) leave frequently throughout the day from Sule Pagoda.

In Thanlyin, motorcycle taxis can take you to Kyaik-Khauk Paya (K1500) and Yele Paya in Kyauktan (K5000).

Bago ပဲခူး

POP 254,424 / 📞052

If it wasn't for Bago's abundance of religious sites and the remains of its former palace, it would be hard to tell that this scrappy town –

OFF THE BEATEN TRACK

TWANTE

Twante (တွံတေး) is a drowsy, spread-out town a 40-minute drive west of Dalah (p51) into the Ayeyarwady Delta past seemingly endless paddy fields. Its main claim to fame is the **Shwesandaw Paya** (ရွှေဆံတော်ဘုရား; K2000; ⊙6am-9pm), a Mon-built *zedi* (stupa) that is believed to be as ancient as the Shwedagon (2500 years old) and is said to contain two hair relics of Buddha. One corner of the compound commemorates King Bayinnaung's defeat of a local rebellion. A 100-year-old sitting bronze buddha in Mandalay style – with eyes staring straight ahead – can be found near the southern entrance. Old bronze buddhas line the western side of the *zedi*.

Also worth checking out are Twante's **Oh-Bo Pottery Sheds** (အိုးဘို အိုးလုပ်ငန်း), which supply much of the delta region with containers of varying shapes and sizes. You can view the process from making the clay, to casting the pots on human-powered wheels and firing in kilns, which can take three to four days. Prices for pots start at K1000 for small ones and up to K35,000 for giant pots used to store rice and water.

Worth a detour on the way to or from Twante is **Mwe Paya**, a temple that is home to scores of sleepy snakes who are tended to by Buddhist nuns. Nearby is a copy of the Mahabodi Pagoda in Bodhgaya, India, where the Buddha gained enlightenment.

To get to Twante, first catch the ferry (K2000/4000 one way/return, 5am to 9pm, every 15 minutes) that shuttles between Pansodan Jetty and Dalah. Twante is a 40-minute drive from Dalah and motorcycle-taxi drivers wait on the jetty and charge K10,000 for a return trip, including stops at the sights. A taxi will cost K30,000. A squashed seat in a minivan to Twante is K1000, but they depart only when full.

50 miles northeast of Yangon on the old highway to Mandalay – was once the capital of southern Myanmar. The opening of Myanmar's main Hanthawady International Airport in 2018 is set to revive Bago's fortunes.

In the meantime, the great density of blissed-out buddhas and treasure-filled temples makes Bago (formerly known as Pegu) an appealing and simple day trip from Yangon, or the ideal first stop when you leave the city behind.

History

Bago was reputedly founded in AD 573 by two Mon princes from Thaton, who saw a female *hamsa* (mythological bird) standing on the back of a male *hamsa* on an island in a huge lake. Taking this to be an auspicious omen, they founded a royal capital called Hanthawady (from the Pali-Sanskrit 'Hamsavati', meaning the 'kingdom of the *hamsa*') at the edge of the lake.

During the later Mon dynastic periods (1287–1539), Hanthawady developed into a walled city of 1 sq mile with 20 gates and became the centre of the Mon kingdom of Ramanadesa, which consisted of all southern Myanmar.

The Bamar took over in 1539 when King Tabinshwehti annexed Bago to his Taungoo kingdom. The city was frequently mentioned by early European visitors – who knew it as Pegu – as an important seaport. In 1740 the Mon, after a period of submission to Taungoo, re-established Bago as their capital, but in 1757 King Alaungpaya sacked and utterly destroyed the city. King Bodawpaya, who ruled from 1782 to 1819, rebuilt it to some extent, but when the river changed its course the city was cut off from the sea and lost its importance as a seaport. It never again reclaimed its previous grandeur.

◉ Sights

To enter Bago's four main sights (Shwethalyaung Buddha, Shwemawdaw Paya, Kyaik Pun Paya and Kanbawzathadi Palace), foreigners must buy the Bago Archaeological Zone ticket (US$10/K10,000). All the other sights are free, although many charge an additional K300 for camera and K500 for video cameras.

Shwemawdaw Paya　　BUDDHIST STUPA
(ရွှေမော်တော်ဘုရား; Shwemawdaw Paya Rd; admission with Bago Archaeological Zone ticket K10,000; ☉ daylight) A *zedi* of washed-out gold

THE HAMSA
In deference to legend, the symbol for Bago is a female *hamsa* (a mythological bird; *hintha* or *hantha* in Burmese) standing on the back of a male *hamsa*. At a deeper level, the symbol honours the compassion of the male *hamsa* in providing a place for the female to stand in the middle of a lake with only one island. Hence, the men of Bago are said to be more chivalrous than men from other Burmese areas. In popular Burmese culture, however, men joke that they dare not marry a woman from Bago for fear of being henpecked.

in the midday haze and glittering perfection in the evening, the 376ft-high Shwemawdaw Paya stands tall and proud over the town. The stupa reaches 46ft higher than the Shwedagon in Yangon.

At the northeastern corner of the stupa is a huge section of the *hti* toppled by an earthquake in 1917. Shwemawdaw is a particularly good destination during Bago's annual pagoda festival, in March/April.

According to murky legend, the original stupa was a small, ramshackle object, built by two brothers, Kullasala and Mahasala, to enshrine two hairs given to them by Gautama Buddha. In AD 982 a sacred tooth was added to the collection; in 1385 another tooth was added and the stupa was rebuilt to a towering 277ft. In 1492 strong winds blew over the *hti* and a new one was raised.

The stupa has collapsed and been rebuilt many times over the last 600 years; each time it has grown a little taller and the treasures mounted in it have grown a little more abundant. The last time it was destroyed was in 1930 when a huge earthquake completely levelled it, and for the next 20 years only the huge earth mound of the base remained.

Shwethalyaung Buddha　　BUDDHIST TEMPLE
(ရွှေသာလျောင်းဘုရား; admission with Bago Archaeological Zone ticket K10,000; ☉ daylight) Legend has it that this gorgeous reclining buddha was built by the Mon king Mgadeikpa in the 10th century. Measuring 180ft long and 53ft high, the monument's little finger alone extends 10ft.

Following the destruction of Bago in 1757, the huge buddha was overgrown by jungle and not rediscovered until 1881, when a

Bago

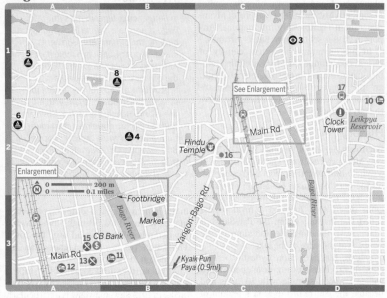

contractor unearthed it while building the Yangon–Bago railway line.

In 1906 an open-sided pavilion was erected over the statue, and in the 1930s a mosaic was added to the great pillow on which the buddha's head rests.

On the rear side of the plinth, in a series of 10 murals, the legend of how the buddha came to be built by Mgadeikpa is depicted. His reign was marked by corruption and violence, but one day his son was out hunting in the forests when his eye fell upon a Mon girl who caused his heart to flutter. Even though she was a Buddhist and he, like everyone in his father's kingdom, worshipped pagan idols, the two became lovers and married after he promised her that she could continue to practise Buddhism.

Back at the court the king was furious when he discovered this and ordered the execution of both the girl and his son. Yet when the new bride prayed in front of the pagan idol it cracked and broke. The king was seized with fear and, realising the error of his ways, ordered the building of a statue of the Buddha and the conversion of the population to Buddhism.

Near the huge head of the image stands a statue of **Lokanat** (Lokanatha or Avalokitesvara), a Mahayana Buddhist deity borrowed by Burmese Buddhism.

A Japanese war cemetery, **Kyinigan Kyaung**, can be seen on the grounds of a monastery just north of Shwethalyaung.

Hintha Gon Paya
BUDDHIST STUPA

(ဟင်္သာကုန်း; ⊙daylight) **FREE** Located a short walk behind the Shwemawdaw (p89), this shrine was once the one place in this vast area that rose above sea level, and so was the natural place for the *hamsa* to land. Images of this mythical bird decorate the stupa built by U Khanti, the hermit monk who was the architect of Mandalay Hill.

You can walk here by taking the steps down from the side of the Shwemawdaw from the main entrance. This paya is a major place of *nat* worship and festivals, and with a bit of luck you'll catch the swirling, veiled forms of masculine-looking *nat* dancers accompanied by the clanging and crashing of a traditional orchestra.

Kyaik Pun Paya
MONUMENT

(ကျိုက်ပွန်ဘုရား; Kyikpon Pagoda Rd; admission with Bago Archaeological Zone ticket K10,000; ⊙daylight) Built in 1476 by King Dhammazedi, the Kyaik Pun Paya consists of four 100ft-high sitting buddhas (Gautama Buddha and his three predecessors) placed back to back around a huge, square pillar, about a mile south of Bago, just off the Yangon road.

According to legend, four Mon sisters were connected with the construction of the buddhas; it was said that if any of them should marry, one of the buddhas would collapse. One of the four buddhas disintegrated in the 1930 earthquake, leaving only a brick outline (since restored) and a very old bride.

Mahazedi Paya
BUDDHIST STUPA

(မဟာစေတီဘုရား; ☉ daylight) FREE The design of the Mahazedi Paya (Great Stupa), with its whitewashed stairways leading almost to the stupa's summit, is unusual for southern Myanmar and certainly one of the more attractive religious buildings in Bago. Originally constructed in 1560 by King Bayinnaung, it was destroyed during the 1757 sacking of Bago. An 1860 attempt to rebuild it was unsuccessful and the great earthquake of 1930 levelled it, after which it remained a ruin. This current reconstruction was completed in 1982.

The Mahazedi originally contained a Buddha tooth, at one time thought to be the most sacred of all Buddha relics, the tooth of Kandy, Sri Lanka. After Bago was conquered in 1539, the tooth was moved to Taungoo and then to Sagaing near Mandalay. Together with a begging bowl supposed to have been used by the Buddha, it remains in the Kaunghmudaw Paya, near Sagaing, to this day.

Shwegugale Paya
BUDDHIST STUPA

(ရွှေဂူကလေးဘုရား; ☉ daylight) FREE A little beyond the Mahazedi Paya, this *zedi* (stupa) has a dark *gu* (tunnel) around the circumference of the cylindrical superstructure. The monument dates from 1494 and the reign of King Byinnya Yan. Inside are 64 seated buddha figures. Many locals venture out here in the early evening.

From the *zedi,* cross a rickety wooden footbridge and you'll arrive at a **nat shrine** with life-sized statues of Ko Thein and Ko Thant, the *nat* of the temple compound.

Kya Kha Wain Kyaung
MONASTERY

(ကြက်ခတ်ဝိုင်းကျောင်း) FREE The sight of some 500 monks and novices filing out in the early morning from one of largest monasteries in Myanmar to collect alms is worth getting up early for. Otherwise, join the tour groups visiting at 10.30am to see the monks eating lunch in a giant hall. You're free to wander around; most of the monks think it's hilarious that tourists come and watch them eat, but the atmosphere is a bit zoo-like.

Maha Kalyani Sima
BUDDHIST TEMPLE

(မဟာကလျာဏီသိမ်တော်ကြီး; Maha Kalyani Thein; ☉ daylight) FREE This 'Sacred Hall of Ordination' was originally constructed in

OFF THE BEATEN TRACK

MOEYUNGYI WETLANDS

About an hour northeast of Bago and close to the village of Pyinbongyi is the **Moeyungyi Wetlands** (မိုးယုန်းကြီးအင်း), a 15-sq-mile lake and marsh that is one of Myanmar's handful of national parks. Sitting on a migration route of birds fleeing the icy Siberian winter and attracting thousands of local waders, the wetlands, which started life as an artificial water-storage reservoir in 1878, will bring a big grin to any birder's face. The last census revealed some 125 different species including great flocks of egrets, cormorants and white storks, and large numbers of the beautiful swamp hen (purple gallinule), plus sarus cranes with their brilliant red heads.

Your best chance of seeing exotic birds is from December to February, either early in the morning or late in the afternoon. During this period, boat tours are available on the lake for US$15 per person. The tour lasts for about two hours and will take you whizzing over to the marshy reed beds in the centre where the birds congregate in vast numbers.

Taxis charge K30,000 for a one-day return trip to the wetlands from Bago.

1476 by Dhammazedi, the famous alchemist king and son of Queen Shinsawpu. Like almost everything in Bago it has suffered a tumbledown history and has been destroyed and rebuilt many a time. Next to the hall are 10 large tablets with inscriptions in Pali and Mon describing the history of Buddhism in Myanmar.

If you can't get enough of buddha statues then across the road from the Maha Kalyani Sima is the **Four Figures Paya**, with four buddha figures standing back to back. An adjacent open hallway has a small reclining buddha image, thronged by followers, and some macabre paintings of wrongdoers being tortured in the afterlife.

Relaxing in the sun next to these two monuments is the serene **Naung Daw Gyi Mya Tha Lyaung**, a reclining buddha sprawled out over 250ft. It was built in 2002 with public donations.

Snake Monastery MONASTERY
(မြွေကျောင်း; daylight) FREE A story goes that a revered monk had a dream that the python you can see snoozing in this monastery was the reincarnation of a *nat;* another is that it is the reincarnation of the monk himself.

Either way, more than 125 years later, the self-same python has grown to be at least 17ft long and a foot wide, making it probably one of the largest snakes in the world. No wonder locals flock here to pay their respects and shower the sleepy snake with gifts of cash.

The **Shwe Taung Yoe Paya** *zedi,* nearby on a small hilltop, is great for watching sunsets; however, you have to cross a festering rubbish dump to reach it.

The monastery and *zedi* are about a mile south of Hintha Gon Paya; locals should be able to direct you there.

Kanbawzathadi Palace PALACE
(ကမ္ဘောဇသာဒီနန်းတော်; admission with Bago Archaeological Zone ticket K10,000; 9am-6pm) At the heart of ancient Hanthawady was the Kanbawzathadi Palace, the remains of which have been excavated just south of Shwemawdaw Paya. The stumps of the huge teak posts that held up part of the palace have been left in situ, while the posts themselves occupy a museum that's a slipshod reconstruction of the Great Audience Hall, originally dating from 1599.

Another reconstructed building in the compound is the Bee Throne Hall.

Festivals & Events

Shwemawdaw Paya Festival RELIGIOUS
(Mar/Apr) This festival attracts huge crowds of worshippers and merrymakers on the full moon of Myanmar's lunar month of Tagu.

Sleeping

Bago's accommodation options are uninspired. That should change after 2018, when Myanmar's new main airport opens near here. For now, the best places to stay are mostly outside central Bago, while the cheapest are located along the busy and very noisy main road through town, so ask for a room at the back of these hotels. Most places don't include breakfast and electricity cuts in and out during the day and night.

Hotel Mariner HOTEL $
(052-220 1034; hotelmariner.hm@gmail.com; 330 Shwemawdaw Paya Rd; r US$35-45;) Newish six-floor property that is the current pick of Bago's budget accommodation offerings. The more expensive rooms are big and

light and some offer grandstand views of Shwemawdaw Paya.

Bago Star Hotel   HOTEL $
(☑ 052-30066; bagostar@myanmar.com.mm; 11-21 Kyaikpon Pagoda Rd; tw US$38; ❄ ⛱ ≋) This self-styled 'country-style, bungalow-type hotel' has a summer-camp feel. Located just off the highway and only a short walk to the ever-watching eyes of the Kyaik Pun Paya, it offers A-frame cabin-like rooms, a murky small pool and – a big plus – bikes for rent (K3000 a day). Generators keep the air-conditioning humming.

San Francisco Guest House   HOTEL $
(☑ 052-22265; 14 Main Rd; r US$10-20; ❄ ⛱) The best of the budget options, if you choose a double room. Small bathrooms, but they are clean, the owner is friendly and you can rent bicycles (K3000 per day) and motorbikes (K8000 per day). There's a curfew from 11pm to 5am.

Mya Nanda Hotel   HOTEL $
(☑ 09 501 9799; 10 Main Rd; r US$10-20; ❄ ⛱) Basic but clean rooms in a central location. The doubles offer a little more space and light.

Han Thar Gardens   HOTEL $$$
(☑ 09 42175 5282; hanthargardens@gmail.com; 34 Bullein Tar Zone Village, Yangon-Mandalay Rd; r US$130-165; ❄ @ ⛱) Overlooking fields and a golf course, this beautifully designed property has environmentally friendly features such as no air-conditioning in the airy 50ft-ceiling rooms of the main building. Run by an overseas-educated Myanmar woman, it also features an excellent restaurant – worth visiting in its own right – serving delicious Burmese food, including local specialities such as *pazun chin* (pickled-prawn salad).

The hotel is a good 20-minute drive out of Bago, on the way to Yangon.

✖ Eating

Hadaya Café   TEAHOUSE $
(14 Main Rd; tea & snacks from K300; ⊘ 3am-10.30pm) This central teahouse is a popular stop for passing truck drivers, hence the long opening hours. It has an English-speaking owner and a reasonable selection of snacks.

Three Five Restaurant   CHINESE, BURMESE $
(10 Main Rd; mains from K2000; ⊘ 7am-9pm; ⛱ ▥) This shabby but friendly place offers a menu spanning Burmese and Chinese cui-

sine, with a few European dishes. At night, it's a popular spot for a beer.

Kyaw Swa   CHINESE $$
(☑ 052-223 0220; 445-446 Yangon-Bago Rd; mains from K4000; ⊘ 9am-9pm; ⛱ ▥) A few miles south of central Bago, this large and popular restaurant serves tasty and reasonably authentic Chinese food in nicer surroundings than most places in Bago.

Hanthawaddy   CHINESE, BURMESE $$
(192 Hintha St; mains from K5000; ⊘ 10am-9pm; ▥) The food here isn't amazing, but it's solid enough, the place is clean and this is the only restaurant in central Bago with a bit of atmosphere. The open-air upper level is breezy and offers great views of Shwemawdaw Paya.

ⓘ Information

CB Bank (Yangon-Mandalay Rd; ⊘ 9.30am-3pm) Has an ATM that takes foreign cards.

Sea Sar (☑ 09 530 0987; myothitsar86@gmail.com; bus station; ⊘ 6am-6pm) The English-speaking owner is helpful and can book onward bus tickets.

ⓘ Getting There & Away

The following table shows travel times and costs between Bago and several main destinations. The range in train fares is between ordinary and upper class.

DESTINATION	BUS	TRAIN
Kyaikto	3hr; K6000	3hr; K650-1300
Mandalay	9-10hr; from K13,000	13hr; K2100-8150
Mawlamyine	6hr; K9000	8hr; K1600-3150
Taungoo	7hr; from K6000	5hr; K1450-2900
Yangon	2hr; K1000	2hr; K600-1150

BUS

Bago's scruffy bus station (Yangon-Mandalay Rd) is about halfway between the town centre and the Bago Star Hotel, located across from the Hindu temple. Many buses passing through Bago can also be waved down from outside your hotel, though unless you have booked a ticket in advance there is little likelihood of getting a seat.

Buses to Yangon leave from along the main road opposite the bus station and depart approximately every 30 minutes from 6.30am to 5.30pm.

Going south, buses to Kinpun, the starting point for Mt Kyaiktiyo (Golden Rock), leave every hour or so from 6am to 3pm. During the rainy season (May to September), most buses go only as far as Kyaikto, 10 miles from Kinpun.

If you're heading north, for Mandalay, Taungoo and Inle Lake, there are a handful of direct services from Bago. It's also possible to hop on services coming from Yangon – book ahead with a local agent, such as Sea Sar (p93), which has an office at the bus station, or ask your hotel to help.

TAXI

A convenient travel option is hiring a taxi for a day trip from Yangon, although it's more expensive than other transport methods. With bargaining this should cost about K80,000 and gives you the additional advantage of having transport between sights once you get to Bago. It also saves traipsing all the way out to the bus station in Yangon.

One-way taxis from Bago straight to your hotel in Yangon cost K40,000.

A guide and driver for a day trip to Mt Kyaiktiyo (Golden Rock) can be hired for K55,000 return.

Ask about any of these options at the town's taxi stand (Yangon-Mandalay Rd) or through any of the central Bago hotels.

TRAIN

Bago is connected by train with Yangon and Mawlamyine and stops north towards Mandalay. Most trains do not run to schedule.

ⓘ Getting Around

Motorcycle-taxi and trishaw – *thoun bein* – are the main form of local transport. A one-way trip in the central area should cost no more than K500. If you're going further afield – say from Shwethalyaung Buddha, at one end of town, to Shwemawdaw Paya, at the other – you should hire a trishaw or motorcycle for the day, either of which will cost around K7000.

Pathein   ပုသိမ်

POP 169,773 / 📞 042

Pathein lies at the heart of an area that produces the finest rice in Myanmar, including *pawsanmwe t'ămìn* (fragrant rice). It's a thriving, busy city, particularly along the riverfront – Pathein is Myanmar's most important delta port outside Yangon – and in the markets near the Shwemokhtaw Paya, the principal religious site.

Most travellers stop here only briefly on their way to nearby beaches, but the workshops in the city's northeast that produce colourful, hand-painted parasols are worth a look. There are also architectural remnants of colonial days in Pathein, which the British called Bassein, including the central jail dating from 1879.

Pathein is the unofficial capital of the Ayeyarwady region and if you're interested in exploring the villages and towns of the delta, this is the logical place to base yourself and to arrange transport, whether boat or car.

History

Pathein was the scene of major clashes during the struggle for supremacy between the Mon and the Bamar. Later, it became an important trading port for goods being moved between India and Southeast Asia. The city's name may derive from the Burmese word for Muslim *(Pathi)* – due to the heavy presence of Arab and Indian Muslim traders here centuries ago; there's still a large Muslim population in the city. The colonial Brits, who set up a garrison here in 1826, corrupted the name to Bassein.

Today, Pathein's population includes large contingents of Kayin (Karen) and Rakhine. Once part of a Mon kingdom, Pathein is now home to only a few Mon. During the 1970s and '80s, the Kayin villages surrounding Pathein generated insurgent activity that has since ended.

◎ Sights

Pathein's central sights can be covered on foot, but to get to Tagaung Mingala Zeditaw, Mahabodhi Mingala Zedi and Leikyunyinaung Paya, it's best to hire a *thoun bein* or motorbike taxi (around K3000).

Shwemokhtaw Paya   BUDDHIST STUPA

(ရွှေမုဋ္ဌောဘုရား; Shwezedi Rd; ⊙ 6am-8pm) **FREE** Looming with grace over Pathein is the golden bell of the Shwemokhtaw Paya. The *hti* (stupa pinnacle) consists of a topmost layer made from 14lb of solid gold, a middle tier of pure silver and a bottom tier of bronze; all three tiers are gilded and reportedly embedded with a total of 829 diamond fragments, 843 rubies and 1588 semiprecious stones.

This large complex is unusually well layered in legend. One states that it was originally built by India's Buddhist King Ashoka in 305 BC. Standing just 7.5ft tall, this original stupa supposedly enshrined Buddha relics and a 6in gold bar.

Another legend says a Muslim princess named Onmadandi requested each of her three Buddhist lovers build a stupa in her honour. One of the lovers erected Shwemokhtaw, the others the less-distinguished Tazaung and Thayaunggyaung Paya.

Whichever story you choose to believe, Bagan's King Alaungsithu is thought to have erected a 46ft stupa called Htupayon over this site in AD 1115. Then, in 1263, King Samodagossa took power, raised the stupa to 132ft and changed the name to Shwemokhtaw Paya, which means Stupa of the Half-Foot Gold Bar.

The southern shrine of the compound houses the Thiho-shin Phondaw-pyi sitting buddha image, which, the story goes, floated to the delta coast on a raft sent from Sri Lanka during ancient times. According to the legend, an unknown Sinhalese sculptor fashioned four different buddha images using pieces from the original Bodhi tree mixed with cement composite. He then placed the images on four wooden rafts and set the rafts adrift on the ocean. One landed in Dawei (Tavoy), another at Kyaikkami (Amherst), another at Kyaiktiyo (this one is now at Kyaikpawlaw), and the fourth landed near Phondawpyi, a fishing village about 60 miles south of Pathein, from where it was transferred to Pathein.

A marble standing buddha positioned in a niche in the fence running along the western side of the stupa marks a spot where Mon warriors once prayed before going off to battle. In the northwestern corner of the compound is a shrine dedicated to Shin Upagot, the Bodhisattva who floats on the ocean and appears to those in trouble. Turtles swim in the water surrounding the small pavilion.

Also in this northwest corner is an unusual golden Ganesh shrine, dedicated to the elephant-headed god worshipped by Hindus as the god of wisdom and wealth.

SOUTHWESTERN MYANMAR PATHEIN

OFF THE BEATEN TRACK

MEINMAHLA KYUN WILDLIFE SANCTUARY

Since 2012, Fauna and Flora International (www.fauna-flora.org), the world's oldest conservation organisation, has been working with the Ministry of Environmental Conservation and Forestry to help promote ecotourism in Myanmar. One of the locations they are focusing on is **Meinmahla Kyun Wildlife Sanctuary** (မိန်းမလှကျွန်းသားတွဲတော; ☑ 045-45578), a swampy, mangrove-covered island in the south of the Ayeyarwady Delta that can make for an adventurous three- or four-day return trip from Yangon.

The 53-sq-mile sanctuary is the premier place in Myanmar to see wild estuarine crocodiles and, if you're lucky, you may also spot rare Irrawaddy dolphins. Between November and February it's also the pit stop for vast numbers of migratory waterbirds on the East Asian–Australasian Flyway. On the aptly named Turtle Island, 7 miles south of Meinmahla Kyun, turtles nest and hatch between October and March. It's possible to take a day trip to this island and camp there overnight.

Aside from the wildlife, the great attraction of this trip is experiencing life in the delta, where the main livelihood activities are rice farming, fishing and crabbing. This also makes it a great destination for fresh seafood.

The sanctuary headquarters is in **Bogalay**, 92 miles southwest of Yangon. The fastest and most comfortable way to get there is by an express boat run by Shwe Pyi Tan Express (p83), which leaves daily at 6am from Phone Gyi Jetty (K11,500, six hours). There is an IWT ferry from Lan Thit Jetty daily at 6pm (deck class/private cabin US$5/25), but it doesn't always run and takes at least 12 hours. Bogalay can also be reached by bus (K4000, five hours) with departures roughly every two hours during the day from Hlaing Thar Yar Bus Terminal.

You must first register with the park headquarters in Bogalay – this process will be much smoother and quicker if you let them know you're coming in advance. From Bogalay, the park staff will organise return boat transport to Meinmahla Kyun (K70,000, up to eight people). You can also book canoe tours along the mangrove-lined creeks on the island (K30,000 per day, up to three passengers). There is basic accommodation available in the sanctuary (US$20 per night).

Specialist tour operators in Yangon, including **SST Tours** (Map p38; ☑ 01-255 536; www.sst myanmar.com; Rm 5-6, 2nd fl, Aung San Stadium, Mingalar Taung Nyunt), can arrange all-inclusive three-day, two-night round trips to the sanctuary from around US$400 per person.

Pathein

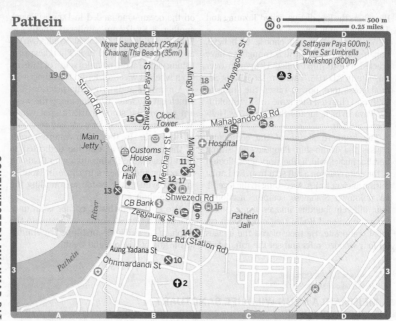

Pathein

◎ Sights

1 Shwemokhtaw Paya	B2
2 St Peter's Cathedral	B3
3 Twenty-Eight Paya	C1

⛱ Sleeping

4 Day to Day Motel	C2
5 Htike Myat San Hotel	C2
6 La Pyae Wun Hotel	B2
7 Myanma Koe Hotel	C1
8 Nay Chi Linn-3 Hotel	C1
9 Pammawaddy Hotel	B2

✖ Eating

10 Myo Restaurant	B3
OK-9	(see 6)
11 Shwe Ayar	B2
12 Shwe Zin Yaw Restaurant	B2
13 Top Star	B2
14 Zone Pan	B3

◉ Drinking & Nightlife

15 Man San Thu	B1

ⓘ Transport

16 Ayer Shwe Zin	C2
17 Bus Company Offices	B2
18 Buses to Chaung Tha Beach	C1
19 Buses to Ngwe Saung Beach	A1

Tagaung Mingala Zeditaw BUDDHIST STUPA
(တကောင်းမင်္ဂလာစေတီတော် (တကောင်းဘုရား);
Tagaung Paya; ⊘daylight) FREE Interesting
from an artistic perspective, this pagoda
is centred on a graceful stupa that sweeps
inward from a wide, whitewashed base to a
gleaming silver superstructure. It's about 2
miles south of the city centre. Look for the
small squirrel sculpture extending from the
western side of the upper stupa, representing a previous life of the Buddha as a squirrel. One of the pavilions at the base of the
stupa contains a large sitting buddha image.

St Peter's Cathedral CHURCH
(စိန့်ပီတာဘုရားကျောင်း; Mingyi Rd) The focal
point of a Catholic educational compound
is this 1872-vintage cathedral distinctively
plastered emerald green. If you're not here
for daily Mass at 6am (also 4pm on Sunday),
the priest will happily let you peek inside.

Shwe Sar Umbrella Workshop WORKSHOP
(☏042-25127; 653 Tawya Kyaung Rd; ⊘8am-5pm)
Sun shades are made in workshops scattered
across the northern part of the city, particularly around the Twenty-Eight Paya (p97),
off Mahabandoola Rd. It's fun to wander the
area, sticking your head into a workshop here
and there to see how they're made. They're
cheap, and the saffron-coloured ones, made

for monks, are waterproof. This family-run workshop is particularly welcoming.

Settayaw Paya
BUDDHIST TEMPLE

(စက်တော်ရာဘုရား; ☉daylight) FREE This charming paya, spread across a hilly green setting, is dedicated to a mythical Buddha footprint left by the Enlightened One during his legendary perambulations through Southeast Asia. The footprint symbol itself is an oblong, 3ft-long impression.

Twenty-Eight Paya
BUDDHIST TEMPLE

(နှစ်ကျိပ်ရှစ်ဆူဘုရား; ☉daylight) This rectangular shrine contains 28 sitting and 28 standing buddha images. None of them are particularly distinguished except that the latter appear in the open-robe style rather than the closed-robe pose that is typical of Mandalay standing images. You may have to ask the caretaker to unlock the building.

At one end of the hall stands a group of crude sculptures depicting a scene from the Buddha's life in which he teaches a disciple the relativity of physical beauty by comparing a monkey, the disciple's wife and a *deva* (celestial being).

Leikyunyinaung Paya
BUDDHIST TEMPLE

(လိပ်ကျွန်းညီနောင်ဘုရား; ☉daylight) This temple, about a mile directly south of Mahabodhi, was renovated by the military regime in the early 1990s to create a facsimile of Ananda Paya in Bagan. Forced labour was used in the renovation, so many locals avoid praying here.

Mahabodhi Mingala Zedi
BUDDHIST TEMPLE

(မဟာဗောဓိမင်္ဂလာစေတီ; ☉daylight) West of Tagaung Mingala Zeditaw, a little way towards the river, stands this temple patterned after the Mahabodhi stupa in Bodhgaya, India.

⚑ Festivals & Events

Vesakha
RELIGIOUS

(☉Apr/May) The people of Pathein celebrate the Buddha's birth, enlightenment and passing away with a huge *paya pwe* (pagoda festival) during the full moon of Myanmar's month of Kason. The festival is held at the Shwemokhtaw Paya (p94).

⌂ Sleeping

Myanma Koe Hotel
HOTEL $

(☎042-21381; myanmarkoehotel@gmail.com; 35 Mahabandoola Rd; r incl breakfast US$35-50; ❉☎) This hotel is the best midrange hotel in town. It has big and bright rooms, decent beds and sizeable bathrooms, all with satellite TV and fridge. There are English-speaking staff. It's worth booking ahead.

Nay Chi Linn-3 Hotel
HOTEL $

(☎042-22844; 6 Mahabandoola Rd; r incl breakfast K10,000-25,000; ❉☎) 'Fresh and clean' is the motto here, and the rooms are spick and span. They're also compact, with smaller bathrooms, and not a lot of light. The cheapest rooms are fan-only. But the price is right and it's fine for an overnight stop.

Day to Day Motel
HOTEL $

(☎042-23368; Jail St; r K13,000-27,000; ❉☎) This motel is in a quieter part of town, opposite the historic Sikh Temple. It has reasonable rooms for the price, although the bathrooms are cramped and dark. A big roof terrace provides a pleasant place to sit and take in the surrounding leafy view. There's a decent wi-fi connection. You can only pay in kyat.

Pammawaddy Hotel
HOTEL $

(☎042-21165; newpammawaddy@gmail.com; 14A Mingyi Rd; r incl breakfast US$15-35; ❉☎) The unremarkable rooms here are a reasonable size, with small bathrooms, and they improve as you go higher up in the building.

La Pyae Wun Hotel
HOTEL $

(☎042-24669; 30 Mingyi Rd; r US$20-30; ❉☎) Friendly hotel whose imposing white exterior shrouds plain but comfortable-enough white-tiled twin rooms, with plainer bathrooms (and cold-water showers). Good wi-fi connection and a central location, but no breakfast.

Htike Myat San Hotel
HOTEL $$

(☎042-22742; htikemyatsan@gmail.com; 8 Mahabandoola Rd; r incl breakfast US$20-55; ❉☎) Rooms here are reasonably modern, spacious and well equipped, a combination that is a rarity in Pathein. But the cheapest ones share (clean) bathrooms. If you want your own bathroom and hot water, you'll need to spend US$35 and up. Efficient staff.

✗ Eating

★ Shwe Ayar
BURMESE $

(32-35 Mingalar Rd; mains from K2300; ☉8am-9pm) It doesn't look like much but this place offers high-quality biryani, which you can supplement with chicken or mutton. The lentil and bean soup is so delicious you'll want a second helping. It also does tasty curry sets. Find it opposite Zaw Optical.

Top Star
CHINESE, BURMESE **$**

(Strand Rd; mains from K3000; ⊘9am-11pm; 📷)
The best of the beer stations and restaurants along the riverfront, Top Star's menu includes a few Thai and Japanese-inspired dishes, and the standard Chinese-Burmese ones. The big windows offer river views and it's fine for an evening beer too.

Zone Pan
BURMESE **$**

(Budar Rd/Station Rd; curries from K2000; ⊘8am-9pm; 📷) This popular curry place has a decent range of tasty curries, soups and salads. To cut the grease, try the mouth-wateringly tart *shauk-thi dhouq* (lemon salad) or a pennywort (a local herb) salad. There's no English sign here; look for the light-blue shopfront opposite Lucky One Tea Shop.

OK-9
TEAHOUSE **$**

(Mingyi Rd; tea & snacks from K300; ⊘5.30am-8.30pm) OK-9 is next to La Pyae Wun Hotel and is perfect for the breakfasts your hotel doesn't provide. This shady teahouse provides plates of freshly baked naan and chickpeas (only until 9.30am), as well as other snacks and a morning caffeine kick.

Myo Restaurant
CHINESE, BURMESE **$**

(5 Aung Yadana St; mains from K3000; ⊘9am-10pm; 📷) It's rather grungy but this beer station and restaurant has a large and solid menu of Chinese-Burmese dishes, as well as beers and some barbecue. It shows the football too.

Shwe Zin Yaw Restaurant
BURMESE **$**

(24/25 Shwezedi Rd; mains from K1500; ⊘8am-9pm; 📷) The menu here has a little more variety than most Bamar curry houses: you'll find goat and beef curries, as well as a sardine salad. It's reasonably priced too.

Drinking & Nightlife

A few beer stations line the riverfront, while teahouses are scattered across the city.

Man San Thu
TEAHOUSE

(3 Shwezigon Paya St; tea & snacks from K300; ⊘6am-11pm; 📶) You can't miss this bustling place, spread over two floors and with a bright orange facade. Inside, there's a small English menu of noodle and rice dishes, plus all the usual teahouse snacks. It has free and functioning wi-fi too.

🛍 Shopping

Aside from the parasol workshops, there is a **night market** that is set up each evening in front of Customs House, where teenagers cruise, flirt and hang out while vendors purvey food, clothing and tools and just about every other requisite for daily life at low prices. Just south of Shwemokhtaw Paya is the **Central Market**, and just south of that the **New Market**, with all manner of goods.

ℹ Information

Young guide **Soe Moe Aung** (📞 09 25032 2368; http://traveltopathein.wordpress.com) is worth tracking down. A mine of local information, he can help arrange all kinds of trips and adventures in the area, including boats along the Pathein River; motorbike taxis to Kayin villages and beaches; and the necessary permits for Mawdin Point.

DON'T MISS

PATHEIN PARASOLS

Pathein is famous throughout Myanmar for the quality of its handmade parasols, used to shade the carrier from the searing sun. Covered in silk or waterproofed cotton, the parasols come in a variety of bright and natural colours.

One type that can be used in the rain is the saffron-coloured monks' umbrella, which is waterproofed by applying various coats of tree resin; a single umbrella may take five days to complete, including the drying process. Parasols and umbrellas can be ordered in any size directly from the workshops, and are a bargain given the amount of work that goes into making them.

Workshops welcome visitors who want to observe this craft, which is a lot more interesting than it might sound. The most centrally located shops are at the southern end of Merchant St, but here you'll only see the finishing decorative steps of the typical 40-stage process needed to make the best parasols.

To see the whole process head to Shwe Sar Umbrella Workshop (p96), the best of several workshops scattered in the vicinity of Twenty-Eight Paya, off Mahabandoola Rd. This workshop has been run by the same family for three generations, and is just around the corner from the Settayaw Paya.

MAWDIN POINT

If you follow the Pathein River until it empties into the Andaman Sea, you'll reach **Mawdin Point**, a place of great religious significance to Myanmar's Buddhists. This is where Buddhism is first believed to have to have been introduced to the country by sailors from the Indian subcontinent; Mawdin Paya has graced the point for centuries.

The best time to visit is during the 15-day Mawdin Paya festival in February or March. Throughout the year, the point can be reached by either bus (K5000, six hours) departing Pathein at noon and returning at 5am the next day; or by boat (K4000, 10 hours) leaving Pathein at 5am and returning at 6pm.

As the point is near a naval base you'll need a permit – Pathein guide **Soe Moe Aung** (p98) can arrange this and provide guiding services to the area (US$30 a day per person), which also includes Thamee Hla (Diamond Island), an important sea-turtle hatchery.

Money can be changed at CB Bank on Shwezedi Rd, where you'll find an ATM accepting international cards. There are also ATMs outside Htike Myat San Hotel and Myanma Koe Hotel.

ℹ Getting There & Around

BUS

If you're bound for Yangon (four hours), head to the bus company offices (Shwezedi Rd) located directly east of Shwe Zin Yaw Restaurant. The cheapest air-con service is offered by **Ayer Shwe Zin** (☏ 09 4974 5191; K3600) and runs three times a day at 4am, 8am and noon, but at six hours it is slower than the many other operators (K7000, four hours, hourly 3am to 3.30pm).

Crowded buses ply the route from Pathein to Chaung Tha Beach (K4000, two hours, 8am, noon and 2pm), departing from an informal **bus station** a couple of blocks northeast of the clock tower.

To Ngwe Saung Beach (K4000, two hours, 8am, 10am, noon, 2pm and 4pm), buses leave from yet another informal **bus station** on the riverfront.

TAXI

Shared taxis for up to four people can be arranged from your hotel in Pathein for Chaung Tha (K45,000), Ngwe Saung (K45,000) and Yangon (K90,000).

TRAIN

Pathein's train station is the terminus of a branch line from Kyankin, 61 miles south of Pyay on the west bank of the Ayeyarwady (Irrawaddy) River.

Chaung Tha Beach
ချောင်းသာကမ်းခြေ

Chaung Tha Beach is the closest thing Myanmar has to a holiday resort for ordinary folks – it's where the locals come to play. At this very Burmese beach party there's bobbing about on rubber rings, plodding along

the beach on ponies, endless guitar playing, boisterous beach football games, happy family picnics and evening fireworks.

Just 25 miles west of Pathein and six-odd hours from Yangon, Chaung Tha gets especially busy at weekends and on holidays. It's not the most awe-inspiring coastline – parts of the beach can get dirty in high season – and the resorts are not aimed at foreigners. But if you're looking to squeeze some sand and sun into your visit to Myanmar, it's a relatively convenient and affordable option and, unlike Ngwe Saung Beach further south, a fair few places stay open year-round.

◉ Sights & Activities

The beach is the main focus here, with the pretty **Kyauk Pahto pagoda** on a rock about two-thirds of the way down. Walk to the far southern end and you can take a boat (K1000 return) to nearby **Aung Mingalar Island** where there's a small fishing village and the **Aung Mingalar Mya Kyunnyo pagoda** up on a hill.

Get up early if you want to browse the village **market** (⊗ 5.30am to 9.30am) located behind Chaung Tha's bus station. The rest of the village lies around here and along the road as it veers left after the Amazing Chaung Tha Resort. Continue to the wooden jetty at the end of the road, where you should be able to persuade one of the fisherfolk to take you up the river and around the **mangroves** (per hr from K10,000). This is also the route to Ngwe Saung.

A modest coral reef lies a short way offshore with reasonable **snorkelling** possible both here and around the headland at the beach's northern end. During rainy season, the water clarity is terrible.

The best snorkelling, though, is about a two-hour boat ride away. Boats, which can

DAY TRIPS FROM CHAUNG THA BEACH

Whitesand Island (The Pyu Kyun), visible from the beach, is a popular snorkelling and swimming spot. Boats (K5000 return, 30 minutes) leave from the jetty at the south end of the village every hour or so from 8am (last one back leaves at 5pm). There's very little shade on the low-lying island; bring plenty of water. Don't attempt to swim over – it's further away than it looks.

About 9 miles north from Chaung Tha is **Chauk Maung Na Ma**, with a white-sand beach similar to Ngwe Saung: it's quiet, and you can snorkel, fish and meet local people. It's also a good place for a picnic. You can walk here in around two hours in dry season.

Whether or not you're not planning to overnight at **Ngwe Saung Beach**, the trip there on a motorbike taxi (K18,000) is highly recommended. The route, which takes about two hours, is through wild and glorious country and involves three river crossings on small wooden boats that have just enough room for a few motorbikes and passengers. You will speed along deserted beaches and through villages amid the forests, bumping along the trail and meeting locals along the way.

be arranged through your hotel or local guide Ko Chit Kaung, cost K50,000 per hour for six people. If you don't have your own gear it's possible to rent a tatty snorkel and mask from some hotels. You can also rent canoes for around K10,000 a day, while you can hire bicycles along the beach (K1000 per hour).

🛏 Sleeping

Chaung Tha offers the most affordable beach accommodation in Myanmar. Some places close during rainy season (mid-May to mid-September), while others slash rates by up to 50%.

You'll only get 24-hour electricity at the more expensive resorts. Elsewhere, you get power from 6pm to 6am. Wi-fi is patchy (if it works, it will be at night when the electricity is on).

There are some off-beach budget guesthouses south of the bus station, along the way to the pier.

★ Hill Garden Hotel   HOTEL $

(☑ 09 4957 6072; www.hillgardenhotel.com; r incl breakfast US$20-45; ❄ 🛜) The Hill Garden's elevated, lush location – the chalets are scattered throughout a large and appealing garden – make this an excellent choice for getting away from it all. The cheaper digs feature a bamboo design, are fan-only and share bathrooms; the more expensive are cement bungalows with air-con. All have balconies. It's more popular with foreigners than locals.

The downside is that it's a good 20-minute walk north along the coast from the centre of Chaung Tha.

Wut Yee Hotel   HOTEL $

(☑ 042-42305; Main Rd; r incl breakfast K30,000-45,000; ❄) You won't hear much English and there's no wi-fi, but this is a sound budget option. It has decent-sized rooms that are more appealing than the price suggests. The open-air, top-floor restaurant does OK Chinese-Burmese and seafood dishes, plus breakfast. It's also close to the shops and market at the heart of the village.

Shwe Ya Min Guesthouse & Restaurant   GUESTHOUSE $

(☑ 042-42126; Main Rd; r incl breakfast US$15-30; ❄ 🛜) Located across the road opposite the beach, this simple but friendly guesthouse has compact and clean rooms with reasonable beds and plain bathrooms. New, posher rooms were under construction at the time of research. The attached restaurant is good.

★ Akariz Resort   RESORT $$

(☑ 042-42116; www.theakarizhotel.com; r K88,000-165,000; ❄ 🛜 ⛱) Beachfronted and brand new in 2016, the Akariz has 59 attractive, spacious rooms with high ceilings, wood floors and excellent beds. The seafront rooms are particularly good, but all rooms have balconies and terraces and proper bathrooms.

New Chaung Tha Hotel   HOTEL $$

(☑ 042-42367; www.newchaungthahotel.com; r US$100-150; 🛜) Rooms at this place are quite stylish – there's almost a vague boutique feel to them – and sizeable, with decent bathrooms and big windows to gaze out to sea. But given the lack of a pool and restaurant, it feels a little overpriced.

Shwe Hin Tha Hotel
HOTEL $$

(☑ 042-42118; Main Rd; r incl breakfast K44,000-88,000; ✴🛜) This long-standing place at the quieter, northern end of the beach is popular with foreign visitors, possibly because of its breezy seaside bar. It has a mix of fan-only rooms with shared bathrooms, housed in an unprepossessing block, and nicer and more spacious beachfront bungalows with air-con. Wi-fi is in the lobby and restaurant only.

Hotel Ayeyawady
HOTEL $$

(☑ 042-42332; Main Rd; r incl breakfast US$30-50; ✴🛜) You're not seafront here – the beach is across the road – but the rooms are big, modern, comfortable and housed in a near-new block fronted by a swimming pool. There's 24-hour hot water, but power only after 6pm. The staff are helpful and it's decent value for the price.

Belle Resort
RESORT $$

(☑ 042-42112; www.belleresorts.com; Main Rd; r US$80-140; ✴🛜🏊) More stylish than most Chaung Tha hotels, the rooms here are understated sophistication with sprawling beds, big bathrooms and massive windows with equally massive ocean views. Staff are efficient.

Azura Beach Resort
RESORT $$

(☑ 042-42324; frontoffice.azura@gmail.com; Main Rd; r K70,000-120,000; ✴🛜🏊) This brand new resort opened in 2016 at the southern end of the beach. It was still putting the finishing touches to the pool and some rooms when we dropped in. Sea-view rooms are very large and comfortable – although the bathrooms are rather small – and equipped with everything you'd need. The staff aren't really used to foreigners.

Grand Hotel
HOTEL $$

(☑ 042-42330; www.grandhotel-chaungtha.com; Main Rd; r K50,000-88,000; ✴🛜🏊) Popular with families, rooms here are mostly housed in the ugly main building, although they are modern with decent beds but small bathrooms. Not all have sea views. The hotel's restaurant, Grand Bistro, is one of the better places to eat in town, while the attached bakery does reliable cakes and coffee.

Golden Beach Hotel
RESORT $$

(☑ 042-42128; www.goldenbeachchaungtha.com; Main Rd; r K77,000-110,000; ✴🛜🏊) This 56-room resort doesn't have the park-like manicured grounds that others do and the

bungalows don't look much from outside, but inside they're comfortable, if not huge. Cheaper rooms are modern, but lack a sea view. Good swimming pool.

★ Amazing Chaung Tha Resort
RESORT $$$

(☑ 042-42346; www.amazing-hotel.com; Main Rd; r US$80-350; ✴🛜🏊) Formerly known as Hotel Max, this is the swishest resort in Chaung Tha by some distance. Villas and rooms are spread around a large, neatly manicured garden facing the southern end of the beach, there's a tennis court and spa, professional staff and a decent restaurant. Note that garden-view rooms have twin beds only.

🍴 Eating

★ Shwe Ya Min Restaurant
CHINESE, BURMESE $$

(Main Rd; mains from K3500; ⊙ 7am-10pm; 🛜📷) This roofed, open-air place across the road from the beach is the best place in town to eat, outside the swish resort restaurants. It has a big menu of reasonably priced Chinese-Burmese dishes and plenty of seafood. Everything is tasty, prepared with care and served with more style than you'd expect.

Grand Bistro
CHINESE, BURMESE $$

(Main Rd; mains from K5500; ⊙ 7am-10pm; 📷) This restaurant inside the Grand Hotel is one of the better places in town to eat, even if it's not exactly an atmospheric venue. The extensive menu includes Chinese-Burmese, Thai and Rakhine dishes, as well as Bamar food. The seafood is predictably good.

ℹ Information

Reliable and friendly guide Ko Chit Kaung can arrange snorkelling trips, day trips and various modes of transport around the area. Find him at his souvenir shop bearing his name close to the Shwe Ya Min Guesthouse & Restaurant (p100) or call him on ☑ 09 42254 4634.

There were no banks or ATMs in Chaung Tha at the time of research. Bring cash.

ℹ Getting There & Around

The twisting 25-mile road between Chaung Tha and Pathein takes two hours to cover by bus. The route passes through rubber plantations spread across the hills – it's a depressing example of the effects of deforestation. More than half the villages passed along the way are Kayin.

BUS

A number of buses leave for Yangon every day (K10,000, six hours). They terminate at Sule

Paya or Aung San Stadium downtown. Book tickets at your hotel. Buses leave from the hotels, or from the bus station opposite Azura Beach Resort. There's also an earlier departure at 5.30am that goes to Hlaing Thar Yar Bus Terminal in the far west of Yangon.

To continue up the coast to Gwa, and from there to Ngapali, you'll first have to return to Pathein by bus (K4000, two hours, 6am, 8am, 10am, noon and 2pm). From there take a bus to Nga Thein Chaung (one hour) where you'll have to change buses for Gwa (two hours). From Gwa, it's around five to six hours to Ngapali, so reckon on having to overnight in Gwa.

BOAT

If it's calm, consider taking a boat (seats six; K70,000, two hours) to and from Ngwe Saung. This is handy if you're in a group but be prepared to wade ashore with your bags. Ask to be dropped as close to your hotel as possible. Bring water and sunblock.

MOTORBIKE

Motorbike taxis can be hired to take you to Pathein (K12,000) or directly to Ngwe Saung Beach (K18,000).

TAXI

Shared taxis for up to four people to Pathein (K45,000), Ngwe Saung (K45,000) and Yangon (K150,000) can be arranged at your hotel.

Ngwe Saung Beach
ငွေဆောင်ကမ်းခြေ

More sophisticated than nearby Chaung Tha Beach, and with finer sand and clearer, deeper water, palm-fringed Ngwe Saung Beach has emerged as a hip destination for Yangon's new rich. These days, the northern end of the beach is home to a succession of upmarket resorts. But backpackers have long found a home here too – the southern end has budget bungalows and an agreeably laid-back vibe. Foreign visitors tend to prefer this to Chaung Tha's more raucous and local atmosphere. Dividing the north and south of the 13 miles of beach here is Ngwe Saung Village, where there is an increasing crop of decent restaurants. Given Ngwe Saung's relative proximity to Yangon – a six-hour bus ride away – this is perhaps the best place in Myanmar for a beach getaway that won't break the bank.

◉ Sights & Activities

Above all else, Ngwe Saung is an indulgent, lie-back-and-do-nothing sort of place, and most visitors are happy to comply. The kind of activities that are common at Chaung

Tha, such as pony rides and beach football, are noticeably absent here. But if sitting around doing nothing more strenuous than wiggling your toes in the sand sounds boring, there are a few calorie-burning activities you can try.

A boat trip out to **Bird Island**, just visible way out on the horizon, for a day of snorkelling and, dare we say it, birdwatching, is the most popular water-based excursion. Boats can be arranged through many hotels for US$20 per person, but don't run in the rainy season (May to September).

If you don't have the stomach or budget for a boat trip, at low tide you can simply walk over to **Lovers' Island** at the southern end of the beach. The water surrounding this island is also a good place to **snorkel** among dancing clouds of tropical fish. Masks and snorkels can be hired from some hotels (Shwe Hin Tha Hotel and Treasure Resort are the most reliable) for K3000 per day. December, January and February are best for water visibility. Diving trips can be arranged via the dive operations based out of Treasure Resort, Eskala Resort and Ngwe Saung Yacht Club and Resort, which also has a marina from where you can go sailing (US$30 per hour).

🛏 Sleeping

The few budget hotels cluster at the southern end of the beach, while the northern end is home to upmarket resorts, which all offer the same facilities: spa, international restaurant, pool. There are a few midrange options scattered along the beach. Most places close in rainy season (May to September). If you want 24-hour electricity, you'll need to check into an expensive resort: everywhere else has power 6pm to 6am only.

Shwe Hin Tha Hotel　　　　　　HOTEL $$
(☑ 042-40340; bungalow incl breakfast US$33-60; ❄) Set at the southern end of the beach, this place has a magnetic pull for backpackers who agonise over whether to choose simple bamboo huts or the more solid bungalows with air-con. Either way, you can be sure that it will be clean and well maintained, and that hot water will appear on request. No wi-fi, and power only after 6pm.

The attached restaurant is beachside and serves up pretty good dishes.

EFR Seconda Casa　　　　　　HOTEL $$
(☑ 042-40282; www.efrsecondacasa.com; Myoma St; r incl breakfast US$80-100; ❄ 🛜) Slap in the

middle of the village strip, with beach access, this midrange place offers compact rattan bungalows and larger cement ones with suntrap flat roofs to bake on. Bathrooms are plain and small, but the rooms themselves are comfortable.

Silver Coast Beach Hotel HOTEL $$

(☑ 042-40324; htoo.maw@mptmail.net.mm; r incl breakfast US$30-55; 🌡🌐) At the southern end of the beach, steps from Lovers' Island, this secluded, peaceful resort is a good budget option with big, if plain, beachside bungalows set in a garden with plenty of space. The cheaper ones are fan-only and have cold-water showers, but all have balconies.

Silver View Resort HOTEL $$

(☑ 042-40317; silverviewresort@gmail.com; r incl breakfast US$55; 🌡🌐🏊) Located south of the village and more popular with vacationing locals than foreigners, this compact compound offers oldish mint-green-coloured bungalows, most offering sea views. They're clean, and there's a small pool and a restaurant.

★ Bay of Bengal Resort RESORT $$$

(☑ 042-40304; www.bayofbengalresort.com; r incl breakfast US$150-240; 🌡🌐🏊) This immense compound dominates the far northern end of Ngwe Saung and is luxurious without being too pricey. The ground-floor Bengal Suites have a spacious sitting area, huge balconies, and bathrooms with a stone tub and open-air shower. Reasons to leave your room include tennis courts, a vast, cascading pool and a spa.

★ Emerald Sea Resort RESORT $$$

(☑ 042-40247; www.emeraldseahotel.com; r incl breakfast US$100-185; 🌡🌐🏊) Located south of the village, this cosy resort isn't as ostentatious as the newer places along the beach, but it has an attractive design and excellent service. The rooms are beautifully created with minimal decor, making the virgin-white and comfortable interiors all the more classy, even if the bathrooms don't quite live up to the price tag.

There's a decent restaurant (advance notice is often required), a spa and a beautiful stretch of beach out front.

Aureum Palace RESORT $$$

(☑ 042-40217; www.aureumpalacehotel.com; r incl breakfast US$160-810; 🌡🌐🏊) Designed in glitzy royal Myanmar style with plenty of gilded traditional carvings and soaring teak pillars, the Aureum caters to the very rich who can gaze out at the strip of beach 20yd in front of the vast, thatched-roof seafront villas. In contrast, the cheapest rooms are rather small for the price. The staff are professional and there's a spa too.

Ngwe Saung Yacht Club & Resort RESORT $$$

(☑ 042-40100; www.ngwesaungyachtclub.com; r incl breakfast US$60-240; 🌡🌐🏊) Built for the 2013 Southeast Asian Games, this resort sprawls across a less-attractive stretch of the beach 5 miles south of Ngwe Saung Village. As the name suggests, there's a nautical theme, with a marina offering boats for hire (US$30 per hour), a diving club and good pool. Rooms are modern, well appointed and comfortable, and the staff are professional.

The cheapest rooms are plain and fan-only and are set in an annex to the side of the main resort (although guests can still use all the resort's facilities). Next to it is a camping site, where two- and four-person tents can be rented (US$50 to US$70).

Eskala Resort RESORT $$$

(☑ 042-40341; www.youreskala.com; r incl breakfast US$110-175; 🌡🌐🏊) This conveniently opened resort just south of Ngwe Saung Village is more reasonably priced than some of its competitors. It offers cooking classes and a dive operation, plus the usual spa, pool and restaurant. Rooms are comfortable, without being distinctive, the seafront bungalows being the best of them. It has keen staff and is walking distance to the village restaurants.

Sunny Paradise Resort RESORT $$$

(☑ 042-40227; www.sunnyparadiseresort.net; r incl breakfast US$75-270; 🌡🌐🏊) Yet another imposing compound north of the village, Sunny Paradise also includes two adjacent properties: Dream Paradise and Ocean Paradise (offering the cheapest rooms with no direct beach access). The attractive, well-equipped wooden bungalows in the Sunny Paradise section are the pick of the bunch.

✗ Eating

Break out of your hotel at least once to eat in the village, where there is a growing number of restaurants. There is little to distinguish one from another – most places offer similar menus focusing on Chinese-style, seafood-based dishes.

★ Ume Restaurant & Bar ASIAN $$

(☑ 09 42532 4652; mains from K4500; ⊙10am-10pm; 🌐📶) Run by a Japanese woman and her Burmese husband, this cool place is lit up spectacularly at night (check out the lights 50ft up at the top of the surrounding palm trees). The menu spans Chinese-Burmese, Thai and Japanese, with pizza as well. There's a nightly fire-dance show and the bar stays open till midnight serving OK cocktails.

Ume is south of the village, close to the Silver View Resort (p103).

Royal Flower
SEAFOOD, INTERNATIONAL $$

(Myoma St; mains from K4500; ⊙10am-10pm; 🖭) The same seafood and Chinese-Burmese dishes offered by all Ngwe Saung restaurants are supplemented here by reasonable pizza and pasta. There's a pleasant atmosphere – there's mellow live music sometimes – and it's consistently popular.

Golden Myanmar
Restaurant
CHINESE, BURMESE $$

(Myoma St; mains from K4000; ⊙7am-10pm; 🖭) Busy with both locals and visitors, this restaurant is located in the middle of Ngwe Saung Village and offers decent and fresh dishes. The seafood is especially good, but the salads are worth sampling too.

West Point
SEAFOOD $$

(Myoma St; mains from K7000; ⊙10am-10pm; 🖭) The closest thing you'll get to seaside dining in the village (the view is distant), West Point has sand for a floor and a nice ambience. But, sadly, the charges for the seafood, Chinese and Thai offerings have jumped considerably in the last couple of

years. The food remains worthwhile, but it is overpriced.

ℹ Information

Sandalwood (⊙7am-7pm), a cafe and information centre, is the place to go for local info. It's located in the market behind the main village strip (accessed off the road on the left heading out of town towards the pagoda).

Local expert and guide **Tom Tom** (📞 09 42246 2904) can arrange a day trip or snorkelling excursion, and rents motorcycles (K10,000 per day). If he's not at the Sandalwood cafe in the market, he can also be found via the Shwe Hin Tha Hotel (p102).

There are a couple of KBZ Bank ATMs in the village and outside the upmarket hotels, including Emerald Sea Resort and Ngwe Saung Yacht Club and Resort, but they're often not working. Bring cash.

ℹ Getting There & Around

Air-con buses to Yangon (K10,000, five to six hours) leave at 6.30am, 8am and noon from Ngwe Saung Village. During rainy season (May to September), only the 8am bus runs. For Pathein (K4000, two hours), buses go at 6.30am, 7.30am, 9am, noon and 3pm. The buses leave and arrive at the junction between the village and the beach resorts.

Taxis can be arranged to Pathein (K45,000) and Yangon (K140,000).

You'll need a motorbike taxi to move between the southern end of the beach and Ngwe Saung Village (K1000). Motorbikes can be hired via Sandalwood or from some hotels for about K10,000 per day.

Southeastern Myanmar

Best Places to Eat

➡ San Ma Tau Myanmar
Restaurant (p123)

➡ Daw Yee (p114)

➡ Shwe Mon (p134)

➡ Bone Gyi (p114)

➡ Zan Pya (p134)

➡ Hla Hla Hnan (p130)

Best Places to Sleep

➡ Hpa-an Lodge (p123)

➡ Cinderella Hotel (p112)

➡ Ngwe Moe Hotel (p112)

➡ Golden Sunrise Hotel
(p108)

➡ Hotel Zayar Htet San
(p129)

Why Go?

Off the beaten track and strangely neglected by many visitors, southern Myanmar offers some of the finest natural sights in the entire country.

In the space of a couple of days, you can descend into the Buddha-packed caves around sleepy Hpa-an and ascend the winding road to the sacred golden boulder perched on Mt Kyaiktiyo (Golden Rock). Then there's the little-known and even less-visited Myeik Archipelago, perhaps Myanmar's most dramatic intersection of water, land and sky.

If that wasn't enough, the historic city of Mawlamyine, once Myanmar's capital, has almost as fine a collection of colonial-era buildings as Yangon, while Dawei and Myeik can boast of centuries of history as ports and mix traditional wooden architecture with brick mansions and buildings constructed during British rule. Best of all, the lack of visitors means there's plenty of space to enjoy the region.

When to Go
Southeastern Myanmar

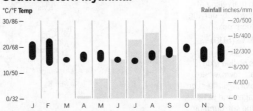

Mar–Apr Temperatures can reach as high as 86°F (30°C) during the summer.

Nov–Jan The days are relatively cool during the winter.

May–Oct Southern Myanmar sees more rain than elsewhere during the wet season.

Southeastern Myanmar Highlights

❶ Myeik Archipelago (p135) Sailing, cruising, snorkelling and diving among the 800-odd islands here.

❷ Hpa-an (p121) Discovering seemingly hidden lakes, hanging Buddhist art and a sparkling spring in the many caves around Hpa-an.

❸ Mawlamyine (p109) Hoping for the inspiration that fired Kipling to compose his most famous opening line in his poem 'Mandalay'.

❹ Myeik (p131) Travelling back in time in this ancient, atmospheric and allegedly haunted port city.

❺ Dawei (p127) Heading to the little-seen golden-sand beaches around this sleepy and historic southern capital.

❻ Mt Kyaiktiyo (p107) Reaching for enlightenment and marvelling at this gravity-defying golden rock.

❼ Ye (p119) Kicking back in this chilled Mon State town, while exploring little-seen villages and temples in the surrounding area.

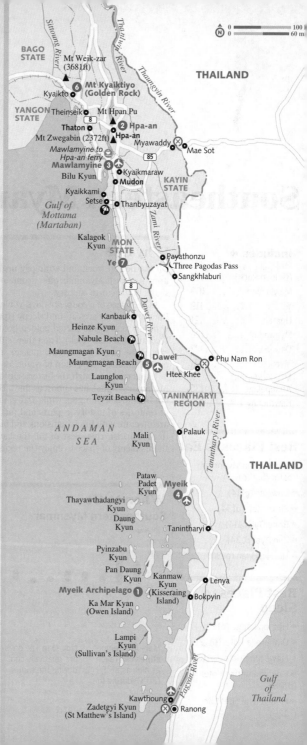

MON STATE

Mon State has a mix of everything that's wonderful and unique about Myanmar: golden temples, a palpable colonial past, charming villages, a mix of different ethnic groups and even some scenic coastline. Travelling in this region is generally easy and the people are friendly, while the distances between key destinations are short. Yet, despite the historic cities and the presence of some of Myanmar's most holy religious sites, relatively few visitors make it down here. That, though, is their loss and travellers who do come have all the more space to enjoy it all.

History

Once native to a broad region stretching from southern Myanmar to Cambodia, the Mon have been absorbed – sometimes willingly, sometimes not – by the more powerful Burmese and Thai cultures in Myanmar and Thailand respectively over the last thousand years.

Though no one knows for sure, the Mon may be descended from a group of Indian immigrants from Kalinga, an ancient kingdom overlapping the boundaries of the modern Indian states of Odisha and Andhra Pradesh. They were responsible for much of the early transmission of Theravada Buddhism in mainland Southeast Asia.

Since 1949 the eastern hills of the state (as well as mountains further south in Tanintharyi Region) have been a refuge for the New Mon State Party (NMSP) and its tactical arm, the Mon National Liberation Front (MNLF), whose objective has been self-rule for Mon State. In 1995, after years of bickering and fighting, the NMSP signed a ceasefire with the Myanmar government. Since then, peace has largely been maintained, and foreign travellers can now venture south of Mawlamyine freely.

Mt Kyaiktiyo (Golden Rock) ကျိုက်ထီးရိုးတောင်

🎵 057

Mt Kyaiktiyo (K6000), the Golden Rock, sounds bizarre: an enormous, precariously balanced boulder covered in gold and topped with a stupa. But this monument is a major pilgrimage site for Burmese Buddhists and it's the presence of so many devotees that makes the place so special.

The atmosphere during the pilgrimage season (November to March) is charged with magic: pilgrims chant, light candles and meditate all through the night, while men (only) are permitted to walk over a bridge spanning a chasm to the boulder to affix gold leaf squares on the rock's surface. And the boulder itself is stunning, especially when bathed in the purple, sometimes misty, light of dawn and dusk.

During the rainy season (June to October), the mountain is mostly covered in a chilly coat of mist and rain, although that doesn't stop people from coming here. The area's hotels are open during this period, but some restaurants shut down.

🏃 Activities

Ascending the Mountain

Kinpun, a busy hub of restaurants, souvenir shops and hotels, is the base camp for Mt Kyaiktiyo. It's from here that large trucks climb the 7 winding miles to the rock (K2500 per person). The truck beds are lined with wooden slats for benches and seat about 40 people. Five passengers are allowed in the much more comfortable front seats (K3000 per person) but these are usually reserved in advance by groups or families. As an individual traveller, it's difficult to secure a front seat, while a group of five has a better chance. The trucks don't leave until they are packed to the brim, so you may have to wait for an hour or more to depart.

The ride takes about 45 minutes and usually includes a brief stop around halfway up to allow trucks coming from the opposite direction to pass. The first truck in the morning leaves at 6am and the last truck down departs at 6pm, though you should try to be at the terminal earlier to avoid the risk of being stranded for the night.

In the old days, trucks only went as high as Yatetaung terminal, leaving pilgrims with a 45-minute, unforgiving and sweaty schlep to the top. Now, the trucks proceed virtually to the peak of Mt Kyaiktiyo, terminating steps from Mountain Top Hotel and the ticket checkpoint, leaving us to ask, 'Where's the sacrifice?'

Perhaps it's the requisite K6000 entrance fee for foreigners, payable a short walk from the truck terminal, just after the Mountain Top Hotel. Tickets are valid for two days. Women wearing shorts or skimpy tops risk being denied entry.

Hiking & Other Activities

If you have the time to extend your stay in the vicinity there are several other rewarding hikes that take in eye-popping views and quiet religious meditation. You can start your journey from Kinpun, the Yatetaung bus terminal, or even the shrine itself.

From Kinpun the most obvious short hike is to **Maha Myaing Pagoda** (မဟာမြိုင်ဘုရား), a miniature Kyaiktiyo, an hour's climb from Kinpun. Any of the Kinpun hotels can point you in the right direction.

From Yatetaung bus station, it's a 45-minute climb to the top of **Mt Ya-The** (ရသေ့တောင်), a 30-minute walk down to **Mo-Baw Waterfall** (မိုးဘောရေတံခွန်) and a 1½-hour walk to the **Sa-ma-taung paya** and **kyaung** (monastery; ဆမတောင်ဘုရား ၊ ဆမတောင်ကျောင်း).

From Kyaiktiyo itself, a trail continues along the crests of the surrounding peaks for another couple of hours to the **Kyauk-si-yo Zedi** (ကျောက်ဆည်ရိုးစေတီ) and **Kyaiktiyo Galay Zedi** (ကျိုက်ထီးရိုးလေးစေတီ), two small, golden, hilltop stupas.

🛏 Sleeping

In terms of value for money, Kinpun and Kyaiktiyo's hotels are some of the worst in Myanmar. Budget options are especially poor, but the high-end places at the summit of the mountain are also grossly overpriced for what you get. If you want to catch the sunrise and sunset, though, this is where you need to be.

Note that foreigners aren't permitted to stay in the many *zayat* (rest shelters) for pilgrims at the mountain summit.

🛏 On the Mountain

Mountain Top Hotel　　　HOTEL **$$**
(☎09 871 8392, in Yangon 01-502 479; www.mountaintop-hotel.com; Mountain Summit; r incl breakfast US$110-135; ❇🛜) The pick of the hotels on the summit, the rooms here are still overpriced but they're clean and well maintained, with good service, and the lo-

cation means stunning views. The attached restaurant is reliable. Wi-fi in the lobby only.

Yoe Yoe Lay Hotel　　　HOTEL **$$**
(☎09 872 3082; www.yoeyoelayhotel.com; Mountain Summit; r incl breakfast US$100-120; ❇) Towering over the pilgrims' village north of the boulder, the Yoe Yoe Lay offers fantastic views from some of its rooms. But it doesn't offer much else, as many of the rooms are small, old-fashioned and have basic bathrooms. At night, the place is lit up like a gaudy Christmas tree.

Kyaik Hto Hotel　　　HOTEL **$$**
(☎09 4981 9196, in Yangon 01-536 003; www.kyaikhtohotel.com; Mountain Summit; r incl breakfast US$85-100; ❇🛜) This former government-owned hotel is where most package tourists stay. There are two wings: the institution-like old block and the better, bungalow-style rooms opposite. None are really worth the price, but they are just a short walk to the boulder.

🛏 Kinpun

⭐**Golden Sunrise Hotel**　　　HOTEL **$**
(☎09 872 3301; www.goldensunrisehotel.com; Golden Rock Rd, Kinpun; s/d incl breakfast US$42/47; ❇🛜) A few minutes' walk outside the centre of Kinpun village in the direction of the highway, the Golden Sunrise is one of the better-value hotels in southern Myanmar. The semi-detached, bungalow-style rooms are undisturbed by noise, decked out with attractive wood furniture, and come with verandahs overlooking a secluded garden.

Bawga Theiddhi Hotel　　　HOTEL **$**
(☎09 4921 6464; www.bawgatheiddhihotel.com; Kinpun; r incl breakfast without bathroom US$20-35, with bathroom US$45; ❇🛜) Kinpun's flashiest hotel has rooms that are clean, spacious

---

LEGEND OF THE BALANCING BOULDER

Legend states that the boulder at Mt Kyaiktiyo maintains its precarious balance due to a precisely placed Buddha hair in the stupa. Apparently King Tissa received the Buddha hair in the 11th century from a hermit who had secreted the hair in his own topknot. The hermit instructed the king to search for a boulder that had a shape resembling the hermit's head, and then enshrine the hair in a stupa on top. The king, who inherited supernatural powers as a result of his birth to a *zawgyi* (an accomplished alchemist) father and *naga* (dragon serpent) princess, found the rock at the bottom of the sea. Upon its miraculous arrival on the mountain top, the boat used to transport the rock then turned to stone. This stone can be seen approximately 270m from the main boulder – it's known as the Kyaukthanban (Stone Boat Stupa).

MT KYAIKTIYO TRANSPORT CONNECTIONS

DESTINATION	BUS	TRAIN
Bago	K5000; 3hr; frequent 8.45am-4pm	K650/K1300 (ordinary/upper class); 3hr; daily noon and midnight
Hpa-an	K7000; 3hr; frequent 9am-3pm	N/A
Mawlamyine	K7000; 4hr; frequent 10am-4pm	K1300/K2550 (ordinary/upper class); 4hr; daily noon & 11.30pm
Yangon	K7000; 5hr; frequent 8.45am-4pm	K1200/K2450 (ordinary/upper class); 5hr; daily noon & midnight

and equipped with TV, fridge and free wi-fi, although only the most expensive come with their own bathroom (the shared bathrooms are well maintained).

Lotus Da Dar　　　　　　　HOTEL **$$**
(☑ 09 2644 92468; reservations@lotusdadar.com; Kinpun; r incl breakfast US$38-60; ❄ ☎) This new hotel has 20 bungalow-style rooms set around an attractive garden. The cheaper rooms are plain; the deluxe ones have better bathrooms. All come with their own verandahs. There's an on-site restaurant and an ATM in the lobby. It's a 10-minute walk from the bus station on the road to Golden Rock.

Golden Rock Hotel　　　　　HOTEL **$$**
(☑ 09 871 8391; www.goldenrock-hotel.com; Mountain; r incl breakfast US$110; ❄ ☎) The Golden Rock Hotel, just a few minutes up from the Yatetaung bus terminal, has comfortable rooms in a secluded location. But you're neither close to the rock itself nor to Kinpun's restaurants, so it's not very convenient. It's normally closed for most of the rainy season (April to September).

✖ Eating

Kinpun has a number of restaurants on the main street with standard Chinese and Burmese menus. At the summit of the mountain, there are many basic restaurants and food stalls.

Yin Yin Pyone　　　　　　　BURMESE **$**
(Kinpun; mains from K3000; ⊙ 5am-8.30pm; 🗒) On the main street in Kinpun, this amiable, Mon-run place cooks up a big selection of reliable curries – fish, chicken, pork and mutton – for lunch, as well as offering Chinese-influenced dishes.

❶ Information

There are no internet cafes in Kinpun, but all the guesthouses and hotels offer wi-fi connections of varying quality.

There is a tiny branch of the KBZ bank in Kinpun with an ATM, but it was closed at the time of research. Another ATM can be found in the lobby of the Lotus Da Dar Hotel. Nearby Kyaikto has branches of the CB and KBZ banks that change money and have ATMs.

❶ Getting There & Away

The major transport hub for Mt Kyaiktiyo is the similar-sounding town of Kyaikto. This is where the train station is, and the town's main street is where you'll board (or disembark from) buses. Frequent pick-ups cruise the road between Kyaikto's train station and Kinpun (from 7am to 4pm, K500, 20 minutes), which is the base camp for Mt Kyaiktiyo.

The one destination you might consider using a train to get to is Kyaiktiyo. Every Saturday, a service using air-conditioned carriages departs Yangon for the Golden Rock at 6.25am (US$10; 4½ hours); it returns on Sunday at noon arriving in Yangon, in theory, at 4.25pm. The air-conditioned carriages are eventually destined to be used on the Yangon Circle Line, once station platforms on that route have been upgraded.

Tickets for relatively comfortable Win Express buses can be purchased in Kinpun across from Sea Sar Hotel and restaurant. The ticket price includes the transfer by pick-up to Kyaikto.

Mawlamyine　　　မော်လမြိုင်

POP C 253,730 / ☑ 057

With a ridge of stupa-capped hills on one side, the Thanlwin River on the other and a centre filled with crumbling colonial-era buildings, churches and mosques, Mawlamyine is a unique combination of landscape, beauty and melancholy. The setting inspired both George Orwell and Rudyard Kipling, two of the English-language writers most associated with Myanmar. Kipling penned his famous poem 'Mandalay' after visiting, while Orwell, whose mother was born here, used Mawlamyine as the backdrop for the stories 'Shooting an Elephant' and 'A Hanging'. Not that much has changed since the days when Orwell and Kipling

Mawlamyine

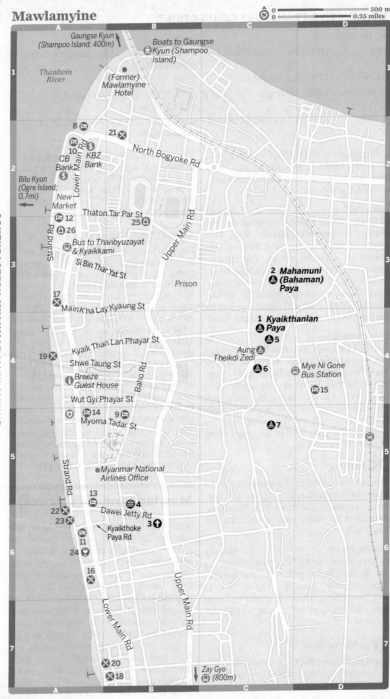

0 ____ 500 m
0 ____ 0.25 miles

Gaungse Kyun
(Shampoo Island; 400m)

Thanlwin
River

Boats to Gaungse
Kyun (Shampoo
Island)

(Former)
Mawlamyine
Hotel

8

21

North Bogyoke Rd

10
CB
Bank

KBZ
Bank

Bilu Kyun
(Ogre Island;
0.7mi)

New
Market

12

26

Thaton Tar Par St

25

Upper Main Rd

Bus to Thanbyuzayat
& Kyaikkami

Si Bin Thar Yat St

Strand Rd

Prison

2 **Mahamuni
(Bahaman)
Paya**

17

Main Kha Lay Kyaung St

1 **Kyaikthanlan
Paya**

5

Kyaik Than Lan Phayar St

19

Shwe Taung St

Aung
Theikdi Zedi

6

Mye Ni Gone
Bus Station

15

Breeze
Guest House

Baho Rd

Wut Gyi Phayar St

14

9

7

Myoma Tadar St

Myanmar National
Airlines Office

Strand Rd

13

22

23

Dawei Jetty Rd

4

3

Kyaikthoke
Paya Rd

11

24

16

Upper Main Rd

Lower Main Rd

20

18

Zay Gyo
(800m)

Mawlamyine

were here and if you've ever wondered what life was like during the Raj, Mawlamyine is about as close as it gets.

But it's not all about history; the area around Mawlamyine has enough attractions, ranging from beaches to caves, to keep a visitor happy for several days.

History

Known to the British as Moulmein, Mawlamyine served as the first capital of British Burma from 1826 to 1852, during which time it developed as a major teak port and saw a major influx of immigrants from India. A fair amount of coastal shipping still goes on, although Yangon and Pathein have superseded Mawlamyine as Myanmar's most important ports. The city is composed roughly of 75% Mon, plus Kayin (Karen), Bamar, Indian, Chinese and other ethnic groups.

⊙ Sights

★ Kyaikthanlan Paya   BUDDHIST TEMPLE
(ကျိုက်သံလန်ဘုရား; Kyaik Than Lan Phayar St; ⊙ daylight hours) FREE Rudyard Kipling's visit to Myanmar spanned just three days, but it resulted in a few lines that turned Burma into an Oriental fantasy: 'By the old Moulmein Pagoda, lookin' lazy at the sea...' The 'Moulmein Pagoda' cited in his poem 'Mandalay' was most likely Kyaikthanlan Paya, the city's tallest stupa.

It's a great spot for views over the city and for watching the sunset. To reach it, approach via the long covered walkway that extends from Kyaik Than Lan Phayar St.

This walkway also had an impact on Kipling, who was later to comment of it: 'I should better remember what the pagoda was like had I not fallen deeply and irrevocably in love with a Burmese girl at the foot of the first flight of steps. Only the fact of the steamer starting next noon prevented me from staying at Moulmein forever...'

★ Mahamuni (Bahaman) Paya   BUDDHIST TEMPLE
(မဟာမုနိ(ဗြဟ္မာ)ဘုရား; ⊙ daylight hours) FREE Directly north of Kyaikthanlan Paya and linked by a covered walkway, this is the largest temple complex in Mawlamyine and easily the most beautiful. It's built in the typical Mon style with covered brick walkways linking various shrines. The highlight is the Bahaman Paya itself, a jewel-box chamber shimmering with mirrors, rubies and diamonds, and containing a century-old replica of its namesake in Mandalay.

Mon Cultural Museum   MUSEUM
(မွန်ယဉ်ကျေးမှုပြတိုက်; cnr Baho & Dawei Jetty Rds; K5000; ⊙ 9.30am-4.30pm Tue-Sun) Unlike most of Myanmar's regional museums, Mawlamyine's is actually worth a visit, even if the collection here is not huge. It's dedicated to the Mon history of the region and the exhibits include stelae with Mon inscriptions, 100-year-old wooden sculptures depicting old age and sickness (used as *dhamma*-teaching devices in monasteries), ceramics, silver betel boxes, royal funerary urns and Mon musical instruments, with most exhibits accompanied by English-language descriptions.

U Zina Paya   BUDDHIST TEMPLE
(ဦးဇိနဘုရား; ⊙ daylight hours) FREE On the southern spur of the ridge overlooking Mawlamyine, this pagoda was named after a former monk who dreamed of finding

gems here, then dug them up and used the proceeds to build a temple on the same site. One of the shrine buildings contains a very curvy, sensual-looking reclining buddha; there are also statues depicting Gautama Buddha's meeting with a sick man, an old man, a dead man and an ascetic – encounters that encouraged him to seek the meaning behind human suffering.

Seindon Mibaya Kyaung   BUDDHIST TEMPLE
(စိန်တုံးမိဖုရားကျောင်း; Kyaik Thank Lan Phayar St; ⊙ daylight hours) **FREE** This 100-year-old monastery is famed for being the place where King Mindon's Mon queen, Seindon, sought refuge after Myanmar's last monarch, King Thibaw, took power.

U Khanti Paya   BUDDHIST TEMPLE
(ဦးခန္တီဘုရား; ⊙ daylight hours) **FREE** This temple was built to commemorate U Khanti, the hermit architect of Mandalay Hill fame. U Khanti supposedly spent some time on this hill as well. It's a rustic, airy sort of place centred on a large buddha image.

Gaungse Kyun (Shampoo Island)   ISLAND
(ခေါင်းဆေးကျွန်း; ⊙ daylight hours) This picturesque little isle just off Mawlamyine's northern end is so named because, during the Ava period, the yearly royal hair-washing ceremony customarily used water taken from a spring on the island. Peace rather than sights is the reason for venturing out here.

You can hire a **boat** (return K3000; ⊙ daylight hours) out here from the pier at the north end of town, not far from the former Mawlamyine Hotel, for K3000 return.

If you're in the mood to explore, you can visit Sandawshin Paya, a whitewash-and-silver *zedi* (stupa) said to contain Buddha hair relics, and a nearby Buddhist meditation centre. Many nuns, with a menagerie of pet dogs, live on the island.

First Baptist Church   CHURCH
(cnr Upper Main & Dawei Jetty Rds; ⊙ daylight hours) **FREE** Founded by American Adoniram Judson in 1827, this was the country's first Baptist church. In addition to this place of worship, Judson's legacy also includes being the first person to translate the Bible into Burmese. As a result of his work, today Myanmar has the third-highest population of Baptists in the world, after the United States and India.

🛏 Sleeping

Mawlamyine's accommodation options have improved, but decent budget places remain elusive. Hotels cluster either in the centre of town close to the riverfront or, less conveniently, near the train and Mye Ni Gone bus station.

Pann Su Wai   GUESTHOUSE $
(☑ 057-22921; 333A Lower Main Rd; r K13,000-26,000; ❇ 🕸) None of the rooms are huge – the singles are tight – and they don't get a lot of natural light, but they are clean and come with OK bathrooms, making them a reasonable deal for the money. The owner speaks English. There's no kitchen here, so no breakfast.

Shwe Myint Mo Tun Hotel   HOTEL $
(☑ 057-27347; r incl breakfast US$35-45; ❇ 🕸 🏊) The pool here is the highlight, because the rooms, located in four-room bungalows or a two-storey poolside structure, are plain and not big. The location outside the city centre on a busy road close to the train station and the Mye Ni Gone bus station is inconvenient, unless you're just passing through for the night.

OK Hotel   HOTEL $
(☑ 057-25097; www.okhotel-mlm.com; cnr Strand Rd & Thaton Tar Par St; s/d incl breakfast US$12/24; ❇ 🕸) As the name suggests, this is an OK budget option, although the old-fashioned rooms aren't big and you'll get some street noise from the nearby market area as well. The cheapest singles are fan-only and very small indeed.

Sandalwood Hotel   HOTEL $
(☑ 057-27253; 278 Myoma Tadar St; r incl breakfast K25,000-30,000; ❇ 🕸) The tile-walled rooms here are spacious and spotless, if a tad institutional and wholly unremarkable. The staff are pleasant and can arrange cars for day trips.

★ Cinderella Hotel   HOTEL $$
(☑ 057-24411; www.cinderellahotel.com; 21 Baho Rd; s/d/tr incl breakfast US$25/55/70; ❇ 🕸) Ignore the shocking purple exterior because inside the rooms are comfortable, spotless, tastefully decorated and well equipped, the staff solicitous and the breakfast one of the best in Myanmar. The one single here books out fast, as do all the rooms in high season.

★ Ngwe Moe Hotel   HOTEL $$
(☑ 057-24703; www.ngwemoehotel.com; cnr Kyaikthoke Paya & Strand Rds; r incl breakfast US$45-60; ❇ 🕸) The spacious, modern rooms here are excellent value with very comfortable beds,

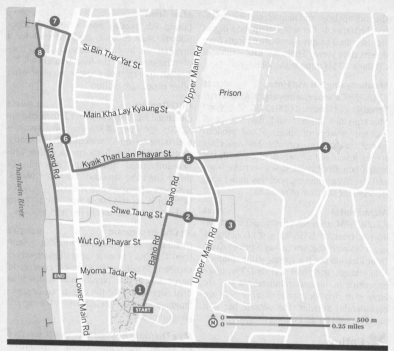

Walking Tour
Colonial Mawlamyine

START BAHO RD
FINISH STRAND RD
LENGTH 2.5 MILES; TWO TO THREE HOURS

Between 1826 and 1852, Mawlamyine served as the first capital of British Burma. An abundance of British residents – from colonial officials to Anglo-Burmese – led to the city being known as 'Little England', a legacy still palpable in Mawlamyine's architecture.

Start your walk near the ❶ **park** on Baho Rd, formerly known as Dalhousie St (after a Scottish administrator of British India). Head north, turning east on ❷ **Shwe Taung St** (look for the corner with the motorcycle taxi drivers), an atmospheric strip of brightly coloured, low-slung houses home to the descendants of Indian civil servants originally brought to Mawlamyine by the British.

Cross Upper Main Rd to ❸ **St Patrick's Cathedral**, founded by the De La Salle brothers in 1829. At the back of the church compound is an overgrown graveyard with headstones, many with British names, some dating back to the mid-19th century.

Continue north on Upper Main Rd. If you haven't already been, turn east on Kyaik Than Lan Phayar St and ascend the covered stairway to ❹ **Kyaikthanlan Paya** (p111) – the inspiration for Kipling's famous poem 'Mandalay'. From here you'll also have a great view of Mawlamyine's prison, built in 1908 and probably the setting for George Orwell's lesser-known 1931 short story 'A Hanging'.

Head west on Kyaik Than Lan Phayar St, veering south into any of the atmospheric side streets and taking in the tiny mosques and colonial-era homes in this predominately Muslim neighbourhood of ❺ **Shwe Taung Quarter**. Emerge on ❻ **Lower Main Rd**, Mawlamyine's main commercial strip, home to many old multistorey shophouses. Continue north until you reach ❼ **Surtee Sunni Jamae Masjid**, a mosque built in 1846 to serve the Muslim officers and civil servants of British Burma.

Then turn west on Phat Tan St. You're now on the riverside ❽ **Strand Rd**, where, heading south, you'll pass the former grand mansions, shipping company offices and theatres from Mawlamyine's former role as a wealthy trading port.

the staff are keen and helpful, and the expansive breakfast buffet sets you up for a day of sightseeing. The more expensive rooms have decent river views. There are KBZ Bank and CB Bank ATMs outside the lobby.

Mawlamyaing Strand Hotel HOTEL $$
(☎ 057-25624; www.mawlamyaingstrandhotel.com; Strand Rd; r incl breakfast US$110-130; ✳ @ 🛜 🏊) Mawlamyine's biggest and flashiest hotel has four storeys of spacious and modern rooms that are on par with business-class rooms just about anywhere else – with the added benefit of great views over the town and river. A swimming pool was under construction at the time of research.

Attran Hotel HOTEL $$
(☎ 057-25764; attranhotelrsvn@gmail.com; Strand Rd; r incl breakfast US$58-90; ✳ 🛜) Looking its age a bit now, the Attran has a prime riverfront location but the rooms, while comfortable enough, are plain and dull. The more expensive are housed in bungalows and are large with river views; the cheaper ones are considerably smaller. The outside bar is a passable spot for an evening libation.

🍴 Eating

⭐ Daw Yee BURMESE $
(U Ze Na Pagoda St; curries from K2500; ⏰ 11am-10pm) Humble Daw Yee does some of the best Burmese food we've come across. It has a great selection of curries, including an insanely fatty prawn curry. Be sure to order one of the vegetable side dishes (K500) that change daily. It's off the southern end of Strand Rd, about 10 minutes' walk south of the Ngwe Moe Hotel; look for the English sign.

Grandfather & Grandmother Restaurant CHINESE, BURMESE $
(Strand Rd; mains from K2500; ⏰ 7am-9pm; 🍴) The money raised at this restaurant goes to a charity helping the town's elderly. No alcohol is served, but they do have decent fruit shakes, reasonable Chinese-Burmese dishes and a riverside location. The sign is written in Burmese only; look for the silhouettes of old people walking with canes.

YKKO BURMESE $
(Strand Rd; mains from K3500; ⏰ 9am-9pm; 🍴) This chain can be found across Myanmar now and is popular both with richer locals and foreigners seeking reliable and clean food. There's a wide range of noodle and rice options, as well as soups and fruit juices.

Maw Shan SHAN $
(Strand Rd; noodles from K1000; ⏰ 7.30am-6.30pm) Maw Shan is a sound spot for a breakfast or lunch of authentic Shan noodles; be sure to try the fried tofu as well. No English spoken, but you can point at what other people are eating.

BBQ Garden BURMESE $
(58 Strand Rd; barbecue from K300, mains from K2500; ⏰ 4-10pm; 🍴) A barn-like space – with a big screen for watching the football – that serves decent barbecue as well as Chinese-influenced dishes and seafood. It's pricer than the streetside barbecue places, but more upmarket and the grilled pork leg (K2500) is great. Choose from the proteins and veggies on display in the refrigerators.

Mi Cho Restaurant BURMESE $
(North Bogyoke Rd; meals from K2500; ⏰ 9am-9pm) This busy hole-in-the-wall place serves excellent Muslim-style Burmese cuisine; in particular, a rich biryani and a delicious dhal soup. Look for the tiny green English-language sign and get here early: the biryani goes quickly.

Mya Thanlwin Restaurant CHINESE, BURMESE $
(Strand Rd; mains from K3000; ⏰ 9am-11pm; 🍴) Standard Burmese-influenced Chinese dishes are available here, but it's as much a place to drink as it is to eat, and the riverside setting and draught beer draw in the locals each night.

Bone Gyi CHINESE, BURMESE $$
(cnr Strand Rd & Main Kha Lay Kyaung St; mains from K3000; ⏰ 9am-9pm; 🍴) There's a huge menu here, mostly featuring Chinese-inspired dishes but also including a few Thai ones and even some spicy Rakhine State–style soups. It's especially good for fish, grilled or steamed. There's a big outside area, efficient service and it's determinedly foreigner-friendly, so a little pricier than other restaurants of its type.

🍷 Drinking & Nightlife

Olala BAR
(383 Strand Rd; ⏰ 2-10pm) Mawlamyine's only genuine bar, Olala serves up reasonable cocktails, as well as local and foreign beers, in a laidback atmosphere and also offers a menu of snack-sized Chinese, Thai and Western food. There's outdoor seating and this is where you will find Mawlamyine's tiny community of foreign residents of an evening.

🔒 Shopping

Mawlamyine has a number of busy markets including the riverside **Zeigyi** (Lower Main Rd; ⊙ 6am-6pm) and the biggest of all, **Myine Yadanar Market** (Thaton Tar Par St; ⊙ 6am-2pm). Though locals distinguish between all of them, you probably won't as they virtually meld into one another and you'll be too engrossed in the melange of smells, sights and tastes to care anyway.

ℹ️ Information

Mawlamyine has branches of the **CB Bank** (Strand Rd; ⊙ 9.30am-3pm) and **KBZ Bank** (Upper Main Rd; ⊙ 9.30am-3pm), with both foreign exchange and ATMs available. There are a number of other ATMs around town too.

Though we'd recommend skipping the basic accommodation at **Breeze Guest House** (☑ 057-22919, 057-21450; breeze.guesthouse@gmail.com; 6 Strand Rd), the staff can arrange reliable guides and trips to Bilu Kyun, as well as renting bicycles (K2000 per day) and motorbikes (K10,000 per day), and chartering boats for the trip to Hpa-an by river (K10,000 per person).

ℹ️ Getting There & Away

At the time of research, **Myanmar National Airlines** (☑ 057-21500, 09 871 8220; www.flymna.com; ⊙ 9am-3pm) was the only domestic airline flying out of Mawlamyine, operating just one flight a week to Yangon (US$91, Monday) and one flight a week to Kawthoung (US$161, Monday). Both these flights are prone to cancellation.

There are no public ferries to Hpa-an, but private boats can be chartered (up to 14 people) at K10,000 per person for the two-hour trip; enquire at **Breeze Guest House**.

Buses for destinations north of Mawlamyine use the **Mye Ni Gone bus station**, located near the train station; a motorcycle taxi to/from the centre should cost K500. For routes south of Mawlamyine, head to the Zay Gyo bus station, a couple miles south of the city centre; a motorcycle taxi to/from here should cost K1000. Vans (actually share taxis) to Myawaddy (K10,000, four to six hours, frequent 6am to 4pm) depart from opposite the entrance to Zay Gyo bus station. Vans to Ye (K3000, four hours) frequently depart between 6am and 1.30pm.

Mawlamyine's train station is 1.5km east of the city centre, a K500 ride on a motorcycle taxi. At the time of writing, trains were not running south of Dawei.

ℹ️ Getting Around

Motorcycle taxis are found on just about every corner in Mawlamyine (short trips K500; longer journeys from K1000).

For destinations outside of town, you'll want a driver. This can be arranged at any hotel. Count on K50,000 to K60,000 for a full day hire. You can also call Ko Min Naing (☑ 057-22247, ☑ 09 2558 42830), a reliable driver who speaks some English.

MAWLAMYINE TRANSPORT CONNECTIONS

DESTINATION	BUS	TRAIN
Bago	K6000; 5hr; daily 8.30am, 9am, 1pm, 2pm, 7pm, 8.30pm, 9pm & midnight	K1660/K3150 (ordinary/upper class); 7hr; daily 8am, 7.30pm & 9pm
Dawei	K11,000-12,000; 8-9hr; 6am, 5.30pm & 6.30pm	K2950/K5900 (ordinary/upper class); 16hr; daily 4.30am
Hpa-an	K1000; 2hr; hourly 6am-4pm	N/A
Kawthoung	K40,000-45,000; 25hr; daily 6am, 5.30pm & 6.30pm	N/A
Kyaikto (for Mt Kyaiktiyo)	K3000; 4hr; daily 8.30am, 11am, 8pm & 8.30pm	K1300/K2250 (ordinary/upper class); daily 8am, 7.30pm & 9pm
Mandalay	K15,500; 13hr; daily 6pm & 7pm	N/A
Myeik	K18,000-20,000; 16hr; daily 6am, 5.30pm & 6.30pm	N/A
Nay Pyi Taw	K10,500; 8hr; daily 6pm	K3400/K6750 (ordinary/upper class); 15hr; daily 6.15am
Pyin Oo Lwin	K17,000; 17hr; daily 5pm	N/A
Yangon	K6000-10,000; 7hr; daily 8.30am, 9am, 1pm, 2pm, 7pm, 9pm, 8.30pm & midnight	K2150/K4250 (ordinary/upper class); 10hr; daily 8am, 7.30pm & 9pm
Ye	K3000; 4hr; daily 7am, 9am, 11am, 1pm, 2pm & 4pm	K1100/K2200; 6hr; daily 4.30am

Around Mawlamyine

If you're finding Mawlamyine a bit too sleepy, you'll be delighted to find that the town functions as a great base for a variety of easy and worthwhile day trips. Visits to Bilu Kyun, a nearby island with handicraft workshops, and to the Buddhist sites south and east of Mawlamyine are the most popular excursions.

Many people save themselves time and hassle by hiring a car (K60,000 per day) and guide (US$20 per day) in order to explore fully. All the hotels can organise this, although the best guides can be found at Breeze Guest House (p115), where Mr Antony and Mr Khaing are both informative and entertaining.

South of Mawlamyine

◎ Sights

Pa-Auk-Taw-Ya Monastery   BUDDHIST MONASTERY
(ဖားအောက်တောရသုန်းကြီးကျောင်း; ☏ 057-22853; www.paaukforestmonastery.org) FREE
Only 8.5 miles south of Mawlamyine, the monastery teaches *satipatthana vipassana* (insight-awareness meditation) and, at 500 acres, is one of the largest meditation centres in Myanmar. Foreigners can visit for the night or several days; sleeping and eating is free but you're up at 3am every day.

Win Sein Taw Ya   BUDDHIST TEMPLE
(ဝင်းစိန်တောရ; ◉ daylight hours) FREE If you thought you'd seen some big old buddhas,
just wait till you get a load of this one. Draped across a couple of green hillsides at Yadana Taung, around 15 miles southwest of Mawlamyine, and surrounded by a forest of other pagodas and shrines, is this 560ft-long reclining buddha. It's easily one of the largest such images in the world.

Many other stupas and standing buddhas dot the area, including 500 statues lining the road to the Win Sein Taw Ya. Aside from inflated buddhas, the area affords some gentle walks with wonderful panoramas.

Every year around the first couple of days of February a festival takes place here to celebrate the birthday of the monk who constructed the buddha. As well as a host of itinerant traders, monks and nuns, magic men and the odd hermit or two, the festival often hosts a major kickboxing tournament, which leads to the slightly surreal sight of hundreds of cheering monks baying for blood in the ring!

Kyauktalon Taung   BUDDHIST TEMPLE
(ကျောက်တစ်လုံးတောင်; ◉ daylight hours) FREE
Kyauktalon Taung is a strangely shaped, sheer-sided crag rising out of the surrounding agricultural land and crowned with stupas. It's a sticky 20-minute climb to the summit. On the opposite side of the road is a similar but smaller outcropping surmounted by a Hindu temple. Kyauktalon Taung is 40-odd minutes south of Mawlamyine, on the road to Thanbyuzayat.

Kandawgyi   LAKE
(ကန်တော်ကြီး; ◉ daylight hours) FREE This lake formed by **Azin Dam** (a water storage

---

NWA-LA-BO PAGODA

A local pilgrimage site, **Nwa-la-bo Pagoda** (နွားလသို့ဘုရား; ◉ daylight hours) FREE is still relatively unknown outside Mon State and, currently, very few foreigners make it out here. This is surprising because the pagoda is a smaller but, geologically at least, far more astonishing version of Kyaiktiyo. Unlike at that shrine, where just one huge boulder perches on the cliff ledge, Nwa-la-bo consists of three sausage-shaped **gold boulders** piled precariously atop one another and surmounted by a stupa.

Nwa-la-bo can't be reached during the rainy season (approximately June to October) and is at its best on a weekend when pilgrims will add more flair to the scene and transport is a little more regular. From Mawlamyine you'll have to wait at the roundabout before the bridge for a northbound bus or pick-up to Kyonka village (K1000), around 12 miles north of town. From here clamber into the back of one of the pick-up trucks that crawl slowly up to the summit of the mountain (K2000 return) in 45 minutes. Allow plenty of time as the trucks don't leave until beyond full, and don't leave your descent too late in the day as transport becomes scarcer after 3pm. Alternatively, motorcycle taxis will do the trip to Kyonka for K8000.

BILU KYUN (OGRE ISLAND)

Not quite as scary as it sounds, **Bilu Kyun** (ဘီလူးကျွန်း) is a beautiful Mon island directly west of Mawlamyine. Roughly the size of Singapore, Bilu Kyun comprises 78 villages that are home to more than 200,000 people. It's a green, fecund place, with palm-studded rice fields and fruit plantations, and has the vibe of a tropical island, only without the beaches.

Some of Bilu Kyun's villages are associated with the production of various handicrafts and household items, from coconut-fibre mats to slate tablets, although the number of workshops has declined in recent years and many of those remaining are now more geared to tourists than anything else.

There's public transport to Bilu Kyun, but the boats run a confusing schedule from a variety of piers. The local authorities also require notice to visit Bilu Kyun. That may change once a new bridge linking the island to the mainland is completed in 2017, but until then the best way to approach the island is via a day tour. Mr Antony or Mr Khaing at Breeze Guest House (p115) lead informative tours, which typically run from 9am to 5pm, circling the island, stopping in at various craft workshops and tacking on a swim stop. The K18,000 fee per person covers transport and lunch.

At research time, foreigners were not allowed to stay overnight on Bilu Kyun.

and flood-control facility that's also used to irrigate local rubber plantations) also boasts a tidy recreation area and is a favourite picnic spot with locals. Don't miss the tasty *buthi kyaw* (deep-fried gourd) sold here. At the northern end of the lake stands the gilded stupa of **Kandawgyi Paya**. The lake is around 18.5 miles southeast of Mawlamyine.

🛈 Getting There & Away

Hop on a Mudon-bound bus from Mawlamyine's Zay Gyo bus station and ask to be dropped at the junctions for any of the southern sights (K800 to K2000, 45 minutes, hourly from 6am to 4pm). Alternatively, a return-trip motorcycle taxi from Mawlamyine to any of the sights will run K8000 to K10,000.

Thanbyuzayat & Around

👁 Sights

Thanbyuzayat   HISTORIC SITE
(သံဖြူဇရပ်; ⊙daylight hours) **FREE** Thanbyuzayat, 40 miles south of Mawlamyine, was the western terminus of the infamous Burma–Siam Railway, dubbed the 'Death Railway' by the thousands of Allied prisoners of war (POWs) and Asian labourers who were forced by the Japanese military to build it. Half a mile west of town lies the **Thanbyuzayat War Cemetery**, containing 3771 graves of Allied POWs who died building the railway.

Most of those buried here were British, but there are also markers for American, Australian and Dutch soldiers. As you walk around this simple memorial, maintained by the Commonwealth War Graves Commission, reading the heart-rending words inscribed on the gravestones, it's impossible not to be moved to the brink of tears.

Death Railway Museum   MUSEUM
(သေမင်းတမန်မီးရထားလမ်းပြတိုက်; ☑09 9716 84627; Thanbyuzayat; K5000; ⊙8am-5pm) This modest new museum in Thanbyuzayat is located at the actual western terminus of World War II's infamous death railway, which connected Myanmar to Thailand and was built under appalling conditions by Asian labourers and Japanese-held Allied prisoners of war. A short stretch of railway track and a Japanese WWII-era locomotive lead to the museum, which has a collection of photos and a dramatic 3D painting depicting a scene from the railway's route but little else on display.

The museum is located about a mile south of Thanbyuzayat's clock tower on the road to Ye. Officially there is a K5000 fee to visit the museum, but it wasn't being charged at the time of research.

Kyaikkami   VILLAGE
(ကျိုက္ခမီ) Located 15 miles northwest of Thanbyuzayat, Kyaikkami was a small coastal resort and missionary centre known as Amherst during the British era. The town is an atmospheric seaside destination, although you'll probably not do any swimming at the rocky and rather muddy beach. Instead, the main focus is **Yele Paya** (ရေလယ်ဘုရား), a metal-roofed Buddhist

THE DEATH RAILWAY

The strategic objective of the Burma–Siam Railway was to secure an alternative supply route for the Japanese conquest of Myanmar and other Asian countries to the west.

Construction on the railway began on 16 September 1942 at existing terminals in Thanbyuzayat and Nong Pladuk, Thailand. At the time, Japanese engineers estimated that it would take five years to link Thailand and Burma by rail, but the Japanese army forced the Allied prisoners of war (POWs) and Asian labourers to complete the 260-mile, 3.3ft-gauge railway in 13 months. Much of the railway was built in difficult terrain that required high bridges and deep mountain cuttings. The rails were finally joined 23 miles south of the town of Payathonzu (Three Pagodas Pass); a Japanese brothel train inaugurated the line. The railway was in use for 21 months before the Allies bombed it in 1945.

An estimated 16,000 POWs died as a result of brutal treatment by their captors, a story chronicled by Pierre Boulle's book *The Bridge on the River Kwai* and popularised by the movie based on the book. Only one POW is known to have escaped, a Briton who took refuge among pro-British Kayin guerrillas.

Although the statistics of the number of POWs who died during the Japanese occupation are horrifying, the figures for the labourers, most from Myanmar, Thailand, Malaysia and Indonesia, are even worse. It is thought that 80,000 Asians, 6540 British, 2830 Dutch, 2710 Australians and 356 Americans died in the area.

shrine complex perched over the sea and said to house 11 Buddha hair relics.

The shrine chamber beneath Yele Paya reportedly contains a buddha image that supposedly floated here on a raft from Sri Lanka in ancient times. A display of 21 Mandalay-style buddha statues sits over the spot where the Sinhalese image is buried. Note that women are not allowed into the main shrine here. One oddity here is that pilgrims standing at the water's edge place clay pots of flowers and milk into the sea in order to 'feed' the spirits.

Adoniram Judson (1788–1850), an American missionary and linguist who has practically attained sainthood among Myanmar Baptists, was sailing to India with his wife when their ship was blown off course, forcing them to land at Kyaikkami. Judson stayed on and established his first mission here; the original site is now a Catholic school on a small lane off the main road.

The only accommodation in town is **Kaday Kywe Guest Villa** (☑ 09 4253 36347, 057-75019; Bogyoke Rd, Kyaikkami; r fan-only/air-con K10,000/50,000; ✱☎), a short walk from Yele Paya. There's a basic restaurant directly across the street.

Setse Beach
BEACH

(စက်စဲမ်းခြေ) This is not a picture-postcard beach by any stretch of the imagination, but as the grime of travel washes away, you probably won't care. This low-key Gulf of Mottama (Martaban) beach, around 50 miles southwest of Mawlamyine, is a very wide, brown-sand strip. The beach is lined with waving casuarina trees and has been a popular spot for outings since colonial times. Though a few locals stop by for a swim, almost no foreigners visit this area and facilities are minimal.

At low tide you can walk along the beach to the small **temple** on the rocks at the northern end.

You can stay at the privately owned **Shwe Moe Guesthouse** (☑ 09 870 3283; Setse; r US$30-60; ✱), which has spacious but run-down beach bungalows. A few modest restaurants offer fresh seafood, including the **Pyay Son Oo Restaurant**, which is very close to the hotel.

❶ Getting There & Away

The same bus runs first to Thanbyuzayat (K1000, two hours, 6am to 4pm) and then Kyaikkami (K1000, three hours, 6am to 4pm). Buses leave from a stall (Lower Main Rd) near Zeigyi market.

During the first half of the day there are regular pick-up trucks from Thanbyuzayat to Kyaikkami (K500) and Setse (K500). The last return departure for both is about 4pm.

East of Mawlamyine

◉ Sights

Kyaikmaraw Paya
BUDDHIST TEMPLE

(ကျိုက်မရောဘုရား; Kyaikmaraw; ☉ daylight hours) **FREE** The small town of Kyaikmaraw

(ကျိုက်မရော), 15 miles southeast of Maw-lamyine, is the site of Kyaikmaraw Paya, a temple of serene, white-faced buddhas built by Queen Shin Saw Pu in 1455. Among the temple's many outstanding features are mul-ticoloured glass windows set in the outside walls, an inner colonnade decorated in mir-rored tiles, and beautiful ceramic tile floors.

Covered brick walkways lead up to and around the main square sanctuary in typi-cal 15th-century Mon style. The huge main buddha image sits in a 'European pose', with the legs hanging down as if sitting on a chair, rather than in the much more common cross-legged manner. A number of smaller cross-legged buddhas surround the main image, and behind it are two reclining buddhas. Another impressive feature is the carved and painted wooden ceiling.

Perhaps as impressive as the temple is the route there, which passes through bright-green rice fields studded with sugar palms and picturesque villages.

Kha-Yon Caves
CAVE

(ခရိုဝ်; ☉ daylight hours) FREE Spirited away in the back of the little-known, dark and dank Kha-Yon Caves are rows of ghostly buddha statues and wall paintings that come lurch-ing out of the dark as the light from a torch catches them. Close by is another, smaller, cave system with an open cavern and a small cave-dwelling stupa. Bring a torch or buy candles from the stall near the entrance. The caves are northeast of Mawlamyine, 30 minutes by bus along the road to Hpa-an.

❶ Getting There & Away

Pick-ups to Kyaikmaraw (K500, one hour, hourly from 6am to 4pm) leave from just south of a roundabout close to Zay Gyo bus station: all motorcycle taxi drivers know the place.

For Kha-Yon Caves, head to Mawlamyine's Mye Ni Gone bus station, take any bus towards Hpa-an and ask to be dropped at the junction for the caves (K1000, 30 minutes, hourly from 6am to 4pm).

Ye
ရေးမြို့

POP C 34,430 / ☎ 057

Charming Ye, pronounced 'yay', has long been off travellers' maps. Until recently, govern-ment restrictions prevented foreigners from moving south of Mawlamyine by road, which left Ye, roughly halfway between Mawlamy-ine and Dawei, isolated. With an attractive,

tree-lined lake at its heart and the Ye River running through it, Ye is a compact town of traditional wooden houses, a hectic, big mar-ket and friendly, curious locals. It's a great place to kick back for a few days and expe-rience small-town Myanmar life, while it's also the ideal base for excursions into the sur-rounding countryside, where you'll find Mon and Kayin villages that rarely see foreigners.

◉ Sights

Most of the sights are outside Ye and you'll need a motorbike to reach them. If you don't want to drive yourself, Starlight Guesthouse (p120) can arrange an English-speaking guide and driver for K25,000 to K30,000 per day. We cover some of the highlights, but you could easily spend a week exploring the area.

Kyaing Ywar
VILLAGE

(ကျိုင်းရွာ) You approach this mixed Mon and Kayin village of wooden stilt houses perched over the Ye River along a road that winds through betel nut, rubber and pineapple plantations, interspersed with golden pago-das half-hidden by trees. The journey is sce-nic enough, but the real reason to come here is to hire a longtail boat (K10,000 return) and head upriver *Apocalypse Now*–style.

After 15 minutes, you'll see a statue of Buddha on a pillar that rises high above the river. The pillar is the cue to stop and climb the stairs to **Kyaing Lakoiw Paya**, a small pagoda funded by the local villagers. You can continue on along the river to oth-er villages (the longer the journey, the more you'll pay the boat captain). Kyaing Ywar is about 8 miles east of Ye, a 40-minute ride on a motorcycle.

Ko Yin Lay
BUDDHIST SITE

(ကိုရင်လေး; off Ye-Mawlamyine Rd; ☉ daylight hours) FREE Known to the locals as 'Banana Mountain', there's no hill to climb here. In-stead, it's an expanding Buddhist complex of shrines and an attractive monastery, all dom-inated by four vast sitting Buddhas grouped around a tower. You can climb the nine-storey tower for great views. The monastery offers a free and tasty vegetarian lunch (a do-nation to the monastery is appreciated). Ko Yin Lay is around five miles north of Ye, off the main Ye–Mawlamyine Rd.

The complex came into being 20 years ago, after villagers noted how a devout novice monk spent weeks alone meditating here. At that time, the area was jungle and the locals swear the now-landscaped site did look like a 'banana mountain' back then.

Shwemawdaw Paya
BUDDHIST TEMPLE

(ရွှေမော်တောဘုရား; Kyaing Ywar village; ⊙ daylight hours) FREE Thirty white-faced standing golden Buddhas rise up the steep track that leads to this peaceful temple, with its own, smaller version of Mt Kyaiktiyo's famous golden rock and a golden *zedi*. Best of all are the stunning views over the surrounding countryside and the Ye River. The temple is at the opposite end of Kyaing Ywar village to the riverfront.

Market
MARKET

(ဈေး; Strand Rd; ⊙ 6am-6pm) Ye is a centre of betel nut production, as well as retailing a lot of fish, and the town's busy market features both products, as well as lots of produce, clothes and imported goods from Thailand. There are also food stalls here. The market sprawls down Strand Rd, running parallel with the Ye River, occupying many blocks.

Shwesandaw Paya
BUDDHIST TEMPLE

(ရွှေဆံတော်ဘုရား; Main Rd; ⊙ daylight hours) FREE Ye's principal shrine sits close to both the lake and the market, its golden pagoda easily visible. There are two main prayer halls, both in the Mon Style; one containing a golden Buddha and the other featuring 20 white-faced Buddhas surrounding six central Buddhas.

Gold Market
MARKET

(ရွှေဈေး; Bo Yint Nawng St; ⊙ 7am-5pm) Ye's small gold market – just to the east of the main market – features mostly jewellery, rather than gold leaf or gold bars. It is worth a stroll and a chat with the vendors, mostly smiley middle-aged ladies who conduct business perched on raised platforms behind metal grilles.

🛌 Sleeping

★ Starlight Guesthouse
GUESTHOUSE $

(☎ 09 2557 13253, 09 2500 88616; www.starlight-guesthouse.com; 13 Yan Gyi Aung Rd; r incl breakfast K21,000-26,000; 🕸🅟) Run by laidback American David and his cheerful Mon wife Winnie, the Starlight is a traveller-friendly guesthouse perched by the lake in the heart of Ye. The six rooms here aren't big, but they are clean and comfortable and some have lake views. Motorcycles can be rented (K7000 per day) and knowledgeable English-speaking guides arranged.

Mya Myint Mo Hotel
HOTEL $

(☎ 057-50527; myamyintmo.ye@gmail.com; 26-28 Duya St; r incl breakfast K30,000; 🕸🅟) On a residential street close to the market, the Mya Myint Mo has compact but modern, well-equipped rooms with decent beds and OK bathrooms. There are good views over Ye from the top floor.

🍴 Eating & Drinking

For a small town, Ye has some decent restaurants, the most atmospheric of which surround the lake. Many serve the Burmese take on Thai food, a consequence of so many locals going to nearby Thailand to work in resorts and restaurants.

There are teahouses and beer stations in the centre of town. One peculiarity of Ye is that the restaurants around the lake don't serve alcohol because the lake is considered holy.

Rot Sar
THAI $

(Lakeside; dishes K600-2500; ⊙ 10am-10pm; 📶) Rot Sar offers the most authentic take on Thai food in Ye – there's a limited English menu – and you get to eat overlooking the lake. It's on the far side of the lake, close to the monastery.

Jasmine Cool
THAI, BURMESE $

(Lakeside; mains from K1500; ⊙ 7am-10pm) Perhaps the most popular teahouse in Ye, the exotically named Jasmine Cool does basic Thai dishes, as well as standard Chinese-Burmese ones, in a lakeside setting. It's busy from the time it opens and is close to the Starlight Guesthouse.

Dream
BEER GARDEN

(Ba Nyar Yan Toe Chae St; beers from K2000; ⊙ 10am-midnight) An unusually sophisticated beer garden for provincial Myanmar, Dream has foreign beers – Thai and Western – as well as Myanmar lager, and a small selection of vodka, gin and whisky. It does reasonable Chinese-Burmese dishes too. It's in the south of town, about 10 minutes' walk from Shwesandaw Paya.

ℹ️ Information

There's a branch of **KBZ Bank** (Main Rd; ⊙ 9.30am-3pm), with ATM, where you can exchange money. There are a couple of other ATMs around town that take foreign cards too.

ℹ️ Getting There & Away

Buses depart from outside the bus ticket offices that can be found along Main Rd, close to the

Shwesandaw Paya (p120). There are five buses daily to Yangon (K8300 to K10,300, 11 hours, 7.30am to 6pm) and seven daily to Mawlamyine (K3000, four hours, 6am to 2.15pm). There's also a daily bus to Dawei at 7am (K6000, four hours), which leaves from the market area close to the riverfront.

Ye's rustic train station is in the west of town. There's a daily train to Yangon at 2.30pm (ordinary/upper class K3250/K6450, 16 hours), two trains daily to Mawlamyine at 4am and 2.30pm (ordinary/upper class K850 to K1100/K2200, six hours) and one train daily to Dawei at 9.30am (ordinary/upper class K1900/K2800, 10 hours).

Getting Around

Ye is a compact place, but motorcycle taxis hop around town for K500 a trip. Drivers congregate by the market and outside Shwesandaw Paya on Main Rd.

Motorcycles can be rented at Starlight Guesthouse (p120) for K7000 per day.

KAYIN STATE ကရင်ပြည်နယ်

The combination of fantastic scenery – tree-covered limestone hills rising above luminous green paddy fields – and a fascinating ethnic mix, makes Kayin State a Myanmar highlight. That's despite the fact that significant parts of the state remain off-limits to foreign visitors, thanks to ongoing tensions caused by what is thought to be the world's longest-running internal conflict.

Almost from the moment Myanmar attained its independence in 1948, the Karen, the main ethnic group in Kayin State, started their battle for autonomy. Since 2012 a fragile ceasefire has been in place between the largest insurgent body, the Karen National Union (KNU), and the Burmese government. That has resulted in the welcome opening of the border with Thailand at Myawaddy. But the KNU's military component, the Karen National Liberation Army (KNLA), continues to control parts of the north and east of the state and foreigners are barred from visiting those areas.

Hpa-an ဘားအံ

POP C 75,140 / ☎058

Hpa-an, Kayin State's scruffy riverside capital, isn't going to inspire many postcards home. But the people are friendly and the city is the logical base from which to explore the Buddhist caves, sacred mountains and rivers and lakes of the surrounding countryside.

Sights & Activities

Khiri Travel (http://khiri.com) offers kayaking excursions through the wetlands around Hpa-an with Kayin guides leading; check its website for more details. There's also some good climbing to be found in the area, although not for beginners. Myanmar Rock Community, based in Yangon, run climbs here. Contact Andrew Riley at andrewkyleriley@gmail.com for more information.

Shweyinhmyaw Paya BUDDHIST TEMPLE
(ရွှေရင်မှော်ဘုရား; off Thida St; daylight hours) FREE Close to the waterfront, this golden pagoda is a popular hang-out around sunset, as well as an easy place to watch the world go by during the day.

Morning Market MARKET
(off Thitsar St; 5am-11am) Hpa-an's vibrant morning market is good for a wander and a chat with the locals.

Clock Tower MONUMENT
(Bo Gyoke St) Now digitised, but not always accurate, Hpa-an's clock tower is lit up at night like a gaudy lollipop.

Sleeping

Accommodation in Hpa-an is a game of two halves, with budget and most midrange options located in town, while upmarket places sit outside the city. Unless you have your own transport, staying outside Hpa-an will leave you stranded in your hotel.

Galaxy Motel GUESTHOUSE $
(☎09 566 1863, 058-21347; cnr Thitsar & Thida Sts; r US$22;) The Galaxy is the sort of guesthouse Myanmar needs more of: tidy and clean with spacious rooms that feature air-con, wi-fi and modern bathrooms. The friendly owner speaks good English and can organise tickets and trips, as well as bicycle (K2000 per day) and motorbike (K7000 per day) hire.

Soe Brothers II Guesthouse GUESTHOUSE $
(☎058-22748, 09 7924 98664; soebrothers05821372@gmail.com; 4/820 Engyin St; r incl breakfast US$15-40;) More upmarket than their original guesthouse (p122), the latest addition to the Soe Brothers family features modern, fresh rooms in pastel pink. The cheaper singles aren't huge and

Hpa-an

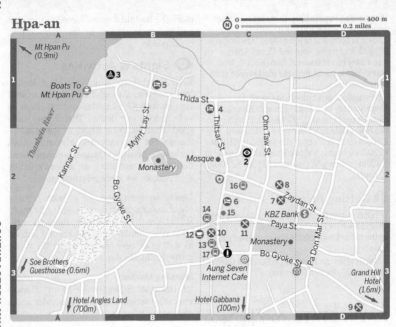

Hpa-an

◎ Sights

🛏 Sleeping

✪ Eating

🍸 Drinking & Nightlife

ℹ Transport

are fan-only, but there's a nice roof terrace for breakfast and the staff are as solicitous as ever. The riverside location means it is a 20-minute walk to the centre of town.

Hotel Angles Land HOTEL $

(☑ 058-21256; angle.landhotel@gmail.com; Padauk Rd; r incl breakfast US$40-45; ❄🛜) This new-ish hotel boasts 22 big, well-maintained and well-equipped rooms, all with equally large bathrooms. It's located about 1 mile south of town, near Hpa-an's City Hall and close to the river.

Golden Sky Guesthouse GUESTHOUSE $

(☑ 058-21510; Thida St; r incl breakfast K20,000-K25,000; ❄🛜) This rough-and-ready, old-school Myanmar guesthouse comes with slightly eccentric owners and an OK communal area. Its biggest rooms, which come with air-con, are acceptable. Trips to the surrounding area can be arranged here.

Soe Brothers Guesthouse HOSTEL $

(☑ 058-21372, 09 4977 1823; soebrothers 05821372@gmail.com; 2/146 Thitsar St; r US$6-25; ❄🛜) A long-standing backpackers' crash pad, the rooms here are basic but the family that runs the place is tuned in to travellers' needs and can arrange many hassle-free excursions. The cheapest rooms are fan-only and share bathrooms; the more expensive ones offer some space. They have another newer, more sophisticated place (p121) close to the river.

Grand Hill Hotel
HOTEL $

(☎058-22286; info@grandhillmyanmar.com; Sin Phyushin St; r incl breakfast US$30-50; ❄🛜) A suburban compound with plain and old-fashioned rooms in the main building and a strip of attached bungalows. None are huge, but the more expensive include air-con, TV and fridge. The cheaper rooms lack windows and are a tight fit. The location, about 2 miles east of the clock tower, isn't convenient.

Hotel Gabbana
HOTEL $$

(☎058-22425; www.hpa-anhotelgabbana.com; Basic Education High School 1 St; r incl breakfast US$45-70; ❄🛜) The best of the midrange options in Hpa-an itself. Rooms aren't huge, but they are comfortable with modern bathrooms and some come with decent views of Mt Zwegabin. Efficient, English-speaking staff and a reasonably central location 10 minutes' walk from the central clock tower.

Hotel Zwekabin
HOTEL $$

(☎058-22556; Hpa-an–Mawlamyine Rd; r incl breakfast US$70-90; ❄🛜) This hotel boasts a park-like atmosphere at the foot of limestone karsts opposite Mt Zwegabin. The best rooms are the vast duplex bungalows with balconies taking in the view; the still-spacious 'Premier' and 'Superior' rooms are in a two-storey condo-like bloc. Located 4 miles outside of town, it's not a very convenient place to stay if you don't have your own wheels.

★Hpa-an Lodge
HOTEL $$$

(☎09 2533 07774; www.hpa-an-lodge.com; base of Mt Zwegabin; r US$200-350; ❄🛜🏊) Set around an attractive, spacious garden with Mt Zwegabin looming overhead, the Hpa-an Lodge is the swishest place in the area. French-run, it features 18 bungalow-style rooms. All are big – the two family rooms are two-storey houses – and very comfortable and superbly maintained. You'll need to book well in advance here, even in the rainy season.

✖ Eating

★San Ma Tau Myanmar Restaurant
BURMESE $

(1/290 Bo Gyoke St; curries from K2000; ⊘11am-9pm; 🏠) This local institution is one of our favourite Burmese restaurants anywhere in the country. The friendly and popular place serves a vast selection of rich curries, hearty soups and tart salads, all accompanied by platters of fresh veggies and herbs and an overwhelming 10 types of local-style dips to eat them with.

Yadanar 2
SHAN $

(Paya St; dishes from K800; ⊘7am-8pm; 🏠) The Hpa-an branch of a famous restaurant in Taunggyi, Shan State, Yadanar 2 serves up tasty Shan noodles, as well as noodle soups, dumplings and a nice lemon fish dish.

Khit Thit Restaurant
CHINESE, BURMESE $

(2/247 Zaydan St; mains from K3500; ⊘8am-10pm; 🏠🏠) Chinese-inspired dishes fill the menu at this friendly, clean place that also shows the soccer. The English-language menu has many options, including plenty of vegetarian ones, or it's OK just for a beer.

Lucky 1
CHINESE, BURMESE $

(Zaydan St; mains from K3500, beers from K700; ⊘8am-11pm; 🏠) This popular place is the closest thing Hpa-an has to a bar – with Kirin and Myanmar lager on tap – and also serves reasonable Chinese-style dishes.

White
TEAHOUSE $

(cnr Thitsar & Bo Gyoke Sts; tea & snacks from K250; ⊘5am-8pm) It's rather grungy but this teahouse serves decent tea and freshly baked naan – great for breakfast. It's just north of the clock tower.

🍷 Drinking & Nightlife

New Day
CAFE

(3/624 Bo Gyoke St; drinks from K600; ⊘8am-4pm) This modern cafe features real coffee, tasty fruit shakes and a variety of baked goods, although its hours are often irregular.

ℹ Information

Slow internet is available at the **Aung Seven Internet Cafe** (Bo Gyoke St; per hour K500; ⊘10am-8pm), just east of the clock tower. All guesthouses and hotels have wi-fi.

Money can be exchanged at the **KBZ Bank** (Zaydan St; ⊘9.30am-3pm), which also has an ATM.

ℹ Getting There & Around

BOAT

There is no official ferry between Hpa-an and Mawlamyine, but private boats that carry 10 to 14 people can be chartered for K10,000 per person. Galaxy Motel (p121) and Soe Brothers Guesthouse (p122) can arrange this.

BUS & PICK-UP TRUCK

Hpa-an's bus station is located about 4 miles east of town, but tickets can be bought and buses boarded at the **ticket stalls** (Bo Gyoke St; ⊙ 6am-9pm) near the clock tower. Buses to Mawlamyine also stop here and at other spots around town. All hotels and guesthouses can arrange tickets.

Vans (share taxis) to Myawaddy (K8000 to 10,000, four to six hours) depart from a **stall** (Bo Gyoke St; K9000; ⊙ hourly 6am-9am) near the clock tower intersection.

DESTINATION	BUS
Bago	K5000; 6hr; daily 6am-9pm
Kyaikto	K5000; 4hr; daily 6am-9pm
Mandalay	K15,000; 12hr; daily 5pm & 6pm
Mawlamyine	K1000; 1½hr; hourly 6am-4pm
Yangon	K5000; 7-8hr; daily 6am-9pm

Around Hpa-an

The real highlights of Hpa-an are all scattered about the divine countryside out of town. While many of these sights are potentially accessible by public transport, you'd need to devote several days to them and be prepared to give your leg muscles a workout. Therefore, almost everyone takes a motorbike (or *thoun bein*; motorised trishaw) tour that circumnavigates Mt Zwegabin, stopping at all of the main sights. A full-day tour costs K30,000 per vehicle (up to six passengers) or K5000 per person, while a half-day tour, hitting destinations of your choice, runs from K15,000 to K20,000. Soe Brothers Guesthouse (p122), Galaxy Motel (p121) and Golden Sky Guesthouse (p122) all organise tours.

⊙ Sights & Activities

★ Saddan Cave
CAVE

(သဒ္ဒန်ဂူ; ⊙ daylight hours) FREE This football-stadium-sized cave is simply breathtaking, its entrance dominated by dozens of buddhas statues, a couple of pagodas and some newer clay wall carvings.

In absolute darkness (bring a torch; otherwise for a donation of K3000, they'll turn on the lights for you), you can scramble for 15 minutes through black chambers as high as a cathedral, truck-sized stalactites and, in places, walls of crystal.

Adding to the general atmosphere, thousands of bats cling to the cave roof. The squealing from them is deafening in places; watch out for bat excrement.

Emerging at the cave's far side, the wonders only increase and the burst of sunlight reveals an idyllic secret lake full of ducks and flowering lilies hidden in a bowl of craggy peaks. There is another cave on the far side of the lake that is actually half flooded, but local fishers occasionally paddle through the cave for 10 minutes to yet another lake. You may be able to persuade one to take you along.

Saddan Cave can be traversed only partially during the rainy season. Come here during the dry season (around November to April) for the full experience. The cave is 17 miles from Hpa-an along the road to Eindu. To get here, take a pick-up to Eindu (K1000). From the village take a motorbike taxi (K2000) for the remaining 2 miles to the cave.

Mt Hpan Pu
HIKING

(ဘားပုတောင်) Mt Hpan Pu is a craggy, pagoda-topped peak that can be scaled in one sweaty morning. To get here, hop on a boat across the Thanlwin River (K500, every 30 minutes from 6am to 6pm) from the informal **jetty** (K500; ⊙ 6am-6pm, every 30min) near Shweyinhmyaw Paya. After reaching the other side, you'll walk through a quiet village before the steep but relatively short ascent to the top.

The views of the river, the surrounding rice fields and limestone cliffs (including Mt Zwegabin) are astounding.

Kyauk Kalap
BUDDHIST MONASTERY

(ကျောက်ကလပ်; ⊙ daylight hours) FREE Standing proud in the middle of a small, artificial lake is Kyauk Kalap, a tall finger of sheer rock mounted by one of the most unlikely pagodas in Myanmar. The rock offers great views of the surrounding countryside and nearby Mt Zwegabin, and is allegedly the best place to see the sunset over this mountain.

A round-trip by motorcycle taxi from Hpa-an will cost K6000, or K10,000 by *thoun bein*.

The compound is a working monastery and is closed every day from noon to 1pm to allow the monks to meditate.

The monastery is also where the highly respected monk U Winaya, whose solid support of democracy leader Aung San Suu Kyi is well known in Myanmar, first resided. U Winaya passed away several years ago and his body was entombed in a glass case at Thamanyat Kyaung, another monastery

MT ZWEGABIN

The tallest of the limestone mountains that ring Hpa-an is **Mt Zwegabin** (ရွှေကပင်တောင်), about 7 miles south of town, which as well as being a respectable 2372ft, is also home to spirits and saintly souls. The two-hour hike to the summit is demanding – up many steps and with aggressive monkeys as constant adversaries – but once at the top the rewards are plentiful.

The summit takes in staggering views, a small monastery and a stupa containing, yes, you guessed it, another hair from the Buddha. If you arrive at the top before noon you can take advantage of a complimentary lunch (rice, orange and tea) and the 11am monkey feeding – different primates, different menus.

The descent down the east side of the mountain takes around 1½ hours. At the time of writing, there was talk of a cable car being constructed in the near future.

You can go to the mountain on a tour from a guesthouse. Alternatively, motorcycle taxis do the return trip for K5000, while a *thoun bein* is K10,000. The hike starts with a 15-minute walk through a village to the base of the mountain on the west side past hundreds (1150 to be precise – don't believe us? Get counting!) of identical Buddha statues lined up row after row.

It is possible to stay at the monastery overnight for a K5000 donation, but sleeping conditions are very simple.

about 25 miles southeast of Hpa-an. On one night in April 2007, the monk's body was stolen (allegedly by soldiers) and has never been recovered.

Kawgun Cave & Yathaypyan Cave   CAVE
(ကော်ဂွန်းဂူ၊ရေသူပြန်ဂူ; Kawgun Cave K3000, camera fee K500, Yathaypyan Cave free; ☉ daylight hours) The 7th-century artwork of the Kawgun Cave consists of thousands of tiny clay buddhas and carvings plastered all over the walls and roof of this open cavern. Just over a mile away is the Yathaypyan Cave, which contains several pagodas as well as a few more clay wall carvings. Both caves are partially inaccessible during the rainy season (June to October). A return-trip by motorcycle taxi is K6000; a *thoun bein* will cost K10,000.

Kawgun was constructed by King Manuaha after he was defeated in battle and had to take sanctuary in these caves. Impressive as it is today, you can only imagine what it was like a few years back, before a cement factory, in its quest for limestone, started dynamiting the nearby peaks – the vibrations caused great chunks of the art to crash to the floor and shatter.

If you have a torch you can traverse Yathaypyan Cave, which takes about 10 minutes, after which you'll emerge at a viewpoint.

Kaw Ka Thawng Cave   CAVE
(ကောကသောင်ဂူ; ☉ daylight hours) **FREE** This area actually consists of three caves, only

two of which are generally open to the public. Kaw Ka Thawng is the first cave you'll come to and has been gentrified with slippery tile floors and numerous buddha statues. Continuing along a path, you'll pass the stairway to another cave that's not normally open. Near the end of the path, you'll reach an inviting spring-fed swimming hole and another water-filled cave that also serves as a swimming hole.

Splitting from the path before the first cave, a long bridge leads to **Lakkana Village**, a picturesque Kayin village, the backdrop to which includes Mt Zwegabin, and which has been featured in numerous Myanmar films and videos.

The countryside here is drop-dead gorgeous and you could easily spend a day walking and swimming.

Kaw Ka Thawng Cave is about 7 miles from Hpa-an along the road to Eindu. From the stall on Zaydan St in Hpa-an, hop on a **pick-up truck to Eindu** (K1000; ☉ 7am-3pm) and ask to be dropped off at Kaw Ka Thawng Cave. A round-trip by motorcycle taxi will cost K6000, or by *thoun bein* it is K10,000.

ⓘ Getting There & Away

Some of the closer attractions can also be reached by bicycle. Bikes (K2000 per day) and motorcycles (K7000 per day) can be rented at the guesthouses or at **Good Luck Motorbike Rent** (Thitsar St; ☉ 8am-8pm).

Myawaddy မြဝတီ

POP C 113,155 / ☑ 058

For decades, Myawaddy, located on the Moei River opposite the Thai city of Mae Sot, alternated between dodgy border town and intermittent battleground. But with the fighting between the Myanmar army and various Karen insurgent groups now largely over, and the 2013 opening of the frontier paving the way for Asian Highway 1 (AH1) to be Southeast Asia's first real transnational conduit, Myawaddy is now a booming trading post. For travellers it remains a transit point and of little intrinsic interest.

☉ Sights

Shwe Muay Wan Paya BUDDHIST TEMPLE

(ရွှေမွေဝမ်းဘုရား; Dar Tu Kalair St; ☉ daylight hours) FREE Within walking distance of the Friendship Bridge, Shwe Muay Wan Paya is Myawaddy's most important temple, a traditional bell-shaped stupa gilded with pounds of gold and topped by more than 1600 precious and semiprecious gems.

Myikyaungon Paya BUDDHIST TEMPLE

(မြေကျောင်းကုန်ဘုရား; Nat Shin Naung St; ☉ daylight hours) FREE Myikyaungon Paya is

a noted Buddhist temple, called Wat Don Jarakhe in Thai, and named for its gaudy, crocodile-shaped sanctuary. The temple is an easy walk from the Friendship Bridge.

🛏 Sleeping & Eating

Restaurants – Burmese and Thai – can be found along AH1, Myawaddy's main drag.

Myawaddy Hotel HOTEL $

(☑ 058-50519; cnr AH1 & Nat Shin Naung St; r incl breakfast US$22-30; ❄ ☎) Conveniently located 0.3 miles from the border, the Myawaddy Hotel has small but clean and well-equipped (air-con, TV, fridge) rooms.

ⓘ Getting There & Away

DESTINATION	VAN (SHARE TAXI)
Hpa-an	K9000; 6hr; hourly 6am-9am
Mawlamyine	K10,000; 4-6hr; frequent 6am-4pm
Yangon	K25,000; 14hr; frequent 6am-5pm

The daily bus to Yangon (K15,000, 16 hours, 5am) departs from a small office on Pattamyar St.

White vans (share taxis) wait on the corner of AH1 and Pattamyar St, a short walk from the border.

ⓘ GETTING TO THAILAND: MYAWADDY TO MAE SOT

You can enter and exit Myanmar to/from Thailand via the Friendship Bridge linking Myawaddy and Mae Sot in northern Thailand's Tak Province. Note that Myanmar visas are not available at the border: they must be obtained in advance. If you have an e-visa, you are able to enter and exit Myanmar here.

Getting to the border Vans (share taxis) and buses linking Myawaddy with Hpa-an, Mawlamyine and Yangon terminate a short walk from the Friendship Bridge.

At the border The **Myanmar immigration office** (☑ 058-50100; AH1, Myawaddy; ☉ 6am-6pm) is at the foot of the Friendship Bridge. After walking across the 0.25 mile bridge, if you don't already have a visa, the **Thai Immigration office** (☑ +066 55 56 3004; AH1, Mae Sot; ☉ 6.30am-6.30pm) will grant you permission to stay in Thailand up to 15 days, or 30 days if you hold a passport from one of the G7 countries (Canada, France, Germany, Italy, Japan, the United States or the United Kingdom).

If you're crossing from Thailand and don't already have a Myanmar visa, it's possible to cross for the day, paying a fee of US$10 or 500B for a one-day visit and leaving your passport at the border. Then you're free to wander around Myawaddy as long as you're back at the bridge by 5.30pm Myanmar time (which is half an hour behind Thai time) to pick up your passport and check out with immigration.

Moving on Mae Sot's bus station is located 2 miles east of the border and has good connections to destinations in northern Thailand and Bangkok. Mae Sot's airport is 2 miles east of the border, from where Nok Air (www.nokair.co.th) operates four daily flights to Bangkok. Both the bus station and airport can be reached by frequent sŏrng·tăa·ou (pick-ups) that run between the Friendship Bridge and Mae Sot from 6am to 6pm (20B).

For further information, head to shop.lonelyplanet.com to purchase a downloadable PDF of the Northern Thailand section from Lonely Planet's *Thailand* guide.

MAUNGMAGAN, NABULE & TEYZIT BEACHES

Dawei's most accessible beach is Maungmagan, a wide, sandy strip spanning approximately 7 miles along a pretty bay. On weekdays, and outside holiday periods, you're likely to have it to yourself, save for the occasional fisher.

Opposite the beach is a collection of three island groups: Maungmagan, Heinze and Launglon, known collectively in English as the Middle Miscos. Due to a natural profusion of wild boar, barking deer, sambar and swiftlets (sea swallows), these islands belong to a marine sanctuary established by the British in 1927 and are still officially protected.

Places to stay at Maungmagan beach include the Burmese/French-run **Coconut Guesthouse & Restaurant** (📞09 42371 3681; www.coconutguesthouse.com; Phaw Taw Oo St, Maungmagan; r incl breakfast US$20-40; ❀🛜), near the village a brief walk from the beach, and the waterfront yet bland **Maungmagan Beach Resort** (📞09 42220 1819; Maungmagan; r incl breakfast K35,000-75,0000,; ❀) at the rocky southern end of the beach. Burmese and European food is available at the former's restaurant. There is also a string of beachside seafood shacks at the road head – on weekends and holidays this end of the beach draws a crowd – as well as restaurants in Maungmagan village itself.

Maungmagan is around 11 miles west of Dawei via a narrow road that winds through villages, rubber plantations and over a high ridge. There's a daily, very crowded truck (Arzarni Rd) that departs from near Dawei's Si Pin Tharyar Zei (p129) at around 7am (K1000 per person); otherwise motorcycles go to Maungmagan for K5000, *thoun bein* for K12,000 and taxis for K25,000. From Maungmagan village, trucks depart for Dawei from the market area when bursting from 7am to 8am (1000K).

As well as Maungmagan, there are a number of stunning and very empty white-sand beaches that can be reached on day trips from Dawei or Maungmagan. For now, facilities are virtually non-existent, bar the odd simple restaurant, and the roads leading to the beaches are bad. You could hire a taxi for a day in Dawei (K60,000) to reach them. But the few travellers who do venture here normally do so on motorbikes that can be hired at Coconut Guesthouse & Restaurant in Maungmagan.

About 13 miles north of Maungmagan is **Nabule**, a lovely strip of sand with a golden pagoda at the north end of the beach. Access is via a bad road; count on a three-hour motorbike ride from Dawei or two hours from Maungmagan.

Around 25 miles south of Dawei is **Teyzit**, a wide white-sand beach that is perhaps the prettiest in the area. There's a small fishing village here, where you can find food, but the last stretch of the road to the beach is poor; allow three hours to get here.

TANINTHARYI REGION
တနင်္သာရီတိုင်း

The deep south of Myanmar, known today as Tanintharyi Region, is a beach bum's dream. The coastline consists of long, sandy beaches fronting a vast archipelago of more than 800 largely uninhabited islands, most of which have seen very few visitors. Away from the beaches, the few significant towns here are all ports, which have centuries of history behind them as trading posts with both the East and West.

Trade brought foreigners to Tanintharyi as far back as 1545, when a Portuguese expeditionary chronicle refers to Tanancarim, somewhere along the northwest coast of the Thai–Malay Peninsula. That Portuguese rendering became Tenasserim in later European records, the name by which the region was known under British rule. These days, Tanintharyi's proximity to Thailand means that there is a constant movement of both goods and people across the border, with many locals going to Thailand as migrant workers.

Dawei

POP C 80,120 / 📞 059

The area near the mouth of the Dawei River has been inhabited for five centuries or more, mostly by Mon and Thai mariners. The present town dates from 1751 when it was a minor port for the Ayuthaya empire in Thailand (then Siam). From this point, it bounced back and forth between Burmese and Siamese rule until the British took over in 1826.

Dawei remains a sleepy seaside town, despite being the administrative capital of

Dawei

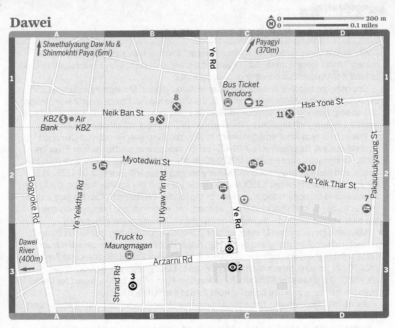

Dawei

Tanintharyi Region. That will change in the next few years as work on the long-delayed Dawei Project, consisting of a deep-sea port set to rival Singapore's and the largest industrial zone in Southeast Asia, gets going properly. Part-funded by Thailand and Japan, the project is controversial, with many locals cit-ing rights abuses such as forced land confis-cations and concerns over the environmen-tal impact. The first phase of the project is expected to be finished in 2018.

⊙ Sights

For a relatively small town, Dawei has a disproportionate amount of interesting ar-chitecture, with many old wooden houses in the two-storey vernacular, with hipped roof lines and plenty of temple-like carved wood ornamentation. Mixed in are more modest thatch-roofed bungalows and colonial-era brick-and-stucco mansions, shophouses and offices, including the pale green, almost church-like 1941 **Division Development Committee** (Arzarni Rd) and the impos-ing 1928 **Office of Tanintharyi Division** (Arzarni Rd).

Payagyi BUDDHIST TEMPLE
(ဘုရားကြီး; Payar Rd; ⊙daylight hours) **FREE**
The main Buddhist monastery in town, col-loquially referred to as Payagyi (Big Pagoda), is an expansive glittering, Disneyland-like compound centred on **Shwe Taung Za Paya**, an immense gilded stupa.

A sculpture of Dharani, the earth god-dess, standing in the corner of one of the compound's main *thein* is a much-venerated object of worship among the people of Dawei, who rub her breasts, thighs and shoulders for good luck.

Shwethalyaung Daw Mu & Shinmokhti Paya
BUDDHIST TEMPLE

(ရွှေသာလျောင်းဒေါ်တော်မူဘုရားကြီးနှင့်ရှင်မုဌိ ဘုရား; ⊙daylight hours) **FREE** Completed in 1931 and measuring 240ft long and 69ft high, Shwethalyaung Daw Mu is the largest reclining Buddha in the country. A couple of miles up the road is Shinmokhti Paya, dating back to 1438 and one of four shrines in the country housing a Sinhalese Buddha image supposedly incorporating pieces of the original Bodhi tree.

Shinmokhti Paya is located about 6 miles from Dawei; a round trip *thoun bein* stopping off at both temples should cost K10,000.

Si Pin Tharyar Zei
MARKET

(Arzani Rd; ⊙5am-6pm) Dawei's main market has the usual selection of food produce, clothes and household goods.

✱ Festivals & Events

Thingyan Festival
CULTURAL

(⊙Apr) During the annual Thingyan festival in April, Dawei's male residents don huge, 13ft-high bamboo-frame effigies and dance down the streets to the beat of the *kalakodaun*, an Indian long drum. The origin of this custom, peculiar to Dawei, seems to be a mystery, but it's most likely linked to a similar custom brought by Indian immigrants many decades ago.

🛌 Sleeping

Garden Hotel
HOTEL $

(☎059-22116; www.gardenhoteldawei.blogspot. com; 88 Ye Rd; r US$20-43; ❇🖿) An attractive, spacious 1940s-era building encompassing both fan-cooled cheapies and several larger, well-equipped, if old-fashioned, air-con rooms. All rooms are well maintained and the staff are helpful.

Shwe Moung Than Hotel
HOTEL $

(☎059-23764; shwemaungthan22@gmail.com; 665 Pakaukukyang St; r incl breakfast K20,000-37,000; ❇🖿) The Shwe Moung Than Hotel is a bright-pink edifice that looks new, even if the rooms feel less fresh. But they're big, clean and comfortable enough. The cheapest top-floor rooms (no lift) are a good deal, but have cold-water showers and no TV.

⭐ Hotel Zayar Htet San
HOTEL $$

(☎059-23902; hotelzayarhtetsan@gmail.com; 566 Ye Yeik Thar St; r incl breakfast US$40-60; ❇🖿) This eye-catching hotel is easily the most stylish and contemporary accommodation in Dawei, as well as the best value. Rooms are decent sized, well equipped and feature the most comfortable beds in southern Myanmar. Good breakfast and helpful staff.

SOUTHEASTERN MYANMAR DAWEI

ℹ GETTING TO THAILAND: HTEE KHEE TO PHU NAM RON

The border crossing from Htee Khee to Phu Nam Ron is the most remote and least-used of Myanmar's open land borders with Thailand. Note that Myanmar visas are not available at the border and that if you have an e-visa, you cannot cross this frontier in either direction.

Getting to the border From Dawei, minivans (K20,000, five hours, 6am and 7am) make the run to the tiny outpost of Htee Khee daily in the morning. Coming from the Thai side, the nearest big town is Kanchanaburi, from where buses go to the Thai border town of Phu Nam Ron (70B, two hours, 10.30am, 11.30am and 12.30pm). It's best to be on the 10.30am bus, as transport on the Myanmar side is scarce in the afternoon.

At the border After being stamped out of Myanmar, catch the shuttle bus (50B) or take a motorcycle taxi (100B) across the six miles of no-man's land that separates the Myanmar border post from the Thai one. On the Thai side, the authorities will issue you permission to stay in Thailand for up to 15 days – 30 days if you hold a passport from a G7 country – or you can enter with a Thai visa obtained overseas. If you're coming from Thailand, you must already have a Myanmar visa, in which case you'll be given permission to enter Myanmar for 28 days.

Moving on From Htee Khee, minivans make the bumpy five-hour journey to Dawei along a partly unsealed road and charge K30,000 or 800B. From Phu Nam Ron, there are four buses daily to Kanchanaburi, from where there are frequent daily buses to Bangkok (120B, 2½ hours).

Golden Guest Hotel
HOTEL **$$**

(☑059-21351; goldenguesthoteldawei@gmail.com; 59 Myotedwin St; r incl breakfast US$40-65; ✳️ 🛜) The single rooms at this new-ish place are tight, but the doubles are spacious and comfortable with decent bathrooms. The rooftop restaurant offers great views over Dawei. Competent staff. Popular with tour groups.

🍴 Eating & Drinking

Hla Hla Hnan
BURMESE **$**

(Neik Ban St; dishes from K200; ⊘noon-9pm) In addition to selling the requisite ingredients for *leq·p'eq thouq* (Burmese tea-leaf salad) this vendor also serves a selection of other equally delicious Burmese-style salads including ginger, tomato, pennywort (a type of herb) and *shauq·thi* (a type of citrus fruit). There's no English-language menu, but orders can be made by pointing to the raw ingredients.

Tha Hto Daw San Family Rice & Curry Shop
BURMESE **$**

(506 Hse Yone St; curries from K1500; ⊘10am-9pm) Daw San has been serving tasty Burmese curry dishes to the people of Dawei for over 40 years. Be sure to add a vegetable dish (K500) to your curry order.

Meik Hswe
BURMESE **$**

(Neik Ban St; snacks from K300, noodles K1200; ⊘5am-5pm) In addition to good snacks and frothy tea, this friendly and popular Muslim teashop does tasty noodles and, on Thursdays, hearty biryani dishes (K2000). It's next door to a mosque: look for the small English sign.

Esso Seafood Restaurant
SEAFOOD **$$**

(☑09-2507 34865; Maungmagan Beach; mains K6000-10,500; ⊘7am-9.30pm; 🅿️) Many of the beachside restaurants at Maungmagan close during the week. This place stays open and offers good baked crab, prawn dishes

and steamed and grilled fish at reasonable prices. You eat on raised platforms under a bamboo roof. It's a few hundred metres east of Maungmagan Beach Resort.

Pearl Princess Restaurant
CHINESE, BURMESE **$$**

(572 Ye Yeik Thar St; mains K4500-8000; ⊘7am-9.30pm; 🅿️) We'd recommend avoiding the same-named hotel, but the attached restaurant offers a decent take on Chinese-style dishes, as well as more pricey seafood, and it's one of the more popular restaurants in town at both lunch and dinner.

Forty Five Bakery
CAFE

(Hse Yone St; drinks from K700; ⊘8am-9pm) This hole-in-the-wall cafe does proper coffee, as well as Thai-style iced green teas. There's a small selection of cakes and sandwiches too.

ℹ️ Information

Currency exchange and an international ATM are available at **KBZ Bank** (Neik Ban St; ⊘9.30am-3pm Mon-Sat).

ℹ️ Getting There & Away

Air KBZ (☑ in Dawei 059-23833, in Yangon 01-372 977; www.airkbz.com; Neik Ban St; ⊘9am-5.30pm), Myanmar National Airlines (www.flymna.com) and Apex Airlines (www.apexairline.com) operate daily flights to Myeik, Kawthoung and Yangon out of Dawei's airport.

Three companies run speedboats from Dawei, with boats bound for Myeik and Kawthoung. Boats depart daily at 4.30am, but the ocean pier is 20 miles downstream from Dawei, so you'll be picked up from your hotel at midnight for the ferry transfer. Tickets are sold at various locations near the main market on Arzani Rd, Si Pin Tharyar Zei, and near the bus ticket vendors on Ye St. Hotels can also book tickets. Note that the boats mostly don't run in the rainy season.

Dawei's bus station is inconveniently located a couple miles northeast of the city centre, but

DAWEI TRANSPORT CONNECTIONS

DESTINATION	AIR (DAILY)	BOAT	BUS
Htee Khee (for Thailand)	N/A	N/A	K20,000 (minivan); 5hr; daily 6am & 7am
Kawthoung	from US$75; 80min	US$70; 12hr; 4.30am	K30,000-35,000; 22hr; 5am
Mawlamyine	N/A	N/A	K12,000-13,000; 8hr; 5am, 1pm & 5pm
Myeik	from US$47; 35min	US$30; 4hr; 4.30am	K8000-10,000; 8hr; 5am
Yangon	from US$105; 70min	N/A	K15,000; 14hr; 5am, 1pm, 2pm, 3pm & 5pm
Ye	N/A	N/A	K6000-8000; 4hr; 5am, 1pm & 5pm

tickets can be purchased in advance from the various vendors near the canal on Ye Rd (although you'll still have to board your bus at the station). Minivans depart from their offices on Ye St, or will pick you up at your hotel.

It is possible to catch a minivan from Dawei to Htee Khee, where you can cross the border to Thailand.

Dawei has a train station, but at the time of writing, trains were not running south of the city.

❶ Getting Around

The centre of Dawei is accessible on foot. To hire a taxi for a day (K50,000 to K60,000, depending on where you are going), ask at your hotel.

Dawei's airport is about 2 miles northeast of town; a motorcycle taxi there should run about K2000. Dawei's bus station is located northeast of the airport; a *thoun bein* to/from will cost about K3000.

Myeik

POP C 115,140 / ☑ 059

Myeik sits on a peninsula that juts into the Andaman Sea. With a location roughly halfway between the Middle East and China, not to mention the safe harbour offered by the peninsula and facing islands, Myeik became an important international port over 500 years ago.

The legacy of that long trading history is a multicultural population, with the descendants of Chinese and Indian Muslim traders joined by Bamar, Mon and Moken (sea gypsies) people. Myeik's intriguing past is also reflected in its buildings, with grand Sino-Portuguese houses jostling with mosques, churches, traditional wooden homes and colonial-era mansions to create a kaleidoscope of architectural styles. Myeik is still a bustling port today. It's home to a large fishing fleet, as well as being the centre of Myanmar's pearl industry, and, along with the port of Kawthoung, is the gateway to the 800-odd islands of the Myeik Archipelago.

History

The Portuguese were allegedly the first Europeans to visit Myeik, while the Siamese (Thais), who ruled the area during the 17th century, installed Englishman Samuel White as harbourmaster. White proceeded to plunder visiting ships at will and to tax the local population for every shilling he could squeeze out of them, exploits described in Maurice Collis' 1936 biography of the man, *Siamese White*. The British, who called the port Mergui, eventually re-occupied Myeik following the First Anglo-Burmese War in 1826, so that along with Sittwe, Myeik became one of the first cities in Myanmar to become part of British India. The city continued to retain its international roots into the 20th century, as this 1901 British census of Myeik indicates:

> A considerable proportion of the population in the town and mines is Baba or half-Chinese, the men retaining the pigtail but talking Burmese or Siamese [...] Of the Musalmans [Muslims], between 2000 and 3000 are Malays and the rest nearly all Zarbadis. Living in boats among the island in a very low stage of civilisation is a wild people of obscure origin, called by the Burmese Salon, by the Malays Orang Basin, by the Siamese Chaunam (waterfolk), and by themselves Maw Ken (drowned in the sea).

The Japanese invaded in 1941, but by 1945 Myeik was back in British hands, until independence was achieved in 1948.

◎ Sights

With a temple-topped hill at its back, a wide harbour at its breast, and a hilly island opposite, Myeik is one of Myanmar's more handsome towns. The town's long trading history means that even today there are still distinct Muslim, Chinese and Catholic quarters.

Despite a 1989 fire that destroyed as many as 3900 buildings, Myeik is still home to some beautiful classic architecture, much of it allegedly haunted. Crumbling Chinese-style godowns (warehouses) line parts of Strand Rd, several grand shophouses can be found in the blocks that surround the Sake Nge Zei market, and some beautiful old Sino-Portuguese mansions can be found along SHS (2) St, east of Assumption Church.

★ **Theindawgyi Paya**   BUDDHIST TEMPLE
(သိမ်တော်ကြီးဘုရား; off Bo Gyoke Rd; ⊙ daylight hours) FREE Myeik's most venerated Buddhist temple, Theindawgyi Paya sits on a ridge overlooking the city and harbour. A beautiful, Mon-style ordination hall of wood, brick and stucco contains an impressive painted and carved ceiling, a 'European pose' buddha towards the front entry, 28 smaller buddhas along its two sides, a large meditation buddha in the centre and a sizeable reclining buddha at the back. A tall gilded stupa stands on a broad platform, allowing excellent views of the city and harbour.

SOUTHEASTERN MYANMAR MYEIK

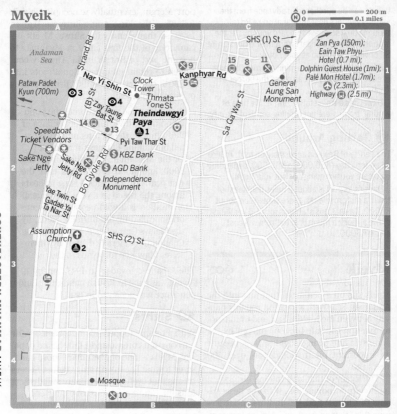

Kadan Island ISLAND

(ကဒန်ကျွန်း) If you want to see an island of the Myeik Archipelago without taking an expensive yacht tour, catch the ferry from Sake Nge Jetty (p134) to Kadan Island, 45 minutes away from Myeik. Don't expect to find any beaches: Kadan is mostly forest and mangrove swamps (good for bird-watching). But the locals are friendly and you'll get a taste of island life. The ferry docks in Kyunsu, the 'capital' of Kadan, where there are restaurants and shops, and you can hire motorbikes (K6000 per day). Note that foreigners are not allowed to stay overnight here, although that may change in the future. There are three ferries a day to Kadan (K1000, 45 minutes, 8am, 11am and 3pm). The last ferry back to Myeik returns at 3.30pm.

Pataw Padet Kyun ISLAND

(ပတောပတတ်ကျွန်း) Located directly opposite Myeik's harbour, this island is named for its two prominent hills. There's no swimming on the island. Instead, it's a short walk from the boat landing to a large, hollow reclining buddha, **Atula Shwethalyaung**, which lies at the foot of rocky, jungle-covered Padet Hill to the south. At 66m it's the third-longest reclining buddha in Myanmar – but with a twist: it's a hollow cement form with an interior walkway lined with comic-strip-like stories of the Buddha's past lives.

Boats can be chartered from the small **jetty** (Strand Rd) at the west end of Pyi Taw Thar St (return trip K3000 to K5000, depending on your bargaining skills).

Myeik Harbour LANDMARK

(Strand Rd) Myeik's vast harbourfront is worth a stroll to watch stevedores loading and offloading cargo from ships and the fishing boats preparing to go to sea. At night, it's pretty when the boats have their lights on.

Myeik

Bu Paya Zedi
BUDDHIST TEMPLE

(ဗုးဘုရားစေတီ; off Bo Gyoke Rd; ⊙ daylight hours)
FREE One of Myeik's many hilltop temples with views over the harbour and town, Bu Paya Zedi also has an appealingly abandoned feel and an abundance of mouldy, crumbling statues.

Sake Nyein Zei
MARKET

(စိတ်ငြိမ်းေဈး; Bo Gyoke Rd; ⊙ 6am-6pm) Myeik's municipal market is a colourful collection of enclosed stalls covering an entire city block.

🏃 Activities

Life Seeing Tours
CRUISE

(☏ 09 7809 80607; www.lifeseeingtours.com; Hotel Grand Jade, 28-30 Kanphyar Rd; ⊙ 9am-6pm) Kawthoung is the main Myanmar-based starting point for tours of the Myeik Archipelago, but there are a few travel companies in Myeik who arrange boat tours and they are normally cheaper than the ones in Kawthoung. This reputable operator offers day tours to outlying islands (US$120 per person), as well as three-day cruises (US$360) and seven-day ones (US$1130).

The most popular destinations include Turtle Egg Island and Dome Island (p135), which offer white-sand beaches and snorkelling, and Mergui Island, where you can hike in the jungly interior. Prices include food, snorkelling equipment and a guide. It's possible to sleep overnight on some islands in tents, although most people sleep aboard the boat.

🛏 Sleeping

Myeik's accommodation scene has improved dramatically in the last couple of years, although foreign visitors are relatively scarce compared to elsewhere in Myanmar. Most hotels and guesthouses are located close to the harbour and seafront. The cheapest places along Strand Rd aren't licensed to accept foreigners.

White Pearl Guesthouse
GUESTHOUSE $

(☏ 09 2528 88812; whitepearlhotelmyeik@gmail.com; 97/98 Middle Strand Rd; r incl breakfast US$14-45; ❄ 🛜) The rooms are compact at this new place, especially the cheapest ones, which are fan-only and share bathrooms, but the price is right and the more expensive rooms offer a small harbour view. The English-speaking owner is around in the mornings and is knowledgeable and helpful, though other staff less so. Motorbikes can be hired (K9000 per day) and boat trips arranged.

Sun Guest House
GUESTHOUSE $

(☏ 059-41745; 1 SHS (1) St; r incl breakfast US$25-40; ❄ 🛜) This guesthouse offers 22 decent-sized and comfortable, if old-fashioned, rooms looked after by two charmingly over-bearing middle-aged ladies who don't speak much English. A good local-style breakfast is served.

Dolphin Guest House
GUESTHOUSE $

(☏ 059-42868; 139 Kanphyar Rd; r incl breakfast K25,000-35,000; ❄ 🛜) Dolphin Guest House is set in a vast cream-coloured villa housing equally spacious and clean rooms – the double rooms nearly echo – with wooden floors. It's inconveniently located a mile or so northeast of the town centre. You won't hear much English here.

★ Eain Taw Phyu Hotel
HOTEL $$

(☏ 059-42055; eaintawphyu.hotel@gmail.com; 42 Kanphyar Rd; r incl breakfast US$65-150; ❄ 🛜 ❄) Eain Taw Phyu is hands-down the best hotel in Myeik and one of the better ones in all southern Myanmar. Its 38 rooms come with their own mini-terraces and are modern, comfortable, spacious and tastefully decorated. Even the cheapest ones are a reasonable size. There's a small swimming pool and efficient, English-speaking staff.

Hotel Grand Jade HOTEL $$

(059-41906; www.hotelgrandjade.com; 28-30 Kanphyar Rd; r incl breakfast US$40-70; ❄ 🛜) This new, Chinese-owned hotel is professional, if anonymous, and good value. Rooms aren't massive, but they are modern and well appointed, and have decent beds. The more expensive have views of the harbour and Theindawgyi Paya. Tickets and boat tours can be booked here and there's a rooftop restaurant serving Chinese and Thai food.

✖ Eating

You'd expect to find a plethora of seafood restaurants in central Myeik. Sadly that is not the case, although the food stalls that spring up nightly along Strand Rd grill prawns, fish and squid.

One local speciality is *kaq kyi kaiq* (scissor-cut noodles): rice noodles that have been cut into short strips and stir-fried with egg and seafood – a lot like *phat Thai*. Try them at the friendly vendor near the mosque in the Muslim quarter.

★ Shwe Mon BURMESE $

(Sake Nge Jetty Rd; curries from K1000; ⏰ 10am-9pm) This Bamar restaurant serves what is one of the richest, tastiest chicken curries we've come across yet, as well as a yummy prawn curry. Be sure to order one of the vegetable side dishes that change daily.

Karaweik BURMESE $

(Kanphyar Rd; mains from K1500; ⏰ 11am-10pm; 🍴) Myeik institution that serves immense bowls of *kyè òu* and other noodle and rice dishes to hordes of locals. Look for the big white villa and the small English sign. There's outdoor seating and an English menu, but no alcohol is served.

Zan Pya BURMESE $

(Kanphyar Rd; mains from K1800; ⏰ 7.30am-6.30pm) Zan Pya is a small place serving heaped plates of delicious chicken biryani that often sell out early. Look for the large aluminum pots a couple doors down from OK Mobile (there's no roman-script sign).

Kaq Kyi Kaiq BURMESE $

(dishes from K500; ⏰ 6am-5pm) This hole-in-the-wall noodle vendor specialises in *kaq kyi kaiq*: scissor-cut noodles fried with seafood or chicken in a wok over a wood fire. The shop is in the Muslim quarter (no roman-script sign), just down the road from a large blue mosque: you'll see people gathered around the wok.

G Apparao Restaurant BURMESE $

(Kanphyar Rd; tea & snacks from K300, noodles from K800; ⏰ 24hr) This Muslim teashop serves good tea and a variety of freshly made snacks, as well as simple rice and noodle dishes. It never closes.

G-Naidu INDIAN $

(Kanphyar Rd; mains from K1200; ⏰ 5am-8pm; 🍴) This teashop-restaurant sells tasty and cheap Southern Indian–style curries, biryanis and dosai. Look for the small English sign.

❶ Information

You can change money at **KBZ Bank** (Bo Gyoke Rd; ⏰ 9.30am-3pm), which also has an international ATM, as does the nearby **AGD Bank** (Bo Gyoke Rd; ⏰ 9.30am-3pm).

❶ Getting There & Away

Air and bus tickets can be bought at **Sun Far** (059-21110; Pyi Taw Thar St; ⏰ 8.30am-5pm) travel agency.

AIR

Air KBZ (www.airkbz.com) and Myanmar National Airlines (www.flymna.com) link Myeik with Kawthoung (from US$47, 45 minutes, twice daily) and Yangon (from US$109, two hours, twice daily), the latter via a stop in Dawei (from US$47, 35 minutes, twice daily).

BOAT

Three companies operate speedboats from Myeik, departing from Sake Nge Jetty (Strand Rd) and bound north to Dawei (US$25, five hours, 11am) and south to Kawthoung (US$40, seven hours, 8am). Tickets are sold from various **vendors** (Sake Nge Jetty Rd; ⏰ 6am-7pm) opposite Sake Nge Jetty. Note that the boats mostly don't run in the rainy season (May to October).

BUS & MINIVANS

Bus tickets for Yangon (K21,000, 22 hours, 3am, 5pm and 6pm) can be bought from the **bus ticket offices** (⏰ 7am-6pm) on Kanphyar Rd. Tickets to other destinations need to be purchased from the **ticket offices** (⏰ 6am-7pm) on Pyi Taw Thar St. Destinations include Dawei

(K10,000, eight hours, 6am, noon and 4pm), Kawthoung (K20,000, 14 hours, 5pm), Mawlamyine (K18,000, 16 hours, 3am, 5pm and 6pm) and Ye (K16,000, 12 hours, 3am, 5pm and 6pm).

Buses depart from Myeik's bus station, 2½ miles from the town centre close to the Myeik Golf Course. A motorcycle taxi to the bus station will cost K2000.

Minivans leave from Pyi Taw Thar St just south of the jetty. Buy tickets here too. Destinations include Dawei (K12,000, six hours, daily morning and afternoon) and Kawthoung (K25,000, 13 hours, daily morning and afternoon).

❶ Getting Around

Most destinations in central Myeik are walkable, but motorcycles taxis do short hops for K500. A motorcycle taxi to Myeik's airport or bus station will cost K2000.

Myeik (Mergui) Archipelago

The beautiful islands of the Myeik Archipelago (also known as the Mergui Archipelago) lie off the Tanintharyi coast in the extreme south of Myanmar. While pearls and marine products from the region are sought after, it is the huge untapped potential of the archipelago as a beach and ecotourist destination that could really transform the area's economy. So far, though, Myanmar has resisted taking advantage of some of its most beautiful assets, although there is talk of opening up a few of the islands in the near future. But most of the islands are uninhabited (and they are much smaller than Thailand's islands), making tourism a challenge. For now, the few islands that do have people remain home to tiny villages with hardly any infrastructure and mixed populations of Burmese and the semi-nomadic Moken, so-called 'sea gypsies' who move from island to island and live by fishing.

The Islands

The Burmese used to say there were more than 4000 islands in the Myeik Archipelago, although British surveyors recognised only 804. The British took the liberty of naming many of the islands, although some are also interchangeably known by their Burmese and sometimes Moken names (some islands are even known by old Thai or Arabic names). Most are uninhabited – some little more than rocky outcrops – some have Navy and Army stations and are off-limits, while others are home to Burmese and, sometimes, small Moken communities.

The more noteworthy islands and diving spots include the following (from north to south).

Daung Kyun (Dome Island) ISLAND

(ဒေါင်းကျွန်း) The islands close to Myeik tend to be less spectacular than the ones grouped near Kawthoung. Dome Island is the exception, with fine white-sand beaches and good snorkelling. It's three hours by speedboat from Myeik.

Kanmaw Kyun (Kisseraing Island) ISLAND

(ကံမော်ကျွန်း) One of the larger islands (158 sq miles) in the Myeik Archipelago and home to Bamar, Karen and Moken villages, as well as big rubber plantations.

Black Rock ISLAND

(ဘလက်ရှော့ကျွန်း) One of the Myeik Archipelago's premier diving sites. This rocky, remote outpost is home to clear water and rich sea life, including manta rays (typically around March).

Lampi Kyun (Sullivan's Island) ISLAND

(လန်ပိကျွန်း; www.lampipark.org) Home to Lampi Island Marine National Park, the only marine park in Myanmar, and thought to be one of the least disturbed island habitats in Southeast Asia. There are Bamar and Moken villages here, and at the time of research there were plans to open a guesthouse; check the website for the latest information.

Bo Cho Kyun (Eyles Island) ISLAND

(ဘိုချိုကျွန်း, Pu Nala) This island is a spiritual home of the Moken, who call it Pu Nala. The island is designated as a Moken resettlement zone, and there is a permanent Moken presence here.

Rocky 1 ISLAND

A rocky outcrop, approximately 10m above water, drawing lots of sea life and home to one of the Myeik Archipelago's largest anemone fields.

Three Islets ISLAND

Home to three notable diving sites: Shark Cave, an underwater canyon with sharks and rich coral; In Through The Out Door, an underwater passage with several species of coral; and OK Rock, supposedly a good destination for diving at any time. The islets are a few miles north of Kyun Philar (Great Swinton Island).

Myeik (Mergui) Archipelago

0   50 km
0   20 miles

ANDAMAN SEA

Mali Kyun

Palauk
Kyaukpa
Palaw

Phetchaburi

THAILAND

Cha-am

Hua Hin

Kadan Kyun (King Island)
Lutlut
Myeik

Thayawthadangyi Kyun

Tanintharyi River

Pran Buri

Pyingyi

Daung Kyun (Dome Island)

Tenasserim

Kui Buri

Thameye
Theinkun

Pyinzabu Kyun

Kanmaw Kyun (Kisseraing Island)

MYANMAR

Prachuap Khiri Khan
Ban Nong Hin

Pan Daung Kyun

Lampon

Black Rock

Lenya

Thap Sakae

Ka Mar Kyun (Owen Island)

Atwin Bokpyin

Myeik Archipelago

Hangapru

Kyun Philar (Great Swinton Island)

Lampi Kyun (Sullivan's Island)

Three Islets

Bo Cho Kyun (Eyles Island)

Myauk Taw Win Kyun (North Twin Island)

Jar Lann Kyun

Ban Thapli
Chumphon

Gulf of Thailand

Taung Taw Win Kyun (South Twin Island)

Nyaung Wee Kyun

Kra Buri
Ban Hat Sai Ri

Bo Wei Kyun (Stewart Island)

Zadetgale Kyun

Kho Yinn Khwa Kyun (Macleod Island)

Thahtay Kyun

Western Rocky

Zadetgyi Kyun (St Matthew's Island)

Kawthoung
Ranong
Lang Suan

Taung Kyun (Christie Island)

Kyun Philar (Great Swinton Island) ISLAND
(ကျွန်းဖိလာကျွန်း) Home to a freshwater spring where passing boats fill up and a small Burmese/Moken village. There's decent snorkelling here and the surrounding islands offer good diving.

Nyaung Wee Kyun ISLAND
(ညောင်ဝီးကျွန်း) A seasonal home for the Moken, this island has beaches, clear water and wildlife, making it a popular stopover for boat tours. Nearby **115 Island** sees a lot of tour groups too and has fine beaches and snorkelling.

High Rock ISLAND
From the surface it's little more than a tree-topped limestone outcropping, but High Rock is home to an abundance of marine life, including at least five types of nudibranch, making it a lauded dive site.

Taung Taw Win Kyun (South Twin Island)/Myauk Taw Win Kyun (North Twin Island) ISLAND
Home to at least three good dive sites including **Pinnacle**, north of Myauk Taw Win Kyun, a known manta ray gathering site during February/March. Taung Taw Win Kyun has clear blue water and fan coral.

Bo Wei Kyun (Stewart Island) ISLAND

(ဗိုလ်ဝှဲ့ကျွန်း) South of this island is a rocky outcrop with above-ground and underwater caves. Nearby **Maccarthy Rock** has a beautiful limestone cliff more than 30m high and good diving. Close-by **Cavern Rock** is another good dive site.

Kho Yinn Khwa Kyun (Macleod Island) ISLAND

(ခရင်းဝွက်ကျွန်း) This horseshoe-shaped island 40 nautical miles from Kawthoung is home to Myanmar Andaman Resort (p138), the only real beach accommodation in the entire Myeik Archipelago. There are at least 20 known dive sites around the island, including **North Rock**, where sea snakes and sea turtles are often sighted.

Western Rocky ISLAND

An underwater cave that has been known to draw sharks makes this arguably the Myeik Archipelago's finest dive site.

Thahtay Kyun ISLAND

(သဘေးကျွန်း) Opposite Kawthoung, this beach-free island, known in Moken as Pulau Ru, is home to Andaman Club (p138). The resort offers trips to beaches on **Zadetgale Kyun** and **Zadetgyi Kyun (St Matthew's Island)**, each about 45-minutes away by speedboat.

🏃 Activities

The vast expanse of the Myeik Archipelago coupled with the area's almost total lack of infrastructure means that to explore the area, you'll have to sign on to a multiday live-aboard diving tour or a boat trip, neither of which come particularly cheap.

Diving

Many visitors approach Myeik Archipelago via diving tours, all of which are based out of Ranong in Thailand. The various outfits run four- to eight-day excursions generally to sites south of Black Rock. Fees for a six-day trip can range from around US$850 to US$1500, which includes accommodation and meals, but generally not the Myeik Archipelago entrance fee (excursions south of Black Rock are US$100 per person for the first five days; excursions north of Black Rock are US$140 per person for the first five days plus US$20 per additional day).

Diving conditions are best November to May. The premier dive sites are Black Rock (p135), where giant manta rays can be found, Western Rocky, which features a swim-through cave, and the Three Islets (p135), where there's an underwater canyon. Divers can expect to see various species of sharks, manta rays and sea turtles, as well as rarer smaller fish like seahorses, frog fish and scorpion fish. The coral in the archipelago is also famed.

Recommended outfits operating out of Ranong include the following:

A One Diving Team DIVING

(☑ in Thailand +66 81891 5510; www.a-one-diving. com; Ranong, Thailand; dive trip 30,900-32,900B) This long-standing dive operation is based out of Ranong, with English-, French- and German-speaking divemasters. They run six- and seven-day trips to the Myeik Archipelago and also **Burma Banks**, a renowned dive area 80 miles west of Kawthoung.

Andaman International Dive Center DIVING

(☑ in Thailand +66 89814 1092, +66 77 834 824; www.aidcdive.com; 97/21 Th Phetkasem, Ranong; dive trip 33,000-46,000B) Six- and eight-day dive trips to the Myeik Archipelago from Thailand.

Smiling Seahorse DIVING

(☑ in Thailand +66 86011 0614, +66 84452 4413; www.thesmilingseahorse.com; 170 Th Ruangrat, Ranong; dive trip 32,000-53,000B; ⊘ 9am-6pm) Six- to eight-day liveaboard diving trips around the Myeik Archipelago, departing from Ranong in Thailand.

Thailand Dive & Sail DIVING

(☑ in Thailand +66 76 485 518; www.thailanddive andsail.com; Khao Lak, Thailand; dive trips from 86,896B) Recommended dive operator based in Khao Lak, Thailand, offering high-end dive trips around the Myeik Archipelago.

Mergui Princess DIVING

(☑ in Yangon 09 42110 7472, 01-401 261; www. merguiprincess.com) Sailing from Kawthoung, *Mergui Princess* runs liveaboard dive cruises in the Myeik Archipelago. Trips range from three to seven days on a variety of different boats and yachts.

Boating

If you'd rather stay above water, various outfits conduct multiday island-hopping excursions, which offer visits to Moken villages, snorkelling, kayaking and beach-bumming, among other activities. Fees for all-inclusive five- to nine-day cruises range from around US$1100 to US$5000. As well as Life Seeing Tours (p133) in Myeik, companies include the following.

Burma Boating
CRUISE

(✐ in Thailand +66 21 070 445; www.burmaboat ing.com; boat cruise US$2600-4950) Six- and eight-day cruises in the Myeik Archipelago from November to May in well-maintained yachts – including the SY *Meta IV*, a beautiful vintage Thai teak sailboat – departing from Kawthoung.

Sailing Charter Phuket
CRUISE

(✐ in Thailand +66 8 1365 5681; www.sailing-phuket. com; per person per day from US$650) Cruises on a catamaran, departing from Phuket in Thailand. You charter the whole boat and so decide on the itinerary.

Mergui Islands Safari
CRUISE

(✐ in Kawthoung 09 509 1672, in Yangon 01-380 382; www.islandsafarimergui.com; boat cruise US$1110-1530) Mergui Islands Safari runs five- and seven-day cruises aboard the MV *Sea Gypsy*, departing from Kawthoung. The *Sea Gypsy* isn't a luxury boat – no private cabins and shared bathrooms – so it's cheaper than other cruises.

Intrepid
CRUISE

(www.intrepidtravel.com; cruise from US$2165) Very reliable operator that offers a nine-day cruise around the Myeik Archipelago departing from Phuket in Thailand.

🛏 Sleeping & Eating

There's long been talk of tourism development in the Myeik Archipelago, yet among the 800-plus islands and hundreds of miles of coastline, there are still only a couple of places to stay.

At the time of research, though, there were plans to open a guesthouse on Lampi Island, a national marine park that is home to both Bamar and Moken people, as part of a community-based tourism project; check the website (www.lampipark.org) for the latest details.

There are no restaurants that we know of on the islands, outside of the two hotels. You eat on board your yacht, or on whichever beach you're anchored off.

Myanmar Andaman Resort
RESORT $$$

(✐ in Kawthoung 059-51046, in Yangon 09 7976 27627; www.myanmarandamanresort.com; Kho Yinn Khwa Kyun (Macleod Island); r incl breakfast & dinner US$150-360; ❄ 🛜) This self-professed 'eco resort' has a picture-postcard location in a beautiful horseshoe-shaped bay on Kho Yinn Khwa Kyun (Macleod Island), 40 nautical miles from Kawthoung. Accommodation takes the form of eight beachfront and spacious but unstylish 'Suite' bungalows and 14 smaller 'Superior' bungalows. Activities include hiking, kayaking and diving (there's an attached dive centre).

Rates include the 1½-hour private transfer to/from Kawthoung every Wednesday and Saturday (from the island at 7am; from Kawthoung at noon). The resort is open from October to April.

Andaman Club
RESORT $$$

(✐ in Thailand +66 2287 3031, in Yangon 01-572 535; www.andamanclub.com; Thahtay Kyun; r incl breakfast US$107-382; 🛜❄) This 205-room luxury resort is located on Thahtay Kyun, an 1800-acre private island directly south of Kawthoung. There's no beach on the island, but there is an 18-hole golf course, spas, pool and gym, while diving trips and excursions to other islands can be arranged. Andaman Club can be reached by boat from Ranong's Saphan Pla Pier or by an hourly shuttle boat from Kawthoung (250B).

ⓘ Getting There & Away

Access to the Myeik Archipelago is by boat tours from Myeik and Kawthoung in Myanmar, or from Ranong in Thailand. The majority of boat tours departing from Myanmar leave from Kawthoung, which is closer to the prettiest islands and the best dive sites, although a few operators run out of Myeik.

There are rumours of ferry services being introduced to certain islands in the future, but at the time of research nothing had been confirmed.

Kawthoung and Myeik both have airports with daily flights to Yangon.

Kawthoung ကော့သောင်း

POP C 57,950 / ☑ 059

This small port at the very end of Tanintharyi Region – the southernmost point of mainland Myanmar (500 miles from Yangon and 1200 miles from the country's northern tip) – is separated from Thailand by a broad estuary in the Pagyan River. It was known as Victoria Point to the British, and to the Thais it's known as Ko Song (Second Island). The Burmese name, Kawthoung (also spelt Kawthaung), is a mispronunciation of the latter.

Kawthoung was one of the earliest British possessions in Myanmar, obtained after the First Anglo-Burmese War in 1826. Today the town is a scrappy border post and jumping-off point for boating and diving excursions to the Myeik Archipelago.

◉ Sights

Cape Bayint Naung
PARK

(ဘုရင့်နောင်ဘုရင်အုပ်; Strand Rd; ⊙24hr) FREE At the southern end of the harbour lies this modest park, named for King Bayinnaung, a Burmese monarch who invaded Thailand several times between 1548 and 1569. A bronze statue of Bayinnaung, outfitted in full battle gear and brandishing a sword pointed at Thailand – not exactly a welcoming sight for visiting Thais – stands at the crest of a hill on the cape.

Anandar Paya
BUDDHIST TEMPLE

(အာနန္ဒာဘုရား; ⊙daylight hours) FREE Towering over Kawthoung is this hilltop temple with great views of the city.

🛌 Sleeping & Eating

A knot of food stalls and restaurants serving standard Chinese-Burmese dishes can be found at the southern end of Strand Rd, opposite the park at Cape Bayint Naung.

Kawthaung Hotel
HOTEL $

(☑059-51474; Bosonpat St; r incl breakfast US$20-45; ❄️🛜) Kawthaung Hotel's deluxe rooms have sea views and are in reasonable condition, while the cheaper rooms are a bit beaten up, with unimpressive beds and bathrooms. It's located about half a mile west of the jetty.

Garden Hotel
HOTEL $

(☑059-51731; www.gardenhotelmm.com; Shwe Minwon Rd; r incl breakfast US$30-40; ❄️🛜) Though it's looking its age a little now, the Garden Hotel is still a reasonable deal, with decent-sized and comfortable-enough rooms. There's a CB Bank ATM in the lobby. One downside is that the hotel is located an uphill hike about 1 mile north of the jetty (K1000 on a motorcycle taxi).

Penguin Hotel
GUESTHOUSE $

(☑09 2605 66762; penguinhotelkt@gmail.com; 339 Sabel St; r incl breakfast US$20-35; ❄️🛜) It's not the friendliest guesthouse in Myanmar,

---

ℹ️ GETTING TO THAILAND: KAWTHOUNG TO RANONG

Kawthoung (also known as Victoria Point), at the far southern end of Tanintharyi Region, is an open border for foreigners to cross to/from Thailand. If you are coming to Myanmar and plan on moving on from Kawthoung, you must obtain a visa in advance: they are not available at the border. If you have an e-visa, you can enter/exit Myanmar here.

Getting to the border The bright green Myanmar border post (Strand Rd; ⊙7am-4pm) is located a few steps from Kawthoung's jetty.

If crossing from Thailand, the Thai border post (Saphan Pla Pier, Ranong; ⊙7.30pm-4.30pm) is at Saphan Pla Pier, located about 6 miles, a 60B motorcycle taxi ride or 20B sŏrng·tǎa·ou (pick-up) ride from Ranong.

At the border If you've arrived in Kawthoung from elsewhere in Myanmar, you're free to exit the country now. After clearing Myanmar immigration, you'll be herded to a boat (100B per person) for the 20-minute ride to Ranong. On the Thai side, the authorities will issue you permission to stay in Thailand for up to 15 days – 30 days if you hold a passport from a G7 country – or you can enter with a Thai visa obtained overseas.

If approaching from Thailand, after passing Thai immigration, board a waiting boat (125B per person) for the 20-minute ride to Kawthoung. Upon arriving at the Myanmar immigration office, you may be greeted by an English-speaking tout who insists on 'helping' by translating and making photocopies in return for an exorbitant fee; you can ignore this. If you haven't already obtained a Myanmar visa, you'll need to pay US$10 for a border pass, which will allow you to stay in a 24-mile radius of Kawthoung for up to 14 days; your passport will be kept at the border. If you already possess a Myanmar visa, you'll be allowed to enter but may be required to show or purchase tickets for onward travel.

Moving on Ranong is a 60B motorcycle taxi ride or 20B sŏrng·tǎa·ou (pick-up) ride from Saphan Pla Pier. Nok Air (☑in Thailand 1318; www.nokair.com) offers daily flights between Ranong and Bangkok (from 1814B, 1½ hours to 1¾ hours, two departures daily), while major bus destinations include Bangkok (445B to 692B, 10 hours), Hat Yai (420B, five hours) and Phuket (250B, five to six hours). If you're bound for points elsewhere in Myanmar, you can move on by bus, boat or plane.

but the smallish rooms are adequate for a night and this is the best deal in town for the price (though with cold-water showers only). Good wi-fi connection. It's located a couple of blocks west of the jetty, behind the market.

Honey Bear Hotel HOTEL **$**
(☏ 059-51352; Strand Rd; r incl breakfast 840B; ❋ ☎) Overlooking the jetty, the Honey Bear consists of 39 relatively modern but simple rooms equipped with TV, air-con, saggy beds and cold-water showers.

Daw Moe BURMESE **$**
(Neikban St; curries from K2000; ◷ 10am-9pm) This tin-roofed restaurant (no roman-script sign) serves up a big spread of Burmese curries, as well as good vegetable side dishes. Located on the uphill portion of Neikban St, about a mile from the pier (K500 on a motorcycle taxi). Most locals can point you in the right direction.

❶ Information

Prices in Kawthoung are often quoted in Thai baht, as well as kyat and US dollars.

You can change money at **KBZ Bank** (Bosonpat Rd; ◷ 9.30am-3pm), which has an ATM that takes foreign cards. There are also moneychangers in the market on Strand Rd.

All hotels offer wi-fi.

❶ Getting There & Away

Sunfar Travels & Tours (off Strand Rd; ◷ 8.30am-5pm) sells air, bus and boat tickets.

It's on the road opposite the jetty, halfway between the jetty and the clock tower.

AIR

Air KBZ (☏ in Kawthoung 09 4306 9018, in Yangon 01-372 977; www.airkbz.com; Bosonpat St; ◷ 7.30am-5pm), Myanmar National Airlines (www.flymna.com) and **Apex Airlines** (www.apexairline.com; 214B Bosonpat Rd; ◷ 8am-5pm) link Kawthoung with Yangon (from US$105, three hours, daily) via stops in Myeik (from US$47, 45 minutes, daily) and/or Dawei (from US$81, 80 minutes, daily).

BOAT

Three companies run speedboats, departing daily at 3am for Myeik (US$45, seven hours) and Dawei (US$65, 12 hours). The boats mostly don't run in the rainy season (May to October).

BUS & MINIVAN

Buses depart from the main highway through town (motorcycle taxis charge K1000 to the departure point). Destinations include Yangon (K49,000, 40 hours, 2pm), Dawei (K35,000, 24 hours, 2pm) and Myeik (K25,000, 15 hours, 2pm).

Minivans go to the same destinations a couple of hours quicker and for similar or slightly higher fares. They leave at 5pm and will pick you up at your hotel. Tickets can be bought at a number of offices around town, or your hotel can get them for you.

❶ Getting Around

Most places are a brief walk from the market and harbour. Kawthoung's airport is approximately 8 miles from the jetty; a *thoun bein* will cost K5000 and a motorcycle taxi K3000.

Bagan & Central Myanmar

Why Go?

This heartland of the Bamar people has been the location of three former Burmese capitals – Bagan, Pyay and Taungoo – plus the latest surreal one, Nay Pyi Taw. Of this quartet, it's Bagan with its wondrous vista of pagodas and stupas, many dating to the 12th century, that's the star attraction. The tallest and most majestic of Bagan's temples, built of brick, decorated inside with beautiful frescoes and topped with gilded *hti* pinnacles, mix Hindu and Buddhist images with locally brewed *nat* (spirits) in nooks and crannies.

Most visitors fly directly to Bagan, but central Myanmar also provides scenic rewards for adventurous travellers. It may be known as the 'dry zone', but the region is far from a desert. Beside highways and rickety train tracks amble ox carts through rice fields and rolling plains, all rimmed by the Shan Mountains to the east and the snaking Ayeyarwady (Irrawaddy) River to the west, creating scenes that hark back centuries.

Best Places to Eat

➜ Black Bamboo (p162)

➜ Weather Spoon's Bagan (p161)

➜ Be Kind to Animals the Moon (p166)

➜ Pleasant Island (p177)

Best Places to Sleep

➜ Blue Bird Hotel (p170)

➜ Ostello Bello (p168)

➜ Lei Thar Gone (p155)

➜ Myanmar Beauty Guest House II (p144)

➜ Win Unity (p176)

When to Go
Bagan

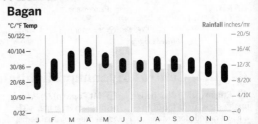

Nov–Feb Most visitors come in 'winter', when temperatures are moderately 'cool' at around 86°F.

Mar–May Hot season, when daytime temperatures boil at up to 100°F (40°C) and higher.

Jun–Oct Rainy season; the landscape is lush and hotel rates are at their lowest.

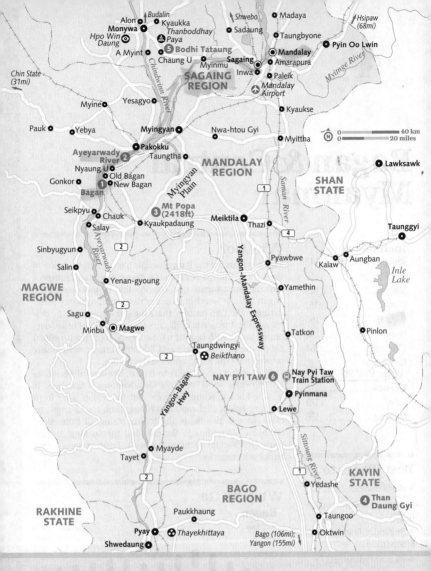

Bagan & Central Myanmar Highlights

1 Bagan (p156) Clambering up the steps to the top of an ancient pagoda for a jaw-dropping view over the temple-studded plain of Bagan.

2 Ayeyarwady River (p165) Taking a sunset boat ride from Old Bagan, enjoying the peaceful rhythms of life along the waterfront.

3 Mt Popa (p172) Paying respects to Myanmar's 37 nat at their spiritual home, the monkey-tastic volcanic mountaintop temple at Mt Popa.

4 Than Daung Gyi (p145) Exploring the peaceful Kayin village of Than Daung Gyi near Taungoo that has only recently opened to visitors.

5 Bodhi Tataung (p179) Pondering what the Buddha would have felt to see his likeness fashioned as a 30-storey concrete statue.

6 Nay Pyi Taw (p146) Discovering Myanmar's surreal 21st-century capital.

History

Conquering armies led by various peoples, including the Pyu, the Mon and the Burmese, have marauded across this central plain, the 'heart of Myanmar', over the centuries. The area around Pyay served as the Pyu capital from the 5th to 9th centuries AD and some historians consider the Pyu to be founders of Myanmar's 'first empire', although little is known of this vanished group.

Bagan's burst of spiritual creativity lasted 2½ centuries, beginning in 1047 and ending as the pounding footfall of Kublai Khan's raiders approached in 1287. The latest empire to lodge in the area is the military junta, which founded the new capital of Nay Pyi Taw in 2005.

While the military still lingers in the background, today Nobel Prize-winner and peace advocate Aung Sang Suu Kyi is running things in Nay Pyi Taw. The sweeping victory of her party, the National League for Democracy, in 2015 is helping to revitalise much of Myanmar, including Bagan, which may receive Unesco World Heritage status in the years to come.

❶ Getting There & Away

Bagan is the main entry point to the region for visitors arriving by air, although Mandalay is also convenient for northern destinations such as Monywa. Yangon is a convenient international entry point for more southerly destinations such as Pyay or Taungoo. Nyaung U is the principal gateway to Bagan, with a train station, a jetty and the airport.

Most visitors by boat come downriver from Mandalay on a fast boat or a slower, luxury cruise.

The majority of long-haul bus routes (eg Yangon–Mandalay) miss Bagan, but there are a few direct bus links between Bagan and Yangon, Mandalay and Inle Lake, including some luxurious sleeper options. Trains to the Bagan area are slow and impractical, with the exception of the Yangon–Bagan sleeper trains. The more interesting road route from Yangon to Bagan is via Pyay and Magwe.

YANGON–MANDALAY HIGHWAY

There are two routes that buses and cars ply between Yangon and Mandalay: the pot-holed old Hwy No 1, which some call the 'high road' (though it runs west of the Shan Hills); and the new Yangon–Mandalay Hwy, dubbed the 'big road'. Neither are particularly gorgeous drives but both provide access to a couple of places of interest en route to the north, including the former capital of Taungoo and the modern-day 'royal capital' of Nay Pyi Taw, a visit to which plunges you into the deepest depths of the bizarre.

Taungoo (Toungoo) တောင်ငူ

POP C 120,000 / ☑ 054

A busy highway town, Taungoo is a popular overnight stop for both tourists and truckers. Sporting several interesting temples, a lively central market and a pretty lake, it has more places of interest than any other town on the Yangon–Mandalay Hwy, but then there's not a lot of competition. A great guesthouse on the town's outskirts makes it easy to stay an extra day, and can also be used as a base for visiting elephant camps in the hills to the west.

The Karen hills to the east are famed for their vegetables and coffee. The area is also known for its numerous areca (betel) palms. In Myanmar, when someone receives unexpected good fortune, they are likened to a betel-lover receiving a paid trip to Taungoo.

A dry-weather road continues east all the way to Loikaw, though it's a rough and slow journey.

History

King Mingyinyo founded his capital here in 1510, and his dynasty ruled the country for the next 150 years. However, WWII bombing wrecked most of Mingyinyo's Katumadi Palace (only sections of the old walls and moat can still be seen). In celebration of the town's 500th anniversary in 2010, a couple of impressive new gates were built, as well as a massive statue of the king, unmissable on the old Yangon–Mandalay road, east of the palace walls.

◉ Sights

Apart from visiting the sights, it's fun to hire a bike and spend half a day pedalling around the town's sights and into the countryside.

Shwesandaw Paya　　　　　　　BUDDHIST TEMPLE
(ရွှေဆံတော်ဘုရား) Taungoo's grandest pilgrimage spot is situated in the centre of town, around 500m west of the main road. The central stupa, a standard-issue bell shape, is gilded and dates from 1597; local legend says an earlier stupa on the site was built centuries before and contains sacred-hair relics. Entering from the north, to your right is a

display of Taungoo kings (and a rather busty queen), and a round building housing a reclining buddha surrounded by *devas* (celestial beings) and monastic disciples.

Nearby, on the western side of the stupa, there's a 12ft bronze, Mandalay-style sitting buddha, given to the paya in 1912 by a retired civil servant who donated his body weight in bronze and silver for the casting of the image. He died three years after the casting at age 72; his ashes are interred behind the image.

On another side (go down one flight of the north stairs and turn right), there's a scruffy garden with a shrine to Thurathati – a goddess borrowed by Buddhists from Hindus – atop a mythical *hintha* (the golden Swan of Burmese legend). Fine-arts students come to pray to her before exams.

Myasigon Paya   BUDDHIST TEMPLE

(မြစည်းခုံဘုရား) About 820ft south of Shwesandaw (p143), off Pagoda St, this lovely modern pagoda features a gold *zedi* (stupa) and many glass mosaics. On the north side, an open building has a faded mural of Taungoo kings.

A nearby squat white building is actually a museum (to have it opened, ask in the pagoda). The dusty interior contains bronze images of Erawan (the three-headed elephant who serves as Indra's mount) and assorted buddha images, but is more interesting for its random secular collection of British colonial-era memorabilia, including an ancient Kodak camera, 80-year-old plates and an old cognac bottle.

Kandawgyi Lake   LAKE, PARK

(ကန်တော်ကြီး) This pretty ornamental lake dates from the days when Taungoo (then known as Katumadi) was capital and Bayin Naung ruled. Strolling or cycling around its perimeter, lined with shady trees, is a pleasant way to pass an hour or so.

On the lake's western flank, sandwiched between the old palace walls and moat, is the **Kyet Minn Nyi Naung Amusement Park**, built by the firm responsible for the neighbouring Royal Katumadi Hotel. Apart from various places to eat and drink here, you can play snooker or hire the karaoke room. There's a free kids' playground, but we were told the pedal boats on the lake were 'not for foreigners'.

🛏 Sleeping

Mother's House Hotel   HOTEL $

(☎ 054-24240;   motherhousehotel@gmail.com; 501-502 Yangon-Mandalay Hwy; s/d US$30/35;

❄ 🞀) This 33-room bungalow complex right on the highway has clean, well-equipped, hotel-style rooms with 24-hour electricity, flat-screen satellite TV, minifridges, wooden floors and muted earth-toned colour schemes. Rooms in back overlook a small garden. Front rooms are rather noisy.

There's also a decent **restaurant** (mains K2500 to K10,000) on-site.

Myanmar Beauty I   GUESTHOUSE $

(☎ 09 535 5555; Bo Muu Pho Kun Rd; s/d/tr US$20/25/30, s/d without bathroom US$8/12; ❄ 🞀) If you're looking for an economical option in the thick of town, this 34-room place is a good choice, with decent rooms within walking distance of eateries and the market. 'Economic class' rooms are clean but bare (fan-only). Pricier 'superior' rooms across the street have tile floors, big TVs and desks (plus air-con and hot water).

★ Myanmar Beauty Guest House II   GUESTHOUSE $$

(☎ 09 78404 0402; Pauk Hla Gyi St; s US$20-40, d US$25-50, tr US$40-60; ❄ 🞀) This 20-room rural complex at the edge of town is reason enough to stop in Taungoo. The Beauty has a pick-and-mix of rustic, all-wood, bungalow-style rooms. Staff are super, and have good recommendations for activities and outings (ask about visiting nearby villages). Another highlight is the wildly local breakfast, with an enormous spread of samosas, sticky rice and exotic fruits.

The best rooms are upstairs and open on to a breezy balcony overlooking the fields; cheaper rooms are in the lower level and have garden views. Plans are underway to add an organic garden (with produce used in the restaurant), and offer cooking classes. It's about 1.5 miles south of the turn-off from the old Yangon–Mandalay Hwy into the centre of Taungoo and is a K2000 trishaw ride from the centre.

Global Grace   HOTEL $$

(☎ 054-26168; www.globalgracehoteltaungoo.com; 20 Mingalar Rd; s US$32-43, d US$35-50; ❄ 🞀) A good midrange option, Global Grace has well-equipped rooms with kettles and minibars, clean-swept wood floors and hot-water bathrooms. Look for the signed turn-off near the vast playing fields along the Yangon–Mandalay Hwy.

Royal Kaytumadi Hotel   HOTEL $$

(☎ 054-24761; www.kmahotels.com; Royal Kaytumadi St; s US$85-110, d US$85-120, ste US$250-950;

THAN DAUNG GYI

Once off-limits to foreigners, Than Daung Gyi is a peaceful hillside village with sweeping views over the lush forests surrounding it. While traditional sights are few, the real appeal of visiting this Kayin village is interacting with the locals and exploring vestiges of old colonial days – with a handful of century-old churches, an old boarding school and a few other tucked-away buildings.

Unlike Kayin villages further afield, the locals have given up traditional dress; they're also largely Christian, which is apparent in attractions such as **Naw Bu Baw mountain**, a Christian pilgrimage site on the edge of town. Here you'll find a magnificent panorama (when the weather cooperates) from a perch 4800ft above sea level. The summit is reached by 374 steps, and lined with small chapels (including one shaped like two giant hands clasped in prayer) along the way.

A good lunch stop is **Amazing Traditional Foods** (Main Rd, Than Daung Gyi; mains around K2000; ◷9am-10pm Mon-Sat; ✓). Located on the main road in Than Daung Gyi, this very welcoming place serves tasty traditional Kayin fare accented with ingredients such as bamboo shoots, fried tofu and spicy fish sauce. You can also buy tea, which is grown in fields nearby. The owners are a good source of info and can advise on walks beyond the village (to hot springs and a waterfall). You can visit for the day, but it's worth staying overnight in one of the new family-run guesthouses that have opened in recent years. There are four or five basic guesthouses on the main road (with rates starting at around US$10) as well as **I Wish** (✆054-45024; s/d from US$20/30), which is set in a 1912 building tucked down a lane, 100yd from the main road.

On the way back from Than Daung Gyi, you can also stop for a swim at **Pathi Chaung**, a creek with lushly lined banks and large boulders. The turn-off is just off the main road when returning to Taungoo (halfway, around 13 miles from Taungoo).

The best way here is by private car, which can be arranged at hotels in Taungoo, including **Myanmar Beauty Guest House II** (p144). There is a strong military presence here, so bring your passport, which you'll need when passing through checkpoints in the area.

✳@⊚✉) Hogging the west side of the lake is Taungoo's fanciest option, with superbly appointed rooms, striking decorative detail and facilities including a swimming pool and spa. The property is owned by a businessman with close links to the generals. The same businessman also bankrolled the city gates and giant statue of Mingyinyo erected to celebrate the city's 500th anniversary in 2010.

Hotel Amazing Kaytu HOTEL $$
(✆054-23977; www.amazing-hotel.com; 8th St Ohtkyauttan; r US$42-58; ✳) 'Hotel Amazing' and 'Simply the Best' are stretching the imagination, but the owners clearly don't lack confidence in their property. Rooms are attractively set and have satellite TV and clean bathrooms (choose a superior or family room for more space and bigger windows). It's just north of the main turn-off from the old Yangon–Mandalay Hwy into the centre of Taungoo. Amazingly, there's no wi-fi.

✗ Eating

Around Taungoo's tea shops, try asking for *yo yo* (normal coffee), which should get you a cup of 'Taungoo coffee', which actually comes from the Karen mountains to the east.

At the **night market**, which convenes next to the central market, vendors specialise in chapatis and meat-stuffed *palata* (fried flatbread). On the old Yangon–Mandalay Hwy, particularly to the south, are many Chinese and Myanmar restaurants.

Stellar Restaurant CHINESE, BURMESE $
(Shwe Kyaung St; mains K2500-5000; ◷9am-11pm; ✓◎) Located near the Myasigon Paya, Stellar is a friendly, buzzing eatery and our favourite spot in town for a meal. Owner Ko Soe Nyi goes out of his way to make you feel at home in his inviting restaurant, and can happily guide you through the menu of chicken, pork and fish dishes – plus ample vegetarian choices.

Like MYANMAR, CHINESE $
(Bo Hmu Po Kun Rd; mains K1500-5000; ◷10am-9pm; ◎) This newish edition to Taungoo serves nicely prepared dishes from a small menu of Chinese and Myanmar classics. It's an open-sided spot located on busy Bo Hmu Po Kun Rd across from Royal Lake. It's a fine

spot to watch the game (European football) when key matches are under way.

ℹ️ Information

Dr Chan Aye (📞 054-23270; drchanaye@gmail. com; Myanmar Beauty Guest House II) Runs a clinic and speaks good English.

ℹ️ Getting There & Around

The narrow but paved 62-mile logging road from Oktwin (9 miles south of Taungoo) to Pauk-khaung provides a shortcut to Pyay. There are no buses between Pyay and Taungoo, but if you have private transport, the road is open to travel (permits no longer required).

BUS

Most buses leaving Taungoo originate elsewhere. Generally stops are at private bus-company offices scattered along the old Yangon–Mandalay Hwy, just south of the turn-off to the 'centre'. It's easiest to have your hotel arrange a seat.

Nay Pyi Taw (K3000, three hours, frequent)
Mandalay (K7500, seven to eight hours, early morning or early evening) Air-con bus.
Yangon (K4500, four to six hours, frequent) Buses with and without air-con.

BICYCLE

Bikes can be rented from some guesthouses, including **Myanmar Beauty Guest House II** (p144) for K2000 a day.

TRAIN

The Taungoo **train station** (📞 054-23308) is located in the centre of town, southeast of the market. Destinations include Mandalay (ordinary/upper K3500/45000, eight hours, 3am, 12.20pm, 2pm and 11pm), Nay Pyi Taw (K500/1000, two hours, 1pm, 4.30pm and 9pm), Thazi (K2000/3500, five hours, 12.20pm) and Yangon (K3000/4000, six hours, 5am, 10.40am, 2pm and 7pm).

Nay Pyi Taw နေပြည်တော်

POP C 925,000 / 📞 067

Absurdly grandiose in scale, Nay Pyi Taw (one translation is 'Royal City of the Sun') is a sprawling, shoddily constructed city with eight-lane highways, 24-hour electricity, and zones for shopping, government housing and hotels, ministry buildings and generals' homes. Apart from the roadblocks that protect the roads leading to the generals' mansions, ministry buildings and the parliament, it's surprisingly open. Visits to some of its sights, including a giant gilded pagoda, allow you to mingle freely with locals while putting a dollar or two into the private econ-

omy. This aside, it can feel soulless – Canberra meets Brasilia with a peculiar Orwellian twist.

History

In 2005, following the tradition of Burma's ancient kings, the military relocated Myanmar's capital to a more strategically central location, about 240 miles north of Yangon. At untold expense (some reports have it at more than US$4 billion), Nay Pyi Taw was built on scrub ground amid rice paddies, villages and small towns such as Pyinmana on the old Yangon–Mandalay Hwy. Most government ministries and their staff have been relocated here but, with a couple of exceptions, the diplomatic community have dug in their heels in Yangon.

⦿ Sights & Activities

You don't come to Nay Pyi Taw for the sights so much as for its surreal atmosphere. Besides, the city is very much a work in progress.

When approaching from the Yangon–Mandalay Hwy, visitors enter Nay Pyi Taw along the 'hotel zone' of Yaza Thingaha Rd. At the road's northern end near the Thabyaegone roundabout (one of the city's several gigantic, grassy road hubs) is the Maniyadanar Kyauk Sein Khanma convention centre. This is the location of the quarterly jade and precious stones fair, Emporium, about the only time Nay Pyi Taw fills with visitors. Next door is the Gems Museum and northeast of the roundabout is the Water Fountain Garden. Another 3 miles or so further north (along Yaza Thingaha) is the impressive National Museum.

Another of Nay Pyi Taw's key sights is the massive gilded pagoda of Uppatasanti Paya (some 3.7 miles east of the National Museum). Several other key sights are a long drive northeast of Nay Pyi Taw, including the curious National Landmark Gardens.

National Landmark Gardens   GARDENS
(အမျိုးသားအထိမ်းအမှတ်ဥယျာဉ်; www.national landmarkgarden.com; adult/child US$10/5; ⊙ 8am-5pm) Spread across 400 acres, these gardens showcase Myanmar's grandest sites in miniature. Hop aboard a golf cart (a one-hour tour is included with admission), and zip from Kachin State to Mandalay, down to Yangon and beyond, while taking in diminutive versions of Golden Rock, Inle Lake and Shwedagon Paya. It's a fun, but undeniably kitschy experience, all the more so given the amusement park rides scattered around – a Ferris wheel, bumper cars, a shooting range and a splashy log ride.

One of the most fascinating exhibitions lies inside a model of Nay Pyi Taw's convention centre, which has an impressive mock-up of all of Nay Pyi Taw, including pagodas, hotels and government buildings (about as close as you'll get to the gated-off epicentre of power), and a levitating train station. There are also two observation towers (one with a restaurant) offering views over the surrounding landscape. It's about 22 miles northeast of the hotel zone (a 40-minute drive).

National Museum
MUSEUM

(အမျိုးသားပြတိုက်; Yaza Thingaha Rd; K5000; ⏲9.30am-4.30pm Tue-Sun; 🖥) After five years of construction, the massive National Museum opened in 2015, and is well worth visiting if you're passing through the capital. Though the building and its empty corridors feel much too large for the contents within, the museum has some beautifully displayed works, particularly from the Bagan period, with lovely 11th-century jewellery, replicas of colourful mural paintings and models of architecturally stunning temples.

Exhibitions cover a huge swath of history: important fossils (such as 40-million-year-old anthropoid jawbones that lend credence to the theory that human ancestors evolved from primates in Asia rather than Africa); Stone Age tools; small figurines of minstrels from Sri-Ksetra (early evidence of musical culture in the region); and intriguing landscape paintings and portraits by 20th-century Myanmar artists. There's also a hands-on room where kids can tinker with musical instruments, try out a hand loom and create their own hand-drawn artworks.

Uppatasanti Paya
BUDDHIST TEMPLE

(ဥပ္ပါတသန္တိစေတီ) An act of merit-making by General Than Shwe and his wife, this 321ft tall golden pagoda – 1ft smaller than Yangon's Shwedagon Paya – is impressive from afar (especially when illuminated at night), but up close betrays its hasty construction with poor finishing. Nevertheless, the vast interior is lined with some vivid carved-stone murals depicting the life and legend of Buddha and key scenes from Myanmar's Buddhist history.

Water Fountain Garden
PARK

(per person/vehicle K700/500; ⏲8.30am-8.30pm) More or less at the heart of Nay Pyi Taw is this government-built, 165-acre grassy park boasting ponds, swinging bridges, gardens, fountains, kitschy sculptures, a playground and a massive water slide (if you have children with you, bring bathing suits).

The gurgling, colourfully lit fountains are usually turned on at around dusk and add to the allure alongside the twinkling fairy lights festooning the (ageing) structures scattered around the grounds.

Teak Spa & Fitness
SPA, SWIMMING

(☑067-810 2067; Shwe Kyar Pin Rd; day pass adult/child US$10/6; ⏲10am-10pm) This peaceful spot feels like an oasis from the concrete-loving capital, with a small grassy yard, koi pond and shimmering pool framed by palms. Aside from spending the day basking poolside, you could come for a spa treatment or dine at the on-site eatery serving Chinese and Thai dishes (mains K7000 to K18,000). It's about 1.2 miles east of Junction Centre (p148).

🛌 Sleeping

Most lodging options are in the hotel zone in the south of the city. Thanks to competition, you'll find some reasonable rates here compared with tourist destinations such as Yangon and Mandalay. ~$20-80

Golden Lake Hotel
HOTEL $

(☑067-434 022; thegoldenlakehotelnpt@gmail.com; 36-37 Yaza Thingaha Rd; r K20,000-80,000; ❄🛜) One of the few cheapies in the hotel zone, Golden Lake has standard rooms with bathrooms outside the room or superior en-suite rooms – the best are bungalow style with parquet floors. Both include similar amenities such as satellite TV and fridge. Friendly, English-speaking staff have a wealth of info on the city. There's also a restaurant (and 24-hour room service).

Hotel Amara
HOTEL $$

(☑067-422 201; www.thehotelamara.com; 11 Yaza Thingaha Rd; s/d US$50/55, ste US$105; ❄🛜) The welcoming Amara is a favourite with visiting diplomats and NGOs. The 104 executive rooms are good value, each with wood or parquet floors, a king-sized bed (in most rooms), modern bathroom and small balcony. For a touch more luxury, opt for the bungalow-style suites.

Royal Lotus
HOTEL $$

(☑067-810 6170; royallotus7sm@gmail.com; 38-39 Yaza Thingaha Rd; d/ste US$38/105; ❄🛜) This large 57-room complex has bright, comfortable rooms with all the usual touches (minibar, air-con, hot water), plus big windows for taking in the surprisingly pastoral landscapes out your window. Staff speak a bit of English.

Nay Pyi Taw

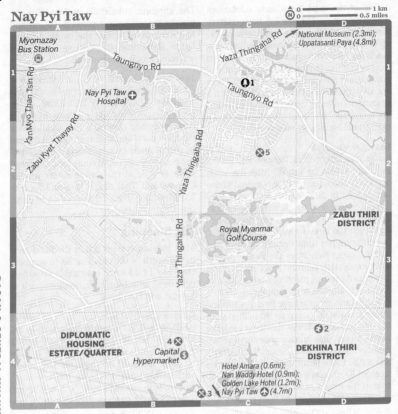

Nay Pyi Taw

◎ Sights
1 Water Fountain Garden.......................C1

⊕ Activities, Courses & Tours
2 Teak Spa & Fitness..............................D4

✖ Eating
3 Café Flight C4
4 Junction Centre B4
5 Maw Khan Nong...................................C2

Nan Waddy Hotel RESORT **$$**
(☎067-419 053; 12 Yaza Thingaha Rd; r US$50, ste US$120; ✳ 🛜) The spacious and sprawling Nanwaddy has a striking lobby to welcome guests and a series of rooms and bungalows set around a pretty lake full of lotus flowers. Rooms are reasonable value and include all mod cons. The suites are pretty impressive for those with the budget and include transfer by golf buggy.

✗ Eating & Drinking

There are a few places to eat and drink atop what is known as Golden Hill. At the foot of the hill, in the evenings, food and tea stalls set up shop. There are also a handful of places to eat in the Junction Centre, where you'll also find a huge Ocean Supermarket and a cinema.

Tai Kitchen THAI **$**
(Yana-Thing; mains K3000-8000; ⊙7am-10pm; 🅿🍽) One of the capital's best restaurants not set in a hotel, Tai Kitchen whips up delicious chicken basil, whole steamed fish with lemon, Shan-style spare ribs and vegetable-filled rice cakes among other hits. It has an attractive wood-filled interior and an outdoor deck when the temperatures aren't too steamy.

Junction Centre FOOD HALL **$**
(Yaza Thingaha Rd; mains from K2000; ⊙10am-9pm; 🅿🍽) This large, modern shopping centre has many temptations for locals and expats alike, including good restaurants such as

YKKO (mains K3500-K5000) that serve hearty plates of pan-Asian cooking. There's also a sprawling supermarket, a movie theatre and an arcade (a fine place to test your footwork on *Dance Dance Revolution*).

Maw Khan Nong BURMESE $
(Golden Hill; mains K1500-2800; ⊙7am-10pm; 🅿🅸) Join government workers at this lively canteen and beer station with a spacious outdoor terrace. Try the tasty fried catfish with bamboo shoots, or a good-value set lunch. Vegetarians can enjoy Shan-style steamed bean curd.

Café Flight ASIAN, INTERNATIONAL $$
(3 Yaza Thingaha Rd; mains K3500-7000; ⊙6.30am-10pm) To experience a Myanma Airways plane, clamber on to this one, parked in front of the Sky Palace Hotel. It's been turned into a cafe-bar serving draught Tiger beer, coffee and other drinks. For something other than drinks, head into the unfussy main restaurant behind, where diners tuck into Thai and Chinese dishes.

Emerald Restaurant ITALIAN, FUSION $$$
(☎067-419 321; www.emeraldpalace.com; 40-41 Yaza Thingaha Rd; mains US$10-30; ⊙11am-10.30pm; 🛜🅿🅸) Located inside the Emerald Hotel in the hotel zone in Nay Pyi Taw's south, this place serves excellent Italian dishes (with executive chef Dario Cattarinich at the helm), including gnocchi with Gorgonzola, veal osso bucco and delicious pizzas – the best in town (Tuesday night features a K10,000 pizza special). There are also appealing curries, Shan-style pork and other traditional plates.

ⓘ Getting There & Away

AIR

Nay Pyi Taw International Airport (NYT; ☎09 79900 0196) is located about 10 miles southeast of the city. There are several domestic flights daily linking Nay Pyi Taw with Yangon (from US$103 one way), plus international services to Bangkok six times a week and Kunming (China) twice a week.

A taxi from the airport to town is about K20,000.

BUS

Nay Pyi Taw has two bus stations. The closest to the hotel zone and other key points is the Myomazay Bus Station, west of the Thabyaegone roundabout. Services from this station depart regularly for Yangon (K6000, five to six hours), Mandalay (K5300, four to five hours) and, less frequently, Bagan (K11,000, around six hours, daily at 7am and 8pm). Other departures include

Kalaw, Taunggyi and Pyay. A taxi to the station from most hotels is about K7000.

TRAIN

Several miles northeast of the Uppatasanti Paya is the massive train station with an old steam locomotive parked just inside the entrance. There are trains to Yangon (ordinary/upper K2800/5600, nine to 10 hours, 11.50am, 8pm, 8.30pm and 10.30pm), Mandalay (ordinary/upper K1850/3700, six to seven hours, 1.50pm, 3.15pm and 11.20pm), Bagan (K2700, 10 hours, 5am) and Kalaw (K1350, 10 hours).

ⓘ Getting Around

Nya Pyi Taw is no place for walking and there's nothing approaching a public bus service. The best way around is by private car, taxi or private motorbike taxi. A taxi from the hotel zone to Myomazay bus station costs around K7000; to/from the train station costs around K15,000. Given the great distances to go anywhere, you're better off hiring a taxi for the day. Rates are around K10,000 per hour and K55,000 for the whole day. A motorbike taxi costs about K3000 per hour (K20,000 for eight hours).

Nay Pyi Taw Taxi & Car Rental Services (☎067-414 994) Run by government-affiliated Max Myanmar group. A taxi from the airport to town is about K20,000.

Meiktila

POP 253,000 / ☎064

The attractive lakeside town of Meiktila, on the crossroads between Yangon, Mandalay, Bagan and Inle Lake, is a busy little trade centre with plenty of locals in uniform from the air-force bases outside town. Legend goes that King Anawrahta, founder of Bagan, had a pond here broadened into the current lake that looms west of town. When the king asked if the lake extended all the way to Mt Popa, the report came back: 'Lord, it doesn't go that far'.

For visitors, Meiktila is a lively city that makes for a fine pit stop when travelling between Nay Pyi Taw and Bagan. While sights are few, the intriguing lakefront and buzzing teahouses just off the main road through town are fine places to soak up the energy of this little-visited crossroads.

History

Between February and March 1945, the British killed 20,000 Japanese soldiers based here in the final WWII battle for control of Burma. Much of the city was flattened. Sadly that trend has continued: town-engulfing fires devastated the city in 1974 and 1991; another big one took out several buildings in 2003.

The name has perhaps become something of a burden, as in 2013 Meiktila once again hit the headlines for all the wrong reasons when internecine rioting broke out between the Buddhist and Muslim communities. Dozens were killed and hundreds displaced and it is still possible to see scars from the violence on the outskirts of town.

⊙ Sights

Lake Meiktila
LAKE

(မိတ္ထီလာကန်) Lake Meiktila is the town's premier attraction. There are no boating options, but you can cycle around some of it. Between the road and rail bridges, west of the city centre, you won't miss **Phaung Daw U Paya** (ဖောင်တော်ဦးဘုရား), a temple housed in a giant floating barge shaped in the form of a golden *karaweik*, a mythical bird.

Cross the road bridge to reach the wooden pier leading to the pretty **Antaka Yele Paya** (အန္တကကျရေလယ်ဘုရား), a small pagoda perched on an island in the lake. Back on the main road is an **Aung San statue**.

Shwe Kyaung
BUDDHIST MONASTERY

(ရွှေကျောင်း) A mile around the west end of Lake Meiktila, Shwe Kyaung is a walled monastery on the inland side of the road with Japanese signs leading to a **WWII monument** that British and Japanese survivors erected in 1972. Monks will show you around. Just past the monument, a picturesque path leads between the lake and (usually) flooded rice fields.

Don't keep going to the south side of the lake, as the path leads into the no-go zone of a military compound.

British Colonial Diplomat House
NOTABLE BUILDING

A few hundred metres southwest of the bridge is a building that was once a British colonial diplomat house. The building was used as an interrogation centre by the Japanese in WWII, and many years later Aung San Suu Kyi and Michael Aris honeymooned here. The house is to the east of the Lakeside Wunzin Hotel.

🛏 Sleeping

Honey Hotel
HOTEL $

(📞 064-25755; Panchan St; s/tw US$30/35; ❄ 🛜) Right on the lake in the southern tip of the town centre, this rambling guesthouse is Meiktila's leading budget option. Rooms

are simple, tiled affairs, with the best of the bunch offering partial views across the lake. Skip breakfast and head to one of the teahouses off the main drag instead.

Floral Breeze Hotel
HOTEL $$

(Wunzin Hotel; 📞 064-23848; 49A Than Lwin Rd; d US$30-50, ste US$60; ❄ 🛜) This long-running spot has comfortably set rooms, painted in ethereal colours (lavender, anyone?). The more expensive suites overlook the lake from a quiet backstreet out of the centre. There's also a scruffy tennis court, though you'll need a racket. It is located near the lakefront, west of the town centre: cross the bridge and head three blocks southwest.

🍴 Eating & Drinking

Honey Restaurant
CHINESE, THAI $

(Panchan St; mains K2500-8000; 🍴) Honey is a friendly spot that serves the usual mix of Thai, Chinese and Western dishes (including fish and chips). It's located near the waterfront, about four blocks south of the bridge. Despite the name, it's not connected with the Honey Hotel a few blocks away.

Champion
BAKERY $

(Mandalay-Yangon Hwy; snacks from K500; ⊘ 7am-9pm) Grab pastries and other baked goods from this popular spot on the main road in the centre of town.

Lekker Corner
THAI $

(mains K3000-5000; ⊘ 10am-9pm; 🍴) A clean and inviting place one block south of the main Mandalay-Yangon Hwy, Lekker Corner whips up catfish with red curry, prawns in tamarind sauce, spicy papaya salad and other zesty Thai dishes.

Golden Rain Tea Center
TEAHOUSE

(tea K200; ⊘ 5am-9.30pm) This popular unsigned place, just north of the Mandalay-Yangon Hwy, has all the usual milky, sweet drinks and filling chicken or steamed pork buns. Mix with locals at the low tables shielded by a rattan roof cover.

ⓘ Getting There & Away

BUS

Buses heading to Yangon, Mandalay and other destinations stop on the main road, just east of the bridge. Along this road you'll find several bus companies heading to the main destinations.

Buses from Meiktila go to Bagan (K5000 to K7000, five hours, 4pm), Mandalay (K3000, three to four hours, several daily), Nay Pyi Taw (K4000, three to four hours, several daily) and Yangon (K9000 to K10,000, eight to 10 hours, twice daily).

TRAIN

There's a small train station in town, catching slow trains heading east–west. A more useful station is in Thazi, about 16 miles east, at the crossroads of the Yangon, Mandalay and Taunggyi lines.

YANGON–BAGAN HIGHWAY

This western route north of Yangon to Bagan is less heavily trafficked than the Yangon–Mandalay route. Sometimes called the 'low road', or 'Pyay Hwy', this route is arguably more attractive than the old Yangon–Mandalay Hwy. It follows the eastern bank of the Ayeyarwady River and rises over lovely hills and valleys north of Magwe. At Pyay, connections to Thandwe (and Ngapali) head west over the mountains.

Pyay   မြည်

POP 136,000 / ☎ 053

With a breezy location on the Ayeyarwady (Irrawaddy) River, Pyay (Prome) is the most interesting stop on the Yangon–Bagan Hwy. The city's glory days date back to the ancient Pyu capital of Thayekhittaya, the partially excavated remains of which lie 5 miles east of Pyay's other stellar attraction: the dazzling Shwesandaw Paya.

Myanmar folk alternate the town's pronunciation between 'pyay' and 'pyi'. The Brits, apparently, couldn't deal with the confusion and called it Prome. The current town site became an important trading centre during the Bagan era. The Mon controlled it when King Alaungpaya conquered it in 1754. Pyay boomed, along with the British Irrawaddy Flotilla Company in the 1890s.

Today, it remains an important transit point for goods between northern and southern Myanmar. Soak up its lively atmosphere along the riverfront and at the roundabout, at the centre of which is a gilded equestrian statue of Aung San.

◉ Sights

Shwesandaw Paya & Around   BUDDHIST TEMPLE
(ရွှေဆံတော်ဘုရား နှင့် အနီးဝန်းကျင်; K3000; ⊙ 5am-10pm) Set on top of a hill in the town centre, the stunning Shwesandaw Paya (and the surrounding pagodas and monasteries) is not only Pyay's major point of interest, but also one of the country's biggest Buddhist pilgrimage sites. Just over 3ft taller than the main *zedi* (stupa) at Yangon's Shwedagon (p45), the Shwesandaw stupa follows the classic Burmese design seen at Bagan's Shwezigon (p195).

Legend goes that it was built in 589 BC, and that the golden *zedi* houses four strands of the Buddha's hair (the Golden Hair Relics). Atop the *zedi* are two *hti* (umbrella-like pinnacles), unusual for Myanmar. The lower, bigger one dates from Pyay's days as a Mon city. The higher, smaller one was added by King Alaungpaya as a symbol of peace between his realm and the Mon, after brutally capturing the city in 1754. In the southwest corner of the complex, the Sacred Tooth Hall is said to house an original tooth from the Buddha. It's in the golden bell (locked) behind the glass. The locks come off once a year for the November full-moon festivities.

The panoramic views from the pagoda are great too. To the east, you'll see the **Sehtatgyi Paya** (ဆယ်ထပ်ကြီးဘုရား; Big Ten Storey), a giant (maybe not 10 storeys, though) seated Buddha, eye-to-eye with the Shwesandaw and watching over it. The smaller gold stupa on the highest hill southeast of Shwesandaw is the **Wunchataung Paya**

BAGAN & CENTRAL MYANMAR PYAY

AKAUK TAUNG

Carved into cliffs overlooking the Ayeyarwady, about 19 miles downstream from Pyay, are dozens of buddha images at **Akauk Taung** (အကောက်တောင်; Tax Mountain). The mountain is named for the crafty toll-takers from the mid-19th century who, when not taxing boats, spent their time carving reclining and meditating buddhas into the steep cliff.

To get there, you'll need to taxi across the Ayeyarwady to **Htonbo** (ထုံးဘို), a village about 90 minutes by road from Pyay, then travel by boat (about K15,000) for the 45-minute look. For some visitors, it's too much travel for minimal payoff. A return taxi to Htonbo from Pyay (sometimes with Shwedaung thrown in) costs about K60,000 for the round trip. Allow about four hours for the whole outing.

Pyay

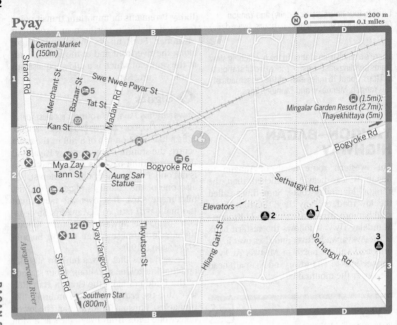

Pyay

(ဝန်ချတောင်ဘုရား; Apology Mountain Pagoda), where people can say 'sorry' for misdeeds. While they're at it, they get the best view of Shwesandaw and the mountains across the river. Reach Wunchataung via Sehtatgyi Rd, east of Shwesandaw.

Central Market MARKET
(⊙7am-4pm) Follow Strand Rd north to catch the action at the lively and colourful central market which spreads over several blocks. As you approach, you'll pass an ornate **Chinese Temple** dedicated to the goddess Guan Yin on the corner of Ya Yoke Tann St. A little further on are giant clay water pots and a row of *thanakha*-wood sellers. Continue along the riverside north of the market to find the Shwepaliamaw Paya.

🛏 Sleeping

Myat Lodging House HOTEL $
(☎053-25695; 222 Bazaar St; s US$20-30, d US$25-35; ❀⊙) This small backstreet guesthouse has bare-bones rooms in a central (but quiet) location within walking distance of the market. Higher-priced rooms have a private bathroom and are set at the back of the maze of buildings. Friendly English-speaking staff give out maps of Pyay and Thayekhittaya.

Smile Motel HOTEL $
(☎053-25142; 10-11 Bogyoke Rd; r US$24-40; ❀⊙) The long corridor leading to the simply furnished rooms may have a shabby carpet and remind you of *The Shining,* but it's clean and the staff are nice, if a bit surprised at your existence. The US$40 family rooms can sleep up to four.

★ **Mingalar Garden Resort** HOTEL $$

(☑053-28662; www.mingalargardenresort.com; Flying Tiger Garden, Aung Chan Tha Quarter; s/d US$70/80; ❄@☎) Near Payagyi Paya and closer to Thayekhittaya than the Ayeyarwady River, this peaceful garden complex of spacious bungalows is set in the beautifully presented grounds of a former cheroot manufacturer. Handsomely appointed rooms have polished wood floors and face either the garden or (better yet) the ornamental lake at the centre of the property. Breakfast is served by the lakeside.

There's also a restaurant and ATM.

Lucky Dragon HOTEL $$

(☑053-24222; www.luckydragonhotel.com; 772 Strand Rd; tw/d/f US$60/65/70; P❄☎☎) Leaving all other town-centre hotels in the shade, this enclave of modern, bungalow-style, wood-floored rooms across from the river is reasonably priced and has pleasant, helpful staff. The small pool is a plus, long enough for a few cooling laps after touring Pyay's sights.

✕ Eating & Drinking

Yes! Coffee & Food House CAFE $

(Strand Rd; mains K2000-5000; ☺7am-10pm; ☑▣) An update on the old-fashioned teahouse, Yes! is awash with a bold vibrant paint job and coloured light bulbs that seem to draw young diners to the low outdoor tables along the riverfront road. There's a big menu with the usual selection of chicken, pork and vegetable dishes, though it's also a fine spot for juices and brewed Brazilian coffee.

Wish River View CHINESE, BURMESE $

(Strand Rd; mains K2000-5000; ☺9am-9pm; ▣) This clean, inviting space is one of the best riverfront restaurants in the area. Stop in for marinated-prawn salad, fiery Thai-style seafood soup or sautéed vegetable dishes. The free peanuts are a nice touch (there's also Carlsberg and a few other beer choices).

Grandma Café KOREAN, INTERNATIONAL $

(Mya Zay Tann Rd; mains K1500-2500; ☺8am-10pm) Owner Banyar Aung learned to make Korean food while working at various restaurants in Kuala Lumpur, then returned home and taught his wife. Together they run this cute place that turns out very tasty *dolsot bibimbap* and *kimchi ramen,* along with more familiar dishes such as sandwiches, burgers and pasta, all at bargain prices.

Hline Ayar CHINESE, BURMESE $

(Strand Rd; dishes K3000-7500; ☺10am-10pm) This popular live-music spot has provincial models singing karaoke from 7pm, but it doesn't have to detract from dinner if you bag a table looking over the Ayeyarwady. Draught beer flows and the menu is predominantly Chinese and Thai.

Night Market MARKET $

(mains around K1000) The night market on Mya Zay Tann St, between the Aung San statue and the river, is atmospheric and well worth browsing for its cheap eats.

Southern Star CHINESE $

(☑053-25484; Strand Rd; mains K3500-7500; ☺10am-11pm) Enjoy river views from this big open-sided restaurant serving a good range of Asian classics from Burma, China, Malaysia and Thailand, close by the Nawade Bridge. In the evenings there's sometimes live music on the small stage, and there are a few private karaoke rooms if you can't contain the urge to sing.

🛍 Shopping

Spectrum Art ART

(off Strand Rd; ☺9am-7pm) Tucked down a sleepy side street off Strand Rd, this tiny traditional house contains a small collection of landscapes, portraits and caricatures by Sooe Lay, who opened the gallery in 1997. Prices for original works cost about US$80 to US$100.

ℹ Getting There & Away

IWT ferries, which used to connect Pyay with Yangon, no longer operate along this route. There is currently no ferry service north or south from Pyay.

BUS

Pyay is located at the junction to Yangon, Bagan and Thandwe (for Ngapali Beach). The highway bus station is about 2 miles east of the centre (just off Bogyoke Rd).

Several companies run buses to Yangon (K5000, seven hours) throughout the day. **Asia Express** (☑053-28145) runs 12 buses per day. There's currently just one bus to Bagan (K14,000, 12 hours), which departs at 5pm. You can also take an early-morning bus to Magwe (K5000, five hours, departs every two hours or so from 6.30am), and catch an onward bus to Bagan.

Heading to Ngapali by bus is possible, but not terribly convenient. There's one bus to Taunggok (K13,000, seven hours) leaving around 5pm.

SHWEDAUNG

The small town of Shwedaung (ရွှေတောင်), about 9 miles south of Pyay via the road to Yangon, contains the famous **Shwemyetman Paya** (ရွှေမျက်မှန်ဘုရား; Paya of the Golden Spectacles), a reference to the large, myopic buddha seated passively here.

Spectacles were first added to the image during the Konbaung era, when a nobleman offered them to the temple in an attempt to stimulate local faith through curiosity. Word soon spread that the bespectacled buddha had the power to cure all ills, especially afflictions of the eyes. The first pair of spectacles was stolen at an early stage, and a second pair was made and enshrined inside the image to protect it from thieves. An English officer stationed in Pyay during the colonial era had a third pair fitted over the buddha's eyes after his wife suffered from eye trouble and the abbot suggested such a donation. Naturally, as the story goes, she was cured. This pair is now in a display case to the left of the image.

Coming south from Pyay, the turn-off for Shwemyetman is located on the right-hand side of the road; a green-and-white sign reads, 'Shwe Myet Hman Buddha Image – 1 Furlong'.

Another few miles south is **Shwenattaung Paya** (ရွှေနတ်တောင်ဘုရား, Golden Spirit Mountain), a hilltop shrine dating back many centuries. A large *paya pwe* (pagoda festival) is held here each year on the full moon of Tabaung (February/March).

To get to Shwedaung, hop on a pick-up truck headed towards Yangon. Pick-up trucks leave frequently from the Pyay bus station and pass by the Aung San statue before hitting the highway.

TRAIN

A lone daily train leaves Pyay's central train station at 11pm for Yangon (K3500 to K5000, nine hours). From Shwethekar station, 3 miles east of the city towards Thayekhittaya, you can also board the Yangon–Bagan train as it takes a three-minute pause at 9.30pm (K1950), before arriving in Bagan at 8am; the Bagan–Yangon train arrives at 2.30am, before continuing on to Yangon.

ⓘ Getting Around

Trishaws and blue taxi pick-up trucks are the main ways of getting around. A trishaw or taxi ride to/from the bus station is around K2000. A regular pick-up truck service runs along Bogyoke Rd to the bus station (K200).

Thayekhittaya (Sri Ksetra) သရေခေတ္တရာ

It's no Bagan, but this ancient site, about 5 miles east of Pyay centre, makes for an enjoyable few hours of laid-back exploration, often in isolation. Known to Pali-Sanskrit scholars as Sri Ksetra (Fabulous City), Thayekhittaya is an enormous Pyu city that ruled in the area from the 5th to 9th centuries AD. Local legend links its origin to the mythical King Duttabaung, who supposedly worked with ogres and other supernatural creatures to build the 'magical city' in 443 BC. The earliest Pali inscriptions found here date to the 5th or 6th centuries.

◉ Sights

Being able to see the 5.5-sq-mile **Thayekhittaya** (သရေခေတ္တရာ; K5000, incl museum K10,000; ⏱9.30am-4.30pm) site means either walking the 7.5-mile loop around it or hopping on the back of an **ox-drawn cart** (per person K7000) for a bumpy, 3-hour dusty journey past the spaced-out temples, most just outside the oval city walls. It's a good idea to have a knowledgeable guide if one is available at the museum. Bicycles aren't permitted, though you can go by car (assuming you've arrived with a driver). Motorbike hire may also be available (K5000).

Before exploring the ancient ruins, it's worthwhile stopping in the small **Sri Ksetra Museum** (သရေခေတ္တရာပြတိုက်; K5000; ⏱9.30am-4.30pm Tue-Sat). Inside, you'll find a posted map of the area and various artefacts from excavations, including sandstone reliefs featuring Hindu deities, 6th-century buddha images, Pyu beads, finely crafted gold and silver jewellery and condensed background details on Pyu architecture, literature and religious beliefs.

Among the most important pieces found at Pyu are small bronze figurines of five performers (a flautist, drummer, clown, dancer and cymbal player), which are among the earliest evidence of Myanmar's musical traditions (and date to between the 4th and 9th century AD). You can see replicas here of the figurines, though the originals are in the National Museum in Nay Pyi Taw.

Behind the museum to the south, the road soon follows the remains of the old palace walls. Ox-cart drivers – at a speed that ebbs and flows according to the mood of the ox – make a counter-clockwise loop of the following sites.

The first stop will be at a recent excavation: a large brick building that is thought to have been a **palace**. After 2.5 miles or so, the road passes **Rahanta Gate**, where fragments of the overgrown brick gate run alongside the dirt road. Immediately south is the **Rahanta cave temple**, thought to date to the Bagan period and last repaired in the 1920s, with eight buddha images lined along the south wall.

About a mile south, the **Bawbawgyi Paya** (Big Grandfather Stupa) is Thayekhittaya's most impressive site: a 50yd cylindrical stupa with a golden *hti* (stupa pinnacle) on its top. It's among the oldest and least obviously renovated Pyu sights, dating to the 4th century. It's the prototype of many Myanmar pagodas.

Around 200yd northeast is the smaller cube-shaped **Bebe Paya**, which has a cylindrical top and a few buddha images inside; it's thought to date to the 10th century. Just east is the squat **Leimyethna Paya**, which has a visible iron frame keeping it together. Inside, four original buddha reliefs (a bit cracked, some faces missing) are visible. On either side of the roads around here, look out for long ruts in the ground, which were once brick moats.

A couple of hundred yards to the north is a fork in the road: to the right (north) is a tin-roofed **cemetery**; to the left (west), on the way to 'Thaungpye Mound', is the better (but bumpier) way back to the museum.

Take the left and after half a mile you'll pass by a gap in the 9ft-thick city walls, which has become a gate. Continue another mile, through a booming farming village of thatch huts with piles of radishes and other produce. Towards the north end of the village is the 13th-century **East Zegu Paya**, a small four-sided temple. It's about 200yd off the main road, but worth visiting for the walk past the fields and farmers.

❶ Getting There & Away

The turn-off here is a couple of miles east of Payagyi Paya. A return taxi between Thayekhittaya and Pyay should cost about K15,000. No direct pick-up truck connects the Pyay town centre with the site. You can ride a bike to the site, but not around it.

Magwe မကွေး

POP 290,000 / ☎ 063

About 155 miles north of Pyay and 93 miles south of Salay, Magwe's locale on the Ayeyarwady River is nice enough, as is the impressive 1.8-mile Magwe Bridge. Beyond this, however, it's a place of dilapidated buildings running along a confusing web of leafy streets. Still, if you're travelling along the bumpy road connecting Bagan and Pyay, you'll probably want to break your journey here and stretch your legs around the 'sights'. Famously, the capital of Magwe Division sat out of the 1988 prodemocracy marches. There's one memorable guesthouse (actually in nearby Yengangyaung) that makes a fine base for exploring the area.

◎ Sights

Nga Ka Pwe Taung   SACRED SITE
(နဂါးပွက်တောင်) Just across the river, a few miles north of the bridge, is the small town of Minbu and the fun Nga Ka Pwe Taung (Dragon Lake), a burping pool of butane gas and mud that has over the years built a few acres of lunar-like terrain with bubbling pools atop four odd mounds. The sludge isn't hot; if your toes slip in, wash them off below at a small pagoda.

Mya Tha Lun Paya   BUDDHIST SITE
(မြသလွန်ဘုရား) Magwe's chief pagoda, the 1929 Mya Tha Lun Paya, is a mile north of the Magwe Bridge. It features a gilded stupa and occupies a hilltop site with great river views.

☆ Festivals & Events

Mya Tha Lun Paya Festival   CULTURAL
(☉ Oct) This month-long fest happens at the Mya Tha Lun pagoda and features food, crafts, traditional dancing and theatre.

⌑ Sleeping & Eating

★ **Lei Thar Gone**   GUESTHOUSE $
(☎ 060-21620; www.leithargone-guesthouse.com; Thit-Ta-Bway Quarter, Yengangyaung; s US$30-60, d US$40-70; ✳ ☎ ☒) ✎ One of the most memorable lodging options south of Bagan is in Yengangyaung, some 30 miles north of Magwe. On a breezy hilltop overlooking a peaceful village, with the winding Ayeyarwady in the distance, is a collection of 15 handsomely designed bungalows with high ceilings, traditional weavings, and bamboo and stone details. The best open on to a terrace with fine views.

A restaurant serves good curries and Western fare. Owner Eric Trutwein uses a portion of the guesthouse profits to fund a primary school he helped create. He can arrange boating or fishing trips on the river and other excursions. Free transport is available from Yengangyaung (pick-up from Bagan can also be arranged).

Rolex Guest House
GUESTHOUSE $

(☑ 09 97447 0618; cnr Mya Than Lun Rd & Ayeyarwady Bridge; s/d with fan K8000/15,000, with air-con K20,000/40,000; ❀) This rambling old guesthouse, on the roundabout facing the bridge entry, doesn't quite live up to the namesake timepiece. It has simple, ageing rooms with cold-water bathrooms attached. It's easy to find and will just about do the trick if passing through for the night. No wi-fi.

Nan Htike Thu Hotel
HOTEL $$

(☑ 063-28204; www.facebook.com/nanhtikethumagway; Strand Rd; r US$50-70; ❀ 🛈 ☀) This riverfront hotel is one of Magwe's best options. Superior river-view rooms are US$70 and are smartly kitted out with flat-screen TV, minibar, bathtubs and small balconies. Facilities include a huge kidney-shaped swimming pool. Across the road on the river's edge is the Elysium Restaurant. The hotel is 1.5 miles south of the bridge.

Mona Liza 2
BURMESE, CHINESE $

(Strand Rd; mains from K1500-6000; ⊙ 7am-10pm) On the river, just north of the bridge, this popular drinking spot also serves great-value food. As the sun dips across the river, locals hit the beer and whisky for the 7pm music and dance show.

❶ Getting There & Around

Magwe's highway bus station is about 1.5 miles east of the central market. Buses from Magwe go to the following destinations: Nyaung U (K5000 to K7000, three to four hours, morning), Pyay (K4800, seven hours, 12.30pm), Yangon (K8500 to K10,500, 12 hours, frequent) and Mandalay (K6000 to K7000, 10 hours, 6.30pm).

Motorised trishaws – with room for you and a few mates – tout their services at the bus station. A ride from the station to Nga Ka Pwe Taung and a stop at a lunch spot costs about K10,000.

BAGAN
ပုဂံ

☑ 061

This temple town is one of Myanmar's main attractions. The area known as Bagan or, as the 'Bagan Archaeological Zone', occupies an impressive 26-sq-mile area, 118 miles south of Mandalay and 429 miles north of Yangon. The Ayeyarwady (Irrawaddy) River drifts past its northern and western sides. For the temples of Bagan, see p180.

The area's most active town and main transport hub is Nyaung U, in the northeast corner. About 2.5 miles west, Old Bagan is the former site of the village that was relocated 2 miles south to New Bagan in 1990. Between the two is Myinkaba, a village boasting a long-running lacquerware tradition. One thing to keep in mind, particularly for travellers exploring the region, is that Bagan is not like Siem Reap or even Luang Prabang. It's an overgrown village and lacks anything resembling a night scene, although it does have basic traveller amenities. Plan your partying somewhere else.

🏃 Activities

Boat Trips

Apart from a sunset boat tour (p165) on the Ayeyarwady, you can also arrange an interesting boat and taxi side trip to mountain-top Tan Kyi Paya, one of four stupas that marked the original edges of the city. Another possible boat trip is to three temples north of Nyaung U.

Ballooning

The best way to truly appreciate Bagan's size and sprawl is from the basket of a hot-air balloon belonging to Balloons over Bagan (Map p159; ☑ 061-60713; www.balloonsoverbagan.com; near Thiripyitsayar St, Nyaung U; per person from US$330). These magical 45-minute rides over one of the world's best ballooning spots operate from October to March. Sometimes sunrise flights are booked up to a month or more in advance, but *if* there's space, any hotel or guesthouse should be able to arrange a ticket.

The well-run company, owned by an Australian-Burmese couple and employing about 100 locals, has 10 balloons that usually fit up to 16 passengers and a pilot. The experience begins with a pick up from your hotel in a lovingly restored, pre-WWII Chevrolet CMP bus, partly made of teak. You can have coffee and snacks while watching the UK-made balloons fill with hot air, and then enjoy sparkling wine and snacks when you land, while watching them get packed up again.

Although sunset flights are offered (depending on weather conditions), the sunrise ones are preferable – the cooler dawn air allows pilots to fly the balloons at lower altitude for a closer view of the temples.

Several other companies offer similar flights, including **Oriental Ballooning** (☎09 25050 5383; www.orientalballooning.com; per person US$395) and **Golden Eagle Ballooning** (Map p159; ☎09 25208 4232; www.goldeneagle balloonig.com; office in Bagan Umbra Hotel; per person from US$320).

🎓 Courses

⭐**Pennywort Cooking Class**　　COOKING
(Map p184; ☎09 25401 0340; www.facebook.com/pennywortcookingclass; Sein Pann St; per person US$20; ⊙classes at 7.30am & 4.30pm) 🍴 Rated highly by travellers is this delightful, hands-on cooking course run by the charismatic May from her family home. The daytime course includes a visit to the market to shop for ingredients (with accommodations made for vegetarians and dietary restrictions), followed by a walk back to May's house for preparation – using charcoal fires to make curries, soups, salads and other dishes.

It's a great way to learn more about Burmese food, customs and culture, and May gives back to the community, with 20% of earnings going towards a town library.

Bagan Thiripyitsaya Sanctuary Resort　　COOKING
(Map p166; ☎061-60048; www.thiripyitsaya-resort.com) This resort offers a variety of courses, including a three-hour cooking course covering four or five traditional dishes for a maximum of four participants (US$100 per person). Other classes include meditation training with a monk (one/two hours US$70/100).

ℹ️ Information

For travel information, try Nyaung U's **Ever Sky Information Service** (Map p159; ☎061-60895; everskynanda@gmail.com; 5 Thiripyitsaya St; ⊙7.30am-9.30pm). The less-helpful government-run **MTT office** (Myanmar Travels & Tours; Map p169; ☎061-65040; ⊙8.30am-4.30pm) in New Bagan has limited information.

The *Map of Bagan* (www.dpsmap.com/bagan; K1000) is sold at most hotels and at the airport. It shows many of the area's paths, but isn't always 100% accurate.

ℹ️ Getting There & Away

The main hub for Bagan is Nyaung U, which is the closest town to the airport and the bus station.

A taxi to/from the Nyaung U airport runs about K6000 (K5000 in low season); to the train station, about 2.5 miles southeast of Nyaung U, drivers charge about K7000.

FROM THE AIRPORT & JETTY

Taxis between Nyaung U airport and hotels in Nyaung U, Old Bagan and New Bagan cost between K5000 and K8000. Horse carts and taxis are cheaper from the Old Bagan or Nyaung U jetties, if you arrive by boat.

BOAT

Operating October to February, three different boat operators travel between Bagan and Mandalay (US$30 to US$35, 10 to 11 hours), with at least one departure daily (between 5am and 6am). You can book tickets through your hotel or an agency such as Ever Sky (p157). Boat operators include **Malikha** (www.malikha-rivercruises.com), **MGRG** (www.mgrgexpress.com) and Shwe Kiennery.

ℹ️ Getting Around

To orient themselves, many visitors opt for a 'greatest hits' tour of the temples on horse cart or by car, then follow it up by checking more remote or lesser-known temples by bike.

E-BIKE & BICYCLE

E-bikes, which operate much like motorbikes but are powered by electric batteries, are widely

WHERE TO STAY

There are three distinct accommodation bases around Bagan. Old Bagan has only high-end hotels, while New Bagan and Nyaung U have a mix of midrange and budget choices.

Old Bagan Closest to the big-time temples, most of Bagan's high-end hotels cluster in and around the riverside and the old palace walls. It's a central location (particularly good for quick visits to Bagan), with plenty of daytime eating options, but less nightlife than Nyaung U. Doubles from around US$100.

New Bagan Only founded in 1990, New Bagan has by far the best midrange choices, with rooms from around US$30 to upwards of US$200. There are also a couple of enticing riverside restaurants – though it's best to come for the view, not the food.

Nyaung U The budget heart of Bagan, with the liveliest restaurant scene and the bulk of the transport connections, Nyaung U is a real town, with guesthouse rooms from US$20. On the downside it's about 2 miles to the temple zone.

ℹ️ GOVERNMENT FEES

All foreign visitors to the Bagan Archaeological Zone are required to pay a K25,000 entrance fee, which goes to the government. (According to an agreement between the Ministry of Culture and the Myanmar Tourism Federation just 2% of the fee goes to conservation and maintenance.) If you arrive by boat or air, the fee will be collected at the river jetty or airport. The fee covers a one-week visit, but it's unlikely you'll be asked to pay again if you stay longer. Entrance fees to the Archaeological Museum and Palace Site also go into government coffers.

available and an ideal way of getting around. Drive slowly on dusty, sandy roads, to avoid an unfortunate spill, and always wear a helmet – available (if not always offered) with every rental. Also, take the phone number of the rental outfit. A good e-bike battery will last eight hours, but if your ride conks out midday, you can call and they'll usually come to replace it with a fresh battery. The going rate is about K8000 per day, with e-bikes available at nearly every hotel and at many travel agencies.

Bicycles are also available from accommodation places, with rates running from K2000 per day to K5000 per day, depending on the condition and model of bike.

Traffic is pretty light on all roads. Early-morning or late-afternoon rides along the sealed Bagan–Nyaung U Rd are particularly rewarding.

HORSE CART

A popular but uncomfortable and slow way of seeing the ruins is from the shaded, padded bed of a horse cart. Drivers speak some English (at least), know where to find the 'keyholders' to locked sites and can point out temples with few or no tourists around. Some might stop by a shop in the hope of securing a commission; it's OK to say 'no thanks'. A cart works best for two passengers, but it's possible to go with three or (for a family with younger children) four.

From Nyaung U or Old Bagan, a day with a horse cart and driver costs about K15,000 to K20,000; a half-day is about K10,000. Prices are sometimes a little higher out of Old Bagan due to the proliferation of high-end hotels.

TAXI

Hiring a shared taxi for the day in Nyaung U costs about US$35 and drivers are usually quite knowledgeable about which temples to visit. Old Bagan hotels will charge anything up to US$75 to hire an unshared taxi. Chartered taxis are also convenient ways of making day trips to Mt Popa and Salay. Taxis between Nyaung U and New Bagan cost about K7000, or K15,000 return.

Nyaung U ညောင်ဦး

POP C 54,000 / ☑ 061

A bustling river town with more action than is on offer elsewhere in Bagan, Nyaung U is where most independent travellers hang their hat (or backpack). Roaming the back roads towards the jetty or stopping at scrappy tea shops will attract friendly wide-eyed looks. There are a handful of temples to see, including Shwezigon Paya, and a lively market. Visitors staying in New or Old Bagan tend to make it here at some stage, either for the restaurant scene (the closest the Bagan area gets to nightlife) or for transport links to other destinations around Myanmar.

Guesthouses and roadside restaurants push a couple of miles west along the road to Old Bagan, reaching the small village of Wetkyi-in (Giant Pig). The town was named for a mythical pig that, according to local legend, inhabited the lake there and was responsible for the deaths of many local people before eventually being killed by a future king of Bagan.

🔘 Sights & Activities

Thanakha Gallery   MUSEUM
(သနပ်ခါးပြခန်း; Map p159; ☑ 061-60179; cnr Yarkintar Rd & Main Rd; ⊙ 9am-9pm) **FREE** Claiming that it's the 'Only One *Thanakha* Gallery in the World', this sizeable complex has a small gallery devoted to the myriad medicinal and cosmetic uses of the *thanakha* tree (*Limonia acidissima*), from its roots to its bark. You can peruse combs, prayer beads and other items made from *thanakha*, as well as paintings depicting royals discovering/introducing this much-loved product. There are also samples on hand, where you can try out *thanakha* on your own skin.

Really, the place is a glorified shop for the *thanakha* cosmetics of Shwe Pyi Nann, as well as a good range of other Bagan and Myanmar souvenirs. A restaurant and a pricey hotel (which doesn't accept foreigners) round out the complex.

Nan Myint Tower   VIEWPOINT
(နန်းမြင့်မျှော်စင်; Map p184; US$5) This silo-shaped building, part of the Tay Za–owned Aureum Palace (p161) hotel has a 9th-floor restaurant and an observation deck on the 12th floor, which affords fine views over the

Nyaung U

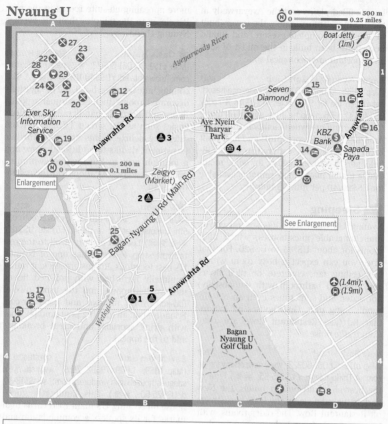

Nyaung U

◎ Sights

1 Gubyauknge B3
2 Kyanzittha Umin B2
3 Shwezigon Paya B2
4 Thanakha Gallery C2
5 Wetkyi-In-Gubyaukgyi B3

✪ Activities, Courses & Tours

6 Bagan Nyaung U Golf Club C4
7 Balloons over Bagan A2
   Golden Eagle Ballooning .... (see 10)

🛏 Sleeping

8 Amazing Bagan Resort D4
9 Bagan Princess Hotel A3
10 Bagan Umbra Hotel A4
11 Eden III Motel D1
12 New Park Hotel B1
13 New Wave Guesthouse A3
14 Oasis Hotel D2
15 Saw Nyein San D1
16 Thante Hotel D2
17 Winner Guest House A3

18 Yar Kinn Tha Hotel B1
19 Z Freeti A2

✖ Eating

20 A Little Bit of Bagan A1
21 Aroma 2 .... A1
22 Bagan Zay A1
23 Black Bamboo A1
   La Terrazza .... (see 22)
24 Mr Bagan A1
25 Myo Myo Myanmar Rice Food B3
26 San Kabar Restaurant & Pub C1
   Sanon .... (see 16)
27 Weather Spoon's Bagan A1

🍸 Drinking & Nightlife

28 Hti A1
29 Shwe Ya Su A1

🛍 Shopping

30 Mani-Sithu Market D1
31 MBoutik D2

temple-filled plains and the Ayeyarwady in the distance. Unfortunately, the tower (built in 2005) is a complete eyesore, and should never have been built in the midst of such an important archaeological zone.

Bagan Nyaung U Golf Club GOLF
(Map p159; ☑061-60035; www.bagangolfresort. net; green fee for 9/18 holes incl clubs & caddy US$40/70; ⊙6am-6pm) Just south of town, this government-owned facility is run by the Amazing Bagan Resort (p161) and has about half a dozen pagodas scattered around its 18-hole, par-72 course, making for some memorable match play. Buggy rental is available for US$20/40 per nine/18 holes.

🛏 Sleeping

Nyaung U's main road has several cheap, interchangeable guesthouses, which offer rooms for about US$15 to US$20. For that price you can expect a boxy room with a lazy ceiling fan, concrete or tiled floors and attached bathroom with (supposedly) hot water, and sometimes even an old air-conditioning unit. Guesthouses off Yarkin-thar Rd (aka Restaurant Row) are away from traffic noise.

New Park Hotel HOTEL $
(Map p159; ☑061-60322; www.newparkmyanmar. com; 4 Thiripyitsaya; r US$15-55; ❋❧) One of the best all-round budget hotels, the New Park is tucked away in the leafy backstreets off Restaurant Row. The older rooms, with bungalow-style front decks, are comfortable, wood-floor set-ups, with reasonable bathrooms. The newer wing brings more space, a fridge, a TV and even a rain shower. The cheapest rooms (US$15 to US$25) are rather cramped.

Eden III Motel GUESTHOUSE $
(Map p159; ☑061-60812; Anawrahta Rd; s US$13-20, d US$17-35; ❋❧) Spread over three buildings (Eden I, II and III) and split in two by the busy road to the airport, Eden isn't exactly paradise. The best rooms are found in the newer Eden Motel III and include a flat-screen TV and a well-appointed bathroom with a bathtub. The young staff are quite attuned to backpacker needs.

Winner Guest House GUESTHOUSE $
(Map p159; ☑061-61069; Nyaung U-Bagan Main Rd, Wetkyi-in; s US$12-15, d US$15-25; ❋❧) This no-frills, family-run guesthouse on the road to Old Bagan has bare-bones rooms with shared bathrooms in front as well as slightly

more appealing en-suite rooms in the rear. It's closer to the temples than the average Nyaung U address.

★**Oasis Hotel** BOUTIQUE HOTEL $$
(Map p159; ☑061-60923; www.oasishotelbagan. com; Anawrahta Rd; r US$40-110; ❋❧❧) A welcoming little boutique hotel, the thoughtfully decorated rooms include parquet wooden floors and Burmese handicrafts, as well as basics such as flat-screen TV and in-room safe. The deluxe rooms are a worthwhile investment thanks to additional space and a location next to the inviting swimming pool. It has a great location near the restaurant strip.

★**Z Freeti** HOTEL $$
(Map p159; ☑061-61003; www.zfreeti.com; 5th Thiripyitsayar St; r US$45-65, ste US$120; ❋@❧❧) Located a short stroll to the restaurant strip, Z Freeti has one of Nyaung U's best locations. Rooms are sleek, if rather minimally furnished with polished floors, modern bathrooms and the usual mix of flat-screen TV, minibar and good air-con. Friendly staff, an inviting pool (and pool bar with drink specials) and great breakfasts add to the appeal.

Saw Nyein San GUESTHOUSE $$
(Map p159; ☑09 79692 7138; www.sawnyein sanguesthousebagan.wordpress.com; s US$18-30, d US$25-50; ❋❧) This family-run guest-house on Nyaung U's main road earns high marks for its spotless accommodation and kind-hearted service. The rooms have tile floors and light pastel colour schemes, although some are a bit on the small side. Staff go out of their way to make you feel at home. Breakfast is served on the breezy rooftop.

New Wave Guesthouse GUESTHOUSE $$
(Map p159; ☑061-60731; www.newwavebagan. com; Bagan-Nyaung U Rd, Wetkyi-in; r US$30-50; ❋❧) This smart guesthouse has attractive, spacious rooms that overlook a back garden. Each has a bright and appealing design with tall ceilings, handcrafted wooden beds and decent bathrooms. A big step up from most of Bagan's guesthouse options.

Bagan Umbra Hotel HOTEL $$
(Map p159; ☑061-60034; baganumbra@ gmail.com; Bagan-Nyaung U Rd; r US$40-120; ❋@❧❧) This vast complex features a chapel-like reception and a wide range of rooms scattered amid several different buildings. The standard and deluxe rooms

are boxy but adequately equipped, while the priciest chambers (grand deluxe) have a boutique feel with stylish design and rain showers.

The pool, complete with a dramatic view of a nearby temple, is the loveliest feature – one of the most appealing of any in Bagan.

Yar Kinn Tha Hotel HOTEL $$
(Map p159; ☏061-60051; Anawrahta Rd; r US$35-65; ✴🛜❄) This long-running hotel provides fair value for money thanks to stable prices, sparkling pool and well-equipped rooms (with satellite TV and minibar). The US$35 rooms with balcony include a garden view, but the US$65 bungalow rooms are more appealing.

Bagan Princess Hotel HOTEL $$
(Map p159; ☏061-60661; www.baganprincessho tel.com; Bagan-Nyaung U Rd; r US$25-50, q US$80; ✴@🛜❄) Built around a small pool, this curiously designed hotel in Wetkyi-in offers amply proportioned rooms, all with separate Jacuzzi bathtubs plus showers in the large bathrooms. Spend a little extra for one of the upper-level deluxe rooms, which have exposed stone walls and beautifully polished wood floors.

The cheapest (standard) rooms are in a separate building around the corner and are too musty to recommend.

Thante Hotel HOTEL $$
(Map p159; ☏061-60315; www.thantenyu.com; Anawrahta Rd; s US$35-50, d US$50-65, tr US$70-90; ✴🛜❄) Just off the main road, this 37-room hotel offers roomy dark-wood bungalows on shady grounds and has an inviting swimming pool. The decor is dated, but the rooms are spacious and have new air-con systems, satellite TV, refrigerator, bathtub, wooden floor and deckchairs on the small porch. There is a good restaurant next door (Sanon).

Amazing Bagan Resort RESORT $$$
(Map p159; ☏061-60035; www.bagangolfresort. net; r from US$140, ste US$210; ✴@🛜❄) The Amazing Bagan is a sprawling resort of impressive design, including a long sparkling pool framed by swaying palms and photogenic brick buildings that mimic old Bagan architecture. The spacious bungalow suites are best and include thoughtful touches such as personal sun hats in the rooms. All rooms are nicely designed with polished wood floors, high-end furnishings and big windows.

There's also a spa and a good restaurant here. The resort is located next to the golf club (p160) and feels a bit isolated – it's a little over 1 mile south of Nyaung U's restaurant strip.

Aureum Palace HOTEL $$$
(Map p184; ☏061-60046; www.aureumpalace hotel.com; r from US$170; ✴🛜❄) One of Bagan's most lavish resorts, the Aureum Palace has high-end rooms and villas, including one on its own little island complete with butler service and a private swimming pool (costing US$1147 per night). Some rooms are too gaudy to recommend. There are two restaurants, two pools and a tower with views over Bagan.

🍴 Eating

Nyaung U's Yar Kinn Thar Hotel Rd (aka Restaurant Row) is a strip of atmospheric open-air eateries geared towards foreign visitors. It's touristy, but easily the epicentre of Bagan action as far as such a thing exists. Many of the restaurants are copycats, with similar 'everything goes' menus (Chinese, Burmese, Thai, Indian, pizza and 'Western' options).

★Weather Spoon's Bagan INTERNATIONAL $
(Map p159; Yarkintar Rd; mains K2200-5000; ⏰9am-11pm; 🛜🍴📶) Brits may be familiar with the name, borrowed from a UK discount-pub chain. The kind-hearted owner Winton, who comes from a peaceful village southeast of Nyaung U, studied balloon piloting in Bristol and clearly honed his cooking skills overseas. His delightful, family-run eatery is justly famous for its decadent burger – easily the best in town.

Other highlights include zesty Thai salads, rich curries, refreshing lassis and the usual mix of other Western fare (pastas, fish and chips, pancakes and other breakfast plates).

Mr Bagan BURMESE $
(Map p159; mains K1000-1500; ⏰10am-10pm; 📶) Tucked down a lane off the restaurant strip, Mr Bagan has rustic charm with its sandy, tree-shaded courtyard and bamboo furniture. It's a great spot to linger over a fresh juice, tea-leaf salad or simple noodle dish. Decent brewed coffee too.

Bagan Zay FUSION $
(Map p159; Yarkintar Rd; mains K3000-7000; ⏰2-10pm; 🛜🍴📶) On Nyaung U's restaurant strip, attractively designed Bagan Zay serves

BAGAN & CENTRAL MYANMAR NYAUNG U

up creative sandwiches and curries, with Asian and Middle Eastern influences. There are ample vegetarian choices, including vegan curry (with pumpkin, cauliflower and broccoli), lentil galettes or a grilled-eggplant sandwich, though you can also dine on caramelised sesame pork or grilled butter fish.

Myo Myo Myanmar Rice Food BURMESE $
(Map p159; Bagan-Nyaung U Rd; small plates K200-500; ⏱8am-8pm) Deservedly popular restaurant that specialises in the personalised tabletop buffets that characterise the national cuisine. But here they really go to town, with 25 small dishes or more appearing at the table, including seasonal specials such as asparagus. English is spoken. Bring a crowd to share. You only pay for what you eat.

Aroma 2 INDIAN $
(Map p159; Yarkintar Rd; dishes K3000-7000; ⏱10.30am-9pm; 🛜🍴) 'No good, no pay' is the mantra of this justifiably confident operation serving delicious veggie and meat curries on banana leaves (or plates) with an endless stream of hot chapatis and five different condiments (including tamarind and mint sauces). The garden-like courtyard adds to the allure.

San Kabar Restaurant & Pub ITALIAN $
(Map p159; Nyaung U-Bagan Main Rd; pizza K5000-6500; mains K3000-6500; ⏱7.30am-10pm; 🛜🍴) The birthplace of Bagan pizza, San Kabar's streetside candlelit courtyard is all about its thin-crusted pies and well-prepared salads. There are three menus, which also include Thai and Chinese-style dishes.

⭐**Sanon** BURMESE, FUSION $$
(Map p159; ☑09 45195 1950; www.facebook.com/sanonrestaurant; Pyu Saw Hit St; mains K4000-8700; ⏱11am-10pm Mon-Sat; 🛜✏🍴) 🍴 A charming addition to the Nyaung U restaurant scene, Sanon has a classy but casual setting, with tropical plants surrounding an open-sided dining room. You'll find inventive Burmese small plates that are meant for sharing: river-prawn and catfish curry, pan-seared squid stuffed with pork, and crispy watercress and onion pakora. It has delicious juices too (try the mint and pomelo freeze).

Head inside to check out the spotless kitchen (with high-end equipment imported from Australia). While the cooking isn't flawless, dining here supports a worthy cause: Sanon is a nonprofit training restaurant that was created to give new opportunities to Myanmar youth.

⭐**Black Bamboo** EUROPEAN $$
(Map p159; ☑061-60782; off Yarkintar Rd; dishes K3000-9000; ⏱10am-10pm; 🛜🍴) Run by a French woman and her Burmese husband, this lush garden-cafe and restaurant is something of an oasis. It's a pleasant place to relax over solid Burmese, Thai and Western dishes, a well-made espresso or a delicious homemade ice cream (the best in Bagan). Service is friendly but leisurely. A new terrace makes a fine spot for an evening drink.

La Terrazza ITALIAN $$
(Map p159; Yarkintar Rd; mains K3000-8000; ⏱noon-10pm; 🍴) Of the Italian joints in Nyaung U, this is the pick of the bunch with decent pizzas, lasagna and pastas, and an abundance of Western and Asian dishes.

A Little Bit of Bagan ASIAN $$
(Map p159; K3000-8000; ⏱10am-10pm) This place on Restaurant Row ought to be called 'A little bit of everything', with its menu of Thai, Chinese, Myanmar and Indian dishes, plus sandwiches, crêpes, pastas and other Western fare. It has slightly higher prices than elsewhere on the street, but remains a popular spot – and rather festive with hanging lamps, potted palms and ambient tunes.

🍷 Drinking & Nightlife

Shwe Ya Su BEER STATION
(Map p159; Yarkintar Rd; mains K3000-6000, BBQ from K500; ⏱7am-10pm) Thanks to endless draught Myanmar Beer, this place with a large outside area and a menu of Chinese-inspired favourites has become quite the local hang-out. A good spot to watch some football (soccer), while the barbecue on offer is tasty too.

Hti BAR
(Map p159; 5 Thiripyitsaya; ⏱10am-11pm) One of Nyaung U's only real bars, Hti is the Burmese name for parasol, and this certainly puts most other would-be bars in the shade. The cocktail list is impressive and food is available including Asian and international dishes, plus a barbecue grill. Shishas on demand.

🛍 Shopping

There is a good selection of souvenirs at the Thanakha Gallery (p158) and at shops along Restaurant Row.

★ **MBoutik**   ARTS & CRAFTS
(Map p159; Anawrahta Rd; ☉9am-6pm daily, to 9pm Nov-Mar) 🖉 This colourful boutique has gorgeous textiles, bags, toys, handicrafts and clothing that are entirely produced by a women's cooperative started by the international NGO ActionAid. Some 600 artisans based in more than 130 villages across the country incorporate traditional designs and patterns in their expertly made works.

Prices are fair, and you can have peace of mind knowing that revenue goes straight to the source.

Mani-Sithu Market   MARKET
(Map p159; ☉6am-5pm Mon-Sat) Near the roundabout at the east end of the main road, this market offers a colourful display of fruit, vegetables, flowers, fish and textiles and is best visited early in the day to see it at its liveliest. There are plenty of traveller-oriented goods (woodcarvings, T-shirts, lacquerware) at its northern end.

ℹ Information

Ever Sky Information Service (p157) Just off the restaurant strip, this friendly place can book tickets and has a secondhand bookshop. Staff can arrange share taxis (to Mt Popa, Kalaw, Salay, around Bagan) for the best available rates.

KBZ Bank (Map p159; 13C Anawrahta Rd) Centrally located bank with an ATM that accepts most international bank cards.

ℹ Transport

AIR

Nyaung U Airport is about 2 miles southeast of the market. Airlines connect Bagan daily with Mandalay (US$50 to US$60, 30 minutes), Heho (US$70 to US$80, 40 minutes) and Yangon (US$100 to US$120, 70 minutes).

Travel agencies sometimes have cheaper tickets than the airline offices. Try **Seven Diamond** (Map p159; 🖉 061-61184; www.sevendiamondtravels.com; Main Rd; ☉9am-8pm).

NYAUNG U (BAGAN) TRANSPORT CONNECTIONS

The following table provides a quick comparison of the various ways of getting to Nyaung U from Yangon and Mandalay.

TO/FROM YANGON	DURATION	COST	FREQUENCY
Air	70min	US$100-110	frequent
Bus	10hr	K13,000-18,000	frequent
Car	9hr	K150,000	charter
Train	16hr	US$35-45	daily

TO/FROM MANDALAY	DURATION	COST	FREQUENCY
Air	30min	US$50-55	frequent
Boat	11hr	US$35	daily in high season
Bus	7hr	K8000-9500	frequent
Car	6hr	K130,000	charter
Train	8hr	US$5-10	daily

BUS TRANSPORT OPTIONS

Destinations from Bagan include the following:

DESTINATION	PRICE	DURATION	DEPARTURES
Kalaw (Taunggyi bus)	K11,000-15,000	9hr	7.30am, 8.30am, 7pm, 8pm
Magwe	K5000	4hr	7am
Mandalay	K8000-9500	4-6hr	frequent
Monywa	K4000	4hr	7.30am
Pyin Oo Lwin	K13,000	7hr	7.30am
Taunggyi	K11,000-15,000	10hr	7.30am, 8.30am, 7pm, 8pm
Yangon	K13,000-18,000	10hr	frequent

BUSES TO MRAUK U

A new overland service connects Bagan with Mrauk U, saving considerable time for travellers wanting to visit this archaeological treasure in Rakhine State. A bus or minivan departs daily at 6.30pm and stops in Kyaukpadaung (one hour), where travellers transfer on to a bus coming from Mandalay. This 45-seat bus then continues on to Mrauk U, arriving at 10am or 11am. You can purchase tickets (K40,000) from Ever Sky (p157).

BOAT

Boats to Mandalay go from either Nyaung U or Old Bagan, depending on water levels. The Nyaung U jetty is about half a mile northeast of the Nyaung U market.

BUS

Shwe Pyi bus station is Bagan's main coach station, located 3 miles southeast of Nyaung U (and half a mile north of the train station), on the highway to Kyaukpadaung. A taxi here costs about K7000. But some of the higher-end bus companies provide transport to the bus station. For this service, it's easiest to book through your hotel or a travel agency such as Ever Sky (p157). If arriving in Bagan, most bus companies provide free transport into town – though you'll have to switch to an open-backed pick-up at the bus station. Ask the driver when arriving.

During peak season, it's wise to book bus tickets for Mandalay, Taunggyi (for Inle Lake) and Yangon a couple of days in advance.

Note: some Mandalay-bound buses go via Myingyan, others via Kyaukpadaung and Meiktila. It is worth paying a little more for the minibuses as they can save two or three hours compared with the slower buses. The Yangon-bound service goes via Meiktila and Nay Pyi Taw. There are lots of different operators serving Yangon, but JJ Express leads the way in comfort with only three seats per row in a sort of business-class-airline configuration.

PICK-UP TRUCKS

The lone daily pick-up service to Mt Popa (K3500 each way, three hours) leaves at 8.30am from in front of the south entrance to the market, and returns at 1pm. From the bus station, half-hourly pick-ups go to Chauk (two hours), where there are onward connections to Salay (one hour).

Pick-ups between Nyaung U, Old Bagan and New Bagan run along the main street, starting from the roundabout outside the Nyaung U market.

TAXI

As Bagan has limited bus connections to other major destinations, many travellers hire shared taxis to destinations around the country. Some vehicles are in better condition than others so check out the car before embarking on an epic journey. Ask at Ever Sky (p157) or at your hotel. Some sample taxi fares: Inle Lake (K150,000, 12 hours), Kalaw (K130,000, 10 hours), Magwe (K70,000, five hours), Mt Popa (K40,000, 1½ hours), Salay (K50,000, two hours), Mt Popa and Salay (K60,000).

TRAIN

The elaborate and over-the-top Bagan train station is located in splendid isolation about 2.5 miles southeast of Nyaung U. The train to Mandalay takes 10 hours and departs at 7am (ordinary/upper class K6200/12,400), while the train to Yangon takes 16 hours and departs at 5pm (ordinary/upper class/sleeper K44,000/K56,000). There is an English-language timetable and prices on display at the station. Train tickets are only sold at the station.

Old Bagan

POP C 2400 / ☎ 061

The core of the Bagan Archaeological Zone contains several of the main temple sites, city walls, a museum, a reconstructed palace, restaurants, a few shops and a cluster of midrange to top-end hotels. It's right on a bend of the Ayeyarwady River and it's well worth wandering down to the waterfront to watch the comings and goings of the river trade.

Sights

Archaeological Museum MUSEUM

(ကာြရှာကျစာသမိုင်းပြတိုက်; Map p166; Bagan-Nyaung U Rd; adult/child under 10yr K5000/free; 9am-4.30pm Tue-Sun) Housed in a sprawling complex, this government-run museum features many fine pieces from Bagan (reclining buddhas, original images, inscribed stones and mural re-creations) and an unexpected room of modern-art renderings of the temples. Other curiosities include a room of 55 kinds of women's hair knots (and five men's hairstyles), models of major temples with architectural details and a model of an 11th-century village.

Bagan Golden Palace PALACE

(ပုဂံရွှေနန်းတော်; Map p166; Bagan-Nyaung U Rd; K5000; 9am-6pm) Following similar government-mandated palace-reconstruction jobs in Bago, Mandalay and Shwebo, this towering concrete-and-steel-reinforced edifice was opened to much fanfare in 2008. Built opposite the excavated site of the actual palace just in from the Tharabar Gate, it's unlikely to bear much resemblance to the original. Either way, it's a sign of the ongoing Disneyfication of Bagan.

🛏 Sleeping

Old Bagan's hotels provide river views, temple proximity and nice pool areas, but don't necessarily offer much more comfort than you get at New Bagan's best – and less-expensive – accommodation. Book ahead, as they fill up months in advance of peak season.

Quoted rates don't include the 10% service charge and 10% government tax, so expect hefty surcharges at peak times. Yangon agents or online hotel booking websites often have discounted rates.

Aye Yar River View Resort   RESORT $$$
(Map p166; ☎ 061-60352; www.ayeyarriverviewresort.com; r US$88-160, ste US$500; ❄ @ 🛜 ⛲) Following a major facelift, this former government hotel offers the best all-round value in Old Bagan. The priciest rooms are set in spacious bungalows with expansive river views, while those closer to the pool are pretty impressive as well, including little details such as rain showers and private balconies.

Bagan Thiripyitsaya Sanctuary Resort   RESORT $$$
(Map p166; ☎ 09 99644 60048; www.thiripyitsaya-resort.com; r US$110-190, with river views US$170-260; ❄ @ 🛜 ⛲) This Japanese joint-venture hotel is located on the river, about 500m south of the Old Bagan walls. It boasts a large swimming pool, but the rooms are mostly set in ageing four-room bungalow-style duplexes with covered decks (the best of which have fine river views).

The restaurant serves up fine cuisine to panoramic river views, and there's a spa and a wide range of activities on offer.

Hotel@Tharabar Gate   HOTEL $$$
(Map p166; ☎ 061-60037; www.tharabargate.com; r US$180-220, ste US$350; ❄ @ 🛜 ⛲) This hotel is a fine option for those who are willing to forgo a river view. Lush gardens of tropical plants and bougainvillea line walkways to the inviting wooden-floor bungalows with decks. The two-room suites at the far end go traditional, with gold-coloured ogres and *naga* spirits on the walls.

It has a great location near some of Bagan's most impressive temples.

Bagan Hotel River View   HOTEL $$$
(Map p166; ☎ 061-60032; www.kmahotels.com; r US$50-250; ❄ @ 🛜 ⛲) This 107-room hotel has bungalows with teak floors in a nice setting. The owner runs the luxurious KMA Hotels group, with hotels in locations from Nay Pyi Taw to Taungoo, and has a history of cosy relations with the generals.

Bagan Thande Hotel   HOTEL $$$
(Map p166; ☎ 061-60025; www.baganthandehotel.net; r US$75-110, with river view from US$160; ❄ 🛜 ⛲) Opened for King Edward VIII in 1922, this riverside hotel carries some dated formality and is arguably overdue a makeover. The simple 'superior' bungalows have decks overlooking the pool and nearby Gawdawpalin Pahto (p183). Best for views, though, are the riverfront deluxe rooms at the river's edge. Breakfast is served under the shade of tropical trees, with a river view.

🍴 Eating

Old Bagan's restaurants (between the Ananda Pahto and Tharabar Gate) make for a convenient lunch stop. The nearby hotel restaurants add a little style (and kyat) to a meal. Alcohol is not served at restaurants within the Old Bagan area as they are in close proximity to the temples. However, this rule does not apply to the luxury hotels and their attached bars and restaurants.

SUNSET ON THE AYEYARWADY

When temple fatigue sets in, take a break from the ancient kingdom and head to the river for a scenic DIY boat trip. Boat operators congregate around the jetty in Old Bagan, near Aye Yar River View Resort, and it's easy to arrange a trip on the spot. The best time to go is before sunset, around 5pm or 6pm depending on the season, when the temperatures drop and you can enjoy the golden light on the riverbanks. It costs around K12,000 per boat for a cruise lasting a little over an hour. You can also head to **Fantasia Jetty & Garden** (Map p166; ☎ 09 97789 15291; www.bagan-boat-trips.com; ⊙ 9am-7.30pm), which offers regular sunset departures at 5pm (per person K4000) in a beautifully restored teak boat. Be sure to bring cold drinks and snacks for the trip.

Old Bagan

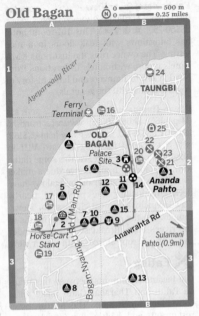

▲ 0 ———— 500 m
N 0 ———— 0.25 miles

Khaing Shwe Wah   VEGETARIAN $

(Map p166; off Bagan-Nyaung U Rd; mains K1500-2500; ⊙10am-9pm; 🖉🍴) This friendly family-run spot serves up delicious plates of vegetarian fare. Start with a papaya or pennywort salad before moving on to noodle soup, golden-pumpkin curry or the much-loved tomato-peanut curry, which goes nicely with coconut rice. Other hits include aubergine salad and guacamole with pappadum.

Starbeam Bistro   INTERNATIONAL $

(Map p166; mains K4000-8000; ⊙10am-10pm; 🛜) Located close to Ananda Pahto, this garden bistro was set up by Chef Tin Myint who spent several years working with the Orient Express hotel group. Dishes include Rakhine fish curry, market-fresh specials, traditional salads such as avocado or tea leaf, and classic baguettes and sandwiches. Best accompanied by a healthy blend or fresh juice.

**Be Kind to
Animals the Moon**   BURMESE, VEGETARIAN $

(Map p166; off Bagan-Nyaung U Rd; mains K2000-4000; ⊙7am-10pm; 🖉) The original among the vegetarian restaurants clustered near Tharabar Gate, this garden-like eatery offers a friendly welcome and delicious food including pumpkin curry with ginger, sautéed vegetables with vermicelli, spicy chapati wraps and creamy lassis. Don't overlook the homemade ice cream for dessert.

Sarabha II   CHINESE, INTERNATIONAL $$

(Map p166; mains K5500-8500; ⊙11am-9pm) Of the two Sarabhas back to back by the Tharabar Gate, we prefer the one behind, away from the road. It's a great midday resting point for shade and its range of food (Chinese, Thai, Burmese, pizza). The food's good, and cheaper than hotel restaurants, but best are the cold towels handed out to wipe the dust from your face. There's an evening 40-minute puppet show at 7.30pm.

Golden Myanmar
BURMESE $$

(Map p166; Bagan-Nyaung U Rd; buffet K4000; ☺10am-10pm) Keep-it-real seekers (and lots of horse-cart drivers) favour this roadside eatery with shaded seats on a brick floor. The 'buffet' (your pick of chicken, pork, fish or vegetable curry) comes with the usual tableful of condiments. There's another location near Ananda Pahto (p187).

 Drinking & Nightlife

You can enjoy drinks with a view at one of the high-end hotel restaurants in Old Bagan. For something less pricey, head to one of the restaurants scattered near Tharabar Gate.

Fantasia Jetty & Garden
CAFE

(Map p166; 09 97789 15291; ☺9am-7.30pm) Aside from running sunset cruises on the river (p165), Fantasia has a peaceful garden with serene views over the river. Order a cold drink, sink into a shaded lounge chair and watch the river traffic slowly drift past.

 Shopping

Shwe War Thein Handicrafts Shop
ARTS & CRAFTS

(Map p166; 061-67032; shi@mptmail.net.mm; ☺9am-9pm) Just east of Tharabar Gate (and well signed off the Bagan–Nyaung U Rd) is this popular treasure trove of Myanmar trinkets. The collection includes antique and new puppets, woodcarvings, chess sets, lacquerware and bronze pieces. Ask to see the antique section at the rear. Lacquerware selections are wider in Myinkaba and New Bagan.

❶ Getting There & Away

Depending on water levels, boats from Mandalay arrive at the ferry terminal (Map p184) near the Aye Yar Hotel.

Myinkaba
မြင်းကပါ

POP C 8500 / ☎ 061

Lacquerware lovers will want to stop at Myinkaba, Bagan's most famous shopping zone. This otherwise sleepy village about half a mile south of Old Bagan has been home to family-run lacquerware workshops for generations. At least a dozen workshops and shopfronts are located around the smattering of choice *pahto* (temples) and stupas from the early-Bagan period. And King

Manuha, respectfully called the 'Captive King', built the poetic Manuha Paya while held here in the 11th century.

 Shopping

Before splashing the cash, it's wise to stop at a handful of places to compare varying styles and prices. Many workshops will show you the stages of lacquerware-making and how lacquer is applied in layers, dried and engraved. There's refreshingly little pressure to buy at any of the workshops. But quality varies; often the best stuff is kept in airconditioned rooms at the back. Most workshops and stores keep long hours (roughly 7am to 9pm during peak season). Generally, it is possible to bargain about 10% off the quoted prices, but not much more.

Golden Cuckoo
ARTS & CRAFTS

(Map p184; ☺6am-8.30pm) Just behind Manuha Paya (p192), Pho Htoo and his brother run this workshop which has been in their family for four generations and focuses on high-quality 'traditional' designs. In addition to exquisite bowls and cylinders, you'll find unusual objects, including a motorbike helmet and guitar (both US$1200). A second branch has opened on the main road a few blocks away.

Art Gallery of Bagan
ARTS & CRAFTS

(Map p184; ☺9am-7pm) English-speaking Maung Aung Myin has two rooms and a busy workshop on the road 200yd north of Manuha Paya. There is a full range of lacquerware, including some beautiful and pricey cabinets and casks.

Family Lacquerware Work Shop
ARTS & CRAFTS

(Map p184; ☺7.30am-5.30pm) This smaller workshop off the east side of the road has some contemporary styles using alternative colours, such as blue and yellow with fewer layers of lacquer.

❶ Getting There & Away

Pick-ups running between New Bagan, Old Bagan and Nyaung U stop here.

New Bagan (Bagan Myothit)
ပုဂံမြို့သစ်

POP C 9200 / ☎ 061

Not as bustling as Nyaung U, even though it's closer to the juicy temples, New Bagan sprung into existence in 1990 when the government relocated the village from the Old Bagan area. The people have done their best to make the most of their new home, with a network of shady, dusty roads away from the river. It's laid-back, friendly and definitely the site of Bagan's best midrange accommodation and riverside restaurants. The morning market (on the main road, three blocks east of the Eight-Faces Paya) offers an interesting glimpse into local life.

🛏 Sleeping

New Bagan has an excellent range of lodgings – mostly at the budget and high end. You'll find the best hostel in the region, simple family-run guesthouses and charming boutique hotels.

★ Ostello Bello
HOSTEL $

(Map p169; ☑061-65069; www.ostellobello.com; Khayea St; dm US$17-25, d US$50; ❋☎) This thoughtfully designed Italian-owned hostel is the best place in town for socialising and meeting other travellers. The buzzing courtyard eatery and drinking space hosts events throughout the week (nights of bingo, trivia), there are loads of activities on offer (sunrise and sunset tours, boat trips), and staff have a wealth of info on Bagan. There's a rooftop lounge with showers, beds and chairs where you can relax – a nice touch for those arriving or leaving early or late.

Bagan Empress
GUESTHOUSE $

(Map p169; ☑09 504 0436; www.baganempress hotel.com; 107 Yuzana St; r from US$25; ❋☎) A few blocks south of the main road, Bagan Empress has minimally furnished spick-and-span rooms that are great value for the area. Staff are friendly and eager to assist travellers (with tickets, tours, transport, bikes, guide service etc). The breezy breakfast room on the top floor is a great place to start the day.

Bagan Central Hotel
HOTEL $

(Map p169; ☑061-65265; www.bagancentralho tel.com; Khaye St (Main Rd); s/d from US$16/35; ❋☎) On the main road, this 26-room place has decent rooms outfitted with bamboo furnishings and Burmese artwork set around a garden with a small and very green ornamental pond. Rooms are clean, but a bit dark.

Mya Thida
GUESTHOUSE $

(Map p169; ☑09 45006 6777; www.facebook. com/myathidahotel; Nwe Ni St; dm/d US$10/25;

❋@☎) One of the cheapest options in New Bagan, Mya Thida attracts a steady flow of budget travellers to its 10 simply furnished bunk rooms (each with four beds) that open on to a narrow courtyard with bristling bamboo and a koi pond. Prices are low, but facilities aren't the cleanest, the wi-fi is weak and breakfast is best avoided.

Kumudara Hotel
HOTEL $$

(Map p169; ☑061-65142; www.kumudarahotel. com; cnr 5th & Daw Na Sts; s/d US$41/47, with view US$56/62, ste US$110; ❋@☎≋) No hotel boasts better balcony views of the mighty sprawl of red-brick temples than Kumudara. Rooms here channel a bit of old-fashioned woodsy charm – its cabin-like rooms have abundant wood panelling and decks poised for taking in the savannah-like scenery filled with birdsong (never mind the old TVs and ageing bathtubs in the cheapest rooms).

It's a friendly spot that feels quite peaceful, being off on its own about half a mile north of the centre. There's also a pool (but not much shade) and a restaurant.

Northern Breeze
GUESTHOUSE $$

(Map p169; ☑061-65472; www.northernbreeze guesthouse.com; 162 Cherry St; r US$25-35; ☎) This friendly new place provides great value for money. Set around a small courtyard, the rooms are a bit on the small side but are nicely maintained and have all the essentials (minifridge, electric kettle with coffee, TV). There are plenty of dining options a short stroll from the guesthouse.

Floral Breeze Hotel
HOTEL $$

(Map p169; ☑061-65072; www.hotelbze.com; Chauk Rd; s/d from US$40/50; ❋☎≋) Built in the classic faux-temple Bagan-style, this friendly, modern hotel offers attractive contemporary rooms complete with squeaky-clean parquet floors, bathtubs and petal-covered bedspreads. The small swimming pool is refreshing after a day on the dusty roads, though it could use a bit more greenery (and shade).

Thazin Garden Hotel
HOTEL $$

(Map p169; ☑061-65035; www.thazingarden.com; r US$80-120; ❋☎≋) Set down a dusty path near a clutch of small temples, this oasis of palms and flowers and shaded walkways is a charming choice. The deluxe 'bungalows' are built in a paya-styled brick complex with a sea of dark luxurious teak inside. Balconies overlook a 13th-century pagoda within

New Bagan (Bagan Myothit)

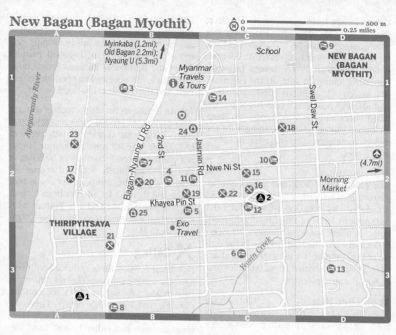

New Bagan (Bagan Myothit)

⊙ Sights
1 Ashe (East) Petleik Paya......................A3
2 Eight-Faces Paya.................................C2

🛏 Sleeping
3 Amata Boutique House.........................B1
4 Areindmar Hotel..................................B2
5 Bagan Central Hotel.............................B2
6 Bagan Empress....................................C3
7 Crown Prince Hotel..............................B2
8 Floral Breeze Hotel..............................B3
9 Kumudara Hotel..................................D1
10 Mya Thida..C2
11 Northern Breeze.................................B2
12 Ostello Bello......................................C2
13 Thazin Garden Hotel...........................D3
14 Thurizza Hotel....................................C1

✗ Eating
15 7 Sisters...C2
16 Black Rose..C2
17 Green Elephant...................................A2
18 Kyaw Kitchen.....................................C1
19 Ma Mae Naing.....................................B2
20 Mingalabar Food Corner.....................B2
21 Mother's House..................................B3
22 Silver House.......................................C2
23 Sunset Garden....................................A2

🛍 Shopping
24 Bagan House......................................B2
25 Tun Handicrafts/Moe Moe's................B2

the grounds; dinner is served on the lawn in front.

The 'superior' rooms are just as inviting with hanging paper umbrellas, a chessboard and deck area. It has a pool, a spa and a billiards table. Nonguests can use the pool for K8000 per day.

Thurizza Hotel HOTEL **$$**
(Map p169; ☎ 061-65229; thirimarlarhotelbagan@
gmail.com; Ingin St; d US$35-53, tr US$75; ❄@

☎) Formerly known as the Thiri Marlar Hotel, teak walkways lead to a mix of rooms wrapped around a small pagoda-style dining room, though most guests eat breakfast on the roof deck with temple views. Standard rooms are small and pokey, while superior rooms are roomier with shiny wood floors and better light – some also have temple views.

The open-air bar is a fine retreat after a day of exploring.

Crown Prince Hotel
HOTEL $$

(Map p169; ☑ 061-65407; www.crownprince hotelbagan.com; Khat Tar St; deluxe US$40-75, ste US$60-100; ❉ 🎅) A smart full-service hotel, the Crown Prince boasts tastefully decorated rooms set with all the essentials (flat-screen TV, minibar, desk, hairdryer and safety-deposit box), plus big windows, wood floors and touches of artwork. Overall a good midrange option, though for the money, some guests prefer staying in a place with a pool.

Arthawka Hotel
HOTEL $$

(Map p184; ☑ 061-60310; www.arthawkahotelbagan.com; 160 Cherry Rd; r US$50-80; ❉ @ 🎅 ⚐) Big glazed clay pots and wicker chairs dot the spacious lobby of this friendly 60-room hotel. It offers spacious rooms with wood floors and white tiled bathrooms. In the centre of the complex is a saltwater pool, shaded by palms. It's located about 0.6 miles east of New Bagan's epicentre.

★ Blue Bird Hotel
BOUTIQUE HOTEL $$$

(Map p184; ☑ 061-65440; www.bluebirdbagan. com; Naratheinka 10; r low/high season from US$87/168; ❉ @ 🎅 ⚐) An absolute charmer, the Blue Bird is one of the most appealing places to stay in Bagan. Rooms are spacious and airy, including contemporary handicrafts and striking bathrooms with an original shower design. The lush gardens conceal a central swimming pool, perfect to cool off after a long day. The restaurant includes impressive fusion food and beautifully made cocktails (for guests only). It's less than a mile southeast of the centre. Take Khayea St east and turn right at the fork.

Bagan Lodge
RESORT $$$

(Map p184; ☑ 061-65456; www.bagan-lodge.com; Myat Lay Rd; r US$160-244, ste from US$425; ❉ @ 🎅 ⚐) The sprawling resort of Bagan Lodge offers something a little different from the high-end hotels of Old Bagan. Rooms are set in stone cabanas with sweeping tented roofs. Spacious and furnished in the colonial style, rooms include huge bathrooms with his 'n' hers sinks. The facilities include two pools, two restaurants, a spa and a fitness centre.

Areindmar Hotel
BOUTIQUE HOTEL $$$

(Map p169; ☑ 061-65049; www.areindmarhotel. com; 2nd St; r US$195; ❉ 🎅 ⚐) Set like a hacienda within private walls, the two-storey

buildings surround a lush courtyard garden complete with lotus-filled pond and twisting acacia trees. The rooms are beautifully decorated with sleigh beds, polished parquet floors and traditional Burmese handicrafts. There's a lovely pool and an open-air restaurant, and the service is top-notch.

Amata Boutique House
BOUTIQUE HOTEL $$$

(Map p169; ☑ 061-65099; www.amatabtqhouse. com; Thiripyitsaya Quarter; r with breakfast US$100-120; ❉ 🎅 ⚐) Amata Boutique House is a sizeable riverside complex in New Bagan that has handsomely designed rooms set around a palm-fringed pool. Service is top-notch and there's a lot on offer here, including a full-service spa and a restaurant with a nightly dance-theatre performance (from October to May).

🍴 Eating

New Bagan's Main Rd is sprinkled with restaurants serving Chinese, Thai and Burmese cuisine. Many foreigners grab a meal on the riverside, just west of the centre. There are several restaurants overlooking the Ayeyarwady and you can either be lost amid the tour groups or have the place to yourself. Bagan's only supermarket, and it's not very super, is Yadanar Mart on Main St.

Ma Mae Naing
BURMESE $

(Map p169; Khayea St (Main Rd); mains around K2500; ⊙ 10.30am-10.30pm; ☑ ◍) On the restaurant-lined main road in New Bagan, Ma Mae Naing (also known as 'Unforgettable') serves delicious fare, with good choices for vegetarians. The small menu consists mostly of curries served with rice and a variety of vegetable side dishes. It all goes nicely with fresh fruit juices (a bargain at K1000 each).

Mingalabar Food Corner
ASIAN $

(Map p169; Bagan-Nyaung U Rd; mains K3000-5000; ⊙ 9am-10pm) Offers the usual combo of Chinese, Thai and Burmese cooking, with ever-flowing draught beer and sizzling barbecue as well. In the evening, an outdoor table on the raised terrace is the place to be.

Mother's House
BURMESE $

(Map p169; Chauk Rd; mains K1500-5000; ⊙ 6am-10pm, closed Sun) Big and busy teahouse with plenty of outdoor seating and an attached restaurant. It's good for a traditional Burmese breakfast before exploring the temples, or after catching sunrise somewhere nearby. Try Shan noodles or deep-fried doughnuts.

Kyaw Kitchen
FUSION $$

(Map p169; ☑09 25975 4811; High School Rd, Hti Min Yin Quarter; mains K4500-8500; ⊕10am-2pm & 5-10pm; ☑️📶) Tucked away a few blocks north of the main road, Kyaw Kitchen earns high marks for its high-quality cooking, friendly service and appealing, garden-like setting. Highlights from the creative and wide-ranging menu include a Burmese-style seafood risotto, butterfish curry, grilled river prawns and a juicy veggie burger.

7 Sisters
BURMESE, ASIAN $$

(Map p169; 79 Nwe Ni St; dishes K4000-12,000; ⊕8am-10pm; ☑️📶) Although it sounds like the title of a fairy tale, the restaurant is indeed run by seven sisters, who do a fine job cooking up prawn curry, Yunnan-style chicken, fried tofu with mushrooms, roast duck and many other dishes of Thai, Chinese and Burmese origin. Set with teak pillars, fine woodwork and a soaring ceiling, the space resembles a Buddhist adoration hall, and tea lights add to the magic in the evening.

Black Rose
ASIAN $$

(Map p169; Khayea St; dishes K1500-8000; ⊕8am-10.30pm; 📶📶) Across from the pagoda in New Bagan's town centre, the Black Rose is a lively, open-sided spot that serves a satisfying assortment of Thai, Chinese and Burmese hits. Fish with ginger, fried vegetable combos, Massaman curry and myriad other curries are all on offer.

Sunset Garden
BURMESE, INTERNATIONAL $$

(Map p169; ☑061-65037; mains K3500-8500; ⊕11am-10pm; 📶) Boasting the best riverside setting of any New Bagan restaurant, Sunset Garden has a huge deck above the Ayeyarwady with memorable sunset views (when the clouds cooperate). Head here for a sundowner before the tour groups pile in for dinner. The menu includes a greatest-hits selection of Burmese, Chinese, Thai and international dishes. Unfortunately, the cooking falls short of the panorama.

Silver House
BURMESE, ASIAN $$

(Map p169; Khaye St (Main Rd); mains K3500-7500; ⊕7am-10pm; 📶) A welcoming family-run restaurant that offers large, tasty portions of dishes such as traditional Myanmar chicken curry with coconut, as well as Thai-style lemongrass chicken.

Green Elephant
BURMESE, ASIAN $$

(Map p169; Yamonar, Thiripissayar Quarter; mains K3000-9000; ⊕11am-4pm; 📶) This open-sided eatery beside the river serves decent curries (including Rakhine-style fish-paste curry), spicy Thai-style soups and Chinese noodle dishes. The setting is the draw, though when we last passed through, the lawn was overgrown, allowing only partial views of the Ayeyarwady River.

🔒 Shopping

Tun Handicrafts/Moe Moe's
ARTS & CRAFTS

(Map p169; Main Rd; ⊕8am-8pm) This family-run local business was one of the first to establish itself in New Bagan and is run by U Kan Tun and her daughter Moe Moe. The large showroom has a mix of traditional and modern lacquerware, and it is possible to see every step of the process in an adjacent workshop.

Bagan House
ARTS & CRAFTS

(Map p169; www.baganhouse.com; 9 Jasmin Rd; ⊕8am-7pm) Worth seeking out on the backstreets, this stylish showroom has a mix of cheap and higher-priced lacquerware, as well as the usual artisans at work. Aung San Suu Kyi visited in 2012. Credit cards are accepted.

Black Elephant Studio
ARTS & CRAFTS

(Map p184; ☑09253205023; https://blackelephant lacquer.com; ⊕8am-5pm) Set up by British-Ukrainian artist Veronica Gritsenko in 1999, this small studio, off the road between Old and New Bagan, produces lacquerware in the traditional style, but with exquisite unique and unusual designs.

ⓘ Information

Exo Travel (Map p169; ☑061-60383; ⊕9am-6pm Mon-Fri, to noon Sat) High-end agent, which can arrange Mt Popa tours or rent imported mountain bikes.

Myanmar Travels & Tours (p157) The government-run tourist office can help organise excursions to visit Chin State (plan on US$100 a day per person).

ⓘ Getting There & Around

Most transport connections are in Nyaung U. There are airline offices on Khayea Pin St as well as abundant agencies that can organise bus tickets, taxis and other transport.

Bicycle rental starts at K3000 per day. E-bikes start at around K6000 per day. Both can be hired from Khayea Pin St.

AROUND BAGAN

Mt Popa ပုပ္ပါးတောင်

♪ 061

Like a Burmese Mt Olympus, Mt Popa is the spiritual HQ to Myanmar's infamous '37 *nat*' and thus the most popular location in the country for *nat* worship.

Mt Popa is now the official name of the famous Popa Taung Kalat, a tower-like 2418ft volcanic plug crowned with a gilded Buddhist temple accessed by 777 steps, on the mother mountain's lower flank. The 4980ft extinct volcano previously known as Mt Popa has been renamed Taung Ma-gyi or Mother Mountain to distinguish it from the more famous Popa Taung Kalat. Covered in lush forests protected within the Popa Mountain Park and home to the exclusive Popa Mountain Resort, the volcano last erupted some 250,000 years ago.

From the temple there are mammoth views back towards the Myingyan Plain and beyond. It's stunning if a little kitsch, but few visitors make the half-day trip from Bagan.

◉ Sights

Popa Taung Kalat Temple BUDDHIST TEMPLE
(ပုပ္ပါးတောင်ကျောင်း) From the nat shrine, start up the many steps under a covered walkway and past the rows of trinket and souvenir shops and shrines to a revered local medicine man, Pomin Gawng. At a steady pace it shouldn't take you more than 20 minutes to reach the summit of this impressive rocky crag crowned with a picturesque complex of monasteries, stupas and shrines. Popa Taung Kalat Temple is but one of several buildings here that you can freely wander through.

Along the way, you'll pass platoons of cheeky monkeys and a small army of locals selling drinks and endeavouring (not always successfully) to keep the steps clean of monkey poo in return for a possible tip. Families with children should take care to keep a distance from the macaques as they have large canine teeth and occasionally pilfer snacks or shiny trinkets from visitors.

The views from the top are fantastic. You may be fortunate enough to spot one of the slow-walking hermit monks called *yeti*, who wear tall, peaked hats and visit occasionally.

Mother Spirit of Popa Nat Shrine SHRINE
(ပုပ္ပါးမယ်တော်နတ်နန်း) Before climbing Popa Taung Kalat, drop by the tiger-guarded shrine in the village at the foot of the mountain (just across from the steps guarded by elephant statues – there are loads of critters around here). Inside you'll find a display extending left and right from an inner hallway door of mannequin-like figures representing some of the 37 official *nat* (spirit beings), plus some Hindu deities and a few necromancers (the figures with goatees at the right end of the shrine).

In the shrine there are also *nat* not counted among the official 37, including three principal figures: the **Flower-Eating Ogress** (aka Mae Wunna, or 'Queen Mother of Popa') and her two sons (to her left and right), **Min Gyi** and **Min Lay**.

A few other interesting *nat* here caught our attention. The plump Pyu goddess **Shin Nemi** (Little Lady) is a guardian for children and is given toy offerings during school exam time. She's the cute little thing clutching a green umbrella and a stuffed animal, midway down on the left of the shrine.

There have been a few Kyawswas in Myanmar spirit history, but the most popular is Popa-born **Lord Kyawswa** (aka Drunk Nat), who spent his few years cockfighting and drinking. He boasts: 'If you don't like me, avoid me. I admit I'm a drunkard'. He's the guardian of gamblers and drunks and sits on a horse decked in rum and whiskey bot-

---

NAT MORAL: FULFIL YOUR DUTIES!

Sometimes it's hard being a *nat*. The namesake figure of the Mother Spirit of Popa Nat Shrine is Mae Wunna. She was famous for her love of Byat-ta, one of King Anawrahta's servants, a flower-gathering Indian with superhuman powers, who neglected his duties and was executed for it. Their two sons, Min Gyi and Min Lay, supposedly born atop Mt Popa, followed their father's tradition. They became servants of the king (often going to China), grew neglectful of their duties, and then *they* were executed. King Anawrahta, however, ordered a shrine built at the place of their execution (at Taungbyone, north of Mandalay), now the site of a huge festival. Many worshippers come to offer a blessing to these three. Mae Wunna and her sons are the central figures facing the entry to the shrine.

FRUIT OF THE PALMS

On the way to or from Mt Popa, stop by one of the several toddy and jaggery (palm sugar) operations that are set up along the road. The operators will give you a basic demo of how the alcoholic drink and sweets are made from the sap of the toddy palm. It's also possible to sample and buy these local products.

tles, to the right. Be sure to pay your respects if you've been partying your way through Southeast Asia up until this point.

Locals pray to **Shwe Na Be** (Lady with Golden Sides) when a snake comes into their house. She's the woman holding a *naga* (serpent) near the corner to the left.

🏃 Activities

Popa Mountain Park   HIKING

A variety of **hiking trails** thread through the Popa Mountain Park, leading to the rim of the volcano crater, and to viewpoints and waterfalls. Along the way, you can observe the difference in the vegetation.

The heights capture the moisture of passing clouds, causing rain to drop on the plateau and produce a profusion of trees, flowering plants and herbs, all nourished by the rich volcanic soil. In fact, the word *popa* is derived from the Sanskrit word for flower.

Trekking here is best done with local guides. Ask at the turn-off, a mile or so back from Popa village (towards Bagan), or enquire at Popa Mountain Resort, halfway up the peak. From the resort, the hike to the crater and back takes around four hours (the resort charges US$24 per group – up to four – for the guided hike).

If you come by taxi, ask the driver to point out bits of **petrified forest**, which are strewn along either side of the road west of Popa village.

✨ Festivals & Events

Mt Popa hosts two huge **nat pwe** (spirit festivals) yearly, one beginning on the full moon of Nayon (May/June) and another on the full moon of Nadaw (November/December). Before King Anawrahta's time, thousands of animals were sacrificed to the *nat* during these festivals, but this practice has been prohibited since the Bagan era. Spirit possession and overall drunken ecstasy are still part of the celebration, however.

There are several other minor festivals, including ones held on the full moons of Wagaung (July/August) and Tagu (March/April), which celebrate the departure and return of the famous Taungbyone *nat* (Min Gyi and Min Lay). Once a year, the Taungbyone *nat* are believed to travel a spirit circuit that includes Mt Popa, Taungbyone (about 14 miles north of Mandalay) and China.

🛏 Sleeping

Popa Mountain Resort   RESORT $$$

(☎02-69169; poparesort@myanmar.com.mm; r US$100-200; ❋@🛜🏊) Some 2.5 miles northwest of Mt Popa's main temple, the lovely, lonely Popa Mountain Resort has lovely all-wood bungalows, dramatically set amid lush gardens with striking views over the mountainside. It sits at 2600ft (798m), and nonguests can take a dip in the infinity pool (US$7) while admiring the panoramic sweep of Popa Taung Kalat (p172).

It has a good **restaurant** (10am-9.30pm; mains US$10-20), overlooking the shimmering spires of Mt Popa's temples. You can also have a spa treatment, go horse riding (US$15 per hour) or take a guided hike to the summit of Popa Mountain Park.

It's owned by Tay Za, a businessman with close links to Myanmar's generals.

ℹ Getting There & Away

Most travellers visit Mt Popa in half a day by shared taxi or organised tour from their hotel. In Nyaung U, guesthouses can usually arrange a space in a shared taxi (without guide); a whole taxi is about K35,000 to K45,000 depending on the quality of the vehicle.

A pick-up truck departs Nyaung U's bus station at 8.30am for Mt Popa (K3000, two hours); on the return leg, it departs Popa for Nyaung U at 1pm. Less conveniently, it is possible to take an hourly pick-up from Nyaung U to Kyaukpadaung (90 minutes) and then another to Mt Popa (45 minutes), but this takes the best part of a day.

Salay   ⊙⊜౧

POP 28,000 / ☎063

The Bagan-era village of Salay, 22 miles south of Bagan, is rooted in the 12th and 13th centuries, when Bagan's influence spread. It remains an active religious centre, with something like 50 monasteries shared among the fewer than 10,000 residents. Day trippers make it here to visit a few of the 19th-century wooden monasteries and some select

Bagan-era shrines, and peek at a handful of untouched British colonial buildings.

It can be paired with Mt Popa on a full-day trip, although the two are in different directions from Bagan.

◉ Sights

An interesting feature in Salay is the faded colonial-era heritage dotted around town and some of the old buildings still feature the Royal Crown high up on their facades. Check out the market area, a few hundred metres west of the museum. This area is especially worth visiting, as few buildings in Myanmar still sport the lion-guarded crown.

Little of the history of Salay's 103 ruins is known outside a small circle of Myanmar archaeologists working with limited funds. It is said that most of the monuments weren't royally sponsored but were built by the lower nobility or commoners – that's why there's nothing on the grand scale of Bagan's biggest structures.

Youqson Kyaung   BUDDHIST MONASTERY
(ရုပ်စုံကျောင်း; K5000; ⊙9.30am-4.30pm) Designed as a copy of the Crown Prince House in Mandalay, and built in 1882–92, the huge wooden monastery is one of Salay's not-to-be-missed sights. Along two of its exterior sides are detailed original carvings displaying 19th-century court life and scenes from the Jataka (stories of the Buddha's past lives) and Ramayana (one of India's best-known legends). Inside, the 17th- to 19th-century pieces are behind glass cases, while the Bagan-era woodcarvings (including a massive throne backdrop) stand in open view.

Paya Thonzu   BUDDHIST TEMPLE
(ဘုရားသုံးဆူ) In the pagoda-filled area just east of Youqson Kyaung lies Paya Thonzu, a small trio of brick shrines with *sikhara* (Indian-style corn-cob-like temple finials) and some faded murals inside. The westernmost shrine (to the left when approaching from the museum) has the most visible murals and also a narrow set of stairs leading to a small terrace. If it's locked, ask at Youqson Kyaung.

Shinpinsarkyo Paya   BUDDHIST TEMPLE
(ရှင်ပင်စာကြိုဘုရား; Temple 88) About 4 miles southwest of town, you'll find the Bagan-era (but renovated over the years) Shinpinsarkyo Paya (Temple 88), which is full of original woodcarvings, some painted afresh in original design. The highlight is inside a glass- and tile-filled pagoda, with two original 13th-century wood Lokanats (Mahayana Bodhisattva guardian spirits).

Near the southern entrance passageway, you'll find several rooms covered with exquisite 19th-century murals (bring a torch to peer around inside the darkened chambers). If the gates are locked, ask one of the attendants to unlock them.

Omwara Paya   BUDDHIST SITE
(ဩဝရဘုရား; Temple 99) Around 1 mile south of Shinpinsarkyo – some taxis won't drive it, but it's an easy 20-minute walk – is the so-called Temple 99, an unassuming 13th-century shrine that features 578 painted Jataka scenes inside. The last 16 paintings on the left represent the '16 Dreams of King Kosala'. Ask at Shinpinsarkyo for a key to the gate (an attendant may even accompany you, helping you in the right direction).

Sasanayaunggyi Kyaung   BUDDHIST MONASTERY
(သာသနာ့ရောင်ခြည်ကျောင်း) The monastery and meditation centre Sasanayaunggyi Kyaung, 0.3 miles north of Paya Thonzu, is a stop-off point for day trippers. It features a lovely 19th-century glass armoire with painted Jataka panels and 400-year-old scripture in Pali inside. The monks are usually happy to show you around, and always appreciate a donation for their on-site school.

Mann Paya   BUDDHIST TEMPLE
(မန်းဘုရား) In the complex about 500yd west of the Paya Thonzu, the Mann Paya is a modern pagoda housing a 20ft gold buddha made of straw lacquer. As the story goes, the buddha image was originally located near Monywa and was washed downstream during an 1888 monsoon, all the way to Salay. Ask for a peek inside from the latched door at the back.

✖ Eating

You can get noodles in the Salay market but otherwise dining options are limited. Bring a picnic from Bagan before setting out, or stop for a bite in Chauk (14 miles north of Salay), which tends to have better eating choices (Chauk is famous for its production of the sweet tamarind flakes that are served at the end of all meals in Bagan).

① Getting There & Away

Salay is 36 miles south of Bagan on a road that's often flood-damaged and occasionally impassable. The route passes through the larger town of Chauk on the way. From Chauk, another road goes east to Kyaukpadaung for alternative access in combination with Mt Popa.

A hired taxi for a four- or five-hour trip to Salay from Nyaung U starts at about K40,000. A day trip combining Mt Popa and Salay costs about 60,000. It's technically possible to come by pick-up truck from Nyaung U in three hours (not including a change in Chauk), but it's not advisable, as some sites in Salay aren't close to the drop-off point.

Pakokku ပခုက္ကူ

POP 130,000 / ☑ 062

A transit point for wayward travellers on the west side of the Ayeyarwady (Irrawaddy) River, Pakokku is a friendly town famed for its tobacco and *thanakha*. Few guests stay here now with the new bridge connecting it to Bagan, 16 miles south, in just 30 minutes. Should you choose to linger, there's a basic riverside homestay, which many guests rank as a highlight of their trip. One of the town's biggest *pwe* (festivals), **Thihoshin**, is held during Nayon in May/June.

History

Pakokku was a quiet backwater until 2007, when it found itself front and centre in international headlines. Monks from the Myo Ma Ahle monastery here kick-started nationwide protests against rising petrol prices that became the 'Saffron Revolution'. While the monks' uprising failed in the short-term, observers argue its brutal suppression was an important watershed and a key element in pushing the generals to kick-start the reform process.

These days, political turmoil resides largely in the past. The only fervour you'll find is at the bustling market, which sprawls for many blocks in the town centre.

◉ Sights

If time is limited, the most rewarding activities in Pakokku include browsing the **market**, checking out some of the **temples** and **monasteries** – including one monastery with a giant clock tower – or just wandering amid the tropical torpor of its picturesquely decrepit side streets, which feature old homes backing on to the Ayeyarwady River.

Pakhangyi   BUDDHIST SITE

(ပခန်းကြီး; K5000) About 17 miles northeast of Pakokku, on the way to Monywa, are the remains of Pakhangyi, a 19th-century wooden monastery. There isn't a lot to see here,

but there are some finely carved wooden doors, and the soaring 65ft teak columns are rather impressive. Admission also gets you access to the Pakhangyi Archaeological Museum, half a mile up the road.

Pakhangyi Archaeological Museum   MUSEUM

(ပခန်းကြီးရှေးဟောင်းသုတေသနပြတိုက်; K5000; ◷ 9.30am-4.30pm Tue-Sun) Half a mile north of Pakhangyi on the main road is this small provincial museum, which has a medley of 19th-century wooden carvings, 11th-century Buddhas made of sandstone, ancient inscribed stone tablets, and some fossils and Neolithic tools thrown in for good measure.

Pakhanngeh Kyaung   ARCHITECTURE

(ပခန်းငယ်ကျောင်း) About 3 miles east of Pakhangyi (take the turn-off just opposite the turn-off to Pakhangyi) is the destroyed frame of Pakhanngeh Kyaung, which was once the country's largest wooden monastery. Many of its 332 teak pillars still stand, and the area, near the fork of the Ayeyarwady and Kaladan rivers, makes for rewarding exploration. A taxi from Pakokku is about K35,000.

🛏 Sleeping & Eating

★**Mya Yatanar Inn**   HOMESTAY $

(☑ 062-21457; 75 Lanmataw St; s/d with fan K10,000/20,000, with air-con K12,000/24,000; ✴) Charming, English-speaking grandma Mya Mya, her daughter and granddaughters will welcome you to your 100-year-old home on the river, a couple of blocks east of the market. Rooms are basic, but bearable once you fall under the hospitable spell of these women. It offers cheap meals and bicycles are available for K2000.

Past guests include a boyishly young David Duchovny, who stayed here in 1983.

Thu Kha Hotel   HOTEL $$

(☑ 062-23077; Myoma Rd; r US$35-70, s with shared bathroom from US$15; ✴ 🛜) This newish hotel has spacious rooms, most with wooden floors, flat-screen TV, stocked minifridge and contemporary bathroom. There is no lift, so rates drop on the higher floors. It's on the busy main road connecting Monywa and Bagan, a few blocks northeast of the market.

Ho Pin Myanmar
Traditional Cuisine   BURMESE $

(☑ 062-22979; 2 St, 11 Quarter; set meals K3500-5000; ◷ 10am-9pm) Recommended by Bagan residents in the know who regularly travel to Pakokku on shopping runs, the Ho Pin prides itself on 'flair and care'. The kitchen is reassuringly visible to diners and hearty Burmese set meals are served to a transient crowd. There's no menu, just pick your dish from the samples in the glass case.

It's located two blocks north of busy Monywa Rd, off Ku Theaina Yone Rd.

ⓘ Getting There & Away

Buses shuttle to and from Bagan (K2000, one hour) and Monywa (K3000, three hours), leaving regularly from Htinn Tann Rd, just north of busy Myoma Rd (and near a hospital). There are three services daily to Mandalay (K6500, seven hours). From Moepip bus station on the west side of town, you can catch one daily bus (K8500, 8.30am) to Mindat in Chin State (handy if you're heading on to India).

Monywa

POP C 185,000 / ☑ 071

Like its neighbour Mandalay, a visit to Monywa is not really about the town itself, but a series of interesting attractions in the surrounding countryside. Pronounced in two syllables (mon-ywa), Monywa is an engaging trade town that makes a sensible stopping point when looping north between Bagan and Mandalay. The town itself is big, hot and flat, with relatively little to see beyond the markets and the pleasant Chindwin riverside setting, though two large, central pagoda complexes, Shwezigon Paya and Su Taung Pye Zedi, are well worth a wander. It is also an embarkation point for the adventurous few who boat-hop the Chindwin to little-visited villages to the north.

🛏 Sleeping

Shwe Taung Tarn　　GUESTHOUSE $
(☑ 071-21478; 70 Station Rd; s US$13-20, d US$20-27; ✺) Budget-minded Shwe Taung Tarn has ageing rooms and an unkempt facade, but it's tolerable for a night.

★ Win Unity　　RESORT $$
(☑ 071-22438; www.winunityhotels.com; Bogyoke Rd; r US$45-60, bungalow US$80-150, ste US$130-300; ✺@☎✺) Easily Monywa's swankiest option, the Win Unity is a series of tile-roofed modern bungalow rooms set on the lakeside, less than half a mile north of the centre. They boast an all-wood design, with porch, big flat-screen TV and spotless bathroom – the best bungalows command a fine view of the lake (and are priced accordingly).

Budget travellers can book a comfortable but simply furnished room in the six-storey building set back from the lake. There's also a good restaurant, an inviting pool, a gym and a spa.

Hotel Chindwin　　HOTEL $$
(☑ 071-26150; www.hotelchindwinmonywa.com; Bogyoke Rd; s US$25-55, d US$30-60; ✺@☎) Towering above the city-centre competition, this high-rise hotel has smart rooms at an affordable price. Standard rooms are small but include many of the features found in the higher-class rooms. Deluxe rooms are almost suites and include a spacious bathroom. Breakfast, served on the 6th floor, has a fine view over Shwezigon and the distant mountains. A lift is available.

Monywa Hotel　　HOTEL $$
(☑ 071-21581; monywahotel@goldenland.com.mm; Bogyoke Rd; s US$35-40, d US$40-45; ✺☎) Set well back from the busy street amid birdsong and creeper-draped trees, this collection of multiroom cabins is popular with small tour groups. Interiors are dated (and painted in surprising colours such as mint or peach), but even the cheaper rooms are fair-sized with effective air-conditioning, desk, fridge, hot showers, satellite TV and reasonable beds.

🍴 Eating

If you want to eat with locals, head to the night market near the clock tower. There are also some casual eateries nearby here along Bogyoke Rd.

Las Vegas　　CHINESE, THAI $
(Bogyoke Rd; mains K2500-8000; ⊙6am-10pm; ☑⑩) Located about 600m north of the bridge over the lake on the main road, Las Vegas is an open-sided tropical-themed eatery serving a fine mix of Chinese and Thai dishes (including a good mixed-vegetable dish with bean curd). There's Tuborg on draught, music videos playing overhead and kind-hearted staff.

Eureka　　BAKERY, CAFE $
(Yonegyi Rd; mains K3000-6000; ⊙7am-9pm; ☎⑩) This pleasant, air-conditioned cafe and bakery serves coffees, iced green tea and other drinks as well as an extensive food menu of curries, sandwiches, cakes and pastries.

Night Market　　STREET FOOD $
(Bogyoke Rd; ⊙5-10.30pm) Various cheap eats are served up nightly between the clock tower and Bogyoke (Aung San) statue. Locals

Monywa

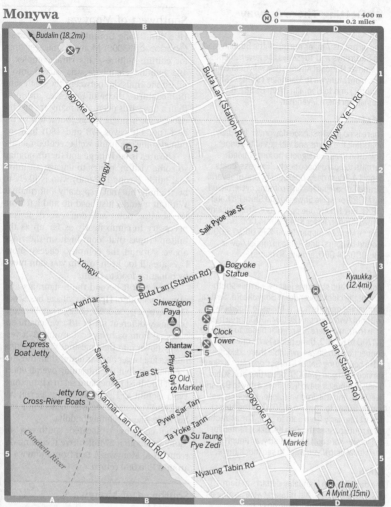

flock here to grab takeaway or chow down while sitting on plastic stools, making it a good place for people-watching.

Pleasant Island   CHINESE $$

(Myakanthar Lake, Bogyoke Rd; mains K2500-10,000; ⏰ 7am-10pm; 📶) Monywa's finest restaurant occupies a tiny lake island across upper Bogyoke Rd from the Win Unity hotel. It's a photogenic spot at sunset, linked to the shore by a rickety wooden bridge. Tasty Chinese, Malay and Thai food is served at open pavilions, but it's also popular with well-to-do locals quaffing beer on a night out.

ℹ Getting There & Away

AIR

The airport is 7 miles north, off the Budalin road. On Saturdays and Tuesdays the government's Myanmar National Airlines (www.flymna.com) flies from Monywa to Mandalay (from US$57, 20 minutes) and to Homalin (from US$81, 65 minutes) in northern Myanmar.

BOAT

There is no public service downriver, but daily boats link the towns and villages of the upper Chindwin River. Foreigners no longer need permits to board these boats. 'Express' boats depart 4.30am daily, operated by one of several Strand Rd companies on a rotating cycle, including MGRG or Ngwe Shwe Oo and Shwe Po Kaba (SPK). Buy tickets one day before. Stops include Kalewa (upper/lower K24,000/14,000, around 13 hours), Mawleik (upper/lower K36,000/18,000, around 18 hours) and Homalin (upper/lower K36,000/24,000, around 30 hours).

BUS

Monywa's bus station is just over a mile southeast of the clock tower down Bogyoke Rd. Several companies operate hourly buses to Mandalay (without/with air-con K2000/3000, three hours, 5am to 4pm). There are regular buses to Pakokku (K1700 to K2500, three hours) with onward connections to Bagan available there, taking an extra hour. Aung Gabar Express operates a direct service to Bagan (K4000) departing at 7.30am. Small minibuses leave five times a day to Bagan (K4000), and will drop you closer to your guesthouse. Buses to Shwebo (K3000, three hours) depart regularly from 5am to 1pm. The attractive rural route passes through Kyaukka, famed for its lacquerware cottage industry, although you'll need local help if you want to see much there.

TRAIN

The daily train to Mandalay departs at 6am (K3500, six hours), but it takes twice as long as the bus in an uncomfortable box car.

ℹ Getting Around

You can get a motorbike or three-wheeler to the centre from the bus station (around K2000). These transport options, along with white, plain-clothed taxis, linger near the northern Shwezigon Paya entrance.

Around Monywa

With only one full day to spare, the most popular option is to visit Hpo Win Daung caves followed by Thanboddhay and Bodhi Tataung. The latter is west-facing, and so is best seen in afternoon sunlight.

Southwest of Monywa

Hpo Win Daung Complex   BUDDHIST SITE

(ရှုဝင်တောင်; K3000) Monywa's biggest draw for culture vultures, this rural complex of 492 buddha chambers was carved into a limestone hillside between the 14th and 18th centuries. None of the 'caves' are more than a few yards deep, and many are just big enough for a single image, but a few of the best (notably caves 478 and 480) have retained some colourful, well-executed murals.

The area is fairly large and there's no map so some visitors prefer to engage an informal guide (around K5000) who is likely to be friendly but not especially informative. Without a guide, just head up and left from the starting point and don't worry, it isn't necessary to climb nearly as far up as the hilltop stupas that loom high on the ridge above. Around the complex, cheeky monkeys are all too keen to help you gain merit by donating food to them.

Some 2000ft beyond the restaurants and souvenir stands of Hpo Win 'village' lies **Shwe Ba Taung** (ရွှေဘတောင်; US$2), a smaller, contrastingly different set of 46 cave chambers accessed from pathways cut around 25ft vertically down into the limestone. The buddha images are larger and far newer than those of the main site but the intriguing overall effect is of a Buddhist Disneyland set in a miniature Petra. Squint at Hpo Win Daung as you return and you might see why locals think the hill looks like a reclining buddha.

The complex is located southwest of Monywa, about a 27-mile drive if coming directly from Monywa. A taxi from Monywa is around K30,000 return.

Southeast of Monywa

When travelling by private vehicle between Mandalay and Monywa, two key sites, Bodhi Tataung and Thanboddhay Paya, can be conveniently visited as a short detour en route. However, for those travelling by local transport, it is wiser to visit on a return excursion from Monywa, (motorbike/three-wheeler around K8000/12,000, three hours).

Thanboddhay Paya   BUDDHIST TEMPLE

(သာမွေဒေဘုရား; ⊘ 6am-5pm) This colourful, modern temple is famed for its staggering number of buddha images as well as its carnivalesque exterior, with a unique roof layered with rows of gilt ministupas. Its flanks burst gaudily bright colours and are offset by 30ft-high concrete obelisks set with uncountable minuscule buddha shapes. The multiarched temple interior is plastered with so many buddha images (5,823,631 according to temple guardians), large and small, that it feels like you're walking through a buddha house of mirrors.

Thanboddhay's kitschfest continues in the surrounding pastel-hued monks' quarters and with two huge, white, concrete elephants at the site's gateway. It's about 1 mile off the Mandalay road, 6 miles from Monywa.

Bodhi Tataung
BUDDHIST MONUMENT

(ဗောဓိတစ်ထောင်) FREE The name of this vast hillside buddha-rama, Bodhi Tataung, translates as '1000 Buddhas'. However, for most visitors, only two of them really count. Opened in 2008, the glimmering 424ft standing Buddha is the second tallest in the world (after Spring Temple Buddha in China), and it utterly dominates the landscape for miles around. Inside the multistorey torso, seemingly interminable stairways link painted galleries, many lower ones depicting gruesome scenes from hell that are not really suitable for young children.

The statue has 31 storeys, said to represent the 31 planes of existence, though access beyond the 25th floor was blocked when we passed through. Lower down the hillside lounges a slightly smaller but still enormous 312ft reclining Buddha. It's hardly refined and the dark interior contains poorly maintained tableaux. Entry is through the right buttock. Under construction is a massive seated Buddha, which will complete the kitschy trifecta. Note that both giant Buddhas face west, so for the best light plan a visit in the late afternoon.

If you're feeling inspired, the Bodhi Tataung site hosts many other minor fascinations, including a whole garden of identical sitting Buddhas under concrete parasols, and the gilded 430ft stupa Aung Setkya Paya, which has lovely views from its upper rim, reached via an inner passageway. Carry your sandals to save your feet from the gravel on connecting roads.

It's located 13 miles southeast of Monywa (and 5 miles east of Thanboddhay, which you'll pass on the way there).

North of Monywa

Wizened old neem trees and many an attractive stupa enliven the busy, well-paved road leading north from Monywa. After 19 miles, Budalin is a small junction settlement with a basic noodle shop, from which it's still rather a slog to reach the area's minor attractions. But you'll certainly be getting far, far off the tourist radar.

Payagyi
BUDDHIST SITE

(ဘုရားကြီး) The large Payagyi stupa and its oversized *chinthe* (half-lion/half-dragon deity) face an abrupt twin-peaked hill, topped with a stupa and castle-like rocky outcrop, and said to have an indelible footprint of Bagan-era King Kyanzittha at its base. Now boxed within concrete walls and a tin roof, the empty front prayer hall retains its 170-year-old teak pillars.

Its carved-stone floor tiles, telling Ramayana tales, have been moved for safekeeping to a museum shed: notice number 274 featuring Hanuman (the monkey god) riding a sheep and smoking a cheroot. The attractive wooden monastery building seems oversized for the handful of resident monks.

It's 18 miles from the central junction in Budalin (marked by a golden horseback Bandula statue, 1640ft north of the Twin Daung turning), where you veer left. Keep left again after 2 miles then continue 14 miles to Ta Kook Ta Nel. Turn right after the little row of teahouses then follow the track 3 miles to Payagyi. It's a long way to come for one monastery, but the rural scenes en route are very attractive. The first six asphalted miles after Budalin pass through cotton fields, sunflowers and Palmyra palms to Nyaung Kai/Ywathar, which has a massive Shwezigon pagoda in a field at its southeast edge.

A Myint

Little visited by foreigners apart from occasional Chindwin cruise groups, A Myint is a charmingly unspoiled riverside village dominated by a series of 336 higgledy-piggledy **ancient stupas** in varying stages of collapse. All are compactly arranged around a little **wooden monastery** and a few retain interior murals. Another minor attraction is the **British-era house** (62 Seidan St) of the former village chief. It's private and still owned by the original family, who might show off their 1920s sepia photos.

A major attraction is the lovely 15-mile ride through agricultural villages from Monywa on a lane that's narrow but unusually well asphalted. Around halfway, look northeast for brief, distant views.

There's no public transport to A Myint. To get here, you'll have to arrange a taxi or motor trishaw from Monywa.

Temples of Bagan

Why Go?

Marco Polo, who may or may not have visited on his travels, described Bagan as 'one of the finest sights in the world'. Despite centuries of neglect, looting, erosion and regular earthquakes, not to mention questionable restoration, this temple-studded plain remains a remarkably impressive and unforgettable vision.

In a 230-year building frenzy up until 1287 and the Mongol invasions, Bagan's kings commissioned more than 4000 Buddhist temples. These brick and stucco religious structures are all that remain of their grand city, with the 11th- to 13th-century wooden buildings long gone. Many restoration projects have resulted in a compromised archaeological site. Often the restorations bear little resemblance to the original building styles. Still, Bagan remains a wonder. Working temples, such as Ananda Pahto, give a sense of what the place was like at its zenith, while others conceal colourful murals and exterior platforms with jaw-dropping views across the plain.

Best Temple Murals

→ Upali Thein (p189)

→ Nandamannya Pahto (p195)

→ Payathonzu (p194)

→ Ananda Ok Kyaung (p189)

→ Abeyadana Pahto (p192)

Best Sunset Spots

→ Shwesandaw Paya (p190)

→ Buledi (p189)

→ Pyathada Paya (p191)

→ Thabeik Hmauk (p191)

→ Tan Kyi Paya (p187)

When to Go

Bagan

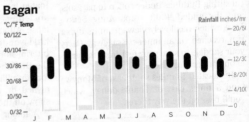

Mar–May Bagan is sizzling; avoid visiting now or you may melt.

Jun–Oct Rainy season; steamy but a good time to go, with cheaper rooms and fewer visitors.

Nov–Feb Best time weather-wise, but temples are crowded and it's hard to find accommodation.

History

According to Pali inscriptions found here, Bagan kings flirted with a couple of different city names in its heyday, including Arimaddanapura (City of the Enemy Crusher) and the less dramatic Tambadipa (Copper Land). The name Bagan may in fact derive from Pyugan, a name first written down by the Annamese of present-day Vietnam in the mid-11th century as Pukam. The British in the 19th century called the site Pagan while the military junta switched it back to Bagan in 1989.

Glory Days

Bagan's 2½ centuries of temple building (from the 11th century to the 13th century) coincided with the region's transition from Hindu and Mahayana Buddhist beliefs to the Theravada Buddhist beliefs that have since

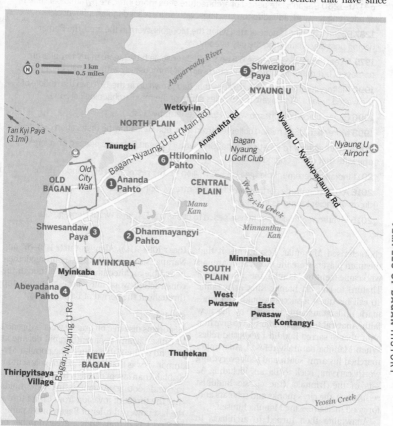

Temples of Bagan Highlights

❶ Ananda Pahto (p187) Marvelling at the perfectly proportioned Ananda Pahto, which houses four giant buddhas carved from teak.

❷ Dhammayangyi Pahto (p190) Speculating on what lies inside the bricked-up inner sanctum of mysterious Dhammayangyi Pahto.

❸ Shwesandaw Paya (p190) Watching a dramatic sunrise over the surrounding expanse of ancient temples.

❹ Abeyadana Pahto (p192) Admiring the intricate murals adorning the dimly lit walls of Abeyadana Pahto.

❺ Shwezigon Paya (p195) Getting acquainted with the 37 *nats* at this beautiful *zedi* in Nyaung U.

❻ Htilominlo Pahto (p189) Taking in the soaring spires, fine carvings and artfully wrought reliefs of photogenic Htilominlo Pahto.

KEY BAGAN DATES

c 950 Evidence from the remains of Pyu-style buildings is the earliest indication of a settlement on this bend in the Ayeyarwady (Irrawaddy).

1057 Temple building speeds up with the sacking of the Mon city of Thaton by Bagan's warrior king Anawrahta, a newly enthusiastic devotee of Buddhism.

c 1100–70 Temples become bigger and are better lit by broader windows, with more of an eye to vertical proportions than horizontal lines.

c 1170–1280 Bagan's late period of architecture sees more intricate pyramidical spires or adorning tile work added to the buildings, with an increased Indian influence.

1287 Bagan's decline is accelerated when the Mongols overrun the area, the Bamar having possibly abandoned the city already.

1975 An earthquake registering 6.5 on the Richter scale hits Bagan; many temples are damaged, but major reconstruction starts almost immediately with the help of Unesco.

1990 Military forcibly relocates a village that had grown up in the 1970s in the middle of the walled area of 'Old Bagan' to 2.5 miles south of the main archaeological zone.

1996 Bagan placed on Unesco World Heritage Tentative List.

1998 More than US$1 million collected from local donations for the restoration of Bagan.

2008 An imaginary re-creation of the 13th-century Bagan Palace is opened on a site opposite that of the original palace.

2011 Indian government pledges US$22 million for the restoration of Ananda Pahto.

2016 A 6.8-magnitude earthquake strikes central Myanmar, causing damage to hundreds of ancient temples in Bagan.

2016 Myanmar officially petitions Unesco to designate Bagan a World Heritage site.

characterised Myanmar. Legend has it that the main players were the monk Shin Arahan who came (sent by Manuha, the Mon king of Thaton) to convert Bamar King Anawrahta. To call his quest a success would be a landmark understatement. Inspired by his new faith, Anawrahta ordered Manuha to give him a number of sacred Buddhist texts and relics. When Manuha naturally refused, Anawrahta marched his army south and took everything worth carrying back to Bagan, including 32 sets of the Tripitaka (the classic Buddhist scriptures), the city's monks and scholars and, for good measure, King Manuha himself.

Anawrahta then turned to architects to create something that befit Buddha. They built and built, and many of the greatest Bagan edifices date from their efforts, including Shwezigon Paya, considered a prototype for all later Myanmar stupas; the Pitaka Taik (Scripture Library), built to house the Pitaka (scriptures); and the elegant and distinctive Shwesandaw Paya, built immediately after the conquest of Thaton. Thus began what the Myanmar people call the First Burmese Empire, which became a pilgrimage point for Buddhists throughout Southeast Asia. King Anawrahta's successors, particularly Kyanzit-tha (r 1084–1113), Alaungsithu (r 1113–67) and Narapatisithu (r 1174–1211), continued their incredible architectural output, although the construction work must have been nonstop throughout the period of Bagan's glory.

Decline

Historians disagree on exactly what happened to cause Bagan's apparently rapid decline at the end of the 13th century. The popular Myanmar view is that hordes of Mongols sent by Kublai Khan swept through the city, ransacking and looting. A contrasting view holds that the threat of invasion from China threw the last powerful ruler of Bagan into a panic. Legend has it that, after a great number of temples were torn down to build fortifications, the city was abandoned so that the Mongols merely took over an already deserted city.

Bagan scholar Paul Strachan argues in *Pagan: Art and Architecture of Old Burma* (1989) that the city was never abandoned at all. Indeed evidence suggests Bagan continued as an important religious and cultural centre into the 14th century and beyond, after which its decay can be blamed on the three-way struggle between the Shan, Mon and Bamar. People began moving back in some numbers only after the British established a presence in the area in the late 19th century, but by that point the plain of temples had fallen victim to frequent earthquakes (there were at least 16 trembles that shook Bagan between 1174 and the big one in 1975), general weathering and neglect.

Controversial Restoration

The enduring religious significance of Bagan is at the heart of the site's recent transformation. It's been changed from piles of picturesque ruins to a practically complete 13th-century city, minus the buildings, such as palaces, homes and monasteries, that would have been made of wood.

In the 1990s and early 2000s, Bagan was massively reworked. Since 1995, more than 1300 Buddhist temples, monasteries and stupas had been speculatively rebuilt from mounds of rubble, and a further 700 damaged buildings received major repairs. This has caused much concern among international preservationists, who have criticised the poor workmanship and historically inaccurate methods and materials often employed.

Putting this into perspective, recent renovations follow a pattern set by early builders. Between 1200 and 1280, construction appears to have begun on new monuments every two weeks. Down history, these hastily built structures have been patched up, repaired and rebuilt. Today's dodgy contractors are only following in the footsteps of their quick-building ancestors.

A Living Religious Site

Following the 1975 quake, Unesco spent 15 years and more than US$1 million on restoration projects. But Bagan's current advanced state of restoration is mainly due to a hugely successful donations program initiated by the government in the mid-1990s and enthusiastically supported by many merit-making locals. The result, according to some international observers, is more akin to a Disney-style version of a great historical site.

Defending the rebuilding program, Culture Minister Win Sein cited the nation's duty to preserve, strengthen and restore all the cultural heritage monuments of Bagan in perpetuity, and emphasised that the temples were still actively used religious monuments much venerated by Myanmar people.

2016 Earthquake

On 24 August 2016, a 6.8-magnitude earthquake struck central Myanmar causing damage to numerous temples in Bagan. Loss of life was limited (no one in Bagan died; several people were killed elsewhere), but nearly four hundred pagodas were affected, including Sulamani, Ananda, Htilominlo, Shwesandaw, Lawkananda and Dhammayazika, along with Ananda Ok Kyaung, whose murals suffered some damage. In the immediate aftermath of the quake, Bagan looked shredded with collapsed walls, piles of rubble and brick debris littering the archaeological zone.

In the weeks that followed, however, it became clear that much of the damage was not to the original centuries-old structures but to renovations added on over the years (from the 1990s until 2005 more than 600 sites were altered, and some experts estimate that 90% of Bagan's pagodas have had significant alterations or have been rebuilt entirely). The foundations and lower parts of temples were undamaged – which is perhaps not surprising given the many other earthquakes these temples have survived over the centuries.

Unlike in earlier days, Myanmar does not want to rush the rebuilding process. The country's de facto leader, Aung San Suu Kyi, has advised the Culture and Religious Affairs Ministry to avoid immediate renovations until thorough assessments have been undertaken. In September 2016, a team from Unesco arrived to work with local experts in the repair process. For visitors, some 33 temples currently remain off-limits until 2018 at the earliest, including Dhammayazika, Htilominlo and Sulamani pagodas.

THE TEMPLES

There are more than 3000 temples spread across the Bagan plain. Despite the 2016 earthquake, which damaged several hundred temples, Bagan's majesty can't be diminished. Seeing the soaring centuries-old structures from a prime spot is dazzling – particularly at sunrise or sunset.

Old Bagan

Old Bagan is the most practical part of Bagan to tour on foot (bring water and a hat). It's best to follow a roughly counterclockwise, 1-mile circuit within the old city walls, starting from Mahabodhi Paya and ending at the Tharabar Gate.

Gawdawpalin Pahto   BUDDHIST TEMPLE
(ကန်တော့ပလ္လင်ဘုရား; Map p184) Standing 197ft tall, Gawdawpalin is one of the largest

Temples of Bagan

See Nyaung U Map (p159)

Ayeyarwady River

Tan Kyi Paya
(3.1mi)

See Old Bagan Map (p166)

33

15

**WETKYI-
IN**

Bagan-Nyaung U Rd (Main Rd)

42
13

Bagan
Nyaung U
Golf Club

NORTH PLAIN

41

14

7

Ferry
Terminal

Old City
Wall

Wetkyi-in Creek

8

Palace
Site

45

**OLD
BAGAN**

19

1 *Ananda
Pahto*

39 **4**

Anawrahta Rd

**CENTRAL
PLAIN**

11

31

29

*Manu
Kan*

21 **27**
26

40

35
37

36

18

Bagan-Nyaung U Rd (Main Rd)

22

32

2 *Dhammayangyi
Pahto*

30

12

48

51

50

MYINKABA

**SOUTH
PLAIN**

20

24

49

**WEST
PWASAW**

3

23

9

34

*Seinnyet
Ama Pahto*

Bagan-Chauk Rd

*Seinnyet
Nyima Paya*

See New Bagan
(Bagan Myothit) Map (p169)

46

THUHEKAN

**THIRIPYITSAYA
VILLAGE**

NEW BAGAN

44

47

10

43

Yeosin Creek

6

5

17

Sittana Paya (0.6mi);
Chauk (19mi);
Salay (22mi)

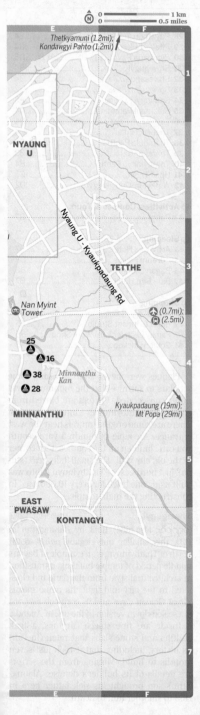

and most imposing Bagan temples, although by no means the most inspiring, with its modernised altar and tile floors inside. Built during the reign of Narapatisithu and finished under that of Nantaungmya, it's considered the crowning achievement of the late Bagan period. The stairs to the top terrace are closed to visitors. The most recent homage was its heavy-duty reconstruction following terrific damage sustained in the 1975 earthquake, as it stands near the site of the quake's epicentre.

Mimalaung Kyaung
BUDDHIST MONASTERY

(မီးမလောင်ကျောင်း; Map p184) A nice set of *chinthe* (half-lion/half-dragon deities) guards the stairway leading up this small, square monastery platform, constructed in 1174 by Narapatisithu. It's about 650ft south of Gawdawpalin, on the other side of the road. In front of the monastery is a brick-and-stucco Tripitaka library next to a large acacia tree. Atop the steps, a tiered roof (with a newer gold-capped *hti,* an umbrella-like decorated pinnacle) contains a large sitting buddha.

Archaeologists discovered an intricately carved 2.5in votive tablet here that contained 78 sculpted figures.

Pahtothamya
BUDDHIST TEMPLE

(ပုထိုးသားများ; Map p184) On the dirt road 500ft east towards the dominating Thatbyinnyu, the Pahtothamya (or Thamya Pahto) was probably built during the reign of Kyanzittha, around the turn of the 12th century, although it is popularly held to be one of five temples built by the little-known king Taunghthugyi (aka Sawrahan; r 931–64). In its prominent vertical superstructure and reconstructed lotus-bud *sikhara* (corn-cob-like temple finial), however, the monument is clearly beginning to move forward from the early period.

The interior of this single-storey building is dimly lit, typical of the early type of Pyu-influenced temples, with their small, perforated stone windows. With a torch you can pick out vestiges of ancient murals along the interior passages, perhaps the earliest surviving paintings in Bagan. Steps lead up to a roomy viewing platform.

Nathlaung Kyaung
HINDU TEMPLE

(နတ်လှောင်ကျောင်း; Map p184) Between Pahtothamya and Thatbyinnyu, this stubby building – the only Hindu temple remaining in Bagan – has a fascinating history. Named 'Shrine Confining Nat', it's where King Anawrahta stored non-Buddhist images, particularly ones for local *nat,* as he tried to enforce Buddhism. The king himself described the temple as 'where

Temples of Bagan

the *nat* are kept prisoner'. Severely damaged in the 1975 earthquake, only the temple's main hall and superstructure (with seven original Gupta-style reliefs) still stand.

A sign dates it to the early 11th century. Some say it was built in 931 by Taunghthugyi; if true, this was about a century before the southern school of Buddhism came to Bagan. The temple is dedicated to the Hindu god Vishnu. The central square of brick supports the dome and crumbled *sikhara,* and once contained freestanding figures of Vishnu, as well as Vishnu reliefs on each of the four sides. The statues were stolen by a German oil engineer in the 1890s, but the badly damaged brick-and-stucco reliefs can still be seen.

Thatbyinnyu Pahto   BUDDHIST TEMPLE
(သဗ္ဗညုထိ်; Map p184) Named for 'omniscience', Bagan's highest temple is built of two white-coloured boxy storeys, each with three diminishing terraces rimmed with spires and leading to a gold-tipped *sikhara,* 207ft high. Its monumental size and looming height make it a classic example of Bagan's middle period. Built in 1144 by Alaungsithu, its terraces are encircled by indentations for 539 Jataka (stories from the Buddha's past lives).

Plaques were never added, leading some scholars to surmise that the monument was never consecrated. Visitors are barred from climbing Thatbyinnyu's inner passages. There are some original murals near the west entrance. A couple of hundred yards south you can climb up on the southeastern corner of the old city wall. The small 'tally *zedi* (stupa)' just northeast of Thatbyinnyu Pahto was built using one brick for every 10,000 used in constructing the main temple.

Shwegugyi   BUDDHIST TEMPLE
(ရွှေဂူကြီး; Map p184) Built by Alaungsithu in 1131, this smaller but elegant *pahto*, 650ft north of Thatbyinnyu, is an example of Bagan's middle period of temple building, a transition in architectural style from the dark and cloistered to the airy and light. Its name means 'Great Golden Cave' and its corn-cob *sikhara* is a scaled-down version of the one at Ananda.

Inside are fine stucco carvings, a teak buddha and stone slabs that retell (in Pali) its history, including that it took just seven months to build. Missing from the scripts are details of its builder's demise: Alaungsithu's son brought his sick father here in 1163 to smother him to death.

Pitaka Taik   BUDDHIST LIBRARY

(ပိဋကတ်တိုက်; Map p184) Following the sacking of Thaton, King Anawrahta is said to
have carted off some 30 elephant-loads of
Buddhist scriptures in 1058 and built this library (just northeast of Shwegugyi) to house
them. The square design follows the basic
early Bagan *gu* (cave temple) plan, perfect
for the preservation of light-sensitive palm-
leaf scriptures. It's notable for the perforated stone windows, each carved from single
stone slabs, and the plaster carvings on the
roof, which imitate Myanmar woodcarvings.

Tharabar Gate   ARCHAEOLOGICAL SITE

(သရဗါတံခါး; Map p184) Do stop on the east
side of this former entrance of the original
palace site. The gate is the best-preserved remains of the 9th-century wall, and the only
gate still standing. Traces of old stucco can
still be seen on the arched gateway and on either side are two niches, home not to buddha
images but to *nat* who guard the gate and
are treated with profound respect by locals.

To the left is Lady Golden Face, and to the
right her brother Lord Handsome. Like most
nat, Tharabar Gate's twosome had a tragic history. A king married Lady Golden Face to lure
her brother Lord Handsome, whom he feared,
out of hiding. When the king had Handsome
burned at the stake, his sister jumped in too;
only her face was saved from the fire.

Superstitious locals don't venture through
the gate by motorbike, car or horse cart without first paying a one-time offering to the *nat*
(usually a bunch of bananas and a couple of
coconuts) to ensure protection against traffic accidents. Don't worry: bicycles are OK,
blessing-free. A number of restaurants are
past the former moat, about 650ft east.

Mahabodhi Paya   BUDDHIST TEMPLE

(မဟာဗောဓိဘုရား; Map p184) Unlike any other
Bagan temple, this monument, located on the
north side of the main road 1000ft west of the
gate, is modelled after the famous Mahabodhi
temple in Bodhgaya, India, which commemorates the spot where the Buddha attained
enlightenment. Built during the reign of
Nantaungmya in 1215, the temple's unusual
pyramidal spire is richly coated in niches en-
closing seated buddha figures, rising from a
square block. The stairway to the top is closed.
Inside is a modern makeover, with tile floor
and carpet.

Bupaya   BUDDHIST TEMPLE

(ဗူးဘုရား; Map p184) On the bank of the Ayeyarwady (reached from the Nyaung U

TAN KYI PAYA

From the Old Bagan jetty you can hire
a private boat to reach Tan Kyi village,
where you can arrange a taxi ride (or
hike) up to **Tan Kyi Paya**, the gold stupa
atop the mountain, visible from much of
Bagan. Views are terrific, looking back
over the river to Bagan's mighty sprawl.
A ride for three or four people, including
wait time, is about K25,000. The trip
takes three or four hours.

road, about 650ft northwest of the Mahabodhi Paya), this cylindrical Pyu-style stupa,
named for *bu* (gourd), is said to date to the
3rd century, older than any Bagan temple.
Most likely it was erected around the same
time as the city walls (around AD 850).

What's seen now – a gold stupa above a
row of crenulated terraces leading down
to the water – is a reconstruction; the 1975
earthquake demolished the original.

Off the road to the southeast is the
Pebinkyaung Paya, a 12th-century pagoda
built in a unique Sinhalese style.

North Plain

The bulk of Bagan's temples are scattered
across the vast northern plain between
Nyaung U, Old Bagan and New Bagan. This
broad area runs between the Old Bagan
walls and Nyaung U, and (mostly) between
the two roads that connect the two.

★ **Ananda Pahto**   BUDDHIST TEMPLE

(အာနန္ဒာပုထိုး; Map p184) With its shimmering
gold, 170ft-high, corn-cob *hti* shimmering
across the plains, Ananda is one of the finest, largest, best preserved and most revered
of all Bagan temples. Thought to have been
built between 1090 and 1105 by King Kyanzittha, this perfectly proportioned temple
heralds the stylistic end of the early Bagan period and the beginning of the middle period.

Ananda Pahto was damaged during the
2016 earthquake, but remains open to visitors.

The central square measures 175ft along
each side. Upper floors are closed to visitors.
The entranceways make the structure a perfect Greek cross; each entrance is crowned
with a stupa finial. The base and the terraces
are decorated with 554 glazed tiles showing
Jataka scenes, thought to be derived from
Mon texts. Look back as you enter to see the

BAGAN IN...

Many visitors set aside just two days in Bagan even though it is easy to spend four or five days here and still leave much unexplored. Consider renting a bike and heading off to view thousands of other random sights – the real pleasure of Bagan comes from a leisurely soaking up of its scale and time-slip atmosphere.

One Day

Stick to the Old Bagan area starting at the **Tharabar Gate** (p187) then heading south to Bagan's most popular temple, **Ananda Pahto** (p187) and west to **Thatbyinnyu Pahto** (p186), near where it is possible to climb up the old city wall.

Just west is where King Anawrahta stored all the non-Buddhist images at **Nathlaung Kyaung** (p185). Back on the main road, backtrack towards Tharabar Gate and detour on the gravel road for a river view from **Bupaya** (p187).

In the afternoon visit lacquerware shops in **Myinkaba** (p167), climb up the hidden stairs in modern Manuha Paya and see the bas-relief figures in **Nan Paya** (p192). Finish up at one of the choice sunset spots, like well-known **Shwesandaw Paya** (p190), near Old Bagan. Unfortunately, less-trafficked viewing platforms like that of Pyathada Paya remain closed following the 2016 earthquake.

Two Days

Having followed the one-day plan, now tick off other highlights starting with **Dhammayangyi Pahto** (p190), Bagan's largest temple. Take the paths east to the gorgeous **Sulamani Pahto** (p190) and escape the crowds at its neighbouring 'mini-me' version, **Thabeik Hmauk** (p191), which is also a good (and generally less-crowded) place for sunset viewing.

In the South Plain area east of Myinkaba, grand **Dhammayazika Paya** (p194) is one not to miss, though it's currently closed for restoration following the 2016 quake. While out this way, visit **Leimyethna Pahto** (p194) for its well-preserved frescoes and **Payathonzu** (p194), which also houses 13th-century murals.

Four Days

On day three many itineraries will see you heading out of the immediate Bagan area to **Salay** (p173), another area sprinkled with old temples and monasteries, and/or **Mt Popa** (p172), famous for its picturesque, *nat*- (spirit-)infested hilltop temple. Both places are interesting, but if you'd rather stay closer to Bagan, schedule visits to **Abeyadana Pahto** (p192) and **Nagayon** (p193) in Myinkaba and the frescoes in **Lawkahteikpan Pahto** (p190). Adventurous half-day boat trips can be made down or across the Ayeyarwady to more remote temples with the chance to sail back into town at sunset.

huge carved teak doors that separate interior halls from cross passages on all four sides.

Facing outward from the centre of the cube are four 31ft standing buddha statues. Only the Bagan-style images facing north and south are original; both display the *dhammachakka mudra* (a hand position symbolising the Buddha teaching his first sermon). The other two images are replacements for figures destroyed by fire in the 1600s. All four have bodies of solid teak, though guides may claim the southern image is made of a bronze alloy. Guides like to point out that if you stand by the donation box in front of the original southern buddha, his face looks sad, while from a distance he tends to look mirthful.

The western and eastern standing buddha images are done in the later Konbaung, or Mandalay, style. If looked at from the right angle, the two lions at the eastern side resemble an ogre. A small, nut-like sphere held between the thumb and middle finger of the east-facing image is said to resemble a herbal pill, and may represent the Buddha offering *dhamma* (Buddhist teachings) as a cure for suffering. Both arms hang at the image's sides with hands outstretched, a *mudra* (hand position) unknown to traditional Buddhist sculpture outside this temple.

The west-facing buddha features the *abhaya mudra* (the hands outstretched, in the gesture of no fear). At its feet sit two life-sized lacquer statues, said to represent

King Kyanzittha and Shin Arahan, the Mon monk who initiated Anawrahta into Theravada Buddhism. Inside the western portico are two symbols on pedestals of the buddha's footprints. Don't leave without taking a brief walk around the outside of the temple, where you can see many glazed tiles and lovely views of the spires and terraced roofs (often away from the hassle of vendors too).

In 1990, on its 900th anniversary, the temple spires were gilded. The remainder of the temple exterior is whitewashed from time to time.

It can feel more like a souvenir stand than a temple given the proliferation of peddlers outside selling books, postcards and oil paintings, but that shouldn't dissuade you from visiting. It's roughly 1600ft east of Thatbyinnyu, 1600ft north of Shwesandaw and 0.6 miles northwest of Dhammayangyi Pahto. Most visitors access it from the northern side, where the highest concentration of hawkers is. For a quieter approach, enter from the east side.

Ananda Ok Kyaung
BUDDHIST, CHAPEL

(အာနန္ဒာအုတ်ကျောင်း; Map p184) Just west of Ananda's northern entry, this small *vihara* (sanctuary or chapel) features some detailed 18th-century murals bursting with bright red and green, showing details of everyday life from the Bagan period. In the southeast corner, you can see a boat depicted with Portuguese figures engaged in trade. Built in 1137, the temple's name means 'Ananda Brick Monastery'. Ananda Ok Kyaung was one of many pagodas damaged in the 2016 earthquake.

Upali Thein
NOTABLE BUILDING

(ဥပါလိသိမ်; Map p184) Just north of the Bagan–Nyaung U Rd, almost midway to Nyaung U, this squat mid-13th-century ordination hall houses some brightly painted frescoes depicting big scenes on the walls and ceilings from the late 17th or early 18th century. Sadly, many pieces crumbled in the 1975 earthquake.

The building, named for a well-known monk from the 13th century, is often locked to protect the art, but you can see in (a bit) from the three gated doorways if the keyholder isn't around. The roof battlements imitate Myanmar wooden architecture, and a small centre spire rises from the rooftop.

Htilominlo Pahto
BUDDHIST TEMPLE

(ထီးလိုမင်းလိုပုထိုး; Map p184) This 150ft-high temple (built in 1218) marks the spot where King Nantaungmya was chosen (by a leaning umbrella, that timeless decider), among five brothers, to be the crown prince. It's more impressive from the outside, with its terraced design, which is similar to Sulamani Pahto (p190). Unfortunately, it's vendor central. Htilominlo Pahto suffered significant damage during the 2016 earthquake.

Have a walk around the 140-sq-ft base to take in the fragments of the original fine plaster carvings, glazed sandstone decorations and nicely carved reliefs on the doorways. Inside are four buddhas on the lower and upper floors, though the stairways are closed. Traces of old murals are also still visible.

Buledi
BUDDHIST TEMPLE

(ဗူးလယ်သိး; Map p184) Great for its views, this steep-stepped, pyramid-style stupa looks ho-hum from afar, but the narrow terrace has become something of an alternative sunset spot. It's about 2000ft south of Htilominlo, across Anawrahta Rd. It's also known as Temple 394 (not correctly labelled on some maps). Unfortunately, Buledi was one of many temples in Bagan badly damaged in the 2016 quake, and remains closed for the interim. If persistent vendors are buzzing around, try the miniature version, **Temple 405**, with several glazed tiles visible, just east of Buledi.

Gubyaukgne
BUDDHIST TEMPLE

(ဂူပြောက်ငယ်; Map p184) Off Anawrahta Rd, almost a mile east of Htilominlo, this early-Bagan-period temple has some excellent stucco carvings on the outside walls (particularly on the north side) and some original paintings visible inside.

Wetkyi-In-Gubyaukgyi
BUDDHIST TEMPLE

(ဝက်ကြီးအင်းဂူပြောက်ကြီး; Map p184) Just west of Nyaung U and about 330ft east of Gubyaukgne, this detailed off-the-main-circuit, 13th-century temple has an Indian-style spire, like the Mahabodhi Paya (p187) in Old Bagan. It's interesting for fine frescoes of scenes from the Jataka but, unfortunately, in 1899 a German collector surreptitiously removed many of the panels on which the frescoes were painted. Those that remain in the entry are in great shape. Steps inside lead to four buddha images and you can see Hindu figures engraved on the spire.

Central Plain

Extending from the edge of Old Bagan, this vast and lovely plain (roughly south of Anawrahta Rd between New Bagan and Nyaung U) is home to a few must-see temples that everyone visits (Shwesandaw Paya and Dhammayangyi Pahto) and many pockets of temples that few ever see. It's a great place to follow your own whims. You'll find goatherds and some village life out here, but no restaurants or lunch options. Some temples are locked but a 'keyholder' should be in the area.

Shwesandaw Paya BUDDHIST TEMPLE

(ရွှေဆံတော်ဘုရား; Map p184) Bagan's most famous sunset-viewing spot, the Shwesandaw is a graceful white pyramid-style pagoda with steps leading past five terraces to the circular stupa top, with good 360-degree views. It's located roughly midway between Thatbyinnyu and Dhammayangyi. Its top terrace is roomy, which is just as well, considering the numbers of camera-toting travellers coming by taxi or bus before sunset. If you go during the day, you'll likely be alone, making it a good spot for temple panoramas.

Shwesandaw means 'golden holy hair': legend has it that the stupa enshrines a Buddha hair relic presented to King Anawrahta by the King of Ussa Bago (Pegu) in thanks for his assistance in repelling an invasion by the Khmers. The terraces once bore terracotta plaques showing scenes from the Jataka, but traces of these, and of other sculptures, were covered by rather heavy-handed renovations. The now-gilded *zedi* bell rises from two octagonal bases, which top the five square terraces. This was the first Bagan monument to feature stairways leading from the square terraces to the round base of the stupa.

The *hti*, which was toppled by the 1975 earthquake, can still be seen lying on the south side of the paya compound. A new one was fitted soon after the quake.

About 500ft north stands **Lawkahteik-pan Pahto**, a small but interesting middle-period *gu* containing excellent frescoes and inscriptions in both Burmese and Mon.

★ Dhammayangyi Pahto BUDDHIST TEMPLE

(ဓမ္မရံကြီးပုထိုး; Map p184) Visible from all parts of Bagan, this massive, walled, 12th-century temple (about 1600ft east of Shwesandaw) is infamous for its mysterious, bricked-up inner passageways and cruel history. It's said that King Narathu built the temple to atone for his sins: he smothered his father and brother to death and executed one of his wives, an Indian princess, for practising Hindu rituals. The best preserved of Bagan's temples, it features detailed mortar work in its upper levels.

Narathu is also said to have mandated that the mortarless brickwork fit together so tightly that even a pin couldn't pass between any two bricks. Workers who failed in this task had their arms chopped off: just inside the west entrance, note the stones with arm-sized grooves where these amputations allegedly happened.

After Narathu died – by assassination in 1170 – the inner encircling ambulatory was filled with brick rubble, as 'payback'. Others quietly argue the temple dates from the earlier reign of Alaungsithu, which would refute this fun legend. It's also likely that this bricking up of the passages was a crude way of ensuring the massive structure didn't collapse.

The plan here is similar to Ananda Pahto, with projecting porticoes and receding terraces, though its *sikhara* (corn-cob-like temple finial) is reduced to a stub nowadays. Walking around the outer ambulatory, under ceilings so high you can only hear the squeaks of bats circling in the dark, you can see some intact stucco reliefs and paintings, suggesting the work had been completed. The mystery goes on.

Three out of the four buddha sanctums were also filled with bricks. The remaining western shrine features two original side-by-side images of Gautama and Maitreya, the historical and future buddhas (it's the only Bagan site with two side-by-side buddhas).

The temple's bad karma may be the reason it remains one of the few temples not to have undergone major restoration. Perhaps in time, one of the great architectural mysteries of Bagan will be solved.

Sulamani Pahto BUDDHIST TEMPLE

(စူဠာမဏိပုထိုး; Map p184) This temple with five doorways is known as the Crowning Jewel and was constructed around 1181 by Narapatisithu. It is one of Bagan's most attractive temples, with lush grounds (and ample vendors) behind the surrounding walls. It's a prime example of later, more sophisticated temple styles, with better internal lighting. Sulamani suffered significant damage during the 2016 earthquake and is likely to remain closed through at least 2017.

Combining the early period's horizontal planes with the vertical lines of the middle period, the receding terraces create a pyramid effect. The stairways to the top are closed.

The brickwork throughout is considered some of the best in Bagan. The gilded *sikhara* is a reconstruction; the original was destroyed in the 1975 earthquake. The

ⓘ KEYHOLDERS & SOUVENIR HAWKERS

Major temples that remain active places of worship such as Ananda Pahto and Shwezigon Paya are always open during the day. For many others you must first find the 'keyholder' who is the caretaker of the site. Often they (or their kids) will find you first and open the gate for you. A bit of 'tea money' (say K500) is appreciated. We're told that the keyholders are assigned by the archaeology department.

The other constant of Bagan temples – even relatively remote ones – are souvenir hawkers, often selling (and sometimes creating) colourful sand paintings. Some of these replicate parts of the murals from inside the temples and are quite skilful, with prices starting as low as K1000 for smaller canvases, but rising sharply for more detailed and larger works; other images are pretty generic and found across all temple sites. Although some hawkers can be persistent, if you're not interested in buying, most will leave you alone.

We're told that official souvenir hawkers at the temples pay a sizeable licence fee, but it's likely that there are many more unofficial vendors, given the potential for relatively easy money. Compared to often arduous work on a farm, selling souvenirs seems like an easy job to some. Unfortunately, a growing number of children in Bagan are quitting school in order to work as hawkers.

interior face of the wall was once lined with 100 monastic cells, a feature unique among Bagan's ancient monasteries.

There's much to see inside. Carved stucco on mouldings, pediments and pilasters represent some of Bagan's finest ornamental work and is in fairly good condition. Glazed plaques around the base and terraces are also still visible, as are many big and small murals.

Buddha images face the four directions from the ground floor; the image at the eastern entrance sits in a recess built into the wall. The interior passage around the base is painted with quite big frescoes from the Konbaung period, and there are traces of earlier frescoes.

Thabeik Hmauk BUDDHIST TEMPLE
(သပိတ်မှောက်; Map p184) Facing Sulamani (p190) from the east, and well worth visiting, this *sikhara*-topped temple looks like a miniature version of its more famous neighbour, but sees far fewer visitors (or vendors). Thabeik Hmauk means 'Boycott Temple', as it was made in response to the similarly designed Sulamani, which was ordered by the brutal king Narapatisithu. Much of its interior was damaged by the 1975 earthquake, but there are multiple stairways up to a wraparound meditation chamber with little light.

There are two outside terraces, reached by narrow stairs, with superb views.

Pyathada Paya BUDDHIST TEMPLE
(ပြသာဒါးဘုရား; Map p184) Dating from the 13th century, during the latter period of temple building at Bagan, this huge, impressive pagoda is a superb sunset-viewing spot, with a giant open terrace (Bagan's largest) atop the steps, and another small deck further

up. Pyathada Paya suffered serious damage in the 2016 earthquake and is currently not open to visitors.

Pyathada's interior arches are still partly open to view. The architects used an inner relieving arch and a second upper arch to support the huge chambers, illustrating the point that temple styles changed in Bagan because the builders improved at arch construction. Note how the top stupa isn't centred on the top platform.

The tour groups have discovered it so you're unlikely to have the place to yourself. It is about half a mile southeast of Sulamani, reached by dirt roads that sometimes get obscured in goat fields.

Myinkaba Area

The sites north and south of Myinkaba village are all just off the main road.

Mingalazedi Paya BUDDHIST TEMPLE
(မင်္ဂလာစေတီဘုရား; Map p184) Close to the riverbank, towards Myinkaba from Old Bagan, Mingalazedi Paya (Blessing Stupa) represents the final flowering of Bagan's architectural outburst, as displayed in its enormous bell-like dome and the beautiful glazed Jataka tiles around each terrace. Although many of the 1061 original tiles have been damaged or stolen, there are still 561 left (in various states of decay). The smaller square building in the *zedi* grounds is one of the few Tripitaka libraries made of brick.

Gubyaukgyi BUDDHIST TEMPLE
(ဂူပြောက်ကြီး; Map p184) Just to the left of the road as you enter Myinkaba, Gubyaukgyi

ⓘ TOP PRACTICAL TIPS

Here are our top practical tips for successfully navigating the temples of Bagan:

➡ Wear sandals, they are much easier to take off at the temples.

➡ Bring a hat to wear when cycling between temple groups, but remember to remove it when entering temple compounds.

➡ Women should cover up to elbows and knees, as these are active religious temples and Bagan is a conservative region.

➡ Drink plenty of water, Bagan is one of the hottest places in the country and dehydration occurs easily.

➡ If on a fleeting visit, take lunch around Old Bagan to maximise time at the temples.

➡ If hiring an e-bike (p157), be careful on the dusty, sandy paths. It's easy to lose control and take a spill.

(Great Painted Cave Temple) sees a lot of visitors who are drawn by the well-preserved, richly coloured paintings inside. These are thought to date from the temple's original construction in 1113, when Kyanzittha's son Rajakumar built it following his father's death. In Indian style, the monument consists of a large vestibule attached to a smaller antechamber. The fine stucco-work on its exterior walls is in particularly good condition. Perforated, Pyu-style windows mean you'll need a powerful torch to see the ceiling paintings clearly. If it's locked during off-season, ask in the village for the keyholder.

Next to the monument stands the gilded **Myazedi** (Emerald Stupa). A four-sided pillar in a cage between the two monuments bears an inscription consecrating Gubyaukgyi and written in four languages – Pyu, Mon, Old Burmese and Pali. It has great linguistic and historical significance – it establishes the Pyu as an important cultural influence in early Bagan and relates the chronology of the Bagan kings, as well as acting as a 'Rosetta Stone' to allow scholars to decipher the Pyu.

Manuha Paya
BUDDHIST TEMPLE

(မနုဟာဘုရား; Map p184) In Myinkaba village stands this active and rather modern-looking pagoda (although it dates from 1059). It is named after Manuha, the Mon king from

Thaton, who was held captive here by King Anawrahta. In the front of the building are three seated buddhas; in the back is a huge reclining buddha. All seem too large for their enclosures – supposedly representing the stress and discomfort the king had to endure.

It is said that only the reclining buddha, in the act of entering *parinibbana* (final passing away), has a smile on its face, showing that for Manuha, only death was a release from his suffering. But if you climb to the top of this paya via the stairs in the back (ask for keys if it's locked), you can see the face of the sitting buddha through a window – from up here you'll realise that the gigantic face, so grim from below, has an equally gigantic smile.

Nan Paya
BUDDHIST TEMPLE

(နန်းဘုရား; Map p184) Just south of Manuha Paya by dirt road, this shrine is said to have been used as Manuha's prison, although there is little evidence supporting the legend. In this story the shrine was originally Hindu, and captors thought using it as a prison would be easier than converting it to a Buddhist temple. It's worth visiting for its interior masonry work – sandstone block facings over a brick core, certainly some of Bagan's finest detailed sculpture.

Perforated stone windows are typical of earlier Bagan architecture – in fact it was probably Bagan's first *gu*-style shrine. In the central sanctuary the four stone pillars have finely carved sandstone bas-relief figures of three-faced Brahma. The creator deity is holding lotus flowers, thought to be offerings to a freestanding buddha image once situated in the shrine's centre, a theory that dispels the idea that this was ever a Hindu shrine. The sides of the pillars feature ogre-like heads with open mouths streaming with flowers. Legend goes that Shiva employed these creatures of Hindu legend to protect temples, but they proved too ferocious so Shiva tricked them into eating their bodies, then fed them flowers to keep their minds off snacking on worshippers. In the centre of the four pillars is an altar on which once stood a standing buddha or (some locals believe) a Hindu god. Ask at Manuha if the temple is locked.

Abeyadana Pahto
BUDDHIST TEMPLE

(အဘိပါယျရတနာပုထိုး; Map p184) About 1300ft south of Manuha Paya, this 11th-century temple with a Sinhalese-style stupa was supposedly built by Kyanzittha's Bengali wife Abeyadana, who waited for him here as he hid for his life from his predecessor King Sawlu. It's famed for its original frescoes, which were cleaned in 1987 by Unesco staff. Ask at the caretaker's house to the south if the temple is locked.

With a torch, you can make out many figures that Abeyadana, believed to be a Mahayanist, would likely have asked for: Bodhisattvas such as Avalokitesvara, and Hindu deities Brahma, Vishnu, Shiva and Indra. The inner shrine contains a large, brick, seated buddha (partly restored); surrounding walls are lined with niches, most now empty. Inside the front wall are many Jataka scenes.

Some visitors enjoy the sunset at the often-overlooked Kyasin across the road.

Nagayon
BUDDHIST TEMPLE

(နဂါးရုံ; Map p184) Slightly south of Abeyadana (p192) and across the road, this elegant and well-preserved temple was built by Kyanzittha. The main buddha image is twice life-size and shelters under the hood of a huge *naga* (dragon serpent). This reflects the legend that in 1192 Kyanzittha built the temple on the spot where he was sheltered while fleeing from his angry brother and predecessor Sawlu, an activity he had to indulge in on more than one occasion.

Paintings also decorate the corridor walls. The central shrine has two smaller standing buddhas as well as the large one. The temple itself – with corn-cob *sikhara,* which some believe to be the Ananda prototype – can be climbed via tight stairs.

Somingyi Kyaung
BUDDHIST TEMPLE

(စိုးမင်းကြီးအုတ်ကျောင်း; Map p184) Named after the woman who supposedly sponsored its construction, this typical late-Bagan brick monastery (about 650ft southwest of Nagayon) is thought to have been built in 1204. A *zedi* to the north and *gu* to the south are also ascribed to Somingyi. Many brick monasteries in Bagan were single-block structures; Somingyi is unique in that it has monastic cells clustered around a courtyard.

New Bagan Area

Sights are a little scarcer heading south of New Bagan.

Lawkananda Paya
BUDDHIST TEMPLE

(လောကနန္ဒာဘုရား; Map p184) At the height of Bagan's power, boats from the Mon region, Rakhine (Arakan) and even Sri Lanka would anchor by this riverside pagoda (about 820ft southeast of the New Bagan crossroads; a sign in Burmese points the way) with its distinctive elongated cylindrical dome. Built in 1059 by Anawrahta, it is still used as a place of worship and is thought to house an important Buddha tooth replica. Lawkananda Paya was one of numerous temples damaged during the 2016 earthquake.

There are lots of benches for wide-open views of the Ayeyarwady, but it's sometimes hard to enjoy hassle-free.

Ashe (East) Petleik Paya
BUDDHIST TEMPLE

(အရှေ့ပလိပ်ဘုရား; Map p184) A short stroll northeast of Lawkananda Paya, this 11th-century temple is best known for the many terracotta Jataka lining the interior.

Anauk (West) Petleik Paya
BUDDHIST TEMPLE

(အနောက်ပလိပ်ဘုရား; Map p184) Just inland to the northeast from Lawkananda Paya lie the excavated remains of this 11th-century paya, and its twin, Ashe Petleik Paya. Found in 1905, the lower parts of the pagodas are hohum from the outside but feature hundreds of terracotta Jataka lining the vaulted corridors (particularly impressive in Anauk Petleik Paya). A keyholder usually appears to unlock the door and turn on the fluorescent lights.

Sittana Paya
BUDDHIST TEMPLE

(စစ်တနာဘုရား) About half a mile south of New Bagan, this large, 13th-century, bell-shaped stupa is one of the most impressive structures in the area. Built by Htilominlo, and showing some Hindu influences, it's set on four square terraces, each fronted by a standing buddha image in brick and stucco. A rather rickety stairway leads up the stupa's southern side to the terraces, where you can circle the structure. At the southwestern corner is a closed-off chamber leading into an inner sanctum.

Eight-Faces Paya
BUDDHIST TEMPLE

(ရှစ်မျက်နှာဘုရား; Map p184; Khayea St) On the main road, this small pagoda makes a handy landmark when navigating New Bagan. It's lit up at night, and best seen from one of the handful of restaurants on its north side.

South Plain

This rural area, along Bagan's southern reaches, follows the main road between New Bagan and Nyaung U Airport, passing Pwasaw and Minnanthu villages on the way. Other than a few places, such as Payathonzu, most sights have few tourists. Many horse-cart drivers will take in the cluster of sights north of Minnanthu and go via dirt paths towards Central Plain sights, such as

Sulamani Pahto. If you want to see the sheer scope of the site, the views west from some of the temples here rival any other in Bagan.

Dhammayazika Paya
BUDDHIST TEMPLE

(ဓမ္မရာဇိကဘုရား; Map p184) Sitting in lush garden grounds with a gilded bell, the Dhammayazika dates from 1196. Set in the south-central end of Bagan on the main road, it also has lovely views from its highest terrace. The pentagonal *zedi* is similar to the Shwezigon (p195) but with a more unusual design. An outer wall has five gateways. Dhammayazika Paya suffered serious damage during the 2016 earthquake, and currently remains closed to visitors through at least 2017.

Up top, five small temples, each containing a buddha image, encircle the terraces; some bear interior murals added during the Konbaung era. Watch out for ghosts here! Supposedly the stupa's construction began under a general who died before its completion. His likeness is said to appear in many photos of the site, including a fairly recent one of government officials. It's possible, with perseverance, to cycle (or motorbike) the thrilling dirt roads here from Dhammayangyi Pahto (p190), a mile north.

Leimyethna Pahto
BUDDHIST TEMPLE

(လေးမျက်နှာဘုရား; Map p184) Built in 1222, this east-facing, whitewashed temple near Minnanthu village (a couple of klicks east of Dhammayazika on the north side of the road) stands on a raised platform and has interior walls decorated with well-preserved frescoes. It is topped by a gilded Indian-style spire like that on Ananda Pahto. The jar-like structures out the front were pillars of a building toppled by the 1975 earthquake.

Tayok Pye Paya
BUDDHIST TEMPLE

(တရုတ်ပြေးဘုရား; Map p184) A couple of hundred yards north of Leimyethna by dirt road, this spired temple gets attention for the views from its upper reaches, although the top level is now closed.

Payathonzu
BUDDHIST TEMPLE

(ဘုရားသုံးဆူ; Map p184) Across the main road from Tayok, this complex of three interconnected shrines (the name means Three Stupas) is worth seeing for its 13th-century murals. It was abandoned shortly before construction was completed. Each square cubicle is topped by a fat *sikhara;* a similar structure appears only at Salay. The design is remarkably like Khmer Buddhist ruins in Thailand. Enter through the middle shrine. To the

right (south) are scratched-up, whitewashed walls. The other two shrines (particularly the northernmost one) are home to lovely, vaguely Chinese- or Tibetan-looking mural paintings that contain Bodhisattva figures. Whether these indicate possible Mahayana or Tantric influence is a hotly debated issue among art historians. Some drawings are rather crudely touched up.

The three-shrine design hints at links with the Hindu Trimurti (triad) of Vishnu, Shiva and Brahma, a triumvirate also associated with Tantric Buddhism. You might also say it represents the Triple Gems of Buddhism (buddha, *dhamma* and *sangha*), except that such a design is uncommon in Asian Buddhist architecture, although it does appear in the Hindu shrines of India and Nepal.

Thambula Pahto
BUDDHIST TEMPLE

(သမ္ဘူလပုထိုး; Map p184) This square temple, surrounded by crumbling walls just north of Payathonzu, is decorated with faded Jataka frescoes and was built in 1255 by Thambula, the wife of King Uzana. It's often locked, but go to the doors (shaded at midday) and peek through the gate to see wall and ceiling murals. A mural of a boat race can be seen from the southern entrance; good ceiling murals are seen from the north side.

TEMPLE FESTIVALS

The following are Bagan's major temple festivals or *paya pwe*, listed in order of their celebration through the year. At all of them, expect religious chanting around the clock, religious-paraphernalia stalls and music and drama performances.

Manuha Paya (⊘ Feb/Mar) The Manuha Paya (p192) temple festival is held on the full moon of Tabaung.

Gawdawpalin Pahto (⊘ Sep/Oct) The Gawdawpalin Pahto (p183) temple festival is celebrated on the full moon of Thadingyut.

Shwezigon Paya (⊘ Oct/Nov) The Shwezigon Paya (p195) temple festival is celebrated on the full moon of Tazaungmon.

Ananda Pahto (⊘ Dec/Jan) This roughly two-week event culminates on the full moon of Pyatho. It's Bagan's biggest festival, when hundreds of monks come to collect alms from thousands of merit-seeking locals.

THREE TEMPLES BY THE AYEYARWADY

From Nyaung U's jetty you can negotiate a fun boat trip to see three temples just off the Ayeyarwady riverbank. Half a mile north is 13th-century **Thetkyamuni**, with a few murals inside (hard to make out) and tight, dark steps leading to a small terrace up top. On the hill nearby is the same-era **Kondawgyi Pahto**, with better-preserved murals and views from the surrounding platform.

Another half a mile or so north is the 11th- and 12th-century **Kyauk Gu Ohnmin** cave temple, built in the side of a ravine. It's said that during WWII Japanese soldiers hid here. The inside tunnels lead about 160ft to blocked-off rubble. Some locals say the tunnel was intended to go, ahem, to Pindaya Cave near Inle Lake. You can climb on top of the temple from the new steps to the right. These sights are accessible, with more difficulty, by road. A boat trip takes about two or three hours, and the driver will show you the temples. It costs about K20,000 for three or four people.

Nandamannya Pahto BUDDHIST TEMPLE
(နန္ဒပညာပုထိုး; Map p184) Dating from the mid-13th century, this small, single-chambered temple has fine frescoes and a ruined seated buddha image. It's about 650ft north of Thambula; a sign leads down a short dirt road. The murals' similarity with those at Payathonzu has led some art historians to suggest they were painted by the same hand.

Nandamannya earns its reputation from its mural of the 'Temptation of Mara', in which nubile young females (vainly) attempt to distract the Buddha from the meditation session that led to his enlightenment. The undressed nature of the females shocked French epigraphist Charles Duroiselle, who wrote in 1916 that they were 'so vulgarly erotic and revolting that they can neither be reproduced or described'. Times change: the topless women can be seen, without blushing, on the back left wall. Just behind the temple is the Kyat Kan Kyaung, a working underground monastery dating from the 11th century. Mats on the tunnel floors are used for meditation.

Kyat Kan Kyaung BUDDHIST TEMPLE
(ကြက်ကန်ကျောင်း; Map p184) This working underground monastery dates from the 11th century. Bring a torch to walk along the cavern-like corridors and see the small chambers where the monks still sleep and pray.

Nyaung U Area

Shwezigon Paya BUDDHIST TEMPLE
(ရွှေစည်းခုံဘုရား; Map p184) At the west end of Nyaung U, this big, beautiful *zedi* is the town's main religious site, and is most famous for its link with the 37 *nat*. Lit up impressively at dusk, the gilded *zedi* sits on three rising terraces. Enamelled plaques in panels around the base of the *zedi* illustrate scenes from the Jataka. At the cardinal points, facing the terrace stairways, are four shrines, each of which houses a 13ft-high bronze standing buddha.

Gupta-inspired and cast in 1102, these are Bagan's largest surviving bronze buddhas.

A 4in circular indentation in a stone slab, before the upwards-heading eastern steps, was filled with water to allow former Myanmar monarchs to look at the reflection of the *hti* without tipping their heads backwards (which might have caused them to lose their crowns).

The most important site here is the small yellow compound called 37 Nat (in English) on the southeast side of the site. Inside are figures of the 37 pre-Buddhist *nat* that were officially endorsed by the Bamar monarchy in a compromising gesture towards a public reluctant to give up all their beliefs for Buddhism. Ask around if the compound is locked. At one end (behind a locked gate) stands an original teak figure of Thagyamin, king of the *nat* and a direct appropriation of the Hindu god Indra. This is the oldest-known free-standing Thagyamin figure in Myanmar.

The site was started by Anawrahta but not completed until the reign of Kyanzittha. The latter is thought to have built his palace nearby.

Kyanzittha Umin BUDDHIST TEMPLE
(ကျန်စစ်သားဥမင်; Map p184) Although officially credited to Kyanzittha, this cave temple may actually date back to Anawrahta. Built into a cliff face 270yd southwest of Shwezigon, the long, dimly lit corridors are decorated with frescoes, some of which are thought to have been painted by Bagan's Tartar invaders during the Mongol occupation after 1287. An attendant will usually greet you with keys to unlock the doors. Bring a torch. It's very quiet in here and you can actually see the 700-year-old brush strokes.

Eastern Myanmar

Best Places to Eat

➡ Thu Maung Restaurant (p220)

➡ Sin Yaw Bamboo Restaurant (p204)

➡ Lin Htett Myanmar Traditional Food (p203)

➡ Live Dim Sum House (p203)

➡ Shwe Let Yar (p233)

Best Places to Sleep

➡ Inle Princess Resort (p210)

➡ Royal Kalaw Hills Resort (p220)

➡ Sanctum Inle Resort (p210)

➡ La Maison Birmane (p202)

➡ Song of Travel Hostel (p201)

Why Go?

Travellers to eastern Myanmar get the chance to experience both beautiful Inle Lake and some of the finest trekking in the country. Then there's the intriguing opportunity of getting right off the tourist trail in areas that see very few foreigners. While much of eastern Myanmar remains closed due to ongoing conflict, more and more places are opening up to visitors. Now, tiny Kayah State and its charming capital Loikaw have joined Shan State's Kyaingtong and its surrounding hill-peoples' villages as one of the least-visited but most rewarding destinations in Myanmar.

So whether you just want to kick back and glide across the placid waters of Inle Lake in a boat, or are up for hiking through remote villages in the region's back hills, eastern Myanmar is an essential stop.

When to Go
Eastern Myanmar

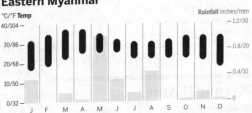

Nov–Jan During winter the daytime temperatures are a comfortable 68°F to 79°F (20°C to 26°C).	**Mar–May** Daytime temperatures can climb close to 104°F (40°C).	**Jun–Oct** If you can, avoid trekking during the rainy season.

INLE LAKE & AROUND

The Inle Lake region is one of Myanmar's most anticipated destinations and all the hype is justified. Picture a vast, serene lake – 13.5 miles long and seven miles wide – fringed by marshes and floating gardens, where stilt-house villages and Buddhist temples rise above the water, and Intha fisherfolk propel their boats along via their unique technique of leg-rowing. Surrounding the lake are hills that are home to myriad minorities: Shan, Pa-O, Taung Yo, Danu, Kayah and Danaw, who descend from their villages for markets that hopscotch around the towns of the region on a five-day cycle.

Nyaungshwe is the accommodation and transport hub of the region. It's a scrappy place, but once you've experienced the watery world that sits right by it and explored the environs of Inle Lake, that won't matter. Few people leave here disappointed with what they've seen and done.

ℹ Information

There is a compulsory K12,500 fee to enter the Inle Lake area, which you must pay on arrival at the **permit booth** (Map p200; ⊙ 6am-9pm) located by the bridge at the entrance to Nyaungshwe. Tickets are valid for one week, although you're unlikely to be asked to pay again if you stay longer.

ℹ Getting There & Away

By far the easiest way to reach the Inle Lake region is to fly. Most long-distance road transport finishes in Taunggyi – to reach Nyaungshwe, you'll have to change at the junction town of Shwenyaung on the highway between Taunggyi and Heho.

AIR

The main airport for the Inle region is at Heho, 25 miles northwest of Nyaungshwe on the way to Kalaw.

Airlines flying out of Heho include **Air Bagan** (☏ Heho 081-63324; www.airbagan.com), **Air KBZ** (☏ Heho 081-63331; www.airkbz.com), **Air Mandalay** (☏ Heho 081-63066; www.airmandalay.com), **Asian Wings** (☏ Heho 081-63327; www.asianwingsair.com) and **Yangon Airways** (☏ Heho 081-63339; www.yangonair.com). The airline offices are in Heho and/or Taunggyi, but several Nyaungshwe-based agents can sell tickets. The airlines have a spider-web-like network of flights across the country with some destinations only reachable via multiple stops; be sure to check if your flight is direct or not.

Taxis waiting at the airport charge K25,000 to Nyaungshwe (one hour). If you're pinching pennies and have the time, a cheaper but much, much less convenient option is to hike the mile to NH4 and wait for a pick-up truck or bus bound for Taunggyi (from K2000, 1½ hours); ask to be let off at Shwenyaung, from where you can charter a *thoun bein,* (motorcycle trishaw) to Nyaungshwe (K6000). You will most likely face a long wait.

Nyaungshwe ညောင်ရွှေ

POP C 80,000 (INCL INLE LAKE) / ☏ 081

Scruffy Nyaungshwe is the main access point for Inle Lake. Located at the north end of the lake, the town was once the capital of an important Shan kingdom (the former palace of the *saophas,* or sky princes, who ruled here is now a museum). These days, Nyaungshwe has become a bustling travellers' centre, with dozens of guesthouses and hotels, an increasing number of restaurants, a few bars and a pleasantly relaxed vibe. If Myanmar can be said to have a backpacker scene at all, it can be found here.

◎ Sights

There are stupas and monasteries all over Nyaungshwe. Most of the latter are clustered around the Mine Li Canal, southeast of the market.

Shwe Yaunghwe Kyaung   BUDDHIST TEMPLE

(ရွှေရောင်ဝဲကျောင်း; Nyaungshwe-Shwenyaung Rd; ⊙ daylight hours) FREE This is probably the most photographed monastery in Nyaungshwe: the unique oval windows in the ancient teak *thein* (ordination hall) create a perfect frame for portraits of the novices. The monastery is 1½ miles north of town on the road to Shwenyaung.

Yan Aung Nan Aung

Hsu Taung Pye Paya   BUDDHIST TEMPLE

(ရန်အောင်နန်အောင်ဆုတောင်းပြည့်ဘုရား; Map p208; Nanthe; ⊙ daylight hours) FREE In the village of Nanthe, this Buddhist temple complex features a 26ft-high sitting buddha surrounded by stucco *deva* (celestial beings) and *chinthe* (half-lion, half-dragon guardians). Although heavily restored, the statue is said to be more than 700 years old. Nanthe is just south of Nyaungshwe.

Yadana Man Aung Paya   BUDDHIST TEMPLE

(ရတနာမာန်အောင်ဘုရား; Map p200; Phoung Taw Site St; ⊙ daylight hours) FREE The oldest and most important Buddhist shrine in Nyaungshwe, this handsome gilded stupa is hidden away inside a square compound south of the Mingala Market. The stepped stupa is unique in Myanmar, and the surrounding

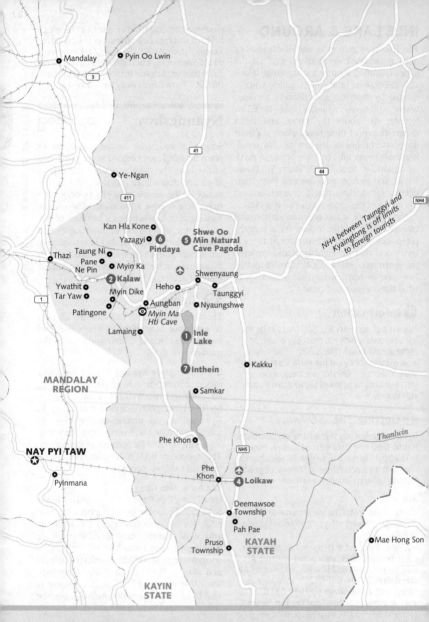

Eastern Myanmar Highlights

1 **Inle Lake** (p206) Drifting around the backwaters, markets, ruined stupas and monasteries of this huge lake.

2 **Kalaw** (p217) Basing yourself in this temperate former hill station and trekking to surrounding villages, or all the way to Inle Lake or Pindaya.

3 **Kyaingtong** (p223) Coming face-to-face with Tai and traditional hill-peoples cultures in this attractive and little-seen city in eastern Shan State.

4 **Loikaw** (p229) Being one of the few independent travellers to visit the atmospheric capital of tiny Kayah State.

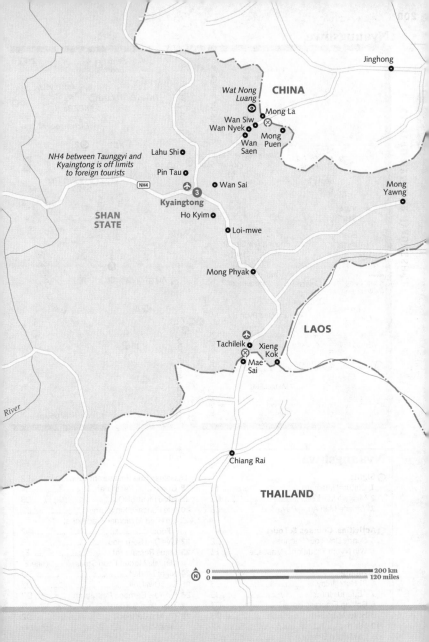

Jinghong

CHINA

Wat Nong Luang

Mong La

Wan Siw
Wan Nyek

Mong Puen

Wan Saen

Lahu Shi

Pin Tau

NH4 between Taunggyi and Kyaingtong is off limits to foreign tourists

NH4

Wan Sai

❸
Kyaingtong

SHAN STATE

Ho Kyim

Loi-mwe

Mong Yawng

Mong Phyak

LAOS

Tachileik

Xieng Kok

Mae Sai

Chiang Rai

THAILAND

0 — 200 km
0 — 120 miles

❺ **Shwe Oo Min Natural Cave Pagoda** (p215) Gazing at the more than 8000 golden buddhas that cover nearly every inch of this temple.

❻ **Pindaya** (p215) Taking the path less travelled and hiking through the tea-tree-studded hills surrounding this town.

❼ **Inthein** (p206) Visiting the five-day rotating market here, or at its other locations around Inle Lake, to pick up unique souvenirs, and perhaps some unique photos.

Nyaungshwe

Nyaungshwe

◉ Sights

◉ Activities, Courses & Tours

◉ Sleeping

◉ Eating

◉ Drinking & Nightlife

◉ Entertainment

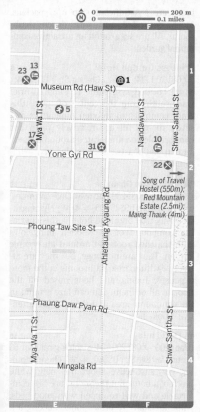

pavilion contains a museum of treasures amassed by the monks over the centuries, including carvings, lacquerware and dance costumes.

Cultural Museum MUSEUM
(ယဉ်ကျေးမှုပြတိုက်; Map p200; Museum Rd (Haw St); K2000; ☺10am-4pm Tue-Sun) This equal parts imposing and melancholy structure is the former *haw* (palace) of the last *saopha* (sky prince) of Nyaungshwe, Sao Shwe Thaike, who also served as the first president of independent Burma. Today, the mostly empty building holds a few dusty displays and is worth visiting more for the stately brick-and-teak structure itself than any educational summary of Shan culture or history.

Mingala Market MARKET
(မင်္ဂလာဈေး; Map p200; Yone Gyi Rd; ☺5am-2pm) At the entrance to town, this busy market is packed with locals every morning, when traders from the lake bring in fresh fish and produce from the floating gardens. The market doubles in size when it hosts the five-day rotating market.

Red Mountain Estate WINERY
(ရက်ဒ်မောင်တိန့်ဝိုင်ခြံ; Map p208; ☎081-209 366; www.redmountain-estate.com; ☺9am-6pm) **FREE** This winery, located in a valley within cycling distance from Nyaungshwe, is open daily for tastings (K3000 for four wines). For many visitors, the views from here are better than the wine.

🏃 Activities

Boat trips (p207) on Inle Lake are the most popular activity here and almost every visitor takes one. Boats set off from several locations along Nan Chaung canal: there's one **jetty** (Map p200) near Teik Nan Bridge, another **jetty** (Map p200) near the western end of Phoung Taw Site St and a third **jetty** (Map p200) at the western end of Phaung Daw Pyan Rd.

Win Nyunt Traditional Massage MASSAGE
(Map p200; off Mya Wa Ti St; massage per hr K7000; ☺9am-8pm) Traditional Myanmar massage to ease aching muscles after a boat trip or a trek.

Sunny Day Tour Services TREKKING
(Map p200; ☎09 4283 72118; htwe.sunny@yahoo.com; cnr Lan Ma Taw St & Yone Gyi Rd; ☺7am-8pm) Reliable, recommended guides for treks around Inle Lake and to Kalaw.

🛌 Sleeping

Nyaungshwe has an increasing number of hotels and guesthouses, spanning everything from budget accommodation, to boutique places, via many anonymous mid-range options. Despite that, finding a bed can be hard during peak season (December to March), so be sure to book in advance, otherwise you could end up sleeping on the floor of one of the town's monasteries.

Like elsewhere in Myanmar, prices have jumped in recent years and many of Nyaungshwe's rooms aren't great value, though discounts are normally available outside of high season.

Almost all rooms have bathrooms with hot showers, but few places offer air-con because of the natural cooling effect of the breeze passing over the lake. Like most of Myanmar, all room rates include breakfast.

★ Song of Travel Hostel HOSTEL $
(☎081-209 731; www.songoftravel.com; Aung Chan Tha 5 St; dm US$13; ❄🤚) Nyaungshwe's only

hostel is brand new and artfully designed with a large roof terrace and a big communal area. There are no private rooms, only identical 14-bed dorms named after Myanmar's states. Dorms aren't huge, but they are light and have lockers, while the communal bathrooms are clean. It's a 20-minute walk to the centre of town, but free bikes are available.

The hostel holds daily events – Burmese language classes, movie nights, group dinners – and can arrange boat trips and treks.

Hotel Maineli
HOTEL $

(Map p200; ☑ 081-209 9589; www.hotelmaineli. com; 66 Maine Li Quarter; r US$35-60; �](✎) Impressive newcomer with very big, well-equipped rooms with comfy beds and decent bathrooms. Professional staff and a peaceful location in a residential area.

Golden Empress Hotel
GUESTHOUSE $

(Map p200; ☑ 081-209 037; goldenempresshotel@ gmail.com; 19 Phaung Daw Pyan Rd; r US$40-45; ✻ @ ✎) An expansive house looked after by friendly owners, the 13 rooms at this place, attractively decked out with blonde wood panelling, are reminiscent of a ski lodge. All come with air-con. The nine upstairs rooms are more expensive and have bigger bathrooms, more natural light and balconies. Book ahead.

Inle Inn
HOTEL $

(Map p200; ☑ 081-209 016; inleinns@gmail.com; Yone Gyi Rd; r US$35-45; ✻ ✎) Newly upgraded, attractive rooms off a courtyard filled with potted plants, and a fine breakfast, are the drawcards here. The cheaper rooms are fan-only; the pricier rooms have more modern fittings and bathrooms, as well as better beds and air-con. The wi-fi connection is strong throughout.

Nawng Kham – Little Inn
GUESTHOUSE $

(Map p200; ☑ 081-209 195; noanhom@gmail.com; Phaung Daw Pyan Rd; r US$15-42; ✻ ✎) The seven fan-only rooms here go quick, but the more expensive rooms with air-con are almost as good a deal. All look out on a pleasant garden. There's a small communal area and the staff are helpful.

Aquarius Inn
GUESTHOUSE $

(Map p200; ☑ 081-209 352; aquarius352@gmail. com; 2 Phaung Daw Pyan Rd; r US$20-50; ✻ ✎) The cheapest rooms at this family-run place are old school, fan-only and share bathrooms. The more expensive ones in the new block are a significant step up: spacious, nicely decorated and with decent bathrooms. All are set around an attractive communal garden.

Princess Garden Hotel
HOTEL $

(☑ 081-209 214; Mine Li Chaung St; r US$25-45; ✎ ✺) Located near Mine Li Canal, a brief walk south from the centre of town, this place combines 15 wooden bungalows and seven rooms. All are relatively plain but comfortable and are located around a shady garden that boasts a reasonable-sized swimming pool.

★ La Maison Birmane
HOTEL $$

(Map p200; ☑ 081-209 901; www.lamaisonbirmane. com; bungalows US$75-105; ✻ @ ✎) Nyaungshwe's only true boutique hotel is this charming compound of 10 wooden bungalows with thatched roofs set around an organic garden. They are not huge, but they are attractive with marble bathrooms in the more expensive rooms, and beds raised off the floor in all of them. You can laze around in the communal area and the staff are attentive. Book ahead.

81 Hotel Inlay
HOTEL $$

(Map p200; ☑ 081-209 904; 81hotel@gmail.com; 56 Phaung Taw Site St; r US$60; ✻ ✎) There's nothing very distinctive about this new, white block of a hotel. But the rooms are big, comfortable and well equipped with good beds, while the staff are professional, making it a decent midrange option.

Paradise Hotel
HOTEL $$

(Map p200; ☑ 081-209 321; www.inleparadise.com; Mya Wa Ti St; r US$65-70; ✻ ✎) Newly relocated, the Paradise is a pretty good midrange choice offering a peaceful location and vibe. Rooms in the main block are modern and well equipped with balconies overlooking a nicely tended garden. The bungalows are bigger and are spread out around the garden.

Viewpoint
HOTEL $$$

(Map p200; ☑ 081-209 062; www.inleviewpoint. com; Yone Gyi Rd; r US$185; @ ✎) Behind the restaurant of the same name are 21 duplex bungalows elevated over the water. Rooms are smart and light, with lots of windows and huge balconies, and all look west to catch the sunset. An eco theme means the rooms utilise natural materials and include interesting quirks such as a Shan-style wooden 'refrigerator'. There's an attached spa and efficient staff.

INLE LAKE'S FIVE-DAY MARKET

A rustic market rotates among several cities and towns in the Inle Lake region. The most touted of these is the so-called floating market at Ywama, but this has become quite touristy in recent years, and the land-based options, where the minorities of the area come down from the hills to trade livestock and produce, are generally much more interesting and 'authentic'.

Towns host the market once every five days; hotels and guesthouses can advise you where the market will be heading next. Keep in mind that markets are not held on full-moon days.

Heho, Thandaung, Thaung Thut Thandaung's market is small and off the beaten track, accessible only via a brief walk from the lakeshore; larger but still rustic is the market at Thaung Thut, located at the far southern end of Inle Lake.

Taunggyi, Floating Market (Ywama) The 'Floating Market' at Ywama has emerged to become the most touristy of the circuit – consider heading elsewhere.

Maing Thauk, Kyauk Taing, Phaung Daw Oo Paya Maing Thauk is close to Nyaung-shwe and reachable by land or boat; while just an hour's bike ride from Nyaungshwe, Khaung Daing's market sees many tourists. The Kyauk Taing market, located at the far southern end of Inle Lake, is largely off the tourist circuit.

Shwenyaung, Khaung Daing, Kalaw, Hmaw Be, Inthein Although Inthein is popular among tourists, it's still worth a visit for its sheer size and photogenic setting; Kalaw's normally tidy market spills over to the streets on market day; Hmaw Be's market, south of Inle Lake, is small but rustic and untouristed. Scrappy Shwenyaung has its own busy market, although it's not of huge interest for visitors.

Nyaungshwe, Pindaya, Nampan On market day Nyaungshwe's normally sleepy market swells to several times its normal size; less-visited Pindaya's central market also bursts at its seams as vendors and buyers come down from the surrounding hills. Nampan's market is extremely photogenic, with vendors in boats, but is also overrun with foreign visitors.

✗ Eating

The restaurant scene in Nyaungshwe is improving, with some Western options joining the Burmese, Chinese and Shan places that dominate. For cheap local eats, check out the **food stalls** (Map p200; Yone Gyi Rd; dishes from K600; ⊗6-9am) in Mingala Market. Local specialities include *shàn k'auq-swèh* (Shan-style noodle soup) and *to·p'ù thouq* (Shan tofu salad), prepared using yellow chickpea tofu, chilli, coriander and chilli oil.

Every evening a very basic **night market** (Map p200; off Yone Gyi Rd; dishes from K800; ⊗5-9pm) unfolds, where you'll find a small selection of basic Burmese dishes.

★**Live Dim Sum House**   CHINESE $
(Map p200; Yone Gyi Rd; mains K2500-4500, dim sum K1700-3700; ⊗10am-9pm; 📶) More and more people – including many Chinese tourists – are making the walk to this laid-back place for the tasty and authentic dim sum, as well as for the other dishes on offer, like Shanghai beef noodles or Kung Pao chicken, a spicy chicken, peanuts and vegetable dish that is a staple in China.

★**Lin Htett Myanmar Traditional Food**   BURMESE $
(Map p200; Yone Gyi Rd; mains from K3500; ⊗10am-9pm; 📶) Hands-down our favourite Burmese restaurant in Nyaungshwe, where the service is as friendly as the food is delicious. Choose from a range of curries and salads, all accompanied by soup, dips and rice. Staff can also arrange cooking classes.

If you haven't yet encountered authentic Myanmar dining, here's the drill: choose a curry or two (refer to the pictures or, better yet, have a look behind the counter) and perhaps a salad (the pennywort salad, made from a slightly bitter fresh herb, is delicious). You'll find the accompaniments (rice, a sour soup, veggies, a fishy dip and three *balachaung,* chilli-based dips) will be supplied as a matter of course.

Htoo Myat BBQ   BURMESE $
(Map p200; Phaung Daw Pyan Rd; mains from K3000, BBQ from K200; ⊗3-9.30pm; 📶) Popular with the locals, this family-run place grills excellent barbecue – the pork ribs and fish especially – and serves up simple, tasty

curries in a congenial atmosphere. Some English spoken.

Thanakha Garden BURMESE, INTERNATIONAL $
(Map p200; ☑ 09 1283 71552; off Museum Rd (Haw St); mains from K3000; ⊙ 11am-9.30pm; ⊕) Set on a peaceful street, this amenable, family-run, bamboo-bedecked restaurant serves clean, fresh food. The Inle fish and salads are recommended, plus a few Western dishes are also available.

Everest Nepali Food Centre 2 NEPALI $
(Map p200; Kyaung Taw Anouk Rd; mains from K3500; ⊙ 7am-9pm; ☑ ⊕) A branch of the long-standing Kalaw-based Nepali restaurant, the Nyaungshwe outlet does hearty curries with rice, chapatti and vegetable side dishes.

Lotus Restaurant INTERNATIONAL, BURMESE $
(Map p200; Museum Rd (Haw St); mains from K2000; ⊙ 10.30am-9.30pm; ⊕) The menu at this affable, bamboo-walled place spans Burmese and Chinese, with a few Western classics. But if you don't like to make culinary decisions, go for the family-style Burmese dinner, which includes soup, salad, curry and a generous fruit plate for only K3500.

Inle Pancake Kingdom CREPERIE $
(Map p200; off Phoung Taw Site St; crêpes from K1000; ⊙ 9am-9pm; ☑ ⊕) Choose from a big range of crêpes and pancakes at this cute little cabin on a narrow alley north of the sports field. Follow the signs from Phoung Taw Site St.

Thukha Caffee TEAHOUSE $
(Map p200; cnr Lan Ma Taw St & Yone Gyi Rd; tea or snacks from K300; ⊙ 5am-4pm; ☑) Nyaungshwe's sole Muslim teahouse, this relaxed place serves good tea and, in the mornings, tasty *pakoda* (deep-fried vegetable dumplings) and Shan noodles.

★ One Owl Grill INTERNATIONAL $$
(Map p200; 1 Yone Gyi St; tapas from K1800, mains from K6800; ⊙ 9am-11pm; ⊛ ⊕) This French-owned bistro has proved a hit with its tapas-style dishes, including the best hummus in Shan State, as well as its breakfasts, salads, burgers and pasta. It's a little more pricey than is usual for Nyaungshwe, but it stays open later than anywhere else. Also does potent cocktails and has a solid wine list. Happy hour is 2pm to 6pm.

★ Sin Yaw Bamboo Restaurant CHINESE, SHAN $$
(Map p200; Kyaung Daw A Shae St; mains from K4000; ⊙ 9.30am-10.30pm; ⊕) The closest thing to an authentic Shan restaurant you'll find in Nyaungshwe, run by a pleasant Shan-Chinese couple. The food is good and flavoursome – they'll tone down the spices for Western palates if you want – and has a distinct hint of the cuisine of neighbouring Yunnan Province in China. They do a passable mojito and rum sour too.

Viewpoint SHAN $$
(Map p200; Yone Gyi Rd; mains from K5000, set meals K15,000-39,000; ⊙ 6am-10pm; ⊛ ☑ ⊕) Taking obscure local cuisines upmarket can be risky, but the self-professed 'Shan nouvelle cuisine' at this, Nyaungshwe's swankiest and most ambitious restaurant, is worth investigating: try a slow-cooked curry. It's also reasonably priced, as are the numerous set menus, which offer a chance to sample Shan dishes you probably won't have encountered before. It's the only air-conditioned restaurant in town. The downstairs lounge-bar has a decent selection of wine and some single-malt whiskies.

Green Chili Restaurant THAI $$
(Map p200; Hospital Rd; mains from K4500; ⊙ 10am-9.30pm; ⊕) This restaurant boasts one of the most pleasant dining rooms in town and the Thai menu here is also one of the more diverse and interesting, although the flavours are spice-light.

Chillax Bistro INTERNATIONAL $$
(Map p200; cnr Kyaung Taw Anouk Rd & Aung Mingalar St; mains from K4200; ⊙ 9am-10pm; ⊛ ⊕) Lame name, but this new place has a big outside terrace and a menu of Western comfort food – pizza, pasta, steaks and burgers – as well as some Asian standards. The food is solid without being spectacular. There's a decent selection of cocktails (from K2000) too, and live music sometimes.

Golden Kite Restaurant ITALIAN $$
(Map p200; cnr Mya Wa Ti St & Yone Gyi Rd; pizza & pasta from K5000; ⊙ 10am-10pm; ⊛ ☑ ⊕) If you're seeking Italian food in Nyaungshwe, consider the pizzas or pasta at this long-standing place, which claims to have sourced its recipes (and fresh basil!) from an Italian lady from Bologna.

Drinking & Nightlife

Pub Asiatico BAR

(Map p200; www.pub-asiatico.asia; Museum Rd (Haw St); ⊙4-11pm; 🕸) If you're looking for an escape from Myanmar for a few hours, this is the place to come. Pub Asiatico is decked out with a pool table and live sport on the TVs, and serves up foreign beers and liquor, as well as highly rated pizzas, in a faintly sterile atmosphere.

Min Min's BAR

(Map p200; Yone Gyi Rd; ⊙9am-10.30pm; 🕸) Long-standing backpacker hang-out that does cocktails, beer and standard Chinese-Burmese dishes.

☆ Entertainment

Aung Myanmar Puppet Show PUPPET THEATRE

(Map p200; Ahletaung Kyaung Rd; tickets K3000; ⊙show times 7pm & 8.30pm) Aung Myanmar Puppet Show has two nightly, 30-minute shows of traditional Myanmar puppetry. It's opposite the Nandawunn Hotel.

Information

There's an international ATM at **KBZ Bank** (Map p200; Lan Ma Taw St; ⊙9.30am-3pm); money can be exchanged at the nearby KBZ Bank **stall** (Map p200; Lan Ma Taw St; ⊙9am-2pm). There are other ATMs that take foreign cards around town too.

Thu Thu (Map p200; 📱081-209 258; thuthua79@gmail.com; Yone Gyi Rd; ⊙7am-8.30pm; 🕸) A friendly, reliable, no-hassle travel agent, who in addition to booking bus and plane tickets, can also arrange boat excursions and guides for treks and visits to Kakku.

ⓘ Getting There & Away

For such a popular destination, not that much transport arrives at, or departs from, Nyaungshwe. Instead, planes, many buses and all trains leave and arrive from nearby places such as Heho (the airport) and Shwenyaung.

AIR

The nearest airport is at Heho, an hour away by car. Taxis charge K25,000 from the airport to Nyaungshwe and K15,000 to go there from Nyaungshwe.

BUSES & PICK-UP TRUCKS

To Inle Lake, any bus bound for Taunggyi can drop you at Shwenyaung – located at the junction for Nyaungshwe/Inle Lake – for the full Taunggyi fare. From Shwenyaung, *thoun bein* drivers will take you the remaining 7 miles to Nyaungshwe for around K6000.

Nyaungshwe-based travel agents such as Thu Thu can sell tickets and arrange hotel pick-up. Otherwise, if you're bound for somewhere else or those times don't work, you'll need to hop on a bus, minivan, pick-up or 'van' (actually a share taxi) in Shwenyaung – all transport that originates in Taunggyi stops at this town

INLE LAKE TRANSPORT CONNECTIONS

Air

DESTINATION	PRICE	DURATION	FREQUENCY
Kyaingtong	from US$118	55min-2¾hr	daily
Lashio	from US$90	45min-1hr	daily via Mandalay
Mandalay	from US$66	30min	daily
Nyaung U (Bagan)	from US$84	75min	daily
Tachileik	from US$118	45min-1¾hr	daily via Mandalay
Yangon	from US$105	1hr-2¾hr	daily

Bus

DESTINATION	PRICE	DURATION	FREQUENCY
Hpa-an	K25,000	19hr	4.30pm
Loikaw	K12,000	10hr	9am
Mandalay	K11,000-18,000	10hr	9am, 7pm & 8pm
Myawaddy	K29,000	22hr	4.30pm
Nyaung U (Bagan)	K11,000-20,000	10hr	8am, 7pm & 8pm
Yangon	K13,000-22,000	12hr	frequent

on NH4. To get to Shwenyaung, hop on any Taunggyi-bound pick-up at the pick-up stand (Map p200; off Yone Gyi Rd) west of the market (K1000), or charter a thoun bein from the stand (Map p200) on Lan Ma Taw St (K6000). Be sure to be at the junction in Shwenyaung early so you don't miss connecting to your bus from Taunggyi (p214).

TAXI

The easiest way to find a taxi in Nyaungshwe is to ask at your hotel. Fares include Shwenyaung (K10,000, 30 minutes), Taunggyi (K30,000, one hour), Heho (K15,000, one hour) and Kalaw (K45,000, three hours). Taxis have room for up to four passengers.

TRAIN

The train rumbling through the hills from Shwenyaung to Thazi is slow but the scenery en route is stunning. From Shwenyaung's tiny station, trains depart at 8am and 9.40am, arriving in Kalaw after three hours (ordinary/upper class K500/1150) and reaching Thazi at least another six hours later (ordinary/upper class K1500/3000). Thoun bein drivers go to Shwenyaung's train station for K6000.

🛈 Getting Around

Several shops on Yone Gyi Rd and Phaung Daw Pyan Rd rent out clunky Chinese bicycles for K1500 per day, as do some guesthouses and hotels.

Motorcycle taxis at the stand (Map p200) near the market go to Shwenyaung for around K6000.

Inle Lake

Almost every visitor to Nyaungshwe takes a boat trip on Inle Lake. But the lake is so large and the villages and temples so spread out that Inle never feels too crowded.

In addition to tourist sights, Inle Lake is also home to many hotels – mostly high-end – which line the lake shore and often feature rooms or bungalows perched right over the water.

🅾 Sights

The sights are spread around the lake and the way to reach them is with a long-tail motorboat.

Inthein   VILLAGE
(အင်းတိမ်; Map p208) A narrow, foliage-cloaked canal winds through the reeds to the lakeside village of Inthein (also known as Indein), dotted with stupas dating back a few centuries.

The *Apocalypse Now* ambience evaporates somewhat when you see the waiting tourist boats and souvenir stalls, but no matter – the pagodas on the hilltop are still incredibly atmospheric. Inthein is on the five-day rotating market circuit and this is one of its busiest and most lively stops.

The first group of ruined stupas is immediately behind the village. Known as **Nyaung Ohak** (ညောင်အုပ်ဘုရား), the crumbling stupas are choked in greenery but you can still discern some ornate stucco carvings of animals, *devas* and *chinthe.*

From Nyaung Ohak, a covered stairway climbs the hill, leading to **Shwe Inn Thein Paya** (ရွှေအင်းတိန်ဘုရား), a complex of 1054 weather-beaten *zedi* (stupas), most constructed in the 17th and 18th centuries. Some of the *zedi* lean at crazy angles while others have been reconstructed. From the pagoda, there are great views across the lake and valley. For even better views, there are two more **ruined stupas** on conical hills just north of the village, reached via a dirt path behind Nyaung Ohak. You could easily spend a few hours exploring the various ruins here.

Nga Hpe Kyaung
(Jumping Cat Monastery)   BUDDHIST TEMPLE
(ငါးဖယ်ကျောင်း; Map p208; ☉ daylight hours) **FREE** On the western side of the lake, Nga Hpe Kyaung monastery was renowned for its jumping cats, trained to leap through hoops during the slow hours between scripture recitals. These days, there is little cat-leaping to be seen, as the new generation of cats here prefers to slumber, unlike their more energetic predecessors who have now sadly moved on to their next lives.

A better reason to visit the pagoda is to see the collection of ancient buddha images. Constructed four years before Mandalay Palace, the huge wooden meditation hall has statues in the Shan, Tibetan, Bagan and Inwa (Ava) styles displayed on ornate wood and mosaic pedestals.

Ywama   VILLAGE
(ရွာမ; Map p208) Ywama was the first village to be developed for tourism and, as a result, it has the greatest number of souvenir shops and restaurants. It's still a very pretty village, with winding channels lined with tall teak houses, but the charm can be diminished by the crowds of tourist boats and paddling souvenir vendors.

SAMKAR

Samkar (ဆမ်ကား), located south of Inle Lake, is best known for its Buddhist ruins. But the real reason to visit is the trip, a boat ride of about three hours that winds south through scenic lakeside villages and beautiful countryside to a second, much less-touristed lake ringed by Shan, Intha and Pa-O villages.

Formerly the seat of a dynasty of Shan princes, today's Samkar has two parts: the old town, a land-bound Shan village home to a small plot of crumbling ruins and a market that is part of the five-day circuit, and a more modern 'floating' village. On the opposite side of the lake, **Tharkong Pagoda** is a collection of *zedi* (stupas) that date back at least 500 years. Nearby, **Tai Arkong** (တိုက်အာကုန်) is a village known for alcohol production. Also close by is **Phaya Taung** (ဖရာတောင့်), a working fishing village with a mixed Pa-O and Intha population that is attracting some visitors.

Pa-O guides are no longer required to visit Samkar. A boat here will run about K60,000. If you choose to stay overnight, there's attractive accommodation at **A Little Lodge in Samkar** (☑ 09 4200 07010; littlesamkarlodge@gmail.com; Samkar; r US$90-125; ☺ ☎), a short walk from Samkar's old town.

Phaung Daw Oo Paya   BUDDHIST TEMPLE
(ဖောင်တော်ဦးဘုရား; Map p208; camera fee K300; ☉ daylight hours) A wide channel leads south from Ywama to the village of Tha Lay and Phaung Daw Oo Paya, the holiest religious site in southern Shan State. Enshrined within the huge tiered pagoda are five ancient buddha images that have been transformed into amorphous blobs by the sheer volume of gold leaf applied by devotees.

During the annual Phaung Daw Oo festival, the images are paraded around the lake in an ornate barge shaped like a *hintha* (the golden Swan of Burmese legend). Local families often bring their children here as part of the ordination rites for the *sangha* (Buddhist brotherhood) – a fascinating spectacle if you happen to be there at the right time.

Thaung Thut   VILLAGE
(သောင်သွတ်; Map p208) At the southern end of the lake, the village of Thaung Thut, about 1½ hours by boat from Nyaungshwe, holds an important market every five days. A long walkway leads uphill from the village to a complex of whitewashed Shan **stupas**.

Further south, the village of **Kyauk Taing** is devoted to pottery-making and is also part of the market circuit. Also in the area, **Kyaing Kan** specialises in weaving robes using lotus threads.

Nampan   VILLAGE
(နံ့ပန်; Map p208) The peaceful village of Nampan is built on stilts over the water. Its main temple, **Alodaw Pauk Pagoda** (အလိုတော်ပေါက်ဘုရား), is one of the oldest shrines on the lake, and the whitewashed stupa enshrines a fabulous gem-encrusted,

Shan-style buddha. Nampan has several small **cheroot factories** and there are some decent restaurants on the edge of the village.

Maing Thauk   VILLAGE
(မိုင်းသောက်; Map p208) Half of the village of Maing Thauk is set on dry land, while the other half sits on stilts over the water, linked to the shore by a 450yd wooden bridge. You can continue walking uphill to a peaceful **forest monastery** (တောရကျောင်း) for good views over the lake.

Maing Thauk is accessible by boat and by road – you can cycle there in an hour or so along a dirt track leading southeast from Nyaungshwe.

Floating Gardens   GARDENS
(ကျွန်းမြော; Map p208) North of Nampan are these famous gardens, where Intha farmers grow flowers, tomatoes, squash and other fruit and vegetables on long wooden trellises supported on floating mats of vegetation. In the morning and afternoon, farmers paddle up and down between the rows tending their crops.

In Phaw Khone   VILLAGE
(အင်းပေါခုံ; Map p208) This tidy village of teak stilt houses is famous for its weaving workshops. Buildings across the village vibrate with the clatter of shuttles and the click-clack of shifting loom frames, and the workshops are a popular stop on the tourist circuit.

🏃 Activities
Motorboat Trips
Every morning, a flotilla of slender wooden canoes fitted with long-tailed outboard

Inle Lake

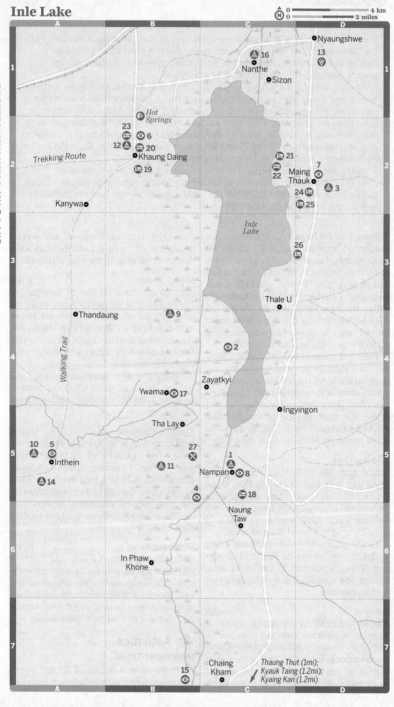

Nyaungshwe

16 Nanthe
13

Sizon

Hot Springs

23
12 6
20
Khaung Daing

21
22 Maing Thauk 7
24 3
25

19

Kanywa

Inle Lake

26

Thale U

Thandaung 9

2

Walking Trail

Zayatkyi

Ywama 17

Tha Lay

Ingyingon

10 5
Inthein 27
11 1
14 Nampan 8
4 18

Naung Taw

In Phaw Khone

15 Chaing Kham

Thaung Thut (1mi);
Kyauk Taing (1.2mi);
Kyaing Kan (1.2mi)

Trekking Route

0 ————— 4 km
0 ————— 2 miles

Inle Lake

motors surges out into the lake, transporting visitors to various natural, cultural, religious, historical or commercial sites.

Every hotel, guesthouse and travel agent in Nyaungshwe can arrange motorboat trips, or you can make your own arrangements directly with the boat drivers at one of the piers or near Teik Nan Bridge – they'll most likely find you before you can find them. Prices for the standard day-long boat trip start at around K15,000 to K18,000, which typically includes visits to the famous sights in the northern part of the lake such as Phaung Daw Oo Paya in Tha Lay, the Nga Hpe Kyaung (Jumping Cat Monastery) in Nga Phe village and the floating gardens. Tacking on a trip to Inthein will raise the cost to K20,000. Other destinations further afield include Thaung Thut (K20,000, 1½ hours), Hmaw Be (K40,000, two hours) and Samkar (K60,000, three hours). The fee covers the entire boat; drivers will carry up to five passengers, who get padded seats and life jackets.

The boats have no roof, so be sure to wear sunscreen. Some people complain of wind chill while on the lake; if that sounds like you, bring a coat or wrap.

Trekking

Inle Lake is the jumping-off point for several treks in the area. The most popular of these is the three-day walk to Kalaw. There are also some interesting day hikes and overnight treks to the east of Inle Lake, typically beginning in lowland rice paddies dotted with Shan stupa ruins and ascending to hillside Pa-O villages with panoramic views over the lake. A common option is a two-day, one-night trek, involving a short boat trip and a stay with a Pa-O family. Guides can talk you through the various treks and itineraries.

Day-hike costs start at K15,000 a day (per person, for groups of two or more), which includes a basic lunch of rice and curry (carry your own bottled or purified water); overnight treks run from K30,000 per person, per day.

Thu Thu (p205) and Sunny Day Tour Services (p201) can both arrange reputable, knowledgeable guides.

🎎 Festivals & Events

Phaung Daw Oo Paya Festival CULTURAL
(Phaung Daw Oo Paya; ⊙ late Sep or early Oct) Inle comes alive during late September or early October for the 18-day Phaung Daw Oo Paya Festival at Phaung Daw Oo Paya. The five revered golden Buddha images from the pagoda are ferried around the lake in a gilded barge shaped like a *hintha* (the golden swan of Myanmar legend) and locals carry out fiercely contested leg-rowing races on the channels between villages. The pagoda festival is closely followed by **Thadingyut**, which marks the end of Waso (Buddhist Lent).

🛏 Sleeping

If cash is no object, there are a growing number of upmarket resorts along the lake shore or, in some cases, built on stilts over it. The majority of Inle Lake's accommodation is near Maing Thauk, although there are also options at Khaung Daing.

Reservations are obligatory during the high season (December to February). All rates include breakfast. All of the hotels can

WORTH A TRIP

KHAUNG DAING

Just because you've been on a boat trip doesn't mean you're finished with Inle Lake. The countryside that surrounds all that water is also worth a visit, and a half-day cycling trip to Khaung Daing (ခေါင်းဒိုင်ရွာ), an Intha village located at the northwestern corner of the lake, is an easy and worthwhile way to experience it.

To get here from Nyaungshwe, cross Teik Nan Bridge and follow the tree-lined, bone-shaking dirt track through the rice fields until you reach the sealed road, then turn left.

The first place you'll reach is Khaung Daing's **hot springs** (ခေါင်းဒိုင်ရေပူစမ်း; Map p208; swimming pool US$7, private pool & bath US$10; ☉5am-6pm). There is no flowing water here: instead there are small pools of very hot water funnelled from the springs themselves. There are public pools (one for men and one for women), or you can opt for your own private pool or bathhouse.

After that, it's a gentle approach to Khaung Daing along a road lined with gold and whitewashed stupas, some perched on the tall hills to the west of the lake. The most interesting is **Phwar Ya Thay Paya** (ဖွားရသေ့ဘုရား; Map p208; ☉daylight hours) FREE, the name of which is said to mean 'Lady Monk' honouring a previous female resident, located close to the hot springs, which offers fine views over Inle Lake.

Just past Khaung Daing, turn left into the gateway that leads to **Hu Pin Inle Khaung Daing Village Resort** (Map p208; ☎081-209 296; www.hupinhotelmyanmar.com; r/ste US$100/250, cottage US$150-200; ※ ⊛). The road here ends in another hilltop temple with views of the lake.

Should you wish to stay in the village, the pick of several upmarket resorts is the attractive, low-key **Inle Lake View** (Map p208; ☎081-209 332; www.inlelakeview.com; r US$200-250; ⊛). The 40 rooms and villas here are spacious, well equipped and tastefully furnished, and all include balconies with great views over the lake. A second option is the airy and sophisticated **Pristine Lotus** (Map p208; ☎081-209 317; www.pristinelotusspa resort.com; bungalows US$200-260; ※ ⊛), located on a landscaped hillside west of Inle Lake. It sports a spa, restaurant and professional staff.

---

arrange pick-ups and return boat trips to/from Nyaungshwe for K10,000.

★ **Sanctum Inle Resort**   BOUTIQUE HOTEL **$$$**
(Map p208; ☎09 2528 18800; www.sanctum-inle-resort.com; Maing Thauk; r US$284-528; ※ ⊛ ⊛) The Sanctum marries a cool, modernist feel with a fantastic upgrade of a building that was once a convent. The monastic theme runs throughout, with the restaurant dubbed a 'refectory', while you imbibe cocktails in the 'Cloister Bar' and unwind in the 'Sanctuary Spa'. Rooms are luxurious, superbly equipped and huge, and the staff and management get rave reviews.

It's worth noting that the resort is by the lake, rather than right over it.

★ **Inle Princess Resort**   BOUTIQUE HOTEL **$$$**
(Map p208; ☎081-209 055; www.inle-princess.com; Magyizin Village; bungalows US$305-335; ※ ⊛ ⊛) Consistently the highest-ranked hotel in the Inle Lake area, the setting here is perhaps the nicest of any hotel on the lake. The stylish wooden cottages are decked out with handmade furniture, designer fireplaces, indoor and outdoor showers and ethnic ar-

tefacts. The more expensive bungalows have lake-facing sun decks. There's a spa and pool and the restaurant and staff get positive reports.

Villa Inle Resort & Spa   HOTEL **$$$**
(Map p208; ☎081-209 870; www.villainle.com; Maing Thauk; bungalows US$300-320; ※ ⊛ ⊛) The 27 wooden villas here are set in 20 acres of grounds and surrounded by some 5000 teak trees. The bungalows themselves feel spacious, boast attractive furnishings and come with inviting balconies that jut out over the lake. It's not exactly a steal, but the friendly service, leg room and ecoconscious vibe make Villa Inle an enticing option.

Golden Island Cottages   HOTEL **$$$**
(Map p208; ☎Nampan 081-209 390, Thale U 09 5210 183; www.gicmyanmar.com; bungalows US$150-170; @ ⊛) Owned by a cooperative of Pa-O people, the bungalows here aren't particularly sexy or well equipped, but they are comfortable and sizeable with high ceilings and balconies and a relatively good deal for the price. The Nampan resort has a great

location over open water while the Thale U resort is closer to shore.

Inle Resort
HOTEL $$$

(Map p208; ☑ 081-209 361; www.inleresort.com; Maing Thauk; r & bungalows US$160-275; ❄ 🖥 ☎) Located on dry land near Maing Thauk, 90 elevated bungalows and duplex villas come together in an attractive, spacious park-like setting. The more expensive bungalows here are huge and have wide balconies offering fine views over Inle Lake; the cheapest rooms are smaller but still big and look out over a pond. Under foreign management, the food here gets good reports.

Sky Lake
HOTEL $$$

(Map p208; ☑ 081-209 128; www.skylakeinleresort.com; Maing Thauk; bungalows US$170-200; ☎) There's nothing very fancy about the 45 bungalows here, but the lakeside ones have balconies and great views and the price is more reasonable than elsewhere on the lake.

✗ Eating

There are numerous floating restaurants in stilt houses on the lake that offer good, if overpriced, Chinese and Shan food, cold beers and English-language menus. The greatest concentration of restaurants is in Ywama, but there are also some decent choices around Nampan.

Inn Thar Lay
CHINESE, BURMESE $$

(Map p208; Tha Lay; mains from K3500; ☉8am-3pm; ◙) This restaurant, with two branches near Phaung Daw Oo Paya, offers a sound take on classic Chinese-Burmese dishes and you get to eat on a platform on stilts overlooking Inle Lake.

❶ Getting There & Away

BUS

From Inle Lake, some bus companies now make stops in Nyaungshwe, or run morning minivans to Hpa-an, Loikaw, Mandalay, Myawaddy, Nyaung U (Bagan) and Yangon.

Taunggyi   တောင်ကြီး

POP C 264,800 / ☑ 081

Perched on top of a mountain, Taunggyi is the capital of Shan State and by far the biggest city in eastern Myanmar. A multicultural town with a majority Shan population and significant Chinese, Muslim and Christian communities, Taunggyi is principally a trading post. Its markets are piled high with Chinese and Thai goods trucked in via the border crossings at Mong La and Tachileik, and destined to be sold on wholesale to markets in Yangon and Mandalay. Unless you're pining for the big city (the Shan State version of it anyway) and/or consumer goods, there's little of interest here for most visitors.

◉ Sights

Myanmar Vineyard
VINEYARD

(မြန်မာ၀ိုင်ခြံ; ☑ 081-208548; www.myanmar-vineyard.com; ☉9am-4pm) FREE Located at Aythaya, 3 miles west of Taunggyi, this vineyard – the country's first – sits at an elevation

---

TAUNGGYI'S RELIGIOUS BUILDINGS

Taunggyi's diverse population is reflected in the town's many religious buildings, which include a number of historic churches such as **St George Anglican Church** (စိန့်ဂျော့ဇမာနွေလလ္လရားကျောင်း; Ganaing Kan St), the main church for Taunggyi's Anglican community, and **St Joseph's Cathedral** (စိန့်ဂျိုးဇက်ဘုရားကျောင်း), which dates back to 1873 and is the principal place of worship for Taunggyi's Roman Catholics. **Myo Le Dhamma Yon** (မြို့လယ်ဓမ္မာရုံ; Bogyoke Aung San Rd; ☉daylight hours) FREE is the town's primary downtown pagoda, while **Yat Taw Mu Pagoda** (ရပ်တော်မူဘုရား; off Circular Rd West; ☉daylight hours) FREE in the southwest is dominated by a 60ft high standing Buddha. Near the market, **Sikh Temple Taunggyi** (Bogyoke Aung San Rd; ☉daylight hours) FREE is the place of worship for Taunggyi's Sikh population. There are also several Burmese-style **mosques** on the alleyways southwest of the market.

On the southern outskirts of town, the huge white **Sulamuni Paya** (စုလာမုဏိဘုရား; ☉daylight hours) FREE has a gilded corn-cob stupa that pays tribute to the Ananda Pahto in Bagan. You can continue a few miles uphill to the ridge-top **Shwe Phone Pye Paya** (ရွှေဘုန်းပြည့်ဘုရား; ☉daylight hours) FREE for dizzying views over Taunggyi and Inle Lake; a round-trip taxi to both temples should run to about K10,000.

Taunggyi

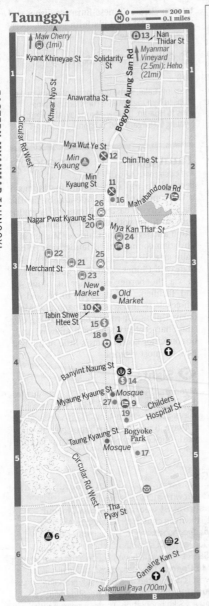

Taunggyi

◎ Sights
1 Myo Le Dhamma Yon	B4
2 Shan State Cultural Museum & Library	B6
3 Sikh Temple Taunggyi	B4
4 St George Anglican Church	B6
5 St Joseph's Cathedral	B4
6 Yat Taw Mu Pagoda	A6

⌂ Sleeping
7 Duwun Motel	B2
8 Golden Win Motel	B3
9 Vision Hotel	B4

⊗ Eating
10 Night Market	A3
11 Sein Myanmar Restaurant	B2
12 Tokyo Cafe	B2

⌂ Shopping
13 Taunggyi Gift Shop	B1

ℹ Information
14 CB Bank	B4
Currency Exchange Stall	(see 18)
15 KBZ Bank	A4
16 Shan Pyi Thar	B2
United Amara Bank (UAB)	(see 27)

ℹ Transport
17 Air Bagan	B5
18 Air KBZ	A4
19 Air Mandalay	B5
Asian Wings	(see 17)
Bus Company Office for Bagan	(see 20)
20 Bus Company Offices for Yangon & Mandalay	A3
21 Minivans to Heho & Kalaw	A3
22 Pick-ups To Nyaungshwe	A3
23 Pick-ups To Thazi & Meiktila	A3
24 Shwe Taung Yoe Express	B3
25 Taxi Stand	A3
26 Taxi Stand	A2
27 Yangon Airways	B4

taxi (K5000), or on any pick-up travelling between Taunggyi and Shwenyaung.

Shan State Cultural Museum & Library
MUSEUM

(ရှမ်းပြည်နယ်ယဉ်ကျေးမှုပြတိုက်နှင့်စာကြည့်တိုက်; Bogyoke Aung San Rd; K5000; ◷ 10am-4pm Tue-Sun) In addition to the usual displays of local ethnic-group outfits, you'll also find a handful of displays of weapons, musical instruments and jewellery. There's also a small section about Shan State's *saophas,* or sky princes, who ruled Shan State until the colonial era. English-language captions are lacking.

of 4290ft on well-watered, limestone-rich soils, providing good growing conditions for shiraz, cabernet sauvignon, sauvignon blanc, chenin blanc and moscato grapes. Open daily for tours and tastings: check the website for details. You can reach Myanmar Vineyard by

Festivals & Events

Fire Balloon Festival   CULTURAL

(☉Oct/Nov) Taunggyi holds a huge and chaotic fire balloon festival every October or November as part of the full moon celebrations during Tazaungmon (the eighth month of Myanmar's lunar calendar). Hundreds of multicoloured, different-shaped hot-air balloons are released skyward to carry away sins. Accommodation is very hard to find at this time.

Note that some of the balloons have fireworks attached and the combination of balloons exploding in flames, rockets going off prematurely and crowded streets results in casualties most years.

Sleeping

Duwun Motel   HOTEL $

(☑081-22355; 112 Mahabandoola Rd; r US$20-34; ❀☏) The best current budget option in Taunggyi, the more expensive rooms here are bright and spacious and come with communal balconies and air-con. The cheaper ones are a little dank and dark and fan-only, but still acceptable. The affable, English-speaking owner is helpful.

Golden Win Motel   HOTEL $

(☑081-200 503; goldenwin.motel@gmail.com; 3 Thanlwin Rd; r US$20-50; ❀☏) There's a range of rooms here, from the cramped, to the spacious with city views, but all are well kept and come with modern bathrooms. Good wi-fi connection and friendly staff.

Vision Hotel   HOTEL $$

(☑081-212 4119; visionhotel.tgi@gmail.com; 120 Bogyoke Aung San Rd; r US$55; ❀☏) A big step up from Taunggyi's other midrange hotels, the Vision has large, modern and comfortable rooms, helpful staff and a breakfast buffet.

Eating

Sein Myanmar Restaurant   BURMESE $

(☑081-212 4255; 15 Bogyoke Aung San Rd; curries from K3500; ☉10am-10pm; ⊡) Locals crowd into this busy restaurant come lunchtime for full-flavoured Burmese-style rice-and-curry sets. In the evening, it's fine for a beer and various fried noodle and rice dishes.

Tokyo Cafe   TEAHOUSE $

(Bogyoke Aung San Rd; dishes from K800; ☉6.30am-9.30pm; ☏⊡) This spick-and-span tea shop has an English-language menu of one-plate dishes.

Night Market   BURMESE $

(Tabin Shwe Htee St; mains from K300; ☉4-10pm) Taunggyi's night market is the place to go for bargain local eats; Daw Than Kyi, at the western end, does excellent *t'ămìn jin*, Shan-style rice (look for the rainbow-coloured plastic sheeting).

EASTERN MYANMAR TAUNGGYI

DON'T MISS

KAKKU

Only a couple of hours' drive from either Taunggyi or Nyaungshwe, the 2478 stupas at Kakku are one of the most remarkable sights in Shan State. Arranged in neat rows sprawling over the hillside, the stupa garden, (according to local legend) was founded by the Buddhist missionaries of the Indian emperor Ashoka in the 3rd century BC. As such, the stupas span a bewildering variety of styles, marking the prevailing architectural trends when they were constructed. Some are simple and unadorned while others are covered in a riot of stucco deities and mythical beasts. Among the tall Shan-style stupas are a number of small square 'monastery style' stupas that are unique to this region. Like most ancient sites across the country, Kakku has been extensively restored using donations from pilgrims, so don't expect an Indiana Jones–style ruin in the jungle.

The annual **Kakku Paya Pwe**, held on the full-moon day of the lunar month of Tabaung (March), attracts Pa-O pilgrims from across Shan State.

Kakku can only be accessed by taxi, either from Nyaungshwe or Taunggyi. A return taxi from Nyaungshwe – including a few hours' waiting time – will run K55,000; from Taunggyi it will cost K40,000. You will also need to be accompanied by a Pa-O guide: Thu Thu (p205) or **Golden Island Cottages** (GIC; Map p200; ☑081-209 551; www.glcmyanmar.com; 89 Phoung Daw Pyan Rd; ☉6am-6pm), both based in Nyaungshwe, can arrange this. There's a US$3 entry fee for the site and a US$5 fee for the guide.

Eating options are very limited at Kakku. Try **Hlaing Konn** (mains from K600; ☉11am-8pm Sep-Apr), a simple Burmese restaurant overlooking the site.

🔖 Shopping

Taunggyi Gift Shop ARTS & CRAFTS
(cnr Bogyoke Aung San Rd & Nan Thidar St; ⊙ 8am-6pm) Stocks a selection of local foods, Shan clothing and handicrafts.

ℹ️ Information

CB Bank (Bogyoke Aung San Rd; ⊙ 9.30am-3pm), **KBZ Bank** (Bogyoke Aung San Rd; ⊙ 9.30am-3pm) and **United Amara Bank** (Bogyoke Aung San Rd; ⊙ 9.30am-3pm) all have ATMs that accept international cards. Exchange is available at the **stall** (27/28 Bogyoke Aung San Rd; ⊙ 9am-2.30pm) attached to the Air KBZ office; money changers can also be found in and around the market.

ℹ️ Getting There & Away

Buses, minivans, pick-ups, 'vans' (share taxis) and taxis leave from several stands around town.

Most long-distance buses depart from the Maw Cherry bus station (off Circular Rd West), a collection of bus company offices about 2 miles north of the town centre; a taxi here will run K2500. The offices (Bogyoke Aung San Rd) of companies running bus and 'van' services

to destinations such as Mandalay (K18,000 to 20,000, 10 hours, departures when full 8.30am to 8pm) and Yangon can be found along the west side of Bogyoke Aung San Rd, close to the Kan-Tone Kan-Sone Hotel. Other bus company offices cluster close to the market. The office (Nagar Pwat Kyaung St) for buses to Nyaung U (Bagan) is on Nagar Pwat Kyaung St. Some companies, including Shwe Taung Yoe Express (Mya Kan Thar St), offer free transport to the bus station.

Minivans to Heho and Kalaw leave from a stop (Merchant St) just off Merchant St.

Pick-up trucks to Nyaungshwe (off Merchant St) wait a block or so north of Merchant St amid the market. Pick-ups to Thazi and Meiktila leave just south of Merchant St.

From the central taxi stand (cnr Bogyoke Aung San Rd & Merchant St), services run to destinations include Nyaungshwe (K20,000, one hour), Kakku (K40,000, 1½ hours) and Kalaw (K40,000, 2½ hours). There is a second, smaller taxi stand (Bogyoke Aung San Rd) on the corner of Nagar Pwat Kyaung St.

Heho functions as the air hub to/from Taunggyi. In Taunggyi, **Air Bagan** (☎ 081-212 4736; www.airbagan.com; Bogyoke Aung San Rd (Main Rd); ⊙ 8am-5pm Mon-Fri & 9am-2pm Sat & Sun), **Air KBZ** (☎ 081-212 4768; www.airkbz.com; 27/28

TAUNGGYI TRANSPORT CONNECTIONS

DESTINATION	BUS & MINIBUS	PICK-UP
Heho (airport)	K2000; minibus; 1hr; 1pm, 2pm & 3pm	K1500; 1hr; departures when full 6am-4pm; from stop off Merchant St
Kalaw	K3000; minibus; 3hr; daily 1pm, 2pm & 3pm; from Merchant St	K2000; 3hr; departures when full 6am-4pm; from stop off Merchant St
Lashio	K15,500; bus; 12hr; daily 1pm	N/A
Loikaw	K7000; bus; 8hr; daily 6.30am; from Maw Cherry bus stand	N/A
Mandalay	K9500-15,000; bus; 10hr; 9am, 7pm & 8pm; from stalls along Bogyoke Aung San Rd and Shwe Taung Yoe Express	N/A
Meiktila	K5500; bus; 6hr; daily 7.30am	K4000; 7hr; departures when full 6am-4pm; from stop off Merchant St
Nyaungshwe	N/A	K1000; 1hr; departures when full 6am-4pm; from stop off Merchant St
Nyaung U (Bagan)	K10,500; bus; 10hr; daily 6.30pm; from stall on Nagar Pwat Kyaung St and Shwe Taung Yoe Express	N/A
Pindaya	K3000; bus; 4hr; daily 1pm; from Maw Cherry bus stand	N/A
Thazi	N/A	K4000; 6hr; departures when full 6am-4pm; from stop off Merchant St
Yangon	K13,500-21,000; bus; 12hr; frequent 3-8pm; from stalls along Bogyoke Aung San Rd and Shwe Taung Yoe Express	N/A

Bogyoke Aung San Rd; ⊙9am-5pm), **Air Mandalay** (☑081-212 1330; www.airmandalay.com; Bogyoke Aung San Rd (Main Rd); ⊙8.30am-5.30pm Mon-Fri & 9am-1pm Sat & Sun), **Asian Wings** (☑081-205 900; www.asianwingsair.com; Bogyoke Aung San Rd (Main Rd); ⊙9am-5.30pm) and **Yangon Airways** (☑081-212 3995; www.yangonair.com; 134 Bogyoke Aung San Rd; ⊙9am-5pm) all have offices, or you can go to **Shan Pyi Thar** (☑081-212 4549; 8 Bogyoke Aung San Rd (Main Rd); ⊙9am-6pm), a travel agent next to the Sein Myanmar Restaurant. A taxi from Heho's airport to Taunggyi costs K25,000; a cheaper but less convenient option is to hike almost a mile to the highway and wait for a pick-up truck or bus to Taunggyi (K2000, 1½ hours).

Pindaya ပင်းတယ

POP C 20,000 / ☑081

The road to sleepy Pindaya cuts across one of the most densely farmed areas in Myanmar – at first glance, the patchwork of fields and hedges could almost be a landscape from central Europe. But it's the Danu, Palaung and Pa-O villages, rather than the farms, around Pindaya that are beginning to draw travellers for treks through less-touristed areas than elsewhere in western Shan State. Another good reason to make the journey here is to visit the famous Shwe Oo Min Natural Cave pagoda, a massive limestone cavern filled with thousands of gilded buddha statues.

◉ Sights

★ Shwe Oo Min Natural Cave Pagoda CAVE

(ရွှေဥမင်သဘာဝလိုက်ဂူဘုရား; Shwe U Min Pagoda Rd; K3000, camera fee K300; ⊙6am-6pm) Set high on a limestone ridge above Pone Taloke Lake, this winding complex of natural caves and tunnels is filled to bursting with buddha images in an astonishing variety of shapes, sizes and materials.

At the latest count, the caves contained more than 8094 statues, some left centuries ago by local pilgrims and others newly installed by Buddhist organisations from as far afield as Singapore, the Netherlands and the USA. The collection of alabaster, teak, marble, brick, lacquer and cement images is still growing – pilgrims arrive in a slow but steady stream, installing new images and meditating in tiny, naturally occurring meditation chambers in the cave walls.

A series of covered stairways climb the ridge to the cave entrance. Most people arrive via the long stairway that starts near the gleaming white *zedi* of **Nget Pyaw Taw Pagoda**, just south of the Conqueror Hotel. You can skip the last 130 steps to the cave mouth by taking the lift.

Two more covered stairways lead north from the lift pavilion. One descends gently back to Pindaya, while the other climbs to a second **cave pavilion** containing a monumental, 40ft-high, gilded, Shan-style sitting buddha. The steps continue along the ridge to a third chamber with a large **reclining buddha** and more shrines and pagodas along the hilltop.

The stairs leading to the cave are about 2 miles south of town on Shwe U Min Pagoda Rd, a 20-minute walk from town. A motorcycle taxi will take you to the top and back for K2000.

Hsin Khaung Taung Kyaung BUDDHIST TEMPLE

(ဆင်ခေါင်းတောင်ကျောင်း; off Shwe U Min Pagoda Rd; ⊙daylight hours) **FREE** This gorgeous temple, with its carved teak panels dating back to the 19th century, is downhill from the Shwe Oo Min Natural Cave Pagoda on the dirt path to Pone Taloke Lake. The path starts just beyond the monastery and is lined with ancient, crumbling *zedi*.

Kan Tu Kyaung BUDDHIST TEMPLE

(ကံတူကျောင်း; Zaw Ti Kar Yone St; ⊙daylight hours) **FREE** At the north end of Pone Taloke Lake, this temple features some heavily restored stupas and a fine teak *kyaung* (Burmese Buddhist monastery) with a large collection of antique buddha images on ornate plinths.

★ Activities

A couple of local guides lead increasingly popular treks in the hill country surrounding Pindaya. Most conduct overnight treks to **Yazagyi** (ရဇကြီး), an attractive and modern Palaung village located in hilly tea-plantation country about four hours' walk east of Pindaya. Some choose to extend this to two nights with a visit to **Kan Hla Kone** (ကန်လှကုန်း) or **Shwe Behto** (ရွှေဘဲတို), which are more remote Danu villages. It's also possible to trek from Pindaya to Kalaw, a trip of three or four days, depending which way you go. Overnight treks start at US$20 per day per person (in groups of two or more), and guides with experience in these areas include U Myint Thoung at Old Home Tour Information Centre (p216) and **Sai Win Htun** (☑09 2507 84688, 09 7883

26316; winhtun123@gmail.com; Golden Cave Hotel, Shwe U Min Padoga Rd).

⭐ Festivals & Events

Shwe Oo Min Paya Pwe CULTURAL
(⊙ Feb/Mar) The main annual *paya pwe* (pagoda festival) at Shwe Oo Min takes place on the full moon of Tabaung. Expect all the usual singing, dancing and hand-operated fairground rides.

🛏 Sleeping

Myit Phyar Zaw Gyi Hotel HOTEL $
(📋 081-66403; 106 Zaw Ti Kar Yone St; r US$15-25; 🛜) Next to the market and right by the lakeshore, Pindaya's one true budget option is clean, tidy, friendly and good value for money.

Global Grace Hotel (Pindaya) HOTEL $
(📋 081-66189; www.globalgracehotelpindaya.com; Shwe U Min Pagoda Rd; r US$40-50; ❄🛜) Sometimes still known by its former name – Pindaya Hotel – this is an old-fashioned but efficient place. The 'deluxe' rooms in the funky main structure are spacious, and have lots of natural light, balconies looking over the lake, TVs and attractive wood flooring and furnishings. The cheaper 'superior' rooms are smaller and at ground level.

Located just south of 'downtown' Pindaya on Shwe U Min Pagoda Rd.

Golden Cave Hotel HOTEL $
(📋 081-66166; www.goldencavehotel.com; Shwe U Min Pagoda Rd; s/d US$42/47; @🛜) A comfortable midrange place near the steps to Shwe Oo Min. The smarter superior rooms have balconies looking towards the caves, and are also equipped with a TV and a fridge.

★ Conqueror Resort Hotel HOTEL $$
(📋 081-66106; www.conquerorresorthotel.com; off Shwe U Min Padoga Rd; r US$70-100; ❄🛜🏊) There isn't a blade of grass out of place at this immaculately maintained resort hotel near the main entrance to the caves. Rooms are set in duplex bungalows around a central restaurant and a large, inviting pool. All are good value for the price, and are equipped with TV, a minibar and balcony, while the 'suite' rooms tack on spacious and stylish bathrooms.

Pindaya Inle Inn HOTEL $$
(📋 081-66029; inleinpdy@gmail.com; Mahar Bandular Rd; r/chalets US$85/120; @🛜🏊) Located at the entrance to town, across the lake from Shwe Oo Min Pagoda, the rooms here are set in either bamboo or stone cottages in a lovingly tended garden centred on a longhouse-style restaurant and bar. The larger, more expensive 'chalets' are a big step up from the overpriced 'bamboo' rooms, equipped with TV, fridge, huge bathrooms with tub, and fireplaces.

🍴 Eating

Good Morning BURMESE $
(Shwe Min U Pagoda Rd; dishes K1000-2000; ⊙ 8am-8.30pm; 📶) There's a small English menu of tasty noodle dishes here, as well as coffee and fruit juices and a pleasant, shaded outdoor area to sit in.

Green Tea Restaurant INTERNATIONAL, BURMESE $$
(📋 081-66345; Shwe U Min Pagoda Rd; mains from K3000; ⊙ 10am-8pm; 🛜📶) Located between the market and Shwe Oo Min Pagoda, this open-air dining room perched over Pone Taloke Lake is Pindaya's poshest and most pleasant place to dine. The pan-Asian menu, with a few Western classics, isn't very exciting but the food is reliable, if less enticing than the setting.

ℹ Information

We're told that there is a US$2 'entry fee' to Pindaya, collected at the entrance to town, although the ticket office has never been staffed when we've visited.

A branch of KBZ Bank was under construction at the time of research, so there should be an ATM and exchange facilities here very soon.

Old Home Tour Information Centre (📋 09 4282 23219, 09 7845 70305; 46 Shwe U Min Pagoda Rd; ⊙ 9am-5pm) Located at the market intersection. Here you'll find friendly local U Myint Thoung, who leads treks and day tours and also sells a small selection of books and antiques.

ℹ Getting There & Away

There's not much direct transport to Pindaya, so you'll probably have to make your way to Aungban, a few miles east of Kalaw along NH4, where transport to Pindaya waits near the clock-tower intersection. Vans make the run to Pindaya from here in the morning (K3000, 1½ hours, 7.30am, 9.30am and 11am), as do two overcrowded pickups (K1500, two hours, 8am and 11am). Waiting motorcycle taxis (K6000 one way, K10,000 round trip) and taxis (K30,000 one way, K50,000 round trip) are another option.

From Pindaya's market intersection, buses bound for Taunggyi and Shwenyaung (for Inle Lake) depart at 5.30am and 5.45am (K3500, three hours). Vans run to Taunggyi and Shwenyaung (for Inle Lake) at 6am and 2pm (K3500 to K4000, 2½ hours). For Aungban, there's a daily pick-up at 7.30am (K1500, two hours) and vans at 10.30am and 1.30pm (K3000, 1½ hours).

Buy tickets for the vans and buses at the shop next to Old Home Tour Information Centre (p216).

Kalaw   ကလော

POP C 57,800 / ☑ 081

Kalaw was founded as a hill station by British civil servants fleeing the heat of the plains. The town still feels like a high-altitude holiday resort: the air is cool, the at-mosphere is calm, the streets are tree-lined, and the surrounding hills are the only place in Myanmar where travellers can trek over-night without prior permission.

One of the few destinations in Myanmar that genuinely caters for backpackers, rather than tour groups, Kalaw is an easy place to kick back for a few days. The town is also no-table for its significant population of Nepali Gurkhas and Indians, whose ancestors came here to build the roads and railway during the colonial era.

⊙ Sights

Thein Taung Paya   BUDDHIST TEMPLE
(သိမ်တောင်ဘုရား; off Union Hwy (NH4); ⊙ day-light hours) FREE For a good view over Kal-aw's market and centre, take the steps on

---

TREKKING FROM INLE LAKE TO KALAW

Instead of enduring yet another crowded, bone-rattling bus ride, consider walking be-tween Inle Lake and Kalaw. There are numerous alternative routes to take you to your destination, and depending on the route that you and your guide agree upon, the journey can take between two and four days.

Although scenic, it's important to understand that this trek is more of a cultural (or even agricultural) experience than a nature walk. The only real forest you'll encounter is just outside Kalaw, and the bulk of the trek passes through relatively modern Pa-O and Danu settlements and extensive wheat, rice, tea, potato, sesame and chilli plantations. At some points you'll be walking on footpaths, while other parts of the trek are on roads (both paved and unpaved) or even along train tracks. You'll most likely spend one night with a Pa-O or Danu family and another at a Buddhist temple.

There are numerous alternate long and short routes; some choose to go by car to Lamaing and walk to Kalaw in one day, while other guides have found ways to extend the trip to four nights. Discuss the options with your guide. If you're doing the standard three-day option, you'll most likely begin at one of the lakeside villages of Inthein, Tha Lay, Thandaung or Khaung Daing. In general, you can expect at least four hours of mostly level walking each day, the only truly steep part being the ascent from Thandaung at Inle Lake. The second day passes through hilly agricultural areas, and as you approach Kalaw on day three, the trek passes through tall mountains fringed with pine trees and tea plantations.

The winter months are the best time to do the trek, the only downside being that you'll almost certainly run into other trekkers – nights with as many as 50 people sleep-ing at the monastery have been reported. During the rainy season many of the roads are irritatingly muddy and slippery. Leeches and mosquitoes can also be a problem.

Guides can arrange to have your bags transported to a hotel in Nyaungshwe, so you carry only what you need for the walk – a towel and a torch (flashlight) are good extras to bring along.

If arranging your trek from Inle Lake, expect to pay K50,000 per person, per day, in groups of two or more. Rates include food, but not the cost of shipping your gear to your destination (per bag K3000), if you want to do so, or the entrance fee at Inle Lake (K12,500). Trekking Kalaw to Inle Lake is normally cheaper, with some guides charging K40,000 per person, per day.

Kalaw

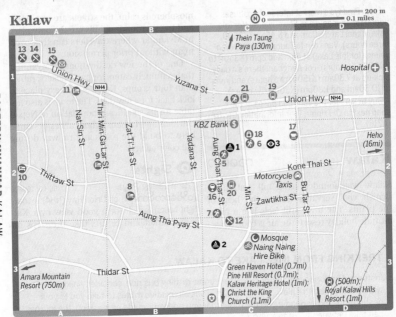

Thein Taung Paya (130m)

the north side of Union Hwy (NH4) to this modest Buddhist monastery with a small congregation of friendly monks.

Aung Chan Tha Zedi
BUDDHIST TEMPLE

(အောင်ချမ်းသာစေတီ; Aung Chan Thar St; ☉ daylight hours) **FREE** Right in the centre of Kalaw, Aung Chan Tha Zedi is a glittery stupa, covered in gold- and silver-coloured glass mosaics.

Market
MARKET

(ကလောမြို့မစျေး; Min St; ☉ 6am-5pm) Kalaw's market is worth a browse – several stalls sell dried fruit and local liqueurs. Every five days, the market is swelled by traders who descend from the hill villages outside town.

🏃 Activities

Almost everyone who comes to Kalaw goes trekking in the hills. The town is surrounded by Buddhist pagodas, hilltop viewpoints and the peaceful villages of the Palaung, Danu, Pa-O, Taung Yo and Danaw peoples, all set in a gorgeous landscape of forest-capped hills.

Popular destinations for one-day treks around Kalaw include the **Myin Ma Hti Cave** (မွ ျံးမ ်တ ိးဂ ူ), the Pa-O villages south of **Lamaing** (လမိုင်း), and the Pa-O, Danu and Taung Yo villages near **Myin Dike** (မွ ျံးတိုက ်) train station. Another common route runs southwest from Kalaw to the Palaung villages of **Ywathit** (ရ ်ာသစ ်) and **Tar Yaw** (တာေယာ), passing the **Viewpoint**, a rustic, Nepali-run restaurant with sweeping views over the hills. The guides at Ever Smile (p219) do visits to **Pane Ne Pin** (ပိန်နဲပင ်) and **Myin Ka** (မွ ျင်ကာ), Palaung and Taung Yo villages respectively, located in a beautiful area north of Kalaw. Alternatively, the guides at **Jungle King** (☎ 09 3601 8340, 09 4283 38036; Aung Chan Thar Pagoda St; ☉ 7am-9pm) lead one-day treks to **Patingone** (ပုတီးကုန်း), a four-hour hike south of Kalaw, where there's a Pa-O/Taung Yo traditional healer.

The most popular overnight trek is undoubtedly the two- to four-day trek to Inle Lake. You can also do a two-day mountain-bike trek along a similar route; contact Naing Naing Hire Bike (p222) for details. A more adventurous overnight route is the multiday trek to Pindaya, via Taung Ni (တေ ာင်ဂ ်ီ). If you're interested in nature more than culture, **Moteh** (☎ 09 7322 1878; Viewpoint) offers a day or overnight 'jungle' trek through a protected forest. Trekkers sleep in the woods or stay overnight at a Taung Yo village.

The level of development varies as you move from village to village. Some hill people still wear traditional clothing and live with-

Kalaw

out electricity or running water, while their immediate neighbours watch European football on satellite TV. The standard of living for hill peoples across the region has been raised by development projects run by the UN and other international NGOs. Most villagers depend primarily on farming, but some subsidise their income by making handicrafts and providing meals and accommodation for visiting trekkers.

On single-day treks, the only equipment you need is a pair of good walking shoes. Meals are usually included in the price of the trek, but you should buy and carry your own drinking water. Trekking goes on year-round, but expect muddy conditions during the rainy season (approximately June to October).

Trekking without a guide is not recommended – the trails are confusing, the terrain challenging and few people in the hills speak English. The going rate for a day hike

is around US\$10 per person (in a group of four); overnight treks start at K30,000 per person, per day, in groups of two or more.

Green Hill Valley   WILDLIFE
(☑09 7310 7278; www.ghvelephant.com; Magway village, Kalaw; per person US\$100, minimum 2 people) 🕬 Seven fortunate elephants no longer fit for work in the government's timber camps have come to retire at this camp founded in 2011 by a family with a history of working with elephants. All visitors, as well as interacting with the elephants, helping to feed and bathe them, get to plant a tree as part of the camp's reforestation project.

Rural Development Society   TREKKING
(RDS; ☑09 7861 16871, 081-50747; http://ruraldevelopmentsociety.wordpress.com; Min St; ⊙9am-6pm) Founded by charity-minded Tommy Aung in 1992, this NGO also leads day and overnight treks in the area and to Inle Lake. Advance notice of three days is requested; email or call Tommy for details. Can also organise mountain-bike trips to Inle Lake (US\$50 per person in a group of four).

Ever Smile   TREKKING
(☑081-50683; thuthu.klw@gmail.com; Yuzana St; ⊙8am-8pm) Friendly, reputable outfit that specialises in the trek to Inle Lake (K40,000 per person in a group of four), as well as day treks within Kalaw township. At the time of research, they were planning to start regular Kalaw–Pindaya treks.

Sam's Trekking Guide   TREKKING
(☑09 4580 40368, 081-50377; samtrekking@gmail.com; 21 Aung Chan Thar St; ⊙7am-7pm) Sam and his family have years of experience leading treks, and conduct day and overnight treks in Kalaw township, as well as multiday treks to Inle Lake and Pindaya. He works out of his eponymous restaurant.

🛏 Sleeping

Kalaw has a generous spread of hotels and guesthouses. Few offer air-conditioning – in this climate they don't need to – but some offer heaters for the winter nights, when the temperature has been known to drop perilously close to freezing.

🛏 In Town

Seint Hotel   HOTEL \$
(☑081-50696; www.seinthotelkalaw.com; Union Hwy (NH4); r US\$25-35; 🕸🛜) Newish, decent-value

hotel with large, well-kept, modern rooms, most with balconies, and reasonable bathrooms. Professional staff.

Pine Breeze Hotel
HOTEL $

(☑ 081-50459; www.pinebreezehotel.com; 174 Thittaw St; r US$35-45; ❄ ☏) Located just west of 'downtown' Kalaw, this baby-blue hilltop structure has four floors of comfortable, well-maintained rooms equipped with TV, fridge, balcony and great views over the town.

Eastern Paradise Hotel
HOTEL $

(☑ 081-50315; easternmotel@gmail.com; 5 Thi-ri Min Ga Lar St; s/d/tr US$20/25/35; ☏) The rooms are old-fashioned, although reasonably sized, and bathrooms a little basic, but the staff are amenable at this long-standing, quiet place and the central location is ideal.

★ Dream Villa Hotel Kalaw
HOTEL $$

(☑ 081-50144; dreamvilla@myanmar.com.mm; 5 Za Ti' La St; r US$50; ☏) A cut above your average Myanmar hotel, and the best mid-range option in Kalaw, the Dream Villa is a spotless, three-storey home with 24 tasteful, attractively decorated wood-panelled rooms with a few local design touches. Efficient, English-speaking staff.

Kalaw Heritage Hotel
HOTEL $$

(☑ 081-50039; www.kalawheritagehotel.com; University Rd; r US$75-120; ❄ ☏) This new hotel has rooms spread across three buildings, two of which date back to 1903 and 1906. Rather more thought has gone into the design here than in some other top-end Myanmar hotels, and the spacious, uncluttered rooms could be in a boutique city hotel, though the bathrooms are a little plain for the price.

🛏 Outside of Town

Kalaw's best and most atmospheric accommodation is located outside of the city centre.

Green Haven Hotel
HOTEL $

(☑ 081-50639; greenhavenhotel@gmail.com; Shwe Oo Min Rd; r K35,000-60,000; @ ☏) The 20 tidy, wood-panelled rooms here are housed in two imposing, two-storey white structures. The family rooms – cute bungalows – are the best and biggest option. To get here, follow Min St south, turning right at the second intersection, or hop on a motorcycle taxi (K1000) near the market.

Pine Hill Resort
HOTEL $$

(☑ 081-50079; www.myanmarpinehill.com; 151 Oo Min Rd; r & bungalows US$95-105; ❄ ☏) Set around a colonial bungalow, this hotel consists of 32 comfortable rooms with proper showers in concrete duplex cottages sprawling through immaculate gardens. 'Deluxe' rooms tack on a safe, air-con and a bathtub. To get here, follow Min St south, turning right at the second intersection, or hop on a motorcycle taxi (K1000) near the market.

★ Royal Kalaw Hills Resort
HOTEL $$$

(☑ 081-50851; www.royalkalawhillsresort.com; r US$150-380; ❄ ☏) Kalaw's swishest hotel. There are only 14 immaculate rooms here (with the best bathrooms in Kalaw), all housed in a beautifully converted colonial-era, mock-Tudor mansion surrounded by an attractive garden. There's a country-house feel to the place, with private dining and sitting rooms, antiques and paintings, a hushed atmosphere and professional staff. There's a spa here too.

Amara Mountain Resort
HOTEL $$$

(☑ 081-50734; www.amaragroup.net/mountain; 10/182 Thidar St; r US$173; ☏) Accommodation here is based in two attractive mock-Tudor buildings in a hilltop garden, one built in 2002 and another a century previously, in 1909. The 11 rooms are equally spacious and attractive regardless of age, with wood floors and lots of natural light, some boasting large bathtubs and fireplace, although no TV. The furnishings add to the neo-colonial vibe. The hotel is about half a mile west of Kalaw.

🍴 Eating

Kalaw has some decent places to eat, many serving food with a distinctive Indian or Ne-pali flavour.

★ Thu Maung Restaurant
BURMESE $

(Myanmar Restaurant; ☑ 081-50207; Union Hwy (NH4); curries from K3500; ⊙ 8am-9pm; 🍴) Newly relocated to a bright green building just past the post office, Thu Maung is one of our fave Burmese curry restaurants in this part of the country, serving up rich, meaty chicken, pork, mutton and fish curries coupled with exceptionally delicious dips, sides, salads, pickles and trimmings. The tomato salad, made from crunchy green tomatoes, is a work of art.

Everest Nepali Food Centre
NEPALI $

(Aung Chan Thar St; curries from K3500; 9.30am-9.30pm;) Ever-popular, convivial Nepali restaurant that serves up tasty curry spreads, complete with a good selection of side dishes.

Thiri Gay Har Restaurant
INTERNATIONAL, BURMESE $

(Seven Sisters; Union Hwy (NH4); mains K2000-4500; 10am-10pm;) Gentrified but relatively full-flavoured Burmese – as well as Chinese, Indian, Western and a smattering of Shan dishes – are served at this cute cottage restaurant that is geared towards foreigners.

Pyae Pyae Shan Noodle
SHAN $

(Union Hwy (NH4); noodles from K600, mains from K1500; 6.30am-8pm;) This cosy, friendly shop sells delicious bowls of its namesake noodles, and has an English-language menu of other one-plate dishes.

Drinking & Nightlife

★ Hi Snack & Drink
BAR

(Kone Thai St; 5-11pm) That rare thing: a genuine bar in a provincial Burmese town, Hi is the size of a closet and boasts a fun, speakeasy feel. If you haven't had its trademark rum sour (K2000), you haven't been to Kalaw. No beer served; just the hard stuff.

Ma Hnin Si Cafe
TEAHOUSE

(Bu Tar St; tea & snacks from K300; 6am-8pm) There's a tiny English-language sign here, but a better way of finding it is to look for the crowd of locals sipping tea, accompanied by plates of *pakoda* (vegetables fried in lentil-flour batter), other tasty deep-fried snacks and solid noodle dishes.

Shopping

A couple of art galleries around the market sell paintings of monks, hill peoples and mountain scenery.

RDS Shop
ARTS & CRAFTS

(http://ruraldevelopmentsociety.wordpress.com; Min St; 9am-6pm) Representing the commercial wing of the Rural Development Society, this shop sells fabrics, clothing and handmade paper produced by local hill villagers. Profits go towards development projects in surrounding Shan and Pa-O villages, and the organisation also arranges treks that get good feedback.

OFF THE BEATEN TRACK

WALKING AROUND KALAW

Although trekking in the hills around Kalaw without a guide is not recommended, there are some interesting and easy-to-find sights just outside town that can be tackled in the form of a self-guided, half-day walk.

Starting at the market, head south on Min St, continuing to University St and turning southwest (right) at the roundabout-like junction (the park will be on your left). Following the hilly, pine-lined road, and veering left at the junction after the Pine Hill Resort, it should take 10 minutes or so to reach **Christ the King Church** (University Rd; daylight hours) FREE, an attractive, historic church dating back to the colonial era, which was run by the same Italian priest from 1931 to 2000.

Return the way you came until you reach the intersection with Oo Min Rd. Turn left and continue about 10 minutes or so until you see a group of pagodas on your left; this is **Shwe Oo Min Paya** (ရွှေဦးမင်ဘုရား; Oo Min Rd; daylight hours) FREE, a natural cave dripping with golden Buddha statues (and also just dripping – watch your footing on the slippery marble pathways).

After exploring the caves, continue along the road until you reach a T-junction. Turn right and follow the wooden signs with gold letters that lead you to **Hnee Paya** (နီးဘုရား; Hnee Pagoda St; daylight hours) FREE, home to a 500-year-old, gold-lacquered bamboo Buddha.

After paying your respects, backtrack along Hnee Pagoda St and turn left at the intersection. Continue along Circular Rd (West) until you reach the T-junction; turn right on Saitta Thukha St and after about 10 minutes or so you'll merge with Thidar St just behind **Hsu Taung Pye Paya** (ဆုတောင်းပြည့်ဘုရား; Aung Tha Pyay St; daylight hours) FREE; it's myriad stupas were restored from ruins using donations from visiting pilgrims.

KALAW TRANSPORT CONNECTIONS

DESTINATION	MINIBUS	PICK-UP	TRAIN
Aungban (for Pindaya)	K1000; minibus; 20min; daily 7am, 7.30am & 8am	K1000; 40min; frequent 7am-6pm	K200/K350 (ordinary/upper class); 1hr; daily 11.30am
Heho (airport)	K3000; minibus; 3hr; daily 7.30am, 8am & 8.30am	N/A	N/A
Loikaw	K4500; minibus; 6hr; daily 5am	N/A	K1550 (ordinary class, no upper class); 13hr; daily 7am
Mandalay	K10,000; minibus; 7hr; daily 9am & 10.30am. K10,000-12,000; bus; 7-8hr; frequent 8-10pm	N/A	N/A
Meiktila	K5000; minibus; 4-5hr; frequent 7am-noon	K3000; 4-5hr; frequent 7am-6pm	N/A
Nay Pyi Taw	K10,000; bus; 7-8hr; frequent 8.30-9pm	N/A	K1750/K3650 (ordinary/upper class); 11hr; daily 12.49pm
Nyaung U (Bagan)	K12,000; minibus; 7hr; daily 8.30am. K11,000; bus; 8hr; frequent 8-9pm	N/A	N/A
Shwenyaung (for Inle Lake)	K3000; minibus; 3hr; daily 7.30am, 8am & 8.30am	N/A	K500/K1150 (ordinary/upper class); 3hr; daily 11.30am
Taunggyi	K3000; minibus; 3hr; daily 7.30am, 8am & 8.30am	N/A	N/A
Thazi	K5000; minibus; 4hr; frequent 7am-noon	K4000; 4hr; frequent 7am-6pm	K850/K1800 (ordinary/upper class); 7hr; daily 12.49pm
Yangon	K12,000-18,000; bus; 10-12hr; daily 9.30am, frequent 5-8pm	N/A	N/A

ℹ Information

KBZ Bank (Min St; ⊙ 9.30am-3pm) has an ATM that accepts international cards, and a currency-exchange counter (9am to 2pm Monday to Saturday).

ℹ Getting There & Away

Several bus ticket offices (Union Hwy; NH4) across from the market, as well as English-speaking Dev Singh at **Sun Shine** (☑ 09 3620 1202; Union Hwy (NH4); ⊙7am-9pm), book seats on the long-distance buses between Taunggyi and various destinations. Air-con buses, fan-cooled minivans and pick-ups to other destinations in and around Shan State also stop along this stretch of the Union Hwy (NH4), but it's worth noting that fares for foreigners are sometimes doubled.

Local minibuses (Kone Thai St) bound for Taunggyi depart every morning from a stop behind the Aung Chang Tha Zedi; these buses can drop you off in Aungban (for Pindaya), Heho (airport) or Shwenyaung (for Inle Lake). Nearby,

the morning minibus to Loikaw (Kone Thai St) departs from in front of Morning Star.

Kalaw's train station is a stop on the slow, winding line that links Thazi and Shwenyaung, as well as the line that links Loikaw and Nay Pyi Taw. Note that trains are almost always delayed by hours.

Kalaw has no airport of its own, but flights are served via Heho, about 16 miles away. Taxis waiting at the airport charge K20,000 to Kalaw (1½ hours); a cheaper option is to hike the near mile to the Union Hwy and wait for a westbound bus or pick-up, although you may face a long wait.

ℹ Getting Around

Kalaw is a compact town but motorcycle taxis at the corner of Kone Thai and Bu Tar Sts can run you to Hnee Paya or the Shwe Oo Min caves and back for around K3000.

Bicycles can be rented at **Naing Naing Hire Bike** (☑ 09 5428 312265; naing.cc@gmail.com; Min St; per day from K3000; ⊙ 8.30am-5pm).

Thazi သာစည်

POP C 20,560 / ☏ 064

Thazi crops up on travellers' itineraries solely because of its location. The town marks the intersection of the Mandalay–Yangon rail line and the railway line that runs through Shan State, and is also where buses from Yangon or Mandalay turn off the Yangon–Mandalay Hwy towards Shan State and Inle Lake.

If you need to stay overnight, the **Moon-Light Rest House** (☏ 064-69056, 09 222 5081; Thazi-Taunggyi Hwy; r US$10-15; ❋ ☏) is a basic, though passable, option. Its cheapest rooms have shared bathrooms and fans only, and there is a friendly English-speaking owner who is helpful when it comes to booking onward bus tickets. There's also a simple attached restaurant.

ⓘ Getting There & Away

Thazi train station is about 300m north of the main road. Buses drop off and pick up passengers along the highway near Moon-Light Rest House. For buses to Nyaung U (Bagan), take any bus to Mandalay or Nay Pyi Taw and change there. To get a seat on one of the more comfortable express buses between Mandalay and Taunggyi, you'll need to make an advance reservation – the staff at the Moon-Light can help.

KYAINGTONG & BORDER AREAS

East of Taunggyi, the landscape rucks up into great folds and is cloaked in dense forest and cut by rushing rivers. This is the heartland of the Golden Triangle, where the production of illicit drugs – opium, heroin and methamphetamines – continues to flourish and where insurgent armies have battled for their own states ever since Myanmar gained its independence in 1948. While some militias have signed ceasefire agreements with the government, parts of the region are still locked in conflict. That, and a myriad of criminal activities, means much of eastern Shan State remains subject to government-imposed travel restrictions.

Kyaingtong (Kengtung) ကျိုင်းတုံ

POP C 44,290 / ☏ 084

Set around an attractive lake, Kyaingtong is one of the most pleasant towns in Myanmar. In culture and appearance, Kyaingtong feels closer to the hill towns of northern Thailand than other cities in Shan State. And whereas most of Shan State is dominated by the Tai Lü and Tai Nuea peoples, Kyaingtong was once the capital of a Tai Khün kingdom

THAZI TRANSPORT CONNECTIONS

Destinations from Thazi include the following:

DESTINATION	BUS	MINIBUS & PICK-UP	TRAIN
Aungban (for Pindaya)	N/A	K5000; 4hr; frequent 7am-11pm	K1150/K2250 (ordinary/upper class); 7hr; daily 6am
Kalaw	N/A	K5000; 5hr; frequent 7am-11pm	K850/K1800 (ordinary/upper class); 6hr; daily 6am
Loikaw	N/A	K8000-10,000; 10hr; daily 5.30pm	K2250 (ordinary class, no upper class); 18hr; daily 6am
Mandalay	K5000; 3hr; frequent 11am-3pm	K5000; 3hr; frequent 11am-3pm	K950/K1950 (ordinary/upper class); 3hr; daily 3am, 6am & 9pm
Meiktila	N/A	K1000; 30min; frequent 4am-6pm	N/A
Nay Pyi Taw	K3000; 4hr; daily 5pm & 6pm	N/A	K900/K1750 (ordinary/upper class); 4hr; daily 11am
Shwenyaung (for Inle Lake)	N/A	K8000; 6hr; frequent 7am-11pm	K1500/K3000 (ordinary/upper class); 9hr; daily 6am
Taunggyi	N/A	K8000; 7hr; frequent 7am-11pm	N/A
Yangon	K10,000; 9-10hr; daily 5pm & 6pm	N/A	K3700/7350 (ordinary/upper class); 11-12hr; daily 9am, 6pm & 8pm

Kyaingtong (Kengtung)

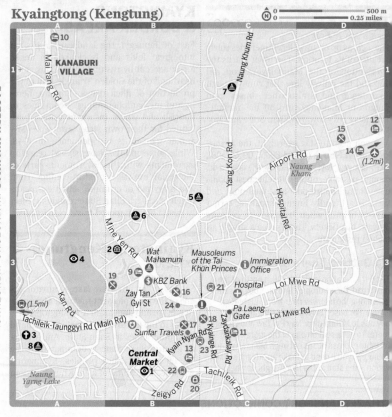

Kyaingtong (Kengtung)

and the majority of its residents still belong to that ethnic group. Kyaingtong was long caught in the crossfire between rival drug

lords, various ethnic armies and the Myanmar military, but the area is now peaceful. The rugged terrain of eastern Shan State contributes to a palpable sense of isolation: Kyaingtong is an outpost of development amid largely deforested mountains that are home to Wa, Akha, Palaung and Lahu villages where little has changed in centuries. This means that hill treks are a major attraction here.

Sights

If there were any more Buddhist monasteries in Kyaingtong, people would have nowhere left to live. The town's 40-odd monasteries are called *wat* rather than *kyaung*, and local monks wear both orange and red robes, reflecting Kyaingtong's close cultural links to Thailand.

★Central Market MARKET
(ဈေး႐ုံ.မဈေး; Zeigyo Rd; 5am-3pm) Kyaingtong's exotic central market is one of our favourites in Myanmar, and plays host to a diverse mix of hill peoples, especially early in the morning, displaying heaps of fresh and unusual produce and delicious breakfast stalls (dishes from K500). You can also find Thai cosmetics and household products here and change money. The market is closed on full-moon days.

Nyaung Toung LAKE
(ညောင်တန်း; Kan Rd) The old British enclave in Kyaingtong was centred on Nyaung Toung, a centrally located lake that is the most happening part of town come nightfall, where locals flock to the surrounding restaurants. Several decaying colonial buildings perch by or close to the lake, including the handsome **Colony House** (Mine Yen Rd). On the road leading towards Taunggyi, the **Roman Catholic Mission** (ရောမကက်သလစ်သာသနာပြုစခန်း) and **Immaculate Heart Cathedral** have been providing an education for hill village orphans since colonial times.

Wat Jong Kham BUDDHIST TEMPLE
(ဝတ်ကျင်ခမ်; off Mine Yen Rd; daylight hours) FREE The gilded stupa of Wat Jong Kham rises majestically above the centre of town. Legend dates the *wat* to a visit by Gautama Buddha but a more likely date for the stupa is the 13th-century Thai migration from Chiang Mai.

Wat In BUDDHIST TEMPLE
(ဝတ်အင်း; off Airport Rd; daylight hours) FREE Just north of Airport Rd, Wat In contains a stunning collection of ancient gilded wooden buddha images in all shapes, sizes and positions.

Yat Taw Mu BUDDHIST TEMPLE
(ရပ်တော်မူ; off Tachileik-Taunggyi Rd (Main Rd); daylight hours) FREE Pointing dramatically towards the mountains on a ridge overlooking Nyaung Toung lake, the 60ft-high standing buddha statue known as Yat Taw Mu is probably the most distinctive landmark in Kyaingtong. Next to the statue is a dusty **Cultural Museum** (US$2 or K2000; 10am-4pm Tue-Sun) with an emphasis on costumes, as well as some farming implements and other tribal objects, some inexplicably painted silver.

Festivals & Events

Water Festival CULTURAL
(Apr) Kyaingtong's big Buddhist calendar event, when everyone gets a dousing, including visitors.

Chinese New Year CULTURAL
(Jan/Feb) Kyaintong's large Chinese community celebrate the Chinese New Year in late January or early February with the usual firecracker-charged festivities.

Sleeping

The accommodation scene in Kyaingtong is fairly limited with just a few realistic places to stay. As is the case elsewhere in Myanmar, breakfast is included in the price. Electricity can be scarce. Most places will accept payment in US dollars, kyat or Thai baht.

Sam Ywet Guest House GUESTHOUSE $
(084-21643; Airport Rd; r US$10-20;) You won't hear much English, and it's a trek from downtown, but this is one of Kyaingtong's few budget options. Big but basic, fan-cooled rooms with cold showers.

TRAVEL RESTRICTIONS

- At research time, foreigners were allowed to travel by road between Tachileik, Kyaingtong and Mong La, and by air between Kyaingtong and Tachileik and the rest of Myanmar, but the 280 miles of Union Hwy (NH4) between Kyaingtong and Taunggyi are off-limits, as is the road from Inle Lake, unless you purchase a very expensive permit.
- If you crossed to this part of Myanmar by land without having obtained a visa in advance, there are a few caveats (p232).

DAY TRIPS AROUND KYAINGTONG

The hills outside of Kyaingtong are dotted with Lahu, Akha, Palaung, Loi, Lisu and Wa villages, as well as those of various Tai groups. Overnight stays are allowed, but you'll need a guide and advance permission from the authorities in Kyaingtong. Recommended guides include **Freddie** (Yot Kham; ☑ 09 4903 1934; yotkham@gmail.com) and **Paul** (Sai Lon; ☑ 09 4903 0464, 084-22812); guide fees run from US$20 to US$25 per day. Transport and guides can be arranged at **Princess Hotel** (☑ 084-21319; kengtung@mail4u.com.mm; 21 Zaydankalay Rd; r US$50-60; ❉ ☎) or **Harry's Trekking House**.

The most popular destination is **Pin Tau**, only 9 miles north of Kyaingtong, where it's possible to visit the villages of several different ethnic groups in a single day. A round-trip taxi here will cost around US$35.

Ho Kyim (ဟိုကင်မ်), approximately 10 miles south of town, is home to several Loi, Akha and Lahu villages. A round-trip taxi here costs around US$40.

The area surrounding the atmospheric Tai Khün village of **Wan Sai** (ဝမ်စိုင်း) is home to several worthwhile sights. From Wan Sai, where many residents still live in traditional wooden homes, it's a brief walk to an Akha village, and another 30- to 40-minute walk to **Ho Lang** (ဟိုလျှမ်း), a hilltop En village. Along the same road, and with great views of the Tai Khün village of **Wan Loi** (ဝမ်လွိုင်) and the river valley, is **That Jom Loi** (သက်ဂျုန်လွိုင်), a hilltop temple. The area is a 45-minute drive east of Kyaingtong; a taxi to these destinations will run about US$40.

Located a 40-minute drive northwest of Kyaingtong is the jumping-off point for **Lahu Shi** (လဟူရှီး), a remote Lahu village accessible only via an arduous three-hour uphill slog. Also north of town, off the road that leads to Mong La, **Wan Nyek** (ဝန်ညက်) and **Wan Saen** are two villages where the Loi people still live in traditional longhouses. A taxi to either of these trailheads costs US$35.

Loi-mwe (လွိုင်မွေ), 20 miles southeast of Kyaingtong, functioned as a second-tier hill station in the British era and you can still see a number of fading **colonial buildings** and a 100-year-old Catholic **church**. The main attraction, though, is the drive up here through a landscape of hills and terraced rice fields. A taxi here should cost around US$40.

If you don't have the time or funds for a trek, a good **self-guided walk** can be had along the former road to Mong La, now colloquially known as Yang Kon Rd. The area is home to several Shan families who earn a living by making **pottery** and *khao sen* (fermented rice noodles), the latter made by a laborious process of boiling, pounding and squeezing a dough of rice flour. Your walk terminates at **Wat Yang Kon** (ဝတ်ရန်ကင်း; Yang Kon Rd; ☉ daylight hours) FREE, known among locals for the decorative robes covering the main buddha statue.

Private Hotel HOTEL $
(☑ 084-21438; privatehotelmyanmar@gmail.com; 5 Airport Rd; r US$39-42; ❉ ☎) The bungalow-style rooms here surround a tidy lawn and come with small balconies. The bathrooms could use some work, but the mattresses are new and the eccentric owner makes every effort to please. It's a long hike, or short motorcycle taxi ride, from the centre of town.

Sam Yweat Hotel HOTEL $
(☑ 084-21235; samywethotel@gmail.com; cnr Kyaing Lan 1 & Kyaing Lan 4 Rds; s/d US$30/35; ❉ ☎) Centrally located Sam Yweat Hotel offers big, clean rooms, OK bathrooms and friendly staff, as well as a handy free map of Kyaingtong.

Harry's Trekking House GUESTHOUSE $
(☑ 084-21418; harry.guesthouse@gmail.com; 132 Mai Yang Rd; r US$10-25; ❉ ☎) It's inconveniently located north of the town centre, but Harry's is a long-standing budget option and the affable owner is knowledgeable about the surrounding area and can organise reliable guides and transport, as well as renting bikes and scooters. Rooms are plain and the mattresses are not the best. The more expensive rooms have air-con, while the cheapest are fan-cooled.

Amazing Kengtung Resort HOTEL $$
(☑ 084-21620; www.amazingkyaingtongresort.com; Mine Yen Rd; r US$69; ❉ ☎ ≋) Set in neatly landscaped grounds that once surrounded the palace of Kyaingtong's *saopha,* or sky prince (demolished in 1991 as revenge

for Shan nationalist activity in the area), there are 108 sizeable and clean, if anonymous, rooms here. All come with balconies and some have lake views. There's a proper swimming pool and an on-site restaurant. Expect 15% discounts in low season.

✖ Eating

Nearly all of Kyaingtong's restaurants serve Chinese food as perceived through a Burmese lens and all shut by 9pm. Nyaung Toung Lake is surrounded by restaurants that come alive in the evening, serving barbecue and claypot noodle dishes, and stay open until 11pm. A couple of places in town serve the local take on classic Western dishes.

★ My Cup   BURMESE $
(Nyaung Toung Lake; mains from K1800; ⊙ 5-11pm; 🖹) Something of a hotspot for young locals, who pack out the outside terrace (inside has air-con) by Nyaung Toung Lake every night. It does its own take on Western food, but the Burmese and Shan salads, curries and soups are rather better. It's also fine for an evening beer.

★ Cafe Twenty One   CAFE $
(✆ 084-21952; 19 Zay Tan Gyi St; mains from K1900; ⊙ 7am-10pm; 🛜 🖹) Pleasant, friendly, chilled-out cafe with a small garden area out back. The big menu mixes Burmese, Chinese and Western dishes and it does reasonable dim sum (K800 per serving), but it's equally good for a coffee or smoothie.

Happy Cafe   TEAHOUSE $
(off Kyain Nyan Rd; tea from K300, noodles from K600; ⊙ 6am-6pm; 🛜) Join the idlers, monks and newspaper-readers at this amenable teahouse with an outside area in the shade. It's a good place to pick up a morning bowl of *mohinga* (noodle and fish sauce soup, K600) or *myishay* (Shan noodle soup, K900). They have wi-fi too.

Best Choice Restaurant   CHINESE, BURMESE $
(Airport Rd; mains from K3000; ⊙ 10am-9pm; 🖹) This Chinese restaurant offers up tasty Chinese-Burmese dishes, and has a cosy dining room at the back and tables under an awning in the yard.

Lod Htin Lu Restaurant   CHINESE, BURMESE $
(Kyainge Rd; mains from K2500; ⊙ 10am-9pm; 🖹) This long-standing restaurant offers the most authentic take on Chinese food in Kyaingtong.

🛍 Shopping

★ U Mu Ling Ta   HOMEWARES
(✆ 084-22611; off Tachileik Rd; ⊙ 8am-5pm) This fifth-generation, family-run shop specialises in lacquerware, from the ubiquitous, multicoloured Bagan style, to the striking, black Kyaingtong style. Pieces start at US$10 and are made on-site, so you can get a peek into the production process. The shop is located at the top of an unmarked driveway on Tachileik Rd – locals should be able to point you in the right direction.

ℹ Information

ATMs have arrived in Kyaingtong, with more being installed at the time of research. You can also find/ exchange US dollars, Chinese yuan and Thai baht with the money-changers at the central market (p225). **KBZ** (Zay Tan Gyi St; ⊙ 9am-3pm) also has an ATM and money-changing facilities.

Immigration Office (cnr Zay Tan Gyi St & Yang Kon Rd; ⊙ 24hr) Down an alley north of Pa Laeng Gate; issues permits for travel around Kyaingtong and to Mong La and Tachileik.

Sunfar Travels (✆ 084-21833; Kyain Nyan Rd; ⊙ 8am-5pm) Sells tickets for all the private airlines.

ℹ Getting There & Away

Shwe Myo Taw Express (✆ 084-23145; Tachileik Rd) and **Thet Nay Win** (✆ 084-23424; Kyain Nyan Rd), with offices in town, run air-con buses to Tachileik, as do three other companies. Shared taxis bound for Tachileik and Mong La depart when full from a forecourt (off Zay Tan Gyi St) just behind the Golden Banyan Restaurant.

Several airlines, including Air Bagan (www. airbagan.com), Air KBZ (www.airkbz.com) and **Yangon Airways** (✆ 084-22798, in Yangon 01-383 100; www.yangonair.com; 36 Zay Tan Gyi St; ⊙ 9am-5pm) connect Kyaingtong and other destinations in northern Myanmar via a confusing, weblike flight map. Note that almost all flights to and from Yangon and Mandalay are not direct and involve one or two stops. Taxis charge K5000 and *thoun bein* K3000 for the 2-mile trip to/from Kyaingtong's airport.

Mong La   မိုင်းလား
POP C 20,745 / ✆ (86) 691

Located on the Chinese border, Mong La lies within Myanmar, but is part of Special Region 4, a mostly autonomous area controlled by the ethnic Shan National Democratic Alliance Army (NDAA), which has long been accused of involvement in the illicit drug trade.

Reliant on China for everything from the electricity supply to mobile-phone connections,

Mong La feels more like a town in neighbouring Yúnnán Province than anywhere in Myanmar. Chinese is the lingua franca here – don't expect to hear any English – and the Chinese yuan (¥) is the local currency. Almost all visitors are from across the border, drawn to Mong La by its dubious reputation for wild nightlife. Gambling and prostitution are the main recreational activities, but Mong La is also notorious for the smuggling and selling of endangered animal species, as well as for being a key node on the people-trafficking route from China to Thailand.

◉ Sights

Most Chinese visitors come to Mong La to gamble, although all the big casinos have moved to **Wan Siw**, a village 10 miles southwest of Mong La. Minivans and cars with individual casino logos on them cruise around town and offer free transport to Wan Siw, although you might have to wait a while for a ride back. The casinos aren't foreigner-friendly, featuring games that most Westerners aren't familiar with, while some also require gamblers to exchange a certain amount of money (usually around US$50) into non-refundable chips upon entry. Photography is not permitted in the casinos, and the security guards don't welcome Westerners, while the people involved in the wildlife trade can get aggressive if you try and take photos.

Perhaps Mong La's most infamous sight is its big and bustling **central market**, a known hotspot for wildlife trafficking. You'll find retailers selling animal parts in the northeast corner of the market.

Museum in Commemoration of Opium-Free in Special Region 4 MUSEUM
(ဘိန်းစိုက်ပျိုးရေးကင်းစင်ရာအထူးဒေသ-၄အထိမ်းအမှတ်ပြတိုက်; ⊙24hr) FREE In 1997, Mong La's ethnic militia ruler declared the region 'drug-free', and this surreal, temple-like museum was opened with much fanfare in a not very convincing attempt to prove that. Dusty, neglected, and staff-free, the museum doesn't appear to have been touched since then. In addition to photos, maps and drug paraphernalia, you'll find creepy life-sized dioramas: one shows long-haired, jeans- and leather jacket–wearing Myanmar youth taking heroin, before being reformed into short-haired, *longyi*-clad respectable citizens.

That Luang Mong La BUDDHIST TEMPLE
(သက်လောင်းမိုင်းလား; ⊙daylight hours) FREE
This attractive, golden hilltop temple is home to around 50 monks and offers fine views over Mong La and towards China. Inside, you'll find an immense Buddha statue and dioramas of famous religious sites across Myanmar.

🏃 Activities

There's huge potential for trekking among various ethnic groups outside Mong La, but for now visitors are not encouraged to venture far out of town.

Destinations outside of Mong La include **Mong Puen** (မုန်ပွအမ်), a Tai Lü village a 30-minute drive east of Mong La where there's a crumbling old Buddhist temple and where most of the 69 families live in traditional wooden houses; **Wat Nong Luang** (ဝတ်နောင်လျှန်), an old Buddhist temple accessible only via a rough four-hour drive; and **Nam Yi** (နမ်ရိ), a village home to a large Buddha image. A car and driver to most destinations around Mong La should cost around Y400 to Y500 per day.

🛏 Sleeping & Eating

Mong La has many hotels, with more being built at the time of research; the most convenient are clustered around the central market. Most places are Chinese-style and more comfortable, if smoky, than Burmese hotels in the same price range. Ignore listed prices: you should be able to get an OK room here for Y150. Very few hotels offer wi-fi, though.

There's good and authentic Chinese food in Mong La, especially Yúnnán and Sìchuān dishes, thanks to the profusion of restaurants run by Chinese immigrants. They can be found in and around the market. At night, many open-air barbecue places get going and stay busy until the early hours.

Kai Xuan Hotel HOTEL $
(☑(+86) 691-556 9111; r Y220-240; ❄) This hotel offers decent-sized rooms with com-

---

ⓘ TRAVEL RESTRICTIONS

➡ At research time, non-Chinese travellers were not allowed to cross to/from China at Mong La.

➡ If you arrived in Myanmar via land at Tachileik and left your passport at the border, a guide and permits are required to visit Mong La. If you haven't already arrived with a guide from Kyaingtong or elsewhere, you'll be required to hire one in Mong La for Y100 per day.

fortable beds and modern bathrooms, although they can be smoky, so check them first. Regular discounts bring prices down to Y150. There's no English-language sign: look for the orange building on the corner opposite the northwest corner of the central market. Like most hotels in Mong La, it doesn't offer wi-fi.

ⓘ Information

Chinese yuan is the currency in Mong La; change in advance at Kyaingtong's central market. You can also change money at Mong La's central market.

ⓘ Getting There & Around

Mong La's bus station, known locally by the Chinese word *chēzhàn*, is a forecourt opposite a PTT gas station about a mile west of town. Shared taxis make the run to Kyaingtong (K13,000/11,000 front/back seat, 2½ hours, from 7am) along a reasonable road when they have enough passengers. Get here in the early morning if you want to avoid a long wait for a ride.

Most of Mong La's sights can be reached by motorcycle taxi. Many drivers congregate around the market and charge Y40 for a round trip to the sights. If you want to hire a car and driver, ask at your hotel or **Shwe Lin Star Tourism** (☑ (+86) 691-556 9331; shwelinstar@ hotmail.com; ⊙7.30am-3pm). Prices start at Y400 per day.

Tachileik   တာချီလိတ်

POP C 51,550 / ☑ 084

Sitting opposite the Thai border town of Mae Sai, Tachileik is a hectic, dusty frontier city. Crossing from Thailand, you'll be struck immediately by the difference in development between Tachileik and Mae Sai. Tachileik, though, is much more prosperous than most Burmese towns of an equivalent size, thanks to it location on the Myanmar–Thai border and the subsequent trade in all manner of legal and illicit items.

There is no reason to stay in Tachileik; for travellers, the town is a transit point only. If you're coming from Thailand and looking to travel onto Kyaingtong, be sure to cross the border early in the morning: the last bus to Kyaingtong leaves at noon.

🛏 Sleeping

If you're stuck overnight in Tachileik, there are a number of hotels close to the border crossing. **Riverside Hotel** (☑ 084-51161; 215 U Aung Zay Ya St; r 700-900B; ❄ 🛜) is accept-

able, but accommodation on the Thai side is better in every respect; the Khanthongkham Hotel, near the border post in Mae Sai, is recommended. Hotels in Tachileik prefer payment in Thai baht, but most places will accept US dollars as well.

ⓘ Information

There are a number of ATMs in Tachileik that accept foreign cards. If you want to exchange Thai baht or US dollars for Myanmar kyat, moneychangers congregate close to the border: the motorcycle taxi drivers who wait for travellers crossing from Thailand will point you in the right direction.

ⓘ Getting There & Away

There are five 'bus stations' in Tachileik, each one for the five different companies offering buses to Kyaingtong. Each company has a couple of daily buses to Kyaingtong (K10,000, four to five hours), at 8.30am and 11.30am or noon. The bus stations are a K1500/50B motorcycle taxi ride from the border. Shared taxis to Kyaingtong (K12,000 to 15,000, three to four hours, frequent 6am to noon) can also be found at the bus stations.

Air Bagan (www.airbagan.com), **Air KBZ** (www.airkbz.com) and **Yangon Airways** (www. yangonair.com) fly to/from Tachileik's airport, as do other airlines, located a couple of miles east of town.

DESTINATION	AIR
Heho	from US$127; 1hr; Mon, Tue, Fri & Sat
Kyaingtong	from US$69; 20min; Wed, Fri & Sun
Mandalay	from US$135; 1½hr; Mon, Wed, Fri & Sun
Yangon	from US$153; 2½hr; daily

KAYAH STATE   ကယားပြည်နယ်

Tiny Kayah State – Myanmar's smallest – is where you can really step off the tourist trail and experience the astonishing diversity of a country that has no fewer than 135 official ethnic groups. Kayah is home to a disproportionate number of Myanmar's minorities, including the Yinbaw, Bre, Kayin (Karen), the eponymous Kayah (Karenni or Red Karen), and perhaps most famously, the 'longneck' Kayan (also known as Padaung).

Wedged between Shan State to north and west, Kayin State to the west and south, and Thailand to the east, Kayah State was long closed to independent foreign travellers. Even now, few foreigners make it down here and visitors are restricted to the capital Loikaw and Deemawsoe Township, to the south-east of Loikaw. But with more of the state expected to open up in the near future and many potential trekking routes in the region, friendly Kayah is set for a tourist boom.

Loikaw

POP C 51,350 / ☏ 083

The capital of Kayah State, Loikaw (လွိုင်ကော်) is a low-key, low-rise town on the Pilu River, dominated by the hilltop pagoda of Taung Kwe Zayde. Loikaw's tidy streets are fine for walking, but the city is really a base for venturing out into the surrounding countryside and villages, where relatively few foreigners have been.

ℹ GETTING TO THAILAND: TACHILEIK TO MAE SAI

Tachileik is one of Myanmar's 'open' land borders for foreign visitors, and it is now possible to enter/exit Myanmar here with an e-visa. But there are a few caveats, and it is possible the following information may change, so be sure to check the situation locally before you travel.

Getting to the border The border is a short walk from 'downtown' Tachileik, or 1.2 miles and a K1500/50B motorcycle taxi ride from the town's five different bus stations.

At the border If you've arrived in Kyaingtong or Tachileik via air from elsewhere in Myanmar, you can freely exit the country at Tachileik. The Myanmar border post is open from 6am to 6pm, and upon crossing to Thailand, the Thai authorities will issue you permission to stay in Thailand for up to 15 days, or 30 days if you have a passport from one of the G7 countries. You can also enter with a Thai visa obtained overseas. Likewise, if you're crossing from Thailand and have already procured a Myanmar visa, you'll be allowed to proceed to Kyaingtong and/or Mong La, or by air to other destinations in Myanmar.

If you're approaching from Thailand and haven't already obtained a Myanmar visa, it's relatively straightforward to cross to Tachileik for the day and slightly more complicated to get a two-week visa and permission to visit Kyaingtong and/or Mong La.

The Thai immigration office (☏ 05 373 1008) is open from 6.30am to 6.30pm. After taking care of the usual formalities, cross the bridge and head to the Myanmar immigration office. There, you must pay a fee of 500B and your picture is taken for a temporary ID card that allows you to stay in town for the day; your passport will be kept at the office.

If you'd like to visit Kyaingtong and/or Mong La, proceed directly to the MTT office. There, you'll need to inform the authorities exactly where you're headed, and you'll need three photos and US$10 or 500B to process a border pass valid for 14 days; your passport will be kept at the border during this time, and you're expected to exit Myanmar at Tachileik. It's also obligatory to hire a guide for the duration of your stay. Guides cost 1000B per day. If you haven't already arranged for a Kyaingtong-based guide to meet you at the border, you'll be assigned one by MTT and will also have to pay for your guide's food and accommodation during the duration of your stay. Recommended Kyaingtong-based guides include **Freddie** (Yot Kham; ☏ 09 4903 1934; yotkham@gmail.com) and **Paul** (Sai Lon; ☏ 09 4903 0464, 084-22812). Note that if you're crossing this way, advance permission from MTT is required to visit other destinations in Myanmar.

Moving on Mae Sai's bus station is 1 mile from the border; pick-ups ply the route between the bus station and Soi 2, Th Phahonyothin (15B, five minutes, from 6am to 9pm). Alternatively, it's a 50B motorcycle taxi ride to/from the stand at the corner of Th Phahonyothin and Soi 4. From Mae Sai, major bus destinations include Bangkok (673B to 943B, 12 hours, frequent from 4pm to 5.45pm), Chiang Mai (182B to 364B, five hours, nine departures from 6.15am to 4.30pm) and Chiang Rai (39B to 69B, 1½ hours, frequent from 5.45am to 6pm).

For further information, head to shop.lonelyplanet.com to purchase a downloadable PDF of the Northern Thailand section of Lonely Planet's *Thailand* guide.

There is no direct transport to Mong La from Tachileik.

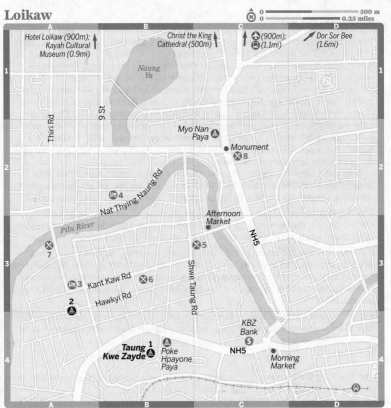

Loikaw

Sights

★ **Taung Kwe Zayde** BUDDHIST TEMPLE

(တောင်ကွဲစေတီ; NH5; camera fee K500; ⊙ daylight hours) Virtually rocketing from the landscape is this explosion of craggy limestone and white and gold stupas. The mountaintop Buddhist temple compound is Kayah State's most famous sight, and the *loi kaw* (Shan for 'island of mountains') are allegedly the origin of the town's name. Even if you're templed out, the wacky Buddhist Disneyland vibe is fun, and the views of the town and countryside really are breathtaking.

Thiri Mingalarpon Kyaung BUDDHIST TEMPLE

(သီရိမင်္ဂလာပုံကျောင်း; Hawkyi Rd; admission by donation; ⊙ daylight hours) Dating back to 1912, this attractive monastery formerly served as the palace of Kayah's *saopha* (sky princes) until 1959. After the last *saopha* passed away in 1987, his children donated the then decaying structure to a local Buddhist organisation.

Loikaw

◉ Top Sights
1 Taung Kwe Zayde B4

◉ Sights
2 Thiri Mingalarpon Kyaung A3

🛏 Sleeping
3 Min Ma Haw A3
4 Nan Ayar Inn B2

🍴 Eating
5 Breakfast Stalls C3
6 Mingala Hin Htoke B3
7 Pho Kwar A3
8 Shan Noodle Shop C2

Had they not done this, the government, at that time keen to do away with symbols of Kayah identity, would probably have allowed the building to fall into disrepair.

AROUND LOIKAW

The area around Loikaw is slowly opening up to visitors, although overnight stays outside Loikaw are still not permitted. At the time of research, Deemawsoe Township, a region 1½ hours south of Loikaw, was mostly open, but for other areas within a day's drive of Loikaw permission from either the local authorities or MTT in Yangon is needed.

Loikaw Travel Infos (p233) can arrange permits with the local government for visits to **Pah Pae** (ပက်ပယ်), the closest 'remote' area to Loikaw. Pah Pae is home to five Kayan (Padaung or 'longneck') villages, including **Rangkhu** (ရန်ကု; donation K10,000), thought to be the largest Kayan village in Kayah State. They can also get permits for **Tawtamagyi** (တော်တမကြီး), another Kayan village in Deemawsoe Township, **Htay Ko** (ဌေးကို), a traditional hill-peoples' area in Pruso Township, southwest of Loikaw, and **Eisan** (အဲဆန်), a Lisu village in Deemawsoe Township.

Note that it takes five days to get permits for the above, so email Loikaw Travel Infos ahead of your visit. They can also arrange transport and the guide you'll need if you want to talk to the villagers. For anything further afield, you'll need to speak to MTT in Yangon.

Dor Sor Bee (ဒေါ်စော်ပီး) Dor Sor Bee, just east of Loikaw, is home to several Kayah animist shrines. The towering logs, whitewashed and topped with decorations meant to symbolise the sun and moon, are gathering points during the Kayah New Year in April.

Pataing Hnyin (ပင်တိုင်းညှင်း) The distinctive tiger-striped head scarves worn by Pa-O women can be spotted as you travel south from Shan State to Kayah State, but you'll see them all over this quiet Pa-O village. It is the most-visited destination in the area around Loikaw but still sees few foreigners. A trip, combining visits to a few other sights, will run around US$90.

Keinari Keinara (ကိန္နရီ ကိန္နရာ; ⊙8am-5pm) This family-run business makes Kayah textiles on traditional looms. It's east of Loikaw and can be combined with a visit to Pataing Hnyin and Dor Sor Bee.

Christ the King Cathedral CHURCH
(Thiri Daw Rd; ⊙daylight hours) FREE Kayah State has long been the stomping ground of Roman Catholic missionaries and is home to many churches. Christ the King was built in 1939 – making it Kayah's oldest-surviving church – and features an intriguing blend of traditional European church architecture and local Buddhist styles, including an attractive bell tower with a bell brought from Italy. Mass is normally held in a larger adjacent building in Burmese, English, Kayan and Latin.

Kayah Cultural Museum MUSEUM
(ကယားယဉ်ကျေးမှုပြတိုက်; off NH5; K5000; ⊙10am-3.30pm Tue-Sun) Like most of Myanmar's regional museums, this oversized hall is home to a disproportionately scanty selection of dusty local relics and the usual display of mannequins wearing ethnic costumes. English-language captions are in short supply.

🛏 Sleeping

Loikaw has few accommodation options but they do include budget, midrange and top-end options. Note that Loikaw is a spread-out town and that the more expensive places are mostly located a 20-minute walk from the town centre.

Kan Thar Yar Hotel HOTEL $
(☎083-22344; kantharyarhotel@gmail.com; 376 U Ni St; r US$35-45; ❄🌐) This new-ish hotel has bright and big, clean and comfortable rooms with modern bathrooms. Some rooms have river views. This is the best midrange option, barring its location: a 20-minute walk north from the 'centre' of Loikaw, close to the Kayah Cultural Museum. Not much English spoken.

Nan Ayar Inn GUESTHOUSE $
(☎083-21306; 112-A Nat Thying Naung Rd; r US$15-25; ❄🌐) An acceptable budget option, this friendly guesthouse close to the river has simple, old-school rooms with small bathrooms. Cheaper ones are fan-only. Free bicycles are offered, but only when they are in working order (which wasn't the case when we visited).

Min Ma Haw GUESTHOUSE $
(☎083-21451; minmahaw96@gmail.com; 120 Kant Kaw Rd; r US$15-40; ❄🌐) The 'economy' rooms here are cubicle-like, have fans only

and share bathrooms. The more expensive ones are a big improvement: spacious, comfortable and quiet, if a little old-fashioned. Good location in the centre of town and the staff speak some English.

★ Kayah Resort   HOTEL $$
(☎083-21374; www.kayahresort.com; 6 U Khun Li St; r US$99-119, f US$249; 🛜 ❄ 💧) Proud possessor of the only hotel swimming pool in Loikaw, this new place is not really a resort but does have the swankiest, most comfortable rooms in town, as well as its own restaurant and efficient English-speaking staff. All the rooms are big, but the family rooms are like mini-houses with two bedrooms and a huge kitchen/living area. It's north of downtown.

Hotel Loikaw   HOTEL $$
(☎083-22946; www.hotelloikaw.com; 9th St; r US$70-80; ❄ 🛜) This quiet riverside hotel is a long walk north of 'downtown' Loikaw and sports a compound of bungalows that house 25 comparatively plain (but large) rooms. Bathrooms are smaller and could do with some TLC. The 'new' five-storey annexe has now been under construction for three years.

🍴 Eating

A few worthwhile restaurants can be found in Loikaw. For a tasty budget breakfast, head to the knot of **noodle stalls and teashops** (Shwe Taung Rd; mains from K500; ⏱6am-3pm) off Shwe Taung Rd.

★ Shwe Let Yar   BURMESE $
(☎083-22528; Kandayawaddy Rd; curries from K3000; ⏱11am-9pm) A couple of miles west of the 'centre' of Loikaw, Shwe Let Yar is considered to be Loikaw's best curry restaurant; check out the photos of visiting Myanmar celebs. Ask for the curry of the day and don't be afraid to try the delicious *balachaung*, a spicy dip. Note there's no roman-script sign.

Mingala Hin Htoke   BURMESE $
(Kant Kaw Rd; dishes from K500; ⏱9am-6pm) Locals come here in their droves for *hìn t'ouq*, an Intha dish of steamed banana-leaf packets of rice with pork or chicken. Also does noodles, good local sausage and addictive deep-fried meatballs. Look for the tiny blue sign (no roman script).

Pho Kwar   CHINESE, BURMESE $
(Thiri Rd; mains from K3500; ⏱10am-10pm; 📶) Loikaw is not a late-night town and this riv-

erside beer garden is one of the few places that stays open after 9pm. There's an English menu of classic Chinese-Burmese dishes and a shaded terrace to drink and eat on. It's located just before the bridge over the Pilu River.

Shan Noodle Shop   SHAN $
(NH5; dishes from K500; ⏱6am-8pm) A friendly Shan family put together tasty bowls of *shàn k'auq-swèh*, Shan noodle soup. The shop is located just south off a corner of NH5, a block south of the town's central white monument; look for the large tree (no roman-script sign).

ℹ Information

You can exchange money at **KBZ Bank** (off NH5; ⏱9.30am-3pm), which also has an ATM.

Loikaw Travel Infos (☎09 4927 8443, 09 42800 1621; loikawtravel.infos@gmail.com) Loikaw natives Htay Aung and Win Naing are the go-to guys for everything Kayah State travel-related. They lead tours of the city and state (per day US$35) and can arrange cars (per day from US$50) and the permission necessary to visit areas outside of Loikaw.

ℹ Getting There & Away

Loikaw's bus station (NH5) is located about 1.5 miles north of the centre of town on NH5; a *thoun bein* to/from here costs K1500, a taxi K2000.

Loikaw's train station is southeast of the centre of town, and is the terminus for a line that runs to Nay Pyi Taw via Shwenyaung (for Inle Lake), Kalaw and Thazi. Trains to and from here are exceedingly slow, even by the tortoise-like standards of Myanmar Railways. You're better off taking the bus.

A daily ferry runs to Nyaungshwe (for Inle Lake) in Shan State (K10,000, eight hours, 9am) from Phe Khon, an hour north of Loikaw. Note that the ferry runs only if it has enough passengers (10 normally) and that it's an uncomfortable ride exposed to the elements. You'll need also to pay the K12,500 Inle Lake admission fee. To get to Phe Khon, catch any bus heading north from Loikaw.

A more relaxing way of reaching Inle Lake by water is to charter your own boat from Phe Khon, which makes the journey less crowded and enables you to stop for sightseeing or a break. The guys at Loikaw Travel Infos can arrange a boat, which costs US$120 and takes about six hours.

Loikaw Airport (NH5) is just north of town. **Myanmar National Airlines** (☎083-21014, in Yangon 01-246 452; www.flymna.com; NH5) has four flights weekly to/from Yangon (US$93).

Mandalay & Around

Best Places to Eat

➡ Aye Myit Tar (p252)

➡ Shan Ma Ma (p252)

➡ Pan Cherry (p252)

➡ Super 81 (p252)

➡ Ko's Kitchen (p251)

Best Places to Sleep

➡ Rupar Mandalar (p250)

➡ Peacock Lodge (p246)

➡ Hotel by the Red Canal (p248)

➡ Shwe Ingyinn Hotel (p249)

➡ Hotel 8 (p249)

Why Go?

The Mandalay region is the major population centre of Upper Burma, itself the cradle of Burmese arts, culture and civilisation. Where Yangon is a diverse microcosm of the nation, Mandalay – for all its traffic and construction – remains an urban expression of Burmese ethnic identity, as seen in local dance shows, puppetry and crafts shops. And that identity is realised not just via considerable cultural capital, but proximity to a host of historical and religious sites. Places such as Inwa and Sagaing offer a green, rural escape from urban congestion, plus access to some of the nation's most evocative religious sites and archaeological ruins.

And one of the world's biggest bells, its longest teak foot bridge and an enormous, failed monument to royal hubris are just around the corner. Throw in Upper Burmese cuisine, friendly locals and sunsets over the Ayeyarwady (Irrawaddy) River, and you have a region worthy of careful exploration.

When to Go
Mandalay

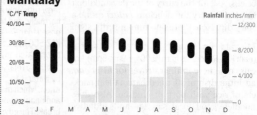

| Nov–Feb Peak tourist season: days hot but bearable, evenings mild and occasionally chilly. | Apr–Sep Extreme heat gives way to serious mid-summer rain; expect widespread closures during Thingyan festival. | Oct & Mar Budget hotels quieter; AC is still useful and rain is still possible. |

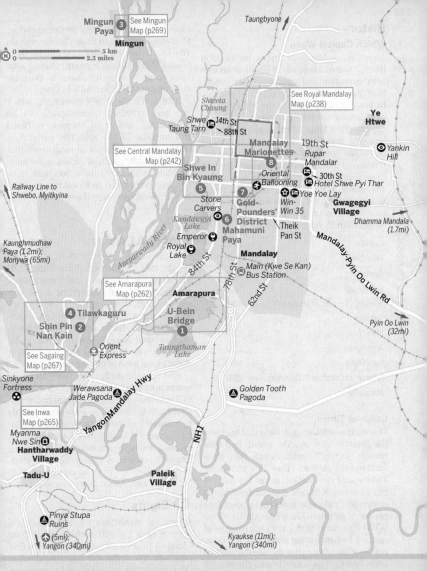

Mandalay & Around Highlights

1 U-Bein Bridge (p261)
Watching sunrise or sunset from the world's longest teak bridge in Amarapura.

2 Shin Pin Nan Kain (p268) Surveying Sagaing's monastery-dappled green hills and endless gilded pagodas.

3 Mingun Paya (p269)
Pondering this king-sized unfinished stupa.

4 Tilawkaguru (p268)
Exploring the ruins and painted frescoes of Tilawkaguru.

5 Shwe In Bin Kyaung (p241) Pottering around Mandalay's lesser-known beautiful teak monastery.

6 Mahamuni Paya (p241) Arriving by 4am at Mahamuni Paya as attendants wash the

face of the country's most famous buddha image.

7 Gold-Pounders' District (p240) Discovering the wealth of crafts being made, including edible sheets of gold leaf, in the Gold-Pounders' District.

8 Mandalay Marionettes (p255) Witnessing a lovely duet of expert royal ballet performed by puppets.

History

Which Capital When

According to Myanmar myths, the Buddha himself visited Mandalay Hill and, in an earlier incarnation, had scuttled up the riverside bluff Shwe-kyet-kya in the guise of a chicken. In less legendary epochs, the Mandalay region hosted several of Burma's post-Bagan capitals. New kings often sought to create a legacy by founding a new capital, transporting whole buildings with them, leaving few remains at older sites. The longest-lasting of these capitals was Inwa, known to Europeans as Ava. Mandalay itself only took shape as a city from 1857 and its brief, if momentous, period as a tailor-made capital city lasted less than 25 years from 1861.

CAPITAL	FROM...
Inwa (Ava)	1364
Taungoo	1555
Inwa (Ava)	1636
Shwebo (then called Mokesbo)	1752
Sagaing	1760
Inwa (Ava)	1764
Amarapura	1783
Inwa (Ava)	1823
Amarapura (after the 1838 earthquake)	1841
Mandalay	1861

Colonial Times

Despite powerful fortress walls that enclosed the gigantic royal city, the British had little trouble ejecting Mandalay's elite from their teak houses in 1885. They deported King Thibaw and demolished part of the original city to create a parade ground, turning the centrepiece palace complex into a governor's residence and club. Much later, during fierce WWII fighting in March 1945, the palace was ravaged by fire, leaving nothing of the original. New Mandalay grew outside the original walls into the vast concrete grid city you see today. The area within the walls was left as a vast tree-shaded army camp. It remains a strange military-controlled dead zone, out of bounds to foreigners apart from the central palace, which was completely rebuilt in the late 1990s, reputedly using forced labour.

Mandalay Today

Since the '90s, Mandalay has been a magnet for Chinese migrants, many of whom have roots in Yunnan Province. This creates an interesting wrinkle in the local Chinese population. Whereas in much of Myanmar, there is a split between generations-deep Chinese-Burmese and those Chinese who arrived in the last few years, in Mandalay there is an additional middle group: Chinese who have spent time acclimatising to Burmese culture, but still have family in China.

The nationalistic 969 movement, which has been criticised internationally for its anti-Islamic and racist rhetoric, is based in Mandalay. In July 2014, 969 leader Ashin Wirathu shared a social-media post that accused Muslim men of raping a Burmese Buddhist woman. In the subsequent riots, two men were killed and local mosques and Muslim businesses were looted and burned.

MANDALAY မန္တလေး

POP C 1,200,000 / ☑ 02 / ELEVATION 244FT

It's the rare traveller who immediately falls for Mandalay. Take every cliché you have of a busy, haphazardly expanding Asian metropolis and then confirm it: Myanmar's second-largest city has many things – concrete buildings, traffic, smog, a level of honking that could give a Vietnamese city a run for its money – but beyond a functional grid, it doesn't have a ton of immediate appeal.

Peer past the surface and you'll find deep reservoirs of Bamar culture, which manifest in countless monasteries, pagodas, workshops and teahouses. As the citizens of this nation revel in their new freedom, Mandalay becomes a loudspeaker for their hopes, dreams, disappointments and desires. If Yangon's nouveau riche dream of the stars, in Mandalay, they're more concerned with building a new nation from the ground up.

⊙ Sights

Several of Mandalay's top attractions are covered by a K10,000 Archaeological Zone ('combo') ticket valid for one week from first purchase. Currently the ticket is checked (and sold) at Mandalay Palace, Shwenandaw Kyaung and two sites at Inwa (Ava).

◉ Royal Mandalay

★ Mandalay Hill LANDMARK
(မန္တလေးတောင်; Map p238; camera fee K1000) To get a sense of Mandalay's pancake-flat sprawl, climb the 760ft hill that breaks it. The walk up covered stairways on the hill's southern slope is a major part of the experience; note that you'll need to go barefoot in places as you pass through numerous temples and pago-

das. The climb takes a good 30 minutes, but much longer if you allow for stops en route. The summit viewpoint is especially popular at sunset when young monks converge on foreigners for language practice.

➡ **South Routes**

There are two southern stairways. The most obvious starts between two giant **chinthe** (half-lion, half-dragon guardian deities) with 1729 steps. There's also an alternative southeastern stairway that is more interesting for glimpsed views, albeit harder on the feet. The two routes converge then climb to a shrine building containing a large **standing buddha**, whose outstretched arm points towards the royal palace. This evokes the legend in which the historical Buddha supposedly visited Burma, accompanied by his disciple Ananda, and on climbing Mandalay Hill prophesied that a great city would be founded below, after 2400 years. Scholars calculated this to mean 1857 AD, the year that King Mindon did indeed decree the capital's move from Amarapura to Mandalay.

Further up, behind the forgettable **Myatsawnyinaung Ordination Hall**, are the windowless ruins of a three-storey stone fortress retaken from the Japanese in a March 1945 battle by Britain's Royal Berkshire Regiment.

Near the summit, on the east side facing the penultimate stupa, a contemporary statue depicts ogress **San Dha Mukhi** offering forth her severed breasts. That's the sort of display that might have alarmed a more squeamish man, but according to legend, her feat of self-mutilation impressed the Buddha so much that he ensured her reincarnation 2400 years later as King Mindon.

➡ **Other Stairways**

Steeper stairways lead up from the north (in 25 minutes) or west (15 minutes) but there's little to see en route apart from canoodling couples (south) or lounging monks (west).

Wear shoes for these stairways and, near the top of the south route, be prepared to clamber across and between a trio of pipes.

➡ **Vehicles**

It's possible to drive most of the way up Mandalay Hill. From the upper car park both a lift and an escalator tower should whisk you up to the hilltop. However, as both are often broken you'll probably need to walk the last five minutes by stairways. From 10th St at 68th St, shared pick-up route 16 (per person K1000) shuttles to the car park. Motorcycle taxis typically charge K3000 up, K2000 down (even though the down route is much further due to a long one-way loop).

Shwenandaw Kyaung   BUDDHIST MONASTERY
(ရွှေနန်းတော်ကျောင်း; Golden Palace Monastery; Map p238; combo ticket K10,000) Lavished in carved panels, this fine teak monastery-temple is noted for its carvings, particularly the interior gilded Jataka scenes (past-life stories of the Buddha). The building once stood within the Mandalay Palace complex as the royal apartment of King Mindon, who died inside it in 1878.

Reputedly unable to cope with Mindon's ghost, his successor, King Thibaw, had the building dismantled, carted out of the palace complex and reassembled outside the fortress walls, where it was converted into a monastery (1880). It's a good thing he did, as all other palace buildings were later lost to WWII bombs.

Mandalay Palace   PALACE
(မန္တလေးနန်းတော်; Map p238; East Gate; combo ticket K10,000; ⊙7.30am-4.30pm) The 1990s reconstruction of Mandalay's royal palace features more than 40 timber buildings built to resemble the 1850s originals. Climb the curious spiral, timber-walled **watchtower** for a good general view. The palace's most striking structure is a soaring multilayered pyramid of

---

ⓘ **NAVIGATING MANDALAY**

Central Mandalay city streets are laid out on a grid system. East–west streets are numbered from 1st to 49th with 12th/26th as the north/south edges of the fortress moat. North–south streets are numbered above 50th, starting from the main Pyin Oo Lwin road in the east but becoming slightly confused west of diagonal 86th where some roads are more crooked and unnumbered.

A street address that reads 66th, 26/27, means a location on 66th St between 26th and 27th Sts. Corner addresses are given in the form 26th at 82nd. The 'downtown' area runs roughly from 21st St to 35th St, between 80th St and 88th St. Across the railway tracks, 78th St, 33/34 has the main new shopping malls while 30th, 35th and 73rd are all developing as busy commercial streets.

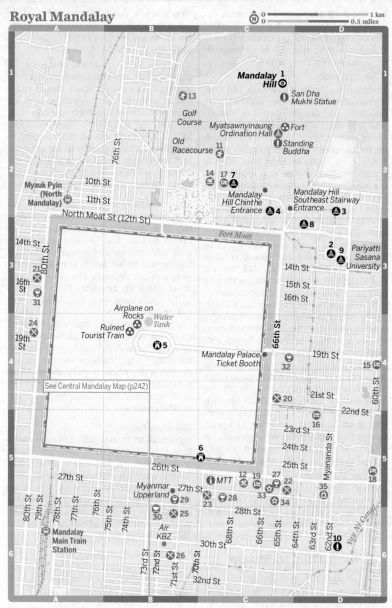

Mandalay Hill 1

San Dha Mukhi Statue

13

Golf Course

Myatsawnyinaung Ordination Hall

Fort

Standing Buddha

Old Racecourse

11

Myauk Pyin (North Mandalay)

10th St

11th St

14

17 7

Mandalay Hill Chinthe Entrance 4

Mandalay Hill Southeast Stairway Entrance 3

North Moat St (12th St)

Fort Moat

14th St

80th St

21

8

16th St

31

2 9

Pariyatti Sasana University

14th St

15th St

16th St

Airplane on Rocks

Water Tank

24

Ruined Tourist Train

19th St

5

66th St

Mandalay Palace Ticket Booth

19th St

15

60th St

See Central Mandalay Map (p242)

32

21st St

22nd St

20

23rd St

16

24th St

25th St

6

Myananda St

26th St

27th St

MTT

12 19 27 22

35

18

Myanmar Upperland

27th St

29

23

33 34

28

Air KBZ

30

25

28th St

Mandalay Main Train Station

66th St

65th St

64th St

63rd St

62nd St

30th St

10

73rd St

72nd St

71st St

70th St

26

32nd St

You Ni Canal

gilt filigree above the main **throne room**. To-day, much of the palace complex outside the front chambers is in serious disrepair, dusted with rubble and bird droppings. Palace access for foreigners is only via the east gate.

If cycling or motorcycling, you must dismount as you pass through the gate and, due to army sensibilities, you are required to stay on the direct access way and palace loop road. From this road you can see (but technically should not approach) the **tomb of King Mindon**, a large **drum-tower**, sheds containing more than 600 stone **inscription slabs** and a small **airplane** on some rocks in the trees.

Royal Mandalay

Top Sights
1 Mandalay Hill....................C1

Sights
2 Atumashi Kyaungdawgyi....................D3
3 Kuthodaw Paya....................D2
4 Kyauktawgyi Paya....................C2
5 Mandalay Palace....................B4
6 Moat & Fortress Walls....................C5
7 Peshawar Relics....................C2
8 Sandamuni Paya....................D3
9 Shwenandaw Kyaung....................D3
10 Skinny Buddha....................D6

Activities, Courses & Tours
11 Asia Centre Driving Range....................C2
12 Mandalay Swan Swimming Pool....................C5
13 Shwe Mann Taung Golf Club....................B1
14 Yatanaban Swimming Pool....................C2

Sleeping
15 Golden Mandalay....................D4
16 Hotel by the Red Canal....................D5
Ma Ma Guesthouse....................(see 18)
17 Mandalay Hill Resort....................C2
18 Peacock Lodge....................D5
19 Sedona Mandalay....................C5

Eating
20 Café City....................C4
21 Golden Duck....................A3
22 Green Elephant....................C5
23 Koffie Korner....................C5
24 Ko's Kitchen....................A4
25 Mingalabar Myanmar Restaurant....................B6
26 Mr BarBQ....................B6

Drinking & Nightlife
27 Cafe JJ....................C5
28 Central Park....................C5
29 Ginki Mandalay....................B5
30 Min Thiha....................B6
31 MR2 Pub....................A3
32 Mya Yi Nandar....................C4

Entertainment
33 Mandalay Marionettes....................C5
34 Mintha Theater....................C5

Shopping
35 Rocky....................D5

The westernmost building within the palace oval contains a minor **culture museum** where the most intriguing exhibit is King Thibaw's dainty, glass-pillared four-poster bed.

Kyauktawgyi Paya BUDDHIST TEMPLE
(ကျောက်တော်ကြီးဘုရား; Map p238; 12th St, 66/68; 6am-8pm) FREE At the heart of this large 19th-century complex is a 900-tonne buddha, 26ft tall and dressed in royal attire. Carved from a single block of marble, it reputedly took 10,000 men 13 days to transport it from a canal to the present site before its dedication in 1865.

The outer halls are edged in mirror tiles. A little subshrine in the southeast courtyard displays a giant marble 'alms bowl' and colourful renderings of King Mindon's 1865 visit. The October temple festival (p246) is so big that stallholders start erecting evening food stalls along the eastern approach roads some two weeks before it starts.

Moat & Fortress Walls FORTRESS
(Map p238) FREE Viewable only from the outside, a 230ft-wide moat and well over 4 miles of crenellated 26ft-high walls form a vast square around the site of the former Mandalay fortress/citadel. Reconstructed in the original 1857 style, the walls are punctuated at regular intervals with gate towers topped by pyramidal creations of fancifully carved woodwork. While artful photography can make much of these scenes, the effect isn't as impressive as you might expect, due to the length and regularity of the walls.

Peshawar Relics BUDDHIST SITE
(ပါရှာဝါရှိဓာတ်တော်မွေတော်ဌာပနာတိုက်; Map p238; U-Khanti Monastery, off 10th St; admission by donation; 7am-7pm) Three tiny shards of bone, believed to be Buddha relics, were discovered in 1908 by British archaeologists at the site of a once-great ancient stupa at Peshawar (in today's Pakistan). For years they were displayed on Mandalay Hill but after thefts of associated gemstones alerted authorities to their vulnerability, the relics were moved to a dusty little museum room in the U-Khanti Monastery.

The bones are normally only displayed on full-moon days, but if you're polite, a monk will bring them out and place them in a hexagonal light stand. You'll be offered a magnifying glass to examine the crystal phial within which the bones are almost invisibly housed.

Central Mandalay

The downtown area is not the city's most beautiful. However, you can easily escape into tree-shaded back alleys further west. And

THE WORLD'S BIGGEST BOOK

Around the beautiful gilt-and-gold stupa of the mid-19th-century **Kuthodaw Paya** (ကုသိုလ်တော်ဘုရား; Map p238; 62nd & 10th Sts; ⏰24hr) **FREE**, you'll find 729 text-inscribed marble slabs, each housed in its own small stupa and together presenting the entire 15 books of the Tripitaka. Another 1774 similarly ensconced marble slabs (collected in 1913) ring the nearby **Sandamuni Paya** (စန္ဒမုနိဘုရား; Map p238; ⏰8.30am-5pm) **FREE** with Tripitaka commentaries. Collectively these slabs are often cited as the 'World's Biggest Book'. Producing the Kuthodaw set alone required an editorial committee of more than 200. When King Mindon convened the 5th Buddhist Synod here, he used a team of 2400 monks to read the book in a nonstop relay. It took them nearly six months. Note that the slabs are placed behind grated entrances in small stupas (and they're written in Pali), so it's tough to make out the text.

amid the smoggy central grid of lacklustre five-storey concrete ordinariness lurk pagodas, striking churches and notable mosques.

Shwekyimyint Paya
BUDDHIST TEMPLE

(ရွှေကြီးမြင့်ဘုရား; Map p242; 24th St, 82/83; ⏰8am-6.30pm) Founded in 1167 by Prince Minshinzaw, exiled son of King Alaungsithu, Shwekyimyint considerably predates Mandalay itself. Minshinzaw consecrated the central sitting Buddha image that's roughly life-sized and crusted with gold and jewelled raiments in an intimately hushed little prayer chamber. The pagoda also hosts other images collected by later Myanmar kings that were relocated here for safe keeping after the British occupied Mandalay Palace.

Jade Market
MARKET

(ကျောက်ဝိုင်း; Map p242; 87th St, 39/40; US$1; ⏰8am-4pm) Rock dust and cheroot smoke fill the air in this heaving grid of cramped walkways, where you'll find a shoulder-to-shoulder mass of jade traders haggling, hawking and polishing their wares. There's a US$1 entry (not always enforced), but you could always sit outside the market and observe craftspeople cutting and polishing jade in the area around 87th St. Be on the lookout for merchants furtively discussing deals over cigarettes and tea at spots such as the Unison Teahouse (p254).

You don't have to want or even like jade to appreciate the timelessness of the scene; merchants may be using their smartphones, but the fierce haggling and individual branding of the jade trade feel like an echo of another era.

Setkyathiha Paya
BUDDHIST TEMPLE

(စက်ကျသိဟာဘုရား; Maha Thakya Thiha Paya; Map p242; 30th St, 85/86; ⏰7am-6pm) Mostly hidden behind shopfronts, this large elevated pagoda complex includes a 'golden rock' lookalike and an enormous sacred bodhi tree planted by U Nu, Myanmar's first post-independence prime minister. However, it is best known for an impressive 17ft-high seated bronze buddha, cast in 1823 by King Bagyidaw.

Flower Market
LANDMARK

(Map p242; 26th & Pulang Sts; ⏰7am-sunset) **FREE** This small market takes up a few blocks worth of space, which by midday become littered with multicoloured clouds of blossoms and piles of cut stems and leaves.

Eindawya Paya
BUDDHIST TEMPLE

(အိမ်တော်ရာဘုရား; Map p242; Eindawya St, 88/89; ⏰6am-late evening) **FREE** Ranged around a sizeable stupa glowing with gold leaf, Eindawa was founded in 1847 by King Pagan Min, whose princely palace once stood here. The complex offers a refreshing dose of relative quiet and serenity, given the bustle of nearby markets. In 1919, Eindawa was the site of a notable cultural battle when a group of Europeans defied the Buddhist ban on shoe-wearing and were forcibly evicted. For their pains, four of the monks who ejected the insensitive foreigners were convicted by a colonial court, one receiving a life sentence. So please take off your shoes!

Gold-Pounders' District
AREA

(Map p242; 36th St, 77/79) Those 1-sq-in goldleaf sheets that worshippers piously place on sacred buddha images are laboriously hand-pounded in dozens of specialist workshops in this two-block area. Two main street souvenir-shop showrooms, King Galon (p256) and Golden Rose (p256), have English-speaking staff who'll patiently talk you through the process while muscled gold-beaters demonstrate. It's free and fascinating, and the sales pitch is pretty casual.

Sri Ganesh Temple
HINDU TEMPLE

(သိရိဂနေ့ရှိဘုရားကျောင်း; Map p242; 27th St, 80/81) This temple's colourful, sculpture-crusted *gopuram* (monumental tower) might excite you if you've never been to southern India or Singapore.

⊙ Greater Mandalay

★ **Shwe In Bin Kyaung**   BUDDHIST MONASTERY
(ရွှေအင်းပင်ကျောင်း; Map p242; 89th St, 37/38; combo ticket K10,000; ⊙ 7am-6.30pm) A meditative departure from the usual Burmese 'douse-it-all-in-gold-and-pastels' aesthetic, this gorgeously carved teak monastery is beloved by tourists and locals. Commissioned in 1895 by a pair of wealthy Chinese jade merchants, the central building stands on tree-trunk poles and the interior has a soaring dark majesty. Balustrades and roof cornices are covered in detailed engravings, a few of them mildly humorous.

★ **Mahamuni Paya**   BUDDHIST TEMPLE
(မဟာမုနိဘုရား; 83rd St; ⊙ complex 24hr, museum sections 8am-5pm) **FREE** Every day, thousands of colourfully dressed faithful venerate Mahamuni's 13ft-tall **seated Buddha**, a nationally celebrated image that's popularly believed to be some 2000 years old. Centuries of votary gold leaf applied by male devotees (women may only watch) has left the figure knobbly with a 6in layer of pure gold...except on his radiantly gleaming face, which is ceremonially polished daily at 4am.

The statue was already ancient in 1784 when it was seized from Mrauk U by the Burmese army of King Bodawpaya. The epic story of how it was dragged back to Mandalay is retold in a series of 1950s paintings in a **picture gallery** across the pagoda's inner courtyard to the northeast of the Buddha image. Bodawpaya also nabbed a collection of Hindu-Buddhist **Khmer bronze figures**, which had already been pilfered centuries earlier from Angkor Wat, and reached Mrauk U by a series

of other historical thefts. Many figures were reputedly melted down to make cannons for Mandalay's 1885 defence against the British. But six rather battered figures remain, which have all been rubbed raw by devotees seeking good health. They're housed in a drab concrete building near the giant gong on the north side of the northwest inner courtyard.

Near Mahamuni's outer northeast exit you'll find a merrily kitsch clock tower and the **Maha Buddhavamsa Museum of World Buddhism**, which is effectively a gallery of paintings about the life of the Buddha, and photos of archaeological sites associated with that saga.

From the central shrine with its multi-tiered golden roof, long concrete passage-ways leading in each cardinal direction are crammed with stalls selling all manner of religio-tourist trinkets. The western passage emerges on 84th St amid fascinating **marble workshops**, where buddha statues are expertly crafted using power tools.

Mahamuni can be conveniently visited en route to Amarapura, Inwa or Sagaing.

Pinya Stupa Ruins   BUDDHIST STUPA
(ပင်းယစေတီပျက်) Possibly Myanmar's most forgotten ancient capital, Pinya rose to prominence in 1303 in the aftermath of the last wave of Mongol attacks. Its founder was upstart governor-king Thihathu, whose son, Athingaraza Sawyun, set up a rival kingdom across the river in Sagaing. The two coexisted for half a century, creating Bagan-style buildings, but today all that remains of old Pinya is a grouping of large brick stupa ruins.

At the time of research, work was being done to improve their structural integrity and clear large amounts of overgrowth. It is still possible to enter the ruins, each of which still has buddha images visible within.

MANDALAY & AROUND MANDALAY

WHITE ELEPHANTS

Legend has it that before giving birth to her auspicious son, the Buddha's mother dreamed of a white elephant presenting her with a lotus flower. In certain Buddhist countries this led to the idea that rare albino elephants were sacred and could not be put to work. Expensive to feed and of no practical use, white elephants were thus seen by 19th-century Western observers to be the embodiment of financial extravagance. The term 'white elephant' came to mean as much in English. However, in Burma/Myanmar and Siam/Thailand, the possession of white elephants was (and is) a potent symbol of kingship. Certain Burmese monarchs referred to themselves as 'golden-footed lord of the white elephant'. In 1885 when one of King Thibaw's white elephants died, it was interpreted as an omen foretelling the king's imminent demise at the hands of a British invasion force. And the Brits' insensitive decision to drag the elephant's carcass unceremoniously out of Mandalay Palace so horrified the pious city folk that the act helped spark 10 years of guerilla resistance.

Central Mandalay

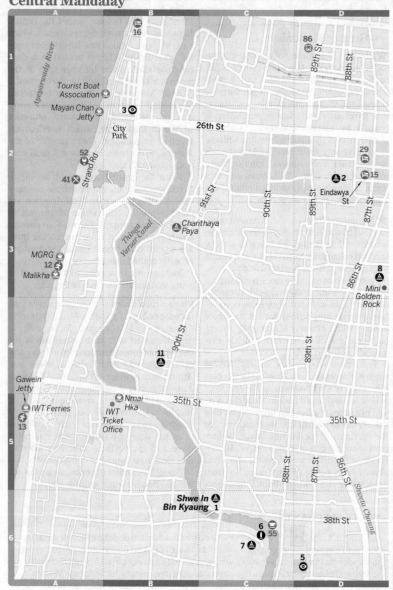

Pinya is an easy 10-minute detour en route to/from Mandalay Airport.

★ **Yankin Hill**　　　　　　　　AREA
(ရန်ကင်းတောင်; ☺ 24hr, stupas close gates around sunset) Staring distantly towards Mandalay Palace, merrily temple-topped Yankin Hill is mostly worth climbing for views of greater Mandalay's rice-field setting and of the Shan foothills behind. After a 10-minute climb via the obvious covered stairway you're likely to encounter a couple of **domesticated stags** –

Lots of hotels!

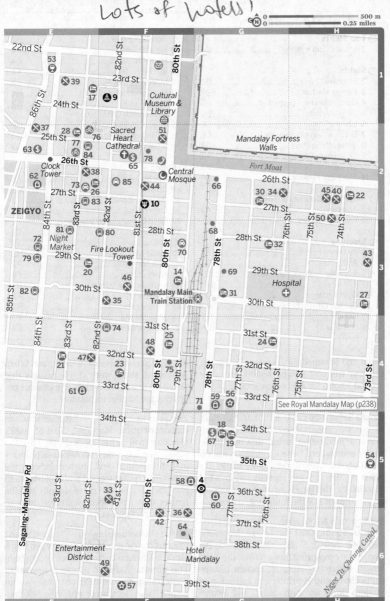

feeding them supposedly brings Buddhist merit. Pagoda walkways turn south along the ridgetop, eventually ducking down into a **rocky cleft** where devotees splash water on tacky gold fish statues that lie at the feet of a Buddha image.

Cars and motorbikes can drive almost to the hilltop from the southeast. Some pick-up 5 (၅) services terminate near the 19th St stairway. Around 300yd back towards Mandalay then 300yd north, **Mya Kyauk monastery** has a dazzlingly distinctive brassy

Central Mandalay

stupa and is famed for its water. A taxi out this way will cost around K5000 return (or around K3000 for a motorcycle taxi).

Skinny Buddha STATUE
(Dokara Sariya; Map p238; 30th St, 60/62) Built in 2011, this remarkable 75ft-tall seated Buddha is a 'meditation image' that falls stylistically somewhere between manga cartoon and Cubism. This Buddha gets marks for being a fairly unique representation amid Mandalay's thousands of almost identical representations of the Enlightened One.

Ma Soe Yein Nu Kyaung BUDDHIST MONASTERY
(မစိုးရိမ်ကျောင်း; Don't be Anxious Monastery; Map p242; 39th St, 87/88; ⊘7am-sunset) **FREE** Across the creek from Shwe In Bin, the city's largest monastery lacks an ancient historical pedigree and is primarily a collection of modern dorm accommodation and lecture halls. It does sport a 'Big Ben' clock and a unique six-storey octagonal library tower topped with a great viewpoint. The monastery has long been noted for the politically forthright views of its monks, and it's the base of controversial monk Ashin Wirathu, figurehead of the 969 movement. While local monks can be friendly, Muslim travellers

may feel uncomfortable in this space. When we visited, there were visible posters that ticked off litanies of Buddhist grievances targeted at the Muslim community.

Thingaza Kyaung BUDDHIST MONASTERY
(သယံဇာကျောင်း; Map p242; 92nd St, 34/35; ⊘6.30am-7pm) This appealingly lived-in monastery has some photogenically dilapidated buildings and, tucked behind the *tagondain* (pillar topped with golden duck) is a shaded open-air trio of sinuous buddha figures that have been weathered into almost abstract ghosts.

Atumashi Kyaungdawgyi BUDDHIST TEMPLE
(အတုမရှိကျောင်းတော်ကြီး; Map p238; off 63rd & 14th Sts; admission by combo ticket; ⊘9am-6pm) This unusually shaped temple is a series of diminishing stupa-dotted terraces over an arched base decorated with peacock motifs. When built in 1857, it housed a famous buddha image with a huge diamond set on its forehead. However, the image was stolen following the 1885 British takeover, and the monastery was gutted by fire five years later. What you see today is a 1996 reconstruction, anchored by a vast (yet oddly empty-feeling) central prayer chamber.

Stone Carvers
WORKSHOP
(⊙ varies, most shops close around 6pm) On the Sagaing–Mandalay road, directly east of Mahamuni Paya, is a whole series of workshops where you can see slabs of rock being blasted, chipped and polished into buddhas of all sizes.

🏃 Activities

The outdoor, Olympic-sized **Yatanaban Swimming Pool** (Map p238; foot of Mandalay Hill & 10th St; K2000; ⊙ 6am-6pm) is OK, but don't use the diving board or you'll pike yourself into a stagnant fountain puddle. For a fee, nonguests can use attractive outdoor pools at hotels such as **Mandalay Swan** (Map p238; ☎ 02-31601; 44, 26th Rd, btwn 66th & 68th Sts; guest/nonguest free/US$5; ⊙ 7am-8pm) and Mandalay Hill Resort ($15).

Amara
BOATING
(Map p242; ☎ 09 40373 5349; www.amaragroup.net; cabins from €1778-4476) Offers upmarket one-week cruises up and down the Ayeyarwady (Irrawaddy) River.

Paukan Cruises
BOATING
(Map p242; ☎ 01-380877; www.ayravatacruises.com; 2-night Bagan cruise, low/high season from US$390/435, 5-night from US$2140/2380) Paukan operates five indulgent classic boat-hotels. One, *Paukan1947*, is a 1947 original with teak and ironwood floors refitted into an upmarket 16-berth cruiser. The others are attractive latter-day re-creations. Most cruises run Mandalay–Bagan or vice versa (note that rates go up if you're travelling from Bagan), but there are five-day, one-week and 10-day options.

Oriental Ballooning
Pricey AF...
BALLOONING
(☎ 02-62625; http://orientalballooning.com; 35th at 71st St; per person US$380; ⊙ Nov-Mar) Predawn balloon flights depart daily in season, weather permitting. Departure points vary.

Asia Centre Driving Range
GOLF
(Map p238; ☎ 02-64583; Mandalay Hill, Aung Myay Thazan Township; per 60 balls K2000; ⊙ 6am-6pm) A central driving range, and good spot to work out your frustrations over the Mandalay bus system. There's a K2000 caddy fee that most locals avail themselves of, but it's not mandatory.

Shwe Mann Taung Golf Club
GOLF
(Map p238; ☎ 02-75898; green fee/caddy/clubs US$30/12/15; ⊙ 5am-6pm) A decent 18-hole course that is handy to Mandalay Hill (p236).

🖝 Tours

Disocvery Rides — MOTORCYCLE TOUR
(☎01-388330; http://myanmarmotorbikes.com)
Discovery, which is run by a mix of expat and local motorcycle enthusiasts, offers motorcycle tours well off the beaten tourism track, giving you a chance to see a Myanmar not often visited by foreigners. It offers a day trip exploring Mandalay and surrounding ancient capitals, and 10- and 15-day treks that explore Bagan, Shan State and Northern Myanmar.

🥢 Courses

Dhamma Mandala — HEALTH & WELLBEING
(☎09 204 4348, 02-39694; www.mandala.dhamma.org; Yaytagon Hill) Rural centre near the base of the Yedagon Hills offers bilingual 10-day Vipassana courses roughly once a month on a donation basis. Book ahead via the website. No visa support.

Festivals & Events

Traditional *pwe* (festivals), big and small, happen often, blocking streets or jazzing up pagoda precincts with all-night music and lively street stalls. Cycle around enough and you'll likely stumble into one.

Mingun Nat Festival — RELIGIOUS
(☺Feb/Mar) Pays homage to the brother and sister of the Teak Tree, who drowned in the river while clinging to a trunk. This fascinating festival takes place from the fifth to 10th days of the waxing moon of Tabaung – the Burmese version of Carnival, complete with all of the associated public drunken behaviour.

Waso — RELIGIOUS
(☺Jun/Jul) The Sagaing Waso festival, followed by the big Paleik festival, takes place in the two weeks following the Waso full moon.

Taungbyone Nat Pwe — RELIGIOUS
(☺Aug) This massive, chaotic festival is held about 12 miles north of Mandalay, and honours two famous Bagan-era *nat* (spirit beings). Celebrations – which consist of lots of loud music, village drinking and more loud music – culminate on the five days leading up to the full moon of Wagaung. A week later worshippers move on to Irinaku (Yadanagu), south of Amarapura.

Thadingyut — RELIGIOUS
(☺Oct) On the full moon of Thadingyut, Myanmar's lights festival celebrates Buddha's return from the celestial sphere. At the south base of Mandalay Hill, the big temple festival at Kyauktawgyi Paya (p239) builds for two weeks beforehand. One day before the full moon, Kyaukse (25 miles south of Mandalay) has its famous two-man 'Elephant Dance' competition.

🛌 Sleeping

Unless otherwise stated, room rates include breakfast. In smaller hotels, air-con may shut off during power cuts as generators can't cope. Note that you will receive a fair price reduction if you opt to pay in kyats, in cash. Many midrange and upmarket hotels offer large discounts (as much as two-thirds off the listed price) if you book online or through a third-party engine.

🛏 Royal Mandalay

Peacock Lodge — GUESTHOUSE $$
(Map p238; ☎09 204 2059, 02-61429; peacocklodge@gmail.com; 60th St, 25/26; r standard/deluxe US$45/70; ❄☎) The main 1960s house of this lovely homestyle inn is set in a tree-shaded yard complete with fairy lights, parasol seating and an old horse cart. Dated if fair-sized standard rooms overlook a lotus-filled canal, while boutique-style 'deluxe' rooms include a few prizes with balconies. Most appealing is the genuine warm and empathetic service.

Hosts treat many guests like part of the family, and may show you their fascinating old photos – 'granddad' was a British-era mayor of Mandalay. A full traditional Burmese multidish dinner is served by advance arrangement. It's rather far from the centre but bicycle hire is available. Bring mosquito repellent.

Hotel Emperor — HOTEL $$
(Map p242; ☎02-68743; www.hotelemperormandalay.com; 74th St, 26/27; r Oct-Mar US$80-100, Apr-Sep US$50-80; ❄☎🅟) Lashings of wood panelling, pretty foliage and the odd carving enliven this superfriendly family-style hotel. Rooms aren't big and some windows stare straight at a wall, but beds are firm, the air-con works well, rooms have fridge, hairdryer, kettle, toiletries etc, and there's decent wi-fi. A modern bistro next door does cocktails and international meals. Bicycle rental is available.

Ma Ma Guesthouse — GUESTHOUSE $$
(Map p238; ☎02-33411; http://mama-guesthouse.com; 60th St, 25/26; r from US$40; ❄☎) This block of high-ceilinged, spare but attractive rooms is good value for money and is graced by helpful owners who are great for booking onward travel.

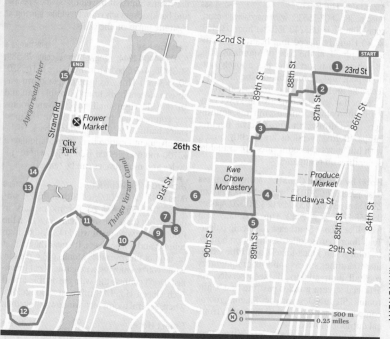

22nd St

START
1 23rd St
2
3
26th St
Flower Market
END
15
Ayeyarwady River
Strand Rd
City Park
14
13
Thinga Yarzar Canal
11
10
12
Kwe Chow Monastery
Produce Market
Eindawya St
4
6
7
8
9
5
91st St
90th St
89th St
88th St
89th St
87th St
86th St
85th St
84th St
29th St

N
0   500 m
0   0.25 miles

MANDALAY & AROUND MANDALAY

Cycling Tour
West Mandalay

START 23RD ST AT 86TH ST
END AYARWADDY RIVER VIEW HOTEL
LENGTH 2.2 MILES; ONE TO THREE HOURS

Keep in mind that even while pedalling Mandalay's web of tree-shaded back lanes, you may have unsettling close encounters with motor vehicles. On a quiet day, turning off bustling, canalside 86th St can feel as though you've suddenly entered a village. If 23rd St is flooded beyond the boxy redbrick-towered **1 Christ Cathedral**, substitute the parallel street a block further south passing some colonial-era government buildings. Briefly follow 87th St. Opposite the large, spired, very pink **2 St Michael's Catholic Church**, turn west again, zigzagging through residential alleys to 88th St. West of the T-junction, 25th St sports a few remnant timber and bamboo-weave homes, and one of Mandalay's **3 workshops** for turning sugar cane into jaggery. Visit grand **4 Eindawya Paya** (p240) then veer west off shady 89th St just before a **5 crocodile bridge** representing Ngamoe Yeik, the faithful servant of tragic Burmese-chronicle hero Min Nandar.

Take the narrow east–west lane between old monastery residences. After **6 Khin Makantaik monastery**, wind past **7 Asumtaik** and **8 Sakutaik** monasteries and spot a **9 house-workshop** that creates Mayuwe rice-puff snack-bars in big sweet-smelling woks.

Where 91st St makes a short dog-leg, a mirror-mosaic colonnade leads into **10 Chanthaya Paya**. Chanthaya's golden stupa looks particularly photogenic in the afternoon light reflecting in lake-like Thinga Yarsar Canal. The best viewpoints are across a long **11 teak footbridge** which could be touted as Mandalay's own mini U-Bein Bridge were it not for the putrid smell of decomposing trash.

Sweep around the big, impressively colourful new **12 Jin Taw Yan Chinese Temple** emerging on to Strand Rd, where the Ayeyarwady riverside includes a series of boat berths with fascinating cargo.

Enjoy riverside scenes with a cheap chilled beer at **13 Cafe YMH**, a meal and show at **14 Mya Nandar** (p253) or a panoramic rooftop cocktail at **15 Ayarwaddy River View Hotel** (p250).

Mandalay Hill Resort
HOTEL $$$

(Map p238; ☑ 02-35638; www.mandalayhillresort. com; 10th St; r US$240-350, ste from US$450; 🏽 ❄ ➋) Handily placed in a beautifully manicured jungle at the base of Mandalay Hill, the city's top resort hotel has a lovely outdoor pool and a breathtaking spa area that feels like an Indiana Jones treasure trove.

'Superior' guest rooms are classy yet cosy with watercolours, timeless mirrors, embroidered bed-throws and nozzle-style reading lamps. 'Deluxe' versions are slightly larger, with hill views. Discount rates are available, depending on occupancy.

Hotel by the Red Canal
BOUTIQUE HOTEL $$$

(Map p238; ☑ 02-61177; www.hotelredcanal.com; 22nd St at 63rd St; r Oct-Mar US$270-320, Apr-Sep US$156-220; 🏽 ❄ ➋ ❄) This intimate gem feels like a cosy Southeast Asia–chic palace. Teak floorboards, toiletries in potion bottles, tasteful Asian knick-knacks and little extras like tea-time snacks and complimentary cocktail hour add to the keen service. An artificial stream gurgles past the best 'Chin' rooms. Slightly less pricey 'Kachin' rooms compensate for low natural light with tropical outdoor showers.

'Rakhine' rooms lack balconies. All in all it's a lovely place but the high-season prices seem extremely steep. Look for online bargains.

Sedona Mandalay
HOTEL $$$

(Map p238; ☑ 02-36488; www.sedonahotels.com. sg; 26th St at 66th St; r/ste from US$200/315; 🏽 ❄) Stroll across ponds through a temple-style gateway to a grand airy lobby overlooking a large open-air swimming pool in a lush semi-jungle setting. Room decor doesn't always live up to the flashy exterior, but better rooms do stare straight down the eastern moat towards Mandalay Hill. Wi-fi is spotty given the price you're paying.

Central Mandalay

The nearest thing to a 'backpacker zone' is a three-block area around the Nylon Hotel in Central Mandalay. Don't imagine Bangkok's Khao San Rd. These are ordinary-looking streets where several cheaper hotels are licensed for foreigners. Places we call 'backpacker hotels' are adept at organising onward and regional transport. You might need to book ahead to get the hotel you want, especially November to January when prices can rise considerably. There's a growing range of high-rise midrange hotels between 79th St and 84th St that offer clean, comfortable, similar rooms aimed at travelling businesspeople and backpackers who don't feel like staring at cigarette burns on the walls.

Yoe Yoe Lay
GUESTHOUSE $

(☑ 09-44404 1944; nanbwe1@gmail.com; 78 58th St, 35/36; 4- & 6-bed dm from US$11, s & d US$20-30; 🏽 ➋ ➋) This excellent proper dorm has air-con, decent beds, knowledgeable staff and an outside communal area. Private rooms are compact but comfortable; the cheapest share bathrooms. The only drawback is the inconvenient location in eastern Mandalay; a K1700 motorcycle-taxi ride to anywhere (bicycles and motorcycles can be rented).

Rich Queen Guesthouse
HOSTEL $

(Map p242; ☑ 02-60172; off 87th St, 26/27; s/d/ tr US$20/25/35; 🏽 ➋ ➋) The rooms vary in quality, but there are some real winners in the front corner with giant windows, fridge, high ceilings and hot showers. It's near the market on a quiet narrow alley. Monks often pass by while you're enjoying a generous local breakfast. Don't confuse this with the double-priced Rich Queen Hotel 1.8 miles east along 26th, where several rooms lack windows altogether.

Smart Hotel
HOTEL $

(Map p242; ☑ 02-32682; www.smarthotelmandalay. com; 28th St, 76/77; r US$30-75; 🏽) This seven-storey tower has clean but small rooms; if you need space to stretch out, this may not be the right spot for you, but otherwise it's great value, especially if you book online. Shoot for upper rooms with balconies that boast distant views of the palace and Mandalay Hill.

Nylon Hotel
HOTEL $

(Map p242; ☑ 02-69717, 02-33460; 25th St at 83rd St; s/d/tr US$20/25/35; 🏽 ➋) There are two annexes at the Nylon; go for the new one, which has reasonably sized, light rooms with modern bathrooms, even if some smell a little of drains. Decent wi-fi connection.

AD1 Hotel
HOTEL $

(Map p242; ☑ 02-34505; ad.1hotel@gmail.com; Eindawya St, 87/88; s/d US$15/25; 🏽 ➋) One of the cheapest deals in town for solo travellers, AD1 offers rooms that are simple and ageing, but functional and clean. It's just off vibrant 'onion market street' in the eastern approach lane to Eindawya Pagoda. Beware if asking a taxi to take you here – to local ears 'AD1' sounds very much like '81' (ie 81st St).

ET Hotel
HOTEL $

(Map p242; ☑ 02-65006, 02-66547; www.ethotel mandalay.com; 83rd St, 23/24; s/d/tr US$20/25/35, with shared bathroom s/d US$15/18; ✳ ☎) A good-value backpacker favourite. Bare fluorescent bulbs on pastel-blue corridor walls can feel a little soulless but rooms are clean and mostly spacious with hot showers. The staff are helpful.

Power points are in short supply but plugs and wi-fi are available in several common areas. Bicycle rental outside is K1500. Odd-numbered rooms have more natural light.

Hotel 8 · HOTEL $$
(Map p242; ☑ 02-31448; 29th St, 82/83; r from US$28; ✳ ☎) This multistorey midrange glass tower is great value for money – scratch that, it's a lovely hotel all around. The ladies at the front desk are friendly and helpful, the staff are attentive (maybe a little too attentive), the vibe is clean and comfortable, and the splashes of colour give the rooms some warm character.

Hotel A1 · HOTEL $$
(Map p242; ☑ 02-67401; http://hotela1mandalay. com; 32nd & 83rd St; r from US$24; ✳ ☎) Buoyant staff, surprisingly light-filled rooms, a decent bar and an efficient, clean and comfortable atmosphere make this a good-value choice for those who want three-star comfort. Be warned that the internet connection can be spotty.

Golden City Light Hotel · HOTEL $$
(Map p242; ☑ 02-60029; www.goldencitylighthotel. com; 77th St, 34/35; r from US$25; ✳ ☎) This friendly spot is located near some cool markets and offers reasonably handsome rooms, chilly air-conditioning, hot showers and decent internet connections. Plus, those red-and black-trim staff uniforms are snappy!

Hotel Yadanarbon · HOTEL $$
(Map p242; ☑ 02-71999; www.hotelyadanarbon. com; 31st St at 76th St; r US$45-93, ste US$135-180; ✳ ☎) All rooms have crisp linens, bed sashes, parquet floors and vague colonial-style bathroom doors. Even the cheapest 'standard' rooms are fair-sized, with fridge, safe, small sitting space, flat-screen TV and bathtub. The location is handy for the train station and there's a wealth of street food right outside, plus a rooftop bar and restaurant.

Gold Yadanar · HOTEL $$
(Map p242; ☑ 02-71048; www.goldyadanarhotel. com; 34th St, 77/78; d/tw/ste/tr US$60/70/80/90; ✳ @ ☎) For a 40-room hotel, a large chandelier dangling from a two-storey foyer might seem a little excessive but it's stylishly done. The rooms are impeccably tidy and well

equipped, and the chunky rounded wooden furniture looks durable. Some rooms have limited natural light, and one is a fully decked-out Hello Kitty suite that will forever haunt our dreams.

Mandalay City Hotel · HOTEL $$
(Map p242; ☑ 02-61700; www.mandalaycityhotel. com; 26th St, 82/83; r US$70-95, ste from US$140; ✳ @ ☎) Walking past you'd never guess this enticing palm-shaded oasis lay just behind all the dreary buildings of 26th St. The airy, tiled lobby is entered across a fish pond and there's an attractive outdoor pool (nonguests US$5). Statuettes, local paintings and some genuinely funky accents add some interest to rooms that are comfortable if not luxurious.

Hotel Queen · HOTEL $$
(Map p242; ☑ 02-71562; www.hotelqueenmandalay. com; 81st St, 32/33; standard/superior/ste/f from US$45/50/60/90; ✳ @ ☎) Good value among similar midrange towers; even the smaller rooms have sitting areas. Superior rooms are more spacious. The foyer is attractive, staff are energetic and there's a bar on the top floor.

79 Living Hotel · HOTEL $$
(Map p242; ☑ 02-32277; http://79livinghotel mandalay.com; 79th St, 29/30; d/family from US$35/65; ✳ ☎) This sensibly priced lower-midrange hotel is handily placed behind the train station with gleaming clean floors, high ceilings, minibar, lift and maybe a (fake) welcome rose on the bed.

My World Hotel · HOTEL $$
(Map p242; ☑ 02-30841; http://hotelmyworld.com; 30th St, 73/74; r US$40-55; ✳ ☎) These rooms have a boutique-like modern design, and the little 5th-floor roof 'garden' has appealing views down busy 30th St. While there's nothing that particularly stands out about My World, it's great value for money.

Royal City Hotel · HOTEL $$
(Map p242; ☑ 02-28299; www.royalcityhotelman dalay.com; 27th St, 76/77; r US$30-55; ✳ @ ☎) This traveller-oriented lower-midrange hotel has a lovely roof garden, helpful staff and decent rooms – nothing too exemplary, but clean and kitted out well for the price.

Shwe Ingyinn Hotel · HOTEL $$$
(Map p242; ☑ 02-73462; www.shweingyinnhotel. com; 30th St at 78th St; r from US$100, ste from US$170; ☎) Shwe Ingyin boasts plenty of style and ranks as one of the nicer top-end hotels in Central Mandalay. A carved

wooden receptionist 'island' dominates the lobby, lantern-lamps and potted plants enliven corridors, and rooms are well kitted out and clean. This hotel offers enormous discounts via online booking engines.

Kyi Tin Hotel
HOTEL, BUNGALOWS $$$

(Map p242; ☑ 02-23715; www.kyitinhotel.com; 80th St, 31/32; r from US$40, bungalow/deluxe US$100-150; ✳) Kyi Tin's defining feature is its series of balcony-fronted bungalows set in a large yet central lawn-and-fountain garden. The whole space has a simple Burma-colonial style with black lacquered wooden floors. It offers fair value, especially if you can seize a promotional rate. Less-interesting 'deluxe' rooms with subdued cream-brown colours are in a partly finished modern block.

Greater Mandalay

Ayarwaddy River View Hotel
HOTEL $$

(Map p242; ☑ 02-64946, 02-72373; www.ayarwaddy riverview-hotel.com; Strand Rd, 22/23; d US$50-130, ste US$170; ✳@☎✉) Luxurious for the price, this sizeable hotel has tasteful, restrained decor in large, fully equipped rooms sporting parquet floors and fashion-neutral bathrooms. Price depends on size and view. And what a view! Upper-floor front-facing rooms look across the river towards distant Mingun, rear-upper ones overlook the city, Mandalay Hill and the Shan uplands. Enjoy the lot from the rooftop bar where marionette shows are staged in high season.

Shwe Taung Tarn
BOUTIQUE HOTEL $$

(☑ 02-75405; www.shwetaungtarnhotel.com; 14th St at 88th St; r from US$80; ✳✳✉) This cosy boutique boasts a tree-shaded pool and rooms with locally flavoured decorative touches and corner bathtubs. Staff are very friendly, and the location is a peaceful, if annoyingly remote, stretch of 14th St – if not for the occasional honk you'd feel as if you'd left the city. Not really, but you get the gist.

Golden Mandalay
HOTEL $$

(Map p238; ☑ 09 40251; shwemdy1974@gmail. com; 60th St at 19th St; r US$35; ✳) Attractively set amid palms with a small dining terrace perched above a canal, this 10-room 'family paradise' is a cluster of relatively simple bungalow-style rooms festooned on the outside with bamboo patchwork designs, temple-style steps, polished stones and carved totem-like designs. It's sweetly unique but lights could be brighter, bathrooms aren't modern, beds are spongy and wi-fi is very limited.

Rupar Mandalar
RESORT $$$

(☑ 02-61552; www.ruparmandalar.com; 53rd St at 30th St; d/ste from US$260/600; ✳@☎✉) This lovely all-teak low-rise complex is set in tropical foliage melding timeless neo-traditional features with modern design flair and lashings of Burma-colonial chic (dark teak, polished wood floors etc). The outdoor swimming pools are remarkably spacious and guests qualify for a free Thai massage in the appealing spa. Serious discounts can be found online. It's hidden away in the far-eastern semirural suburbs so you'll need wheels to get virtually anywhere.

Hotel Shwe Pyi Thar
HOTEL $$$

(☑ 02-74402; www.hotelshwepyithar.com; 51st St, 31/32; r US$140-300, ste US$700-2500; P✳☎✉) All the carvings, marble, polished parquet, greenery, views and black-lacquered bedsteads don't necessarily compensate for the isolated out-of-town location of this six-storey complex, which is popular with the wealthy set.

✗ Eating

There's no main restaurant area; many better choices require cycling down dark roads, such as 27th St, south of the moat. But if you persist for a few minutes in any direction you're likely to find some good street-food areas. For inexpensive barbecue snacks (notably spicy whole fish for around K2500) and K800 draught beers, visit one of the countless beer stations.

Hours vary; if business is slow, many restaurants will close early, or stay open if busy.

Upper Burmese are sometimes nicknamed 'bean eaters' by their coastal cousins, which speaks to the importance of beans as a regional staple. While rice remains the main source of caloric intake, bean salads and curries are a common accompanying dish. The city of Mandalay is also strongly associated with *nan gyi thoke* (nahn-jee-thoke) a delicious noodle and chicken salad mixed with onion, turmeric, chilli and oil, served at room temperature.

✗ Royal Mandalay

Mingalabar Myanmar Restaurant
BURMESE $

(Map p238; ☑ 02-60480; 71st St, 28/29; mains K1500-6000; ⊙6am-9pm; ✳🍴🍶) This large, clean and friendly locals' favourite is a traditional Burmese pick-and-pig-out kind of spot: select your soup or curry or salad (really, any sort of yummy thing that can be spooned on

LOCAL KNOWLEDGE

MANDALAY STREET FOOD STALLS

Along with beer-station barbecues, the best-value dining is usually at street stalls, many of which plonk down their plastic stools for only a few hours a day. Certain corners or street sections have culinary specialities, but knowing which takes some insider knowledge.

Morning Only

➡ Shan noodles with bean paste – 29th St, 80/81 before 10am.

➡ *Mohinga* (fish noodle soup) – Try the three-wheel street-trolley stall at 32nd St at 81st St, from 6.30am to 9.30am. There's another fantastic *mohinga* station with similar hours just to the left as you pass the entrance gate to Mahamuni Paya.

Daytime

➡ Point-and-pick multicurries – several inexpensive family snack outlets are dotted along an unnamed lane between 74th and 75th Sts.

➡ Burmese sweets – takeaway from near 85th St at 27th St in Zeigyo Market.

➡ Sweet tea and fresh *nanbya* (tandoor bread) at **Min Thiha** (p254).

Night-time Only

➡ Indian chapatti and curry – 28th St at 82nd St.

➡ Indian/savoury 'pancakes' and biryanis at **Karaweik** (Map p242; 26th St at 83rd St; pancakes K500-750; ⊘ 5.30pm-midnight).

➡ Chinese food stalls – 34th St at 76th St with a night market (vegetables) stretching along 34th St.

➡ A night market at 84th & 29th St offers a grab bag of all of the above.

to rice), have it served with a veritable forest of side dishes, feel full for the rest of the day.

Ko's Kitchen   THAI $$
(Map p238; ☑ 02-31265; 80th St at 19th St; mains K3500-8500; ⊘ 11am-2.30pm & 5.30-9pm; ❋ ⓘ) You'll find an intimidatingly large menu of authentic (read: spicy and very good) northern-Thai food served in an attractive art-deco building with simple, peach-coloured decor. Eat early to avoid evening tour groups, which can overwhelm this relatively modest-sized place.

Green Elephant   BURMESE $$
(Map p238; ☑ 02-61237; www.greenelephant-restaurants.com; 27th St, 64/65; mains K8000-13,000; set menus from K8500-15,000; ⊘ 10am-10pm; ❋ 🛜 ⓘ) This is basically Burmese cuisine for tour groups, although individuals can usually get a slightly adapted version with six or so dishes on request. The food is good, so if you're nervous about trying Burmese outside on the street, this is a solid bet, but otherwise it's local cuisine with significantly marked-up prices.

A few tables are tucked within an air-conditioned Pyin Oo Lwin–style colonial-era building full of period relics (ask). Others spill out into a bamboo-tufted garden lit by lanterns and a less-impressive pavilion space beside it.

Café City   INTERNATIONAL $$
(Map p238; ☑ 02-61237, 02-61484; East Moat Rd/66th St, 20/22; meals K5500-10,200, draught beer K1500; ⊘ 9am-11pm; ❋ 🛜 ⓘ) Red-'leather' booths and classic vintage signs add to the feeling of a comfortable, latter-day American diner transplanted into Myanmar. The menu ranges from steaks and English triangular sandwiches to 'lobster' and delicious coconut-basted fish kebabs. Oh, and the coffee is great. It's popular with wealthy local families.

Koffie Korner   INTERNATIONAL $$
(Map p238; ☑ 02-68648; 27th St at 70th St; mains K3500-9000; ⊘ 9am-10.30pm; ℗ ❋ 🛜 ⓘ) This gently buzzing lounge-style cafe-restaurant is set behind palms. The predominantly Western menu has lots of coffee drinks (imagine that), quesadillas, Russian salad, pasta, steak and some imaginative sauce flavours such as lime-caper-butter, spicy raisin-orange or garlic-mint. This spot is popular with young, moneyed Mandalay folks, and a large cocktail menu makes it a trendy night-time hang-out.

Golden Duck   CHINESE $$
(Map p238; ☑ 02-36808; 80th St at 16th St; veg/nonveg dishes from K2000/4000, duck K12,000;

⊙10.30am-2.30pm & 6-9.30pm; ✱ⓘ♿) This large bustling Chinese restaurant is a veritable local institution. That sweet view across the moat is well complemented by some perfectly roasted duck and chilli-lashed noodles. Service can be slow.

✗ Central Mandalay

Aye Myit Tar
BURMESE $

(Map p242; 81st St, 36/37; full meal K2200-6500; ⊙8.30am-9.30pm; ✱ⓘ) Brightly lit, this simple but historic thick-walled colonial-era merchant's building now houses a popular multicurry eatery. Choose the main dish and four sides; four condiments, soup, rice and salad are included.

Pan Cherry
INDIAN $

(Map p242; ☎02-39924; 81st St, 26/27; curry K1500-4000; ⊙8am-9pm) Sit at plastic chairs in a floral-ceilinged box room for great-value, belly-straining Indian meals complete with dhal, condiments, veg, rice and pappadam.

Super 81
CHINESE $

(Map p242; 81st St, 38/39; mains K3500-13,000; ⊙9.30am-11pm) Excellent, beautifully presented Chinese food in very generous portions, plus typical barbecues and cheap draught beer in frosted glasses. Downstairs is a convivial beer station but prices are the same upstairs in the pleasantly appointed air-con restaurant. Handy place if you're waiting for a Moustache Brothers (p255) performance.

Shan Ma Ma
SHAN $

(Map p242; ☎02-71858; 81st 29/30; dishes K1500-7000; ⊙11am-9.30pm; ✐ⓘ) Low plastic stools? Check. Delicious smell of frying oil? Check. And the friendly sisters who run it will offer you a taste of what's on offer before you decide. This is Southeast Asian budget dining at its best, all home-cooked curries and noodle dishes made to order. Eat like royalty while spending the change you found between your couch cushions.

Shwe Khaing Barbeque
BARBECUE $

(Map p242; 82nd St at 33rd St; mains K1500-7000; ⊙11am-10pm; ⓘ) This excellent little barbecue spot is popular with locals, who pack in to watch football, sink beers and order everything from land and sea grilled to order – be it tomatoes, shrimp, skewers, or whole fish. If you can think of it, these guys can cook it over an open flame, and it comes out great.

Lashio Lay
SHAN $

(Map p242; ☎02-22653; 23rd St, 83/84; per plate K500-2500; ⊙10am-9.30pm; ⓘ) This simple, long-running restaurant is known for consistently good, Shan-inspired dishes. Point and pick and pay per dish – a couple of curries and some rice ought to fill you up. Popular for cold beers as the evening goes on.

Rainforest
THAI $

(Map p242; ☎09 4316 1551, 02-36234; lane off 27th St, 74/75; mains K2500-6000; ⊙10am-10pm; ⓦⓘⓘ♿) Climb through a treasure-packed family 'antique' shop to a covered balcony with tinkling wind chimes and assorted handicrafts to dine on Thai food that's creamy and mildly spiced for Western palates. This place feels the most backpacker-oriented in Mandalay (except perhaps Marie-Min next door), as reflected by the linen-clad clientele.

Too Too Restaurant
BURMESE $

(Map p242; 27th St, 74/75; meals K2800-5000; ⊙10am-8.30pm) Respected home-style local fare, precooked and served in a bright bland box room. Pick your main curry (prawn recommended) from the display; two sides, two condiments, soup and rice come free.

Pakkoku Dawlaymay
BURMESE $

(Map p242; 73rd St, 27/28; mains K1300-3000; ⊙10am-8.30pm; ⓘ) This basic, archetypal local restaurant is a garage-style room with whirring fans and light panels that indicate (in Burmese) which of some three dozen possible curries are available (printed list usually available in English on request). Curries come with a panful of rice and accompaniments, usually salad herbs, tomato-bean curry, peanut salad and a semi-sweet dhal.

Marie-Min
VEGETARIAN $

(Map p242; off 27th St, 74/75; mains K2000-3000; ⊙9am-10pm; ⓦⓘⓘ) An all-vegetarian menu fits the owners' stated principle: 'Be kind to animals by not eating them', which has an admirable logical consistency. Highlights of the menu, which largely references Sri Lanka, India and Myanmar, include tofu curry, a meal-sized aubergine 'dip' and avocado milkshakes (K2000) that are as 'fabulous' as promised. Very popular with backpackers.

SP Bakery
BAKERY $

(Map p242; ☎02-64213; www.spbakery-myanmar. com; 32nd St, 80/81; baked goods K700-2000; ⊙8am-10pm; ✱) This branch of a beloved national chain dishes out decent and cheap baked goods – sweet and savoury pies, buns and the rest. If you need to fuel up before some day tripping, it's a good option.

Fried Grasshopper Vendors
STREET FOOD $

(Map p242; 86th St, 24/25; bag of grasshoppers K350) Looking for something strange? 'Hop' on over to these stalls for fried grasshopper.

Nova Coffee
INTERNATIONAL $$

(Map p242; ☏ 9 40276 6721; 37th St, 79/80; mains K2000-12,000; ☉ 10am-10pm; ❄ ☎ ▨) Frigid air-conditioning, friendly staff and excellent coffee greet you at Nova, which is popular with Mandalay's young and hip things. The menu runs an eclectic gamut from bacon carbonara to deep-fried prawns; we're fans of the desserts, which range from chocolate puddings to enormous waffles.

BBB
INTERNATIONAL $$

(Map p242; ☏ 02-73525; 76th St, 26/27; mains K4000-11,000; ☉ 10am-10.30pm; ❄ ▨) This Mandalay classic is a regular hang-out for the expat/NGO-employed/businessperson crowd, who pack in for stiff cocktails and good Western food. It's one of the more attractive restaurants in town, and manages to recreate the 'cosy-restaurant-meets-pub' vibe quite well in the heart of Mandalay.

Cafe House
INTERNATIONAL $$

(Map p242; ☏ 02-32771; 37th St, 78/79; mains K1500-7000; ☉ 8am-10pm; ❄ ▨) Easily missed in the gold-pounders' area, Cafe House is comfy with forgettable decor but strong air-con. The big draw is the superb fried wanton wheel with ginger sauce, a great snack for two to share; that said, the menu draws from an eclectic array of cuisines (Thai, Chinese and Western).

V Cafe
INTERNATIONAL $$

(Map p242; ☏ 02-24688; 25th St at 80th St; mains K2500-8000; ☉ 9am-10.30pm; ❄ ☎ ▨) V's prices are noticeably cheaper than most of Mandalay's air-conditioned Western cafe-bars. While the dangling hearts and mood-lit flower cut-outs are more cutesy than trendy, there's a top-floor rooftop bar with close-up views of the moat and fortress walls.

Bistro at 82nd
INTERNATIONAL $$$

(Map p242; ☏ 09 25012 1280; www.bistro82nd mandalay.com; 82nd St, 30/31; mains K9000-17,000, grill K10,000-33,500; ☉ 11am-10pm, limited menu 2-6pm; ❄ ☎ ▨) This smart little restaurant is all the rage with the Mandalay jet-set crowd. Pack in for strong coffees, creative cocktails and continental European cuisine, ranging from Italian pasta dishes to French-style roast chicken. It sets aside special nights for mixed grills featuring big cuts of steak and chops imported from Australia. Reservations aren't a bad idea.

Greater Mandalay

Mr BarBQ
BURMESE $

(Map p238; 71st St at 31st St; barbecue K600-8000; ☉ 11am-11pm) This garden-style beer station is hard to beat for quality barbecue with many less-common options including whole squid and delicious fish-wrapped prawns. A popular spot for a beer, several packs of cigarettes and football on the TV.

Mya Nandar
BURMESE, CHINESE $$

(Map p242; ☏ 02-66110; www.myanandarrestau rant.com; Strand Rd, 26/28; mains K4000-13,000; ☉ 9am-11pm; ▨) Smart open-sided pavilions in a great tree-shaded riverside location with good and varied food. The bigger draws (October to February) are the free puppet shows (1pm) and traditional dances (7.30pm to 9pm) performed even when tour groups fail to show up. Bring mosquito repellent.

Drinking & Nightlife

The drinking scene in Mandalay is roughly divided into three camps: hip bars for the city's young elites (with the odd expat thrown in), loud, bare-bones beer stations serving frosty brews for the working man (and we mean men), and drinks at more upmarket Western-fusion-style restaurants. Women are welcome at each of these, but will stand out at beer stations.

Central Park
BAR

(Map p238; 27th St, 68/69; beer from K900, cocktails from K3000; ☉ 10am-11pm) This convivial open-sided bar-pavilion cleverly combines the best points of a beer-and-barbecue station with a low-key, musically eclectic cocktail bar adding a tourist-friendly food menu to boot. It's a sociable place to unwind and some of the decorative Myanmar artefacts are a century old.

Ginki Mandalay
BAR

(Map p238; ☏ 09 79780 2600; cnr 71st & 28th Sts; beer from K2000, cocktails K3500-8000; ☉ 10.30am-11pm; ☎) A branch of the same-named Yangon bar-restaurant, at Ginki you can imbibe on its large terrace shaded by palm trees; a step up from drinking in your typical, scruffy beer station. The menu (mains from K3000) mixes Chinese, Thai and Indian dishes, with a few Western ones.

Mya Yi Nandar
BEER STATION

(Map p238; 19th St, 65/66; draught beer from K700) One of Mandalay's more appealing beer stations with fairy lights, balloon-shaped lanterns and foliage including a row of mature palms.

Royal Lake
BEER STATION

(☑ 09 100 9445; Kandawgyi Lake; mains K400-12,000; ⏱ 9am-11pm, music from 7pm) This lakeside complex has a boardwalk seating area with stage for live music. What's far more remarkable, however, is a gilded wooden 'royal barge' moored 650ft around the shore. Once a feature of the central moat, the barge is far more boatlike than the bigger, concrete Yangon version. When it's quiet, you can have a beer without eating a meal.

MR2 Pub
COCKTAIL BAR

(Map p238; ☑ 02-22955; 80th St, 16/17; espresso/juice/cocktails K1500/2000/5000; ⏱ 9am-10pm) The animated youthful clientele don't seem quite poised enough for the cutting-edge music and design of this smooth bar that softens its neo-Bauhaus architecture with fountain pool, coloured lights and giant floral paintings. It's a restaurant by day.

Min Thiha
TEAHOUSE

(Map p238; 28th St at 72nd St; tea/nanbya K350/300; ⏱ 6am-4pm) Three trees grow through the roof of this archetypal unsophisticated older teahouse, its walls pasted with Buddhist aphorisms, bread pictures and English Premier League lion symbols.

Cafe YMH
BEER STATION

(Ya Mone Hlaing; Map p242; Strand Rd, 26/28; draught beer K600; ⏱ 9am-10pm) This slightly tatty beer station has a terrace with a brilliant view overlooking the riverboat activity, plus an astonishingly wide-ranging menu.

Cafe JJ
BAR

(Map p238; ☑ 02-74349; www.cafejj.com; 26th St at 65th St; coffee K1200-3000, cocktails K3000-7000; ⏱ 9am-10.30pm; 🛜) Distinctive 'caged' lamps provide character in this comfortably hip cafe with Casadio espresso machine and chilled Athaya Burmese red wine on tap.

Uncle Chan Beer Station
BEER STATION

(Map p242; 35th St, 72/73; barbecue items from K800, mains K3000-5000; ⏱ 8am-10pm) A cut above most typical beer barns and a little less male-dominated, there's a wide range of eating possibilities here, but the prime attractions are the polar-cold brews in superfrosty mugs. Stretching several blocks up

73rd St from here are several equally lively eating and drinking spots.

Unison Teahouse
TEAHOUSE

(Map p242; 38th St at 88th St; tea K300; ⏱ 5am-1am) This octagonal teahouse is a fun place to retreat to after visiting the jade market. You can watch furtive-looking gem merchants discussing deals over a cuppa.

Emperor
BEER STATION

(Kandawgyi Pat Rd at 85th St; draught beer K1000) This simple beer station comes to life after dark when the trees are beautifully lit with orange paper lanterns. Snooker tables are available; live acoustic music sets start at around 7pm.

Rainbow
BEER STATION

(Map p242; 83rd St at 23rd St; beer K700, barbecue/small plates from K800/2000; ⏱ 9am-11pm) This lively beer station draws in the crowds for football-watching; it serves reasonable food too.

☆ Entertainment

Evening shows, professionally performed but aimed squarely at tourist audiences, have helped rekindle interest in traditional dance and puppetry. The most authentic performances are set to a six-piece 'orchestra' led by a distinctively wailing *hneh* (an oboe-like instrument). The other musicians are percussionists notably playing gamelan-style arrangements on gongs and tuned circles of minidrums known as *sai-wai*. You can see a selection of performances during dinner shows at several upmarket hotels, and at Mya Nandar (p253) riverside restaurant.

Yoke thé, or Burmese marionette puppetry, has been a performing art since at least the late 18th century. The skill of *yoke thé* masters, and the beauty of their handcrafted puppets, is the stuff of folklore. Characters ranging from *nagas* to princes, and from ogres to magicians caper and dance on a raised stage, moving their limbs and heads in a sinuous, oddly expressive manner. Ever read about the 'uncanny valley', the point where an artificial representation of a human begins to resemble an actual human in an almost unsettling way? You can see the point reached at a Burmese puppet show, although we mean this in a good way – the performers are simply that skilled. The entire affair is buoyed by an energetic orchestra (*hsaing-waing*) that adds clashing cymbals, tinkly percussion, and plenty of

MOUSTACHE BROTHERS – FROM SLAPSTICK TO SATIRE

The internationally celebrated **Moustache Brothers** (Map p242; 39th St, 80/81; K10,000; ☺8.30pm) perform *a-nyeint* – a form of vaudeville folk opera with dance, music, jokes and silly walks. In 1996 the brothers performed an Independence Day show at Aung San Suu Kyi's Yangon compound, telling politically tinged jokes about Myanmar generals. For two of the three 'brothers' (Par Par Lay and Lu Zaw), the result was arrest and seven years' hard labour. Several Hollywood comedians (including Rob Reiner and Bill Maher) wrote to the government in protest while the third brother, Lu Maw, kept the Mandalay show going with the help of his wife.

After their release in 2002, the reunited Moustache Brothers remained 'blacklisted' from playing at outside events (marriages, funerals, festivals and so on). However, they played a series of gala performances at home attended – inevitably – by government agents, nicknamed 'KGB' by Lu Maw. The regional commander soon summoned Par Par Lay and demanded that all performances stop, even in his house. But when Par Par Lay got home, some Westerners had already gathered for that night's show. Imaginatively the troupe decided to go ahead without costumes and make-up, arguing that a costume-less show would be a 'demonstration' not a real 'performance'. Somehow, it worked. Following the September 2007 troubles (the Saffron Revolution monk protests), the group's original leader Par Par Lay (who passed away in August 2013) suffered another month in jail. But the shows – now entirely in English – have never stopped. Costumes have reappeared, at least for the dancers, adding colour to the concrete-box theatre room that's adorned with photos of the brothers' glory days and their many celebrity encounters.

The show can be tough to follow. The levels of English aren't phenomenal, and Burmese humour itself relies on a sense of slapstick and cultural references that will understandably soar over a foreigner's head. On the flip side, the political satire isn't exactly subtle, and there are plenty of 'Take my wife, please' riffs. This isn't a critique – simply an acknowledgement that the show, for all its foreign attendance, still hews to Burmese humour conventions, and some audiences may struggle to keep up. But approach with an open mind and an appreciation for the show's deep empathy, and you'll walk away with a grin as big as Lu Maw's.

good-natured back and forth banter with the puppet handlers. To enjoy a show try Mandalay Marionettes.

⭐ **Mandalay Marionettes**   PUPPET THEATRE
(Map p238; ☏02-34446; www.mandalaymarion ettes.com; 66th St at 27th St; K10,000; ☺8.30pm; 🐾) On a tiny stage, colourful marionettes expressively recreate snippets of traditional tales. Occasionally a curtain is lifted so that you can briefly admire the deft hand movements of the puppeteers (one an octogenarian) who have performed internationally. You can also buy puppets here.

Mintha Theater   DANCE
(Map p238; ☏09 45897 4512 09 680 3607; www. minthatheater.com; 58th St, 29/30; K14000; ☺8.30pm Jul-Mar) 🐾 Colourfully costumed dancers perform around 10 dances from a larger repertoire. Some give human form to traditional stories of local folklore, while others are examples of typical Burmese slapstick – perhaps a comedic drunkard or the jokily incompetent moustachioed U Shwe

Yoe, tumbling off the stage as he fails to impress his beau.

The Mintha Theater is now the public venue of the Inwa School of Performing Arts, a new high school for youth who aspire to be professional stage artists. Proceeds from the theatre benefit the school and preservation of Myanmar performing arts, which face low funding from state sources. To learn more about and support these efforts, check out www.artsmandalay.org.

Minglar Diamond Cineplex   CINEMA, CONCERTS
(Map p242; ☏02-765641; 5th fl, Diamond Plaza, rear bldg, 33rd St, 78/77; tickets from K1500) Hidden on the 5th floor of this big shopping centre are a three-screen cinema, several fast-food eateries and a concert hall with occasional Myanmar rap and pop gigs.

Win-Win 35   LIVE MUSIC
(35th St, 60/62; draught beer from K750; ☺9am-11pm, music from 7.30pm) A small stage in the garden of this spacious beer station provides live music from talented local

bands. The show we enjoyed featured *Hotel California*–esque chords and a singer with a Joe Cocker rasp. No cover, cheap beer and sizzler-plate meals where the main vegetable is roast garlic.

🛍 Shopping

Mandalay is a major arts and crafts centre. It's probably the best place in Myanmar for traditional puppets and handwoven tapestries. Beware: items may be deliberately scuffed or weathered to look older than they are. Handicraft places generally have to pay commissions to drivers or guides, so prices may prove better if you visit alone.

Rocky GIFTS & SOUVENIRS
(Sein Win Myint; Map p238; ☑02-74106; 27th St, 62/63; ⊙8.30am-8pm) One of Mandalay's better handicrafts shops; the goods include lacquer, puppets, carvings and stuffed 'gold-thread' appliqué tapestries, plus gems and jade – basically, the full gamut of traditional arts and crafts.

King Galon ARTS & CRAFTS
(Map p242; ☑02-32135; 36th St, 77/78; ⊙8am-6pm) The most sophisticated of Mandalay's gold-leaf workshops, King Galon offers patient explanations of the gold-pounding process without sales pressure. Also stocks a range of souvenir handicrafts.

> ### ⓘ WHERE TO FIND HANDICRAFTS & ANTIQUES
>
> ➡ Buy puppets at Moustache Brothers (p255) and Mandalay Marionettes (p255).
>
> ➡ Monks' accoutrements (alms bowls, robes, fans etc) are sold in the street west of Eindawa Paya.
>
> ➡ Some gold-leaf-pounding workshops have souvenirs.
>
> ➡ There's a popular antiques and souvenir shop below Marie-Min (p252), which keeps the same hours as the restuarant.
>
> ➡ There are numerous silk workshops and handicraft emporia along the main Sagaing road in Amarapura.
>
> ➡ Good-value souvenirs can be found in the approach passages to Mahamuni Paya and from peddlers around Inwa.
>
> ➡ Mingun has numerous 'art' galleries, mostly inexpensive.

Sut Ngai FABRIC
(Map p242; 33rd St, 82/83; ⊙8am-8pm Mon-Sat) Sells Kachin fabrics and costumes, aimed mainly at Kachins themselves rather than tourists.

Shwe Pathein GIFTS & SOUVENIRS
(Map p242; 141 36th St, 77/78; parasols from US$15; ⊙8am-5pm) Pathein-style parasols. Next door there's a leather workshop and a gold-leaf shop.

Ocean Super Center SUPERMARKET
(Map p242; Diamond Plaza basement, 78th St, 33/34; ⊙9am-9pm) Central Mandalay's best-stocked supermarket is in the basement of the city's biggest shopping mall.

Zegyo MARKET
(Zaycho; Map p242; 84/86th, 26/28th; ⊙hours vary by shop) The 25-storey tower that overpowers the Mandalay skyline balances atop one of three horrendous, neighbouring concrete 'malls', stiflingly crammed full of fabric sellers. However, the surrounding older market areas are fascinating places to wander amid piles of dried fish, sacks of chilli and giant clusters of bananas. The area begins busting around 8am, and most shops close by 7pm.

Golden Rose ARTS & CRAFTS
(Map p242; 36th St, 78/79; ⊙7am-8pm) A row of four gold-leaf beaters thump away at the back of the Golden Rose shop-workshop with visitors welcome to drop in and watch or get a full explanation of the beating process.

Aurora ARTS & CRAFTS
(Map p242; 78th St, 35/36) Handicrafts gallery.

ⓘ Information

INTERNET ACCESS
Wi-fi is available in better cafe-bars and in most hotels, including budget lodges. Internet cafes are dotted every few blocks throughout the city centre. Speeds are moderate at best, and at worst annoyingly slow. Don't count on downloads or streaming internet.

MONEY
Pristine euro, US dollar and Singapore dollar banknotes can be changed for excellent rates at Mandalay Airport and at downtown money changers, such as **Faith Moneychanger** (Map p242; 26th St, 81/82; ⊙9am-5pm), and several branches of **KBZ Bank** (Map p242; 34th St at 78th St; ⊙9.30am-3pm Mon-Fri) and **CB Bank** (Map p242; ☑02-22176; 26th St, 84/85; ⊙9.30am-3pm Mon-Fri). Both banks (and numerous other

financial institutions) have 24-hour ATMs for Visa, MasterCard, Maestro, Plus and UnionPay.

Midrange and high-end hotels, and some higher-end restaurants, may accept credit cards, but you'll need cash elsewhere.

POST

DHL (Map p242; ✆ 02-39274; Hotel Mandalay, 78th St, 37/38; ⏰ 8.30am-5.30pm Mon-Fri, to 12.30pm Sat) International courier.

Main Post Office (Map p242; ✆ 02–27755; 22nd St, 80/81; ⏰ 10.30am-4pm Mon-Fri)

TELEPHONE

Calls cost K100 (local) or K200 to K500 (in-ternational) per minute from street stands. Mobile-phone SIM cards typically cost around US$1.50 from ever-multiplying phone shops.

Central Telephone & Telegraph (CTT; Map p242)

TOURIST INFORMATION

MTT (Myanmar Travel & Tours; Map p238; ✆ 02-60356; 68th St, 26/27; ⏰ 9.30am-6pm) The government-run travel company doubles as a tourist office, giving away multicity maps as well as selling transport tickets and places on tours that require government permits.

TRAVEL AGENCIES

Green Myanmar (Map p242; ✆ 09 42007 7655, 09 96991 0109; www.green-myanmar. com; cnr 78th & 26th Sts) Can arrange boat tours and sightseeing excursions.

Mandalay Palace Ticket Booth (Map p238; east entrance, Mandalay Palace, 19th St) Sells tickets to Mandalay Palace and combo tickets to local temples and archaeology sites.

Myanmar Upperland (Map p238; ✆ 02-65011; www.myanmarupperland.com; 27th St, 71/72; ⏰ 9am-6pm Mon-Sat) Arranges tours of the city and surrounding region.

Nice Style (Map p242; ✆ 02-64103; www. travelsmyanmarservices.com; 25th St, 82/83;

⏰ 9am-8pm Mon-Fri, to 3pm Sat & Sun; ☎) Professional travel and tour agent.

Seven Diamond (Map p242; ✆ 02-72939, 02-72868; www.sevendiamondtravels.com; 82nd St, 26/27; ⏰ 8.30am-6pm, closed Sun) Helpful, major agency that can prebook flights and hotels by email request and organise airport-bound shared taxis.

Tour Mandalay (✆ 02-62625; www.tourman dalay.travel; cnr 35th & 71st Sts; ⏰ 9am-6pm Mon-Fri, to 1pm Sat & Sun) Professional agency that can arrange cruises and other tours.

❶ Getting There & Away

AIR

All flights use **Mandalay International Airport** (MDL; ✆ 02-27048, 02-27027), which is just over 20 miles south of the city. International and domestic routes expand on an almost monthly basis.

Major airlines operating from Mandalay in-clude **Air Bagan** (Map p242; ✆ 02-61791; www. airbagan.com; 78th St, 27/28; ⏰ 9am-5pm Mon-Fri, to 1pm Sat), **Air Mandalay** (Map p242; ✆ 02-61513; www.airmandalay.com; 78th St, 29/30; ⏰ 9am-5pm, to 1pm Sun), **Asian Wings** (Map p242; ✆ 02-74791; www.asianwingsair. com; 30th St at 78th St; ⏰ 9am-5pm Mon-Fri, to 2pm Sat & Sun), **Golden Myanmar** (✆ 09 97799 3000; www.gmairlines.com), **Yangon Airways** (www.yangonair.com), **Air KBZ** (Map p238; ✆ 02-24861; www.airkbz.com; 30th St, 71/72; ⏰ 9am-5pm Mon-Fri, to 1pm Sat & Sun), **Myan-mar National Airlines** (Map p242; ✆ 02-36221; www.flymna.com; 81st St, 25/26; ⏰ 8.30am-3pm), **Mann Yadanarpon** (www.airmyp.com), **China Eastern** (✆ 02-01172; http://en.ceair. com; 70th St, 34/35), **Bangkok Airways** (Map p242; ✆ 02-36323; www.bangkokairways.com; 78th St, 33/34) and **Air Asia** (www.airasia.com).

You'll find frequent daily flights to Yangon, Tachileik, Nyang U (Bagan) and Heho (Inle Lake),

MANDALAY TRANSPORT CONNECTIONS OVERVIEW

DESTINATION	BUS	TRAIN	AIR	BOAT
Bagan	9hr, US$10	8hr, K4000-10,000	US$60-68, 30min	10-14hr, from US$40
Bhamo	N/A	N/A	US$58-134, 50min	N/A
Hsipaw	5-6hr, US$5	11hr, K5000-10,000	US$95-108, 45min to Lashio +2hr taxi	N/A
Inle Lake	11-13hr, US$12-25	N/A	US$75 30min via Heho +1hr taxi	N/A
Nay Pyi Taw	5hr, US$8	1hr, K10,000-20,000	US$100-120, 30min, twice weekly	N/A
Yangon	9-10hr, US$15-20	15½-16½hr, K4650-18,000	US$79-150, 90min	N/A

and several flights a week to towns such as Lashio, Putao and Myitkyina. International connections link Mandalay to Bangkok, Chiang Mai and Kunming; while some of these flights are direct, others connect through Yangon.

BOAT

Taking a boat on the Ayeyarwady River is one of Mandalay's delights. Flits to Mingun (US$8, one hour) or all-day rides to Bagan (from US$40, 10 hours) are most popular, though a return service to Inwa is a great alternative. Prebooking one day ahead is usually fine for Bagan – bring plenty of drinking water.

Boats to Mingun depart at 9am; boats to Bagan leave around 7am.

IWT Ferries (Map p242; ☏ 01-381 912, 02-36035; www.iwt.gov.mm/en; Gawein Jetty) In the past, operated slow boats to Katha and Bhamo, but these routes were closed at the time of research. If they resume, expect the trip to take three/four days to Katha/Bhamo. Tickets can be purchased from the **IWT Ticket Office** (Map p242; 35th St).

Malikha (Map p242; ☏ 02-72279; www.malikha-rivercruises.com; to Bagan/Mandalau US$47/33) Comfy tourist boats do the Bagan run. Buy tickets through hotels, agencies or online.

MGRG (Map p242; ☏ 011-202 734; www.mgrgexpress.com; Strand Rd; to Bagan US$42) Bagan express ferries (October to March). Tickets from a booth at the **jetty** (Map p242).

Nmai Hka (Map p242; ☏ 02-700 072, 09 3311 5588; www.nmaihka.com; A-15, 2nd fl, train station; to Bagan US$40) Shwei Keinnery ferries to Bagan (tourist season) and Bhamo (summer) plus seasonal Tharlarwaddy to Mingun and Inwa. Ticket office is 100yd east of the IWT ferry. Departures from Gawein Jetty.

Tourist Boat Association (Mayan Chan Jetty; Map p242; Mingun US$8) Departs for Mingun at 9am from a jetty at the end of 26th St. No prebooking; just show up.

If you want a full cruise there are plenty of very upmarket options, notably with Paukan (p245), Amara (p245) and **Orient Express** (www.orient-express.com/web/rtm/voyages_in_myanmar.jsp) boats. Exact offerings change every year so consult the websites and expect to spend thousands of dollars.

BUS & SHARED TAXI

Two of Mandalay's three major bus stations are infuriatingly distant from the city centre and there

MANDALAY BUS & ROAD TRANSPORT OPTIONS

Bus stations: TM (Thiri Mandalar bus station); PGMS (Pyi Gyi Myat Shin bus station); Main (Kwe Se Kan Highway bus station). Agents: AY (Aung Yedana); ChM (Cherry Myay); Duh (Duhtawadi); LM (Lwin Mann); MM (Meisho Mann); ShMT (Ko Htay/Shwe Mann Thu). For shared taxis have your hotel book by phone and get picked up at your door. Higher fares will net you air-con and (slightly) adjustable seats.

DESTINATION	TYPICAL FARE (K)	DURATION	DEPARTURE TIME	DEPARTURE POINT	TYPE
Amarapura	500	45min	frequent	84th at 29th	pick-up
Bagan	8000-11,000	6hr	many	Main	bus
Hsipaw	5000	8hr	2pm	PGMS	shared taxi
Inle Lake	12,000-17,000	6-8hr	9am, 5pm & 10pm	Main	bus
Kalaw	12,000	8hr	use Taunggyi buses	Main	bus
Kyaukse	5000	4½hr	1pm	PGMS	bus
Lashio	7500	11hr	6pm	PGMS	bus
Nay Pyi Daw	from 6000	4hr	frequent 7am-9pm	Main	bus
Shwebo	2500	3½hr	hourly 8am-3pm	TM	bus
Pyin Oo Lwin	8000	2hr	hourly 6am-4pm	hotel	shared taxi
Pyin Oo Lwin	2500	2½hr	5am-5pm	83rd at 28th	pick-up
Sagaing	500	1hr	around 3 per hour till 7pm	84th at 30th	pick-up
Taunggyi	10,000-13,000	7-8hr	9am, 10pm, 11pm	Main	bus
Taungoo	8000	7hr	9pm	Main	bus
Yangon	from 11,000 (standard) to 24,000 (air-con)	8hr	frequent	Main	bus

are proposals to move the main highway bus station even further south. **Thiri Mandalar bus station** (Map p242; 89th St, 21/22) is relatively central. Pyi Gyi Myat Shin bus station is 2 miles east of the centre and has buses for Hsipaw and Lashio. Kwe Se Kan Highway bus station (also known as Chan Mya Shwe Pyi, or main bus station) is 5 miles south of the centre, and it can take 45 minutes for the K3000/6000 motorbike/taxi ride from central Mandalay, even more by pick-up. Allow plenty of time once you're there to find the right bus in the mayhem.

Prebooking bus tickets for longer-distance routes (over four hours) is wise. Booking through backpacker hotels will usually incur a commission but that's rarely more than the motorbike-taxi fare you'd incur when buying your own.

Academy (02-78699 02-78885; K25,300) provides a bus service connecting Bagan and Mandalay with Mrauk U. The bus departs daily at 4pm – no arrival time is given, but if the trip goes without a hitch (Ha!), you should get there at around 1pm. Buses depart from Kwe Se Kan.

Bus-company and ticket-agency contacts include **Aung Yedana** (Map p242; 02-24850; 79th St, 27/28), **Cherry Myay** (Map p242; 02-73571; 27th St at 83rd St; air-con car/minivan per person from K6000; 6.30am-4pm) and **Duhtawadi** (Map p242; 02-66073, 02-61938; 31st St, 81/82).

Long-distance shared taxis, where available, are worth considering as most offer door-to-door

service, saving potentially long trips to/from bus stations at either end of your journey.

TRAIN

As the train station (30th St, 78/79) is relatively central, rail travel has the advantage of saving the long commute to an outlying bus station.

🛈 Getting Around

TO/FROM THE AIRPORT

Much of the one-hour drive into town from Mandalay Airport is through fields and scrubland swaying with mango trees and palmyra palms and liberally dotted with gilded pagodas. If you're arriving in Myanmar for the first time it's a great first taste.

There are free shuttle buses for some hotel guests. Otherwise, it's taxi time! There's a fixed rate of US$10/K12,000 for a private taxi, or US$5/K4000 for a shared taxi. Cheaper guesthouses will order you an airport car for about the same price as a shared taxi, but big hotels ask for a fair bit more. Taxis on the street typically want double fare, as they'll find it hard to get a return ride.

BICYCLE

Mandalay's vast size can rapidly become overwhelming, but the city is very flat, so if you're not intimidated by the traffic, renting a bicycle or moped can be a great solution. Several rental agents in the central backpacker area charge around K2000/10,000 per day for bicycles/

MANDALAY FERRY OPTIONS

DESTINATION	PRICE	DURATION (HR)	DEPARTURES	BOAT
Bagan	US$42	10	7am daily Oct-Mar	Nmai Kha, MGRG
Bagan	US$47	10	7am daily Oct-Mar then sporadic	Malikha
Bagan	US$40	11	6am Mon & Fri	IWT Hanthawaddy
Bhamo*	US$100-120	34	7am thrice weekly Jul-Sep	IWT
Inwa	US$8	1	noon daily Oct-Mar	multiple operators
Mingun	US$8	1	8.30am daily Oct-Mar	multiple operators

* Boats to Bhamo were not running at the time of research.

MANDALAY TRAIN ROUTES

Sample foreigner fares (from ordinary to sleeper class):

DESTINATION	PRICE (K)	DURATION (HR)	DEPARTURE
Hsipaw	5000-10,000	11	4am
Monywa	10,000-20,000	5¼	2.30pm
Myitkyina	15,000-20,000	20	10am, 1.30pm, 4pm, 4.45pm, 6.30pm
Nyaung U (Bagan)	4000-10,000	8	9pm
Pakkoku	4000-6000	11	6pm
Yangon	4650-18,000	15½-16½	multiple departures

motorbikes including long-established **Mr Jerry** (Map p242; ☑ 02-65312; 83rd St, 25/26; ⊙ 8am-8pm) and **Mr Bean** (Map p242; ☑ 02-31770; 83rd St, 24/25). Several hotels rent bicycles too. Cyclists are advised to carry a head torch at night.

To go further afield, expat-run **Mandalay Motorcycle** (Map p242; ☑ 09 44402 2182; www.mandalaymotorbike.com; 32nd St, 79/80; per day city bike from K10,000, trail bike from K40,000) and **Myanmar Bike Rental** (☑ 09 4211 30276; www.myanmarbikerental.com; 59th St, 22/19; city bikes K5000-15,000, 200cc K25,000, motorcycle K50,000) have city bikes and trail bikes. Call ahead or shoot them an email to set up your rental and plan your route.

MOTORCYCLE & TAXI

Motorcycle taxis lurk near hotels and on city corners. Expect to pay K1000 for a short hop, K1500 across the centre, and K10,000 for all-day hire within Mandalay (or K15,000 including Amarapura, Inwa and Sagaing); double these rates for a regular taxi. The following drivers speak decent English.

Aung-Aung (☑ 09 40264 8306) Friendly, helpful driver.

Ko Zaw (☑ 09 40251 2327; mandalay.city. tour@gmail.com) Thoughtful, English-speaking motorcycle-taxi driver.

Seven Diamond Express (Map p242; ☑ 02-22365; 32nd St, 82/83) Local taxi service.

Zin Mi (09 4315 9591; zinmehtunshinshin1987@ gmail.com) Daughter of Moustache Brother comedian Lu Maw, Zimi is probably the only female motorcycle-taxi driver in Mandalay. Also puts together her own recommended tours.

BUS & PICK-UP TRUCKS

The public transport system uses pick-up trucks that make regular lengthy stops, rarely leaving till jammed full. Route numbers are displayed above the cab in local script. Different coloured boards sometimes denote variant routings, but the entire system seems to get upended every few months. If you're willing to brave it, the bus fare is around K500.

From 25th/83rd diagonally opposite Nylon Hotel (p248):

➠ ၁ (1), ၅ (5), ၁၉ (19) via 78th St, south to the train station, east on 30th. 5 and 19 then head east on 19th while 1 heads north up 62nd.

➠ ၁၆ (16) goes to the base of Mandalay Hill; blue sign goes via the train station.

From 84th St at 29th St:

➠ ၈ (8) passes Mahamuni Paya en route to Amarapura.

➠ ၁၀ (10) heads to the Kwe Se Kan Highway bus station.

TRISHAW

Traditionally the main form of city transport, pedal trishaws are now relatively rare except around the markets. A K4000 return fare takes you from the city centre to the base of Mandalay Hill; all-day hire from around K10,000. Give an extra tip, because these guys work hard for the money.

AROUND MANDALAY

For many visitors, the historic sites around Mandalay trump anything in the city itself. Iconic attractions include U-Bein Bridge in Amarapura, Sagaing's temple-studded hills and horse-cart rides around the rural ruins of Inwa.

Entry to Inwa's two main sites and Amarapura's Bagaya Kyaung are included in Mandalay's K10,000 'combo' ticket. A separate K3000 ticket for Mingun and Sagaing is

---

ELEPHANT DANCING IN KYAUKSE

Bagan was not the only place to benefit from King Anawrahta's remarkable 11th-century building spree. According to legend, one of Anawrahta's relic-carrying elephants took a liking to Webu Hill, above today's Kyaukse. Anawrahta took that as a sign to found a city at its base, starting with an irrigation system created using a stone dam (*kyauk se*). Nearly a millennium later, the attractive small town (around 40 miles south of Mandalay) remains elephant mad. Naive elephant masks and toys are sold at numerous kiosks, and white elephant statues guard the **gigantic golden Buddha** halfway up Webu Hill's north slope. A nationally famous **elephant dance** competition forms the centrepiece of Kyaukse's main festival. The dancing 'elephants' are actually two humans in wonderfully idiosyncratic costumes. The competition is held one day before Thadingyut full moon (October), but for a day or two beforehand you might see 'elephants' practising their prancing around town.

Kyaukse is about 22 miles south of Mandalay on Hwy 1. Pick-up trucks run from 84th St at 29th St in Mandalay (front/back K1000/500); depending on the passenger situation, it can take up to two hours to get there. You can hire a taxi from Mandalay for around K20,000 to K30,000; expect some bargaining.

TA MOKE SHWE GU GYI

The enormous temple complex of **Ta Moke Shwe Gu Gyi** (တမုတ်ရွှေဂူကြီး; GPS 21.644556, 96.055727; ⏰8am-6.30pm) FREE is one of the finest archaeological sites in the country outside Bagan or Mrauk-U, but its remoteness and lack of English signage on-site make a visit challenging. Still, even without interpretive help, this is a fascinating spot, anchored by a two-storey temple marked by sturdy brickwork and magnificent stucco reliefs. Some of the latter include scenes from the life of the Buddha, as well as depictions of animals, plants and mythological beings.

The complex consists of eight buildings that date back as far as the 8th century, with the 'youngest' constructed in the 14th century. Be on the lookout for an 'encased' Buddha image: three concentric Buddha statues arranged like Russian dolls around each other. There are a lot of other impressive artworks, but it's difficult to appreciate without interpretive signs. If you don't mind some academic language, download the paper 'Ta Mok Shwe-gu-gyi Temple: Local Art in Upper Myanmar 11th–17th Centuries', by Elizabeth Moore, Win Maung and Htwe Htwe Win, available for free online, to learn more about the site.

It can be a trick getting here. The ruins are decidedly off the beaten path, and there was no pick-up-truck path here at the time of research.

The ruins are about 11km west of Kyaukse, an hour's drive south of Mandalay. From there you'll want to take the first road outside the northern city entrance that leads west to the Yangon–Mandalay Hwy. Be on the lookout for signs (in Burmese and English) for Ta Moke Shwe Gu Gyi, located roughly halfway between Kyaukse and the highway. Bargain hard with a taxi driver, and expect to pay at least K20,000 for a there-and-back excursion.

patchily enforced. No one checks for tickets at the other sites.

A popular option is to combine Amarapura, Sagaing and Inwa into a full-day trip by motorcycle taxi (K20,000) or taxi (around K50,000). For most taxi drivers, 'Inwa' means dropping you at the Myitnge ferry, assuming you'll cross then tour by horse cart. However, Myanmar Upperland (p257) offers an all-day tour by air-con minibus (US$28 per person, hotel pick-up 8am) that includes driving into and around Inwa plus sunset at U-Bein Bridge, lunch, water and several interesting workshop visits.

Motorbike taxis typically charge around K2000 extra to drive around the Inwa ruins (if you insist). Add another K2000 to see Paleik en route, and K5000 to include Mingun. Beware that doing the whole lot in one long day will feel very rushed. Ideally, make two or three day trips.

Amarapura   အမရပုရ

POP C 35,000 / ☎02

Myanmar's penultimate royal capital, Amarapura (amu-*ra*-pu-*ra*) means 'City of Immortality', though its period of prominence lasted less than 70 years (from 1783). In 1857 King Mindon began dismantling most of the palace buildings, shipping them 7 miles north to Mandalay, which was to become the new capital according to a Buddhist prophecy. These days leafy Amarapura is essentially a spread-out suburb of Mandalay, attractively set on a wide, shallow lake, named for an ogre who supposedly came looking for the Buddha here.

The wide roads and twisting alleyways make Amarapura feel less aggressively modern than Mandalay, and killing a day here is a pleasant undertaking. The main attraction is an iconic wooden footbridge that crosses the lake. Several other minor sights are widely scattered – you'll need a bike or taxi to see them all.

⊙ Sights

★**U-Bein Bridge**   BRIDGE
(ဦးပိန်တံတား) FREE The world's longest teak footbridge gently curves 1300yd across shallow **Taungthaman Lake**, creating one of Myanmar's most photographed sites. In dry season it feels surreally high and mostly crosses seasonal vegetable gardens. But after the summer rains, the area becomes a big lake and water laps just below the floor planks. Just a few of the 1086 poles on which it stands have been replaced by concrete supports.

A great time to visit the bridge is just after sunrise when hundreds of villagers and monks commute back and forth across it.

Amarapura

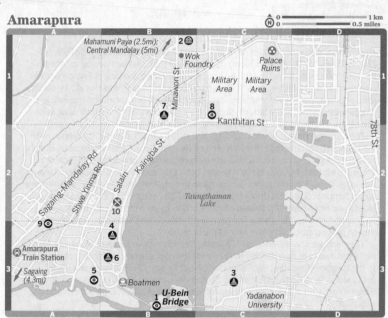

The light is often best around an hour before sunset, but by then there will be a lot of tourists and trinket sellers. However, while the bridge gets very busy, it rarely feels like a commercial gauntlet.

Bagaya Kyaung MUSEUM
(ဘားကရာကျောင်း; admission by combo ticket; ☉8am-6.30pm) If you want to squeeze full value out of your Mandalay 'combo' ticket, head to this 1996 concrete-pillared reconstruction of an early-19th-century monastery. It has plenty of flying wooden filigree roof work,

a substantial ancient library of Pali scripts, plus a museum of 19th-century buddha images, but few travellers are greatly impressed. Nearby there are several distinctive **tobacco drying barns**, and, further east, the hefty ruins of two former **palace** buildings.

Kyauktawgyi Paya BUDDHIST TEMPLE
(ကျောက်တော်ကြီးဘုရား; ☉8am-7pm) FREE
Around 200yd beyond the eastern end of U-Bein Bridge, this 1847 pagoda, built by Pagan Min, was supposedly modelled on the larger Ananda Pahto at Bagan, but its five-tiered roof makes it look more like a Tibetan/Nepali temple. While the paya doesn't have the perfectly vaulted roofs or the finer decorations of the original, it does have some fairly well-preserved life-scene frescoes in the four approaches.

Werawsana Jade Pagoda BUDDHIST PAGODA
(Hsin Ywa hill, Myinhmu Village; ☉24hr) FREE
Werawsana is reputedly the world's first pagoda built entirely out of jade. It's a sight to behold in the evening, when it radiates a soft green glow that's almost otherworldly (seriously, it looks like a piece of Buddhist kryptonite). But it is also a carnival scene – hawkers, teenagers and party people camp out here, which gives this religious site a surprisingly raucous feel. The Jade Pagoda

stands outside Amarapura, about 9 miles to the south.

Maha Ganayon Kyaung BUDDHIST MONASTERY

(မဟာဂန္ဓာရုံကျောင်း; ⊙7am-evening) FREE Just west of U-Bein Bridge, this sprawling monastery is a pleasantly meditative place for most of the day. But you may want to avoid the monastery at about 11am, when busloads of tourists arrive to gawp while the whole monastery sits down to eat, their silence pierced by the endless rattle of camera shutters.

Kyo Aung Sanda BUDDHIST MONASTERY

(ကြို့အောင်စန္ဒာ; ⊙ sunrise-sunset) FREE Little visited, this curious latter-day monastery features a mini 'Golden Rock', a prayer hall full of monk-posture statues and several surreal *Alice in Wonderland*–style staring Tweedledum and Owl figures.

Shwe Linmin Paya NOTABLE BUILDING

(ရွှေလမင်းဘုရား; Kanthitan St; ⊙ sunrise-sunset) FREE This attractive 19th-century square-based stupa has a gold spire and white/ice-blue lower sections from a 2006 makeover. It's set in a nursery of flowering shrubs beside the lake road.

Pahtodawgyi BUDDHIST STUPA

(ပုထိုးတော်ကြီး; ⊙ sunrise-sunset) FREE This vast bell-shaped pagoda, erected by King Bagyidaw in 1820, is the tallest structure for miles around (185ft). Men only are allowed to climb halfway to the upper terrace to appreciate views over the plethora of *hti* (stupa pinnacles) glittering through Amarapura's lush foliage.

Shwe Sin Tai WORKSHOP

(⊙7am-6pm) FREE Hand-worked silk-weaving workshop that welcomes visitors without sales pressure.

Lin Zin Kone Cemetery CEMETERY

(လင်ဇင်းကုန်း) When Inwa-based King Hsinbyushin sacked Ayuthaya in today's Thailand, he reputedly returned with thousands of prisoners including the Ayuthayan King Udombhara who became a local monk. When Udombhara died nearly 30 years later, was buried in a grand tomb whose location has long been disputed. In 2013 archaeologists claimed 'with 90% certainty' to have identified the grave in Lin Zin Kone Cemetery.

It's currently just a pile of old bricks backing onto rubbish-strewn waste ground, and Thai-backed efforts to restore it have been stalled by diplomatic hectoring between Myanmar and Thailand.

✖ Eating

Near either end of U-Bein Bridge there are eateries and food stalls where you can buy noodles, tea and roasted crab.

Renaissance Cafe BURMESE, THAI $$

(3 Salain; set meals K7500-13,000; ✳) Partly a showcase for the company's attractive modern rattan furniture and tableware, this friendly restaurant offers a variety of multi-dish Thai, Burmese or European meals; your guide or driver eats for free, which is nice, as the food is good but a bit overpriced.

ℹ Getting There & Around

Crammed-full pick-up trucks leave from 84th St at 29th St in Mandalay (K500, 45 minutes) and pass along the main Sagaing road. For U-Bein Bridge, get off just after it crosses the railway and walk east or take a horse cart (K2000).

A return taxi from Mandalay with an added 90 minutes of sightseeing should run around K10,000, or K7000 on a motorbike.

Boatmen can ferry folks across the water if you're not into crossing the U-Bein Bridge on foot.

Inwa (Ava) အင်းဝ

Since 1364, Inwa has taken four turns as royal capital of the Burmese people. Indeed, upper Burma was often referred to as the 'Kingdom of Ava', even well after the royal court abandoned Inwa for Amarapura in 1841. Despite its rich history, the site today is a remarkably rural backwater sparsely dotted with ruins, monastic buildings and stupas. It's a world away from the city bustle of Mandalay, which is a big part of its charm. Many visitors like to explore by horse cart, and while this can be charming, cycling allows more flexibility, village stops and human interactions.

The Mandalay 'combo ticket' is theoretically required to visit Inwa but it's only checked if you enter Bagaya Kyaung or Maha Aungmye Bonzan.

◉ Sights

You'll find persistent drinks vendors and postcard peddlers at the major sites. But much of Inwa's charm is in simply finding your own viewpoint or village encounter amid the pagodas.

★ Bagaya Kyaung MONASTERY

(ဗားကရာကျောင်း; combo ticket; ⊙ sunrise-sunset) This lovely 1834 teak monastery is Inwa's most memorable individual attraction.

It's supported on 267 teak posts, the largest 60ft high and 9ft in circumference, creating a cool and dark prayer hall that feels genuinely aged. Stained timbers are inscribed with repeating peacock and lotus-flower motifs. Despite the constant flow of visitors, this remains a living monastery with globes hung above the little school section to assist in the novices' geography lessons. Beware of protruding floorboard nails.

Daw Gyan
BUDDHIST PAGODA

(☉sunrise-sunset) **FREE** Within the green patchwork of paddies that forms a quilt over Inwa, a small temple perches on a tiny artificial island. This is Daw Gyan, a collection of several rust-red brick stupas arranged under enormous shade trees. On-site, a small flooded arcade leads to a buddha seated above the reflective waters. The entire place is supremely serene, especially given the verdant pastoral backdrop.

Maha Aungmye Bonzan
MONASTERY

(မဟာအောင်မြေဘုံစံ; ☉sunrise-sunset) **FREE** Built, unusually, of stucco-covered brick, this 1822 royal monastery temple is a rare survivor from the Ava era. The faded, sturdy structure looks very attractive in cleverly taken photographs, but in the harsh midday sun the main attraction is the cool afforded

by its ultra-thick walls and the bats flitting through its empty undercroft. Directly east, forming a fine background, is **Htilaingshin Paya**, an attractive array of gilded stupas, some dating to the Bagan period.

Behind, near the crumbling former monks' residence, a footpath leads to seasonally flooded river gardens and views to Sagaing.

Shwezigon Paya
BUDDHIST SITE

(ရွှေစည်းခုံဘုရား) This golden stupa rises photogenically above the overgrown south-west corner of Inwa's city walls. The best view is from across the moat, especially in September when the water level is high. The main access is from the northwestern city gate, but there is also a small pathway at the back of the associated monastery, allowing you to continue east by bicycle or motorbike.

Yedanasimi Paya
RUINS

This small but photogenic ensemble brings together three sitting buddhas and a handful of old brick stupas shaded by a giant flame tree.

Nanmyin
TOWER

(အင်းဝနန်းမြင့်မျှော်စင်) **FREE** All that remains of King Bagyidaw's palace complex is this 90ft 'leaning tower of Inwa', shattered but patched up and still standing after the

---

ALTERNATIVE INWA

Get a little off the beaten track at some of Inwa's minor sights and viewpoints.

➡ In dry season you can visit a row of disintegrating brick stupas west of Bagaya Kyaung, leading towards a mysterious array of overgrown temple ruins.

➡ Don't miss the view of the Shwezigon Paya golden stupa across the moat from near the overpriced two-hall **Archaeological Museum** (အင်းဝရှေးဟောင်းသုတေသနပြတိုက်; foreigner K5000; ☉9am-4.30pm Tue-Sun).

➡ Enjoy tree-framed views of several small pagodas from the rough track that gives a false short cut between gigantic **Nogatataphu Paya** (Lawkatharupha Paya) and the Sagaing Ferry jetty.

➡ The short restored sections of city wall near the three whitewashed pagodas of **Shwe Myauk Taung** are best viewed across the moat looking north.

➡ There are great Ayeyarwady River views from the square inner bastions of the 1874 **Sinkyone Fortress**, plus you'll find numerous stupas down weather-damaged lanes directly south.

➡ Fascinating **Hantharwady Village**, around a mile south of the moat, has countless stupas including the large, gilt, bell-shaped **Sandamuni Paya** (စန္ဒမုနိဘုရား, Maha Myamuni) and the four-storey stub of the once huge **Le-htat-gyi Paya** (လေးထပ်ကြီးဘုရား), now dangerously fissured by earthquakes. The charmingly uncommercial lacquerware company, **Myanma Nwe Sin** (☉roughly 8am-5pm), makes monks' alms bowls in the backstreets.

Inwa

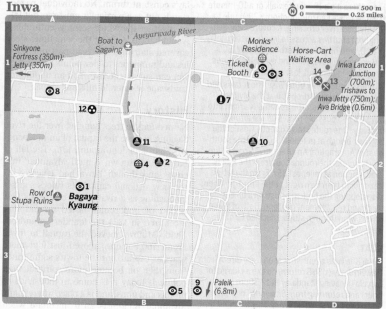

Inwa

⊙ Top Sights

⊙ Sights

⊗ Eating

1838 earthquake. The watchtower is neither beautiful nor especially high, but wide views from the top are great for getting your bearings amid the widely scattered sights; at least if it's open. It was closed for safety at the time of research due to damaged timber.

Htilaingshin Paya   PAGODA

(ထီးလိုင်ရှင်ဘုရား) This whitewashed pagoda complex, topped with the occasional gold-leafed stupa, dates back to the Bagan period.

✖ Eating & Drinking

There are basic local tea shops at Maha Aungmye Bonzan and Nogatataphu, plus at each of the villages and at the main (eastern) jetty, where you'll find some appealing tourist-friendly options.

Ave Maria   CHINESE, BURMESE $

(📞 09-26328; mains K2000-4500; ⊗ 8.30am-6pm) Follow the signs to this slightly hidden garden restaurant with attractive river views and good curry dishes.

Small River Restaurant   INTERNATIONAL $$

(📞 09 9100 1921; mains K3500-7000; ⊗ 8am-6pm; ✔) A popular tourist retreat near Inwa jetty, Small River has tables dotted throughout a tree-shaded garden backing on to a modest colonial-era wooden house (not part of the restaurant). It has some nice vegetarian options.

ⓘ Getting There & Away

Sagaing–Mandalay pick-ups can drop you at Inwa Lanzou junction just west of Ava Bridge.

From there it's a 15-minute walk or a 10-minute **trishaw** (Inwa Lanzou Junction; K200) ride to the Myitnge river crossing. A covered wooden longboat shuttles across to Inwa's eastern jetty (K800, with bicycle/motorbike K1000/1500 return, two minutes) around every 15 minutes according to demand, last at 6pm.

Unless you specify otherwise, most taxis and motorbike taxis will drop you at the Myitnge Jetty. However, motorbikes can drive right into Inwa via two possible routes off the airport highway. One route starts directly west of the big river bridge at milepost 357.8, to the south-west of Amarapura. An alternative access lane starts across the roundabout from the Paleik road junction at milepost 357. From the latter, head north then turn right at the first T-junction, sidestepping the broken bridge on a bike-wide track and replacement pontoon. Both of these routes wind through stupa-speckled Hanthar-wady Village.

BOAT

Nmai Kha runs a tourist-season ferry direct from Gawein Jetty (US$8 return, no extra charge for bicycles) leaving Mandalay at 12.30pm (one hour) and returning from Sinkyone Fortress at 4pm (two hours). While giving only a limited time in situ, it is a great way of getting to/from Inwa by bicycle. The return journey passes Sagaing's golden stupas at sunset.

ℹ Getting Around

There are no taxis or motorbike taxis (unless you hire your own from Mandalay).

The most popular way to visit Inwa is by horse cart (K9000). Dozens of carts wait at Inwa's eastern jetty. Horse-cart tours are a major part of the Inwa experience – carriages avoid noise pollution and create picturesque scenes along the tree-lined tracks. However, cart drivers typically stick to a fixed route, and some of their ponies look to be in sad condition. Whether this is due to slow business or the actions of the horse-cart driver is tough to determine – most cart drivers are friendly and honest, but this isn't a universal standard.

Bringing your own bicycle or motorbike from Mandalay will allow you to explore thoroughly. Walking is possible, but less efficient.

Sagaing   စစ်ကိုင်း

POP C 70,000 / ☏ 072

A crest of green hills studded with white and gold pagodas marks the 'skyline' of Sagaing, a religious pilgrimage centre that resembles Bagan with elevation. This pretty, friendly town is a major monastic centre and a somewhat serene escape from Manda-lay's constant thrum. No individual pagoda stands out as a particular must-see, but tak-en together the whole scene is enthralling. A highlight is walking the sometimes-steep covered stairways that lead past monaster-ies and nunneries to viewpoints from which you can survey the river and an undulating landscape of emerald hills and stupas.

History

Named for the trees hanging over the river, Sagaing became the capital of an independ-ent Shan kingdom around 1315. The fall of Bagan had thrown central Myanmar into chaos and though Pinya had emerged as the new regional capital, its ruler's son set up Sagaing as a rival power centre. Its first period of importance lasted around half a century: in 1364 the founder's grandson, Thado Minbya, moved the capital to Inwa. From 1760 Sagaing enjoyed just four more years as capital, but the town's significance from then on became more spiritual than political. Today it is home to thousands of monks and nuns, and is a place where many Myanmar Buddhists go to meditate when stressed.

◉ Sights

To enter Sagaing and Mingun, you must technically buy a K3000 combo ticket, sold at many sights or by inspectors. In Mingun, collection of this ticket seems rarely en-forced. We've heard that officials in Sagaing are more demanding, but we were never asked for a ticket here either.

◎ Sagaing Hill & Around

Stupa-topped hillocks coalesce into Sagaing Hill, a long tree-dappled north–south ridge that starts around 1½ miles north of the market area. A narrow, driveable lane winds up or you can take the 350-step stairway from **One Lion Gate**.

★ Soon U Pon
Nya Shin Paya   BUDDHIST TEMPLE
(ဆွမ်းဦးပုညရှင်ဘုရား; camera fee K300; ⊙ sunrise-sunset) This 'early offering shrine' is the most important of the temples on Sagaing Hill's southern crown and the first you'll come to on climbing the One Lion stairway. Notice the bronze frogs that serve as a collection box in the rather gaudy Buddha hall – the hill was originally thought to resemble a giant toad, a superstitious blessing which inspired Sagaing's development in the 14th

century. The central 97ft-high gilded stupa was originally conceived in 1312.

Legends claim that it magically appeared overnight, built by the local king's faithful minister Pon Nya in a superhuman flurry of activity inspired by a magical Buddha relic that he'd found in a betel-nut box. The myth fancifully claims that Pon Nya himself was of supernatural parentage, his father having 'flown' to Sagaing from the Himalayas

millennia before, arriving to a curious communion with the Buddha, seven hermits and a flower-bearing orangutan. Burmese genealogy is never boring.

★ **Tilawkaguru** BUDDHIST TEMPLE
(တိလောကဂုရု; ⊙9.30am-4.30pm) FREE At the foot of the great temple-studded hills of Sagaing, you'll find this little-visited cave monastery. Supposedly built around the

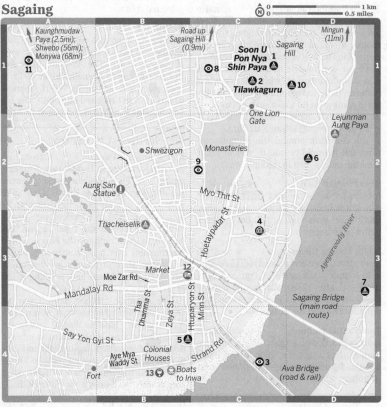

Sagaing

◎ Top Sights
1 Soon U Pon Nya Shin Paya...................C1
2 Tilawkaguru..C1

◎ Sights
3 Ava Bridge...C4
4 Buddha Museum....................................C3
5 Htuparyon Paya.....................................B4
6 Shin Pin Nan Kain.................................D2
7 Shwe-kyet-kya.......................................D3
8 Sitagu Buddhist Academy....................C1
9 Thakya Dita Nunnery............................C2
10 U Min Thonze Caves............................D1
11 Ubamin Silverware...............................A1

⌂ Sleeping
12 Shwe Pyne Sone..................................B3

⌂ Drinking & Nightlife
13 Minsuyek...B4

1670s, Tilawkaguru is filled with some of the most impressive preserved cave paintings in the country. Vivid frescoes depict the life (and past lives) of the Buddha, animals, warriors, battles, merchants, courtesans, kings, peasants and vivid menageries of mythological creatures. Finding the keyholder can be challenging, but a good bet is the **Buddha Museum** (ဗုဒ္ဓပြတိုက်; K5000; ⊘ 9.30am-4.30pm).

While visiting is free, it's nice to give the keyholder a few thousand kyats as a tip.

Sitagu Buddhist Academy   UNIVERSITY
(သီတဂူကမ္ဘာ့ဗုဒ္ဓတက္ကသိုလ်; ⊘ 24hr) FREE Set up in 1994 to educate the brightest young monks, this academy is a major intellectual centre for Theravada Buddhism. The centrepiece is a Sanchi-style hemispherical stupa, gilded and embossed with dharma-wheel patterns. In the surrounding arcade are photos of Asia's great Buddhist sites, often shown as holiday-style snaps featuring the university's founder-monk U-Nyan Nate Tara.

You can walk around the campus anytime, but it would be odd to visit at night, after the monks turn in (around 8pm).

Shin Pin Nan Kain   BUDDHIST PAGODA
(ရှင်ပင်နန်ကိုင်; ⊘ 8am-7pm) FREE Shin Pin Nan Kain's brass-clad stupa sits on a hilltop that's lower than Sagaing Hill but has even better panoramas.

U Min Thonze Caves   BUDDHIST SITE
(ဥမင်သုံးဆယ်; ⊘ sunrise-sunset) FREE Around a 10-minute walk north of Pon Nya Shin (p266), U Min Thonze Caves (literally '30 Caves') is famed for its crescent-shaped colonnade of 45 buddha images.

Thakya Dita Nunnery   NOTABLE BUILDING
(သက်ကျဒိဿဒီလရှင်ကျောင်း) This modern nunnery has a 16ft, 6in, gilded woven-cane buddha figure in an air-conditioned glass chamber.

⊙ Town Centre & Ayeyarwady River

The flat market area has little charm but further south it's pleasant to cycle along Strand Rd with a few old **colonial-era buildings** lining its north side and views across to Inwa from the Ayeyarwady riverfront.

Shwe-kyet-kya   BUDDHIST STUPA
(ရွှေကျက်ကျ; ⊘ sunrise-sunset) FREE One of the best places from which to appreciate Sagaing is from across the river at this little bluff with a cascade of small stupas. It's

part of a pair with the bigger Shwe-kyet-yet on a gentle rise across the road. The name, meaning Golden Fowl's Run, relates to curious legends from one of Buddha's supposed past lives...as a chicken.

Htuparyon Paya   BUDDHIST STUPA
(ထူပါရုံဘုရား) FREE This gigantic stupa, originally built in 1444, is unusual for having three circular storeys each incorporating arched niches. Across the street, a garden of garish statues includes a particularly fearsome red cobra.

Ava Bridge   BRIDGE
Linking Sagaing and Amarapura are two parallel bridges, each with multiple metal-framed spans. The 16-span 1934 Ava Bridge was partly demolished in 1942 to deny passage to advancing WWII Japanese troops. It wasn't repaired until 1954. The big new Sagaing Bridge was completed in 2005.

⊙ Northwest of Centre

Kaunghmudaw Paya   BUDDHIST STUPA
(ကောင်းမှုတော်ဘုရား; Monywa Hwy; ⊘ sunrise-sunset) FREE Five miles northwest of central Sagaing, Kaunghmudaw Paya is a vast gilded pudding of a stupa rising 150ft high. It was built in 1636 to commemorate Inwa's re-establishment as the royal capital. According to local tradition, the king agonised interminably over how to shape the stupa. His queen, tired of hubby's indecisiveness, ripped open her blouse and, pointing to her breast, said: 'Make it like this!'

Less romantic scholars claim it was actually modelled after the vast Suvarnamali Mahaceti (Ruwanwelisaya) stupa in Anuradhapura, Sri Lanka. Kaunghmudaw is distantly visible from Sagaing Hill and easy to spot as you drive past en route to Monywa. The surrounding area has many other stupas and is well known for silversmiths.

Ubamin Silverware   WORKSHOP
(☏ 072-21304, 09 203 1564; Monywa Hwy) FREE Behind their shop (2 miles northeast of Sagaing market), Ubamin's artisans hammer, tap and polish remarkable detail into silver pots, repoussage vases and animal figures. Fascinating, and no sales pressure.

⊨ Sleeping & Eating

There are some cheap Burmese restaurants and teahouses strung along Mandalay Rd and Strand Rd; none stand out as particularly stellar, but they're all decent value.

Shwe Pyne Sone HOTEL **$$**

(☏ 072-21384, 072-21942; shwepyaesonehotel.sgg@gmail.com; 20 Aoe Tan Lay Rd; r US$25-50; ❄️📶) It has basic, clean rooms arranged around generously spacious common sitting areas on each landing. The wi-fi can be unreliable. Bicycle/motorbike rental costs around K4000/10,000 per day.

🍷 Drinking & Nightlife

Minsuyek BEER STATION

(Strand Rd; draught beer K800; ☺8am-9pm) It's scruffy, but this stilted riverside beer station has great views towards Inwa.

ℹ️ Getting There & Away

Pick-ups from Mandalay (K500, one hour) drop off passengers in the market area, but return from outside Aye Cherry Restaurant by the Ava Bridge's south slip road.

If the river is behaving, **longboats** (Strand Rd; per person/boat K400) will shuttle you across to Inwa from the end of Zeya St. Charter one or be prepared to wait hours.

Mingun မင်းကွန်း

☏ 072

Home to several unique sites – as well as the footer foundations for what would have been the largest temple *and* mythological lions' butts in the world – Mingun is a compact riverside village that makes a popular half-day excursion from Mandalay. The journey is part of the attraction, whether puttering up the wide Ayeyarwady or rollercoastering along a rural lane from Sagaing.

A Sagaing–Mingun fee (K3000) is half-heartedly collected on the east side of Mingun Paya. In peak season this might be checked at the Mingun Bell, but we weren't asked for it.

From November to February little Mingun can feel overloaded with visitors (especially before 1pm, when most tourist boats return to Mandalay). But drinks sellers and oil-painting vendors are easily avoided by walking behind the monuments on the dusty paths to the west. Views from these paths are most attractive in the afternoon when sunlight illuminates the west-facing side of Mingun Paya.

👁️ Sights

While there are no real opening hours for the pagodas, you definitely don't want to attempt the climb up Mingun Paya in the dark.

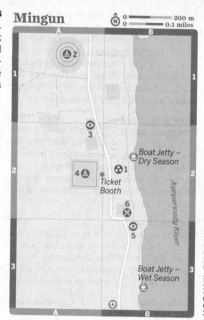

Mingun

👁️ Sights
1 Chinthe Ruins	B2
2 Hsinbyume Paya	A1
3 Mingun Bell	A2
4 Mingun Paya	A2
5 Pondaw Paya	B3

🍴 Eating
| 6 Point | B2 |

Mingun Paya BUDDHIST STUPA

(မင်းကွန်းဘုရား) **FREE** Started in 1790, Mingun Paya (or Pahtodawgyi) would have been the world's biggest stupa had it been finished. In fact, work stopped when King Bodawpaya died in 1819. That left only the bottom third complete. But the result is still a huge structure – a roughly 240ft cube on a 460ft lower terrace. It is often described as the world's largest pile of bricks. There's a steep staircase to the top where you can enjoy amazing views of the countryside.

For added drama, there are several deep cracks caused by the massive 1838 earthquake.

Mingun Bell HISTORIC SITE

(မင်းကွန်းခေါင်းလောင်း) **FREE** In 1808 Bodawpaya continued his biggest-is-best obsession

MANDALAY & AROUND MINGUN

by commissioning a bronze bell weighing 55,555 *viss* (90 tonnes). It's 13ft high and more than 16ft across at the lip and was the world's biggest ringable bell for many decades, albeit now surpassed by the giant bell of Pingdingshan, China. You can duck beneath and stand within the bell while some helpful bystander gives it a good thump.

Hsinbyume Paya   BUDDHIST STUPA

(ဆင်ဖြူမယ်ဘုရား) FREE Built in 1816, possibly using materials pilfered from Mingun Paya (p269), this unusual pagoda rises in seven wavy, whitewashed terraces representing the seven mountain ranges around Mt Meru – the mountain at the centre of the Buddhist universe.

Chinthe Ruins   RUINS

(ချင်္သဲ) Across the road from Mingun Paya lie two house-sized brick-and-stucco ruins. These are just the haunches of what would have been truly gigantic *chinthe* (the pagoda's half-lion, half-dragon guardian deities).

Pondaw Paya   NOTABLE BUILDING

(ပုံတော်ဘုရား) FREE To see what Mingun Paya (p269) would have looked like had it ever been completed, have a quick look at diminutive Pondaw Paya, 200yd south at the end of the tourist strip.

Eating

There are half a dozen snack shacks around the Mingun Paya entrance. **Point** (mains K2000-5000), near the ferry jetty, has a river view and serves draught Spirulina beer (K700).

Getting There & Away

Mingun is a pleasant 35-minute drive from Sagaing, easily added to an 'ancient capitals' motorcycle or taxi tour from Mandalay.

You can also get here by boat (one hour out, 40 minutes back, passport required). From Mandalay's 26th St 'tourist jetty' (Mayan Chan), boats depart at 9am (foreigner US$8) returning at 1.30pm.

Another option is taking a bicycle on the boat then riding down to Sagaing (roughly two hours). There are no major hills en route but there are plenty of undulations that can be a little testing for rental bikes without gears. Sagaing–Mandalay pick-ups will transport you and your bike back to Mandalay for K3000 or less.

Paleik   ပလိပ်

The main reason to come to Paleik, about 12 miles south of Mandalay, is to view its **Snake Pagoda** (Yadana Labamuni Hsu-Taung-Pye; ⊙7am-9pm) FREE. This modest and rather kitschy attraction earned its name from its three resident giant pythons. They appeared from the nearby forest in 1974 and never left. Much of the statuary replicates a scene from the Buddha's life when he sought shelter from the rain under the hood of a *naga* (a cobra-like water dragon), but for many, the main attraction is the pythons' 11am daily washing and feeding ceremony.

Off-season it's delightfully low-key, attracting a handful of local families. But the whole atmosphere changes dramatically when, as commonly occurs in peak season, a tourist bus arrives.

Less than a five-minute walk south of the snake pagoda is Paleik's 'mini-Bagan', an almost entirely overlooked collection of more than 300 closely packed stupas in varying states of repair. Many date from the Konbaung period.

Getting There & Away

Riding a motorbike along the busy Mandalay–Yangon road is an unpleasant chore, mitigated slightly by a brief stop at the **Golden Tooth Pagoda** (ရွှေသွားဘုရား; ⊙ sunrise-sunset). There are contrastingly pleasant, well-asphalted rural lanes running cross-country to Inwa and, with a brief double-back, to Sagaing: turn west at the petrol station just north of the big river bridge.

Otherwise, the best way of getting out here is via a Kyaukse-bound pick-up, or adding a side trip here while exploring the area on a taxi or motorbike tour (expect to pay an extra K2000).

Northern Myanmar

Best Places to Eat

➡ Taj (p279)

➡ Mrs Popcorn's Garden (p286)

➡ Lake Front Feel (p279)

➡ Club Terrace (p286)

➡ Jing Hpaw Thu (p295)

Best Places to Sleep

➡ Hotel Pyin Oo Lwin (p277)

➡ Mr Charles Guest House (p285)

➡ Putao Trekking House (p305)

➡ Hotel Maymyo (p277)

➡ Hotel Katha (p300)

Why Go?

Rugged and remote, northern Myanmar offers a fascinating mix of ethnic minority peoples and the prospect of travel through some of the least-visited areas of the country. While much of this vast region remains off-limits, two main routes are accessible. One climbs rapidly from Mandalay to the British-era summer capital of Pyin Oo Lwin, and then continues across the rolling Shan Plateau to Lashio. The crisp evenings are a great relief from the heat of the plains, while hikes take visitors into timeless Palaung and Shan hill villages.

Another other option is taking a ride along the mighty Ayeyarwady (Irrawaddy) River, stopping off at Katha, the setting of George Orwell's *Burmese Days*. The lazy, meandering journey provides great opportunities for genuine interaction with the locals.

Far beyond Myitkyina lie the rarely seen, snow-capped peaks of Myanmar's Himalaya where trekking and whitewater rafting are taking off around Putao.

When to Go
Northern Myanmar

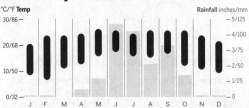

°C/°F **Temp**   **Rainfall** inches/mm

Nov–Feb The best time for trekking or river travel, with temperatures comfortable and water levels high.	**Mar–May** The Shan Plateau's cooler days offer an escape from the ferocious hot season.	**Sep & Oct** Despite the rain, the best time for serious far-north climbing expeditions.

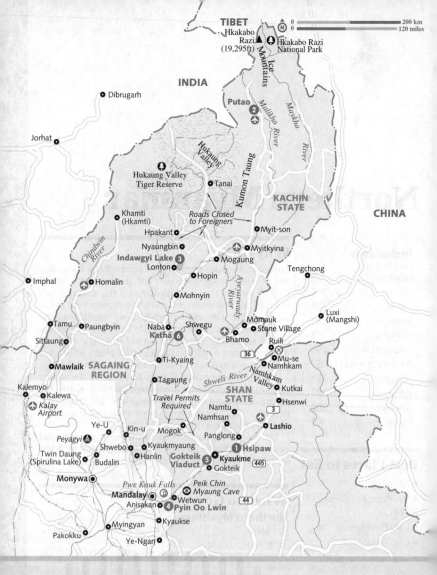

Northern Myanmar Highlights

① Hsipaw (p282) Walking into unspoilt Shan and Palaung villages from this delightful laid-back plateau town with royal connections.

② Putao (p304) Heading to the far north and the Himalaya region, where tough trekking and exhilarating whitewater rafting are taking off.

③ Indawgyi Lake (p296) Cycling around this serene lake and then taking a boat to the mystical Shwe Myitsu Paya.

④ Pyin Oo Lwin (p273) Enjoying the cool upland air and colonial-era architecture of the old British summer capital of Myanmar.

⑤ Gokteik Viaduct (p280) Riding the bouncing train across this mighty viaduct, Myanmar's highest railway bridge.

⑥ Katha (p300) Spending lazy days drifting down the mighty Ayeyarwady River, including George Orwell connections in sleepy riverside Katha.

People

The north is sparsely populated and ethnically complex, with many minority groups dominating a series of pro- and anti-government local administrations and regional armed militias.

Northeast of Mandalay you'll find many Shan people (as in eastern Myanmar), divided into five sub-groups all prefixed 'Tai', along with the Wa and the Palaung, who regard themselves semi-religiously as the guardians of Burmese tea production. Lashio and several other border areas have large Chinese populations, who speak Mandarin as well as the Yunnan dialects spoken across the frontier.

In Kachin State, north of Mandalay, 'minorities' (notably Kachin and Shan) form an overall majority. As an ethnic term, Kachin is generally synonymous with speakers of the Jingpaw (Jingpo) language. But by Myanmar's official definition, it also covers at least five other groups, including Rawang and Lisu. The Lisu language is written in a sci-fi capitalised Latin script with many inverted letters and 'vowel-free' words (hello is 'hw hw'). Over the past century, many Kachin and a majority of Lisu have converted to Christianity, their former animist beliefs now largely reduced to colourful folklore as seen in two great festivals at Myitkyina.

In the Himalayan foothills are minuscule populations of various Tibetan tribal peoples including the Taron, Asiatic pygmies who now number fewer than 10 and are limited to Naungmun in Myanmar's northernmost tip.

❶ Dangers & Annoyances

Since Burma's independence, the north has witnessed a whole smorgasbord of low-level uprisings and ethnic separatist movements in what is arguably the world's longest-running civil war. Tourists aren't allowed too close to any flash points, so for most visitors these issues are more a political curiosity than a serious danger, although the closure of whole parts of the region is an obvious annoyance. Despite ongoing efforts to broker ceasefires, fighting still continues between the Kachin Independence Army and the Tatmadaw (the Myanmar military), especially in eastern Kachin State. Shan rebels and the United Wa State Army are active in northern Shan State, along with the smaller Palaung State Liberation Front. Who's fighting who, and where, can change dramatically, so check with the locals to see what the current situation is in more remote areas. Foreigners are never targeted, but there is always the chance of being in the wrong place at the wrong time. The Tatmadaw, too, do not take kindly to travellers wandering into conflict zones.

MANDALAY TO LASHIO

Pyin Oo Lwin (Maymyo)
ပြင်ဦးလွင်

POP C 158,783 / ☏ 085 / ELEVATION 3445FT

Founded by the British in 1896, Pyin Oo Lwin was originally called Maymyo ('May-town'), after Colonel May of the 5th Bengal Infantry and was designed as a place to escape the Mandalay heat. After the construction of the railway from Mandalay, Maymyo became the summer capital for the British colonial administration, a role it held until the end of

NORTHERN MYANMAR PYIN OO LWIN (MAYMYO)

❶ TRAVEL RESTRICTIONS

Several parts of the north are essentially closed to foreign visitors without special permission. The main exceptions are areas along or close to the Mandalay–Lashio road and towns along the Ayeyarwady between Mandalay and Bhamo. You can link Mandalay and Myitkyina by railway but not by road, unless you have a guide and a private car. Permits are no longer required for flights into Putao town, but you still need them to trek to rural villages beyond. Permits are also still required for the gem-mining centre of Mogok. You can drive, accompanied by a guide, from Lashio to Mu-se for the Chinese border crossing. However, you cannot currently travel to the trekking and tea centre of Namhsan due to insurgent activity. Travel between Myitkyina and Bhamo, whether by boat or road, is impossible for foreigners (and difficult even for the locals thanks to ongoing fighting). Foreigners are seriously discouraged from visiting the jade-mining sin city of Hpakant (Pakkan).

The situation remains highly changeable with the government, at times, stopping the issuing of permits and adding previously open places to the list of those off-limits; always check with local tour operators for the situation at the time of travel and be prepared to alter your travel plans.

Pyin Oo Lwin (Maymyo)

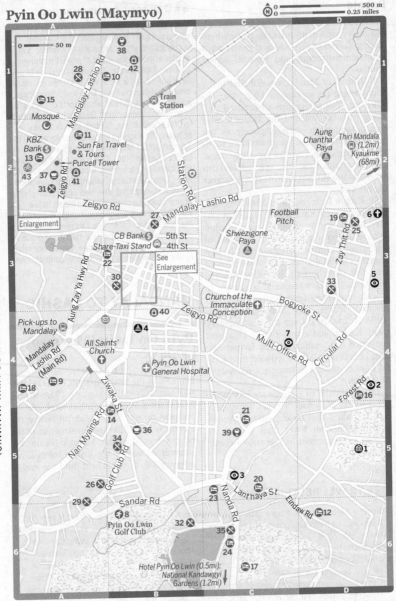

British rule in 1948. The name was changed after the British departed, but numerous colonial mansions and Christian churches remain, as do the descendants of the Indian and Nepali workers who came here to lay the railway line. More recently, Pyin Oo Lwin has become famous for its fruit, jams and fruit wines. With the rise of the Myanmar version of the nouveau riche, Pyin Oo Lwin is once again a popular weekend and hot-season getaway, so get here sharpish to experience what's left of the old charm and calm.

Pyin Oo Lwin (Maymyo)

◎ Sights
1 Candacraig Hotel D5
2 Chan Tak D4
3 Former Croxton Hotel C5
4 Maha Aung Mye Bon Thar
  Pagoda B4
5 Number 4 High School D3
6 Seventh Day Adventist Church D3
7 Survey Training Centre C4

❸ Activities, Courses & Tours
8 Pyin Oo Lwin Golf Club B6

⊖ Sleeping
9 Aureum Resort at Governor's
  House A4
10 Bravo Hotel B1
11 Cherry Guesthouse A2
12 Dahlia Motel D6
13 Golden Dream Hotel A2
14 Grace Hotel 1 .... B5
15 Hotel Maymyo A1
16 Hotel Shwe Nann Htike D4
17 Kandawgyi Hill Resort C6
18 Nan Myaing Hotel A4
19 Royal Jasmine Hotel D3
20 Royal Parkview Hotel C5
21 Royal Reward Resort Hotel C5
22 Ruby Hotel B3

23 Tiger Hotel C5
24 Win Unity Hotel C6

❽ Eating
25 Aung Padamyar D3
26 Club Terrace A5
27 Daw Khin Than B3
28 Family Restaurant A1
29 Feel Cafe A5
30 Ko Zaw's Krishna B3
31 La Yone A2
32 Lake Front Feel B6
33 Sain Mya Ayar D3
34 San Francisco B5
35 Taj C6

◎ Drinking & Nightlife
36 Barista-Khine Coffee Shop B5
37 December Cafe A2
38 Win Thu Zar B1
39 Woodland C5

◎ Shopping
40 Central Market B4
41 Liqueur Corner A2
42 Pacific World Curio B1

❸ Transport
43 Crown Bicycle Rental A2

◎ Sights

★ **National Kandawgyi Gardens** PARK
(အမျိုးသားကန်တော်ကြီးဥယျာဉ်; Nanda Rd; adult/
child under 12yr US$5/3; ⊗ 8am-6pm, aviary 8am-
5pm, orchid garden & butterfly museum 8.30am-5pm,
Nan Myint Tower lift operates to 5pm) Founded in
1915, this lovingly maintained 435-acre botanical garden features more than 480 species of
flowers, shrubs and trees. The most appealing
aspect is the way flowers and overhanging
branches frame views of Kandawgyi Lake's
wooden bridges and small gilded pagoda. Admission includes the swimming pool, **aviary,
orchid garden and butterfly museum** and
the bizarre **Nan Myint Tower.**

Looking like a space rocket designed for
a medieval Chinese Emperor, the 12-storey
tower offers panoramic views, which are
better appreciated from the external stair-
case than through the grease-smeared windows of the observation deck.

Unfortunately, you can't use a bicycle to
get around the grounds, so bring walking
shoes and allow around two hours to do it
justice. Using the southern entrance slightly
reduces the walking you have to do. By 6pm
both gates will probably be locked, so watch
the time, as there are no closure warnings.

The garden's two entrances are both on
the eastern side of Kandawgyi Lake, around
a mile south of smaller Kandawlay Lake.

National Landmarks Garden MUSEUM
(အမျိုးသားကန်တော်ကြီးဥယျာဉ်; adult/child
US$4/2; ⊗ 8am-6pm) This extensive hilly park
is dotted with representations of famous
landmarks from around Myanmar. Some
are pretty tacky, but if you haven't got time
to tour the entire country... The entrance is
opposite the National Kandawgyi Gardens,
near the southern (main) entrance. There is
also an **amusement park** just to the north:
one ticket includes admission to both sites.

Chan Tak TEMPLE
(ချန်တပ်; 134 Forest Rd) This large, classically
styled, if mostly modern, Chinese temple
comes complete with ornate stucco dragons,
rock gardens, a vegetarian buffet restaurant, landscaped ponds and a seven-tiered
Chinese-style pagoda.

Candacraig Hotel HISTORIC BUILDING
(သီရိမြိုင်ဟိုတယ်, Thiri Myaing Hotel; ☎ 085-22047;
Anawrattha Rd) Formerly the British Club, this
classic colonial pile comes complete with side
turrets and is set in attractively manicured

COLONIAL BUILDINGS

Most of Pyin Oo Lwin's trademark colonial-era buildings are dotted amid the southeastern woodland suburbs on and off Circular Rd. Many look like classic 1920s British homes, while the biggest have the feel of a St Trinian's–style boarding school. There are also a number of decaying but still impressive mansions on Nan Myaing St heading towards the Naval College.

Check out the splendid **Former Croxton Hotel** (Gandamar Myaing Hotel; Circular Rd), as well as the **Number 4 High School** (Circular Rd) and the **Survey Training Centre** (Multi-Office Rd). Up near the Shan Market, a fine half-timbered mansion is a **Seventh Day Adventist Church** (Cherry St).

gardens. There's a slightly spooky air to the place, and many locals believe it's haunted. It was closed for a major renovation during our recent visit. Previously there was a restaurant but, sadly, no raj-redolent bar.

Maha Aung Mye Bon Thar Pagoda BUDDHIST TEMPLE
(မဟာအောင်မြေဘုံသာဘုရား) FREE Around 6am the pretty Maha Aung Mye Bon Thar Pagoda broadcasts Buddhist *suttas* (lectures) through its loudspeakers, just in case you need a free wake-up call. It is one of the busiest temples in town on festival days.

🏃 Activities

Pyin Oo Lwin Golf Club GOLF
(☑ 085-22382; Golf Club Rd; green fee US$10, caddy US$5, shoe hire US$1, club hire K10,000; ⊙ 6am-6pm) The 18-hole Pyin Oo Lwin Golf Club is one of Myanmar's better courses and is popular with the many army officers based in town. There's a strict dress code – collars, caps and no jeans – and a caddie is compulsory. You can hire clubs and golf shoes.

🛌 Sleeping

Some of Pyin Oo Lwin's cheaper hotels aren't licensed to accommodate foreigners. Staying in the leafy gardens area south of the centre is a distinctively Pyin Oo Lwin experience, but consider renting a bike – with which you'll need a torch (flashlight), as the pot-holed roads get very dark at night. Staying

centrally is less atmospheric, but more convenient for transport, restaurants and shops.

Golden Dream Hotel GUESTHOUSE $
(☑ 085-21913; goldendreamhotel@gmail.com; 64 Mandalay-Lashio Rd; r incl breakfast US$6-24; ※) This is the best-value cheapie in town, with rooms that share bathrooms from just US$6. An extra dollar earns you a sink, and rooms from US$12 and up include a full bathroom and the chilled breeze of air-con.

Hotel Shwe Nann Htike HOTEL $$
(☑ 085-28288; www.hotelshwenannhtike.com; 71 Forest St; r incl breakfast US$40-80, ste US$55-140; ⊜ ※ 🕾) Having just opened when we were in town, this is a classy addition to the accommodation offerings in Pyin Oo Lwin. All 40 rooms are large and include tasteful wooden trim and well-presented bathrooms with tubs. Suite rooms start at just US$55 and rise to US$140 for the 'Royal Suite Room'.

Tiger Hotel HOTEL $$
(☑ 085-21980; tigerhotelpol.com; 13/243 Sandar Rd; r incl breakfast US$40-100; ※ 🕾) This expanding hotel has a range of rooms spread across different buildings. The best all-round rooms are the bungalows suites in the garden (from US$50 to US$60). More expensive suites are set in a cluster of new houses, but the furnishings are a little on the bling side. There is also an al-fresco cocktail bar.

Royal Jasmine Hotel HOTEL $$
(☑ 085-29737; royaljasminehotel.myanmar@gmail.com; 5 Thu Min Galar Quarter; r incl breakfast US$40-55; ⊜ ※ 🕾) Run by popular Burmese crooner Nay Ye Mun (you might even be in town when he gives a performance at the rooftop terrace), it's a clean and cared for midrange business hotel and good value at these rates. Like many of the new hotels in town, it includes a lift.

Win Unity Hotel HOTEL $$
(☑ 085-23079; www.winunityhotels.com; 3 Nanda Rd; r incl breakfast US$40-110; ⊜ ※ 🕾) Under the same ownership as Win Unity in Monywa, it's a friendly, family-run hotel near the lakeside. Rooms have recently been upgraded with new TVs and some smarter touches, including Jacuzzi-style tubs in the two suites (US$110).

Royal Reward Resort Hotel HOTEL $$
(☑ 085-28271; www.royalrewardresort.com; 36 Circular Rd; r incl breakfast US$54-80, ste US$153-180; ※ @ 🕾) This resort hotel is designed in

faux-British colonial style and set in extensive grounds. Rooms feature wooden floors, local textiles and generous detail. Suites are like studios and are a good option for families.

Town Centre

★ Hotel Maymyo
HOTEL $

(☑085-28440; hotelmaymyo@gmail.com; 12 Yadanar St; r incl breakfast US$25-45; ⊖※☎) Arguably the best-value hotel in town, this slick business-style hotel has 40 spick-and-span rooms with all the amenities of a more expensive property, including flat-screen TV, minibar, safe, and swish bathrooms. Breakfast is included at the rooftop restaurant, which offers panoramic views of town.

Bravo Hotel
HOTEL $

(☑085-21223; bravohotel.pol@gmail.com; Mandalay-Lashio Rd; s/d incl breakfast US$20/30; ※☎) Although the rooms are a little dated now, earthenware amphorae, ornate teak chests and carved gilded panel-work reveal that some thought has gone into the design here, thanks to the owner's sister business Pacific Tribal Handicrafts. It's a reliable option with helpful staff.

Ruby Hotel
HOTEL $

(☑085-21909; rubyhotel@gmail.com; Block 4, 32/B Mingalar St; r incl breakfast K25,000-30,000; ※☎) Tucked down a quiet side street, but close to the centre of town, this hotel has bright clean rooms with attached bathrooms.

ⓘ WANDERING BY WAGON IN PYIN OO LWIN

Clip-clopping around town in the picturesque, colourfully painted horse-drawn carriages that stand in for taxis here is a long-established Pyin Oo Lwin tradition. Known locally as 'wagons', they congregate close to the market and the clock tower. Wandering the mansion-lined streets of the southern part of town by wagon is especially evocative, and they can also be positioned artfully to act as foreground props for photos.

Increasing traffic, though, means the wagons are less plentiful than they once were. Always establish the price before you set off, and pick a driver who speaks some English. Reckon on K1500 to K2000 for a short trip across town and K15,000 for an all-day tour.

Cherry Guesthouse
GUESTHOUSE $

(☑085-21306; 19 Mandalay-Lashio Rd; s/d incl breakfast US$10/20; ☎) This small guesthouse is pretty basic, but the prices reflect the rooms. Small singles are cells with shared bathrooms, but doubles and twins offers more space and some include a bathroom.

Palace Hill

Nan Myaing Hotel
HISTORIC HOTEL $

(☑085-22118; www.nanmyainghotel.com; Mandalay-Lashio Rd; dm incl breakfast US$11, r US$25; ☎) Currently the top backpacker place in town, this hotel is set in an old British building dating from 1922. Room 101 is reputed to be haunted – in a very Orwellian coincidence. Staff are super-helpful with travel information. Orchid Hotel Group has taken the place over and will upgrade it to a luxe property in the future.

Aureum Resort at Governor's House
HOTEL $$$

(☑085-21902; www.aureumpalacehotel.com; off Mandalay-Lashio Rd; bungalows/ste incl breakfast US$90/250; ⊖※☎) This painstakingly precise recreation of the former British governor's mansion is an impressive statement, but only five suites are within the main half-timbered mansion, with the remaining accommodation being in stylish bungalows in the extensive grounds (electric buggy links). The governor's house is also open to nonguests as a small museum complete with waxwork figures (US$3 entry for foreigners).

Gardens Area

Grace Hotel 1
GUESTHOUSE $

(☑085-21230; 114A Nan Myaing Rd; s/d incl breakfast US$10/20; ☎) The high-ceilinged rooms are showing their age and the share bathrooms are primitive, but the staff are obliging and there's a leafy garden with sun-loungers. Bicycle hire is K2000 a day.

Dahlia Motel
GUESTHOUSE $

(☑085-22255; 67 Eindaw Rd; s/d/tr incl breakfast US$20/35/45; ※) A cluster of concrete buildings, the Dahlia offers the cheapest beds in the leafy 'burbs, but is somewhat short on atmosphere. Rooms vary wildly in quality, so ask to check a few options first.

★ Hotel Pyin Oo Lwin
BOUTIQUE HOTEL $$

(☑085-21226; www.hotelpyinoolwin.com; 9 Nanda Rd; deluxe r/ste incl breakfast from US$100/120; ※@☎✉) This is a gorgeous boutique hotel with bungalows scattered around a 5-acre site that feels like a suburban cul-de-sac and comes with a mini-version of the Purcell Tower. The roomy and smart bungalows all have terraces and working fireplaces. Efficient, English-speaking staff, Asian fusion restaurant and a heated indoor swimming pool complete the perfect picture.

Kandawgyi Hill Resort HOTEL $$
(☑085-21839; www.myanmartreasureresorts.com; Nanda Rd; d/tr incl breakfast from US$45/50; ❀❉ ❧) Boasting a splendid setting, with five of the 15 rooms inside a 1921 British-era house that was British Military Intelligence HQ after the war, the key attraction is a delightful terrace commanding a large sweep of garden leading down to the lakefront road. Other rooms are in bungalows in the gardens. Rooms have heating – important in the winter.

Royal Parkview Hotel HOTEL $$
(☑085-22641; www.royalparkview.hotelspyinoolwin. com; 107 Lanthaya St; r incl breakfast US$40-80; ❀❉❧) Still a reliable midrange option, there's neither royalty nor park views here, but long ceiling drapes add a sophisticated style to the restaurant and the wide range of rooms are attractive and comfortable and come with mini-terraces.

✖ Eating

Pyin Oo Lwin's culinary choices reflect its different communities, with Indian- and Chinese-themed places, as well as many restaurants serving a fusion-like mix of dishes. Standard, cheap teahouses and eateries are scattered throughout the city centre, both along the main road and around the Central Market – where a night market fills three blocks of Zaigyo St with snack-food stands – as well as close to the Shan Market.

If you're willing to spend a little more, a handful of stand-out restaurants can make dining in Pyin Oo Lwin a real pleasure.

Feel Cafe BURMESE $
(☑085-23170; Sandar St; mains K2000-5000; ❧7am-9pm; ❧▣) Not to be confused with the superbly located Lake Front Feel (p279), this is the Bamar budget experience compared with the international offerings at the lake branch. Choose from a tasty array of Burmese favourites. This place is justifiably popular with Mandalay visitors.

Ko Zaw's Krishna INDIAN $
(☑094-5003 7289; 50 Gurkha Rd; mains K2000-3000; ❧11am-9.30pm; ▣) On a back street near the town centre, this cheap and cheerful South Indian restaurant offers simple yet flavoursome curries. Choose from vegetarian, chicken or mutton – the rice, chapati and sides are all included in the price.

Aung Padamyar INDIAN $
(Zay Thit Rd; curries K5000; ❧11am-6.30pm) One of the most popular Indian restaurants in Pyin Oo Lwin, this is a secluded, friendly, family-run eatery with a range of curries, all of which come with side dishes to create a veritable feast. Take the first right off Circular Rd after the Shan Market and then the first left down a small alley. Only kyat is accepted here.

San Francisco SOUTHEAST ASIAN $
(Golf Club Rd; mains K2000-7000; ❧5.30am-9.30pm; ❧▣) A long way from the Bay Area, this airy joint attracts many locals with its mix of Chinese and Thai dishes, along with a few Kachin and Western specialities. The servings are generous. It's equally good for a beer.

La Yone CHINESE $
(Zeigyo Rd; mains from K3000; ❧8am-9pm; ▣) Almost every restaurant in Pyin Oo Lwin features Chinese-influenced dishes, but La Yone is run by immigrants from Fujian and so the flavours are authentic. At night, it also acts as an unofficial beer station.

Daw Khin Than BURMESE $
(Mandalay-Lashio Rd; curries K3000; ❧7am-7pm) With so many foreign-themed eateries in town, proper Bamar food is hard to find. This place satisfies lunchtime curry cravings, as well as offering Shan noodles for breakfast.

Sain Mya Ayar CHINESE $
(Zay Thit Rd; dim sum & noodles K500-3000; ❧6am-8.30pm) A cute, Chinese-style, open-air restaurant run by a Shan family serving tasty dim sum in the front yard of a modest half-timbered colonial-era house. It does noodle dishes and juices too.

Family Restaurant BURMESE, THAI $
(off Mandalay-Lashio Rd; mains K1800-6800; ❧9am-9.30pm) The decor is bland and there's no alcohol served, but the delicious curry spread comes with complimentary veggie side dishes, salad, rice, soup, pappadams and chutneys and dips.

Snack-Food Stands STREET FOOD $
(snacks K500-1500; ❧5.30-9pm) A night market with snack-food stands fills three blocks of Zaigyo St in the vicinity of the Central Market.

★Taj
INDIAN $$

(☑ 09 78404 9880; 26 Nanda Rd; mains K3000-10,000; ⊙10am-10pm; ❄ 🛜 🗐) The standout Indian restaurant in town, this opulent lakeside eatery is much more reasonably priced than its extravagant look suggests. Best by night, the fish and prawn tikka are some of the best we have ever tasted and quite literally melt in the mouth. Beer, wine and cocktails are available, and the friendly staff deliver a high standard of service.

★Lake Front Feel
EUROPEAN, PAN-ASIAN $$

(☑ 085-22083; off Nanda Rd; mains K3000-10,000; ⊙8.30am-9pm; 🛜 🗐) The upmarket yet casual lakeside setting is an obvious attraction. Its menu spans Europe and a fair chunk of Asia, making it the only place in town where you can sate your sushi craving. The waterside terrace is a relaxed spot for a sundowner. During busy weekends or holidays, dinner reservations are advisable.

Club Terrace
SOUTHEAST ASIAN $$

(☑ 085-23311; 25 Golf Club Rd; mains K2500-7000; ⊙8am-10pm; 🗐) One of the most popular of Pyin Oo Lwin's restaurants, this place occupies a gorgeous half-timbered colonial bungalow with tables spilling out onto the garden terrace. The food favours a tasty combination of Thai and Chinese flavours, as well as a small selection of Shan and Western options. Extensive wine selection, including local fruit vintages.

🍸 Drinking & Nightlife

Barista-Khine Coffee Shop
CAFE

(Ziwaka St; ⊙7.30am-7.30pm; 🛜) The best coffee shop in town. The baristas really know how to present the coffee with an artistic flourish. As well as a caffeine kick, there are also light snacks available.

December Cafe
CAFE

(Zeigyo Rd; ⊙6am-9pm) Popular with officer cadets (wear green to blend in), this place occupies the ground floor of an old colonial building and has good cheap coffee, juices, milkshakes and Burmese-style snacks.

Woodland
BAR

(53 Circular Rd; cocktails from K3500; ⊙11am-11pm; 🛜) Electric-blue panelling, a glass wall that reveals an aviary, as well as a spacious garden area, make this a stylish if self-conscious venue for an evening libation. It has live music, cocktails, foreign beers and an extensive menu of Asian and Western favourites.

Win Thu Zar
BEER STATION

(Mandalay-Lashio Rd; ⊙9am-9pm) A standard male-dominated beer hall notable purely because it serves tastily smooth spirulina 'anti-ageing' beer on draught. It's better than it sounds, as the bitter flavour of the spirulina is subtle.

🛍 Shopping

Fruity is the word that springs to mind. Burmese tourists come here to buy fresh fruit, fruit jams and fruit-infused wines, which is all produced locally.

Central Market
MARKET

(Zeigyo Rd; ⊙6.30am-5.30pm) Sample Pyin Oo Lwin's famous (if seasonal) strawberries and other fruit, fresh, dried or as jams and wine. It also has cheap Western clothes and *longyi* (sarong-style garments). There are tailors on the 1st floor if you need alterations or something knocked up.

Pacific World Curio
ANTIQUES, CRAFT

(⊙8am-7pm) Decent selection of Shan puppets, as well as other 'antiques' and local craft items. Test your haggling skills.

Liqueur Corner
ALCOHOL

(Zeigyo Rd; ⊙8.30am-8.30pm) Sells local fruit wines (bottles from K5000), as well as Burmese rum and whisky.

ℹ Information

For an overview of all things Pyin Oo Lwin, including lots of photographs of sights around town, check out the website www.pyinoolwin.info. Most of the major banks are strung out along the Mandalay-Lashio Rd in the centre of town.

CB Bank (135 Mandalay-Lashio Rd) Pristine dollars can be changed here, plus there is a debit/credit card–compatible ATM.

KBZ Bank (65 Mandalay-Lashio Rd) Main branch of KBZ. Includes a cluster of international ATMs.

Sun Far Travel & Tours (☑ 085-28373; cnr Merchant & Zeigyo Rds; ⊙9am-6pm Mon-Sat) Pyin Oo Lwin branch of a nationwide travel agency, it's a useful stop to book airline tickets out of Mandalay or Lashio.

ℹ Getting There & Away

Yangon and Nay Pyi Taw buses leave from the inconvenient main bus station Thiri Mandala, 2 miles east of the Shan Market.

All other buses leave from behind the San Pya Restaurant, 600m south of the bus station, as do some shared taxis and pick-ups to Mandalay.

Pick-ups to Mandalay leave from near the gas station at the roundabout at the entrance to town, as well as less frequently from outside the train station, north of the town centre.

Shared taxis to Mandalay leave from 4th St.

If arriving at Mandalay International Airport and planning to transfer to Pyin Oo Lwin, direct taxis are available for around US$35.

The only way to go to the gem-mining district of Mogok is by private car with a tour guide, and you need official permission to visit, best arranged in advance through a Yangon- or Mandalay-based tour operator.

ⓘ Getting Around

Crown Bicycle Rental (46 Mandalay-Lashio Rd; bicycles/motorbikes per day from K2000/8000; ⊘7.30am-6.30pm) rents bicycles and motorbikes. It also has some automatic motorbikes for K15,000 per day.

Motorcycle taxis are easy to find close to the Central Market and the Bravo Hotel. Expect to pay K1500 to Kandawgyi Gardens. For longer hires, consider engaging an English-speaking driver. Rates are around K20,000 for a full day.

Three-wheel pick-ups congregate outside the market; plan on paying around K2000 to Kandawgyi Gardens.

Pyin Oo Lwin to Kyaukme

If you're driving to Kyaukme/Hsipaw, there are several interesting sights that are just a short detour from the main road, and are awkward to visit via public transport. A round-trip half-day tour by motorcycle-taxi to all of the following from Pyin Oo Lwin should cost around K12,000.

Aung Htu Kan Tha Paya BUDDHIST TEMPLE
(အုံ့ထွးကံ့သာဘုရား) Finished in March 2000, this dazzling pagoda is by far the region's most impressive religious building. It enshrines an enormous 17-ton white marble Buddha statue that fell off a truck bound for China in April 1997. After several attempts to retrieve the Buddha failed, it was decided that the statue 'had decided to stay in Myanmar'.

Eventually cranes were used to yank him up the hill and a dazzling new golden pagoda was built for him. He is now draped in gilt robes and sits in a temple interior that's an incredible overload of gold. The pagoda is on a hilltop, just south of the Lashio-bound highway, around 15 minutes' drive beyond Pyin Oo Lwin's vast Defense Forces Technological Academy compound. If you reach the toll gates, you've gone half a mile too far.

Pwe Kauk Falls WATERFALL
(ပွေးကောက်ရေတံခွန်; K500, camera fee K300; ⊘6am-7pm) Called Hampshire Falls in British times, Pwe Kauk is a fan of small weirs and splash pools rather than a dramatic waterfall, but the forest glade setting is pretty. A series of little wooden bridges, souvenir stands and children's play areas add to the attraction for local families but undermine any sense of natural serenity. It's a two-minute drive down a steep, easily missed lane excursion off the Hsipaw road that starts directly north of Aung Htu Kan Tha Paya.

Myaing Gyi MONASTERY
(မြိုင်ကြီး) FREE After descending a loop of hairpins from Pyin Oo Lwin, the Hsipaw road reaches attractive Myaing Gyi where a rickety monastery climbs a wooded hillside. Two minutes' drive further on, the roadside **Wetwun Zaigone Monastery** is more photogenic with a fine array of stupas and Balinese-style pagodas behind a giant old banyan tree.

DON'T MISS

GOKTEIK VIADUCT

A highlight of the long, slow Mandalay–Lashio train ride is the mighty **Gokteik Viaduct** (ဂုတ်ထိပ်တံတား). It spans the Gokteik Gorge, a densely forested ravine 34 miles northeast of Pyin Oo Lwin that cuts an unexpectedly deep gash through the otherwise mildly rolling landscape. At 318ft high and 2257ft across, it was the second-highest railway bridge in the world when constructed, and remains Myanmar's longest. From aboard the train, the best views are from north-facing windows (the left side if you're heading towards Lashio).

The viaduct is visible through the trees for some time as the train winds down from the plateau, and there are fine views from parts of Gokteik station (near the viaduct's western end), but be aware that the train only stops there very briefly. Trains slow to a crawl when crossing the viaduct to avoid putting undue stress on the ageing superstructure. Despite some 1990s renovation work, the viaduct – built in 1901 by contractors from the Pennsylvania Steel Company – still creaks ominously as trains edge their way across.

ANISAKAN FALLS

Just north of **Anisakan** village, the plateau disappears into an impressive, deeply wooded amphitheatre, its sides ribboned with several **waterfalls**. The most spectacular of these is the gorgeous three-step Dat Taw Gyaik, whose last stage thunders into a shady splash pool beside a small pagoda on the valley floor. It's best visited in the early morning or late afternoon.

To get here from Pyin Oo Lwin, take the main Mandalay highway (a motorbike taxi is about K8000 return). In Anisakan town take the second asphalted turn right (signposted) and keep right past the first large pagoda. At the end of this road a pair of basic shack-restaurants mark the start of a steep, twisting, rocky forest trail about 40 minutes' trek from the waterfall. It's treacherous in the rainy season (wear proper walking shoes), although you'll get to see the falls in magnificent, full flow. Local girls will follow you with drinks; they make good guides (K1000).

Should you wish to stay there's **The View** (☑ 085-22881; www.theviewpyinoolwin.com; Anisakan; bungalows incl breakfast US$250; ☻✳@🛜🚗). Under the same ownership as Hotel Pyin Oo Lwin (p277), this new resort has a dramatic setting overlooking the Dat Taw Gyaik Falls. The bungalows are pricey, but from their steep hillside location you get to-die-for views. There's also a terrace restaurant open to nonguests.

NORTHERN MYANMAR KYAUKME

Peik Chin Myaung
CAVE

(ပိတ်ချင်းမြောင်; camera fee K300; ⊙6.30am-4.30pm) FREE About 5 miles east of Myaing Gyi is this Buddhist cave complex. Many Buddhist caves are little more than rocky niches or overhangs, but **Peik Chin** is much more extensive. It takes around 15 minutes to walk to the cave's end, following an underground stream past a series of colourful scenes from Buddhist scriptures interspersed with stupas and Buddha images.

There are a few sections where you'll need to bend over to get beneath dripping rocks, but most of the cave is high-ceilinged and adequately lit, so you don't need a torch. It can feel sweaty and humid inside. No shorts or footwear permitted.

The access road is around 2½ miles east of Myaing Gyi, just beyond the green sign announcing your arrival in Wetwun town. Turn right through a lion-guarded gateway arch, then descend inexorably for another 2 miles to the large parking area thronged with souvenir stalls.

Kyaukme
ကျောက်မဲ

POP C 39,930 / ☑ 082 / ELEVATION 2950FT

Pronounced 'Chao-may', Kyaukme is a lowrise, bustling market town with a smattering of colonial-era architecture, bracketed by monastery-topped hills, each only 15 minutes' walk away using steep, covered stairways. The main attraction here is hiking into surrounding Shan and Palaung hill villages. The town sees far fewer travellers than Hsipaw and there's only a few foreigner-licensed places to stay. Kyaukme means 'black stone'; local legend has it that its citizens were dishonest traders of precious (or not so precious) gems.

🏃 Activities

Trekking

The typical walking destinations have an unspoilt charm that challenges even those around Hsipaw. However, Kyaukme itself is pretty spread out, so most treks start with a motorcycle ride to a suitable trailhead. This is typically included in guide fees, which cost around K30,000 for a couple. For longer motorbike trails you'll need to add K10,000 per day for bike rental plus petrol.

Do not stray from market paths when trekking around Kyaukme, as two German tourists were injured by shrapnel during a landmine explosion in April 2016. Stick to marked paths and always trek with a local guide.

Naing-Naing (☑09 4730 7622; naing ninenine@gmail.com), nicknamed '9-9', is Kyaukme's best-known guide. He speaks good English, has a fascinating background and an extensive knowledge of the entire area. He prefers to take groups of four.

🛏 Sleeping

Northern Rock Guesthouse GUESTHOUSE $
(☑082-40660; northernrock.kme@gmail.com; 4/52 Shwe Phe Oo Rd; r US$6-25; ☻✳🛜) Sister hotel to the Northern Rock in Hsipaw, this friendly guesthouse offers very basic cubicle rooms in the old house at the front, the cheapest options

with shared bathroom only. However, the US$20 to US$25 rooms are much nicer and include a bathtub and air-conditioning.

One Love Hotel
HOTEL $

(📞 082-40943; 1 Pinlon St; r incl breakfast US$30-40; 😊❄🛜) Not a Bob Marley tribute hotel, but the smartest all-rounder in Kyaukme, the new rooms here have flat-screen TV and a minibar. Family rooms include a double and single bed. Wi-fi is included in the rates.

A Yone Oo Hotel
GUESTHOUSE $

(📞 082-40183; Shwe Phi Oo Rd; r US$8-70; ❄🛜🍴) This sprawling complex has a dizzying array of rooms in a variety of buildings. Cheapest rooms are very basic with a shared bathroom. Best value are the rooms with bathroom attached, including some large bungalow rooms for US$20/25 per single/double. There are large family rooms from US$50 to US$70.

🍴 Eating

There's a strip of Yunnan-style Chinese restaurants close to the cinema, three blocks south of Shwe Phi Oo Rd, as well as snack stalls in the market.

Shwe Mate Sone Restaurant
CHINESE $

(📞 082-40360; Aung San Rd; mains K1500-5000; ⏱7am-9pm; 📶) This hole-in-the-wall restaurant near the market offers a good range of Chinese classics in a clean and comfortable environment. Plastered with Myanmar Beer posters, it also offers draught for K800 a glass.

Thiri Pyitsaya
BURMESE, CHINESE $

(4/54 Shwe Phi Oo Rd; dishes K1500-4000; ⏱7am-9pm; 📶) One of only two places in town with an English-language menu, this is an amiable little place for basic noodle and rice dishes, as well as juices and beers.

❶ Getting There & Away

Buses leave from the southwest corner of the market. Minibuses pick up from A Yone Oo Hotel

(which can book tickets). Other Lashio- and Mandalay-bound buses can be caught on the main highway, a K1500 motorbike taxi ride away.

The train station is a 10-minute walk northwest from the guesthouse.

Hsipaw
သီပေါ

POP C 20,897 / 📞 082 / ELEVATION 2300FT

Increasing numbers of foreigners are finding their way to delightful Hsipaw (pronounced 'see-paw' or 'tee-bor'), drawn by the possibilities of easily arranged hill treks that are more authentic than those around Kalaw or anywhere in northern Thailand. Many people, though, find the town's laid-back vibe and intriguing history as a Shan royal city as much of an attraction and spend far longer here than they intended. With just enough tourist infrastructure to be convenient, Hsipaw remains a completely genuine northern Shan State town. Be sure to check it out before this changes.

There are insurgents operating in some rural areas around Hsipaw, so certain destinations like Namhsan are now off-limits to foreigners. Local businesses in Hsipaw are 'taxed' by insurgents from the Shan State Army (SSA) from time to time, but there have been no incidents involving foreigners to date.

Because of ongoing security problems, be sure to check with local travel agents before planning a trekking trip around Hsipaw.

⊙ Sights

The present town centre, Tyaung Myo, dates back only to the early 20th century. The main monasteries, stupas and former palace lie on higher ground around a mile further north in Myauk Myo.

Myauk Myo
AREA

(မြောက်မြို့,) FREE At the northern edge of town, Hsipaw's oldest neighbourhood has a village-like atmosphere, two delightful old teak monasteries and a collection of ancient

KYAUKME TRANSPORT CONNECTIONS

DESTINATION	BUS	MINIBUS	TRAIN
Hsipaw	K2000; 1hr; frequent	N/A	ordinary/upper class K300/650; 3hr; 1.50pm
Lashio	K4000; 3hr; 7am	back/front seat K5500/6500; 3hr; 2 daily noon-1pm	ordinary/upper class K600/1300; 6hr; 1.50pm
Mandalay	K3500; 6hr; 4 daily 4.30am-7am	back/front seat K6500/7500; 4½hr; 5 daily 7am-2pm	ordinary/upper class K950/2150; 11½hr; 11.25am

HSIPAW'S SHAN PALACE

Hsipaw was ruled by a *sawbwa* (sky prince) until the military junta seized power in 1962, ending the centuries-old tradition of the different regions of Shan State being run as separate kingdoms by 32 sky princes. The last *sawbwa* of Hsipaw disappeared during the army takeover (the book *Twilight over Burma: My Life as a Shan Princess,* written by his wife Inge Sargent, describes the tragic events), leaving his nephew Mr Donald in charge of the family palace. Imprisoned for a number of years and then placed under effective house arrest, during which time the palace was closed, Mr Donald is now free thanks to the reforms Myanmar has undergone since 2011, and people can once again visit the palace.

In truth, it's not a palace in the traditional sense. Built in 1924, it's a fading, although still impressive, English-style mansion set in run-down grounds. But if the building is infused with a melancholic air, then the charming Mr Donald and his wife, Fern, make gracious hosts. They welcome visitors in their sitting room decorated with family photos and will relate the fascinating history of their ancestors and the sad fate of the last *sawbwa.*

While there is no admission fee, a donation (given respectfully) is expected and goes towards maintaining the palace. Mrs Fern is also a keen reader and always appreciates new books in English. In theory, the palace is open for a few hours each day, from 9am to noon and 4pm to 6pm. If the gates are chained, they're not receiving visitors. It had been closed for a few months at the time of our last visit. To reach the palace, cross the bridge at the northern end of Namtu Rd, turn right at the police station and then left at the monastery. The palace is up the track past the immigration office.

brick stupas known locally as **Little Bagan**. The multifaceted wooden **Madahya Monastery** looks especially impressive when viewed from across the palm-shaded pond of the **Bamboo Buddha Monastery** (Maha Nanda Kantha).

The 150-year-old buddha is made from lacquered bamboo strips, now hidden beneath layers of gold. Around and behind lie a few clumps of ancient brick stupas, some overwhelmed by vegetation in vaguely Angkorian style. The nickname for this area, Little Bagan, blatantly overplays the size and extent of the sites but the area is undoubtedly charming.

To get here cross the big bridge on Namtu Rd heading north. Turn first left at the police station, then first right and fork left. Take this lane across the railway track then follow the main track as it wiggles.

To return by an alternative route, take the unpaved track east behind the Bamboo Buddha monastery, rapidly passing **Eissa Paya** (where one stupa has a tree growing out of it). You'll emerge near **Sao Pu Sao Nai**, a colourful shrine dedicated to the guardian *nat* of Hsipaw. Rather than turning left into the shrine, turn right and you'll reach Namtu Rd a little north of the railway.

Sunset Hill　　　　　　VIEWPOINT

FREE For sweeping views across the river and Hsipaw, climb to **Thein Daung Pagoda**, also known as Nine Buddha Hill or, most popularly, Sunset Hill. It's part of a steep ridge that rises directly behind the Lashio road, just over a mile south of Hsipaw.

Cross the new river bridge, follow the main road left then take the laterite track that starts with a triple-crowned temple gateway around 300m beyond. There's a small English sign at the gateway. The climb takes around 15 minutes.

Bawgyo Paya　　　　BUDDHIST TEMPLE

(တော်ကြီးဘုရား) FREE Five miles west of Hsipaw, beside the Hsipaw–Kyaukme road, this pagoda is of great significance to Shan people and gets overloaded with pilgrims who arrive en masse during the annual **Bawgyo Paya Pwe**, culminating on the full moon day of Tabaung (February/March). The pagoda's current incarnation is an eye-catching 1995 structure of stepped gilded polygons, within which the dome supposedly incorporates genuine rubies.

The name translates loosely as 'Dad come and get me', referencing the original pagoda, which was built centuries earlier by a heartbroken Shan king who had married off his daughter, warrior-princess Saw Mun La, to the Burmese king as part of a Shan-Burma peace deal. The Burmese king adored her but, as the seventh wife in his harem, her presence and growing favour caused trouble. Jealous concubines set about denouncing her as a spy. The king didn't fall for the lies but realised that he'd better get her out of his court before the other wives murdered

Hsipaw

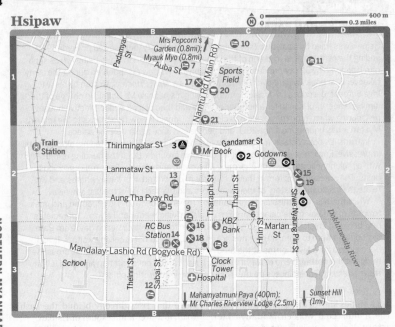

Hsipaw

◉ Sights
1 Banyan Tree Nat Shrine	C2
2 Central Market	C2
3 Central Pagoda	B2
4 Produce Market	D2

🛏 Sleeping
5 La Residence	B2
6 Lily The Home Hotel	C2
7 Mr Charles Guest House	B1
8 Nam Khae Mao Guesthouse	C3
9 Northern Land Hotel	B2
10 Red Dragon Hotel	C1
11 Riverside @ Hsipaw Resort	D1

12 Tai House	B3
13 Yee Shin Guesthouse	B2

🍴 Eating
14 A Kaung Kyite	B3
15 Club Terrace	D2
16 Law Chun	B3
17 Pontoon	B1
18 San	B3

🍸 Drinking & Nightlife
19 Black House Coffee Shop	D2
20 La Wün Aung	C1
21 Mr Shake	C1

her. The plan should have worked, but on the long, arduous route back to her father's court she fell ill. The Shan king was sent for but arrived to find her already dead of a mystery sickness. The point where she died became the site of a pagoda to underline Shan-Burmese friendship. You'll get a brief glimpse of the temple from the right-hand side of any Kyaukme- or Mandalay-bound bus.

Mahamyatmuni Paya　　BUDDHIST TEMPLE
(မဟာမြတ်မုနိဘုရား; Namtu Rd) FREE South of the central area, Mahamyatmuni Paya is the biggest and grandest pagoda in the main town. The large brass-faced Buddha image

here was inspired by the famous Mahamuni Buddha in Mandalay. He's now backed by an acid-trip halo of pulsating coloured lights that would seem better suited to a casino.

Central Pagoda　　BUDDHIST PAGODA
(Namtu Rd) FREE The principal Buddhist temple in the heart of Hsipaw, it has a shimmering golden stupa visible from several blocks away.

Produce Market　　MARKET
(⊘4.30am-1pm) Most interesting before dawn when the road outside is jammed with hill villagers selling their wares; all will have

cleared away by 7am, although the market continues until 1pm.

Central Market MARKET
(⏱6am-5pm) The main market in town is a busy affair in the morning when locals come to shop for produce. By the afternoon, it is usually pretty sleepy.

Banyan Tree Nat Shrine SHRINE
(ညောင်ပင်နတ်စင်) FREE This is an important local shrine for traditional *nat* worship.

Activities

Trekking

The Palaung and Shan villages dotting the hills surrounding Hsipaw are perhaps the main reason to visit the area, and treks to them are deservedly popular. The most visited village is **Pankam**, a Palaung settlement nestled on a ridge about five hours' walk from Hsipaw. It's a gentle trek that takes you through a number of timeless Shan villages with stilt houses. Note how each hamlet has a *kin-gyiao*, a wooden phallus placed above a buried urn of vegetable oil to ensure fertile fields. Gateways with crossed-wooden-knife symbols are present to protect the settlements from evil spirits. Pankam itself has a fascinating shrine commemorating the 12th-century legend of how a powerful *nat* spirit bestowed tea seeds on the Palaung. Tea remains the principal source of income for the Palaung, who regard themselves as the guardians of tea cultivation in Shan State.

Pankam can be visited as part of a multi-day trek, hiking out and back in two days, or you can hitch a lift one way on a motorbike (K5000 from Hsipaw, but K10,000 coming back) if you don't want to stay overnight. Going with a guide will enable you to communicate with the locals and ensure you don't accidentally stumble into insurgent territory.

But with Pankam now firmly on the tourist route, some travellers are seeking alternative treks to more remote locations. Options include a two-day hike to Kyaukme that takes you through fields and forests. Bear in mind that some of these treks are only possible between October and March; during the rainy season, the trails become very difficult.

If you want something less arduous, then the guides at Mr Charles Guest House can take you to local waterfalls, or arrange combined trekking and boat trips, which will spare your knees.

Each of the guesthouses can organise guides (from K10,000 per day; K20,000 for an overnight trek) to take you on a range of fascinating walks into the hills above town visiting Shan and Palaung villages. Mr Charles Guest House is especially well organised and most evenings will have guides sitting on the front terrace to answer questions about the various options. Generally a next-day departure is possible if you don't want anything too adventurous.

Workshop Visits

If you don't fancy trekking, there are various workshops and mini-factories around town, where you can see locals carrying out cottage industries like weaving, noodle-making, cheroot rolling and even popcorn popping. All these are marked on the map in the reception at Mr Charles Guest House. Or find a guide via a guesthouse to combine a few workshop visits with, perhaps, a field-stroll to Parpeit village and hot springs.

Sleeping

⭐**Mr Charles Guest House** HOTEL $
(☏082-80105; www.mrcharleshotel.com; 105 Auba St; dm incl breakfast US$7-12, r US$18-45; ❄🌐) Still the most efficient, comfortable and traveller-friendly guesthouse in town, the large Mr Charles operation encompasses everything from simple mattresses on the floor in the dorms to swish suites with heating and air-con. Expect to pay US$18 and up for a room with its own bathroom, but book ahead in peak periods.

The helpful staff at this Shan-owned guesthouse can arrange transport, treks and tours. It has bicycle (K2000 per day) and motorbike (K10,000 per day) hire and communal upstairs balconies where guests swap travel stories late into the evening.

La Residence GUESTHOUSE $
(☏09 25602 8188; laresidencehsiipaw@gmail.com; 27 Aung Tha Pyay Rd; r K19,000-22,000; ❄❄🌐) Set in an attractive wooden home in the middle of town, this small guesthouse has plenty of charm and character, if not quite the comfort level of the smarter competition. Rooms in the main house are shared bathroom, but the garden bungalows include a private bathroom. There is an atmospheric bar-restaurant downstairs with draught Myanmar Beer.

Yee Shin Guesthouse GUESTHOUSE $
(☏082-80711; Namtu Rd; r US$5-30; ❄🌐) Centrally located and run by a very helpful family. Rooms with shared bathrooms at the Yee Shin are tiny, but also have a tiny impact

on your wallet. There are spacious air-con rooms in a newer building that come with private bathroom and hot water. Facilities include table tennis, and staff can even arrange a take away pizza from one of the only resident foreigners in town.

Lily The Home Hotel
GUESTHOUSE $

(082-80318; www.lilythehome.com; 108 Aung Tha Pyay Rd; r US$9-70; ⊖✳🛜) This smart and friendly hotel just keeps on expanding and now offers 33 rooms spread across a jumble of buildings. Cheapies involve a shared bathroom, but all are meticulously clean. Rooms for US$15 include air-con, and rooms from US$40 and up are in the new main building with Hsipaw's only lift. Treks can be organised and there's bike hire (K2000 per day).

Northern Land Hotel
HOTEL $

(082-80713; www.northernlandhotel.com; Namtu Rd; r US$25-28; ⊖✳🛜) This relatively new guesthouse is clean and well run, offering rooms with capacious beds and all the trimmings like flat-screen TV, minibar and hot-water showers. It's in a very central location with lots of restaurants nearby.

Red Dragon Hotel
HOTEL $

(082-80740; Mahaw Gani St; r incl breakfast US$7-30; ⊖✳🛜) One of the more high-rise buildings in town, so you might want to request a room on a lower floor as it doesn't have a lift. Cheapest rooms involve a shared bathroom, but there are also lots of air-con units with private bathroom. There is a rooftop restaurant for breakfast (included) and extensive views over the town.

Nam Khae Mao Guesthouse
GUESTHOUSE $

(082-80077; namkhaemaoguesthouse@gmail.com; 134 Mandalay-Lashio Rd; s/d without bathroom US$5/10; ✳@🛜) This central guesthouse has pretty much the cheapest beds in town, but as with everything in life, you get what you pay for. The rooms are small, but the shared bathrooms are clean and include hot water.

Mr Charles Riverview Lodge
LODGE $$

(082-80105; http://mrcharlesriverviewlodge.com; r US$55-65; ⊖✳🛜) Beautifully set on the Dokhtawady River about 2.5 miles from town, this is boutique bliss amid ricefields. Rooms are stylishly finished with ample river-facing balconies and the bathrooms include a rain shower. The restaurant is a peaceful place for lunch if trekking or cycling in this area, and Shan set meals are available.

Riverside @ Hsipaw Resort
BOUTIQUE HOTEL $$

(082-80721; www.hsipawresort.com; Myohaung village; r US$65-90; ⊖✳🛜) Located across the river from Hsipaw itself, this is an impressive boutique resort from the Amata group of hotels. The bungalow rooms are among the most spacious in town, and some have good views of the countryside. It is possible to cross the river by local boat, or you have a fairly circuitous drive back to town.

Tai House
HOTEL $$

(082-80161; www.taihouseresort.com; 38 Sabai St; s incl breakfast US$30-50, d US$40-60; ⊖✳🛜) This lovingly designed resort boasts a lush garden brimming with orchids. The deluxe bungalows are spacious and stylish and include TV and minibar. Cheaper superior rooms don't include these extras and also lack a bathtub.

🍴 Eating

Hsipaw's dining options have improved as the number of visitors has increased. While there are many simple places strung out along Namtu Rd, more sophisticated restaurants can also be found.

Street vendors sell *moun-ou-khalei* (rice-flour balls) and *kauk-pout* (pronounced 'cow-po'), rounds of pounded sticky brown rice that are barbecued then sprinkled with jaggary and sesame.

★ Mrs Popcorn's Garden
CAFE $

(snacks K1000-3000; ⊙7am-7pm; 🖋) Run by the irrepressible Mrs Popcorn, this place is a definitive stop on a tour of the Myauk Myo area of town where 'Little Bagan' is located. Choose from homemade snacks, some traveller favourites and, of course, popcorn. Cold beer is available, so it's easy to kick back and while away a couple of hours in the late afternoon.

★ Club Terrace
SOUTHEAST ASIAN $

(35 Shwe Nyaung Pin St; mains K3000-5000; ⊙10am-10pm; 🖋) Dine al-fresco in a gorgeous 90-year-old teak house with a lovely riverside terrace. The menu mixes Thai and Chinese flavours, with a few Shan dishes like minced chicken curry with basil leaves. It has a decent wine list, splendid service and a peaceful, evocative setting.

It's an offshoot of the restaurant of the same name in Pyin Oo Lwin (p279).

Law Chun
CHINESE $

(Mr Food; Namtu Rd; dishes K1500-6000; ⊙9am-8.30pm; 🖋) Nicknamed 'Mr Food', this restaurant offers Chinese dishes for Burmese and Western palates, so it's light on the spices. Law Chun stands out from the pack thanks to its bright and breezy interior. Draught beer is available, so it usually draws a few backpackers by night.

A Kaung Kyite BURMESE $

(cnr Namtu & Mandalay-Lashio Rds; mains K2000-4000; ☺9am-8pm) This is the best place in town for authentic Bamar food, as the curries come with an array of side dishes. Do as the locals do and sample them at lunchtime when they are fresh off the stove.

San SHAN, CHINESE $

(Namtu Rd; dishes K1500-4500, barbecue from K300; ☺10am-midnight; 🗈) With its retro interior and small terrace, San is popular with travellers who come for the many barbecue options and the Chinese-style mains. Dali beer from China is available, as well as the usual Burmese beers.

Pontoon CAFE $

(Namtu Rd; mains K2000-4000; ☺8am-6pm; 🛜🗈) This place has homemade sandwiches, salads, cakes and banana pancakes. It also offers some decent Shan coffee, but locals say the service has been a bit spotty since the foreign owner packed her bags and returned home.

🍷 Drinking & Nightlife

Mr Shake JUICE BAR

(Namtu Rd; fruit shakes K1000-1500) It does what is says on the sign, and that is wholesome fruit shakes blended up by a friendly family, plus some naughty but nice options like oreo shakes. Also known as Yuan Yuan Fruit Shake, this place even rustles up some alcoholic options, including a zesty mojito.

Black House Coffee Shop CAFE

(23 Shwe Nyaung Pin St; coffee from K800; ☺6am-6pm) An airy, 75-year-old teak shophouse backed by a wide river-facing yard, this is an easy place to linger over a coffee made from Shan-grown beans, or sup a late-afternoon beer as sunset approaches.

La Wün Aung TEAHOUSE

(Namtu Rd; ☺24hr) One of several teahouse bars that hide the sports field but make amends by screening international football matches. It never closes and has motorbikes available for rent.

ℹ Information

KBZ Bank (139 Tharaphi St; ☺9am-3pm) A bank with a Visa and Mastercard-friendly ATM.

The guesthouses are the best sources of reliable advice about things to do and see. Another mine of local information and history is Ko Zaw Tun, who is known as Mr Book, as he runs a small **book stall** (Namtu Rd; ☺9am-7pm) opposite the entrance to the Central Pagoda, which his family helped to build.

ℹ Getting There & Away

Buses and minibuses leave from the RC bus station on the Mandalay–Lashio road and the Duhtawadi Cafe on Lammataw St opposite the market. Lashio-bound buses can be picked up from the Mandalay–Lashio road opposite the RC bus station.

The train station is in the west of town.

ℹ Getting Around

Trishaw rides start from K500 and they wait by the market. Bicycles (K2000) and motorbikes (K10,000) can be rented from guesthouses around town.

HSIPAW TRANSPORT CONNECTIONS

DESTINATION	BUS	MINIBUS	SHARED TAXI	TRAIN
Bagan	K17,300; 10hr; 7pm	N/A	N/A	N/A
Kyaukme	K1000; 1hr; noon & 3.30pm	K1500; 7am	N/A	ordinary/upper class K300/650; 3hr; 9.40am
Lashio	N/A	N/A	K40,000 private hire	ordinary/upper class K700/1650; 4hr; 3.15pm
Mandalay	K4500-6000; 5½hr; 5.30am, 7am, 8am, 10am, 7pm & 8pm	K8000; 5hr; 7am & 9am	back/front seat K12,000/14,000, whole car K50,000	ordinary/upper class K1700/3950; 13hr; 9.40am
Pyin Oo Lwin	K5000; 3hr; 7pm & 8pm	N/A	N/A	K1200/2750; 7hr; 9.40am
Taunggyi	K15,500; 12hr; 3 daily 3.30-5pm	N/A	N/A	N/A

Lashio လားရှိုး

POP C 174,335 / ☑ 082 / ELEVATION 3120FT

Lashio (pronounced '*lar*-show') is a booming and sprawling market town with a significant Chinese population. You're most likely to come here for the airport, as it is the nearest to Hsipaw, or if you've managed to organise the necessary permits for the five-hour drive to the Chinese border at Mu-se.

Once the seat of an important Shan *sawbwa* (Shan prince), Lashio played a pivotal role in the fight against the Japanese in WWII as the starting point of the Burma Road, which supplied food and arms to Chiang Kai-Shek's Kuomintang army. Little evidence of that evocative history remains today, thanks to a disastrous 1988 fire that destroyed most of the city's old wooden homes.

◉ Sights & Activities

A few decrepit old wooden buildings and an eye-catching central mosque aren't quite enough to bring a photogenic quality to predominantly concrete central Lashio. However, the pre-dawn morning market is particularly endearing when many vegetable sellers light their wares with flickering candles.

Maha Bodayaong   BUDDHIST TEMPLE

(မဟာဗောဓိ) If you walk towards the Hsipaw bus stand you'll pass the pretty 1994 Maha Bodayaong temple, whose unrefined seven-storey church-like tower offers decent townscape views, assuming you can find a monk who'll let you climb it.

Mahamyatmuni Paya   BUDDHIST TEMPLE

(မဟာမြတ်မုနိဘုရား; Lanmataw St) FREE Between the large main market and the Nannhaewon Amusement Park is the eye-catching Mahamyatmuni Paya, an open-sided pavilion enshrining a dazzle-faced seated Buddha along the lines of Mandalay's Mahamuni.

Lashio Golf Club   GOLF

(9/18 holes K10,000/20,000; ⊙9am-6pm) This is quite a smart golf course for this part of the country and offers very low rates. Add K10,000 for a buggy and K5000 for a caddy for nine holes.

🛏 Sleeping

Most hotels in Lashio are Chinese-owned and overpriced compared with the better options in nearby Hsipaw, so few foreigners stay here.

★ Mansu Hotel   HOTEL $

(☑082-25249; mansuhotel@gmail.com; Theinni Rd; r incl breakfast K36,000-52,000; ⊖❄🛜) The smartest hotel in town, the Mansu also deserves credit for being the only hotel to charge a flat kyat rate for both locals and foreigners. Rooms have some decorative flourishes, flat-screen TVs and slick new bathrooms. Deluxe rooms are more like mini-suites.

Lashio Motel   MOTEL $

(☑082-23702; lashiomotel@gmail.com; r incl breakfast US$30-35; ❄🛜) This 49-room hotel is a hangover from the earlier days of MHT government-owned properties, but is in reasonable shape after some renovations. Baby-blue bathrooms have been upgraded, as have the TVs, and rates include breakfast.

Ya Htaik Hotel   HOTEL $

(☑082-22655; yahtaiklso@gmail.com; Bogyoke Rd; s US$35-55, without bathroom US$15; ❄🛜) The only place in Lashio where you'll find a budget bed. The cheapest rooms are perfectly acceptable, but the shared bathrooms have squat toilets and tiny showers. More expensive rooms are much bigger and come with a somewhat smarter trim.

🍴 Eating

Food stalls serving Shan noodles, hotpots and barbecue can be found at the junction of Theinni Rd and Bogyoke St. Many more

LASHIO TRANSPORT CONNECTIONS

DESTINATION	BUS	MINIBUS	SHARED TAXI	TRAIN
Hsipaw	K2000; 3hr, 6 daily	N/A	back/front seat K5000/7000; 2hr; frequent	ordinary/upper class K700/1650; 4hr; 5am
Mandalay	K6000; 8hr, 6 daily	K10,000; 7hr; 4 daily	back/front seat K15,000/17,000; 7hr; frequent	ordinary/upper class K2400/5550; 16hr; 5am
Pyin Oo Lwin	K5500; 6hr, 6 daily	N/A	back/front seat K12,000/15,000; 5hr; frequent	ordinary/upper class K1900/4400; 11hr; 5am
Taunggyi	K15,000; 14hr; 2pm	N/A	N/A	N/A

appear after 5pm when the busy night market (5pm to 9pm) gets going.

Ngwe Hnin Phyu
SHAN $

(12/8 Thukha Rd; mains K1500-4000; ⊘10.30am-9pm) A great little Shan restaurant in the middle of downtown Lashio, this place has a tabletop counter filled with 20 or more pots and pans offering a mix of Shan and Chinese dishes. Just point and eat. The bathrooms downstairs are like a furnace if you want a free sauna.

Shwe Lawon
CHINESE $

(Theinni Rd; mains from K2500; ⊘9am-9pm; 🝖) The 2nd-floor terrace is swish by Lashio standards and the locals rate it as the best Chinese food in town. It offers a generous selection of meat, fish and veggie dishes.

ⓘ Getting There & Away

Lashio offers flight connections to Mandalay (US$90, 45 minutes, three weekly), Yangon and Kyaingtong, plus road and rail links to Hsipaw, Pyin Oo Lwin and Mandalay.

The main bus station is a mile north of the city centre. Minibuses and shared taxis leave from here too.

Lashio's miniature train station is 2 miles northwest of the market.

The airport is 3 miles north of town. A taxi costs K3000 to the airport and K5000 when heading into town.

ⓘ Getting Around

Three-wheel pick-ups and motorbike taxis charge K500 to K1000 for short hops around town.

Mogok

POP C 77,609 / 🕾 086

Welcome to Rubyland. Long closed to foreigners, the ruby-mining town of Mogok is now open to visitors with the necessary permits. With 90% of the world's rubies coming from Myanmar, Mogok and the surrounding area is a key hub of the ruby trade, with much of the mining done by hand.

As well as rubies, you'll find sapphires, emeralds, and lapis lazuli and other semi-precious gems on sale in the markets. Many of the traders are Chinese or Indian. If you're interested in purchasing any stones, be sure you know what you are doing, as this isn't a place for rookie gem-buyers.

In addition to rubies, Mogok has a beautiful mountain setting with a significant Shan population, as well as Palaung and Lisu.

ⓘ GETTING TO CHINA: MU-SE TO RUILI

Getting to the border While no documents are required to travel to Mu-se itself, people planning to cross the border need a permit from MHT, which will take 10 days to two weeks to process and is most easily arranged via a recommended tour operator. Border crossers will also need a pre-booked guide and car (US$200) to make the four-hour journey from Lashio to Mu-se.

At the border You must have a Chinese visa already, as they are not available at the border.

Moving on From Ruili in China, semi-regular buses run daily to Yunnan's capital, Kunming (14 hours).

There are a number of eye-catching pagodas and a WWII cemetery containing the remains of British soldiers who died fighting nearby.

In early 2017 Myanmar's government temporarily stopped issuing permits for travel to Mogok; check with local travel agents for the latest situation.

⦿ Sights

★Cinema Hall Market
MARKET

(⊘6-11am) As the epicentre of the gem trade in Myanmar, Mogok has many marketplaces for gems. The early-morning market is known as the Cinema Hall Market, as it is outside the old cinema, and involves local dealers pushing rough uncut stones. In the afternoon, the action shifts to the Paik Swae market, where the high-rollers hang out.

Paik Swae
MARKET

(ပိတ်စွယ်ရေး; ⊘1-6pm) At the afternoon market, there are tables for buyers and sellers, while brokers mingle in between trying to establish a sale. It's very interesting to witness the scene even if you are not in the market for a purchase.

Phaung Daw U Paya
BUDDHIST TEMPLE

(ဖောင်တော်ဦးဘုရား; ⊘6am-6pm) FREE The holiest of the many temples dotting the Mogok skyline, Phaung Daw U Paya has a dais that conceals some ornate pedestals encrusted with priceless gems, which are on display in a glass case behind the seated Buddha. Once a year in March, they are brought out for a spring equinox festival, which attracts thousands of the faithful.

Pada Myar Zeidy
BUDDHIST TEMPLE

(ပတ္တမြားစေတီ) FREE Forget the golden spire of this temple – you are up here for the classic calendar view over Mogok and its central lake, created from the remnants of an abandoned open-pit ruby mine from the colonial period.

British War Cemetery
CEMETERY

FREE The British War Cemetery at Ywar Thar Yar, about 12 miles from Mogok, is a stark reminder of the remote battle sites that once dotted the world during the days of the British Empire. The cemetery is rather neglected these days, but is a very atmospheric spot in the Shan Hills. The cemetery contains the dead from the Third Anglo-Burmese War of 1886–93.

King Chaung Waterfall
WATERFALL

(မင်းချောင်းရေတံခွန်; K2000; ⊘7am-5pm) This pretty waterfall has been turned into a bit of a circus with the establishment of an amusement park below. Choose from bumper cars, a vomit-inducing 5-D ride and other arcade games or head straight to the waterfall instead.

🏃 Activities

One of the most popular activities in Rubyland is visiting an active gem mine. There are both open-pit and underground mines, but open-pit mines operate in the dry season only, as they are flooded in the wet season. Underground mines operate year-round, but it is only possible to get access to enlarged tunnels above ground. Permission is required from Myanmar Gem Enterprises, arranged by your local guide.

🛏 Sleeping

⭐ Kingbridge Hotel
HOTEL $$

(☑086-20088; www.kingbridgehotel.com; Mintadar Quarter; r US$75-200; ❄❋🛜🛆) Built over a hillside on the edge of town, this is the most stylish hotel in Mogok. Rooms are extremely spacious and include large bathrooms with tubs and rain showers. Cable TV is on tap, plus there's a minibar and safe. Facilities include an impressive infinity pool for laps and a reliable restaurant.

Golden Butterfly Hotel
HOTEL $$

(☑094 40253 4366; www.goldenbutterflyhotel mogoke.com; Kyatpyin Rd; r US$75-120; ❄❋🛜) This all-wooden resort is located on a hilltop pass about 3 miles above Mogok and is easily distinguishable by the giant golden butterfly on the gate. The 25 rooms are set in Swiss-style alpine chalets that slope down the hill and include hot water and wi-fi access.

Mogok Motel
MOTEL $$

(☑086-20118; Kanthayar Rd; standard/superior/VIP r US$40/60/90; ❋🛜) Looking rather forlorn from the outside, this former government hotel has better than expected renovated superior rooms inside. Avoid the unrenovated standard rooms for now or go VIP with a panoramic lake view from the rooftop penthouse.

🍴 Eating

Many visitors end up eating at their hotel restaurants, as the better hotels are a little way from the centre of town. There are a handful of local restaurants around town and there's a lively night market.

Ah Kaung Kyaik Restaurant
BARBECUE $

(☑09 4924 4226; Kanthayar Rd; mains K2500-9000; ⊘6.30am-9.30pm) Overlooking the lake near Mogok Motel, this is the liveliest restaurant in town. Outside is a huge selection of skewers to point at and barbecue. Inside the menu is predominantly Chinese. It doubles as the town bar, with draught Myanmar Beer and a pretty good local spirit selection available.

Night Market
STREET FOOD $

(Kanthayar Rd; mains K500-2000; ⊘5-9pm) Spread out along the spur road to Mogok Motel, this is a bit of a social hub for the Mogok community after dark. Steam and smoke rises into the cooling air and locals chow down on barbecue, noodles, dim sum and more.

Lu Htu Restaurant
ASIAN $

(☑086-20399; Bogyoke St; mains K2000-7000; ⊘7am-9pm) Located on the main street, this is a popular lunchtime stop for Chinese classics and Burmese curries. The small roadside diner is more atmospheric than the new hangar-like hall out the back.

U Bein Tea Shop
TEAHOUSE $

(Paik Swae Market; mains K250-1000; ⊘7am-6pm) This popular Burmese teahouse is a great place to observe the Paik Swae gem market and some deals are even made over or under the tables. Piping hot teas and homemade cakes.

ℹ Information

KBZ Bank (Bogyoke St; ⊘9am-3pm Mon-Fri) The only ATM machine in town is located here.

Sai Sein Win (☑09 25626 9867; saiseinwin510 @gmail.com) is a Mogok resident of 25 years and a tour guide, making him a font of knowledge on the attractions of Rubyland.

❶ Getting There & Away

Mogok can only be visited with an official permit (US$40) from MHT, which takes about 10 days or two working weeks to process. This means you effectively have to travel here in a private car with an approved guide, so two-day packages quickly run into several hundreds of dollars for the trip from Mandalay or Pyin Oo Lwin. Best is probably to combine the two and make a loop from Mandalay to Pyin Oo Lwin via Mogok. Book through a reputable agent in Yangon or Mandalay.

It takes about six hours to Mogok from Mandalay (124 miles), four hours from Shwebo (99 miles) and four hours from Pyin Oo Lwin (82 miles). The old road via Kyaukme is not in the best of condition, and so is less frequently used these days.

Should travel restrictions be lifted at some point, local transport prices from Mogok include Mandalay (car front/back K13,000/10,000), Pyin Oo Lwin (minivan, K8500) and Shwebo (car front/back K12,000/10,000). There is usually a surcharge for uphill sectors from Mandalay and Shwebo, plus expect to be hit with a small foreigner surcharge.

UPPER AYEYARWADY

Snaking across Kachin State like an enormous python, the mighty Ayeyarwady River provides the main transport route between a series of gently interesting port towns, isolated villages and gold-panning camps. While no individual sight is jaw-dropping, the journey itself involves an immersion in local life that many visitors find unforgettable. Unlike boat rides from Mandalay to Bagan, ferries on the upper Ayeyarwady are used almost entirely by locals and the slow days drifting along the river provide an opportunity to interact with people in a way that is often impossible on dry land. A phrase book and a bottle of Grand Royal whiskey can be useful tools to help break the ice.

Note that the Ayeyarwady isn't scenically dramatic in the way of, say, the Nam Ou in neighbouring Laos, but the landscape does reach several modest crescendos as rolling fields and distant sand banks alternate with forest-dappled defiles.

Myitkyina

POP C 243,031 / ☑ 074

The capital of Kachin State, Myitkyina lacks much in the way of headline sights. Nonetheless it's an engaging, multicultural place, home to Kachin, Lisu, Chinese and Burmese, and hosts two of Myanmar's most important 'ethnic' festivals. A low-rise town with a fair scattering of part-timber houses, its residents seem keen to assist visitors, with local Christians particularly eager to practise their English. Quiet at the best of times, the town is especially sleepy on Sundays when the churches fill up. Few foreigners make it here, and those who do are mostly missionaries or NGO workers.

◎ Sights

The town sprawls for miles, but the central area is a manageable compact grid. Walking out of the train station, Waing Maw St heads east, reaching the river bank in five short blocks. Parallel but four blocks further north is Zei Gyi Rd, the junction marked by one of Myitkyina's two clock towers. Zei Gyi runs east to the market and river, west across the tracks passing very close to the YMCA (follow the tracks north), the Hotel United (second block then north) and plentiful restaurants. Parallel to Ze Gyi, and four blocks further north, Si Pin Thar Yar St also crosses the railway. The main road then swerves northwest to become Pyi Htaung Su Rd, the road to the airport and Sinbo ferry jetty. Or continue in a northerly sweep on Thakhin Phay Net St to reach the museum and, eventually, Manao Park, Jing Hpaw Thu restaurant and Palm Spring Resort.

Produce Market   MARKET
(☺5am-5pm) This riverside market specialises in colourful heaps of Chinese fruit and local vegetables. Many of the latter arrive by canoe and are then lugged up the rear stairway on shoulder poles. At dawn this creates an unforgettable spectacle with boats gliding in across shimmering golden water backed by a rising sun. Directly southwest is the architecturally drab **Myo Ma Market** (☺8.30am-5pm).

Hsu Taung Pye Zedidaw   BUDDHIST TEMPLE
(ဆုတောင်းပြည့်စေတီတော်) **FREE** This gilded 'wish-fulfilling' pagoda is the town's most eye-catching religious building, sitting on the banks of the Ayeyarwady River at the north end of Zaw John (Strand) Rd. Opposite its stupa, a 98ft-long **reclining buddha** and a nearby standing equivalent were funded by a Japanese soldier who served here in WWII, in part to commemorate 3400 of his comrades who died.

Kachin State Cultural Museum   MUSEUM
(ကချင်ပြည်နယ်ယဉ်ကျေးမှုပြတိုက်; Yon Gyi St; US$2; ☺9am-4pm) Displays Kachin and Shan costumes and the usual assortment of

ⓘ UPPER AYEYARWADY RIVER TRIP PLANNING

At the time of writing, foreigners were barred from taking IWT ferries and fast boats north from Bhamo to Myitkyina. However, foreigners can now take fast boats between Bhamo, Katha and Mandalay if the IWT schedule is too slow-paced. Several international companies offer luxury cruises along the Upper Ayeyarwady, albeit rarely more than a few times a year.

Which Boat?

Travellers cruising the Ayeyarwady can choose between the slow IWT ferries or the much quicker fast boats. While the fast boats inevitably save a lot of time, in truth the fast boats are more uncomfortable than the IWT ferries and are often dangerously overcrowded. One such fast boat sank in 2012, prompting a ban on foreigners using the fast boats for a couple of years.

IWT Ferries

These two- or three-storey craft are the cheapest option and the best for interacting with locals, but they're slow, unreliable and not very comfortable for long journeys.

Routes They run three times a week between Bhamo and Mandalay (Monday, Wednesday and Friday) with stops in Shwegu, Katha, Ti-Kyaing, Tagaung and Kyaukmyaung. Ferries can be a day or more late, so don't be in a hurry.

Tickets Ticket-purchasing procedures vary by port, but foreigners always need to pay with pristine US dollar bills, sometimes at the relevant IWT office. Agency bookings aren't possible and there are no seat reservations – indeed, no seats whatsoever, just cold metal decks.

Comfort and provisions You'll generally need to sleep aboard at least one night, and maybe three nights northbound from Mandalay to Bhamo. A few simple cabins are available (US$60, shared toilet), but most folk travel deck class (maximum fare US$12), for which you'll need your own mat and bedding. Snacks and drinks are sold aboard, but are comparatively pricey. Food can also be bought at the boat stops.

Fast Boats

These are long, covered motorboats carrying between 30 and 80 passengers. Departures are regular.

Routes Fast boats make daily one-day hops along the following sections, always travelling by day (each sector will be in a different boat): Bhamo–Shwegu–Katha and Katha–Mandalay.

Tickets These are usually purchased just before departure, or one day before for Katha–Mandalay.

Comfort and provisions The wooden bench seats are small and often partly broken. Life jackets may not be available. You'll need to sleep at local guesthouses, which are very basic in Shwegu and Katha. Bring plenty of drinking water. You can buy food at the brief intermediate halts.

When to Go?

Boats run all year between Mandalay and Bhamo.

➡ Journeys are fastest in autumn when water levels are high. By February, sandbanks mean that the IWT ferry will have to moor overnight, adding up to a day to southbound journey times.

➡ April is difficult due to Burmese New Year, with boats packed full of local travellers and ferries seriously overloaded.

➡ In summer, rain and high winds can make the passage very uncomfortable.

Where to Start & Finish?

North of Mandalay there are currently only three realistic start/finish points for foreigners on the Ayeyarwady adventure:

Bhamo No rail or road link to Mandalay or Myitkyina, so the only way in is by air. But accommodation is good and Bhamo to Katha is the most popular single section of river due to the (brief) drama of the second defile. Shwegu, in between Bhamo and Katha, is an offbeat highlight.

Katha Popular for its George Orwell connections. Some people like to travel by boat between Katha and Mandalay. Four daily trains also connect with Mandalay, albeit some at antisocial times and from the railhead of Naba about 16 miles away. River scenery south of Katha is initially lovely, but there's no easy jump-off point till Kyaukmyaung.

Kyaukmyaung Getting off at this interesting pottery town makes sense if you're heading for Bagan, which you can reach across country via Shwebo, Monywa and Pakokku. Continuing by boat to Mandalay you'll pass Mingun, but IWT ferries won't stop there.

How Long Will It Take?

The minimum time from Bhamo to Mandalay by IWT ferry will be two to three days, assuming the boats are running to schedule. You can save time by jumping ship at Katha and catching the express boat or train to Mandalay. Bear in mind that it takes two days longer to travel northbound, upriver, than it does going in the other direction.

How Much Will It Cost?

IWT ferries are far cheaper than the other options. A deck ticket from Bhamo to Mandalay is US$12 (about K17,000), whereas the express boat from Katha to Mandalay alone costs K25,000.

What to See

Travelling between Bhamo and Shwegu, the scenery reaches a modest climax in the short second defile where the Ayeyarwady passes through a wooded valley with a rocky cliff face at one point, often described misleadingly as a gorge.

IWT ferries tend to travel the section south of Katha in the dark, but this stretch has some of the Ayeyarwady's more appealing landscapes, with several pagoda-topped hills and thatched villages. The first stop is Ti-Kyaing (pronounced 't'chine'; Htigyaing) where on the riverfront a double row of thatched wooden stilt houses leads north from the jetty, a monastery hill rises directly above and a large Buddha reclines on the next hill northeast.

If and when foreigners are again allowed to take the river route between Bhamo and Myitkyina, it is necessary to spend a night in the delightfully carless riverside village of Sinbo. Founded as a teak station for the Scottish firm Steel Brothers, Sinbo is a neat grid of unpaved streets, the mostly wood and part-timber houses set amid coconut and toddy palms. There are no must-see sights, but river views are mesmerising from the muddy lane that climbs between the trio of old stupas and the 1919 British Officers' Bungalow at the south end of town.

Buying Provisions

Even if you don't disembark along the way, you'll have no problem meeting the people who live there. The IWT ferries and fast boats are the principal source of income for many people residing along the banks of the Ayeyarwady, and the moment they come into sight, villagers jump into their wooden longboats laden with everything from home-cooked curries and grilled fish to beer and cigarettes to sell to the passengers. Others wade out to the ferries, their wares balanced precariously on their heads. These impromptu markets not only make great photo opportunities, but also are generally cheaper and tastier than the monotonous diet of noodles and oily curries sold aboard the IWT ferries. And you'll soon get used to shopping on water.

MYIT-SON

About 25 miles north of Myitkyina, **Myit-Son** (မြစ်ဆုံ) marks the point where the Mayhka and Malikha Rivers come together to form the Ayeyarwady. It's considered a local 'beauty spot', although it's not the most picturesque location on the Ayeyarwady.

The confluence is distantly overlooked by a series of rough snack places and teahouses, a big dumpling-shaped golden pagoda and a traditional Kachin longhouse rebuilt as a 'cultural emblem'.

The road north of Myitkyina (bound eventually for Putao) has been partly rebuilt, but the last 7 miles to Myit-Son are horrendously bumpy. You'll need a photocopy of your passport and visa to hand to a police checkpoint en route. A motorbike/taxi from Myitkyina costs around K20,000/50,000 return (1½ hours each way).

instruments, farming tools and ethnological artefacts. There are English captions.

Aung Ze Yan Aung Paya   BUDDHIST TEMPLE
(အောင်ဇေရန်အောင်ဘုရား) FREE Just east of the airport, this pagoda is noteworthy for its arcing ranks of about 1000 little buddhas sitting in the grounds.

⚘ Festivals & Events

Lisu New Year   CULTURAL
Started in 2011, this big three-day bash unites Lisu folks from all across Kachin State and Xishuangbanna (China) in a very colourful, if comfortably slow-moving fair. The event is entirely untouristy, unless you count the many costumed Lisu villagers snapping photos of one another, as the varied regional Lisu costumes are markedly different. Highlights include barefoot climbing of a knife tower and have-a-go stalls to test your prowess on a traditional crossbow. Held before the February full moon.

Manao Festival   CULTURAL
Originally a way to propitiate the local *nat*, this is now a nationally important gathering of the six Kachin tribes for feasting and costumed dances. It's performed in Manao park (north of centre), where the large Native American–style totem poles remain in place year-round. Accommodation is at a

premium at this time. Observers get into the festival mood by drinking copious quantities of rice beer. Held on and around 10 January, Kachin State Day.

🛏 Sleeping

In Myitkyina, nowhere with 'Guesthouse' in its name accepts foreigners, but the YMCA doubles as the closest thing to a hostel. There are now several upmarket hotels in town.

Xing Xian Hotel   HOTEL $
(☑ 074-22281; yadanarpaing@mptmail.net.mm; 127 Shan Su North; r US$16-33; ✱) Two giant vases welcome you into this quiet, friendly, long-standing and centrally located hotel. Even the cheapest rooms are spacious and well equipped, adding up to one of the better budget deals in town.

YMCA   HOSTEL $
(☑ 074-23010; maran.nemra@gmail.com; YMCA St; r US$10-28; ⊜✱🛜) Budget prices and helpful English-speaking staff ensure that the 10 rooms here book up fast. Conditions, however, are pretty basic. The cheapest rooms, without bathrooms or air-con, are especially grungy, so it is worth investing US$15 and up for a private bathroom. No breakfast, but free tea and coffee.

Hotel United   HOTEL $
(☑ 074-22085; hotelunitedmyitkyina@gmail.com; 38 Thit Sa St; s/d/tr US$30/35/45; ✱🛜) A reliable old-timer, United has 36 well-kept rooms. Doubles and twins include a shower, while family rooms have a bathtub. Friendly staff speak some English.

★ Hotel Nan Thida   HOTEL $$
(☑ 074-22362; myitkyinariverview@gmail.com; cnr Strand & Zaw Jun Rds; r incl breakfast US$40-60; ⊜✱🛜) Recently taken over by the owners of the Putao Hotel, the rooms in the main building are spectacularly spacious and come with impressive and colourful Kachin motifs all over the walls. A rain shower in the slick bathrooms completes the picture. It overlooks the Ayeyarwady River next to Hsu Taung Pye Zedidaw.

Hotel Madira   HOTEL $$
(☑ 074-21119; www.hotelmadira.com; 510 Pyayhtaungsu Rd; r US$42-74; ⊜✱🛜) Kachin-owned, this classy hotel offers quality rooms and service at an affordable price. The rooms are big and bright, plus there's even a

gym if you want a workout. It's on the road into town from the airport.

Hotel Myitkyina
HOTEL **$$**

(📞 074-21306; www.hotelmyitkyinakachin.com; 111 Si Pin Tar Yar St; r US$45-80; 😊 ❄ 🐕) One of the newer hotels in town, this smart business block offers clean, crisp rooms with flat-screen TV, minibar and hot-water showers. It's about 500m north of the railway station.

Palm Spring Resort
RESORT **$$$**

(📞 074-22938; www.palmspringresort.com.mm; 7/8 Sitarpu Quarter; r/bungalow US$120/150; 😊 ❄ @ 🐕 ☁ ⛵) An infinity pool overlooking the Ayeyarwady River was not something we expected in provincial Myitkyina. Rooms at Palm Spring are superbly finished in teak and some include a hot tub, but it is worth shelling out a little extra for the bungalows in the lush garden. Facilities include a river-view restaurant and a small gym.

✕ Eating

Traditionally, Kachin food uses less oil than Burmese cuisine. Classic dishes include *chekachin* (steamed chicken pasted with spices and wrapped in a banana leaf), *sipa* (freshly steamed vegetables sprinkled with sesame powder) and *nakoo-che* (hot-sour fish with bamboo shoots). Wash it down with *kaung-ye*, a cloudy semi-sweet pink-brown beer made from sticky rice.

A wide range of standard, accessible eateries are along Zaw Gyi St, west of the rail tracks.

★ Jing Hpaw Thu
BURMESE **$**

(dishes K2000-5000; ⏰ 9am-10pm) Be sure to head out to this attractive riverside restaurant, considered the top spot for real Kachin food. The specialities here are superb, tangy dried beef with a spicy dipping sauce, as well as the fish dishes and chicken or pork served in a banana leaf. No English is spoken, so just point at the dishes that take your fancy.

A three-wheeler will charge about K5000 return from the centre of town. Or try the rather bland city-centre sibling located on Tha Khin Net Phay Rd.

Orient Restaurant
KACHIN, JAPANESE **$**

(YMCA St; mains K2000-5000; ⏰ 7am-9pm, closed Sun morning; 🍴) A meeting place for Myitkyina's tiny foreign community, the menu here is an intriguing blend of local dishes, international comfort food and some unexpected Japanese classics like sushi and ramen, as the Kachin owner previously lived in Japan.

Italian N'Dream
CAFE **$**

(📞 094-2105 2226; 17 Myo Thit St; cakes K500-2000; ⏰ 7am-9pm; ❄ 🐕) This cosy little corner cafe serves cheap and cheerful home-made cakes and locally produced ice cream, which isn't world-beating but is good value at K1000 for two scoops. Coffees and teas are also available, all in an air-con environment.

Night Market
STREET FOOD **$**

(Aung San Rd & Wai Maw St; dishes K500-2000; ⏰ 4.30-9.30pm) This is a lively place to come and street surf after about 4pm when the stalls set up, complete with Shan hotpots, steaming noodles, smoking barbecues and bubbling curries. Locals come here to dine on the way home or pick up takeaway.

Mya Ayer
CHINESE **$$**

(71 Shan Su North; mains K3000-12,000; ⏰ 9am-10pm; 🍴) This is the most authentic Chinese option in a town with a sizeable Chinese population. The big menu includes some spicy hot and sour dishes from Szechuan, making it a great place to dine in communal Chinese style.

Kiss Me
BURMESE **$$**

(Zaw John Rd; dishes K2000-10,000; ⏰ 6am-9pm; 🐕 🍴) A hotspot for Myitkyina's youngsters, this riverside pavilion turns out some fine food. Try the *gyin tok* (a crunchy ginger salad) or the zesty curries. There are fresh shakes and juices too, but no alcohol is served if you are planning a sundowner, as it is curiously located in the grounds of Hsu Taung Pye Zedidaw.

Bamboo Field Restaurant
ASIAN **$$**

(313 Pyi Htaung Su Rd; mains K3000-10,000; ⏰ 9am-10pm; 🐕 🍴) On the main airport road, this barn-like place has a rotating crew

NORTHERN MYANMAR MYITKYINA

ⓘ MYITKYINA TRAVEL RESTRICTIONS

At the time of writing, travel to and from Myitkyina was severely restricted due to ongoing fighting between the Kachin Independence Army and the Myanmar military. Foreigners are barred from taking either buses or boats to or from Myitkyina, meaning the only way in or out of the town is by train or plane (unless you are prepared to hire an expensive private car and guide, and even then you can only travel south to Indawgyi Lake and Katha).

of singers belting out Burmese pop songs on weekends. The menu mixes Chinese, Thai and Vietnamese with Western classics. Check out the ambitious cocktail list, or sample the draught beer on tap. It shows English Premier League games.

River View Restaurant   CHINESE **$$**
(☑ 074-28152; mains K2000-10,000, dim sum K500-1500; ⊙ 6am-10pm; ▣) Get your morning nourishment from this riverside terrace joint with the tastiest dim sum in town, making it a popular breakfast stop. By night it reinvents itself as a beer garden and is a great place to watch sunset over the Ayeyarwady while nursing an ice-cold Myanmar Beer.

ⓘ Information

Free maps are available at the YMCA (p294) and Xing Xian Hotel (p294), although they are light on any useful detail. There are now several major banks in Myitkyina with ATMs.

Aya Bank (64 Bogyoke Aung San Rd; ⊙ 9am-3pm Mon-Fri, to noon Sat) ATM that accepts international debit and credit cards.

KBZ Bank (Munkhrain Rd; ⊙ 9am-3pm Mon-Fri) Main branch of KBZ with a Visa/Mastercard-friendly ATM.

Snowland Tours (☑ 074-23499; www.snowlandmyanmar.com; Wai Maw St) Two blocks east of the station, this helpful agency with English-speaking staff can book flights and arrange customised tours.

ⓘ Getting There & Away

At the time of writing, foreigners were only allowed to arrive and leave Myitkyina by plane or train, or by private car with a guide, and only to the south (Indawgyi Lake and Katha).

Myitkyina's airport is a couple of miles from the town centre. A three-wheeler costs K3000. Air-conditioned taxis are available for K5000 per person. On arrival at the airport, you will need to present your passport to the immigration police.

The train station is close to the clock tower in the centre of town.

Boats leave from the Talawgyi Pier, a K5000 ride from town in a three-wheeler.

ⓘ Getting Around

Motorised three-wheelers (called *thoun bein*) carrying up to four people charge K3000 to/from the airport, or K5000 to the boat jetty for Sinbo.

Bicycles (K2000 per day) and motorbikes (K10,000 per day) can be rented at the Orient Restaurant next to the YMCA.

Indawgyi Lake
အင်းတော်ကြီး

About 110 miles southwest of Myitkyina, placid Indawgyi is the largest natural lake in Myanmar and one of the most special, serene places in the entire country. The lakeshore is ringed by rarely visited Shan villages, and the surrounding Indawgyi Wetland Wildlife Sanctuary provides a habitat for around 200 species of birds, including shelducks, pintails, kingfishers, herons, egrets, Myanmar peacocks and the rare sarus crane, the world's tallest flighted bird. Very remote and tranquil, it's a great place to kick back for a few days.

⊙ Sights & Activities

Shwe Myitsu Paya   BUDDHIST TEMPLE
(ရွှေမြစ်ဆုံဘုရား; ⊙ 6am-6pm) The mystical Shwe Myitsu Paya, on an island off Nam Tay village, seems to float on the surface of the lake. The central, gilded stupa was constructed in 1869 to enshrine Buddha relics transported here from Yangon. It costs K1000 for a boat to the island from the nearby pier. Women are not allowed to enter the temple itself.

Pilgrims visit in droves for the **Shwe Myitsu Pwe**, held during the week before the full moon of Tabaung (March), at which time the lake waters are low enough for a walk along a seasonal causeway to the pagoda. The temple is about 7 miles from Lonton. Head 5 miles north and then turn off east

---

MYITKYINA TRANSPORT CONNECTIONS

DESTINATION	AIR	TRAIN
Bhamo	US$75; 1hr	N/A
Hopin (for Indawgyi Lake)	N/A	ordinary/upper class K900/1750; 5hr; 4 daily
Mandalay	US$85; 70min; daily	depending on class K4150-11,350; 24hr; 4 daily
Naba (for Katha)	N/A	K1600-4900; 12hr; 4 daily
Putao	US$100; 1hr; daily	N/A
Yangon	US$160; 2hr 40min; daily	N/A

towards the lake at the village of Nam Tay, where you see a large sign in Burmese script.

Inn Chit Thu Tourism Centre KAYAKING

(⊙7am-6pm) Just north of the Indaw Mahar Guesthouse, the Inn Chit Thu Tourism Group is a locally run organisation that puts its profits into community projects. It rents out kayaks (K15,000 per day), which are a great way to explore the lake. You can also rent bicycles here (K7000 per day) to explore the pretty villages around the lake, including the picturesque village of **Lwemun**.

🛏 Sleeping & Eating

There's not a whole lot of choice when it comes to accommodation around Indawgyi Lake, as only one guesthouse in Lonton is approved to host foreigners.

There is a handful of simple local restaurants located opposite the Inn Chit Thu Tourism Centre where you can get basic meals cooked on a wood stove, including fish curry. Mercifully cold Myanmar Beer is also available. The stall opposite Indaw Mahar Guesthouse offers 'Genius Coffee' in a French press and homemade American-style pancakes for breakfast.

Indaw Mahar Guesthouse GUESTHOUSE $

(☑ 097-325 9692; r K10,000) The only licensed guesthouse in the Indawgyi Lake area is in the village of Lonton on the lake's southwestern shore. Indaw Mahar is near the end of the village close to the army checkpoint and has eight very simple rooms in a stilt building right at the water's edge.

ℹ Getting There & Away

TAXI & PICK-UP TRUCK

From Hopin, there is a good new road to Lonton (one hour) and Indawgyi Lake. A taxi will cost about K25,000 one way. Motorbike taxis are available for K10,000 to K15,000, depending on your negotiating skills, although some Indawgyi Lake residents may take you for as little as K6000 if they are heading home. Overloaded pick-ups leave a few times a day (K4000, two hours or more), but are slow as they stop to drop off goods.

A very rough road continues all the way to Khamti via the casino-filled jade-mining boom town of Hpakant (Pakkant), but foreigners can't go anywhere beyond Nyaungbin without hard-to-score permits.

TRAIN

Four daily Myitkyina–Mandalay trains stop in Hopin, which is roughly halfway between Myitkyina and Katha. Time your arrival to avoid a forgettable overnight in Hopin. It costs K1300 for an upper-class seat south to Naba (for Katha), K1750 for an upper-class seat to Myitkyina, or K9000 for a sleeper to Mandalay.

Bhamo (Banmaw) ဗန်းမော်

POP C 58,696 / ☑ 074

For many travellers, Bhamo ('ba-more') used to be a staging post on the river journey to Myitkyina or Mandalay. However, with river travel north to Myitkyina not currently permitted, it's rather fallen off the map in recent years. If you do make it here, you'll discover one of Myanmar's more relaxed and attractive towns. The central riverfront is especially lively on Friday, when villagers flood in for the market. It's lined with several old stained-teak houses and is overhung with magnificent mature 'rain trees', so named because their lovely pink flowers bloom in the monsoon season.

◉ Sights

It is more about the languid riverside atmosphere than the sights in Bhamo, but there are a couple of attractive temples.

At the southern end of the riverfront are dealerships selling great stacks of claypots including simple water carriers from Shwegu and giant glazed amphorae from Kyaukmyaung. Two short blocks east then one north on Lammataw Rd brings you to the main market (Thiri Yadana), from which Sinbyushin St leading west becomes the main road to Myitkyina and China. It quickly passes Post Office St (for Grand Hotel, turn right after one block), the pre-dawn vegetable market and Letwet Thondaya Rd (for the Friendship Hotel, turn left after the second block). Around 500m further is the large, photogenic complex of Theindawgyi Paya.

Shwe Kyina Paya BUDDHIST TEMPLE

(ရွှေကျီးနားမဟာစေတီတော်) About 3 miles north of town, beyond the military enclave, the historic Shwe Kyina Pagoda has two gold-topped stupas and marks the site of the 5th-century Shan city of Sampanago (Bhamo Myo Haung, Old Bhamo). Almost nothing remains of the old city, though locals remember numerous remnant bricks and posts remaining into the 1950s.

Theindawgyi Paya BUDDHIST TEMPLE

(သိမ်တော်ကြီးဘုရား; Sinbyushin St) FREE Around 4 miles from town is the large,

NORTHERN MYANMAR BHAMO (BANMAW)

photogenic complex of Theindawgyi Paya, which features a gilded stupa with an elongated bell-shape. It's best admired from the southeast across a pond lined with concrete monk statues.

Bamboo Bridge BRIDGE
(return toll with bicycle K500) It is worth checking out this rickety but spectacular bamboo bridge that allows you to cross the wide Tapin River.

🏃 Activities

For a nice bicycle ride continue west over the bamboo bridge for 30 minutes through timeless Sinkin village and on to a brickworks. From here a 10-minute stairway climb takes you up Theinpa Hill past a meditation hall to a stupa with very attractive panoramas.

Rent bicycles from **Breeze Coffee & Cold** (Letwet Thondaya Rd; per day K2000; ⊙8.30am-7pm), a small shop almost opposite Friendship Hotel.

🛏 Sleeping

★ Friendship Hotel HOTEL $
(☑074-50095, in China 0086-692 687 6670; Letwet Thondaya Rd; s/d/tr incl breakfast US$25/30/40, without bathroom US$10/20/30; ❄🛜) This hotel is large, comfortable and excellent value for money. Even the shared bathrooms are well maintained, while the better rooms have decent mattresses, and all qualify you for one of the best buffet breakfasts in Myanmar. Helpful manager Moe Naing speaks fluent English and offers a useful free map.

Hotel Paradise HOTEL $
(☑074-50136; hotelparadisebanmaw@gmail.com; Shwe Kyaung Kone St; s/d/tr US$15/30/35; ❄@) All the rooms here are a decent deal: reasonably sized and clean with OK bathrooms. It's past the southern end of the riverfront in a strip of lively restaurants.

Grand Hotel HOTEL $
(☑074-50317, in China 0086-692 688 1816; Post Office Rd; r US$20-35; ❄) Grand, indeed, is its modern lobby and blue-glass facade, but the rooms are altogether more down-to-earth and rather austere. Keen staff and some English spoken.

🍴 Eating

Sut Ngai BURMESE $
(Sinbyushin St; mains K1500-4000; ⊙9am-9pm) Popular with the locals, there's fine barbecue, as well as Kachin specialities like lime-flavoured pork served in a banana leaf and draught Myanmar Beer. No English spoken; point at what others are eating.

Shamie Restaurant BURMESE $
(Mingone Junction; curries K2000; ⊙7am-10pm) Excellent spot for proper curry spreads, with eight different types available (including beef, a rarity in Buddhist Myanmar). They come with rice and veggies and fantastic homemade tamarind chutney.

Sein Sein CHINESE $
(Kannar Rd; mains K2000-5000; ⊙9am-9pm; 📷) The rough round tables and beer-poster decor promise little. But the reliable Chinese food is considered the best in town, and there's draught Dagon beer. It's near the IWT office.

ℹ Information

Free town maps are available for guests at the Friendship Hotel. They are extremely useful, if misleadingly out of scale towards the edges.

The prefix ☑0086-692 denotes 'China numbers', which should be dialled from another China-line phone (☑0086-692 numbers) to avoid paying international call rates.

BHAMO TRANSPORT CONNECTIONS

DESTINATION	AIR	IWT FERRY	FAST BOAT
Katha	N/A	deck/cabin US$5/30; 12hr; Mon, Wed & Fri	K12,000; 6hr; 1 daily
Kyaukmyaung	N/A	US$12; 24hr; Mon, Wed & Fri	N/A
Mandalay	US$100; 50min	deck/cabin US$12/60; 40-48hr; Mon, Wed & Fri	N/A
Myitkyina	US$75; 1hr	N/A	N/A
Shwegu	N/A	US$5; 6hr; Mon, Wed & Fri	K6000; 3hr; 1 daily
Yangon	US$155 (via Mandalay); 2½hr	N/A	N/A

ⓘ Getting There & Away

At the time of writing, foreigners were not allowed to enter or exit Bhamo by bus.

IWT ferries leave from a jetty 2½ miles south of town. Fast boats leave from a pier on the central riverfront.

The airport is a 10-minute ride from the centre of town. Immigration police will register you on arrival.

ⓘ Getting Around

Motorcycle/three-wheeler taxis cost K1000/ 2000 to the airport, or K2000/3000 to the IWT ferry dock.

Intervillage pick-ups (called 'Hilux' after the vehicle model name) devote the rear section to goods and fix seats high on the roof as though for a safari. Dangerously top-heavy.

Shwegu   ရွှေကူ

POP C 18,894 / ☎ 074

Every year only a handful of travellers jump ship at historic Shwegu, a long ribbon of township that stretches for 3 miles along the Ayeyarwady's southern bank. It's best known for its elegantly unfussy pottery and for the fabled Shwe Baw Kyune monastery on mid-river Kyundaw ('Royal') Island. Few locals speak English.

⊙ Sights

Shwe Baw Kyune   BUDDHIST MONASTERY
(ရွှေတော်ကျွန်း) At first glance this monastery looks 20th-century. Historians, though, say it was built in the 13th century, while monastic fables suggest it was founded two millennia ago when an Indian prince turned up with seven holy bone fragments of the Buddha. These are now encased within small buddha statuettes decorated over the centuries with layers of gold leaf.

While they form the monastery's priceless main treasure *(dattaw)*, for non-Buddhists the monastery is far more interesting for its extraordinary array of over 7000 closely packed stupas, ancient and modern, which fill the eastern end of the island. Some are whitewashed, others gilded and many more are mere piles of antique bricks with just traces of former stucco detail. Most appear to have been suffocated for years by foliage, Angkor Wat style. The bushes were recently cut back to reveal the spectacle, but getting to the outlying stupas is very uncomfortable barefoot given all the stubble and thorns (carry your sandals).

Hidden here and there are dozens of tiny buddha statues and the odd brick-and-stucco lion. The whole scene is made even more photogenic by a series of *pyatthat* (stepped towers) that flanks the monastery's central golden-tipped stupa. And the island setting, with its tree-shaded village of wooden stilt houses, makes for a wonderfully peaceful environment. There's a big local festival here in the week leading up to full moon of Tabaung.

Old Shwegu   AREA
(ရွှေဂူအဟောင်း) Around 400m west of the central jetty is a stretch of relatively old wooden houses. Further inland is an area of tree-shaded footpaths and alleys that forms an intriguing pottery district. Here, in household compounds, Shwebo's archetypal *tau ye-u* (drinking water pots) and *subu* (football-sized piggy banks) are formed and fired in kilns of carefully heaped rice-husks.

An Daw Paya   BUDDHIST TEMPLE
(အံတော်ဘုရား) This eye-catching ornate pagoda lies in a rural mainland field, directly across the river from Shwe Baw Kyune and around 2 miles east of central Shwegu. Motorcycles charge K1000 to get there, but finding one to come back can be tricky.

🛏 Sleeping & Eating

There's only one place in Shwegu that accepts foreigners, and it is very basic.

There are teahouses and simple restaurants clustered near the jetty.

Sag Guesthouse   GUESTHOUSE $
(☎ 074-52647; s K16,000, without bathroom K6000) The only place that accepts foreigners, Sag Guesthouse is opposite where the Bhamo–Mandalay buses stop and behind the Mingala Monastery. The rooms are small, with hard beds and cold showers, but this is the only option. It's a 10-minute motorbike ride (K1000) from the jetty.

ⓘ Getting There & Around

IWT ferries leave Monday, Wednesday and Friday for Katha (US$5). Foreigners are technically barred from the fast boats that leave daily between 11am and noon (K7000), but you may be allowed on here. An afternoon bus to Mandalay via Katha leaves at 2pm but won't take foreigners.

From a logging jetty 300m west of An Daw Paya, an open longboat ferries passengers across to Shwe Baw Kyune (K500/4000 per person/boat, five minutes). A much more convenient option is to charter your own boat directly from Shwegu's central jetty, taking around 15 minutes each way. A K10,000 return charter should include several hours' wait while you explore the island.

Katha ꩫ꩜꩜

POP C 26,732 / ☏ 074

Literature lovers and boat bums will enjoy the small but lively Ayeyarwady port town of Katha, the setting for George Orwell's *Burmese Days*. It makes a pleasant break from the IWT ferry, and there's a rail link to Mandalay if you're fed up with going with the flow. Budget guesthouses, a couple of local restaurants and various boat ticket sales booths are close together along three short central blocks of Strand Rd, the attractive curving riverside road.

◎ Sights

In 1926 and 1927 Katha was home to British colonial police officer Eric Blair, better known by his pen name George Orwell. Much of *Burmese Days* is based on Orwell's time here, and several buildings that feature in the book are still standing. None, though, are marked as such or are commercial tourist attractions (although the Katha Hotel has a helpful brochure with key buildings identified), so ask politely before trying to barge in. The half-timbered former **British Club**, now used as an association office (and much rebuilt since Orwell's time), is tucked away 100m behind the 1924 **Tennis Club** on a street appropriately called Klablan (Club St). A block north, the 1928 **DC's House** was actually completed just after Orwell's stay, but its unmistakable style would fit McGregor. Three families now live there and Daw Wei Wei Dwin sometimes shows visitors into the original (much decayed) drawing room. Two blocks south, Orwell would have lived at the comfy, two-storey **police commissioner's house**, which is still used as such, so it's not advisable to knock on the door. Directly northwest, the Orwell-era **St Paul's Anglican Church** collapsed in 2007 and has been replaced by a new church part-sponsored by troops from the Princess of Wales's Royal Regiment in appreciation of the hospitality they received in Katha during Christmas 1944.

🛏 Sleeping

Only three places in Katha accept foreigners, including a riverfront budget guesthouse, a guesthouse-restaurant in the centre and a smart boutique hotel.

Eden Guesthouse GUESTHOUSE $
(☏ 074-25429; Shwe Phone Shein St; s/d K15,000/25,000; ❋ 🛜) This guesthouse has small air-con rooms with attached bathroom, but they are showing their age. Downstairs are a lively restaurant and beer garden, which draw a local crowd. It's close to the cluster of George Orwell–related sites.

Ayarwady Guest House GUESTHOUSE $
(☏ 074-25140; Strand Rd; r per person K9000, without bathroom K7000; ❋) This riverfront guesthouse is good value for solo travellers, offering solid air-conditioned rooms with attached bathroom. The rooms with shared bathroom are fairly primitive by comparison. The owners speaks good English and are a useful source of travel advice.

★ Hotel Katha BOUTIQUE HOTEL $$
(☏ 075-25390; www.hotelkatha.com; 4 Landamaw St; r incl breakfast US$18-43; ❃ ❋ 🛜) This classy new budget boutique hotel is the best lodging in town and is set in a building redolent of Orwell's *Burmese Days*. Rooms are well appointed with flat-screen TV, fridge and hot-water showers. The main difference between standard, superior and deluxe is the room size. Breakfast is included in the

KATHA TRANSPORT CONNECTIONS

DESTINATION	IWT FERRY	EXPRESS BOAT	TRAIN
Bhamo	deck/cabin US$5/30; 16hr; Tue, Fri & Sun 9pm	N/A	N/A
Kyaukmyaung	US$5; 12hr; Mon, Wed & Fri 5pm	N/A	N/A
Mandalay	deck/cabin US$9/45; 24-40hr depending on the season; Mon, Wed & Fri 5pm	K25,000; 14hr; 5am	K2550-6950; 12hr; 4 daily
Myitkyina (via Naba)	N/A	N/A	K1600-4900; 9hr; 4 daily
Shwegu	US$5; 6hr; Mon, Wed & Fri 5pm	N/A	N/A

attached restaurant, which has an extensive Asian menu (mains K3000 to K10,000).

Eating

Shwe Sisa
BURMESE $

(Strand Rd; mains K2000-6000; ⊙9am-10pm) For a brew with a view, try this riverside restaurant perched over the Ayeyarwady. The location makes Shwe Sisa good for a sunset beer. Also try the fresh barbecued 'Slavia' fish.

Sein Family Restaurant
CHINESE $

(Strand Rd; mains K2000-5000; ⊙7am-8pm; 🖼) Run by the descendants of Chinese immigrants, this river-facing restaurant serves consistently good Chinese fare, including sweet-and-sour dishes and steaming noodles.

ⓘ Getting There & Away

IWT ferry tickets are only available an hour before departure and can be bought from opposite the main jetty. Buy tickets for the Katha–Mandalay express boat from the office on the riverfront a day before departure. The boat leaves from the office.

The nearest train station on the Mandalay–Myitkyina line is at Naba, 16 miles west of Katha. The most convenient option is to take a three-wheeler into town, which costs about K10,000 to charter or K1000 to share. There are two afternoon buses to Naba (K1000, 2pm and 5pm). A daily train connects Naba to Katha (K200, 6.30am), returning to Naba at 3pm.

Bus travel is now permitted to and from Katha, but it is advisable to take a night bus (K10,000, 10 hours) given the long journey time.

Kyaukmyaung
ကျောက်မြောင်း

POP C 10,703 / 🖊075

The last major IWT ferry stop before Mandalay is Kyaukmyaung (pronounced 'Chaomiao'), famous for its distinctive glazed pottery. The pottery is produced in the delightful Ngwe Nyein district, a 20-minute stroll south along the riverside from central Kyaukmyaung's attractive triple-stupa, Nondo Zedi. Traffic en route is mainly a procession of ox carts carrying firewood or rice husks for pot-firing.

⊙ Sights

Pottery Workshops
WORKSHOP

The pottery district stretches a mile south of town beyond the Ayeyarwady bridge site. A block or two inland, several 'factories' are housed in bamboo-thatched barns, which

---

IRRAWADDY DOLPHINS

The Irrawaddy dolphin is one of Myanmar's most endangered animals. This small cetacean has a short, rounded snout like a beluga whale and hunts in lakes and rivers using sonar. In the past, dolphins and humans were able to coexist quite peacefully, and there are even reports of dolphins deliberately herding fish into nets, but the use of gill nets and the poisonous run-off from gold mining has driven the dolphin onto the critically endangered list. Only an estimated 50 to 75 remain in the river for which they are named. Yet sightings do still occur, and a 45-mile stretch of river south of Kyaukmyaung has been designated as a dolphin-protection zone.

---

shelter as many as 60 potters working at hand- or foot-turned wheels. Visitors are welcome to nose around and you'll also see kilns, drying yards and piles of rough clay being chopped.

Beyond Letyway Kyaunggyi monastery you'll see almost every open space filled with large amphorae waiting to be shipped on river barges. Homes, many of them old wooden affairs with distinctive portal-arches, double as shopfronts selling vases, jugs and mustard pots (from K200). While some are vivid green (notably big owl-figure vases), archetypal Kyaukmyaung designs are usually glazed a rich glossy brown that's casually daubed with swirls of beige-yellow, the latter apparently taking its colour from old batteries.

🛏 Sleeping & Eating

Kyaukmyaung has one ultra simple guesthouse (r per person K1500), but it isn't licensed for foreigners, so you're normally expected to sleep in nearby Shwebo, 18 miles west. However, the local police will usually make exceptions if your ferry arrives at a late hour. The guesthouse, unmarked in English, is down an alley just inland from the river.

Almost at the ferry jetty, the restaurant marked with a diamond graphic is run by local character Sein Win who speaks some English.

ⓘ Getting There & Away

Southbound Katha–Mandalay express boats usually arrive around 2pm, docking at a central

WORTH A TRIP

HANLIN

An almost imperceptible rise means that the attractive village of Hanlin (Halingyi, Halin, Halim) sits very slightly above the pan-flat surrounding plains. For centuries this geographical advantage was deeply significant and the site was home to a large city over 1600 years ago.

The few visitors who brave seriously rough roads to get here come to explore the area's various **archaeological remains** (ဟန်လင်းရှေးဟောင်းသုတေသနပြတိုက်). But unless you're an enthusiast, the archaeological site is a disappointment.

Luckily Hanlin village is a magical place in its own right. Unpaved ox-cart tracks link an incredible plethora of decaying old **stupas** that create the feeling of an untouched mini-Bagan. It's best appreciated when the area is viewed from behind Maung San Monastery with its obvious golden *zedi*.

Near the market is a collection of **inscribed steles** and **stone slabs** in now-forgotten Pyu script. Within the Nyaung Kobe Monastery, a **museum room** displays various ancient, but unlabelled, archaeological finds. Another minor attraction is the little **hot spring area**, where villagers collect water from circular concrete-sided well-pools and bathe in two bigger basin-pools.

Hanlin is about 12 miles southeast of Shwebo. There are two routes here. One follows the canal beside the bus station for 6 miles to Bo Tè village. From there, turn left (across the canal) on the first significant road. This soon degenerates into a bumpy ox-cart track. Fork left at the only other junction. The other, quicker route takes you south of the bus station, before turning left and travelling for 6 miles down an unsealed rocky track that leads to Site 29 and the village. Going either way by car or three-wheeler would be excruciatingly uncomfortable. It's better by motorcycle: with a driver you'll pay at least K10,000 return from Shwebo.

jetty three minutes' walk north of Nondo Zedi. IWT river ferries stop here mid-afternoon too and cost US$5 for a deck ticket to Mandalay or Katha. Pick-ups meet the boats and charge K500 for the 45-minute ride to Shwebo, where buses leave for Mandalay hourly (K2000, three hours).

Shwebo ရွှေဘို

POP C 69,036 / ☑ 075

Between 1752 and 1755, the leader of little Moksobo village, Aung Zeya, revived Burmese prestige by fighting off both Manipuri and Bago-Mon armies. Rebranding himself King Alaungpaya (or Alaungmintayagyi), his short reign transformed formerly obscure Moksobo into glittering Shwebo ('Golden Leader'), which became, until his death in 1760, the capital of a newly reunified Burma. These days, Shwebo makes relatively little of its royal history and few foreign tourists bother making a special excursion to see its reconstructed palace. However, if you're jumping off an Ayeyarwady ferry at Kyaukmyaung, Shwebo makes a pleasant enough staging point from which to reach Bagan (via Monywa and Pakokku) without returning to Mandalay. Shwebo is locally famed for snakes and *thanakha* (p303) and some visitors consider it good luck to take home some earth from 'Victory Land', as Shwebo has been known since Alaungpaya's time.

◉ Sights

Most of the sights in Shwebo are related to its prominence as a former royal capital, including the reconstructed palace and a handful of gleaming payas. Nearby Hanlin Archaeological Zone is an active excavation site in what was an important Pyu-era city from the 4th to 9th centuries.

Shwebon Yadana PALACE
(ရွှေဘုံရတနာ; admission incl Hanlin US$5; ☉ 7.30am-5pm) The city's most striking buildings are a pair of towering gold-painted wooden throne rooms, nine tiers high, once part of King Alaungpaya's 1753 palace. What you see today, though, are reconstructed, empty structures and the exhibits formerly on display are now in the National Museum in Nay Pyi Taw. Come here to pick up a ticket for Hanlin.

Shwe Daza Paya BUDDHIST TEMPLE
(ရွှေတန်ဆာဘုရား) FREE As you approach from the south, central Shwebo's skyline is

given an alluring dazzle by a collection of golden pagoda spires. These cluster around the extensive, 500-year-old Shwe Daza Paya. Close up, however, the complex feels a little anticlimactic.

Old City Moat
AREA

During its 18th-century heyday, the palace was at the heart of an enormous walled city. The walls are now almost entirely gone, but some parts of the wide **moat** are well preserved. The most attractive is the section around 2 miles north of town near **Maw Daw Myin Tha Paya**, a pagoda built by Alaungpaya and guarded by giant *chinthe* (half lion, half dragon deity).

🛏 Sleeping

Pyi Shwe Theingha Hotel
HOTEL **$**

(☏075-22949; Shwe Daza Paya St; r US$22-44; ❀❄🛜) Conveniently located opposite the bus station, this is the best hotel in town – although there's not a lot of competition. Rooms are large and comfortable if a tad musty, and include TV, fridge and hot-water bathrooms.

Sann Tinn Hotel
HOTEL **$**

(☏075-22128; Yan Gyi Aung St; r K25,000-35,000; ❄🛜) Located in the north of town on the road to Kyaukmyaung, this cheap hotel has basic but comfortable rooms with attached bathroom. K35,000 will secure a bathtub, although whether there is enough hot water to fill the bath is debatable.

🍴 Eating

Open-air food stalls set up shop around the market, especially after dusk. There's a

LOCAL KNOWLEDGE

SHWEBO THANAKHA

Wherever you go in Myanmar you'll find hawkers selling *thanakha*, the sandalwood-like logs that are ground to a paste and smeared on the skin as sunblock. Shwebo's *thanakha* is considered the country's sweetest-smelling and forms the subject of a famous folk song, so if you want a gift to delight guesthouse grandmas elsewhere in Myanmar, you won't do better. It's sold on the southern approach cloister to Shwe Daza Paya.

Shwebo

(map)

sprinkling of restaurants along Aung Zeya St, with many beer stations in the northern quarter and along Yan Gyi Aung St.

Shwe Paing
BURMESE, CHINESE **$**

(Yan Gyi Aung St; mains K1500-4000; ⊙6am-9pm) An airy, neighbourhood Chinese joint with a Burmese flavour to the generous dishes, which come with soup and salad. It's located on the main drag through town, but there is no English sign or menu.

Eden Culinary Garden
CHINESE **$**

(Aung Zeya St; dishes K2000-4000; ⊙6am-9pm; 🖉📶) The staff fall over themselves at the sight of a foreigner here, and the spacious garden setting is pleasant if a little ramshackle as its renovated and extended. The predominantly Chinese menu is fine, with some good vegetarian options. Draught Myanmar Beer is K800 a cup.

ℹ Getting There & Away

The main bus station is a mile south of the town centre with connections to Mandalay, Monywa and Kyaukmyaung. The train station is in the west of town with connections to Mandalay, Myitkyina, Naba (for Katha) and Hopin (for Indawgyi Lake).

SHWEBO TRANSPORT CONNECTIONS

DESTINATION	TRAIN	BUS	PICK-UP TRUCK
Mandalay	K800-1700; 4hr; 4 daily	K2000; 3hr; every 30min 5am-3pm	N/A
Myitkyina	K6700-13,400; 18-20hr; 4 daily	N/A	N/A
Monywa (for Bagan)	N/A	K1500; 3hr; every 30min 5am-3pm	N/A
Kyaukmyaung	N/A	K500; 45min; regular	K500; 45min; frequent until 4pm

🛈 Getting Around

A trishaw or motorbike ride from either the bus or train station to the centre costs around K1000. Hotel staff may be able to arrange informal bicycle hire.

THE FAR NORTH

Myanmar's far northern range of Himalayan 'Ice Mountains' is one of the world's least-known 'last frontiers'. **Hkakabo Razi** (19,295ft), the nation's loftiest summit, was not conquered until 1996, but that's not surprising given the trek to reach its base camp takes several weeks. The surrounding **Hkakabo Razi National Park** is considered a treasure trove of biodiversity. Landscapes here include steep forests, ridges of peaks bursting through the snowline and deep valleys carved by fast-flowing mountain rivers.

It is no longer necessary to have a permit to fly into the town of Putao, but you do require a permit for all destinations beyond the town, which means trekkers effectively need a permit to visit.

Allow ample time for organising practicalities, as securing a permit via a travel agent typically takes between 10 days and two weeks. In early 2017 Myanmar's government temporarily stopped issuing permits for travel to destinations outside of Putao; check with local travel agents for the latest situation.

Putao
ပူတာအို

POP C 15,978 / ✆ 074

Set in a beautiful green valley below snow-capped peaks, Putao is the only town of any size in this far north Himalayan region of Myanmar. It sprawls across several hills and the action gravitates around two markets: the Central Market and the Airport Market. This was the site of the isolated British WWII military outpost, Fort Hertz, but there is no actual fortress to visit.

The area around Putao is home to sparse populations of Rawang, Lisu, Kachin, Shan and the last remaining Taron on earth, the only known pygmy group in Asia. The population is heavily Christian and most villages have more churches than temples.

The best time to visit for trekking is from October to April, when daytime temperatures are quite pleasant and nights are cool. Conversely the mountaineering season for conquering Hkakabo Razi is August and September when there is minimal snow on the route to the summit.

◎ Sights

Central Market MARKET
(◷ 6am-6pm) The Central Market is a lively place to explore if you get here early when all the locals arrive from out of town. Doors open at 6am, so get here from 5.30am to see the crowds forming. It stays busy until around 8am when locals drift back to their villages. Friendly food stalls sell noodles, soups and more.

🏃 Activities

Hkakarbo Golf Club GOLF
(K2000; ◷ from 3pm) Arguably the cheapest golf course in the world, it is also one of most beautifully situated, with the mountains all around. That said, it's not the best tended, and between the cows, water buffaloes, dung and more, it's more like adventure golf. With club rental and a caddy, the total bill will come in at K10,000.

Trekking

The Putao region still feels (and genuinely is) entirely cut off from the rest of Myanmar. The main draw around Putao is trekking or mountaineering. Compared with Hsipaw or Kalaw, the trekking is pretty expensive and averages out at about US$100 to US$200 per day, depending on specific routes, group size and the level of accommodation. Although it is an expensive destination, it remains pretty exclusive, making Bhutan look like a veritable Benidorm.

Popular treks include two-day/one-night treks to nearby Lisu or Rawung villages, a four-day trek to the 'last village' and 10- to 12-day treks to conquer Phongun Razi (11,483ft), Phangram Razi (14,199ft) or Phonyin Razi (14,098ft), all mountain peaks near the Indian border. For an excellent visual impression of trekking routes in the mountains around Putao, see www.hsdejong.nl/myanmar/putao.

Even for just a two-day walk you'll probably get porters, a good cook and accommodation provided en route whether camping or in a very basic village homestay or cabin.

Most treks include some photogenic suspension footbridges and some unspoilt rural villages, although the latter aren't markedly different from similar settlements elsewhere in rural north Myanmar. Unless you trek many days further, the Himalayan horizon will remain fairly distant, and might stay hidden altogether by rain clouds.

Don't underestimate the rigour of hiking here. Even the shortest loop includes long days of fairly strenuous gradients and a high chance of leeches, and you'll need to be prepared for damp, cold weather.

Forget conquering Hkakabo Razi, Southeast Asia's tallest mountain at 19,295ft, unless you are a professional mountaineer with six weeks to spare. Two Burmese climbers disappeared on the mountain in August 2014 and a rescue helicopter crashed during the search operation.

Most trekkers come on an organised 'tour' through tour operators in Yangon. Recommended operators include the following:

Icy Myanmar TREKKING
(☏ 09 97135 2778, 09 4934 8766; japha.michael@gmail.com; trekking & whitewater-rafting day trip US$100) ✈ Run by experienced local guide Japhase, Icy Myanmar offers trekking and whitewater rafting day trips on the rivers around Putao. He also offers multiple day treks and longer whitewater rafting trips for those who want to explore in depth.

Putao Trekking House TREKKING
(www.putaotrekkinghouse.com) ✈ The original trekking operator in the far north, Putao Trekking House offers multiple day treks from its base in town. Treks include a stay in its upmarket village houses along the way or camping in tents if ascending the peaks on the Indian border.

Discovery DMC TREKKING
(☏ in Yangon 01-388330; discoverydmc.com) ✈ This Yangon-based tour operator offers a selection of original trekking itineraries around Putao and is a good choice to arrange your permit for the trekking destinations beyond Putao.

Whitewater Rafting

Putao is also home to the only whitewater rafting outfit in Myanmar. Icy Myanmar operates one-day rafting and trekking combinations for US$100 per person. The rivers are extremely beautiful and most of the rapids are grades 3 or 4, allowing you appreciate the scenery without worrying too much about flipping. Rafting trips run on the Mula Creek, the Malikha River and the Maykha River. Multiday trips are also available, although it is better to have some whitewater experience for the longer trips.

🛏 Sleeping

Only three accommodation options are available to foreigners in Putao, and they're relatively upmarket compared with lowland Myanmar. There are two guesthouses in town that currently do not accept foreigners, but are hoping to get their licence in the near future. Nights can be quite warm in summer, and power is usually available only from 6pm to 9pm. Resorts may run a generator if they have good occupancy.

★ Putao Trekking House LODGE $$
(www.putaotrekkinghouse.com; s/d incl breakfast US$110/120; ❄) The first lodge established in Putao and still the most atmospheric place to stay. Rooms are set in handsome wooden houses arranged around a meticulously tended garden. Some rooms include balcony views over the surrounding rice fields and mountain peaks. Set lunches (US$12) and dinners (US$15) are available in the welcoming restaurant.

Hotel Putao RESORT $$
(☏ 09 4711 1111; www.hotelputao.com; Putao Airport Market St; dm US$30, r US$60-80; ❄) This beautiful lodge is now exceptional value thanks to the management slashing the rates by half. Rooms are spacious – the deluxe rooms, in particular, are positively enormous. The only drawback is they are not really positioned to

take advantage of the views. The restaurant includes Thai and international dishes and very occasional live music.

Malikha Lodge
HOTEL **$$$**

(www.malikhalodge.net; r per night from US$700, packages per person from US$3000) Owned by Burmese billionaire Tay Za, this lodge is the most exclusive accommodation in the far north. The problem is that it's so exclusive, it's often impossible to secure a room if Tay Za and his buddies are in town. Bungalows are stunningly set in jungle in Mulashidi village or on the banks of the Nam Lang River.

Rooms are available on a nightly basis, but most guests are travelling on all-inclusive packages that include meals, trekking and whitewater rafting.

Eating

There are few restaurants in Putao. Two popular places share a street corner near the Central Market. The market itself is a good place for a local breakfast, against a backdrop of colourful commerce.

Tha Wan Razi
CHINESE **$**

(☑ 09 8400 186; Central Market; mains K2000-5000; ⊙ 7am-9pm; 🖾) A popular restaurant in the middle of town, this place has electricity all day via batteries. The food is predominantly Chinese with a few Burmese and Kachin dishes on the modest menu. By night it is probably the closest thing to a bar in town, and some locals and the occasional traveller gather here for cold beer.

The owners also operate a small guesthouse with the cheapest rooms in town at US$20, but were not allowed to accept foreigners at the time of writing.

Kham Su Ko
CHINESE, BURMESE **$**

(☑ 09 8401 082; Central Market; mains K1500-4500; ⊙ 7am-9pm; 🖾) Located on a corner near the Central Market, this friendly place offers Chinese and Burmese dishes throughout the day. The family also runs an attached guesthouse, but were not allowed to take foreigners at the time of writing, although it is worth checking if the situation has changed if you're on a budget.

ⓘ Getting There & Away

The only way to get in and out of Putao is to fly with Myanmar National Airlines (www.flymna.com), Golden Myanmar Airlines (www.gmair-lines.com) or Asian Wings Airways (asianwing-sair.com). There is usually at least one flight per day from Yangon and Mandalay via Myitkyina. It costs US$100 to Myitkyina, US$165 to Mandalay and US$229 to Yangon. No permit is required to fly to Putao, but you will still need a permit if you plan to do any trekking.

The road from Myitkyina to Putao is not open to foreigners.

ⓘ Getting Around

Cars and 4WDs are available for hire in Putao and are normally included in the organised tour packages offered via tour operators and trekking companies. Local transport is mainly limited to three-wheelers and these are available from the airport to the Central Market area or Putao Trekking House for K5000.

Hotel Putao has a fleet of original BMW mountain bikes available for rent for a somewhat hefty US$30 per day.

Western Myanmar

Best Places to Eat

➡ Aung (p317)

➡ Htay Htay's Kitchen (p313)

➡ Pleasant View Islet Restaurant (p312)

➡ Green Umbrella (p312)

➡ Moe Cherry (p324)

Best Places to Sleep

➡ Ngapali Bay Villas & Spa (p311)

➡ Yoma Cherry Lodge (p310)

➡ Bayview Beach Resort (p311)

➡ Nawarat Hotel (p324)

➡ Hotel Memory (p317)

Why Go?

Remote, rugged and rewarding, Myanmar's westernmost states – Rakhine (also known as Arakan) and Chin – remain staunchly untouristed.

Those travellers who make it to Rakhine State tend to confine themselves to the pristine sand and turquoise waters of Ngapali Beach on the Bay of Bengal: Myanmar's premier beach destination. Far fewer venture further north to the old Rakhine capital of Mrauk U, an amazing archaeological site studded with hundreds of temples, and the current capital, scrappy Sittwe.

But if you really want to get off the grid, then head to largely unknown and undeveloped Chin State, where breathtaking mountains, forests and traditional villages await. The south of Chin is already seeing a tentative increase in visitors, drawn by treks to and around Mt Victoria. But the perhaps more stunning hills in the north of the state – close to Myanmar's border with India – still see only a handful of foreigners a year.

When to Go
Western Myanmar

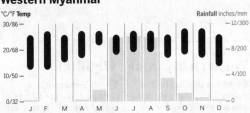

Nov–Mar Many of Ngapali Beach's hotels are only open during the high season.

Mid-May–mid-Oct Monsoon season in both Rakhine and Chin states.

Mid-Dec Rakhine State Day, in Sittwe and Mrauk U, is one of the region's biggest celebrations.

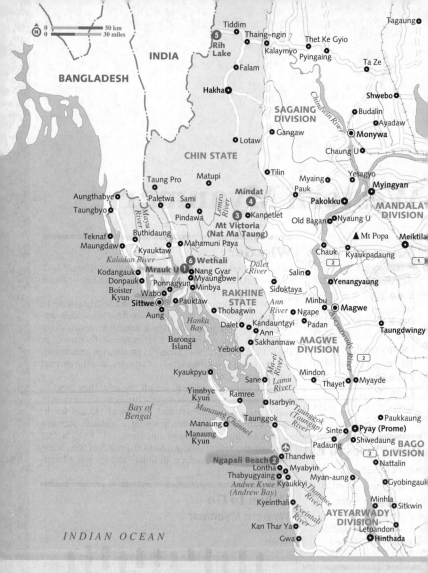

Western Myanmar Highlights

❶ Mrauk U (p318) Drifting around the hundreds of ruined temples and fortifications in the former grand capital of Rakhine State.

❷ Ngapali Beach (p309) Savouring the seafood, sand and sunsets at Myanmar's most sophisticated beach destination.

❸ Mt Victoria (p326) Climbing Myanmar's third-highest mountain in southern Chin State.

❹ Mindat (p327) Striking out for treks through timeless Chin villages from this hilltop town.

❺ Rih Lake (p331) Getting way off the map at this heart-shaped lake on the Myanmar–India border.

❻ Wethali (p325) Taking in both the emerald-green Rakhine countryside and the state's ancient history on a half-day trip here from Mrauk U.

RAKHINE STATE

The interchangeable terms Rakhine (sometimes spelled Rakhaing) and Arakan refer to the people, the state and dialect of Myanmar's westernmost state. Isolated from the Burmese heartland by mountains, home to a long coastline and the seat of at least four former kingdoms, Rakhine feels very different from the rest of Myanmar and the Rakhine remain staunchly proud of their unique identity. This has led to much strife over the centuries between both the Rakhine and the Bamar and the minority Muslim residents of the state, known in the west as the Rohingya. Serious sectarian violence between the Rakhine and the Rohingya erupted in 2012, while there were further clashes in 2016 near the closed border with Bangladesh.

For visitors, Rakhine offers two contrasting experiences: the remarkable temples of the ancient capital Mrauk U in the north of the state and the palm tree-fringed beach resort of Ngapali in the south of Rakhine.

History

Even today there remains a debate over whether the Rakhine are actually Bamar with Indian blood, Indians with Bamar characteristics or a separate race (as is sometimes claimed locally). Although the first inhabitants of the region were a dark-skinned Negrito tribe known as the Bilu, later migrants from the eastern Indian subcontinent developed the first Hindu-Buddhist kingdoms in Myanmar before the first Christian millennium. These kingdoms flourished before the invasion of the Tibeto-Burmans from the north and east in the 9th and 18th centuries. The current inhabitants of the state may thus be mixed descendants of all three groups: Bilu, Bengali and Burmese.

Regardless, Rakhine's historical roots are linked to those of northern India, which held political and cultural sway over the region for centuries before the land fell under Bagan's dominance during Western medieval times. In 1430 the local king Naramithla returned after three decades in exile in the Bengali city of Guar to establish a new capital at Mrauk U from where Rakhine was ruled for the next 400 years. When the British annexed the state in 1826, the capital was moved to Sittwe.

In 2012 sectarian riots in Sittwe led to the expulsion of that city's Muslim community (known in the Western press as the Rohingya). The unrest was seen as at least partially responsible for sparking widespread anti-Muslim sentiment across Myanmar. At the time of writing, around 100,000 Rohingya remain confined to squalid 'resettlement' camps across Rakhine State.

Ngapali Beach ငပလီကမ်းခြေ

♪ 043

With its pristine, palm-tree-fringed white sand, the clear waters of the Bay of Bengal, and a host of sophisticated accommodation, Ngapali – supposedly named years ago by a homesick Italian reminiscing about Napoli – has a justified reputation as Myanmar's premier beach getaway.

But for all the swish resorts, Ngapali maintains a laid-back fishing village vibe, as evidenced by the small boats that head out nightly to catch the bounty that is served up to visitors just hours later. The locals remain smiley, and despite the increasing number of hotels, the 15 miles of coast here means there's still a lot of space on the beach.

Peak season is from November to March. Even then, Ngapali is an early-to-bed place rather than a rip-roaring beach-party destination. During the rainy season (May to October), things are almost comatose, with many hotels closing for renovations or just opening a few rooms.

⊙ Sights & Activities

South of the hotels, and easily reached barefoot by the beach, is the rustic fishing village of **Gyeik Taw**, where small fish dry on bamboo mats across the beach. Even further south is the bigger village of **Lontha** and an inlet of the same name, backed by a sweeping curve of mangrove and sand facing south.

On a bayside hill east of Lontha is a modest white **stupa**. It's worth seeing for its glorious panoramic views – and for the adventure to reach it. To get there, turn left at the town junction (near the market). The road runs parallel to the boat-filled bay and quickly degenerates into a path too sandy to ride on; if you're on a bike, leave it with a local. About five minutes or so after passing a small bridge, you reach the hill steps to the stupa.

Four-hour snorkelling trips, arranged by any hotel or directly with boat owners on the beach, usually depart at 7am or 8am to catch the day's clearest water. Most trips take in a few spots around (private) 'Pearl Island' off the south end of the beach. The coral isn't

Ngapali Beach

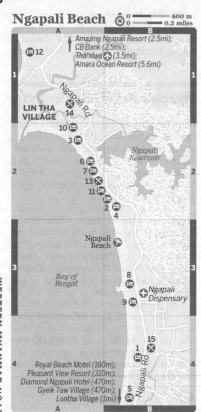

Ngapali Beach N 0 — 400 m / 0 — 0.2 miles

Amazing Ngapali Resort (2.5mi);
CB Bank (2.5mi);
Thandwe (3.5mi);
Amara Ocean Resort (5.6mi)

LIN THA VILLAGE

Ngapali Rd

Ngapali Reservoir

Ngapali Beach

Bay of Bengal

Ngapali Dispensary

Royal Beach Motel (160m);
Pleasant View Resort (310m);
Diamond Ngapali Hotel (470m);
Gyeik Taw Village (470m);
Lontha Village (1mi)

vember to March). All hotels include free airport transfer.

★ Yoma Cherry Lodge HOTEL $$

(☎043-42339; www.yomacherrylodge.com; off Ngapali Rd; r incl breakfast US$115-140; ❄️🖥🛜) Just north of Lin Tha Village, this excellent-value boutique place has handsome, Burmese-influenced, thatched-roof structures set around a well-tended garden. Rooms are very comfortable and big, with equally spacious balconies and attractive furniture. It has a beach side restaurant and bar too. Book well in advance.

Laguna Lodge HOTEL $$

(☎043-42312, in Yangon 01-501 123; www.lagunalodge-myanmar.com; Ngapali Rd; r incl breakfast US$60-80; 🛜) A rare 'budget' option in Ngapali, but on a prime strip of the beach, the laid-back Laguna goes rustic with its simple but spacious rooms with open-shuttered windows and huge balconies. Mosquito nets hang over the big beds and a giant circular window in the bathrooms offers views through the room to the beach. All rooms are fan-only.

Royal Beach Motel HOTEL $$

(☎043-42411, in Yangon 01-393 458; www.royalbeachngapali.com; Ngapali Rd; r incl breakfast US$80-115; ❄️🖥🛜) More personable than the other midrange places, Royal Beach boasts

---

super, but there are plenty of bright red and blue fish to follow. Some people bring along fishing rods to drop a line.

Ngapali Concierge ADVENTURE SPORTS

(☎09 42173 1079; www.ngapaliconcierge.com) Run by the ebullient Gunter, a Costa Rican married to a local woman, Ngapali Concierge offers treks (from US$30 per person per day) and mountain bike tours (from US$49 per person per day) of the surrounding area, as well as rafting and sea-kayaking trips.

🛏 Sleeping

Hotels straggle north to south along Ngapali Beach, with the main road through the area running parallel to the beach, which is best at the southern end. At the northern end, the beach narrows and is more rocky, although it's still pleasant.

Plan ahead, as some places book up months in advance of high season (from No-an almost village-like atmosphere. The 22 rooms are decent-sized and many sport huge balconies. While it's a good strip of beach here, the rooms are plain, a little old-fashioned and lack TVs. Only six of the rooms have sea views; the rest look out on a garden.

Memento Resort
HOTEL $$

(☑ 043-42441; ngapalimementoresort@gmail. com; Ngapali Rd; r incl breakfast US$45-90; ❄ ☎ ☏) Budget by Ngapali standards, the beach-front rooms at this long-standing place aren't sexy or new, but they are spacious and are located steps from a rocky and scenic strip of beach. The cheapest rooms lack both sea views and air-con.

Lin Thar Oo Lodge
HOTEL $$

(☑ 043-42426, in Yangon 01-861 0279; www.linthar oo-ngapali.com; Ngapali Rd; r incl breakfast US$90-110; ❄ ☎) There's a mix of older, garden-view rooms and newer seafront bungalows at this midrange place. The rooms are big enough and the bathrooms OK, but you're paying for the location right on the beach.

Silver Beach Hotel
HOTEL $$

(☑ 043-42652, in Yangon 01-381 898; Ngapali Rd; r incl breakfast US$123-213; ❄ ☎) At the north-ern end of the beach, Silver Beach features prim, red-roofed duplex cottages that con-jure up the look of a 1950s British holiday camp, with dated furnishings to match.

★ Ngapali Bay Villas & Spa
RESORT $$$

(☑ 043-42301, in Yangon 01-230 0932; www. ngapalibay.com; villas incl breakfast US$285-565; ❄ ☎ ☏) Our favourite of the high-end re-sorts in Ngapali, and one of the most luxu-rious hotels anywhere in Myanmar. The 32 huge sea-view villas here feature stunning high arched ceilings and are decorated with real style in dark wood. Sixteen of the villas have their own plunge pools too, while the restaurant and spa are highly rated.

Aureum Palace
RESORT $$$

(☑ 043-42412, in Yangon 01-399 341; www.aureum palacehotel.com; Ngapali Rd; bungalows incl break-fast US$220-550; ❄ @ ☎ ☏) How's this for decadent: 42 free-standing bungalow suites interspersed throughout a jungly, isolated-feeling compound, and equipped with hand-some wood and stone furnishings and private Jacuzzi. The only thing more ostentatious is the hotel's single 'Executive Room', complete with its own private pool.

Jade Marina Resort
RESORT $$$

(☑ 043-42430, in Yangon 01-660 112; www.jade marinaresort.com; r incl breakfast US$180-350; ❄ ☎ ☏) This place has 56 rooms, 20 of them substantial two-storey affairs, but all sizea-ble and set around a very pleasant garden that sits behind a good strip of sand.

Amazing Ngapali Resort
RESORT $$$

(☑ 043-42011, in Yangon 01-203 500; www. amazing-hotel.com; r incl breakfast US$180-468; ❄ ☎ ☏) The spacious and well-equipped rooms and 49 villas all come with balconies and many have sea views. The only let-down are the beds, which are rather small and hard for a place of this quality. The resort is close to Ngapali village and the airport, but away from the majority of restaurants further south.

Bayview Beach Resort
RESORT $$$

(☑ 043-42299, in Yangon 01-504 471; www.bay view-myanmar.com; Ngapali Rd; r incl breakfast US$180-220; ❄ ☎ ☏) One of the more af-fordable top-end options in Ngapali, the Bayview occupies a nice strip of beach. The 45 'bungalows' are actually linked rooms that are very comfortable without being super-flash and come with semi-outdoor shower, lots of space, and lounge chairs on the private deck. Guests can rent out wind-surfers, kayaks and catamarans (US$5 to US$20 per hour).

Amara Ocean Resort
RESORT $$$

(☑ in Yangon 01-721 869; www.amaragroup.net; bungalows incl breakfast US$290-400; ❄ @ ☎ ☏) Fancy 3 miles of almost entirely undevel-oped white-sand beach? If you can afford one of the 26 beautiful teak villas at this re-sort north of the airport, then it's all yours. Rooms are steps from the beach, although it is not as good for swimming here as it is further south, and all have sea views.

Sandoway Resort
RESORT $$$

(☑ 043-42233, in Yangon 01-294 612; www. sandowayresort.com; Ngapali Rd; r & bungalows incl breakfast US$190-410; ❄ @ ☎ ☏) Along with palm-shaded walkways leading past well-tended gardens and ponds, the high-light at this Italian-Myanmar joint venture is the free-standing two-storey 'villas' and 'cottages', which feature lofty ceilings and appealing craft details. You get no TV, but there's a massive communal screening room for movies, comfortably set out with padded armchairs for nightly screenings.

Amata Resort & Spa · RESORT $$$

(☑043-42177, in Yangon 01-665 126; www.amata resort.com; r incl breakfast US$200-230, bunga-lows US$320-440; ✽@🛜☒) This complex of two-storey cabanas and rooms (request rooms 701 and 702 for their brilliant beach views), set back from the beach in lush gardens, is one of Ngapali's most stylish resorts. The eponymous spa is highly rated and the staff are pleasant and professional.

Diamond Ngapali Hotel · RESORT $$$

(☑043-42089, in Yangon 01-502 894; www.dia mondngapali.com; Ngapali Rd; r incl breakfast US$90-180; ✽🛜☒) Located at the far southern end of Ngapali's main beach, the 24 spacious, pebble-dash bungalows here come with simple furnishings and alternate between pool and sea views.

Pleasant View Resort · RESORT $$$

(☑043-42251, in Yangon 01-393 086; www.pvrnga pali.com; Ngapali Rd; r & bungalows incl breakfast US$130-220; ✽🛜☒) Being expanded at the time of research, the Pleasant View has an attractive location at the far southern end of the beach. Accommodation ranges from free-standing and duplex bungalows to rooms in a two-storey structure, all of which are simply decorated but spacious.

Thande Beach Hotel · RESORT $$$

(☑043-42278, Yangon 01-546 225; www.thande beachhotelmyanmar.com; Ngapali Rd; r incl breakfast US$110-250; ✽🛜☒) The least stylish of the upmarket resorts, the Thande is nevertheless a pleasant place to bunk, offering duplex bungalows and rooms in a two-storey building surrounded by gardens, all located in a handy mid-beach location.

✖ Eating & Drinking

Restaurants line the main road through Ngapali, with a dozen and more places offering similar menus at similar prices. This is probably the best place in Myanmar for fresh seafood, while all the restaurants offer a few Rakhine specialities.

There's also a strip of sand-in-your-toes-type beach restaurants between Memento Resort and Thande Beach Hotel, which have near-identical menus to the restaurants on the main road.

Zaw-II · BURMESE $$

(Ngapali Rd; mains from K5000; ⊙9am-9pm; 🖾) Popular with the locals, the Rakhine food here comes with a kick, but the spices can be toned down if you ask. Also does good grilled seafood, as well as curries and salads.

Green Umbrella · BURMESE $$

(mains from K3500; ⊙10am-10pm; 🖾) The pick of the beach restaurants, this long-established and reliable place offers super-fresh seafood and curries, and you can gaze out on the Bay of Bengal while eating.

Pleasant View Islet Restaurant · SEAFOOD $$

(Pleasant View Resort, Ngapali Rd; mains from K5000; ⊙9am-10pm; 🖾) Set on a rocky islet at the beach's southern end (you may have to wade through knee-deep surf to get to it, or catch the free boat service at high tide), this stylish eatery serves Western-influenced seafood dishes at a better price than most hotel restaurants. It's also perfect for sunset cocktails.

Catch · INTERNATIONAL $$

(Bayview Beach Resort, Ngapali Rd; mains US$8-25; ⊙7am-11pm) The restaurant of the Bayview Beach Resort (p311) is located away from the

---

OFF THE BEATEN TRACK

THANDWE

Located about 4 miles inland from the northern end of Ngapali Beach, **Thandwe** (သံတွဲ) and its low-key streets occupy a valley. It's been a key Rakhine town for many centuries. When the British stationed a garrison here around the turn of the 20th century – the former colonial jail is today Thandwe's central **market** (သံတွဲဈေး; ⊙6am-4pm) – they twisted the name into Sandoway.

While not an essential destination, Thandwe makes for an interesting visit if you fancy a change of scene from the beach.

Three golden stupas stand on hilltops around Thandwe, each offering excellent view-points of the town's tin roofs peeking out of a sea of palms and hills. The tallest is **Nandaw Paya** (နန်းတော်ဘုရား; ⊙daylight hours) FREE, followed by **Sandaw Paya** (ဆံတော်ဘုရား; ⊙daylight hours) FREE and **Andaw Paya** (အံ့တော်ဘုရား; ⊙daylight hours) FREE.

Frequent pick-up trucks to/from Ngapali run from 6am to 6pm (K500).

beach, but everyone eats from the Catch's menu by dining at Sunset Bar, which *is* by the beach. It's good for fillets of barracuda, burgers and pizzas.

Htay Htay's Kitchen BURMESE $$
(Ngapali Rd; mains from K4000; ⊙7am-10pm; 🖭) At the northern end of the beach in Lin Tha Village, this attractive restaurant is run by a friendly couple. Expect tasty, if gentrified, Rakhine soups (if you want your food local-style – ie spicy – just ask), as well as decent curries and salads.

Sandoway Resort Restaurant ASIAN, EUROPEAN $$$
(Sandoway Resort, Ngapali Rd; mains US$9-48; ⊙7am-10pm; 🖭) An elegant place to dine by the beach, with one of the more creative menus among the big resort restaurants. The Italian co-owners ensure that the pasta is made *al dente* and you can also dip into local dishes, such as *laphet thoke* (tea-leaf salad).

Sunset Bar BAR
(Ngapali Rd; ⊙6am-11pm; 🖭) As the name suggests, this is a fine place for a drink while watching the sun sink into the Bay of Bengal. The cocktails and beers are reasonably priced (happy hour is from 6pm to 7pm), and you sit overlooking a wide strip of sand. It's inside the Bayview Beach Resort (p311).

ℹ Information

There are ATM's that take foreign cards outside many of the hotels, as well as a branch of **CB Bank** (Ngapali village; ⊙9.30am-3pm), which changes money, close to the Amazing Ngapali Resort (p311). There is also a **KBZ Bank** (Thandwe Market; ⊙9.30am-3pm) in Thandwe that changes money and has an ATM.

All hotels offer wi-fi, although connections can be patchy in the rainy season.

ℹ Getting There & Away

AIR

Thandwe airport is named for the town 4 miles inland, but is closer to Ngapali village and the north end of the beach. The hotels meet all flights and offer free transport to/from the airport.

Asian Wings (🗹043-42037, in Yangon 01-515 259; www.asianwingsair.com; 112 Ngapali Rd), **Air Bagan** (🗹in Yangon 01-513 322, 043-42429; www.airbagan.com; 407 Ngapali Rd), **Air KBZ** (🗹in Yangon 01-373 787; www.airkbz.com), **Air Mandalay** (🗹in Yangon 01-501 520, 043-42404; www.airmandalay.com) and **Yangon Airways** (🗹in Yangon 01-383 100; www.yangonair.com) serve Yangon (from US$111,

55 minutes to 2¼ hours, daily), sometimes via Sittwe (from US$72, 45 minutes, daily). There are fewer flights in the rainy season (May to October), but Myanmar National Airlines (www.flymna.com) keeps flying daily.

BOAT

Taunggok, 50 miles or so north of Thandwe, is the jumping-off point for travellers catching boats to Sittwe. Carriers include **Shwe Pyi Tan** (🗹in Sittwe 043-65130, in Taunggok 043-60704) with departures at 6.30am on Tuesday, Friday and Sunday (US$35, 10 to 11 hours); and **Malikha Travels** (🗹in Taunggok 043-60127), leaving at 6.30am on Wednesday and Saturday (US$30, 10 to 11 hours). The boats don't always run in the rainy season (May to October).

There are daily buses to Taunggok from Thandwe's bus station (K4000, three to four hours, 1pm).

BUS

There are daily air-con buses to Yangon (K15,000, 11 to 12 hours, 7am and 3pm) via Gwa, as well as a daily bus to Yangon via Pyay (K15,000, 13 hours, 1pm). For Mandalay, take the Yangon bus via Pyay and change buses in Pyay (K15,000, nine hours, 1pm). There's also a daily bus from Thandwe to Sittwe (K18,000, 18 hours, noon). Buy tickets at **Aung Thit Sar** (🗹043-65363) in Lon Tha village, or from your hotel. The bus will pick you up from your accommodation.

Kan Thar Ya Beach
ကမ်းသာယာ ကမ်းခြေ

If Ngapali's ever-expanding resort scene is too slick for you, try Kan Thar Ya, a far less developed beach area 64 miles south. The sand isn't as fine as Ngapali's, although it's still pretty good and fringed by palm trees, while the location between the mouths of two rivers means the water isn't always clear. But if you don't like seeing anyone else on the beach, then this is the place for you. There are other untouched beaches nearby too. This is still mostly virgin territory for foreigners, so don't expect much in the way of comfort or facilities.

🛏 Sleeping

For now, there are only a couple of very basic guesthouses approved to take foreigners; they're both in or near the town of Gwa, approximately 15 miles south of Kan Thar Ya. Further north, about 30 minutes' drive past Kan Thar Ya, is a new and better option.

Yaewaddy Motel   MOTEL $
(☑ in Yangon 01-642 740; www.yaewaddymotel.com; Zee Gone village; r incl breakfast US$35; ❋)
It isn't in Kan Thar Ya, but this new place is about 30 minutes' drive north of the beach on its own strip of OK sand. Rooms are in concrete bungalows and come with air-con and TVs. You'll have to make your own way here from Gwa by car or motorbike.

Sakawar Guest House & Restaurant   GUESTHOUSE $
(☑ 09 4966 6029; Main Rd; r US$10-15) Closer to the beach than the other guesthouse licensed for foreigners in the area, the Sakawar has basic fan-only rooms and a shared bathroom. It does have a restaurant, though.

❶ Getting There & Around

To reach Kan Thar Ya, hop on one of the two daily buses that run from Thandwe to Yangon via Gwa, and get off in Gwa (K15,000, five hours, 7am and 3pm). You'll have to pay the full fare to Yangon. From Gwa, motorcycle taxis charge K10,000 to K15,000 for return trips to Kan Thar Ya Beach.

Sittwe (Aykab)   စစ်တွေ

POP C 100,748 / ☑ 043

Rakhine State's capital, Sittwe (still known sometimes by its former name Aykab), sits in an incredible spot where the wide, tidal Kaladan River kisses the big fat Bay of Bengal. It's a historic place, although there's little of that past still around or accessible. There are some lively markets, and when the new port is finished, an economic boom might liven things up, but for now there's little of real interest here. The impact of sectarian violence in 2012, along with the town's generally scrappy vibe, means that most visitors approach the city as little more than a transit point to the ruins at Mrauk U.

History

Sittwe was little more than a village prior to the Burmese invasion of the Mrauk U kingdom in 1784. Fifty years later, Sittwe's economy underwent a boom when British forces took over during the First Anglo–Burmese War. The British moved the state capital here from Mrauk U and named the place Akyab after the nearby Akyattaw Ridge.

Incoming wealth from trade with Calcutta fuelled the construction of some fine colonial mansions, but Sittwe suffered badly during heavy WWII fighting between the British and Japanese forces.

Today, the town's economy is set to benefit from the new harbour – a joint venture between Myanmar and India – being constructed (and obscuring views of the Kaladan River from parts of Strand Rd) next to the municipal market.

The sectarian violence that erupted in Sittwe in 2012 has had a huge impact, effectively turning the city into an overwhelmingly Rakhine and Buddhist town overnight. With most of the Muslim Rohingya former residents confined to 'resettlement' camps outside the city, Sittwe's once vibrant Muslim quarter is virtually empty and strictly off-limits and, like the town's oldest mosque, protected by armed guards.

◉ Sights

Most of Sittwe's action runs along the Main Rd, which parallels the Kaladan River. Along this route, don't miss the **Fruit Bat Trees** (Main Rd), where during the day hundreds of noisy fruit bats fight with equally noisy crows before heading off at dusk – there's a great view of their migration from the roof of the Shwe Thazin Hotel (p317).

Central Market   MARKET
(မြို့ ဈေး; Strand Rd; ⊘ 6am-6pm) Focused on the 1956 municipal market building, there's lots going on here from dawn up to noon and beyond – it's well worth popping by before your boat or plane leaves. Head straight past *longyi* (sarong-style garment), fishing-net and vegetable stands to the fish and meat area, where stingrays, gutted eels and drying sharks make quite a scene. In the bay small boats jostle for space to unload their catch.

Shwezedi Kyaung   BUDDHIST TEMPLE
(ရွှေစေတီ ကျောင်း; U Ottama St; ⊘ daylight hours) Partly housed in a picturesque, ramshackle colonial-era building on a back street, this was the monastery of U Ashin Ottama (1880–1939), a leader of the Burmese independence movement during British colonial rule, who died while imprisoned for his political activities. In September 2007, monks at this monastery followed in his footsteps

and took part in the protest marches then happening across the country. More recently the monastery served as a shelter for those displaced by the anti-Muslim riots in 2012.

View Point   LANDMARK
(စစ်တွေျမူးဝိုင်; Strand Rd) **FREE** Strand Rd leads about 1.5 miles south to a location called View Point, where you can watch the sun set over **Sittwe Beach**, a broad brown strip of sand, and the Bay of Bengal. The site has been undergoing redevelopment for over a year now, but there are still no restaurants here (although there is a handsome sculpture of two Rakhine wrestlers). That may change in the future.

Thoun bein (motorised trishaws) will take you there and back for K5000 and taxis for K10,000.

Lokananda Paya   BUDDHIST TEMPLE
(လောကနန္ဒာဘုရား; May Yu St; ⊙ daylight hours) You can't miss this big golden pagoda between the airport and the centre. Its cavernous gilded worship hall, held aloft by decorated pillars, is pretty spectacular.

On the west side of the compound is a small ordination hall, which houses the intriguing Sachamuni Image, a bronze buddha with its surface entirely encrusted with mini-buddhas. Apparently the image dates from 24 BC and is said to have been found by Mrauk U fishermen.

Jama Mosque   MOSQUE
(ဂျမားဝလီ; Main Rd) This impressive 1859 building – the oldest mosque in Sittwe – could have been lifted out of the pages of *Arabian Nights*. Sadly, since the 2012 sectarian riots, it's been strictly off-limits, with barbed wire and armed guards preventing access, and has fallen into a state of disrepair. But its impressive white minarets still poke above the trees and the wall that surrounds it.

Rice Market   MARKET
(ဆန်ဈေး; ⊙ 6am-6pm) A few blocks north of the main market is the Rice Market, with tiny lanes between the Kaladan River and Strand Rd filled with simple wood homes, where traders hawk brown and sticky rice – some bound for Bangladesh.

Maka Kuthala Kyaungdawgyi   MUSEUM
(မဟာကုသလကျောင်းတော်ကြီး; Main Rd; ⊙ 6am-7pm) **FREE** Monk U Bhaddanta Wannita spent 49 years collecting old coins and buddha images from monasteries to protect them from thieves. Some of his collection is displayed in his former monastery, which is housed in a grand, century-old British colonial mansion just north of the centre. The dusty, eclectic museum contains cases of old banknotes, buddhas, votives (candleholders) and coins from the Mrauk U and other ancient periods, plus many bone relics of head monks, kept in small tins.

Rakhine State Cultural Museum   MUSEUM
(ရခိုင်ပြည်နယ်ယဉ်ကျေးမှုပြတိုက်; Main Rd; K5000; ⊙ 9.30am-4.30pm Tue-Sun) This museum features two floors of dusty Rakhine cultural goodies. On the 1st floor are displays on local customs such as models showing off some of the 64 traditional Mrauk U royal hairstyles, and drawings illustrating key moves you may need for Rakhine wrestling. The 2nd floor features diagrams and artefacts that detail Rakhine's origins (around 3000 BC) and four key periods (Dhanyawadi, Vesali, Lemro and Mrauk U), complete with useful renderings and models.

🛏 Sleeping

Hotels in Sittwe aren't great value, although there is an increasing number of sleeping options. Almost all places are on or off Main Rd.

Yuzana Aung Guest House   GUESTHOUSE $
(☎ 043-24275; Nga Pain St; r incl breakfast US$25-35; ❋ ☎) This new guesthouse spread over four floors is the best budget option in Sittwe. Rooms are compact, but they are light, clean and well equipped and come with comfortable beds. The staff are keen and there are good sunset views from the roof terrace.

Kiss Guest House   GUESTHOUSE $
(☎ 09 45116 5896; kissguesthouse@gmail.com; 145 Main Rd; r US$20; ❋ ☎) The small rooms, and even smaller bathrooms, are in reasonable condition and are clean enough to make this an adequate crash pad for an overnight stay.

Motel Shwe Myint Mho   HOTEL $
(☎ 09 77979 9533; shwemyintmho2014@gmail.com; 56 Main Rd; r US$25; ❋ ☎) Tight and plain rooms with smaller bathrooms, but they are clean and OK for an overnight pit stop. No breakfast here.

Mya Guest House   HOTEL $
(☎ 09 45307 2866; 51/6 Bowdhi Rd; r US$25-35; ❋) Foreigners are now directed to a newer block of spacious rooms that have hot water

Sittwe (Aykab)

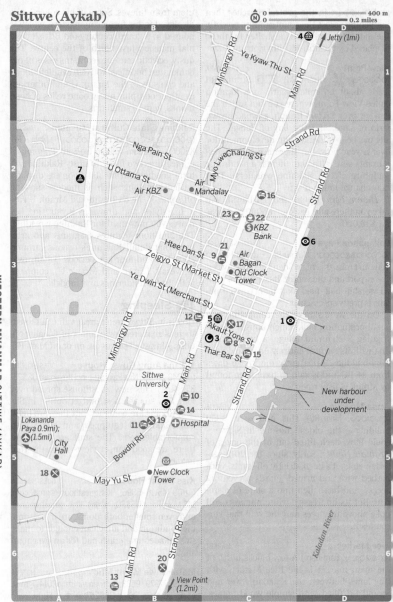

and air-con, but no wi-fi. Acceptable for a short-term stay. It's just off Sittwe's Main Rd.

Strand Hotel   HOTEL $$
(☏043-22881; strandhotelsittwe@gmail.com; 9 Strand Rd; r incl breakfast US$45-95; ❈ 🛜) It's

not as flash as its namesake hotel in Yangon, but the 21 rooms here are modern, decent-sized and comfortable, although some bathrooms can be a little musty, so check them first. Helpful English-speaking staff and a reasonable breakfast. Despite its loca-

Sittwe (Aykab)

tion on Strand Rd, there are no river views here: the new port gets in the way.

Hotel Memory   HOTEL $$
(☎ 043-21794; www.hotelmemorysittwe.com; 19 Akaut Yone St; r incl breakfast US$55-80; ☀❄🛜) Standard rooms here aren't big – something of a Sittwe theme – but they are modern and well equipped and the bathrooms are a cut above the local competition. The professional staff can book onward tickets and the restaurant does OK Rakhine and Chinese-Burmese dishes.

Royal Sittwe Resort   RESORT $$
(☎ in Yangon 01-393 458, 043-23478; www.royalsittweresort.asia; r incl breakfast US$80-115; ❄🛜⛱) The pool was half-full of dirty green water, and the rooms old-fashioned, worn, and overpriced. But they are the only ones in town that can boast a beach view. Popular with aid workers who have drivers, which you'll need as it's 1.5 miles south of town.

Shwe Thazin Hotel   HOTEL $$
(☎ 043-22314; www.shwethazinhotel.com; 250 Main Rd; r incl breakfast US$45-60; ❄🛜) The rooms here are clean but old-fashioned, despite a seemingly never-ending refit to this long-standing place (it now has a lift). The bathrooms are OK, but the rooms are generally overpriced. The staff can book bus, boat and plane tickets.

Noble Hotel   HOTEL $$
(☎ 043-23558; anw.noble@gmail.com; 92 Main Rd; r incl breakfast US$40-53; ❄🛜) The rooms here are small, but they are comfortable and come with desk, satellite TV, safe and fridge. It's often booked out, so reserve ahead.

✖ Eating

★ **Aung**   BURMESE $
(off Ye Dwin St; curries from K3000; ⏰10am-9pm; 🍴) Located on a small street directly behind the museum, this popular, friendly place does Burmese-style set meals with an emphasis on Rakhine-style spice and tartness. You could work from the English-language menu, but pointing to whatever looks tastiest is an equally good strategy. The fish curries are ace, but you can skip the bear curry.

Móun·di Stand   BURMESE $
(May Yu St; mains K300; ⏰6am-6pm) *Móun·di*, thin rice noodles in a peppery, fish-based broth, is Rakhine State's signature noodle dish. Sittwe's best – many claim – is served at this stall (look for the green awning) facing the city hall.

Mya Teahouse   TEAHOUSE $
(51/6 Bowdhi Rd; tea/snacks from K300; ⏰6am-5pm) Sit under shady trees amid the potted plants and flowers at this pleasant teahouse. Good for a breakfast of fried rice, or *mohinga*, a fish-flavoured noodle soup (K600).

River Valley Seafoods Restaurant   CHINESE, BURMESE $$
(☎ 043-23234; www.rivervalleyrestaurantsittwe.com; Strand Rd; mains from K5000; ⏰9am-10pm; 🍴) Popular among foreign visitors and the local gentry, Sittwe's fanciest restaurant has a prime location on Strand Rd facing the river. There's a big garden lit up at night to eat in and the menu is reasonably priced with many seafood options. There's a less atmospheric branch on Main Rd, close to Shwe Thazin Hotel.

DAY TRIPS FROM SITTWE

Have a day to spare? Consider taking one of the following boat trips. The most potentially interesting is to the weaving village **Wabo**, a 90-minute boat ride from Sittwe, where you can see Rakhine-style *longyi* (sarong-style garments) being made; the Rakhine are known in Myanmar as skilled weavers who can produce intricate designs in their cloths. The other boat trip is to hilly **Baronga Island**, across the wide Kaladan River, to see a typical fishing village. Boat hire to either will run about K100,000, and you'll also need a guide: try the recommended Naing Naing or ask at your hotel for one (K30,000 per day).

ⓘ Information

KBZ Bank (Main Rd; ⏱9.30am-3pm Mon-Fri) Bank offering foreign exchange and an ATM. There are other ATMs that take foreign cards on Main Rd.

May Flower Travels & Tours (Main Rd; ⏱9am-5.30pm) Can book air tickets.

ⓘ Getting There & Away

Foreigners are now allowed to travel overland to and from Sittwe.

AIR

Sittwe's airport is about 1.5 miles west of the centre. *Thoun bein* (K3000 to K4000) and motorcycle taxis (K2000) await flights.

Air KBZ (☎ in Yangon 01-373 787, 043-22779; www.airkbz.com; U Ottama St; ⏱8am-5pm), **Air Mandalay** (☎ in Yangon 01-501 520, 043-21638; www.airmandalay.com; U Ottama St; ⏱8am-6pm), **Air Bagan** (☎in Yangon 01-513 322, 09 852 2256; www.airbagan.com; Htee Dan St; ⏱9am-5pm) and Myanmar National Airlines (www.flymna.com) connect Sittwe with Yangon (from US$91, 1¼ hours) and Thandwe (from US$72, 45 minutes). There are fewer flights in the rainy season (May to October).

BUS

Sittwe's bus station is about 3 miles northwest of the centre. A *thoun bein* will cost K4000, and a motorcycle taxi K2500.

There are daily buses to Mrauk U (K4000, 3½ hours, 6.30am and noon), Yangon (K20,500, 28 hours, 6am) and Mandalay (K25,300, 24 hours, 6am).

BOAT

Sittwe's jetty is 1 mile north of town, a K2000 ride in a *thoun bein*.

To Mrauk U

To reach Mrauk U by boat there a few options.

The slowest is the double-decker boats run by the government's **Inland Water Transport** (IWT; ☎ 043-23382). There's an office west of Sittwe's jetty, though there's no need to buy tickets in advance. Ferries depart Sittwe Tuesday and Friday at 8am, and return from Mrauk U on Wednesday and Saturday at 8am (US$7, four to seven hours).

Slightly faster is a chartered private boat (K150,000, four to seven hours), a simple tarp-covered boat with a flat deck, a few plastic chairs and a very basic toilet. Generally a boat can fit four to six people, with a driver who will wait at Mrauk U with the boat for two or three nights.

By far the quickest and best option is the 'speedboats' run by **Shwe Pyi Tan** (☎ 09 4959 2709, 043-22719; cnr Main Rd & U Ottama St; ⏱8am-8pm), with departures from Sittwe on Wednesday, Friday and Sunday at 7am, and from Mrauk U on Monday and Thursday at 7am (K25,000, two hours).

To Taunggok

Fast boats to Taunggok, the jumping-off point for Ngapali Beach, are run by **Malikha Travels** (☎043-24248, 043-24037; Main Rd; ⏱9am-5pm), with departures on Monday and Thursday at 6am (US$30, 10 to 11 hours), and Shwe Pyi Tan, with departures on Wednesday, Friday and Sunday at 6am (US$35, 10 to 11 hours).

Mrauk U ⟨ မြောက်ဦး⟩

POP C 36,139 / ☎043

Myanmar's second-most-famous archaeological site, Mrauk U (pronounced 'mrau-oo') is very different from Bagan. The temples – previously mistaken for forts due to thick bunker-like walls built for protection from the fierce Rakhine winds – are smaller and newer and, unlike Bagan's, are predominantly made from stone, not brick. Mrauk U's temples, too, are dispersed throughout a still-inhabited and fecund landscape of small villages, rice paddies, rounded hillocks and grazing cows, whereas Bagan's temples stand in somewhat sterile isolation. Beyond its temples, Mrauk U remains a rough and ready riverside town surrounded by some beautiful countryside, where you'll find Chin villages and other significant archaeological and religious sites. Best of all, you're likely to have the temples all to yourself: only about 5000 foreigners make it to Mrauk U annually. That will change if a long-delayed airport opens in the next few years, so get here before the rush.

History

Mrauk U was the last great Rakhine capital, from 1430 to 1784, when it was one of the richest cities in Asia. In its heyday, it served as a free port, trading with the Middle East, Asia, Holland, Portugal and Spain. The Portuguese Jesuit priest, A Farinha, who visited in the 17th century, called it 'a second Venice', while other visitors compared it to London or Amsterdam. Little remains of the European quarter, Daingyi Phat (about 3 miles south of Mrauk U's current centre), other than ruins and a Hindu temple.

The Mrauk U dynasty was much feared by the peoples of the Indian subcontinent and central Myanmar. Japanese Christians fleeing persecution in Nagasaki were hired as bodyguards for the king. At Mrauk U's peak, King Minbin (1531–53) created a naval fleet of some 10,000 war boats that dominated the Bay of Bengal and Gulf of Martaban. Many of Mrauk U's finest temples (Shittaung, Dukkanthein, Laymyetnha and Shwetaung) were built during his reign.

Mrauk U was a successor to three earlier kingdoms in the area: Dhanyawady (c 1st to 6th centuries AD); Wethali (3rd to 11th centuries AD), the remains of which are still visible to the north; and Lemro (11th to 15th centuries AD). All four kingdoms blended elements of Theravada and Mahayana Buddhism with Hinduism and Islam. In the late 18th century, the Konbaung dynasty asserted its power over the region and Mrauk U was integrated into the Burmese kingdoms centred on Mandalay.

After the First Anglo–Burmese War of 1824–26, the British Raj annexed Rakhine and set up its administrative headquarters in Sittwe, thus turning Mrauk U into a political backwater virtually overnight.

◉ Sights

The original site of Mrauk U is spread over 17.5 sq miles, although the town today and bulk of the temples to visit cover a 2.7-sq-mile area. Most of the temples in the North Group and all of the Palace Site can be reached by foot, but you'll most likely want to hire a bike or truck to see the more remote temples in the North Group or those in the East Group.

The sights are not always marked – in English or any other language – and this is where an experienced guide can come in handy. Not only do many of the guides in the **Regional Guides Society – Mrauk U** (☑ 09 78240 4790, 09 25024 2844; jimes.htun@gmail.com; per day US$35) speak English well and have a good grasp on local history and culture, but they're also locally based, work independently and are dedicated to the principles of community-based tourism.

A torch (flashlight) is necessary to see some of the more interesting stone carvings – in particular those at Dukkanthein Paya, Andaw Paya and Mahabodi Shwegu.

◉ North Group

For many, this area is the best of the bunch in Mrauk U, with all sites within walking distance. There are a couple of tea shops, food stalls and a gift shop below Shittaung Paya.

★ Shittaung Paya   BUDDHIST TEMPLE
(ရှစ်သောင်းဘုရား; K5000; ⊘ 7am-5pm) Shittaung means 'Shrine of the 80,000 Images', a reference to the number of holy images inside. King Minbin, the most powerful of Rakhine's kings, built Shittaung in 1535. This is Mrauk U's most complex temple – it's a frenzy of stupas of various sizes; some 26 surround a central stupa. Thick walls, with windows and nooks, surround the two-tiered structure, which has been highly reconstructed over the centuries – in some places rather clumsily.

Outside the temple, beside the southwest entrance stairway, and inside a locked mint-green building, is the much-studied **Shittaung Pillar** (ရှစ်သောင်းဘုရားသမိုင်းကျောက်စာတိုင်; ⊘ daylight hours) FREE, a 10ft sandstone obelisk brought here from Wethali by King Minbin. Considered the 'oldest history book in Myanmar' (by the Rakhine at least), three of the obelisk's four sides are inscribed in faded Sanskrit. The east-facing side likely dates from the end of the 5th century. The western face displays a list dating from the 8th century, outlining Rakhine kings from 638 BC to AD 729 (King Anandacandra).

Lying on its back next to the pillar is a cracked, 12ft-long **sandstone slab** featuring an engraved lotus flower (a Buddhist motif) growing from a wavy line of water

MRAUK U FEES

Foreign visitors to Mrauk U are required to pay an archaeological site 'entry fee' of K5000. There's only one place to pay it – Shittaung Paya – but it is sometimes collected at the boat jetty when you arrive or depart. On the government ferry, you may be asked to show proof of payment before leaving.

and touching an intricately engraved *dhammacakka* (Pali for 'Wheel of the Law').

Along the outer walls, several **reliefs** can be seen (some are hard to reach); a few on the south side are rather pornographic.

Inside the temple's prayer hall you'll see several doors ahead. Two lead to passageways that encircle the main buddha image in the cave hall (which can be seen straight ahead).

The far left (southwest) doorway leads to the **outer chamber**, a 310ft passageway with sandstone slabs cut into six tiers. More than 1000 sculptures depict Rakhine customs (eg traditionally dressed dancers, boxers and acrobats), beasts of burden and hundreds of Jataka (scenes from Buddha's past 550 lives). At each corner are bigger figures, including the maker King Minbin and his queens at the southwest corner. The passage opens in the front, where you can step out for views.

Next to the outer chamber entry is a coiling **inner chamber** leading past scores of buddha images in niches, passing a Buddha footprint where – it's said – the Buddha walked during his post-enlightenment. Once you get to the dead end, double back to the hall, and see if you can feel the passageway becoming cooler. Some claim it does, symbolising the 'cooling effect' of Buddhist teachings.

Andaw Paya BUDDHIST TEMPLE
(အံတော်ဘုရား; daylight hours) FREE Andaw Paya takes the form of an eight-sided monument with a linear layout: rectangular prayer hall to the east, multispired sanctuary to the west. Sixteen *zedi* (stupas) are aligned in a square-cornered U-shape around the southern, northern and western platforms. Two concentric passageways are lined with buddha niches; in the centre of the shrine, an eight-sided pillar supports the roof.

The original construction of the shrine is ascribed to King Minhlaraza in 1521. King Minrazagyi then rebuilt Andaw in 1596 to enshrine a piece of the Buddha tooth relic supposedly brought from Sri Lanka by King Minbin in the early 16th century.

★ **Dukkanthein Paya** BUDDHIST TEMPLE
(ထုတ်ခံသိမ်ဘုရား; daylight hours) FREE Built by King Minphalaung in 1571, Dukkanthein Paya smacks of a bunker (with stupas). Wide stone steps lead up the south and east side of the building considered to be an ordination hall; take the east side steps to reach the entrance. The interior features spiralling cloisters lined with images of buddhas and ordinary people (landlords, governors, officials and wives) sporting all of Mrauk U's 64 traditional hairstyles. The passageway nearly encircles the centre three times before reaching the sun-drenched buddha image.

★ **Mahabodhi Shwegu** BUDDHIST TEMPLE
(မဟာဗောဓိရွှေဂူ; daylight hours) FREE The highlight of this squat, little-visited temple is its passageway with bas-relief illustrations of the *tribumi* – Buddhist visions of heaven, earth and hell – including acrobats, worshippers and animals. At the end there's a 6ft central buddha and four buddhas in niches; the throne of the former includes some erotic carvings. Mahabodhi Shwegu is largely hidden behind shrubbery on a hilltop northeast of Ratanabon Paya. To get here, proceed up the barely discernible uphill path that starts behind the covered water well.

Ratanabon Paya BUDDHIST STUPA
(ရတနာပုံဘုရား; daylight hours) FREE This massive stupa (sometimes called Yadanapon) is ringed by 24 smaller stupas. It was apparently built by Queen Shin Htway in 1612. During WWII a bomb nailed it, but it had already been picked at by treasure hunters attracted by the name, which means 'accumulation of treasure'. Renovations later repaired the enormous bomb-made crack and reinserted the tall *chattra* (spire).

Laungbanpyauk Paya BUDDHIST TEMPLE
(လောင်ပွန်းပြောက်ဘုရား; daylight hours) FREE This octagonal, slightly leaning *zedi* (stupa) was built by King Minkhaungraza in 1525. An unusual feature is its outer wall, adorned with Islamic-inspired glazed tiles in the shape of large flowers.

Pitaka Taik HISTORIC SITE
(ပိဋကတ်တိုက်; daylight hours) FREE This compact, highly ornate stone building is one of the seven Mrauk U libraries remaining

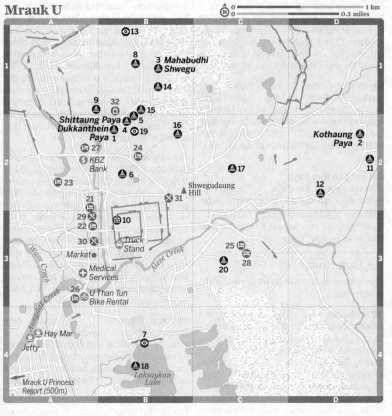

Mrauk U

⊙ **Top Sights**

⊙ **Sights**

🛏 **Sleeping**

✖ **Eating**

🛍 **Shopping**

WESTERN MYANMAR MRAUK U

from the original 48. Today protected by a blue-and-maroon shelter, it was built in 1591 by King Minphalaung as a repository for the Tripitaka (Three Baskets; the Buddhist canon), which was received from Sri Lanka in the 1640s. It's wee – only 13ft long and 9ft high.

Laymyetnha Paya
(လေးမျက်နှာဘုရား; ⊙ daylight hours) FREE
This poorly restored temple looks a bit like a squashed-up version of the nearby Dukkanthein but was actually built 140 years earlier, making it the oldest temple of the Mrauk U period.

Ratana San Rwe Paya & Ratana Hman Kin Paya
BUDDHIST STUPA
(ရတနာစံရွှေဘုရား ရတနာမှန်ကင်းဘုရား; ⊙ daylight hours) FREE Directly south of Mahabodhi Shwegu, these two adjacent hilltop stupas have been recently restored.

⊙ East Group

This area stretches a mile or so east of the palace walls.

★ Kothaung Paya
BUDDHIST TEMPLE
(ကိုးသောင်းဘုရား; ⊙ daylight hr) FREE One of Mrauk U's star attractions, Kothaung Paya is also the area's largest temple. It was built in 1553 by King Minbin's son, King Mintaikkha, to outdo his dad's Shittaung by 10,000 images ('Kothaung' means 'Shrine of 90,000 Images').

Kothaung Paya is located a mile or so east of the palace; follow the road directly north of the market, veering left on the much smaller road before the bridge.

Much of Kothaung Paya was found in fragments. Legends vary – that lightning or an earthquake destroyed it in 1776, that

ⓘ BOOKS ABOUT MRAUK U

There are several useful books on Rakhine history and Mrauk U. Myar Aung's paperback *Famous Monuments of Mrauk-U* (2007) has lots of photos, but its poorly translated text isn't the easiest to follow. Far better are Pamela Gutman's scholarly *Burma's Lost Kingdom: Splendours of Arakan* (2006), Tun Shwe Khine's artful *A Guide to Mrauk U* (1993) and U Shwe Zan's more detailed *The Golden Mrauk U: An Ancient Capital of Rakhine* (1997), all of which are worth searching out before heading to Mrauk U.

jewel-seekers overturned walls, or that it was built with inferior stones by a superstitious king bent on beating a six-month deadline. Regardless, the structure as it looks today is the result of a rather heavy-handed 1996 reconstruction. Recalling Borobudur in Indonesia, the exterior is coated with bell-like stone stupas. The 90,000 images in question line the outer passageway, the entrances to which are guarded by grimacing ogres. Stairways lead up to a top terrace, once dotted with 108 stupas.

Peisi Daung Paya
BUDDHIST PAGODA
(ပေစီတောင်ဘုရား; ⊙ daylight hours) FREE Sitting on a hilltop, this unrestored four-door pagoda is thought to predate the Mrauk U period. Climb to the top, push your way past the rubble and cobwebs and inside you'll find four sandstone buddha images, three of which have marble eyes – ostensibly added later by merit-seeking monks. The view from the top, of seemingly endless hillocks that allegedly were each home to some sort of Buddhist monument, puts Mrauk U's former wealth and glory in perspective.

Pharaouk Paya
BUDDHIST TEMPLE
(ဘုရားအုပ်ဘုရား; ⊙ daylight hours) FREE The name of this hilltop temple can be interpreted as meaning 'holding control of the people'. Its 29 niches with sitting buddha statues are a reference to Mrauk U's 29 former townships.

Sakyamanaung Paya
BUDDHIST STUPA
(သက္ကကြမြှန့်အဓေပျုဘုရား; ⊙ daylight hours) FREE Roughly half a mile northeast of the palace walls, and behind Shwegudaung hill, this graceful Mon-influenced *zedi* was erected in 1629 by King Thirithudhammaraza. At this later stage, stupas were built more vertically and ornately than before.

The lower half of the well-preserved 280ft *zedi* features a multitiered octagonal shape, as at Laungbanpyauk Paya, but beyond this the bells revert to a layered circular shape mounted by a decorative *hti* (umbrella-like top). You'll see brightly painted, half-kneeling giants at the west gate.

Ratanamanaung
BUDDHIST TEMPLE
(ရတနာမာန်အောင်; ⊙ daylight hours) FREE There are good views westward from this temple looking over Shwegudaung hill.

⊙ Palace Site & Around

Just east of the main strip of Mrauk U village, the one-time royal palace of Mrauk U now is mostly crumbling walls (though the outer walls still stand 11.5ft high).

Legend has it that King Minbin's astrologers advised a move here in 1429 after the palace at Launggret had been invaded by 'poisonous snakes and evil birds'. His representatives witnessed some strange things at this spot – an old man playing a flute pointed to a cat-chasing rat and then a snake-biting frog – apparently suggesting its soil as being worthy of a king. Construction began in 1430 (though some sources say 1553).

Haridaung Paya
BUDDHIST TEMPLE

(ဟာရိတောင်ဘုရား; ⊘ daylight hours) FREE Built around 1750, this small white temple with fine westward views is on a hilltop just north of the palace walls. It's a good place to get your bearings or to view the sunset.

Palace Museum
MUSEUM

(နန်းတော်ပြတိုက်; K5000; ⊘ 10am-4pm Tue-Sun) Just inside the palace's western walls is the Department of Archaeology's insufficiently illuminated but worthwhile museum. Inside you'll find an interesting selection of buddha images, inscribed stone slabs, cannons, floor tiles, Wethali-era coins and a helpful model of the Mrauk U site. Old photos on the walls include a pre-restoration shot of Ratanabon's crack (p320). Items are signed in English, although foreign scholars note that the dates on some pieces should be taken with a pinch of salt.

◎ South Group

South of the palace site and across the river are evocative back lanes through thatched-hut villages and a host of pagodas. About half a mile south, the **Laksaykan Gate** leads to the eponymous lake, a source of clean water.

Sanda Muhni
Phara Gri Kyaung Taik
BUDDHIST TEMPLE

(စန္တာမုနိဘုရားကြီးကျောင်းတိုက်; ⊘ daylight hours) FREE The highlight at this hilltop monastery, and the temple's namesake, is the **Sanda Muhni**, a buddha statue said to have been cast from the precious metal left over from making the Mahamuni buddha. Legend has it that this 4ft image was encased in concrete in the 1850s to protect it from pillaging British troops, and then forgotten about for over a century. In April 1988 one of the glazed eyes dropped out, revealing the metal statue beneath.

The **main hall** is packed with more ancient buddha images that the monks will happily explain to you. They will also point out a large copper roof tile (now used as a table top), saved from Mrauk U's palace after the Burmese carted the rest off to Mandalay back in the 18th century.

Next door, a small elevated structure – not open to the public – is home of Buddha's many scattered molars: **relics** brought here from Sri Lanka in the 16th century.

Shwetaung Paya
BUDDHIST PAGODA

(ရွှေတောင်ဘုရား; ⊘ daylight hours) FREE Southeast of the palace, the 'Golden Hill Pagoda' is the highest in Mrauk U. Built by King Minbin in 1553, it's accessed by a few trails largely lost under thick vegetation. This is a good spot from which to view the sunrise.

✦ Festivals & Events

One of the most interesting times to visit Mrauk U is during the huge weeklong **paya pwe** (pagoda festival) held near Dukkanthein Paya in mid-May. It includes music, dance, traditional Rakhine wrestling and boat racing.

⌂ Sleeping

The accommodation scene in Mrauk U is uninspired. Few places are worth the prices being charged or have wi-fi, although hot water is more or less standard now. Electricity comes and goes here, but all hotels and guesthouses have generators.

Mrauk U Palace
HOTEL $

(☎ 09 42175 1498; www.mraukupalaceresort.com; r US$45; ❄ ☎) The 22 identical and sizeable yellow duplex bungalows are comfortable for Mrauk U, if unexciting, and are equipped with fridge, hot-water shower, air-con and small balcony. Staff are helpful and efficient. It also has wi-fi, sometimes.

Laymro River Guest House
GUESTHOUSE $

(☎ 09 44008 1577; r K10,000-15,000) Newish, no-frills place with compact, plain, slightly musty but still acceptable fan-only rooms. The owner speaks some English and the 2nd-floor balcony is OK for an evening beer.

Royal City Guest House
HOTEL $

(☎ 09 850 2400, 043-24200; r US$10-25, bungalows US$40-55; ❄) Clean and reasonably comfortable rooms with cold-water showers in the main building for the budget crowd (the cheapest are very small indeed and lack bathrooms), and bungalows with air-con (if the electricity is working) and hot water across the road for those who can afford a bit more. The staff give out a map of the main sites.

Prince Hotel
GUESTHOUSE $

(📞 09 4958 3311, 043-50174; www.mraukuprince hotel.com; r US$30-50; ❄️ 📶) Located half a mile east of the market and set around a pleasant garden. An ongoing renovation sees the larger, more expensive rooms being given a bit of life, but the bathrooms need work. It's run by a pleasant family.

Golden Star Guest House
GUESTHOUSE $

(📞 09 4967 4472; r US$10-30; ❄️) Mrauk U's long-standing backpacker crash pad offers basic and cramped fan-cooled rooms, all with showers and all needing a lot of TLC. There are a couple of more expensive rooms in better shape that come with air-con.

★ Nawarat Hotel
HOTEL $$

(📞 043-50073, in Yangon 01-298 543; mraukoona warathotel@gmail.com; r US$55-98; ❄️ 📶) It's neither new nor sexy, but this is probably Mrauk U's best-value digs. Located a short walk from the main sights, the semi-detached concrete bungalows here are big and comfortable with decent beds and are well kitted out with satellite TV, fridge and balcony. There's also an OK attached restaurant.

Shwe Thazin Hotel
HOTEL $$

(📞 043-50168, 09 850 1844; www.shwethazinhotel. com; r US$65-80; ❄️) A little more thought has gone into the design here than in other Mrauk U hotels. The 23 chalet-style rooms feel spacious and comfortable and are well equipped, but the bathrooms are rather plain for the price. There's an attached restaurant.

Vesali Resort Hotel
HOTEL $$

(📞 043-50008, in Yangon 01-703 048; vesaliresort @gmail.com; r US$40-65; ❄️) Inconveniently removed from the bulk of the temples and town, the Vesali's 28 semi-detached bungalows are set around an attractive garden and come with dark-wood floors, vaulted ceilings, private decks and OK bathrooms. But the beds and fittings need an upgrade and there's no wi-fi.

Mrauk U Princess Resort
HOTEL $$$

(📞 09 850 0556, 043-50232; http://mraukuprin cess.com; bungalows from US$250; ❄️ @ 📶) Mrauk U's most luxurious digs, the Princess offers handsome, large, well-equipped wooden villas, as well as a restaurant and bar. We liked the vast, tub-equipped bathrooms, and the attractive gardens and ponds that make up the grounds, but you're isolated away from the centre of town and the sights, and it feels a little overpriced for what you get.

✖ Eating

Mrauk U's culinary options are pretty limited. There are a few local restaurants serving Bamar and Chinese-Burmese dishes to the west of Mrauk U's market. For something more upmarket, consider the restaurants at the Mrauk U Princess Resort, Nawarat Hotel or the Shwe Thazin Hotel.

Happy Garden
CHINESE, BURMESE $

(dishes from K2500; ⊘ 8am-10pm; 🍴) This beer-garden joint is the most lively spot in town come nightfall. The Chinese-sounding dishes are tasty enough, and there are a few Burmese options as well. Fine for a beer too. It also rents a few basic bungalows (K8000 to K30,000).

Kaung Thant
BURMESE $

(curries from K2500; ⊘ 9am-10pm) A bare-bones Burmese-style curry shop at the foot of the bridge just north of the market, 'Good and Clean' does Rakhine-style set meals, which are served by an affable local family. Look for the partially hidden English sign.

For You
CHINESE, BURMESE $

(mains from K1500; ⊘ 8am-8pm; 🍴) Simple, clean, reliable but uninspired Chinese-style dishes at this homely place. A good spot for morning noodles.

Moe Cherry
BURMESE $$

(mains from K4500; ⊘ 9am-9.30pm; 🍴) More sophisticated than the other restaurants in Mrauk U – a shaded terrace to eat on and tablecloths! – this is also the best place in town for both Rakhine-style curries and Chinese-Burmese fusion food. There's an extensive English menu and beer as well.

🛍 Shopping

A couple of gift shops outside the Shittaung Paya sell souvenirs.

L'amitie Art Gallery
ART

(⊘ 7am-6pm) This simple hut is hung with attractive canvases in oils and pastels created by Khine Minn Tun, whose now deceased father Shwe Maung Thar painted the ceiling panels in the central hall of Shittaung Paya.

ℹ Information

There's a branch of the **KBZ Bank** (⊘ 9.30am-3pm). It has an ATM and you can change money. It's on the main road through town, close to the Shwe Thazin Hotel.

Only some hotels in Mrauk U have wi-fi, and it doesn't always work.

In case of an emergency, the hospital at Sittwe is your best bet. For minor ailments visit the friendly English-speaking **doctor** (☏ 043-50032, 043-24200), south of the market.

ℹ Getting There & Away

Foreigners can now travel overland to/from Mrauk U.

BUS

There are two buses daily to Sittwe (K4000, 3½ hours, 6am and 7am), although you can always try to get a ride on the buses passing through later from Mandalay and elsewhere.

A daily bus leaves for Mandalay (K25,000, 20 hours, 8.30am). If you're heading to Bagan or Pakokku, take this bus and get off in Magwe, spend the night there and then catch one of the many vans or buses from Magwe to those destinations.

A sole minivan runs daily to Thandwe, for Ngapali Beach, (K35,000, 22 hours, 4pm).

BOAT

Mrauk U's jetty is about half a mile south of the market. Come here on the day of departure to buy tickets, or to the adjacent Hay Mar teashop, where Aung Zan can assist in buying tickets, and offers private boat rides back to Sittwe (from US$20 per person).

Double-decker boats run by the government's Inland Water Transport (p318) depart from Mrauk U for Sittwe on Wednesday and Saturday at 8am (US$7, four to seven hours). The faster 'speedboats' run by Shwe Pyi Tan (p318) leave Mrauk U for Sittwe on Monday and Thursday at 7am (K25,000, three hours).

ℹ Getting Around

Thoun bein cruise Mrauk U's bumpy streets for K2000 a local trip. They congregate on the south side of the palace site.

TRUCK

Small trucks can be hired from the stand on the south side of the palace site. A day hire, taking in the sites in and near Mrauk U, should cost about K35,000.

BICYCLES

Bicycles can be hired from **U Than Tun Bike Rental** (per day K2000; ⊘ 7am-7pm), just south of the bridge leading to the central market.

Around Mrauk U

The temples are only a part of the area's attractions. Tack on a few extra days here to enjoy a relaxing boat ride down the Lemro River to Chin villages, or to venture out to Wethali and Mahamuni Paya, two important archaeological and religious sites north of Mrauk U of which the locals are very proud.

Wethali   HISTORIC SITE
(ဝေသာလီ; ⊘ daylight hours) FREE About 7 miles north of Mrauk U are the barely discernible remains of the kingdom of Wethali. Founded in AD 327 by King Mahataing Chandra, according to the Rakhine chronicles, archaeologists believe that the kingdom lasted until the 8th century. Today, in addition to the walls of the 1650ft by 990ft central palace site, the main attraction for visitors is the so-called **Great Image of Hsu Taung Pre**, a 16.5ft Rakhine-style sitting Buddha said to date from AD 327.

The elevated track that runs adjacent to Wethali is in fact an abandoned railway line. A rare incidence of the former military government bowing to popular opinion occurred here in late 2010, when a few brave locals protested against the planned route of a new railway linking Sittwe with Minbu, the construction of which was damaging temples and sites within the archaeological area. The project was halted and the railway's route changed.

Mahamuni Paya   BUDDHIST TEMPLE
(မဟာမုနိဘုရား; ⊘ daylight hours) FREE Twenty miles north of Wethali, just beyond the former ancient capital of Dhanyawady, is Mahamuni Paya, the alleged first home of the Buddha image now housed in the temple of the same name in Mandalay. The legend goes that the image was cast when Buddha visited the area in 554 BC. Even now, some Rakhine recount with fiery passion how the Burmese King Bodawpaya sent soldiers to dismantle and remove the Mahamuni Buddha in 1784.

Today 'Mahamuni's brother' – a smaller statue allegedly cast from the same materials – is now one of three fine golden images resting inside. A replica of the original, commissioned 100 years ago by a wealthy resident of Sittwe, sits to the left. The temple structure dates from the 19th century, as earlier ones were destroyed by fire. Down the steps, near the south walls of the shrine, is a museum (admission US$5) with a couple of dozen relics and some beautiful engraved stones.

There is a strip of good Burmese restaurants across from Mahamuni Paya, so it's a clever idea to combine this trip with lunch.

ⓘ Getting There & Away

The trip out to Mahamuni Paya can be arranged via the Regional Guides Society – Mrauk U (p319). It spans about half a day, including a visit to Wethali, and car hire costs about K60,000, plus US$35 for a guide.

CHIN STATE   ချင်းပြည်နယ်

Wild, mountainous and remote, Chin State is Myanmar's poorest and least-developed state. Scrunched up against the borders with Bangladesh and India, Chin is sparsely populated and lacking in infrastructure. But it makes up for that with densely forested hills and mountains that soar above 10,000ft and are separated by vast valleys through which rivers rage. Home to traditional villages inhabited by the friendly Chin people, a Tibeto-Burman group which has largely adopted Christianity, this is the perfect place to take the road less travelled.

Southern Chin State is already attracting visitors intent on hiking up Mt Victoria, the state's highest peak, and trekking to the villages around the hilltop town of Mindat. But northern Chin State remains mostly virgin territory for foreigners. Don't expect much in the way of comfort here. Instead, revel in a land that looks like it's barely been touched by human hands.

The rainy season in Chin State lasts longer than elsewhere in Myanmar, running from May to October. During this period, landslides block muddy roads, the mountains are obscured by cloud and mist, and journey times lengthen. The best time to visit is between November and March.

ⓘ Information

Myanmar's central government has declared several destinations in Chin State – including Mindat, Mt Victoria and the state capital Hakha – 'open', meaning that permits are no longer necessary to visit these areas. But some places, like Paletwa and Matupi, do still require advance permission, and if you're up on the Myanmar–India border, the local immigration officials will likely join you for a cup of tea to inquire what you're up to. Saying you're just visiting as a tourist normally satisfies them.

There are very few banks in Chin State. At the time of research, the only place you'll find one that can change money and has a working ATM is in the state capital, Hakha.

The Chin people are 80% Christian and they take the Sabbath seriously. On Sundays, almost all restaurants shut and no buses, minivans or jeeps run. Plan ahead accordingly.

ⓘ Getting There & Away

There are no airports in Chin State, and roads are largely unsealed and in poor condition. In the rainy season (May to October), journey times get much longer. Remember that no public transport runs on Sundays.

Southern Chin State is accessed by bus and minivan from Bagan or Pakokku, or by boat from Mrauk U if you're heading to Paletwa.

The jumping-off point for northern Chin State is Kalaymyo, in neighbouring Sagaing Division. Kalaymyo has an airport with daily flights to Yangon and Mandalay, and you can catch daily buses, minivans and jeeps from there to the Chin State capital of Hakha and the other major towns in the north: Falam and Tiddim.

Mt Victoria (Nat Ma Taung) ဝိတိုရိယတောင်

The most popular destination in Chin State is Mt Victoria, roughly 80 miles west of Bagan. The 10,016ft (3053m) mountain is the highest in Chin State and the third-highest in Myanmar. The peak stands amid a 279-sq-mile national park and is a prime spot for birdwatching. It's best visited November to February when the rhododendron bushes that cover the slopes are in full bloom. During the rainy season (May to October), the mountain is normally inaccessible and hotels shut down.

Most people come to Mt Victoria from Nyaung U, a six-hour drive. The starting point for the trek to the summit is the village of Kanpetlet: it's an easy hike that anyone in reasonable physical condition can accomplish. After that, options include camping on Mt Victoria, staying at the base of the mountain, or the more demanding three-day trek to Mindat on the opposite side of the mountain.

Permits are not required to visit Mt Victoria, but for all intents and purposes a guide is, which means that everybody approaches Mt Victoria on a tour. A typical trip to Mt Victoria spans from four to six days, and the cost for two people, including accommodation and transportation, starts at about US$900. Several tour agencies have itineraries covering Mt Victoria, including the Yangon-based **Tours Myanmar** (☑09

42006 0272; www.toursmyanmar.com), which offers both vehicle and bicycle tours to the area led by experienced guide Mr Saw; while **Go-Myanmar** (www.go-myanmar.com) and **Bike World Explores Myanmar** (www.cyclingmyanmar.com) offer cycling tours.

🛏 Sleeping & Eating

There are an increasing number of eco-lodges outside the village of Kanpetlet. Otherwise you can camp or stay in a local villager's house. Most people eat where they stay, either in the village homes or the restaurant of their hotel. There are a couple of simple restaurants in Kanpetlet.

Mountain View Hill Resort HOTEL $
(Mt Victoria St; r incl breakfast US$45) This new-ish place has 25 concrete bungalows with wooden floors and OK beds that are more comfortable than other similarly priced places around Mt Victoria, although still not warm. There's an attached restaurant and it's also walking distance to the village of Kanpetlet.

Pine Wood Villa Resort GUESTHOUSE $$
(☎09 7308 2783; r incl breakfast US$60-80) About an hour's walk outside Kanpetlet, this guesthouse has rooms in the main building, or nicer, if rustic, bungalows. None are worth the price, but you're paying for fine views of Mt Victoria. There's an attached, reasonably priced restaurant. Electricity only in the evenings, and there's no heating here – it gets cold at night.

❶ Getting There & Away

Tours to Mt Victoria start in Bagan, a six-hour drive away, where your transport will meet you. But it's also possible to hike here from Mindat, a three-day journey.

Mindat   မရေးတပျိုမြို့

POP C 10,000 / ☎070

Sitting at almost 5000ft above sea level, Mindat is strung out along a ridge top, with its houses perched above and below the single road running through the town. It's a stunning setting and Mindat is a jumping-off point for treks to the surrounding traditional hill villages and Mt Victoria. The town itself is unremarkable, although it offers an immediate contrast to neighbouring Magwe Division far below. Churches far outnumber pagodas – a reflection of the Christian majority population – while the higher altitude means this is one of the few places in Myanmar where you'll see people wearing socks (with flip-flops). In the rainy season especially, the locals wrap up in woolly hats like it's the Arctic, but most Westerners find the cooler weather (bring a fleece) a huge relief after the baking central plains.

◉ Sights

Sanminedidisiv Paya   BUDDHIST PAGODA
(စံမင်းသိရိဘုရား; off Main Rd; ☉daylight hours) Climb the steep steps up to this small golden *zedi* (stupa) perched above Mindat for awesome views over the surrounding area.

WESTERN MYANMAR MINDAT

WORTH A TRIP

CHIN VILLAGES

An interesting contrast to the temples at Mrauk U is a day trip to the Chin villages along the Lemro River.

These boat trips don't reach Chin State, but seven or so of the traditional Chin villages along this stretch of the river have dwindling numbers of elderly women who have tattooed faces, a practice that ended among the Chin a couple of generations ago.

Visiting here is a chance to get a sense of Chin village life if you're not heading to Chin State proper. The women in the villages are used to foreigners and are normally happy to have their photos taken. But be sure to ask their permission and expect to pay K5000. Simple handicrafts are sold in the villages as well, and buying them is a good way of putting some cash into the local economy. The villages here are poor even by Myanmar standards, so you might want to consider making a donation too, either of school supplies or a few thousand kyat, but it's not obligatory. In addition to the Chin villages, there's the busy morning market at the village of **Pan Mraung**.

Typical trips, which the Regional Guides Society – Mrauk U (p319) or your hotel can help arrange, include a half-hour car transfer to the jetty, an approximately two-hour boat trip upstream, an hour or so at a couple of villages and lunch. The total cost will run US$80 to US$100 per person. It's advisable to bring water and snacks as well.

KEEP YOUR BUS TICKETS

One peculiarity of Chin State is that guesthouses will ask you for your bus ticket when you check in, so hang onto them. Apparently immigration officers in Chin State need to know what bus you arrived on when the guesthouse staff register you with them.

It's at the far end of town, 15 minutes from the market.

Activities

Almost everyone who comes to Mindat goes trekking, with the prime time to hit the hills being November to April. In the rainy season (May to October), the fantastic views are often obscured by rain and clouds. There are many, many villages out there, some still animist and with their own shaman, all set amid beautiful, rolling countryside.

Treks can last from three to 10 days, but typically run four days and three nights, with stops each night to eat and sleep in a village home. Conditions are simple, but the people are very friendly.

A guide is more or less essential, both to stop you getting lost and to get over the language barrier: all villagers speak the various Chin dialects – you won't hear much Burmese, let alone English, once you're outside Mindat. One recommended guide is Naing Kee Shing (p329).

Another option is to head about 100 miles northwest from Mindat along a rough road to the town of **Matupi**. This town is surrounded by hill villages, which see even fewer visitors than the ones around Mindat, as well as dense forests that are still home to leopards, bears, monkeys and, supposedly, tigers. But to visit Matupi you'll need a permit and a 4WD vehicle, which will cost at least US$100 a day to hire in Chin State, as well as a guide.

If you're really adventurous, it's also possible to trek all the way to Mrauk U in Rakhine State, via Kanpetlet and Paletwa. Again, permits are required and the trip will take eight days, the last day and half spent on a boat floating down the Lemro River to Mrauk U.

Almost all travellers arrange their treks through Yangon-based tour operators, who can arrange the necessary permits. Uncharted Horizons (p421) is a specialist in getting

off the tourist trail in Chin State, including the trek to Mrauk U, but other recommended operators include **Myanmar Trekking** (Map p52; ☎ 01-667 948; www.myanmartrekking. com; Rm 7, 4A Parami Rd, Mayangone) and **Ayarwaddy Legend Travels & Tours** (Map p38; ☎ 01-252 007; www.ayarwaddylegend.com; 104 37th St, Kyauttada).

Sleeping

There are only a handful of guesthouses in Mindat. Electricity comes and goes here, but the guesthouse generators get going after 6pm.

Se Naing Family Guest House GUESTHOUSE $
(☎ 070-70149, 09 44200 2645; mindatfgh@gmail. com; Main Rd; r incl breakfast K15,000-40,000) Run by the charming Monica, who speaks reasonable English, this cosy guesthouse has simple but clean rooms. The more expensive have their own small bathrooms, but there is hot water for everyone here, a luxury in Chin State, and fine views from the roof. The guesthouse is close to the village entrance.

Tun Guest House GUESTHOUSE $
(☎ 070-70166, 09 4717 0090; off Main Rd; r K12,000-25,000) Cheaper rooms are small with thin mattresses and share a bathroom. The more expensive ones have their own basic bathrooms. Some travellers have complained of being overcharged for treks and transport organised here. The guesthouse is about 200yd downhill from the main road – a 10-minute walk from the market. Look for the signs pointing the way.

Victoria Guest House GUESTHOUSE $
(☎ 070-70127; Main Rd; r K10,000-20,000) Rooms at this place almost opposite the market are basic and plain, and all share bathrooms. But the owner is friendly and helpful.

Eating

Myo Ma Restaurant CHINESE, BURMESE $
(Main Rd; mains from K2500; ⊙ 7am-9.30pm) The best and most popular place in Mindat to eat (there's not much competition), Myo Ma does reasonable Chinese-Burmese dishes and serves up draught beers. It does takeaway as well. Find it five minutes' walk uphill from market: look for the blue building with the Myanmar Lager sign.

Noodle Shop NOODLES $
(Main Rd; noodles from K700; ⊙ 6am-5pm) This no-name noodle shop is busy all day serving

up bowls of Shan-style noodles. It's opposite Victoria Guesthouse.

🛍 Shopping

Market MARKET

(off Main Rd; ⊘6am-5pm) Mindat's small market is just off the main road. It's mostly produce – you'll see old women with tattooed faces bent double under their food shopping – but there are a couple of shops selling traditional Chin clothes, bags and purses, which make good souvenirs.

ℹ Information

There are no banks or ATMs in Mindat. Bring cash.

A recommended guide to the area around Mindat and beyond, Naing Kee Shing speaks excellent English, can arrange permits and is a mine of information about the region. He charges US$60 per day, excluding food, transport and accommodation. He can be contacted on ☑ 09 45463 1280, but is often away on treks, so email him first at chinlion93@gmail.com.

ℹ Getting There & Away

Remember public transport doesn't run on Sundays in Chin State.

Buses and minivans go to Mindat from Pakkoku, Magwe Division. They leave from the Moe Pi bus station, which is 500yd from the main bus station, between 6am and 8am (K7000, six hours).

Going in the opposite direction, buses and minivans depart from near the market in Mindat for Pakokku between 6am and 8.30am (K7000, six hours). There's also a daily bus to Mandalay (K12,000, 12 hours, 8am).

If you're heading to northern Chin State, catch the daily minivan to Gangaw (K8500, six hours, 7am), from where you can pick up another minivan to Kalaymyo in Sagaing Division (K8000, four hours, 8am, 10am and 2pm), where there is daily transport into northern Chin State. There is a very rough road from Gangaw to Hakha, the Chin capital, but it's normally closed due to landslides.

Kalaymyo (Kalay)
ကလေးမြို့

POP C 130,506 / ☑ 073

Kalaymyo, mostly known by its former name of Kalay, has a claim to be the true capital of Chin State, even though it is located just across the border in neighbouring Sagaing Division. Over half its population are Chin, far outnumbering the people who live in the actual Chin capital, Hakha, and the estimated 500-plus churches in Kalaymyo – some no more than houses with a cross catering to tiny congregations, and others sizeable – are testimony to the Chin influence. Sitting in a valley close to the confluence of three rivers and with the Chin Hills looming over the city, Kalaymyo is also notable geographically because the Tropic of Cancer passes through it. During WWII the town was an important staging post in the battles against the Japanese. These days it's a low-key place with many wooden houses and the gateway to northern Chin State.

Kalaymyo's hotels, restaurants, banks, bus station and airport are all strung along Bo Gyoke Rd, which runs all the way to the border with Chin State.

🛏 Sleeping & Eating

If you're heading to or from Chin State, then you'll almost certainly spend a night or two here. You'll find reasonable accommodation along Bo Gyoke Rd, close to the airport and bus station.

Majesty Hotel HOTEL $

(☑073-22010; info@majestymyanmar.com; Bo Gyoke Rd; r incl breakfast K55,000; ✳🏠) The smartest option along Bo Gyoke Rd, the Majesty has big, bright white-tiled rooms with high ceilings and bathrooms with a tub. Staff can book air and bus tickets too.

Shin Hong Hotel HOTEL $

(☑073-22714; shinhonghotel.kalay@gmail.com; Bo Gyoke Rd; r US$30; ✳🏠) The closest hotel to the bus station, the Shin Hong feels a little institutional but has large, comfortable enough rooms with small bathrooms. Wi-fi and power come and go, but if you're coming from Chin State, you'll consider the 24-hour hot water to be worth the price alone.

Beer Garden Restaurant CHINESE, BURMESE $

(Bo Gyoke Rd; mains from K3000; ⊘10am-11pm; 🗐) This busy, no-name beer-garden restaurant next door to the Shin Hong Hotel serves up reasonable Chinese-Burmese food and good barbecue, as well as offering draught beer and football on the TV.

ℹ Information

KBZ Bank (Bo Gyoke Rd; ⊘9.30am-3pm) You can exchange money here and it has an ATM that takes foreign cards (there are other ATMs around town too). It's 10 minutes' walk east of the Majesty Hotel.

ⓘ Getting There & Away

Kalaymyo is the closest place with an airport to northern Chin State. **Air KBZ** (Bo Gyoke Rd; ⊙ 9am-5pm) and **Myanmar National Airlines** (www.flymna.com; Bo Gyoke Rd; ⊙ 9am-5pm) fly on alternate days to Yangon (from US$171) and Mandalay (from US$109). Their offices are across the road from the KBZ Bank, about 10 minutes' walk east of the Majesty Hotel.

Kalaymyo's scruffy bus station is off Bo Gyoke Road, a 10-minute walk from the Shin Hong Hotel. There are daily, crowded minivans Monday to Saturday to Hakha (K10,000, eight hours), Falam (K5000, four hours) and Tiddim (K7000, four hours). Most leave between 6am and 8am.

There are also daily buses to Yangon (K25,000, 22 hours, 2pm) and Mandalay (K15,000, 10 hours, 2pm).

If you're heading directly to Rih Lake, uncomfortable jeeps to Rihkhawdar (K15,000, nine hours) leave daily Monday to Saturday when full from an office about a mile west of the bus station on Bo Gyoke Rd. They depart between 6am and 9am.

Tiddim တီးတိန်မြို့

POP C 15,000 / ☑ 070

About two hours' drive from Kalaymyo into the Chin Hills, the road forks: south to Falam and Hakha, north to Tiddim and the Myanmar–India border. This part of northern Chin State is even less visited than the regions further south, despite the fact that the area around Tiddim is home to Kennedy Peak, Chin State's second-highest mountain. Tiddim, also known as Tedim or Teddim, is the ideal place to break the arduous journey to mystical Rih Lake. The town itself is small and scrappy with many churches – although some nearby villages are still animist – and is inhabited by curious, welcoming locals. And like the rest of this part of Myanmar, it is set amid stunning countryside that is ripe for exploration.

◉ Sights

Kennedy Peak   MOUNTAIN
(ကနေဒီတောင်) Kennedy Peak stands 8868ft high, making it Chin State's second-highest mountain. The site of a battle between the British and Japanese in WWII, the peak is as yet untouched by tourism, so there are no known hiking routes up it. Instead, a rough road leads to the summit from Sozang village, about 15 miles from Tiddim on the road back to Kalaymyo, which hugs the base of the mountain.

The hike up is an easy couple of hours and the views are great along the way, but, unfortunately, there's now a TV tower at the top.

Siang Sawn   VILLAGE
(ရှန်တောန်း) This village is an oddity in that it remains predominantly animist, despite its proximity to heavily Christian Tiddim. Many inhabitants still wear Chin costume and this is the closest village to Tiddim where you can experience something of traditional Chin village life. It's about 2 miles north of Tiddim: follow the main road out of town and it's the first village you come to.

🛏 Sleeping & Eating

There are only a couple of guesthouses in Tiddim. Expect electricity only after 6pm and on alternate days!

Ciimnuai Guest House   GUESTHOUSE $
(☑ 070-50037, 09 7323 3562; Kam Hau Rd; r K10,000) One of the better guesthouses in Chin State, Ciimnuai has great views of Kennedy Peak from its terrace and 2nd-floor communal area. Rooms are compact and share a clean bathroom with a sit-down toilet. Hot water can be provided on request. The owners can provide some information about the area. It's just to the side of the clock tower.

Asian Restaurant   CHINESE, BURMESE $
(off Kam Hau Rd; mains from K1500; ⊙10am-10pm; 🖉) There's a small English menu of Chinese-Burmese dishes, most rice and noodle-based, at this restaurant set up in the front room of the owner's house. It's the only place that serves alcohol and that stays open in the evening. Find it down some steps just off the main road, close to the junction with the Tiddim–Rihkhawdar road. Look for the English sign.

Mangala Restaurant   BURMESE $
(Kam Hau Rd; curries from K2500; ⊙5am-6pm) Right at the junction of the main road and the Tiddim–Rihkhawdar road, this place does OK Burmese curry sets, as well as noodles. No English menu.

ⓘ Getting There & Away

Minivans and jeeps to/from Tiddim run Monday to Saturday only.

There are daily minivans to Tiddim from Kalaymyo's bus station (K7000, four hours), most leaving 6am to 9am.

From Tiddim, there are a number of minivans to Kalaymyo (K7000, four hours) at 7am from the bus ticket offices opposite Mangala Restaurant at the junction of the main road through town and the road to Rihkhawdar.

If you're heading to Rih Lake, daily and very uncomfortable jeeps to Rihkhawdar (K8000, four hours) pass through Tiddim from Kalaymyo 9am to noon. Be sure to reserve a seat the day before at the stall at the junction of the main road and the road to Rihkhawdar.

❶ Getting Around

You're on your own when it comes to travelling up here, but Ciimnuai Guest House (p330) can organise a car and driver (K150,000 per day) or a motorbike (K50,000 per day) should you need one.

Rihkhawdar ရိဟ်ဟောဒါ

Way up on the Myanmar–India border, Rihkhawdar is a small but hectic border town and the gateway to mystical Rih Lake. Separated from Mizoram State in India by a 100yd-long bridge, Rihkhawdar sees trucks from India and Myanmar move in both directions carrying cargo, while the shops here are full of Indian goods and the Indian rupee is as much the currency as the Myanmar kyat. This is a closed frontier for both ordinary Burmese and foreigners, although local residents can cross the border during the day. Instead, the main reason to come here is to visit nearby Rih Lake, an idyllic lake that sits almost on the border with India.

◉ Sights

★ Rih Lake   LAKE

(ရိဟ်ရေအိုင်) This small, heart-shaped lake has huge spiritual significance to the Mizo people, who inhabit both sides of the nearby Myanmar–India border and for whom the lake is the traditional pathway for the dead to reach their final resting place. Rih Lake certainly has a magical, tranquil setting: the water shines a deep blue and the lake is surrounded by rice paddies and forested hills. Rih Lake is accessed from nearby Rihkhawdar, a 15-minute ride away on a motorcycle taxi (K5000 return).

Although the Mizo have largely been converted to Christianity, Rih Lake is part of their ancient animist traditions: the gateway to the Mizo version of heaven, known as Piairal, through which all the dead must

pass to reach their eternal home. These days the concept of Piairal has been blended with the Christian idea of paradise, allowing Rih Lake's mystical status to continue. The lake's aura is enhanced by its remoteness and it remains a key pilgrimage site for Mizo people in both Chin State and Mizoram State in India, as well as a favourite hang-out for the people living nearby, who come to swim, drink and make merry on weekends. During the week, the lake is much more peaceful and you'll have it mostly to yourself.

⬛ Sleeping & Eating

There are only two sleeping options in Rihkhawdar for foreigners: one in town and one by Rih Lake itself, which we don't recommend.

A few basic noodle and fried-rice restaurants can be found on the main road through Rihkhawdar, as well as a better, more sophisticated place serving Chinese-Burmese dishes by Rih Lake. Most places are closed on Sundays.

Rih Shwe Pyi Guest House   GUESTHOUSE $ (☑ 09 647 2400; r K15,000-25,000; ☀) This is the best place to stay if you're overnighting in Rihkhawdar after visiting Rih Lake. The more expensive rooms are large and comfortable for Chin State, although it's still cold-water showers. The cheapest rooms share DIY showers and squat toilets. It's about three minutes' walk from the bridge that leads to India, just off the main drag through town.

🍸 Drinking & Nightlife

Rih Lake Bar   BEER GARDEN

(Rih Lake; beers from K2500; ☉ 6am-6pm) Join the locals who flock to this shaded, open-air bar right on the shore of Rih Lake on the weekends; it's open on Sundays. During the week, you'll have it largely to yourself. You can order food from the nearby Rih Restaurant.

ℹ️ Getting There & Away

There is no transport to/from Rihkhawdar on Sundays.

From a bus ticket office a mile west of Kalaymyo's main bus station, jeeps (K15,000, nine hours) leave when full for the very uncomfortable drive to Rihkhawdar. Get here at 6am to look for a ride and preferably buy a ticket the day before.

A much better option is to catch one of the daily minivans to Tiddim (K7000, four hours) that leave around 7am from Kalaymyo's bus station and break the journey there. From Tiddim there are daily jeeps (K8000, four hours) to Rihkhawdar from 9am to noon.

From Rihkhawdar jeeps return to Kalaymyo daily from 7am to 9am (K15,000, nine hours).

It is also possible to visit Rih Lake on a very long day trip from Tiddim, but you'll need to hire a vehicle and driver, which will cost K150,000 per day. The staff at Ciimnuai Guest House (p330) can arrange a car.

Falam   ဖလန်း

POP C 15,000 / ☎ 070

Perched on a hilltop, with still higher and thickly forested hills rising above it, Falam has a spectacular setting and was the British headquarters in the Chin Hills during the colonial era. It remained the capital of Chin State until 1965, and is still Chin's second 'city'. It's a mellow, predominantly Christian town with many churches, a smattering of pre-independence architecture and wooden houses on stilts rising up and down the hillsides. If you're heading to and from Hakha, you'll pass through Falam anyway, but it's worth stopping for a night or two. And like the other towns in northern Chin State, Falam is surrounded by countryside wholly untouched by tourism.

◎ Sights

Yanpaymanpay Paya   BUDDHIST TEMPLE

(ရန်ပြေမာန်ပြေဘုရား; ☉ daylight hours) This temple with a golden *zedi* (stupa) and a sitting, white-faced Buddha surrounded by five disciples looms over Falam from almost the highest point above the town. There are absolutely sublime, panoramic views across the countryside from here: on a clear day you can really see for miles and miles. It's a steep 20-minute walk from the centre of town: take the road past the Holy Guest House and KBZ Bank and keep walking uphill.

Falam Baptist Church   CHURCH

(Bo Gyoke Rd; ☉ daylight hours) It's not very old – dating back only to 1983 – but this is possibly the largest church in Chin State and it dominates Falam. It's worth checking it out on a Sunday, when it's packed out and the sound of the congregation singing hymns can be heard throughout the centre of town.

**Former District
Commissioner's House**   HISTORIC BUILDING

Back when the Chin Hills were part of British Burma, they were administered from this red-brick house, the former home of the District Commissioner. The house is around 100 years old, but it's still a government building today, so you can't go inside. It's fine, however, to take photos outside. It's downhill from the main road and close to the Moon Guest House.

🛏️ Sleeping

Falam has a handful of basic guesthouses, most along or off Bo Gyoke Rd, the main road winding through town.

Beautyland Guest House   GUESTHOUSE $

(☎ 09 77955 1046; r K15,000) It's a stiff, 15-minute walk uphill from the centre of town, but the rewards are great views over Falam and the hills. Rooms are reasonably sized and plain and share an OK bathroom. To get here, take the road past the KBZ Bank and keep climbing.

Holy Guest House   GUESTHOUSE $

(☎ 09 40030 5703; Bo Gyoke Rd; r K15,000) Rooms here are bigger and in better condition than other places in Falam, while still being simple and plain. The shared bathroom is the cleanest and best in town and has a hot-water shower. English-speaking owner. It's opposite the Baptist church.

Emanuel Guest House   GUESTHOUSE $

(☎ 09 40030 5573; Bo Gyoke Rd; r K15,000) Compact but clean rooms at this place, but you won't hear any English. It's on the main road, a two-minute walk north of the bus ticket offices.

Moon Guest House GUESTHOUSE $

(☑09 45959 4750; 123 Thi Sar Rd; r K15,000)
The granddaddy of Falam guesthouses, the Moon has small, beaten-up and tatty rooms, all sharing a primitive bathroom (although it does have a Western toilet). The upside is that the owner is friendly and helpful, and will discount the rooms by 33%, and there's a rickety wooden balcony offering fine views over the hills at sunrise and sunset.

It's downhill from the main road through town; go down the steps by the bus ticket offices.

✗ Eating

Chinese Restaurant CHINESE, BURMESE $

(off Bo Gyoke Rd; mains from K2500; ⊙11am-7.30pm; 🎨) This no-name place is really the front room of the owner's house. There's a small English menu of Chinese-Burmese dishes, but you'll do better pointing at what the locals are eating. It's down an alley to the west of the Baptist church, next door to the large white building with a blue sign.

U Lay BURMESE $

(Bo Gyoke Rd; curries from K3000; ⊙10am-9pm)
This is the most popular restaurant in town, serving up Burmese curry sets at lunch and simple Chinese-Burmese dishes in the evening. It's also the only place that serves alcohol. No English menu, no English spoken and no English sign, but it's a two-minute walk north of the bus ticket offices.

ⓘ Information

KBZ Bank (off Bo Gyoke Rd; ⊙9.30am-3pm)
One of only two banks that we are aware of in Chin State. You can't change money here but we were told that an ATM will be installed at some point in the future. It's to the side of the Holy Guest House, east of the Baptist church.

ⓘ Getting There & Away

Minivans to Falam (K5000, four hours) leave from Kalaymyo's bus station Monday to Saturday.

From Monday to Saturday, there is a daily bus (K3000, 1pm) and minivan (K5000, 3pm) from Falam to Hakha. They leave from the bus ticket offices in the centre of town close to the Baptist church. You can also try for a place on the minivans that start passing through from Kalaymyo around 11am, but they are often full.

There are daily minivans (K8000, 7am) and one bus (K5000, 7am) to Kalaymyo. They leave from the bus ticket offices in the centre of town and also don't run on Sundays.

Hakha ဟားခါးမြို့

POP C 24,926 / ☑070

Hakha, the capital of Chin State, is precariously located along a series of shifting hillsides above and beneath Bo Gyoke Rd, the main drag through town. Landslides are a regular occurrence, especially in the rainy season (May to October). Indeed, so perilous is Hakha's position that in 2015 a team of German geologists said Hakha was too dangerous to live in and recommended moving the capital. That isn't going to happen. Instead, trees and grass are being planted in an effort to stop erosion. Falling rocks and earth apart, Hakha is a friendly, scruffy place dominated by its many churches. Surrounding the town is some gorgeous, almost completely unknown countryside, which is home to many villages. Best of all, the locals are uniformly happy to see foreigners. With only around 50 to 100 Westerners visiting annually – almost all of whom are missionaries or aid workers – you're guaranteed some attention here.

⦿ Sights

Tourism isn't in its infancy here: it is nonexistent. That will change in the next few years, but for now you are on your own when it comes to exploring.

View Point VIEWPOINT

Fine views over Hakha and the surrounding hills from this viewing platform about a mile outside town. To find it, follow Bo Gyoke Rd south past the football stadium and head uphill for 25 minutes.

Hakha Baptist Church CHURCH

(⊙daylight hours) With its fine stone steeple and red roof, this is the most distinctive and historic of Hakha's many churches. Funded by American missionaries, it dates back to 1908, but was extensively rebuilt in the early 1960s. It's about 400yd downhill from the football stadium.

In the nearby compound of the Hakha Baptist Association is a grey 1907 bungalow that houses a **Missionaries Museum**, although it was closed and lacking exhibits when we dropped by.

🛏 Sleeping

At the entrance to town is the posh Pyi Taung Su Guest House. Don't get excited as you can't stay here; it's for government officials only. Foreigners are restricted to a handful of places, all basic and located along Bo Gyoke Rd close to the clock tower.

Rung Guest House
GUESTHOUSE **$**

(✆ 070-22524; Bo Gyoke Rd; r K15,000-20,000; ☎) The best place in town. The more expensive rooms here come with their own small bathrooms, Western toilets and TVs. Hot water is delivered each morning by hand. Cheaper rooms share bathrooms and are rather more basic. The staff speak English and there's wi-fi, although it wasn't working when we were there.

Grace Guest House
GUESTHOUSE **$**

(✆ 070-21301; Bo Gyoke Rd; r K15,000-20,000) The 'special' rooms out the back in a new wooden block are eccentrically arranged so that the beds occupy almost all the space, but they are comfortable enough and have their own bathrooms. 'Normal' rooms are dark and cramped and share squat toilets. The staff speak some English.

✕ Eating & Drinking

A few restaurants straggle along Bo Gyoke Rd, and share similar menus of Chinese-Burmese dishes. Most close on Sundays. Prices tend to be a little higher than elsewhere in Myanmar, a consequence of the relative isolation of Hakha, and Chin State, from the rest of the country.

Hakha is a heavily Christian place and you won't find beer stations here. Head to the restaurants for alcohol. Tea shops are scattered around town.

Shwe Myo
Daw Restaurant
CHINESE, BURMESE **$$**

(off Bo Gyoke Rd; mains from K4000; ☉10am-10pm, closed Sun; ▣) The best and liveliest place to eat in Hakha, with decent Chinese-Burmese dishes – large portions – and beer on tap. Find it on the left-hand side of the street that runs off Bo Gyoke Rd, opposite Grace Guest House.

Hakha Kitchen
CHINESE, BURMESE **$$**

(Bo Gyoke Rd; mains from K7000; ☉9am-10pm, closed Sun; ▣) More expensive than other restaurants in town, but the food is pretty good (the fried rice and noodle dishes are cheaper). It's just past the clock tower, below Bo Gyoke Rd: look for the English sign. Serves alcohol.

Chin Taung
Taan Food Centre
CHINESE, BURMESE **$$**

(Bo Gyoke Rd; mains from K3000; ☉8am-4pm Mon-Sat, 4-9pm Sun; ▣) Facing the clock tower, this 2nd-floor restaurant has an English menu of Chinese-Burmese classics, and curtained cubicles to eat in. Unusually it's open on Sunday evenings.

ⓘ Information

CB Bank (Bo Gyoke Rd; ☉9.30am-3pm) One of the only two banks, that we're aware of, in all Chin State. You can change money here and it has an ATM, although we wouldn't rely on it.

Friends of Nature (✆ 070-21083; fonhakha@ gmail.com; 362 Bo Gyoke Rd; ☉8am-5pm) The English-speaking staff here can organise a car (K50,000 per day) and a tour guide (US$40 per day), but aren't as helpful with information about the countryside surrounding Hakha.

ⓘ Getting There & Away

From Kalaymyo's bus station, daily buses (K8000, 10 hours) and quicker and more comfortable, if cramped and crowded, minivans (K10,000, eight hours) run to Hakha Monday to Saturday.

From Hakha, buses (K8000, 10 hours) and minivans (K10,000, eight hours) run to Kalaymyo via Falam (K5000, four hours). All leave at 7am from a variety of bus-company offices on the road behind the football stadium, which is off Bo Gyoke Rd.

There are also daily buses Monday to Saturday to Yangon (K35,000, 18 hours, 9am) and Mandalay (K15,000, 14 hours, 8pm).

Understand Myanmar

Myanmar Today

State Counsellor Aung San Suu Kyi and her colleagues have their work cut out for years to come tackling Myanmar's key problems, not least of which are stopping civil insurrections and securing peace, curbing human rights abuses and rectifying the impact of decades of economic mismanagement and corruption. There are some bright spots: sanctions have been dropped and the ancient city of Bagan may gain Unesco World Heritage status by 2019.

Best on Film

The Monk (2014) Low-key coming-of-age drama about a boy raised in a monastery who has to decide whether to further embrace Buddhism or move into the secular world.

Kayan Beauties (2013) Thriller about four Kayan girls who travel from their village to Taunggyi, where one of them gets kidnapped by human traffickers.

Yangon Calling (2013) Documentary about Myanmar's punk-rock scene directed by Berlin-based filmmakers Alexander Dluzak and Carsten Piefke.

Best in Print

Burma's Spring (Rosalind Russell; 2016) Lively memoir with a broad cast of characters from girl band singers and domestic workers to opposition politicians.

Golden Parasol (Wendy Law-Yone; 2013) An insider's view on key events in modern Myanmar's history; her father, Ed Law-Yone, an influential newspaper editor, was exiled from the country in the 1960s.

River of Lost Footsteps (Thant Myint-U; 2006) Must-read historical review, by the grandson of former UN secretary general U Thant.

21st-century Panglong Conference

Since taking office in April 2016, the National League for Democracy (NLD) government has prioritised bringing about sustainable peace for Myanmar following nearly 60 years of civil insurrections. On 31 August 2016, the 21st-century Panglong Conference (named after the Panglong Agreement of 1947 between Suu Kyi's father Aung San and major ethnic group leaders), convened in Nay Pyi Taw. Representatives of 19 ethnic groups sat with top government and army (Tatmadaw) leaders, as well as the UN Secretary-General, to air their grievances and hopes for the future.

Offended by organisational hiccups and a perceived lack of inclusiveness, the Wa delegation, representing the country's most powerful ethnic armed group, stormed out on day two of what was to be a five-day conference, but which ended up lasting four. Not a brilliant start, but Suu Kyi's achievement of persuading so many rebel and ethnic groups to attend the conference (more than had signed up to the previous government's Nationwide Ceasefire Agreement) was still generally applauded.

Reforming the Army

A key stumbling block for peace is that distrust of the Tatmadaw is ingrained among ethnic minorities following decades of conflict. Although sidelined, the military continues to wield significant political and economic power in Myanmar. In the 2016–17 annual budget, the defence ministry received the largest share, with 1.24 trillion kyat appropriated.

However, there are signs that the military's top brass is adapting to the more democratic times. In September 2016 Commander-in-Chief Senior General Min Aung Hlaing warned the army to follow the Geneva Convention and respect human rights. Earlier in the month, in a groundbreaking ruling, a court martial found seven soldiers, including four military officers, guilty of murdering five civilians in Shan State's Lashio township during a botched interrogation. The soldiers were sentenced to five years in prison with hard labour.

Restoring Myanmar's Reputation

It's not just the army that Suu Kyi has to keep onside. Powerful neighbours China and India cannot be ignored, alongside the US and others keen to do business in Myanmar. In a symbolic gesture, Suu Kyi chose China for her first visit as State Counsellor, perhaps in an effort to mend bridges strained over issues such as the Myitsone Dam. Funded by China, the US$3.6 billion project was suspended in 2011 and continues to be a major source of friction between the two countries. China is also considered key in helping bring some of the more belligerent factions in the civil war to the negotiating table.

Suu Kyi continued her foreign tours in the US in 2016. In a meeting with President Obama, he announced the end to his country's final set of targeted economic sanctions on Burma. Later, speaking at the UN, Suu Kyi pledged to promote human rights in Rakhine State, at the same time as carefully avoiding mentioning the persecuted Rohingya by name. In 2016 she visited India to partake in the Brazil, Russia, India, China, South Africa (BRICS) summit in Goa.

Rebuilding Bagan

The 6.8-magnitude earthquake that struck central Myanmar on 24 August 2016 was a painful reminder that whatever progress the country may be making, it remains hostage to geological and geographical factors beyond its control. The damage to hundreds of temples across the plains of Bagan appeared devastating, but for some this has been seen as a chance to fix the poorly executed past restorations of the temples, and put the country's most important archaeological site in a better position for achieving Unesco World Heritage recognition by 2019. This prize had been denied to the military junta for over two decades thanks to dodgy restorations and lax supervision at the site. Now there's a chance to do things properly.

Unesco Myanmar is coordinating an international team to work on the monuments and is supporting the government in its bid to apply for World Heritage status. But to achieve ranking alongside other Southeast Asian cultural treasures, such as Angkor Wat, it's likely that 40 odd hotels and other businesses will have to be demolished or moved away from the proposed heritage zone. In the meantime, on the government's long list of new laws to enact are bills increasing the protection of Myanmar's cultural heritage, with tougher punishments, including jail terms of up to seven years for anyone found to have damaged, removed or destroyed heritage buildings.

POPULATION: **51.41 MILLION**

AREA: **261,228 SQ MILES**

GDP: **US$64.86 BILLION**

GDP GROWTH: **7% (FOR 2015)**

INFLATION: **10.8%**

if Myanmar (Burma) were 100 people

68 would be Bamar
9 would be Shan
7 would be Kayin (Karen)
4 would be Rakhaing
3 would be Chinese
2 would be Indian
2 would be Mon
5 would be other

belief systems
(% of population)

88 Buddhist
6 Christian
4 Muslim
2 Hindu, Animist & Other

population per sq km

MYANMAR   USA   UK

≈ 30 people

History

A succession of major ethnic groups have held sway down the ages across the territory that now makes up Myanmar, with the Bamar only coming into prominence in the 11th century. Civil war erupted between minority groups after independence from British colonial rule in 1948; on the fringes of the nation, the unrest continues today. The country is now emerging from nearly 50 years of military rule into an era of democracy and economic growth.

Pre-Colonial Burma

Earliest Inhabitants

Archaeologists believe humans have lived in the region as far back as 75,000 BC.

In 2003 a 45-million-year-old fossil (possibly the anklebone of a large ape-like animal) was found in central Myanmar that might just prove the area to be the birthplace of *all* humans. The implication of this research is that our primate ancestors may have had Asian rather than African origins.

There's no debate that 2500 years ago the area was a key land link between traders from China, India and the Middle East. Ancient Greeks knew of the country, too.

The First Burmese Empire

Bagan was nearly 200 years old when its 'golden period' kicked off – signalled by the energetic, can-do King Anawrahta taking the throne in 1044. His conquest of the Mon kingdom and the adoption of Buddhism inspired a creative energy in Bagan. It quickly became a city of glorious temples and the capital of the First Burmese Empire.

Anawrahta's successors (Kyanzittha, Alaungsithu and Htilominlo) lacked his vision, and the kingdom's power slowly declined. In 1273 King Narathihapate made the diplomatic mistake of offending the growing power of Kublai Khan by executing his envoys. When the Mongols invaded in 1287, Narathihapate fled south to Pyay (Prome) where he committed suicide.

The limestone Padah-Lin Caves in western Shan State contain paintings that could be 13,000 years old, and there's evidence that local farmers had domesticated chickens and made bronze by 1500 BC.

Legend has it that Buddha gave eight of his hairs to a couple of visiting Burmese merchants 3000 years ago. They are enshrined in Yangon's Shwedagon Paya.

TIMELINE	850 BC	3rd century BC	1st century BC
	According to Burmese chronicles, Abhiraja of the Sakyan clan from India founds Tagaung, 127 miles north of Mandalay; his son travels south and founds a kingdom at Rakhine (Arakan).	The Mon, who migrated into the Ayeyarwady Delta from present-day Thailand (and from China before that), establish their capital, Thaton, and have first contact with Buddhism.	Possible founding of Beikthano (named after the local word for Vishnu), a Pyu town east of current-day Magwe; it's believed to have flourished for about 400 years.

ORIGINAL KINGDOMS

Four major precolonial ethnic groups peppered Burma's flatlands with their kingdoms for centuries, while smaller ethnic groups lived – mostly untouched – in the remote hills beyond. The early histories that are attached to these groups are a mix of fact and legend.

Pyu Arriving from the Tibeto-Burman plateau and/or from India around the 1st century BC, the Pyu established the first major kingdom of sorts, with city-states in central Myanmar, including Beikthano, Hanlin and Sri Ksetra (Thayekhittaya). In the 10th century Yunnanese invaders from China enslaved or scared off most Pyu.

Rakhine Also known as Arakanese, these people claim their kingdom was well under way by the 6th century BC. Certainly it was in full force by the 15th century, when their Buddhist kingdom was based in Mrauk U and their navy controlled much of the Bay of Bengal.

Bamar Also known as Burmans, these people arrived from somewhere in the eastern Himalaya in the 8th or 9th century, supplanting the vanquished Pyu and establishing the cultural heartland of Myanmar as it's still known. Centuries of conflict with the Mon erupted after their arrival. Although the Bamar came out on top, the result was really a merger of the two cultures.

Mon This race, who may have originated from eastern India or mainland Southeast Asia, settled fertile lowlands on the Ayeyarwady (Irrawaddy) River delta across Thailand to Cambodia. They developed the area as Suvannabhumi (Golden Land), with their Burmese kingdom, centred on present-day Thaton, coming into existence around the 9th century.

In the ensuing chaos, Shan tribes (closely related to the Siamese) from the hills to the east grabbed a piece of the low country, while the Mon in the south broke free of Bamar control and re-established their own kingdom.

The Second Burmese Empire

It would be another 200 years before the Bamar were able to regroup to found their second empire. During this time, a settlement of Bamar refugees in central Taungoo survived between the Mon to the south and the Shan to the north and east, by playing the larger forces off against each other.

In the 16th century, a series of Taungoo kings extended their power north, nearly to the Shan's capital at Inwa, then south, taking the Mon kingdom and shifting their own capital to Bago. In 1550 Bayinnaung came to the throne, reunified all of Burma and defeated the neighbouring

Remembered as *tayokpyay min* ('the king who ran away from the Chinese'), Narathihapate was also known for his gluttonous appetite, demanding 300 varieties of dishes at his banquets.

AD 754	849	1044	1057
Nanzhao soldiers from Yunnan, China, conquer the hill tribes in the upper reaches of the Ayeyarwady (Irrawaddy) River and challenge the Pyu who ruled from the city of Sri Ksetra.	Bagan is founded on the site of a once-thriving Pyu city; its first name may have been Pyugan, something recorded 200 years later by the Annamese of present-day Vietnam.	Anawrahta slays his brother, takes the throne in Bagan and starts organising his kingdom to kick off the 'golden period' of the First Burmese Empire.	Having subdued the Shan Hills, Anawrahta's armies sack the ancient Mon city of Thaton and bring back 30,000 people to Bagan, including the Mon king, Manuha.

Siamese so convincingly that it was many years before the long-running friction between the two nations resurfaced.

Following Bayinnaung's death in 1581, the Bamar's power again declined. The capital was shifted north to Inwa in 1636. Its isolation from the sea – effectively cutting off communication around the kingdom – ultimately contributed to Myanmar's defeat by the British.

The Third Burmese Empire

With all the subtlety of a kick to the groin, King Alaungpaya launched the third and final Burmese dynasty by contesting the Mon when the latter took over Inwa in 1752. Some say Alaungpaya's sense of invincibility deluded the Burmese into thinking they could resist the British later on.

After Alaungpaya's short and bloody reign, his son Hsinbyushin charged into Thailand and levelled Ayuthaya, forcing the Siamese to relocate their capital to what would eventually become Bangkok. Hsinbyushin's successor, Bodawpaya (another son of Alaungpaya), looked for glory too, and brought the Rakhine under Burmese control. This eventually led to tension with the British (who had economic interests in Rakhine territory) that the dynasty would not outlive.

Colonial Burma
Wars with the British

With eyes on fresh markets and supply sources in Southeast Asia, Britain wrested all of Burma in three decisive swipes. In the First, Second and

Published in 1925, GE Harvey's *History of Burma* gives a chronological rundown of Myanmar's kingdoms from the Pyu era until 1824, faithfully recounting many fanciful legends along the way.

One of the biggest meteor showers in modern history filled Burma's sky in 1885. Locals saw it as an omen of the end of their kingdom.

THREE KINGS

Lording it over a military parade ground in Myanmar's capital of Nay Pyi Taw are giant statues of the three kings considered the most important in Burmese history:

Anawrahta (1014–77) The creator of the First Burmese Empire ascended the throne in Bagan in 1044. He unified the Ayeyarwady Valley and held sway over the Shan hills and Rakhine at the same time as introducing key religious and social reforms that form the basis of modern Burmese culture.

Bayinnaung (1516–81) Aided by Portuguese mercenaries, this king of Taungoo is famed for unifying Burma for its 'second empire' and conquering Ayuthaya, the capital of Siam (Thailand), in 1569. Since 1996 his likeness has ominously looked over Thailand from near the border at Tachileik.

Alaungpaya (1714–60) With no royal roots, this hometown hero of Mokesebo (Shwebo) founded the Konbaung dynasty and created the second largest empire in Burmese history. His reign lasted only eight years, ending when he died – some say from poisoning – on retreat from Siam, after being turned back by rains.

1084	1273	1290s	1315
Kyanzittha continues the reforms started by his father, Anawrahta, including developing the Burmese written language; he's succeeded in 1113 by his grandson Alaungsithu, who rules until 1167.	In a curious gesture of diplomacy against far-superior forces to the north, the Burmese in Bagan slay Tartar ambassadors, prompting a peeved Kublai Khan to invade 14 years later.	Marco Polo becomes possibly the first Westerner to travel in central Burma (then known to foreigners as Mien), and publishes an account of his travels in 1298.	After the collapse of Bagan, Sagaing becomes the capital of a Shan kingdom. The capital moves to Inwa in 1364 and stays there intermittently until 1841.

Third Anglo-Burmese Wars they picked up Tanintharyi (Tenasserim) and Rakhine (Arakan) in 1824, Yangon (Rangoon) and southern Burma in 1853, and Mandalay and northern Burma in 1885.

The first war started when Burmese troops, ordered by King Bagyidaw, crossed into British-controlled Assam (in India) from Rakhine to pursue refugees. General Maha Bandula managed some minor victories using guerrilla tactics, but eventually was killed by cannon fire in 1824. Burmese troops then surrendered. The Treaty of Yandabo, helped by missionary translator Adoniram Judson (whose name is still on many Baptist churches in Myanmar), gave Rakhine and Tenasserim to the British.

Two Burmese kings later, Bagan Min started his reign in the same manner that many did: with mass executions to rid the capital of his potential rivals. An 1852 incident involving the possible kidnapping of two British sea captains (some argue it never happened) gave the British a welcome excuse for igniting another conflict, and an opportunity for more land. The British quickly seized all of southern Burma, including Yangon and Pathein (Bassein). They then marched north to Pyay (Prome), facing little opposition.

The Burman (1882) and Burma: A Handbook of Practical Information (1906) by colonial adventurer Sir J George Scott remain in print today and still provide an insight into the nation's culture.

The Final Two Kings

The unpopular Bagan Min was ousted in favour of the more capable and revered Mindon Min, who moved the capital to Mandalay. Palace intrigues, including the murder of Mindon's powerful half-brother by Mindon's own sons, stayed the king's hand in naming his successor. When Mindon suddenly died following an attack of dysentery in 1878, the new (rather reluctant) king, Thibaw Min, was propelled to power by his ruthless wife and scheming mother-in-law. The following massive 'massacre of kinsmen' (79 of Thibaw Min's rivals) made many British papers. Alas, previous kings hadn't had to face the consequences of world media attention, and this act did little to generate public backlash in the UK against Britain's final, decisive war against the Burmese.

In 1885 it took Britain just two weeks to conquer Upper Burma, exile Thibaw and his court to India, and establish control over all the country. Direct colonial rule was implemented only where the Bamar were the majority (ie in the central plains). The hill states of the Chin, Kachin, Shan, Kayin and Kayah were allowed to remain largely autonomous – a decision that would have ramifications in the run-up to independence in 1948 and beyond.

The 1885 conflict between Burma and Britain is sometimes called 'the war over wood', as Britain's victory allowed it to secure rights to Burma's plentiful teak forests.

The Impact of British Rule

Burma was henceforth administered as part of 'British India'. Indian immigrants flooded into the country, acting like second colonisers, building businesses and taking rare, low-level government jobs from the hostile

1433	1472	1527	1540
Rakhine's ruler, Naramithla, establishes a new capital at Mrauk U, which, over the course of the next few centuries, grows into a grand city of temples and international commerce.	The great Mon king, Dhammazedi, takes the throne, unifies the Mon, moves the capital from Inwa to Bago (Pegu), and sets up diplomatic contact with Europe.	The Shan, who had exercised increasing control over the area following the fall of Bagan, defeats the kingdom at Inwa and rules Upper Burma for 28 years.	Lower Burma is reunified after Tabinshwehti, the ambitious and young king of Taungoo, defeats the Mon kingdom at Bago – helped by Burmans fleeing the Shan in Inwa.

indigenous population. In 1927 the majority of Yangon's population was Indian. Chinese immigration was also encouraged, further subjugating and marginalising the Burmese people.

Cheap British imports poured in, fuelled by rice profits. Many key cities and towns were renamed by the British with Yangon becoming Rangoon, Pyay becoming Prome and Bagan renamed Pagan.

Much of Burma was considered a hardship posting by British colonial officials, who found the locals difficult to govern. On the other hand, many of the British officials were incompetent and insensitive, and refused to honour local customs such as removing shoes to enter temples, thus causing grave offence to the majority Buddhist population. Inflamed by opposition to colonial rule, unemployment and the undercutting of the traditional educational role of Buddhist monasteries, the country had the highest crime rate in the British Empire.

> Despite a British-held ban against visiting Buddhist sites (because of the tradition of visitors being asked to remove their shoes), aviator Amelia Earhart visited them anyway (and took off her shoes).

Rise of Nationalism

Burmese nationalism burgeoned in the early days of the 20th century, often led by Buddhist monks. University students in Yangon went on strike on National Day in 1920, protesting elitist entrance requirements at British-built universities. The students referred to each other as *thakin* (master), as they claimed to be the rightful masters of Burma. One *thakin* – a young man called Aung San – was expelled from university in 1936 for refusing to reveal the author of a politically charged article.

Growing demands for self-government and opposition to colonial rule eventually forced the British to make a number of concessions. In 1937 Burma was separated administratively from India and a new legislative council including elected Burmese ministers was formed. However, the country continued to be torn by a struggle between opposing political parties and sporadic outbursts of anti-Indian and anti-Chinese violence.

> **WWII Sites in Myanmar**
>
> Start of Burma Road (Lashio, Northern Myanmar)
>
> Taukkyan War Cemetery (North of Yangon)
>
> Thanbyuzayat War Cemetry (Mon State)
>
> Meiktila (Central Myanmar)

Aung San & WWII

More famous in the West as Aung San Suu Kyi's father, Bogyoke (General) Aung San is revered as a national hero and his likeness is seen throughout the country. He was born in Natmauk in Burma's central zone on 13 February 1915, the youngest of six children in a farming family.

An intelligent child, Aung San went on to study at Rangoon University. Here he edited the newspaper and led the All Burma Students' Union. At 26 years old, he and the group called the Thirty Comrades looked abroad for support for their independence movement. Although initially planning to seek an alliance with China, they ended up negotiating with Japan and receiving military training there. The Thirty Comrades became the first troops of the Burmese National Army (BNA) and returned to Burma with the invading Japanese troops in 1941.

1551	1599	1760	1784
Bayinnaung becomes king and, having conquered the Shan in 1557, reunifies all of Myanmar as the Second Burmese Empire; his forces take the Siam capital of Ayuthaya in 1569.	Following his defeat of Bago, the King of Rakhine grants the Portuguese mercenary Filipe de Brito e Nicote governorship of the port of Syriam (Thanlyin), which he controls until 1613.	Burmese King Alaungpaya, having conquered Inwa, Pyay (Prome), Dagon (which he renames Yangon) and Tenasserim (Tanintharyi), fails to take Ayuthaya in Siam and dies during the retreat.	Alaungpaya's son Bodawpaya defeats Rakhine, hauling off the revered Mahamuni Buddha image (supposedly cast during Buddha's legendary visit to the area in 554 BC) to Inwa.

By mid-1942 the Japanese had driven retreating British-Indian forces, along with the Chinese Kuomintang (KMT), out of most of Burma. But the conduct of the Japanese troops was starting to alienate the Burmese. Aung San complained at Japan's 15th Army headquarters in Maymyo (now Pyin Oo Lwin): 'I went to Japan to save my people who were struggling like bullocks under the British. But now we are treated like dogs'.

Aung San and the BNA switched allegiance to the Allied side in March 1945. Their assistance, along with brave behind-enemy-lines operations by the Chindits, an Allied Special Force, helped the British prevail over the Japanese in Burma two months later. Aung San and his colleagues now had a chance to dictate postwar terms for their country.

Post-Colonial Burma

Towards Independence

In January 1947 Aung San visited London as the colony's deputy chairperson of the Governor's Executive Council. Meeting with British Prime Minister Clement Attlee, a pact was agreed, under which Burma would gain self-rule within a year.

A month later, Aung San met with Shan, Chin and Kachin leaders in Panglong, in Shan State. They signed the famous Panglong Agreement in February 1947, guaranteeing ethnic minorities the freedom to choose their political destiny if dissatisfied with the situation after 10 years. The agreement also broadly covered absent representatives of the Kayin, Kayah, Mon and Rakhine.

In the elections for the assembly, Aung San's Anti-Fascist People's Freedom League (AFPFL) won an overwhelming 172 seats out of 225. The Burmese Communist Party took seven, while the Bamar opposition,

Armed Forces Day (27 March) commemorates the Burmese soldiers' resistance against the Japanese army in WWII.

REVOLUTIONARY MONKS

In 1919, at Mandalay's Eindawya Paya, monks evicted Europeans who refused to take off their shoes. The British, sensing that this 'Shoe Question' was the start of a nationalist movement, sentenced the monk leader, U Kettaya, to life imprisonment. This would not be the last involvement of the *sangha* (Buddhist brotherhood) in politics.

U Ottama, a monk who had studied in India and returned to Burma in 1921, promoted religious liberation as a way to bring the independence movement to the attention of the average local Buddhist. After numerous arrests, U Ottama died in prison in 1939. Another monk, U Wizaya, died in prison in 1929 after a 163-day hunger strike, which began as a protest against a rule that forbade imprisoned monks from wearing robes.

In the footsteps of these martyrs to the nationalist cause strode the brave monks who, risking arrest and worse, marched the streets in 2007.

1813	1826	1852	1857
Adoniram Judson, a Baptist missionary from Massachusetts, arrives to convert souls and translate the Bible; thanks to his influence, Myanmar has the third-largest number of Baptists worldwide.	The Treaty of Yandabo concludes the First Anglo-Burmese War that had begun two years previously; the British annex Rakhine and Taninthayri (Tenasserim) and demand an indemnity of £1 million.	Following the possible kidnapping of two of its nationals, Britain starts the Second Anglo-Burmese War for control of Lower Burma; Mindon Min overthrows his half-brother and sues for peace.	Mindon Min moves Upper Burma's capital from Inwa to a newly built city at the foot of Mandalay Hill, thus fulfilling a purported 2400-year-old prophecy by Buddha.

Patricia Elliott's *The White Umbrella* (www. whiteumbrella. com) is the fascinating true story of Shan royal Sao Hearn Hkam, wife of Burma's president and founder of the Shan State Army.

led by U Saw, took three. (U Saw was Burma's prime minister between 1939 and 1942, and was exiled to Uganda for the rest of WWII for secretly communicating with the Japanese following a failed attempt to gain British agreement to Burmese home rule.) The remaining 69 seats were split between ethnic minorities, including four seats for the Anglo-Burman community.

On 19 July 1947, 32-year-old Aung San and six aides were gunned down in a plot ascribed to U Saw. Some speculate that the military was involved, due to Aung San's plans to demilitarise the government. Apparently U Saw thought he'd walk into the prime minister's role with Aung San gone; instead he took the noose, when the British had him hanged for the murders in 1948.

U Nu & Early Woes

While Myanmar mourned the death of a hero, Prime Minister Attlee and Aung San's protégé, U Nu, signed an agreement for the transfer of power in October 1947. On 4 January 1948, at an auspicious middle-of-the-night hour, Burma became independent and left the British Commonwealth.

Almost immediately, the new government led by U Nu had to contend with the complete disintegration of the country, involving rebels, communists, gangs and (US-supported) anticommunist Chinese KMT forces.

The hill-tribe people, who had supported the British and fought against the Japanese throughout the war, were distrustful of the Bamar majority and took up armed opposition. The communists withdrew from the government and attacked it. Muslims from the Rakhine area also opposed the new government. The Mon, long thought to be totally integrated with the Burmese, revolted. Assorted factions, private armies, WWII resistance groups and plain mutineers further confused the picture.

U Nu, Burma's first prime minister, was also a devout Buddhist who banned the slaughter of cows after winning the 1960 election. His autobiography *Saturday's Son* was published in 1975.

In early 1949 almost the entire country was in the hands of a number of rebel groups, and there was even fighting in Yangon's suburbs. At one stage the government was on the point of surrendering to the communist forces, but gradually fought back. Through 1950 and 1951 it regained control of much of the country.

With the collapse of Chiang Kai-Shek's KMT forces to those of Mao Zedong, the tattered remnants of the KMT withdrew into northern Burma and mounted raids from there into Yunnan, China. But being no match for the Chinese communists, the KMT decided to carve their own little fiefdom out of Burmese territory.

The First Military Government

By the mid-1950s the government had strengthened its hold on the country, but the economy slipped from bad to worse. U Nu managed to remain in power until 1958, when he voluntarily handed the reins over to

1862	1866	1885	1886
Bahadur Shah Zafar, the last emperor of India, is exiled with his family to Yangon, which the British call Rangoon. He dies in 1858, and is buried in secrecy.	Mindon's sons conspire against the heir apparent – beheading him in the palace – prompting Mindon to choose Thibaw, who showed no interest in the throne, as his successor.	The Third Anglo-Burmese War results in the end of the Burmese monarchy, as Britain conquers Mandalay, sending Thibaw and his family into exile in India.	Burma becomes an administrative province of British-ruled India, with its capital at Rangoon; it takes several years for the British to successfully suppress local resistance.

a caretaker military government under General Ne Win. Considering the pride most of the country had in the Burmese army, which had helped bring independence, this was seen as a welcome change.

Freed from the 'democratic' responsibilities inherent in a civilian government, Ne Win was able to make some excellent progress during the 15 months his military government operated. A degree of law and order was restored, rebel activity was reduced, and Yangon was given a massive and much-needed clean-up.

In *The River of Lost Footsteps*, Thant Myint-U writes that Ne Win's first period of government was considered by some 'the most effective and efficient in modern Burmese history'. Sadly, the same would not be true for the general's second, much more extended, stint at Burma's helm.

The Burmese Road to Socialism

Free elections were held in December 1960 and the charismatic U Nu regained power with a much-improved majority, partly through a policy of making Buddhism the state religion. This, and politically destabilising moves by various ethnic minorities to leave the Union of Burma, resulted in an army coup in March 1962.

U Nu, along with his main ministers, was thrown into prison, where he remained until he was forced into exile in 1966. Ne Win established a 17-member Revolutionary Council and announced that the country would 'march towards socialism in our own Burmese way', confiscating most private property and handing it over to military-run state corporations.

Nationalisation resulted in everyday commodities becoming available only on the black market, and vast numbers of people being thrown out of work. Ne Win also banned international aid organisations, foreign-language publications and local, privately owned newspapers and political parties. The net result was that by 1967 a country that had been the largest exporter of rice in the world prior to WWII was now unable to feed itself.

Riots & Street Protests

Opposition to Ne Win's government eventually bubbled over into a strike by oil workers and others in May 1974 and, later that year, riots over what was seen as the inappropriate burial of former UN secretary-general U Thant in Yangon. Responding with gunfire and arrests, the government regained control and doggedly continued to run the country – further impoverishing the people with successive demonetisations.

In late 1981 Ne Win retired as president of the republic, retaining his position as chair of the Burmese Socialist Programme Party (BSPP), the country's only legal political party under the 1974 constitution. But his successor, San Yu, and the government remained very much under the influence of Ne Win's political will.

Following Ne Win's military coup in 1962, the country started closing off the outside world, limiting foreigners' visits to just 24-hour visas, later extended to a week.

As many as 250,000 people of Indian and Chinese descent left Burma in the 1960s. Anti-Chinese riots in Yangon in 1967 also resulted in hundreds of Chinese deaths.

1920	**1937**	**1939**	**1941**
Students across Burma strike in protest against the new University Act, seen as helping to perpetuate colonial rule; the strike is celebrated today by National Day.	A new constitution for Burma sets up a legislative council, giving locals a larger role in the running of the country; it's not enough to stem calls for independence.	Still under British watch, the leader of Burma's government, U Saw, holds office until his arrest in January 1942 for communicating with the Japanese.	After training with the Japanese, Aung San – Aung San Suu Kyi's father – founds the Burmese Army, and marches into Burma with his benefactors to oust the British.

In 1988 the people again took to the streets en masse, insisting that Ne Win had to go. Public protests reached a climax on the auspicious date of 8 August 1988 (8-8-88), after which the government steadily moved to crush all opposition, killing an estimated 3000 and imprisoning more. Tens of thousands, mainly students, fled the country.

Slorc Holds an Election

In September 1988 a military coup (widely thought to have had the blessing of Ne Win) saw the formation of the State Law & Order Restoration Council (Slorc) and the promise to hold a multiparty election within three months.

Although 235 parties contested the election (which was delayed until May 1990), the clear front runner from the start was the National League for Democracy (NLD). The NLD was led by several former generals, along with Aung San Suu Kyi (daughter of hero Aung San), who had made such a public impression at rallies during the 1988 protests.

In the run-up to the election, Slorc tried to appease the masses with construction programs, adding a coat of paint to many buildings in Yangon and abandoning socialism in favour of a capitalist economy. In 1989 it changed the name of the country to Myanmar, then placed Aung San Suu Kyi under house arrest and detained many other prodemocracy leaders.

Convinced it had effectively dealt with the opposition, the government went ahead with the country's first election in 30 years. The voter turnout – 72.59% – was the highest in Myanmar's history. The result was a resounding victory for the NLD, which took 392 of the 485 contested seats (or about 60% of the vote), with the military-backed National Unity Party gaining just 10 seats with just over 25% of the vote.

> The 1988 demonstrations were sparked by a students' fight at the Rangoon Institute of Technology (that's right, RIOT) that ended with police intervening and some students being killed.

Post-1990 Myanmar

NLD under Attack

Slorc barred the elected members of parliament from assuming power, decreeing that a state-approved constitution had to be passed by national referendum first. In October 1990 the military raided NLD offices and arrested key leaders. Five years later Slorc deemed it safe enough to release Aung San Suu Kyi; at the same time, many other high-level dissidents, including the NLD's Tin U and Kyi Maung, were also released from prison.

In May and September 1996, a congress of NLD members was held in a bold political gambit to show that the party was still an active force. The military junta responded by detaining hundreds who attended the congress; the street leading to Suu Kyi's residence was also blockaded, prohibiting her from making speeches at her residence.

In 1998 Suu Kyi attempted to leave Yangon to meet with supporters, but was blocked by the military and forcibly returned to the city. A

1945	1947	1948	1958
Aung San turns his army against the Japanese to support the British; later he forms the Anti-Fascist People's Freedom League (AFPFL) to fight for Burmese independence.	Having gained independence from Britain and rallied ethnic groups to a 10-year deal where they could secede from Burma by 1958, Aung San and six colleagues are assassinated by rivals.	On 4 January the country gains independence as the Union of Burma with U Nu as the prime minister; immediately it is destabilised by various ethnic and political conflicts.	A split in the AFPFL causes parliamentary chaos; U Nu barely survives a no-confidence vote and invites General Ne Win to form a 'caretaker government', which lasts until 1960.

second attempt to drive to Mandalay in September 2000 again saw the Lady (as she is affectionately known) detained at a military roadblock and later placed under house arrest. Save for barely a year (between 6 May 2002 and 30 May 2003), she would spend the next decade shut away from the public.

Than Shwe Takes Over

Due to the tourism boycott launched by the NLD and others, there was a disappointing turnout for the junta's official 'Visit Myanmar Year 1996'. Increased sanctions from the West led the government to seek other sources of income: namely trade with China, India and Thailand.

Khin Nyunt, feared head of military intelligence, became prime minister in 2003. The man known as the Prince of Darkness took the lead on the junta's seven-step 'roadmap towards discipline-flourishing democracy'. But only a year later hard-liner Senior General Than Shwe ousted Khin Nyunt and many of his fellow intelligence officers; at a secret trial, Khin Nyunt was sentenced to 44 years in jail.

Than Shwe initially promised to continue the transition to democracy, but instead his activity showed a focus on negotiating multimillion-dollar trade deals with China, India and Thailand, and importing weapons and military know-how from Russia and North Korea.

In 2005 an entirely new capital city was created in the arid fields near Pyinmana. The junta named the city-in-the-making Nay Pyi Taw (Royal Capital), leaving little doubt that Than Shwe's strategies and inspirations were aligned less with the modern world than with Burmese kings of centuries past.

Than Shwe: Unmasking Burma's Tyrant by Benedict Rogers is an unauthorised biography of the secretive senior general who called the shots in Myanmar between 2004 and 2010.

MIXED FEELINGS ABOUT THE TATMADAW

From a small and disunited force at the time of independence, Myanmar's army, the Tatmadaw, has grown to nearly half a million soldiers. It takes care of its troops and their dependants by providing subsidised housing and access to special schools and hospitals. The military also owns two giant corporations – the Union of Myanmar Economic Holdings (UMEH) and Myanmar Economic Corporation (MEC) – whose dealings extend into nearly every corner of the economy.

Small wonder that for many families, having a son (it's rarely a daughter, although there are some roles for women in the army) who is a solider results in much appreciation for the financial security it brings. Many other people in Myanmar live in fear of the army, but there are others who continue to respect the institution for the role it originally played in securing independence for the nation – not least of whom is Aung San Suu Kyi whose father was a general.

1962	1964	1978	1988
Following the coup by Ne Win, a peaceful student protest at Rangoon University is suppressed by the military, with more than 100 students killed and the Student Union building blown up.	All opposition political parties are banned, commerce and industry are nationalised, and Ne Win begins the process of isolating Myanmar from the rest of the world.	General San Yu succeeds Ne Win as Burma's president but Ne Win remains the ultimate ruler, even after his resignation from the Burmese Socialist Programme Party in 1988.	Civilian unrest grows as living standards continue to fall. On 8 August huge nonviolent marches end with the military killing more than 3000 protestors; the military promises to hold democratic elections.

The 'Saffron Revolution'

In mid-2007 natural gas prices rose by 500% (and petrol by 200%), leading to price hikes for everything from local bus tickets to rice. In late August a group of '1988 generation' protestors were arrested for staging a march against the inflation. On 5 September, when monks denounced the price hikes in a demonstration in Pakokku, the protests escalated. The military responded with gunfire and allegedly beat one monk to death.

In response, the All Burma Monks Alliance (ABMA) was formed, denouncing the ruling government as an 'evil military dictatorship' and refusing to accept alms from military officials (a practice called *pattam mikkujana kamma*). By 17 September, marches were happening daily, swelling in numbers across major cities, including Yangon, Mandalay, Meiktila and Sittwe.

Unexpectedly, monk-led crowds were allowed to pray with Aung San Suu Kyi from outside her house gates on 22 September. Two days later, anything from 50,000 to 150,000 protestors marched through the streets of Yangon in what would become known as the Saffron Revolution. All the while the government watched, photographing participants.

On 26 September, the army began shooting protestors and imposed a curfew. By the end of the week, monasteries had been raided, around 3000 people had been arrested and over 30 were dead, including a Japanese photographer whose killing in central Yangon was captured on video.

Cyclone Nargis

In the aftermath of the 2007 demonstrations, Than Shwe finalised the long-delayed new constitution, which had been under discussion since 1993, and announced a national referendum for it on 10 May 2008. But on 2 May, Cyclone Nargis – the second-deadliest cyclone in recorded history – tore across the Ayeyarwady Delta.

A DIFFERENT KIND OF REVOLUTION

As David Steinberg points out in *Burma/Myanmar: What Everyone Needs to Know*, the Saffron Revolution was neither saffron nor a revolution. Burmese monks wear maroon (not saffron) coloured robes for a start. The revolutionary part of the events of 2007 was that, for the first time, they were broadcast via smuggled-out videos on satellite TV or the internet. For a nail-biting account of how incendiary video evidence was captured of the army violently cracking down on the people during the so-called 'Saffron Revolution', watch the Oscar-nominated documentary *Burma VJ* (https://vimeo.com/33160416).

1990	1995	1997	2000
In May the National League for Democracy (NLD), led by Aung San Suu Kyi, conclusively wins the first nationwide election in three decades, but the military refuses to relinquish power.	Aung San Suu Kyi is released from house arrest. The government uses forced labour to ready some sites for 'Visit Myanmar Year'; NLD and other activist groups launch a tourism boycott.	US and Canada impose an investment ban on Myanmar. State Law & Order Restoration Council (Slorc) changes name to the State Peace & Development Council. Myanmar joins Asean.	The EU intensifies its economic sanctions against Myanmar, citing continued human rights abuses in the country. Aung San Suu Kyi again under house arrest until May 2002.

Cyclone Nargis' 121mph winds, and the tidal surge that followed, swept away bamboo-hut villages, leaving over two million survivors without shelter, food or drinking water. Damages were estimated at US$2.4 billion. Yangon avoided the worst, but the winds (at 80mph) still overturned power lines and trees, leaving the city without power for two weeks.

The government was widely condemned for its tepid response to the disaster. Outside aid groups were held up by a lack of visas and the Myanmar military's refusal to allow foreign planes to deliver aid. Locals stepped into the breach, heroically organising their own relief teams. In the meantime, the government kept the referendum more or less on schedule, outraging many locals and outside observers.

A New Constitution

Even before the cyclone, activist groups and NLD members had urged the public to vote 'no' at the referendum to change the constitution. They feared that it would enshrine the power of the generals. Others worried that not voting would only deepen the military hold on the government and leave no wiggle room for other political parties to contribute.

Voting took place in two rounds during May 2008, while a reported 2.5 million people still required food, shelter and medical assistance. The military announced that 98.12% of those eligible had voted and that 92.48% had approved the new constitution (p373) – even though very few would have even seen the document in advance of the referendum.

With Than Shwe's roadmap towards discipline-flourishing democracy in place, and yet another reason found to keep his nemesis, Aung San Suu Kyi, under house arrest (beyond her scheduled release in 2009), Myanmar's first general election in 20 years went ahead in November 2010.

Roadmap to Democracy

Over 30 different political parties jumped through a considerable number of hoops to contest the 2010 election, including the National Democratic Force (NDF), a breakaway group from the NLD that, unlike its parent party, decided to participate in the poll. As expected, the USDP triumphed in an election the UN called 'deeply flawed'. Not surprisingly, many considered the change of government to be largely cosmetic, but one good result was that, with victory in the bag, Aung San Suu Kyi was released from house arrest and was permitted contact with the international media.

In February 2011 a quasi-civilian parliament convened for its initial sessions, replacing the military regime's State Peace and Development Council (SPDC). A new president, former general and old prime minister

> According to research by Asean and the UN, Cyclone Nargis caused 84,537 deaths and 53,836 missing people – 138,373 in all, 61% of whom were female. Other estimates are even higher, suggesting 300,000 were lost. Children, unable to withstand the inflow of water, were most vulnerable to drowning.

> *Everything is Broken* by Emma Larkin is an eye-opening account of the regime's response to the worst natural disaster to befall Myanmar in modern history.

2002	2003	2004	2006
In March Ne Win's son-in-law and three grandsons are arrested for plotting to overthrow the junta; Ne Win is placed under house arrest and dies on 5 December, aged 91.	Aung San Suu Kyi and NLD members are attacked by pro-government mobs in northern Myanmar; up to 100 are killed. 'The Lady' is again placed under house arrest.	Having brokered a ceasefire agreement with Karen insurgents, Prime Minister Khin Nyunt, the moderate voice in the military who outlined a seven-point 'roadmap' for democracy, is arrested.	General Than Shwe and the government move the capital from Yangon to Nay Pyi Taw, a new city in central Myanmar.

Thein Sein, was 'chosen' by the elected reps to take over from Senior General Than Shwe, Myanmar's supreme ruler for the past two decades. Than Shwe has since quietly faded into the background and in December 2015 even met with Aung San Suu Kyi, his former nemsis.

After the 2010 Election

Given how glimmers of democratic hope for Myanmar had been so cruelly snubbed in the recent past, many could be forgiven for taking with a pinch of salt Thein Sein's inaugural address to the new parliament, which promised meaningful reforms for the country, including tackling corruption and poverty.

However, a year later, after the president had met with Aung San Suu Kyi, started to release political prisoners, diminished state censorship and enacted various laws to begin liberalising the economy (including allowing the kyat to float), it was becoming clear that positive changes really were afoot in Myanmar. International sanctions were dropped, world leaders flew into Yangon, and it seemed the country might well be on the way to coming in from the cold.

A ceasefire in 2012 with Karen rebels also provided a hiatus to the longest-running insurrection in contemporary history. However, inter-ethnic and religious violence in Rakhine State and central Myanmar has since tempered the feel-good factor about Myanmar's reforms, reminding everyone that there are significant difficulties for the country to overcome.

NLD in Parliament

By-elections in April 2012 saw a landslide victory for 42 NLD candidates, including Aung San Suu Kyi, who became de facto leader of the opposition. The economy developed rapidly as foreign investors rushed to gain a foothold in a market largely cut off from the world for nearly half a century. The easing of censorship also witnessed an explosion in new media, largely unafraid to document the country's multiple failings as well as its successes. In 2014 Myanmar chaired the Association of Southeast Asian Nations (Asean), a privilege it had been denied in 2006.

However, initially cordial relations between Suu Kyi and Thein Sein soon turned sour. The president appointed the new member of parliament as chair of a commission to investigate a dispute at the Letpaudaung copper mine that had resulted in the authorities injuring many protesters. There was a public outcry when the commission's report in 2013 allowed mining at the site to continue and included only mild criticism of the police's actions.

Suu Kyi and the NLD's near silence about the violence that had broken out between Buddhists and Muslims, initially in Rakhine State

Ne Win died, disgraced and living in obscurity, in 2002. His protégé Khin Nyunt was charged with corruption and placed under house arrest until January 2012, when he was released as part of the amnesty on political prisoners; he now runs a gallery in Yangon.

Outrage: Burma's Struggle for Democracy by Bertl Lintner is one of several works by the long-time Bangkok-based foreign correspondent and Burma expert, exploring the machinations of Myanmar's military government.

2007	2008	2010	2011
Following fuel price hikes, monk-led protests hit Myanmar's streets; after 50,000 march in Yangon in September, the government brutally cracks down on this 'Saffron Revolution', killing at least 31.	Cyclone Nargis tears across the delta, killing an estimated 138,000 and leaving many more without homes. Two days later (sticking to schedule), a referendum on constitutional reform takes place.	NLD boycott the October elections but many other parties decide to take part; few are surprised when the military-backed USDP wins. Aung San Suu Kyi is released in November.	The seventh and final step on the military's 'roadmap to democracy' is ticked off when former general Thein Sein is sworn into office as president, heading up a quasi-civilian government.

and later in other parts of the country, also drew criticism. The party's decision not to include any Muslims among the over 1000 candidates they put up for the 2015 national and regional election didn't help and has cast the NLD as neither so democratic nor anti-discriminatory as previously thought.

Nationwide Ceasefire Agreement

On coming to power, Thein Sein made putting an end to the civil wars that have plagued Myanmar in the modern era a top priority. In October 2015, weeks before the national elections, a ceasefire deal was signed with eight out of the 16 main rebel ethnic groups that had participated in the previous four years of negotiations. The door was also left open for political dialogue and inclusion of other ethnic groups at a later point in time.

Thein Sein claimed the so-called Nationwide Ceasefire Agreement (NCA) an 'historic gift from us to the generations of the future'. This neatly ignored the fact that the Kachin Independence Army, Shan State Army and United Wa State Army had refused to sign and that these key rebel armies continued to control the most territory and arms. As the date of the election approached, the Tatmadaw was still fighting these rebel groups on several fronts.

2015 Election

The government's cancellation of a bi-election in 2014 and the purge in August 2015 of Shwe Mann as speaker of the lower house of parliament and USDP party chair (he'd become too conciliatory to Aung San Suu Kyi in the eyes of serving and fellow former generals) rang warning bells about the November 2015 general election. However, despite a last-minute government attempt to delay the poll under the pretext of flooding in Chin State, the election went ahead as scheduled.

While far from perfect, local and international observers agreed that this election was free and fair. Everyone had expected the NLD to do well, but when the results began to come through, the scale of that victory became apparent. Aung San Suu Kyi's party had secured a landslide, winning 79% of the elected seats (235 in the lower House of Representatives and 135 in the upper House of Nationalities) and giving it an outright majority in both houses. Celebrations broke out across the country as the president and military accepted defeat and indicated they would honour the result.

Built during British rule of Burma, Yangon's infamous Insein prison was the Empire's largest penitentiary. It is still in use and has been the unwelcome home of political dissidents including, on three occasions, Aung San Suu Kyi.

The Rebel of Rangoon: A Tale of Defiance and Deliverance in Burma by Delphine Schrank (2015) is a gripping portrait of three regime opponents by the *Washington Post*'s Burma correspondent between 2007 and 2011.

HISTORY POST-1990 MYANMAR

2012	2015	2016	2017
Aung San Suu Kyi and 42 other NLD candidates win parliamentary seats in by-elections. Clashes between Buddhists and Muslims in Rakhine State leave hundreds dead and tens of thousands of Rohingya displaced.	The NLD wins just under 80% of all seats in parliament in the general election, enabling the party to choose Myanmar's president and form the government.	A 6.8-magnitude earthquake strikes central Myanmar, causing damage to hundreds of ancient temples in Bagan.	The UN releases a report on alleged human rights abuses against the Rohingya in the Rakhine state.

People & Religious Beliefs of Myanmar

Multicultural Myanmar is more salad bowl than melting pot. The government recognises 135 distinct ethnic groups that make up eight official 'major national ethnic races': Bamar, Shan, Mon, Kayin (Karen), Kayah, Chin, Kachin and Rakhine. Freedom of religion is guaranteed under the country's constitution, but Buddhism is given special status by both government fiat and demographic preponderance. Myanmar's ethnic patchwork of people also embraces a variety of other faiths, of which Islam and Christianity have the most adherents.

Main Ethnic Groups

Historically, Myanmar's diverse ethnic make-up has been delineated by its topography. The broad central plain, with the Ayeyarwady (Irrawaddy) River and Myanmar's most fertile soil, has been populated by whichever group was strongest – usually the Bamar (Burmese) in the past few hundred years. Most ethnic groups continue to live in some sort of isolation in the mountains lining much of Myanmar's international border, notably the Shan, Kayah and Kayin in the east; the Kachin to the north; and the Chin and Rakhine to the west.

In larger cities such as Yangon and Mandalay, there exist significant minority populations of ethnic Chinese and Muslims. These groups, particularly the Chinese, are often well represented within the fields of commerce and trade, which leads to some tension with the local ethnic majority – usually, Bamar.

As in many other ethnically (and religiously) diverse countries, feelings of pride and prejudice cause friction between Myanmar's ethnic groups. Ask a Bamar (or a Shan or a Kayin) for an opinion about their countryfolk of different ethnic or religious backgrounds and you'll get an idea of the challenges Myanmar governments have faced in their efforts to keep the peace and preserve the borders. While urban migration and technology do some work to speed integration, most citizens of Myanmar are acutely aware of their ethnicity and the position such an identity has within the nation's baked-in demographic power structures.

Bamar

Also known as Burman or Burmese, the Bamar make up the majority (more than two-thirds) of the population. Thought to have originally migrated from the Himalaya, the Bamar ruled much of what is now Myanmar from Bagan (Pagan) by the 11th century. When the British conquered Myanmar in the 19th century, it was the Bamar who had to relinquish the most. Many ancient court customs and arts were lost when the Bamar monarchy was abolished.

Despite an enduring attachment to older animist beliefs in *nat* (spirits), the Bamar, from trishaw drivers to senior generals, are devout Theravada Buddhists. Monks are highly respected and the media reports daily on the merit-making of top officials at the country's principal

When Myanmar locals go on holiday it's often in the form of a pilgrimage. Ma Thanegi describes one such trip in *The Native Tourist: In Search of Turtle Eggs*.

For a deep (English language) dive into the world of Myanmar's young and wealthy urban class (and the expats who hang out with them), plus the occasional good listicle and news reporting, check out Coconuts Yangon (http://yangon.coconuts.co).

Buddhist places of worship – continuing a tradition of patronage started by Burmese monarchs.

Coming of age (*shinbyu*) is a major event in Bamar/Buddhist culture, with parades around villages and towns for boys about to enter monasteries as novice monks, and both girls and boys having their ears pierced.

The military and current government stopped short of making Buddhism the state religion (as Prime Minister U Nu did in 1960). However, nation-building efforts have included establishing the Bamar language (Burmese) as the language of instruction in schools throughout Myanmar, so most non-Bamar speak Burmese as a second language.

Chin

Of Tibeto-Burman ancestry, the Chin people call themselves Zo-mi or Lai-mi (both terms mean 'mountain people'), and share a culture, food and language with the Zo of the adjacent state of Mizoram in India. Making up around 2.2% of Myanmar's population, they inhabit the mountainous region (mostly corresponding with Chin State) that borders India and Bangladesh to the west. Outsiders name the different subgroups around the state according to the district in which they live, for instance Tiddim Chin, Falam Chin and Hakha Chin.

In the past the Chin, as with most highland dwellers, led labour-intensive lives, and their relatively simple traditional dress reflected this. Men wore loincloths in the warmer months and draped blankets over themselves when the weather turned cool. The women wore poncho-like garments woven with intricate geometric patterns. These garments and Chin blankets are highly sought after by textile collectors today.

Traditionally the Chin practise swidden (slash-and-burn) agriculture. They are also hunters, and animal sacrifice plays a role in important animistic ceremonies: the state has the largest proportion of animists of any state in Myanmar. Even so, some 80% to 90% of Chin are believed to be Christian, mainly following the efforts of American missionaries during the British colonial period. Present-day activities of government-sponsored Buddhist missions in the region are seen as a challenge to both animism and Christianity among the Zo or Chin groups. Many Chin have fled west to Bangladesh and India.

Intha

Although they follow Buddhism and wear modern Myanmar costume, the Intha people of Inle Lake are culturally quite distinct from their Shan neighbours.

As Myanmar has opened to the world, there has been a massive influx of Chinese people (tourists and migrants) into northern Burma, evident in Mandalay and certainly in border towns such as Mong La, where the yuan is the local currency.

The Chin National Front (www.chin land.org) would like to create a sovereign 'Chinland' out of parts of Myanmar, India and Bangladesh.

THE WOMEN WITH TATTOOED FACES

The most extraordinary (but no longer practised) Chin fashion was the custom of tattooing women's faces. Chin facial tattoos vary according to tribe, but often cover the whole face – starting at just above the bridge of the nose and radiating out in a pattern of dark lines that resemble a spider's web. Even the eyelids were tattooed. A painful process, the tattooing was traditionally done to girls once they reached puberty.

Legend has it that this practice was initiated to keep young Chin maidens from being coveted by Rakhine princes whose kingdom bordered the southern Chin Hills. But it's just as likely that the tattoos were seen as a mark of beauty and womanhood. One proud old Chin woman we met told us that she was just seven when she started pestering her parents to have her own facial inking.

Efforts by Christian missionaries and a government ban on facial tattoos in the 1960s have resulted in the practice dying out. But in some Chin villages (particularly in the more traditional southern areas) live a handful of tattooed grannies.

The ancestors of the Intha are thought to have migrated to Inle from Dawei in southern Myanmar. According to the most popular legend, two brothers from Dawei came to Yaunghwe (the original name for Nyaung-shwe) in 1359 to serve the local Shan *sao pha* (sky lord). The chieftain was so pleased with the hard-working Dawei brothers that he invited 36 more families from Dawei; purportedly, all the Intha around Inle Lake, who number around 70,000, are descended from these migrant families.

A more likely theory is that the Intha fled southern Myanmar in the 18th century to escape wars between the Thais and Bamar.

Kachin

For more about the struggle of the Kachin, from a certain Kachin perspective, see the website of the Kachinland News (http://kachinlandnews.com).

Like the Chin, the Kachin (1.5% of the population) are part of the Tibeto-Burman racial group. Based mainly in Kachin State, they are divided into six ethnic subgroups (Jingpaw, Lawngwaw, Lashi, Zaiwa, Rawang, Lisu), among which the Jingpaw are the most numerous. Also tradition-ally animist, the Kachin were heavily targeted by Christian missionaries during colonial times (about 36% of the population are Christian, mostly Baptist and Catholic).

As much of Kachin State lies above the Tropic of Cancer, the climate is more extreme – stiflingly hot in the summer months and downright cold in the winter – and the Kachin seem to have abandoned their traditional dress for Western clothes that can be easily changed to suit the seasons.

About the only vestige of Kachin dress still commonly worn are men's *longyi* (sarong-style lower garment) of indigo, green and deep-purple plaid. During festive occasions, Kachin women sport finely woven wool skirts decorated with zigzag or diamond patterns, and dark blouses fes-tooned with hammered silver medallions and tassels.

Conservationist and author Alan Rabinowitz relates much about local life in the Kachin hills in his fascinating *Life in the Valley of Death*.

Following independence from Britain, Kachin relations with the Burmese-run government were increasingly precarious. After the mil-itary coup in 1962, the Kachin Independence Army (KIA) was formed under the Kachin Independence Organisation (KIO). These two organi-sations effectively ran the state on an economy based on smuggling and narcotics until a ceasefire agreement was struck in 1994.

After 17 years, the ceasefire broke, and in July 2011, fighting with the Tatmadaw (Myanmar army) broke out in the state again; as of 2016, more than 100,000 people have been displaced by the conflict and are currently living in refugee camps.

Kayah

Also known as the Karenni or Red Karen, the Kayah are settled in the mountainous isolation of Kayah State.

Visit Karenni People (www.karennirefugees.com) to find out more about the Kayah/Red Karen people living in one of the poorest and least accessible parts of Myanmar, written from the perspective of refugee-rights activists.

As with many of Myanmar's ethnic groups that traditionally prac-tised animism, the Kayah were targeted for conversion to Christianity by Baptist and Catholic missionaries during the colonial period. The name 'Red Karen' refers to the favoured colour of the Kayah traditional dress and the fact that their apparel resembles that of some Kayin (Ka-ren) tribes – a resemblance that caused the Kayah to be classified by colonisers and missionaries as 'Karen'.

Today the Kayah make up a very small percentage of the population of Myanmar – around 0.75% – and the vast majority lead agrarian lives. A sig-nificant number of Kayah also live in Thailand's Mae Hong Son Province.

Kayan

Perhaps the most recognisable – and enigmatic – of Myanmar's ethnic groups is the Kayan. Known in English as 'longnecks' and in Burmese as Padaung (actually a Shan term meaning 'wearing gold' – a moniker generally considered pejorative by the Kayan), the tribe is best known for the women's habit of wearing brass rings around their necks. Over time, the rings lower the women's collarbones and ribcage, making their necks appear unusually long. A common myth claims if the coils are removed, the women's necks will fall over and the women will suffocate. In fact, the women attach and remove the coils at will and there is no evidence that this deformation impairs their health at all.

Nobody knows for sure how the coil custom got started. One theory is that it was meant to make the women unattractive to men from other tribes. Another story says it was so tigers wouldn't carry the women off by their throats. Most likely it is nothing more than a fashion accessory.

In recent years some claim that the rings are applied with a different purpose – to provide women from impoverished hill villages with the means to make a living posing for photographs. Some souvenir shops on Inle Lake employ Kayan women to lure passing tourist boats. And there are claims that Kayan women have been ferried across the border to villages in neighbouring Mae Hong Son, in Thailand, to provide a photo opportunity for visiting tour groups. These villages are often derided as human zoos, but are actually refugee camps that also function as rural markets, with the women earning money by selling souvenirs and drinks.

At the time of research, the bulk of Myanmar's accessible 'traditional' (ie ringwearing) Kayan villages in Kayah State were in Deemawsoe township, southwest of Loikaw. Rangkhu is the largest village in the area.

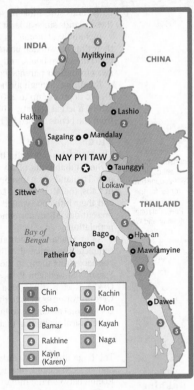

1	Chin	**6**	Kachin
2	Shan	**7**	Mon
3	Bamar	**8**	Kayah
4	Rakhine	**9**	Naga
5	Kayin (Karen)		

Kayin (Karen)

No one knows for sure how many Kayin (also known as Karen) there are in Myanmar. This ethnic group numbers anything between four and seven million and is linguistically very diverse, with a dozen related but not mutually intelligible dialects. Originally animists, it's now reckoned that the majority are Buddhists, with around 20% Christian and a small percentage Muslim.

The typical dress of both the Kayin men and women is a *longyi* with horizontal stripes (a pattern that is reserved exclusively for women in other ethnic groups). A subgroup of the Kayin lives on both sides of the Thailand–Myanmar border.

For a long time, the independence-minded Kayin were the only major ethnic group to never sign peace agreements with the Myanmar military. But in 2012, the Karen National Union (KNU), best known of the diverse Kayin insurgency groups, signed a ceasefire (p351) with the Myanmar government.

Moken

Also known as sea gypsies, or Salon in Burmese, the Moken live a nomadic life drifting on the ocean winds around the Myeik Archipelago, Tanintharyi (Tenasserim) Division. Numbering around 2000 to 3000

Like almost every ethnic minority in Myanmar, the Moken suffered greatly under military rule; reports from the late 1990s talk of how almost all Moken were subjected to forced relocations to onshore sites. For more information, see www.survival international.org.

individuals, the Moken, scientists believe, have been floating around these islands since at least 2000 BC.

Incredibly at home on the water, Moken families spend almost all their time on wooden boats, called *kabang*. As the boys come of age they build their own boats, and as the girls come of age and marry, they move away from their parents' boat.

Breathing through air hoses held above the water surface, the Moken dive to depths of up to 200ft in search of shellfish. For all their skill, this can be a lethal activity, with divers dying in accidents each year, mainly from the bends caused by rising too quickly to the surface.

Mon

Myanmar's constitution has set aside 'self-administered zones' for the Naga, Danu, Pa-O, Palaung, Kokang and Wa peoples.

The Mon (also called the Tailing by Western historians) were among the earliest inhabitants of Myanmar and their rule stretched into what is now Thailand. As happened with the Cham in Vietnam and the Phuan in Laos, the Mon were gradually conquered by neighbouring kingdoms and their influence waned until they were practically unknown outside present-day Myanmar, where they currently make up some 2% of the population.

As in Thailand, which also has a Mon minority, the Mon have almost completely assimilated with the Bamar and in most ways seem indistinguishable from them. In the precolonial era, Mon Buddhist sites, including Yangon's Shwedagon Paya, were appropriated by the Bamar (though the Golden Rock is still in Mon State), and Mon tastes in art and architecture were borrowed as well. To this day, the Bamar regard the Mon in a way that is somewhat analogous to European regard for Hellenic Greece – as bearers of a classical civilisation that laid the groundwork for the modern era.

Naga

The Naga are mainly settled in a mountainous region of eastern India known as Nagaland, but significant numbers live in the western Sagaing Region between the Indian border and the Chindwin River.

Rakhine Cultural Relics

Temple ruins (Mrauk U)

Mahamuni Buddha image (Mandalay)

Rakhine State Culture Museum (Sittwe)

When the British arrived in the mid-19th century, the Naga were a fragmented but fearsome collection of tribes. Headhunting was a tradition among them and for many decades they resisted British rule, though a lack of cooperation between the tribes hindered their efforts to remain independent. After nearly 17,000 Naga fought in WWI in Europe, a feeling of unity grew, which led to an organised Naga independence movement.

The Naga sport one of the world's most exotic traditional costumes. Naga men at festival time wear striking ceremonial headdresses made of feathers, tufts of hair and cowry shells, and carry wickedly sharp spears. Several tour companies organise trips to the region during the Naga new year in January when such ceremonies are performed.

Rakhine

The Rakhine (also spelled Rakhaing and formerly called Arakanese) are principally adherents of Buddhism; in fact, they claim to be among the first followers of Buddha in Southeast Asia. Their last ancient capital was centred at Mrauk U in Rakhine State, which borders Bangladesh. Today, they constitute around 3.5% of the population.

The Rakhine language is akin to Bamar, but due to their geographical location, the Rakhine have also absorbed a fair amount of culture from the Indian subcontinent. In the eyes of most Bamar, the Rakhine are a Creole race – a mixture of Bamar and Indian – a perception that the Rakhine strongly resent. With that said, it is true that the local culture exhibits a strongly Indian flavour, particularly when it comes to food and music. The Rakhine have a reputation for skilled weaving and are known in Myanmar for their eye-catching and intricately patterned *longyi*.

Rakhine State also has a minority population of Muslim Rakhine, as well as the Rohingya, another Muslim people.

Shan

The biggest ethnic group in Myanmar after the Bamar, the Shan account for around 9% of the population. Most Shan are Buddhists and call themselves Tai ('Shan' is actually a Bamar word derived from the word 'Siam'). This name is significant, as the Shan are related ethnically, culturally and linguistically to Tai peoples in neighbouring Thailand, Laos and China's Yunnan Province. In fact, if you've spent some time in northern Thailand or Laos and learnt some of the respective languages, you'll find you can have a basic conversation with the Shan, who nonetheless must write in the Burmese alphabet.

Traditionally, the Shan wore baggy trousers and floppy, wide-brimmed sun hats, and the men were known for their faith in talismanic tattoos. Nowadays Shan town-dwellers commonly dress in the Bamar *longyi*, except on festival occasions, when they proudly sport their ethnic costumes.

> To find out more about the Shan and issues in Shan State, read the Shan Herald Agency for News (http://panglong.org).

PEOPLE & RELIGIOUS BELIEFS OF MYANMAR MAIN ETHNIC GROUPS

ROHINGYA

Even in a nation synonymous with ethnic strife, the Rohingya stand out as perhaps Myanmar's most besieged and beleaguered group. However, to Myanmar's lawmakers, the general public and even the prodemocracy avant-garde, the Rohingya don't even exist.

Myanmar's officialdom are loathe to use the term 'Rohingya'. Instead, this contingent of 800,000 Muslims are considered invaders from neighbouring Bangladesh. Myanmar officials routinely describe them as pests, though they constitute as much as 20 percent of the population of coastal Rakhine State.

Animosity against the Rohingya runs so deep that even basic details of their origins and demographics are hotly disputed. Broadly speaking, the Rohingya have darker complexions than their Buddhist neighbours and generally speak a dialect of the Bengali language readily understood in Chittagong, Bangladesh's major seaport.

Those lucky enough to possess government identification are classified as 'Bengali', the dominant ethnicity in Bangladesh. But this tends to rile Rohingya activists, who resent the implication that they are wholly indistinct from their cousins across the border. Rohingya scholars cite historical evidence — including the logs of European explorers — that suggests a Rohingya presence in modern-day Myanmar that dates back centuries.

Along with various other groups of South Asian Muslims, many Rohingya descend from families led to Myanmar in the 19th century by the British Empire. During colonisation, historical borders were blurred, mass migration ensued and many Muslims (Bengali and otherwise) were brought over to toil on farms or serve as second-tier administrators.

For hardline Myanmar nationalists, the Rohingya are an undesirable outcome of colonial occupation that needs correcting. Myanmar's current citizenship law, widely derided by global human-rights groups, seeks to deny citizenship to any group who arrived after (or because of) British invasion.

This thinking is crucial to understanding widely held beliefs in Myanmar that the Rohingya are a fictitious ethnicity. An extremist screed titled *Rohingya Hoax*, written by a former Myanmar foreign diplomat, describes the word 'Rohingya' as a Bengali Muslim linguistic invention designed to convince the world that they are native to Myanmar.

As the 2012 Rakhine State riots, 2013 riots in Meiktila, Lashio, Kantbalu and Thandwe, the 2014 Mandalay riots, and ongoing violence in Rakhine state (p377) have demonstrated, this disdain for Rohingya is hardly limited to rhetoric.

Patrick Winn is Southeast Asia correspondent for Public Radio International/GlobalPost.

MYANMAR'S CYCLE OF LIFE

Rural dwellers make up about three-quarters of Myanmar's population, so much of local life revolves around villages and the rhythms of rice cultivation. Here, national politics or dreams of wealth can pale in comparison to the season, the crop or the level of the river (used for bathing, washing and drinking water). Everywhere, people are known for helping each other when in need, and call each other 'brother', 'sister' and 'cousin' affectionately.

Families tend to be large; you might find three or four generations of one family living in a two- or three-room house. The birth of a child is a big occasion. Girls are as welcome as boys, if not more so, as they're expected to look after parents later in life. Some thatched huts in the countryside have generators, powering electric bulbs and pumping life into the TV a couple of hours a night; many don't. Running water outside cities and bigger towns is rare, yet even in the deepest jungle hamlet, you may see the glow of a smartphone illuminating an otherwise electricity-free night.

There is a widespread belief in ghosts, which are created when an individual passes without accompanying funerary rituals; this is a trope that harks back to folk belief, and cuts across many religious practices in Asia. With this in mind, it is fair to say death is a big deal, and entire charities exist to provide funeral services for the poor. To miss a funeral is an unimaginable faux pas. If a heated argument goes too far, the ultimate capper is to yell: 'Oh yeah? Don't come to my funeral when I die!'

In former times the Shan were ruled by local lords or chieftains called *sao pha* (which translates, somewhat fantastically, to sky lords), a word that was corrupted by the Bamar to *sawbwa*. Many Shan groups have fought the Bamar for control of Myanmar, and a few groups continue a guerrilla-style conflict in the mountains near Thailand.

In Andrew Marshall's *The Trouser People* the intrepid author goes in search of the Wa's creation myth lake of Nawng Hkeo.

Wa

The remote northeastern hills of Shan State – the homeland of the Wa – are off-limits to tourists. During British colonial times, these tribal people – living in fortified villages, speaking dozens of dialects and having an (unfair) reputation for being permanently unwashed and frequently inebriated – were hated and feared: a status they have yet to throw off.

The British distinguished two main groups of Wa according to how receptive they were to the colonisers' attempts to control them. The 'Wild Wa' were headhunters, and decorated their villages with the severed heads of vanquished enemies to appease the spirits that guarded their opium fields. (Apparently they only stopped the practice in the 1970s!)

The so-called 'Tame Wa' allowed the colonisers to pass through their territory unimpeded, yet the area inhabited by the Wa – east of the upper Thanlwin (Salween) River in northern Shan State – was never completely pacified by the British.

White Lotus Press (www.white lotuspress.com) publishes books in English on the various people of Myanmar, including titles on the Kachin, Mon, Moken and Shan.

For decades, the United Wa State Army (UWSA; estimated at 20,000 to 25,000 soldiers) has controlled this borderland area, gathering power and money through the production of opium and methamphetamine; the US labelled the UWSA a narcotics trafficking organisation in 2003. Nevertheless, the UWSA struck a ceasefire deal with the military regime in 1989 and the territory under their control looks set to be designated a special autonomous region for the Wa in the future.

Women in Myanmar

Myanmar stands as a challenge to the Western trope that holds poorer nations are somehow inherently sexist. Here, the birth of a daughter is celebrated and lauded – a daughter, after all, is often considered more dutiful than a son. Girls are educated alongside boys, and women outnumber men in university and college enrolment. Most white-collar professions grant women six weeks of paid maternity leave before birth and one or two months afterwards.

Myanmar women enjoy equal legal rights to those of men, can own property, do not traditionally change any portion of their names upon marriage and, in the event of divorce, are legally entitled to half of all property accumulated during the marriage. Inheritance rights are also equal.

Rights on paper, however, don't always translate into reality. In the current parliament only 43 out of 433 MPs are women, although this number represents a jump from previous years. Still, apart from Aung San Suu Kyi – herself constitutionally barred from the presidency on the pretext of a law that punishes her for her past marital status – there is no doubt men dominate the political sphere.

When it comes to religion, women also take a back seat. Many people in Myanmar – women as well as men – believe the birth of a girl indicates less religious merit than the birth of a boy, and that only males can attain *nibbana* (for a woman to do so, she first has to come back as a man!). Buddhist shrines, including Mandalay's Mahamuni Paya and Yangon's Shwedagon Paya, have small areas around the main holy image or stupa that are off-limits to women.

In the private sector, there is a bit more equality at play. While men dominate the largest commercial interests in the nation, many small, midsized, and even a few large businesses are managed by women. In both villages and cities, women often manage family finances, a fiduciary role that also serves to somewhat bridge the gender gap. In addition, women are a noticeably vocal presence within the country's growing print and social media community.

Just as boys between the ages of five and 20 usually undergo a pre-puberty initiation as temporary novice monks, girls around the same age participate in an initiatory ear-piercing ceremony (often called 'ear-boring' in Burmese English). Some also become temporary nuns at this age, but nuns are not as venerated in Myanmar as monks.

While men dominate the nation's beer stations (and women are often sidelined as karaoke entertainment), women do engage in Myanmar nightlife.

Religion & Belief

About 88% of the people of Myanmar are Buddhist, but many also pay heed to ancient animist beliefs in natural spirits *(nats)*. Locals are proud of their beliefs and keen to discuss them. Knowing something about Buddhism in particular will help you better understand life in the country.

Buddhism

The Mon were the first people in Myanmar to practise Theravada (meaning Doctrine of the Elders) Buddhism, the oldest and most conservative form of the religion. King Asoka, the great Indian emperor, is known to have sent missions here (known then as the 'Golden Land') during the 3rd century BC. A second wave is thought to have arrived via Sinhalese missionaries between the 6th and 10th centuries.

By the 9th century, the Pyu of northern Myanmar were combining Theravada with elements of Mahayana (Great Vehicle) and Tantric Buddhism brought from their homelands in the Tibetan Plateau. During the early Bagan era (11th century), Bamar King Anawrahta decided that the Buddhism practised in his realm should be 'purified' from all non-Theravada elements. It never completely shed Tantric, Hindu and animist elements, but remains predominately Theravada.

Officially Myanmar is 0.8% animist, 0.5% Hindu, 6% Christian and 4% Muslim; others believe that non-Buddhists may account for 30% of the population.

During the U Nu period (1948–62), Buddhism functioned as a state religion, as embodied in such catchphrases as 'the Socialist Way to Nibbana'.

Theravada vs Mahayana

Theravada Buddhism (also followed in Cambodia, Laos, Sri Lanka and Thailand) differs from Hinduism, Judaism, Islam and Christianity in that it is not centred on a god or gods, but rather a psycho-philosophical system. Today it covers a wide range of interpretations of the basic beliefs, which all start from the enlightenment of Siddhartha Gautama, a prince-turned-ascetic who is referred to as the Buddha, in northern India around 2500 years ago.

In the Theravada school, it's believed that the individual strives to achieve *nibbana* (nirvana), rather than waiting for all humankind being ready for salvation as in the Mahayana (Large Vehicle) school. The Mahayana school does not reject the other school, but claims it has built upon it via practices such as recognising *bodhisattva*, individuals who have delayed *nibbana* to facilitate the enlightenment of mankind.

Some argue Mahayana Buddhism is simply the faith as reflected and interpreted by the cultures of China, Korea, Japan and elsewhere, just as Therevada Buddhism reflects the cultural milieu of Southeast Asia. Clearly, there is a chicken-and-egg conundrum at play when considering this hypothesis, but it is safe to say that, theologically, Theravadins place a heavier emphasis on the *sangha* (community of monks); it is almost unthinkable for a Myanmar Buddhist male to finish his life without spending at least some time as a shaven-headed initiate at a monastery.

The Theravadins see Mahayana as a misinterpretation of the Buddha's original teachings. Of the two, Theravada Buddhism is more austere and ascetic and, some might say, harder to practise.

Buddhist Tenets

Buddha taught that the world is primarily characterised by *dukkha* (suffering), *anicca* (impermanence) and *anatta* (insubstantiality), and that even our happiest moments in life are only temporary, empty and unsatisfactory.

The ultrapragmatic Buddhist perception of cause and effect – *kamma* in Pali, *karma* in Sanskrit, *kan* in Burmese – holds that birth inevitably leads to sickness, old age and death, hence every life is insecure and subject to *dukkha*. Through rebirth, the cycle of *thanthaya* (samsara in Pali – a term for the cycle of birth, death and rebirth) repeats itself endlessly as long as ignorance and craving remain.

Only by reaching a state of complete wisdom and nondesire can one attain true happiness. To achieve wisdom and eliminate craving, one must turn inward and master one's own mind through meditation, most commonly known in Myanmar as *bhavana* or *kammahtan*.

Devout Buddhists in Myanmar adhere to five lay precepts, or moral rules (*thila* in Burmese, *sila* in Pali), which require abstinence from

Buddhism Resources

DharmaNet (www. dharmanet.org)

Access to Insight (www.accessto insight.org)

World Dharma (www.world dharma.com)

Buddhist Studies (www.buddhanet. net)

FOUR NOBLE TRUTHS & THE EIGHTFOLD PATH

THE BUDDHA TAUGHT FOUR NOBLE TRUTHS	THE EIGHTFOLD PATH
1 Life is *dukkha* (suffering).	1 Right thought
2 *Dukkha* comes from *tanha* (selfish desire).	2 Right understanding
3 When one forsakes selfish desire, suffering will be extinguished.	3 Right speech
4 The 'eightfold path' is the way to eliminate selfish desire.	4 Right action
	5 Right livelihood
	6 Right exertion
	7 Right attentiveness
	8 Right concentration

BUDDHA'S HAND SIGNS

At temples and shrines, look out for the following hand signs of buddha images, each with a different meaning:

Abhaya Both hands have palms out, symbolising protection from fear.

Bhumispara The right hand touches the ground, symbolising when Buddha sat beneath a banyan tree until he gained enlightenment. By touching the Earth, the Buddha drew on its stability as a base of his own knowledge and resolve.

Dana One or both hands with palms up, symbolising the offering of *dhamma* (Buddhist teachings) to the world.

Dhyana Both hands rest palm-up on the buddha's lap, signifying meditation.

Vitarka or Dhammachakka Thumb and forefinger of one hand forms a circle with other fingers (somewhat like an 'OK' gesture), symbolising the first public discourse on Buddhist doctrine.

killing, stealing, unchastity (usually interpreted among laypeople as adultery), lying and intoxicating substances.

In spite of Buddhism's profound truths, the most common Myanmar approach is to try for a better future life by feeding and caring for monks (the *sangha*), donating to temples and performing regular worship at the local paya (Buddhist monument) – these activities are commonly known as 'merit making'. For the average person everything revolves around the merit (*kutho*, from the Pali *kusala*, meaning 'wholesome') one is able to accumulate through such deeds.

Only a minority of Myanmar's Buddhists are vegetarians, and this applies to monks as well. Despite Buddhism's philosophical stance against worldly pleasure, many Buddhists enjoy food, cigarettes, even alcohol (the latter is rejected by monks); to appreciate *dukkha*, one must know that which is given up on the road to self-denial.

Monks & Nuns

Myanmar's monkhood, numbering around 500,000, is collectively known as the *sangha*. Every Buddhist Myanmar male is expected to take up temporary monastic residence twice in his life: once as a *samanera* (novice monk) between the ages of 10 and 20, and again as a *hpongyi* (fully ordained monk) sometime after the age of 20. Almost all men or boys aged under 20 'take robe and bowl' in the *shinpyu* (novitiation ceremony).

All things possessed by a monk are offered by the lay community. Upon ordination a new monk is typically offered a set of three robes (lower, inner and outer). Other possessions a monk is permitted include a razor, a cup, a filter (for keeping insects out of drinking water), an umbrella and an alms bowl.

In Myanmar, women who live the monastic life as *dasasila* ('10-precept' nuns) are often called *thilashin* (possessor of morality) in Burmese. Burmese nuns shave their heads, wear pink robes and take vows in an ordination procedure similar to monks. Generally, nunhood isn't considered as 'prestigious' as monkhood, as nuns generally don't perform ceremonies on behalf of laypeople, and keep only 10 precepts – the same number observed by male novices.

Both men and women will take on monastic vows at important junctures in their lives, such as the death of a loved one, a painful break-up, or even after achieving some form of worldly success. During these periods, an individual may remain a monk or nun for as long as is required to achieve some form of spiritual perspective – a week, a month or, sometimes, a lifetime.

In mornings, you'll see rows of monks and sometimes nuns carrying bowls to get offerings of rice and food. It's not begging. It's a way of letting even poor locals do the deed of *dhana*, thus acquiring merit.

Bright red robes are usually reserved for novices under 15, darker colours for older, fully ordained monks. Myanmar eschews the orange and yellow robes so commonly seen in Thailand and Laos.

Temples & Monasteries

Paya (pa-*yah*), the most common Myanmar equivalent to the often misleading English term 'pagoda', literally means 'holy one' and can refer to people, deities and places associated with religion. Often it's a generic term covering a stupa, temple or shrine.

There are basically two kinds of paya: the solid, bell-shaped *zedi* and the hollow square or rectangular *pahto*. A *zedi* or stupa is usually thought to contain 'relics' – either objects taken from the Buddha himself (pieces of bone, teeth or hair) or certain holy materials.

The term *pahto* is sometimes translated as temple, though shrine would perhaps be more accurate as priests or monks are not necessarily in attendance. Mon-style *pahto*, with small windows and ground-level passageways, are also known as a *gu* or *ku* (from the Pali-Sanskrit *guha*, meaning 'cave').

Both *zedi* and *pahto* are often associated with *kyaung* (Buddhist monasteries), also called *kyaungtaik* and *hpongyi-kyaung*. The most important structure on the monastery grounds is the *thein* (a consecrated hall where monastic ordinations are held). An open-sided resthouse or *zayat* may be available for gatherings of laypeople during festivals or pilgrimages.

Building a paya or monastery, or contributing to their upkeep, is a major source of merit for Myanmar's Buddhists. Even the poorest villager can usually afford to spend a few thousand kyats on gold leaf, which can be pressed on a Buddha statue, or flowers that can adorn a shrine, which all counts towards good merit. Such practices are themselves a manifestation of traditional folk religion, which blends with Buddhism into a syncretic worship that turns an older animistic reverence for sacred spaces into a means of honouring the Buddha and the *sangha*.

Many Buddhist temples in Myanmar have their own *nat-sin* (spirit house) attached to the main pagoda.

Nat Worship

One of the most fascinating things about Myanmar is the ongoing worship of the *nat* (spirit being). Though some Buddhist leaders downgrade them, the *nat* are very much present in the lives of the people of Myanmar, and you'll often find them sharing space with Buddha in their own *nat-sin* (spirit house) at temples, private residences and even corporate offices. Be on the lookout for a coconut, sometimes wrapped in a *gaung*

THE WATER FESTIVAL

Occurring at the height of the dry and hot season, around the middle of April, the three-day Thingyan (Water Festival) starts the Myanmar New Year. As in Thailand's Songkran, the event is celebrated in a most raucous manner – by throwing buckets of cold water at anyone who dares to venture into the streets. Foreigners are not exempt!

On a spiritual level, Myanmar people believe that during this three-day period the king of the *nat* (spirit beings), Thagyamin, visits the human world to tally his annual record of the good deeds and misdeeds humans have performed. Villagers place flowers and sacred leaves in front of their homes to welcome the *nat*. Thagyamin's departure on the morning of the third day marks the beginning of the new year, when properly raised young people wash the hair of their elder kin, buddha images are ceremonially washed, and *hpongyi* (monks) are offered particularly appetising alms food. On a physical level, it's nice getting a little soak amid sweltering April weather.

Although the true meaning of the festival is still kept alive by ceremonies such as these, nowadays it's mainly a festival of fun and a period when the country's rather rigid social order is briefly upended. In cities, temporary stages called *pandal* (from the Tamil *pendel*) are erected along main thoroughfares, with water barrels ready to douse all passers-by.

ATTENDING A NAT PWE

You arrive at a typical Burmese village, or wander through a residential neighbourhood, a suburb of a city that's firmly off the tourist trail. There's a commotion; stalls are set out, crowds are rushing in one direction, and the general vibe is one of simmering excitement.

You follow the masses toward the tinny clang of what sounds like a mass execution of cats, and turns out to be a bad sound system with all volume controls turned to max. Everyone is laughing, joking and – noticeably in a country that tends to frown on public inebriation – drinking. And then you see what all the fuss is over: a woman or transgendered individual dressed in a drag costume slugging back whiskey, chain smoking cigarettes, engaging in a mix of classical dance, stand-up comedy, slapstick vaudeville and shamanic spiritual summoning.

Welcome to a *nat pwe*.

The term roughly translates to 'nat dance/festival', although it refers to a spectacle that is part dance, carnival, ritual and sacred ceremony all at once. During a *nat pwe*, a *nat gadaw* – the aforementioned woman or transgendered person – is possessed by a *nat*. The *nat gadaw*, accompanied by an orchestra, disrupts the local social hierarchy, bringing the spirit world to the people and giving license to bawdy behaviour, jokes and the public airing of grievances. In the meantime, the *nat gadaw* asks the audience for donations, which ward off bad spirit attention, pay off the orchestra and, of course, fund the *nat gadaw*.

While the jokes, commentary and deeper theology of a *nat pwe* will likely soar past those foreigners lucky enough to find one, their atmosphere and social impact are easy enough to grasp. For a time, the borders between spirit and physical worlds breaks down, and the rules and routines that often define life in Myanmar are cast away. On one level, setting aside a time for breaking rules is a societal rule in and of itself, but that doesn't make the wild abandon encountered at a *nat pwe* any less deeply felt.

baung (turban), hanging above a small offering plate or bowl; this is a shrine intended for the *nats*.

History of Nat Worship

Worship of *nats* predates Buddhism in Myanmar. *Nats* have long been believed to hold dominion over a place (natural or human-made), person or field of experience.

Separate, larger shrines were built for a higher class of *nat*, descended from actual historic personages (including previous Thai and Bamar kings) who had died violent, unjust deaths. These suprahuman *nat*, when correctly propitiated, could aid worshippers in accomplishing important tasks, vanquishing enemies and so on.

Early in the 11th century in Bagan, King Anawrahta stopped animal sacrifices (part of *nat* worship at Mt Popa) and destroyed *nat* temples. Realising he may lose the case for making Theravada Buddhism the national faith, Anawrahta wisely conceded the *nat's* coexistence with Buddha.

There were 36 recognised *nat* at the time (in fact, there are many more). Anawrahta sagely added a 37th, Thagyamin, a Hindu deity based on Indra, whom he crowned 'king of the *nat*'. Since, in traditional Buddhist mythology, Indra paid homage to Buddha, this insertion effectively made all *nat* subordinate to Buddhism. Anawrahta's scheme worked, and today the commonly believed cosmology places Buddha's teachings at the top. With that said, the *nats* still occupy an important role as sources of potential good luck and fortune; in this regard, they are similar to Catholic saints, although they do not occupy the same intercessionary position between a worshipper and a higher power.

The written Burmese word *nat* is likely derived from the Pali-Sanskrit *natha*, meaning lord or guardian.

Worship & Beliefs

In many homes you may see the most popular *nat* in the form of an un-husked coconut dressed in a red *gaung baung* (turban), which represents the dual-*nat* Eindwin-Min Mahagiri (Lord of the Great Mountain Who is in the House). Another widespread form of *nat* worship is exhibited through the red-and-white cloths tied to a rear-view mirror or hood ornament; these colours are the traditional *nat* colours of protection.

Some of the more animistic guardian *nat* remain outside home and paya. A tree-spirit shrine, for example, may be erected beneath a particularly venerated old tree, thought to wield power over the immediate vicinity. These are especially common beneath larger banyan trees *(Ficus religiosa)*, as this tree is revered as a symbol of Buddha's enlightenment.

A village may well have a *nat* shrine in a wooded corner for the propitiation of the village guardian spirit. Such tree and village shrines are simple, dollhouse-like structures of wood or bamboo; their proper placement is divined by a local *saya* (teacher or shaman), trained in spirit lore. Such knowledge of the complex *nat* world is fading fast among the younger generations.

Spirit possession – whether psychologically induced or metaphysical – is a phenomenon that is real in the eyes of locals. The main fear is not simply that spirits will wreak havoc on your daily affairs, but rather that one may enter your mind and body and force you to perform unconscionable acts in public.

> Those with a general fear of *nat* will avoid eating pork, which is thought to be offensive to the spirit world.

Nat Festivals

On certain occasions the *nat* cult goes beyond simple propitiation of the spirits (via offerings) and steps into the realm of spirit invocation. Most commonly this is accomplished through *nat pwe* (spirit festivals), special musical performances designed to attract *nat* to the performance venue.

To lure a *nat* to the *pwe* takes the work of a spirit medium, or *nat-gadaw* (*nat* wife), who is either a woman or, more commonly, a male transvestite who sings and dances to invite specific *nat* to possess them. The *nat* also like loud and colourful music, so musicians at a *nat pwe* bang away at full volume on their gongs, drums and xylophones, producing what sounds like some ancient form of rock and roll.

Every *nat pwe* is accompanied by a risk that the invited spirit may choose to enter, not the body of the *nat-gadaw*, but one of the spectators. One of the most commonly summoned spirits at *nat pwe* is Ko Gyi Kyaw (Big Brother Kyaw), a drunkard *nat* who responds to offerings of liquor imbibed by the *nat-gadaw*. When he enters someone's body, he's given to lascivious dancing, so a chance possession by Ko Gyi Kyaw is especially embarrassing.

Once possessed by a *nat*, the only way one can be sure the spirit won't return again and again is to employ the services of an older Buddhist monk skilled at exorcism – a process that can take days, if not weeks. Without undergoing such a procedure, anyone who has been spirit possessed may carry the *nat* stigma for the rest of their lives. Girls who have been so entered are considered unmarriageable unless satisfactorily exorcised.

> Myanmar residents – including the urban educated elite – will usually cop to their belief in traditions, such as the power of lucky numbers and talismans, and the subsequent ill effects of unlucky numbers and artefacts.

Superstition & Numerology

Superstitions run deep in Myanmar. Many people consult astrologers to find mates and plan events. According to Benedict Rogers, author of a biography of Than Shwe, the retired senior general has seven personal astrologers at his call, several of whom were once tasked with focussing their darker arts on his chief nemesis, Aung San Suu Kyi.

On a less dramatic level, Myanmar astrology, based on the Indian system of naming the zodiacal planets for Hindu deities, continues to be an important factor in deciding proper dates for weddings, funerals, ordinations and other events. Burma became independent at 4.20am on 4 January 1948, per U Nu's counsel with an astrologer.

Numerology plays a similar role with both eight and nine being auspicious numbers. The Burmese word *ko* (nine) also means 'to seek protection from the gods'. General Ne Win was fascinated with numerology, especially that relating to the cabalistic ritual Paya-kozu (Nine Gods). In 1987 he introduced 45-kyat and 90-kyat notes, because their digits' sum equalled nine.

While many monks and religious Buddhists may dismiss the above as, well, superstition, even wealthy, educated locals, as well as Myanmar people who have emigrated, will bless a car with holy water before a road trip that may be calculated to fall on a lucky number day.

Islam

Although official statistics say that 4% of Myanmar's population follow Islam, the Burmese Muslim Association claims the number is between 8% and 12%. Either way, Muslims have been part of Myanmar's religious fabric from at least the 9th century, and possibly as far back as the 6th century in Rakhine State. Today, Myanmar's Muslims represent a wide swath of ethnicities, which can include those of Chinese, Indian and Rohingya descent.

Waves of Indian immigration under British colonial rule boosted the local Muslim population. This was slashed during WWII when many Indians fled the country, and again from the start of military rule in 1962 when ethnic Indians were expelled from the army and marginalised in society.

In subsequent years, Muslims – in particular the Rohingya – have been targeted as illegal immigrants, stirring up ethnic and religious intolerance, which continues to linger dangerously in Myanmar society.

Local Buddhists often point to historical incidents of violence instigated by Muslims (for example, the murder of Buddhist Rakhines during WWII) as proof that Muslims cannot integrate into Buddhist communities, despite the obvious counterpoint of years of peaceful coexistence.

Contemporary issues related to terrorism and ISIS inflame these prejudices; for example, when the Taliban destroyed the famed Bamiyan Buddha images, Myanmar's Buddhists were incensed.

Christianity

Officially, some 6% of Myanmar's population are Christians. Anglican, Baptist and Catholic missionaries have been active in Myanmar for over 150 years. Going even further back there were communities of Christians among the Japanese who fled to Arakan (Rakhine State) in the 16th century and the Portuguese Catholics (and later Dutch and French mercenaries and prisoners of war) who arrived in the early 17th century. The presence of missionaries in the hill country has led to many upland minorities converting to Christianity, particularly in areas such as Chin and Kachin states.

Other Religions

Hinduism is practised among locals of Indian descent who settled in the country during colonial times. However, the religion's influence and reach in Myanmar stretch back many centuries, as Hindu temples in Bagan attest. Burmese adaptations of Hindu deities are worshipped as *nat*.

Other faiths you'll come across include the various traditional religions of Chinese immigrants, and animism among the small tribal groups of the highlands.

Yangon has a tiny Jewish community of about 20 people (buttressed by expats as of late). The Jewish community in pre-WWII Rangoon numbered around 2500 and the city once had a Jewish mayor (as did Pathein). Burma was also the first Asian country to recognise Israel in 1949. However, the military coup and its aftermath encouraged most to leave. Even so, the city's 19th-century Moseah Yeshua Synagogue is beautifully maintained.

Hinduism and Buddhism have deep historical and philosophical ties, and in many archaeological sites, including Bagan and the ancient capitals that ring Mandalay, you'll find evidence of old Hindu shrines and temples.

Ethnic groups that traditionally practised animism have proved more receptive to conversion to Christianity, especially the Kayin, Kachin and Chin.

Aung San Suu Kyi

Her life reads like a contemporary fairy tale. Wife of an Oxford academic and mother of two, daughter of a national hero, Aung San Suu Kyi came to international attention as a prisoner of conscience in Burma. Five years after her release from house arrest in 2010 she would lead her party, the National League for Democracy (NLD), in a landslide electoral victory, vanquishing the military junta who had held her captive for 15 years.

Family & Influences

Aung San Suu Kyi was born just two years before the assassination in July 1947 of her father, Aung San, leader of the Burma Independence Army and the key architect of the country's independence. Aung San had met Suu Kyi's mother, Ma Khin Kyi, a nurse, while recuperating from malaria in Rangoon General Hospital in 1942.

Her father's premature death was not the only family tragedy: in 1953 Suu Kyi's elder brother Lin drowned accidentally at the age of eight (there was also an elder sister Chit, but she had died when only a few days old in 1946, a year before Suu Kyi's birth). Later, Suu Kyi would become estranged from her eldest brother Aung San Oo, an engineer who emigrated to the US; in 2001 he unsuccessfully tried to sue her for a share of their mother's home – 54 University Ave, Yangon (Rangoon), where Suu Kyi spent the many years of her house arrest.

Her parents' political activism and example of public service had an enormous influence on Suu Kyi. 'When I honour my father, I honour all those who stand for the political integrity of Burma', she writes in the dedication to her book *Freedom from Fear*. In the essay 'My Father', she says he was 'a man who put the interests of the country before his own needs' – something Suu Kyi has also done.

Suu Kyi's mother was also a prominent public figure in newly independent Burma, heading up social planning and policy bodies, and briefly acting as an MP, before being appointed the country's ambassador to India in 1960. Suu Kyi finished her schooling in New Dehli, then moved to the UK in 1964 to study at Oxford University. It was in London at the home of Lord Gore Booth, a former ambassador to Burma, and his wife that Suu Kyi met history student Michael Aris.

Suu Kyi's interviews in 1995 and 1996 with journalist and former Buddhist monk Alan Clements, described in *The Voice of Hope* (www.worlddharma.com/items/voice-of-hope), often intermingle politics and Buddhism.

Marriage, Children & the Oxford Years

When Aris went to Bhutan in the late 1960s to work as a tutor to the royal family and continue his research, Suu Kyi was in New York, working at the UN; they corresponded by post as their love bloomed.

However, when they married on 1 January 1972 in London, neither Suu Kyi's mother or brother attended the ceremony, heightening the perception that the union was not approved of in Burmese circles. Daw Khin Kyi was soon won around to her new son-in-law, especially once Suu Kyi gave birth to her first son, Alexander, in 1973. By 1977 the family were living in Oxford, where Aris was teaching at the university and Suu Kyi had given birth to her second son, Kim.

Friends remembers the future leader of Burma's democracy movement from the Oxford period of her life as a thrifty housewife making do on Aris' meagre salary.

It's true to say that there are few indications from this period of her life of the political interests or ambitions that would later set Suu Kyi on such a different path. However, a clue lies in one of the 187 letters Suu Kyi wrote to Aris in the eight months before their marriage. In his introduction to *Freedom from Fear*, Aris reveals that his future wife asked '...that should my people need me, you would help me do my duty by them'. That moment came in March 1988. Suu Kyi's mother had suffered a stroke.

Return to Burma

Suu Kyi immediately packed her bags to return to Yangon.

Meanwhile there was growing turmoil in Burma as students and others took to the streets calling for a change of government. Back in Yangon, where injured protestors were brought to the same hospital that her mother was in, it was something Suu Kyi could not ignore, especially when political activists flocked to her mother's home on Inya Lake to seek her support.

It was at this point, as the street demonstrations continued to mount, that Suu Kyi decided to join the movement for democracy. Her speech at Shwedagon Paya on 26 August 1988, with her husband and sons by her side, electrified the estimated crowd of half a million, and sent ripples of excitement and hope throughout the country. Elegantly attired, the trademark flowers in her hair, the 43-year-old Suu Kyi brought a hitherto-unseen sophistication to Myanmar politics as she launched what she called 'the second struggle for national independence'. The brutal reaction of the military brought the protests to an end a month later.

Braving the Generals

Suu Kyi, however, was just getting started, and in September 1988 she joined several former generals and senior army officers (including Tin Oo, army chief of staff in the 1970s, who had been jailed for his role in an abortive coup in 1975) to form the NLD. As the party's general secretary, she travelled around the country attending rallies.

Her assistant at the time, Win Htein, a former army captain, recalled in an interview with the *New Yorker* how easily she was able to connect to the people. The Burmese were fascinated by the daughter of national hero General Aung San, but Suu Kyi soon also proved her own courage and strength of will. In April 1989, while campaigning in the town of Danubyu, she came up against soldiers who threatened to shoot her and her supporters; courageously she continued to move forward and calmly asked that they be allowed to pass. Only at the last minute did a senior officer step in and order the men to lower their guns (it's a scene reimagined in the films *Beyond Rangoon* and *The Lady*).

LIFE OF AUNG SAN SUU KYI

19 June 1945

A baby girl is born in Yangon (Rangoon) and named after her father (Aung San), paternal grandmother (Suu) and mother (Khin Kyi); the name means 'a bright collection of strange victories'.

1960

Daw Khin Kyi is appointed Burma's ambassador to India. Suu Kyi accompanies her mother to New Delhi, where she continues her schooling.

1964

Suu Kyi moves to the UK to study at Oxford University. Meets future husband, Tibetan scholar Michael Aris, at London home of her 'British parents', Lord Gore Booth and his wife.

1967

Graduates with a third-class degree in politics, philosophy and economics. Daw Khin Kyi retires to Yangon.

1969–71

Moves to New York for post-graduate studies, but ends up working for the UN alongside family friend and 'emergency aunt' Ma Than E and Secretary-General U Thant.

1972

Marries Aris and joins him in Bhutan, where he's tutoring the royal family. Suu Kyi works as research officer in Bhutan's Royal Ministry of Foreign Affairs.

1973–77

The couple return to the UK for the birth of their first son, Alexander. They take up residence in Oxford, where their second son, Kim, is born in 1977.

In July 1989 Aung San Suu Kyi, who by now had become the NLD's primary spokesperson, was placed under house arrest for publicly expressing doubt about the junta's intentions of handing over power to a civilian government, and for her plans to lead a march in Yangon to celebrate Martyrs' Day. Her status as Aung San's daughter saved her from the fate of many other NLD members, who were imprisoned in the country's notorious jails.

With her husband and sons by her side, Suu Kyi went on a hunger strike for 12 days to gain an assurance that her jailed supporters would not be tortured. None of this stopped the NLD from decisively winning the general election of May 1990.

A Prisoner of Conscience

According to local custom, Aung San Suu Kyi's name, like that of all Burmese, should be spelled out in full. It's also commonly preceded by the honorific title Daw. We follow the international convention of shortening her name to Suu Kyi.

Aris left Yangon with their sons on 2 September 1989. Suu Kyi would not see either Alexander or Kim for more than two and a half years. Her husband was allowed to spend one more fortnight with her over Christmas in 1989, a time he described in *Freedom from Fear* as 'among my happiest memories of our many years of marriage'.

At any moment during her years of arrest, Suu Kyi knew that the authorities would let her walk free to board a flight to return to her family in the UK. But once she left Burma she knew she would never be allowed to return, and she would not accept permanent exile. It was a sacrifice in which her family supported her, acting as her proxies to accept from the European Parliament in January 1991 the Sakharov Prize for Freedom of Thought and the Nobel Peace Prize in October of the same year.

As the international honours stacked up (the Simón Bolivar Prize from Unesco in June 1992; the Jawaharlal Nehru Award for International Understanding in May 1995), Suu Kyi maintained her strength and spirits by meditating, reading (in *Letters from Burma* she writes how she loves nothing more than relaxing over a detective story), exercising, practising piano and listening to news on the radio. From May 1992 until January 1995, she was also permitted regular visits from her husband and sons.

AUNG SAN SUU KYI BOOKS & MOVIES

Freedom from Fear (1991) is a collection of writings by Suu Kyi and supporters on topics ranging from her father to the Nobel Prize acceptance speech delivered by her son Alexander. *Letters from Burma* (1997) features a year's worth of weekly essays Suu Kyi wrote on Burmese culture, politics and incidents from her daily life for the Japanese newspaper *Mainichi Shimbun*.

One of the most comprehensive biographies is *The Lady and the Peacock: The Life of Aung San Suu Kyi of Burma* (2011), by Peter Popham, which includes extracts from Suu Kyi's private diaries. Popham also authored *The Lady and the Generals: Aung San Suu Kyi and Burma's Struggle for Freedom* in 2016, covering the period from her release in 2010 until the election victory of 2015.

Justin Wintle's *The Perfect Hostage* (2007) is an impressively researched account of Suu Kyi's life and times, and of modern Burmese history, which paints a very believable, likeable 'warts and all' portrait of the Lady. A more up-to-date biography is Rena Pederson's *The Burma Spring: Aung San Suu Kyi and the New Struggle for the Soul of a Nation* (2015).

On the cinematic front, Luc Besson's *The Lady* (2011) is a romantically inclined biopic based on Suu Kyi's life between 1988 and 1999 when her husband Michael Aris died; it stars Malaysian actress Michelle Yeo as Suu Kyi.

Covering similar ground, but in documentary format, is *Lady of No Fear* (www.ladyofnofear.com), directed by Anne Gyrithe Bonne, which was finished before Suu Kyi's release in 2010 and includes interviews with close friends and colleagues about the famously private woman.

Five Years of Freedom

Much to the joy of her supporters at home and abroad, as well as her family, the government released Suu Kyi from house arrest in July 1995. She was allowed to travel outside Yangon with permission, which was rarely granted. During her subsequent five years of freedom, she would test the authorities several times with varying degrees of success.

The last time she would see her husband was in January 1996. A year later he was diagnosed with prostate cancer, which would prove to be terminal. Despite appeals from the likes of Pope John Paul II and UN Secretary General Kofi Annan, the generals refused to allow Aris a visa to visit his wife, saying that Suu Kyi was free to leave the country to tend to him. Aris died in an Oxford hospital on 27 March 1999, his 53rd birthday; over the telephone he had insisted Suu Kyi remain in Burma where many political prisoners and their families also relied on her support.

The following decade was marked by more extended periods of house arrest punctuated by shorter spells of freedom. A couple of intercessions by UN special envoys resulted in talks with military leaders and the release of hundreds of political prisoners, but no real progress on the political front – nor release for the woman who had become the world's most famous prisoner of conscience.

Run-Up to Elections & Release

On 22 September 2007, at the height of the failed 'Saffron Revolution', the barricades briefly came down along University Ave, allowing the protestors to pass Aung San Suu Kyi's house. In a powerful scene, later recounted by eyewitnesses and captured on mobile phone footage, the jailed NLD leader was briefly glimpsed at the gate of her compound, tears in her eyes, silently accepting the blessing of the monks.

A couple of meetings with a UN envoy, Ibrahim Gambari, and members of the military later that year failed to result in Suu Kyi's release. Her house arrest was extended by a year in 2008 and then by a further 18 months in August 2009 (conveniently sufficient to keep her out of the way during the 2010 elections) following her encounter with John Yettaw. The 53-year-old Vietnam vet had strapped on homemade flippers and paddled his way across Inya Lake to the democracy leader's home. Suu Kyi took pity on the exhausted American and allowed him to stay, even though she knew such a visit violated the terms of her house arrest.

Six days after the 2010 election, the regime finally saw fit to release her, announcing in the *New Light of Myanmar* that she had been pardoned for 'good conduct'. Ten days later she was reunited with her son Kim, who brought her a puppy as a present. Kim returned again in July of 2011 to accompany his mother on a trip to Bagan, her first outside of Yangon since 2003.

AUNG SAN SUU KYI FIVE YEARS OF FREEDOM

1985–87

At Kyoto University Suu Kyi researches her father's time in Japan; she also registers at London's School of Oriental and African Studies for a doctorate in Burmese literature.

1988

Returns to Yangon in March to care for her mother, who has suffered a stroke; in September becomes secretary-general of National League for Democracy (NLD).

1989

At her mother's funeral in January she swears to serve the people of Burma until her death. Stands for election in February; placed under house arrest in July.

1991

Wins Nobel Peace Prize; sons accept it on her behalf. Pledges she will use US$1.3 million prize money to establish health and education trust for Burmese people.

1995

Released from house arrest, resumes campaigning for the NLD, but her movements are restricted. At year's end, she sees Aris for what will be the final time.

1996

In November her motorcade is attacked in Yangon, the windows of the car she is travelling in are smashed by a mob; despite presence of security forces no one is arrested.

1999

Suffering terminal prostate cancer, Aris is refused entry to Burma and dies in the UK. After his funeral, sons Kim and Alexander are allowed to visit their mother briefly.

Aung San Suu Kyi in November 2016

Reconciliation & Election

Emerging from house arrest, Suu Kyi addressed a jubilant crowd: 'I'm going to work for national reconciliation. That is a very important thing. There is nobody I cannot talk to. I am prepared to talk with anyone. I have no personal grudge toward anybody.'

The Daw Aung San Suu Kyi Pages (www. dassk.org) gathers together links to many online features about the Lady and Myanmar, including videos.

Initially, Suu Kyi's offer fell on deaf ears. However, in August 2011 the regime began to take a more conciliatory approach. Suu Kyi had talks with President Thein Sein and the government began to release political prisoners and legalised trade unions. In November 2011 the NLD announced its intention to re-register as a political party so it could contest the by-elections of April 2012 – Suu Kyi would be one of 45 NLD candidates.

In the run-up to the poll, Suu Kyi greeted a steady stream of international dignitaries to Yangon, including US Secretary of State Hillary Clinton in December 2011. She also toured the country campaigning for the NLD, battling exhaustion and ill health. The effort was rewarded by an almost clean sweep in the April election for the NLD, giving the opposition party an 8% block in the national parliament.

However, before they could take their seats, Suu Kyi and her NLD colleagues were faced with a dilemma: whether to swear an oath to 'safeguard' the very constitution they had been campaigning against. On 2 May political pragmatism won out as all the NLD MPs made the oath to become lawmakers.

International Accolades & Alliances

For 24 years Suu Kyi had refused to leave Burma for fear she would not be allowed to return. But in May 2012 all that changed when she packed her bags for a series of high-profile international visits, including to Oslo to accept her Nobel Peace Prize, 21 years after winning it; to her old home Oxford, to accept an honorary degree; and to London for a historic address to both houses of parliament. At every stop she was treated as if she was the visiting head of state.

Long before the 2015 election, Suu Kyi made it plain that her goal was the presidency of Myanmar. But to achieve this ambition would require reform of the constitution which, in turn, would mean an accommodation with the military – something unthinkable to many of her supporters.

Even so, in 2014, Suu Kyi forged a working relationship with Shwe Mann. The powerful former general and speaker of the lower house of parliament was also in favour of constitutional change. This was all the more surprising as Shwe Mann, too, had designs on Myanmar's presidency. This disloyalty to the army didn't go unnoticed and in August 2015, Shwe Mann paid the price when he was unceremoniously sacked as leader of the USDP and confined to his home.

Above the President

Shwe Mann still ran as a USDP candidate in the November 2015 general election. Along with hundreds of his USDP colleagues, he found himself without a job as Suu Kyi led the NLD to a landslide victory, securing ruling majorities in both houses of the national parliament. Unlike in 1990, the generals knew the game was up and let the result stand, allowing a smooth transition of power in February 2016.

The flawed constitution remained intact, however, so rather than taking the top job, Suu Kyi who had already declared herself 'above the president' before the election, had her proxy Htin Kyaw create the new post of State Counsellor. With this prime ministerial-style role Suu Kyi, along with her responsibilities as minister for foreign affairs, education and energy, is effectively running the country – albeit still with 25% of the parliamentary seats occupied by serving military.

It's not all been plain sailing. Suu Kyi's refusal to speak up for the persecuted Rohingyas has drawn criticism, the *Economist* noting how Suu Kyi's halo had slipped in the eyes of human rights advocates over the issue. The NLD's decisions to field no Muslim candidates in the 2015 election and reject other long-standing supporters who were viewed as too independent also saw Suu Kyi and party elders branded as imperious and authoritarian.

Many have noted that it was inevitable that, once Suu Kyi escaped the shadows of incarceration, aspects of the fairy-tale princess image crafted around her by the media and her supporters would start to crumble. The time has now come for the world to judge Suu Kyi in the full glare of the democratic freedoms she has so long campaigned for.

2000
Begins second period of house arrest in September; a month later starts secret talks with the junta, facilitated by UN special envoy Rizali Ismail.

2002
Released in May; returns to campaigning around Yangon and in late June makes a triumphant visit to Mandalay, her first trip to Myanmar's second-largest city since 1989.

2003
In May, while touring northern Myanmar, Suu Kyi and 250 NLD members are attacked by a pro-junta mob; at least 70 people are killed. Another period of house arrest follows.

2007
In September she makes a fleeting appearance, greeting protesting monks at her gate. In October a meeting with UN envoy Ibrahim Gambari is followed by talks with NLD and regime reps.

2011
Freed from house arrest in November 2010, Suu Kyi commences talks with the government during 2011, leading to the release of political prisoners and recognition of the NLD.

2012
In April Suu Kyi is elected to the lower house of the Burmese parliament, representing the constituency of Kawhmu. She travels abroad for first time in 24 years.

2016
Following the NLD's landslide win in the 2015 election, Suu Kyi takes up newly created role of State Counsellor (de facto prime minister) as well as reins of several ministries.

Government, the Economy & Human Rights

Since the election victory of the National League for Democracy (NLD) in 2015, compared to other nations in Southeast Asia, such as Thailand, Vietnam and Laos, Myanmar appears a beacon of democratic freedoms. However, that 'democracy' is compromised by a flawed constitution imposed by the previous military government and the ongoing civil conflicts that plague parts of the country. Here we look at who is part of Myanmar's government and how it is tackling the country's poor human rights record.

Politics

Myanmar's national parliament is made up of the 440-seat People's Assembly (Pyithu Hluttaw) and the 224-seat Upper House (Amytha Hluttaw). Each of the country's seven states and a further 14 administrative divisions (which include seven regions, six self-administered zones and one self-administered division) also has its own state or regional legislature, made up of elected civilian members and representatives of the armed forces.

National League for Democracy

Founded on 27 September 1988, the National League for Democracy (NLD) is the best known of Myanmar's political parties, thanks to its leader Aung San Suu Kyi. The 2015 election was a game-changer for the NLD. With around 60% of the seats in both houses of the national parliament, the party is firmly in the driving seat, able to propose, draft and approve new laws. With a couple of exceptions, the NLD also secured power in of all the state and regional legislatures.

However, on key issues, such as defence and home affairs, the military still retains control. This power-sharing situation will continue while the terms of the military-drafted constitution remain in force.

This same constitution made Suu Kyi ineligible for the presidency – that is the reason her long-time political ally U Htin Kyaw now occupies a role that has become one of a figurehead. Real power resides with Suu Kyi, who is State Counsellor, as well as Minister of Foreign Affairs of Myanmar and head of the president's office. Suu Kyi's wide-ranging powers, coupled with her authoritarian style of leadership, have lead to concerns about lack of checks and balances in the parliamentary system.

Much has changed since its publication in 2011, but David Steinberg's *Burma/Myanmar: What Everyone Needs to Know* still sheds some light on many aspects of the country's complex situation via a series of concise and understandable Q&As on history and culture.

The Military & USDP

Although it no longer wields the total power in Myanmar that it once did, the role of the military in politics and governing the country cannot be discounted. In the run-up to the 2010 election, many in the upper echelons of the military, including President Thein Sein, resigned their posts to become candidates for the military-backed Union Solidarity & Development Party (USDP), which, to nobody's surprise, was the victor.

The scale of the USDP's loss in the 2015 election was severe – it now has just 41 MPs spread across both houses of parliament. However, it is still Myanmar's second-largest political party. Also, there's the 25% blocks of unelected seats in both houses reserved exclusively for military appointees. It is impossible for the NLD to alter any aspect of the constitution without some of those appointees breaking ranks.

Military figures hold command of the key ministries of border affairs, defense and home affairs. All are crucial in the government's top priority of securing an end to the civil wars that have raged in parts of Myanmar since independence. USDP lawmakers are in charge of the ministries of labour, immigration and population, and religious affairs and culture. Ti Khun Myat, an ethnic Kachin national MP from the USDP, is vice speaker of the lower house.

Other Political Parties & Opposition Groups

After the NLD and USDP, the next largest opposition party in parliament is the Arakan National Party (ANP) with 10 seats in the upper house and 12 in the lower house. The ANP also holds the most number of seats (22) but not a controlling majority in the Rakhine State Parliament.

The Shan Nationalities League for Democracy (SNLD) has three seats in the upper house and 12 in the lower, putting it in fourth place. The Shan vote was split over several parties with the similar-named Shan Nationalities Democratic Party having lost its position prior to the 2015 election as the third-largest party nationally, and now holds just one seat in the Shan State Parliament.

Other parties with single-figure representation at the national level include the Pa-O National Organisation (PNO), Ta'ang National Party (TNO), Zomi Congress for Democracy (ZCD) representing Chin State, and Lisu National Development Party (LNDP). There are numerous other ethnic parties, some of whom didn't win seats or are unregistered opposition groups. All of this is an indication of how complicated and potentially divisive ethnic politics is in Myanmar.

The Economy

In the light of recent financial and legal reforms, Myanmar's economic prospects are bright. The country is rich in natural resources, including gas, oil, teak, and precious metals and gems. The potential for the agriculture sector (under colonial rule, Burma was the world's largest exporter of rice) is huge. In 2016 economic growth is likely to be over 8%. With the new NLD government, investment is also flooding into the country.

Since the introduction of mobile phone service competition and the explosive growth of smartphones and internet usage, there's much talk of

The 2008 constitution contains provisions to stop attempts to prosecute former general Than Shwe and other top military brass for crimes committed under their watch.

THE 2008 CONSTITUTION

Under the 2008 constitution, Myanmar is divided into seven regions (where the Bamar are in the majority) and seven states (minority regions, namely Chin, Kachin, Kayah, Kayin, Mon, Rakhine and Shan states). In addition there are six ethnic enclaves (Danu, Kokang, Naga, Palaung, Pa-O and Wa) with a degree of self-governance.

A quarter of the seats both at the national and state level are reserved for unelected military candidates; this gives the military a casting vote on any constitutional change because these require a parliamentary majority of more than 75%. There are provisions that the military cannot be legally held to account for crimes against the population committed during its governing period. Key cabinet positions are reserved for serving military, and the Commander-in-Chief of the armed forces has far-reaching reserve powers.

There are also the conditions that must be met for a person to assume the office of president; these clauses effectively barred Aung San Suu Kyi from the presidency and is the reason why she created the new post of State Counsellor.

HISTORY OF SANCTIONS

From the late 1980s, economic sanctions by mainly the US, EU, Canada and Australia were applied in an attempt to force political and social change in Myanmar. It was a controversial policy: while the NLD, the leading democracy group of the time, insisted they were necessary as a way of maintaining pressure on the military junta, others pointed out the harm that sanctions did to Myanmar's citizens, who in the main were struggling to make a living.

In 1995 the NLD also called for a tourism boycott, which led to criticism of Lonely Planet's continued coverage of the country. In 2010 the travel boycott was officially dropped by the NLD, who now welcome independent tourists who are mindful of the political and social landscape.

During 2012, as the pace of reform in Myanmar continued, the EU, Australia and the US all largely suspended their economic sanctions against the country. In May 2016 the US lifted sanctions on 10 state-owned companies in the banking, timber and mining industries, but kept others such as the ban on the import of jade and rubies in place. Four months later, when President Obama met with Aung San Suu Kyi in the US, he pledged to lift all remaining sanctions 'soon'.

For further information on Myanmar's economy read the reports compiled by the Harvard Ash Centre (http://ash.harvard.edu/myanmar-program).

Myanmar making a digital 'leapfrog' as new technology boosts the economy. Set against this, however, is the crippling impact of decades of poor economic management and rampant corruption. Basic infrastructure and services, including roads, electricity supply, education and healthcare, all urgently need upgrading. Myanmar's people are among the poorest in Southeast Asia, with over 25% of the population living beneath the poverty line. Poverty is over 50% in rural areas where 70% of the population live.

Inflation is also a problem hitting an average of 7.4% in 2014–15 and predicted to be almost double that in 2016. The country's budget deficit in the first six months of the 2015–16 financial year was of K3.1 trillion (US$2.4 billion), up 27% year-on-year.

2014 Census

Sound national economic planning is based on accurate population data. The problem for Myanmar was that for much of the 20th century, such data didn't exist. Censuses were carried out, but the results, with the military in charge and significant areas of the country excluded from the survey because of armed conflicts, were always cast into doubt.

In a country with over 135 ethnic groups, at least 19 major languages and ongoing civil wars, undertaking a census is no simple exercise. However, in March 2014 one was finally carried out under the auspices of the United Nations Fund for Population Activities (http://myanmar.unfpa.org). Even so, around 1.2 million people in parts of northern Rakhine, Kachin and Kayin states were not counted. There was also criticism that the poll did not recognise Rohingya Muslims in the list of the country's 135 official ethnic groups.

Where China Meets India – Burma and the New Crossroads of Asia by Thant Myint-U is about the historic and current connections between the three countries.

When the results (www.themimu.info/census-data) started to come in six months later, there were a few surprises. With a population of 51.41 million, Myanmar was discovered to have around nine million fewer people than previously thought. Yangon (Rangoon), with 5.2 million residents, has four times the population of the country's second-biggest city, Mandalay, and 70% of the population live in rural areas.

Further analysis revealed some other striking facts: life expectancy is among the lowest in the region (for men 63.9 years, for women 66.8 years). An average of only 32.4% of households use electricity for lighting, but slightly more (32.9%) own a mobile phone. Underlining how rural a country Myanmar is, 21.6% rely on bullock carts for transportation; just 3.1% own a car, truck or van.

Noticeably absent from the results published in May 2015 were stats on religion. This was because of fears that a confirmation on the number of Muslims in Myanmar could exacerbate religious tensions. These figures were released in July 2016 showing that Muslims make up 2.3% of the population, a fall from a previous census figure of 3.9% that had widely been believed to have undercounted Muslim citizens. Even with the uncounted Muslims in Rakhine State added to this, Myanmar's total Muslim population is likely to be much lower than previously estimated.

Bribery & Corruption

Bribery and corruption are common in Myanmar. In a country where salaries are very low and providing 'tea money' or 'gifts' to facilitate goods and services is pretty much par for the course, it's no surprise that Myanmar consistently ranks close to the bottom of Transparency International's Corruption Perception Index.

However, the Berlin-based antigraft organisation noted that, in 2015, Myanmar had made tiny steps forward, reflecting some improvements made under President U Thein Sein's administration. The situation is likely to improve further as the NLD has made stamping out corruption a core of its policies. Under Aung San Suu Kyi's government, civil servants have been banned from accepting gifts worth more than K25,000. New rules also forbid government officials from hiring their relatives as assistants. In April 2016 the government publicly shamed a media company for giving a K5 million gift to the assistant of a high-level government official.

Also helping to educate businesses and make a change to this culture is the Yangon-based Myanmar Centre for Responsible Business (www.myanmar-responsiblebusiness.org). A joint initiative of the Institute for Human Rights and Business (IHRB) and the Danish Institute for Human Rights (DIHR), the centre was set up in 2013 and has the promotion of human rights across business in Myanmar as one of its core values.

Human Rights

There have been improvements in human rights in Myanmar in recent years, not least because of the freedom the press now has to report on such issues. However, there is still much work to be done, including on issues such as political prisoners and child labour.

Those living in rural communities risk losing their land or being made homeless by ethnic conflict, exploitative laws and unscrupulous businesspeople. Across the country, Muslims are under attack and, as Human Rights Watch and many others point out, the Rohingya (p357) continue to face statelessness and systematic persecution.

Political Prisoners

The NLD has pledged to release all political prisoners, and create no more prisoners of conscience. Aung San Suu Kyi's first official act as State Counsellor in April 2016 was to free 113 political prisoners. However, the Assistance Association for Political Prisoners (AAPP; www.aappb.org), which keeps a running tally of the detainees, believes as of August 2016 there are 206 political prisoners: 86 in prison, 35 awaiting trial in prison and 85 awaiting trial outside prison.

Prodemocracy groups point out that the Peaceful Assembly Act introduced in 2012 is being used to arrest political activists as it only grants the right to protest under strict conditions. Under this law unauthorised gatherings of just two people are illegal.

In May 2016 the AAPP and the Former Political Prisoners Society (FPPS) released a joint report, *After Release I Had to Restart My Life from the Beginning: The Experience of Ex-Political Prisoners in Burma and the Challenges of Reintegration*. The report, which took two years to compile

Fiery Dragons: Banks, Money lenders and Microfinance in Burma by Sean Turnell explains how Myanmar went from one of the richest countries in Southeast Asia to one of its poorest within the space of a century.

Guy Delisle's *Burma Chronicles* is a graphic novel based on the experiences of the Canadian cartoonist in Myanmar with his wife, an administrator for Médecins Sans Frontières (MSF) during 2007. It's both amusing and horrifying, covering topics ranging from electricity outages to the heroin-shooting galleries in jade-mining towns.

and includes information gathered from 1621 former prisoners, provides details of failings in Myanmar's judiciary; torture and misconduct in the prison system; and barriers to reconciliation and treatment.

Child Labour

Child labour is a massive issue in Myanmar: the 2014 census counted more than 1.5 million children aged 10 to 17 (21%) as working. The NLD government plans to crack down on the practice and warned businesses in June 2016 that if they hired children under 14 years they would face fines of up to K10 million, six months in prison, or both. Teens aged 14 to 16 are only supposed to work a maximum of four hours a day.

Travellers will most often come across teenage and pre-teen boys working in teashops, but it's also an issue for girls who are sent by their impoverished families to work in homes as maids, in factories or – worse – in karaoke bars and massage parlours. Children can work anything up to 13 hours a day, seven days a week. If they're lucky, they will be allowed home to see their families once a year. Some are forced to work in hazardous environments and others are little more than indentured slaves, their families having taken the child's wages in advance. Terrible stories of abuse have recently been highlighted by local media.

One of the few ways for children to escape this situation is to have access to education – it's extreme poverty and lack of access to quality schools that force families to send their kids to work. The Myanmar Mobile Education Project (www.facebook.com/myMEproject) is a charity that provides free informal education to 1500 children working in teahouses in five cities, including Yangon and Mandalay. It helps provide a win-win situation for everyone: the children continue earning an income and the employers benefit from having more confident, educated kids.

In 2011 unions became legal for the first time since 1962. Employers also now have to comply with agreements made before a conciliation body. But with penalties for non-compliance being a maximum fine of US$100 or less than a year in jail, critics claim the law has no teeth.

Land Confiscation

Democracy and human rights groups concerned with Myanmar point to land confiscation as one of the biggest problems the country needs to tackle. As Myanmar's economy has opened up, there has been an increase in grabs of resource-rich land by the military, corrupt officials and business cronies, particularly in border areas where ethnic communities report being dispossessed by various industrial development projects.

Critics say that laws relating to land ownership enacted in 2012 have failed to provide adequate protection for farmers from having their land requisitioned by the authorities. Among the cases that it has reported on recently are those associated with the expansion of the Letpadaung copper mine (p402) in Monywa township.

THE GEM BUSINESS

Myanmar generates considerable income from the mining of precious stones – including rubies, jade and sapphire – and metals such as gold and silver. There is controversy surrounding this mining, however, with reports of forced labour and dangerous working practices. At Hpakant, ground zero for Myanmar's billion-dollar jade industry, working and living conditions are appalling. The area is notorious for high levels of heroin addiction and HIV rates. The anti-corruption organisation Global Witness estimated the total value of the country's jade production at US$31 billion in 2014, almost half of the country's GDP. Most taxes on that income are avoided, and very little of the revenue from the trade is shared by miners or others in Kachin.

If you are looking to buy gems and jewellery while in Myanmar, one project worth looking into is that of the nonprofit charity Turquoise Mountain, which has collaborated with the British ethical jeweller Pippa Small (http://www.pippasmall.com). Her Burma Collection sources semi-precious stones from small traders, mainly women, in Mogok.

Several civil society groups, including the Karen Human Rights Group and the Land in our Hands network (LIOH or Doe Myay in Burmese), have published reports detailing land conflicts and grabbing across the country. The 2015 LIOH report *Destroying People Lives: The Impact of Land Grabbing on Communities in Myanmar* reflected the experiences of more than 2000 people in 62 townships in six states and seven regions.

Ethnic Conflicts

Fighting between different ethnic groups within Myanmar began in 1948 after the nation's independence and has yet to cease. Thein Sein's government agreed a ceasefire in October 2015, but with only eight out of 15 armed ethnic groups. Fighting subsequently flared in eastern parts of the country between the military, non-signatories and groups that did not take part in the negotiations.

The NLD has made achieving national reconciliation one of its top priorities. The stakes are high. Many of the most egregious human rights abuses levelled at Myanmar, including massive displacement of people, rape, the use of forced labour and child soldiers and torture, are inextricable from the conflicts between ethnic groups and the army. There are entrenched interests in maintaining the status quo on both sides, not least because of the US-billion-dollar black economy fuelled by smuggling and drug running in the wartorn areas.

Religious Conflicts

Since 2011, battles between religious groups in Myanmar have flared up, as witnessed particularly in Rakhine State where the government's non-recognition of the Muslim Rohingya minority is the flash point. There have also been outbreaks of violence between Buddhist and Muslim communities in Meiktila, Mandalay, Lashio and Bago.

In recent years, Myanmar's religious hate speech law has also been used to protect ultra-nationalists rather than religious minorities. This and other laws 'to protect race and religion' enacted by the previous government under pressure from powerful Buddhist nationalists have been widely condemned by Myanmar civil rights groups and the international community for discriminating against non-Buddhists.

Relations between the religions hasn't been helped by the fact that there are more higher-ranking Buddhists in government than those of any other religion. There has also been a program of building pagodas in border regions, including the Christian area of Kachin State bordering China and the Muslim areas of Rakhine State bordering Bangladesh.

In 2016 the US Commission on International Religious Freedom (US-CIRF) called on the new NLD government to end abuses of religious freedom.

Press Freedom

In August 2012, the government abolished prepublication censorship of the media – something that had been routine since the 1962 military takeover. This move radically changed Myanmar's media landscape. Previously exiled media organisations, including the Democratic Voice of Burma (www.dvb.no), the Irrawaddy (www.irrawaddy.org) and Mizzima (www.mizzima.com), have all re-established bureaus in Myanmar, one of the clearest indications of an improved reporting environment.

It's not a clear-cut improvement, though. Hundreds of laws still exist under which journalists can be punished for publishing or broadcasting material that offends the government. Other methods have also be used to curtail press freedom. A BBC reporter was jailed in June 2016 for allegedly striking a policeman while covering a student protest in the previous year; a month later his appeal against the conviction was upheld.

The Transnational Institute (www.tni.org) has many scholarly articles and reports about the political situation and ethnic conflict in Myanmar.

Nowhere to Be Home, edited by Maggie Lemere and Zoë West, presents 22 often heartbreaking oral histories of Myanmar citizens gathered from those living in the country and those in exile.

GOVERNMENT, THE ECONOMY & HUMAN RIGHTS PRESS FREEDOM

Even though it has reached its best ever position, in 2016 Myanmar still ranked 143 out of 180 nations on the Reporters Without Borders' index on media censorship. The press freedom organisation noted, 'Burmese-language state media...continue to censor themselves and avoid any criticism of the government or the armed forces'.

Activist Websites

Burma Campaign UK (http://burmacampaign.org.uk)

Network Myanmar (www.networkmyanmar.org)

US Campaign For Burma (http://uscampaignforburma.org)

Karen Human Rights Group (http://khrg.org)

Burma Partnership (http://www.burmapartnership.org)

Print

The dissolution of the censorship board meant that private daily newspapers could be published for the first time since the early 1960s. Thirty-one companies gained licences to print daily newspapers; few of them either made it to print or survived in business for a year.

The country's only privately owned English-language newspaper is the *Myanmar Times*, which is published Monday to Friday. It faces competition from the English weekly news magazines *Mizzima Weekly* and *Frontier Myanmar*. All of these print media publish the kind of critical news and features that would have been impossible a few years ago.

Even the once notorious propaganda sheet *New Light of Myanmar* is moving with the times; rebranded the *Global New Light of Myanmar,* it hired three expat reporters in 2015 in its efforts to liberalise, improve reporting ethics and appeal to new readers. The NLD's aim is to eventually privatise state-run media such as this paper, but at the time of research it remains the exclusive print platform for announcements from government departments.

TV & Radio

Free-to-air TV channels in Myanmar include MRTV, Myawady TV and Myanmar International, but many locals prefer to get their news from overseas radio broadcasts by the BBC's World Service, Voice of America (VOA) and RFA (www.rfa.org), or from satellite-TV channels such as BBC World, CNN and DVB. The NLD government has said existing TV companies will have to reapply to keep their broadcasting licences and that companies in the private sector will be given an equal chance to compete. It has also vowed not to interfere in or influence state-run media.

Internet

Relaxation in press censorship has had a dramatic impact on internet access. Previously blocked international and exile media news sites and blogs are now freely available. The 2014 launch of two new mobile phone networks led to an explosion in the number of people using such devices to connect to the internet.

However, in 2015, the watchdog Freedom House (https://freedomhouse.org) pushed back Myanmar's 'Freedom on the Net' ranking from 'partly free' to 'not free', because of increased government intimidation of internet users during social protests and a surge in the conflicts in ethnic minority regions.

Blood, Dreams and Gold: The Changing Face of Burma (2015) by Richard Crockett is a wide-ranging account of the momentous changes in the country between 2010 and 2104 by the former *Economist* correspondent.

In 2012 Nay Phone Latt, recipient of the PEN/Barbara Goldsmith Freedom to Write award, was released after four years behind bars for blogging. He has since founded the independent Myanmar Bloggers Society and the Myanmar ICT for Development Organization (MIDO), which disseminates information about the internet and holds training sessions on how to blog.

Such education is necessary if internet liberalisation is to have any real lasting impact in Myanmar. In March 2016, activists launched a Facebook page dedicated to addressing the rising number of hate-speech cases and how best to deal with hate speech on social media.

Eating in Myanmar

Burmese food suffers from a bad rap – a rather unjustified bad rap in our opinion. While it can be oily, and lacks the diversity of that of neighbouring Thailand, with a bit of pointing in the right direction and some background knowledge, we're confident you'll return from Myanmar having savoured some truly tasty and memorable meals.

A Burmese Meal

T'ămìn (rice), also written as *htamin,* is the indisputable core of any Burmese meal. Second in importance, and providing the grains with some flavour, are *hìn,* Burmese-style curries. Those who've been burned by the spiciness of Thai food will be pleased to learn that Burmese curries are probably the mildest in Asia. The downside is that Burmese curries are often oily, largely due to a cooking process that sees them cooked until the oil separates from all other ingredients and rises to the top. The Burmese term for this cooking method is *s'i pyan* (oil returns), and the process ensures that the rather harsh curry paste ingredients – typically chilli, turmeric, tomatoes, ginger, garlic, onions and shrimp paste – have properly amalgamated and have become milder. Some restaurants also add extra oil to maintain the correct top layer, as the fat also preserves the underlying food from contamination by insects and airborne bacteria while the curries sit in open, unheated pots for hours at a time.

Accompanying the curries is a unique repertoire of side dishes that blend Burmese, Mon, Indian and Chinese influences, predominantly plant- and seafood-based ingredients, and overwhelmingly savoury, salty and sometimes tart flavours. Indeed, one of the pleasures of eating an authentic Burmese meal is the sheer variety of things to eat at a single sitting. Upon arriving at any *Myanma sà thauq sain* (Burmese restaurant), and after having chosen a curry, a succession of sides will follow. One of these is invariably soup, either an Indian-influenced *peh·hìn·ye* (lentil soup, or dhal), studded with chunks of vegetables, or a tart, leaf-based broth. A tray of fresh and parboiled vegetables, fruits and herbs is another obligatory side dish; they're eaten with various dips, ranging from *ngăpí ye* (a watery, fishy dip) to *balachaung* (a dry, pungent combination of chillies, garlic and dried shrimp fried in oil). Additional vegetable-based salads or stir-fries, unlimited green tea and a dessert of pickled tea leaves and chunks of jaggery (palm sugar) are also usually included.

Burmese Specialities

One of the culinary highlights of Burmese food is undoubtedly *ăthouq* – light, tart and spicy salads made with vegetables, herbs, fruit or meat tossed with lime juice, onions, peanuts, roasted chickpea powder or chillies. Among the most exquisite are *maji·yweq thouq,* made with tender young tamarind leaves, and *shauq·thi dhouq,* made with a type of lemon-like citrus fruit. In fact, the Burmese will make just about anything into a salad, as *t'ămìn dhouq,* a savoury salad made with rice, and *nan·gyi dhouq,* a salad made with thick rice noodles, prove.

Food is so enjoyed in Myanmar that standard greetings to friends and foreigners include *sà pyi bi la?* (Have you eaten your lunch yet?) and *ba hìn ne sà le?* (What curry did you eat?).

Burma: Rivers of Flavour by Naomi Duguid (http://naomiduguid.com) is the most expansive book on Burmese food to have been published in English.

A BURMESE NOODLE PRIMER

Myanmar's noodle dishes, known generally as *k'auq·s'wèh*, are quite unlike those found elsewhere in Southeast Asia. Often eaten for breakfast or as snacks between the main meals of the day, they can be divided into three general categories:

'Dry' Noodles

S'i jeq Meaning 'cooked oil', this refers to noodles (rice or wheat) slicked with oil, topped with roast meat, and served with a side of broth and small salad of cucumber (in Yangon) or onions (in Mandalay).

Nàn·gyì dhouq/móun·di These two, virtually identical, dishes consist of thick, round rice noodles served with chicken, slices of fish cake, parboiled bean sprouts and sometimes slices of hard-boiled egg. The ingredients are seasoned with toasted chickpea flour, drizzles of turmeric and/or chilli oil, and served with sides of pickled vegetables and a bowl of broth.

Nàn·byà·gyì thouq In Mandalay, this is a dish similar to the above, but made with flat, wide wheat noodles.

'Soup' Noodles

Kya·zin hin Mung bean-vermicelli served in a clear broth with wood-ear mushrooms, lily flowers, slices of fish cake, and pork or chicken. Typically garnished with hard-boiled egg, coriander, chilli flakes and thinly sliced shallots, and seasoned with lime juice and fish sauce.

Kyè òu Meaning 'copper pot', this dish with Chinese origins combines thin rice noodles, egg, pork, seasoned pork balls, pork offal and greens in a hearty broth.

Móun·hìn·gà The most ubiquitous noodle, and Myanmar's unofficial national dish, consists of fine, round rice noodles served in a thick fish- and shallot-based broth. Made hearty with the addition of pith from the stalk of the banana tree, the dish is often served topped with crispy deep-fried veggies or lentils.

Óun·nó k'auq·s'wèh This dish unites pale wheat noodles, a mild coconut-milk-based broth, shredded chicken, slices of hard-boiled egg, deep-fried crispy bits and a drizzle of chilli oil. Served with sides of chopped green onion, thinly sliced shallots and lime.

Shàn k'auq·s'wèh Possibly the most famous Shan dish, this takes the form of thin, flat rice noodles in a clear broth with chunks of marinated chicken or pork, garnished with toasted sesame and a drizzle of garlic oil, and served with a side of pickled vegetables. A dry version, in which the broth is served on the side, is also common.

Rakhine móun·di This state's signature dish unites thin rice noodles, flaked fish and a peppery broth. Served with a spicy condiment of pounded green chilli.

Somewhere In-Between

To·hù nwe k'auq·s'wèh Literally 'warm tofu', this dish is similar to *shàn k'auq·s'wèh*, except that the clear broth is replaced by a thick porridge made from chickpea flour. The mixture is supplemented with pieces of marinated chicken or pork, a drizzle of chilli oil, and sides of pickled veggies and broth.

Myì shay Thick rice noodles served with chicken or pork and parboiled bean sprouts, and united by a dollop of sticky rice 'glue' (actually the same batter used to make the noodles). The dish is seasoned with chilli oil and vinegar (in Mandalay) or tamarind (in Mogok), and served with sides of pickled veggies and broth.

A popular finish to Burmese meals, and possibly the most iconic Burmese dish of all, is *leq'p'eq* (often spelled *laphet*), fermented green tea leaves mixed with a combination of sesame seeds, fried peas, fried garlic, peanuts and other crunchy ingredients. A popular variant of the dish is *leq·p'eq thouq,* in which the fermented tea and nuts are combined with slices of tomato and cabbage and a squeeze of lime. The salad is a popular snack in Myanmar, and the caffeine boost supplied by the tea leaves makes the dish a favourite of students who need to stay up late studying.

Regional & Ethnic Variations

Burmese cuisine can be broadly broken down into dishes found in 'lower Myanmar' (roughly Yangon and the delta), with more fish pastes and sour foods; and 'upper Myanmar' (centred at Mandalay), with more sesame, nuts and beans used in dishes.

In Mandalay and around Inle Lake, it's fairly easy to find Shan cuisine, which is relatively similar to northern Thai cuisine. Rice plays an important role in Shan cuisine, and in addition to Shan-style rice noodles, *ngà t'ǎmìn jin* (rice kneaded with turmeric oil and topped with fish) is worth trying.

Mon cuisine, most readily available in towns stretching from Bago to Mawlamyine, is very similar to Burmese food, with a greater emphasis on curry selections. While a Burmese restaurant might offer a choice of four or five curries, a Mon restaurant will have as many as a dozen, all lined up in curry pots to be examined. Mon curries are also more likely to contain chillies than those of other cuisines.

Rakhine food is often likened to Thai food for its spiciness. *Ngǎyouq-thì jiq,* a 'dip' of grilled chillies mashed with lime and shrimp paste, is an obligatory side that embodies this, and sour soups and seafood-based curries are also constants. The region's signature noodle dish is *móun-di,* thin rice noodles served in a peppery fish-based broth, often with a side of a spicy chilli paste.

In towns large and small throughout Myanmar, you'll find plenty of Chinese restaurants, many of which do a distinctly Burmese (ie oily) take on Chinese standards. Despite being the most ubiquitous type of dining in Myanmar (upcountry, this is often the only kind of restaurant you'll find), it's probably the least interesting. Indian restaurants are also common, although much more so in the big cities than elsewhere. Excellent chicken *dan·bauq* (biryani), as well as all-you-can-eat vegetarian *thali* served on a banana leaf, can be found in Yangon and Mandalay.

Sweets

The typical Burmese dessert is often little more than a pinch of pickled tea leaves or a lump of palm sugar (jaggery). More substantial sweet dishes, generally referred to as *móun* (sometimes written *moun* or *mont*), are regarded as snacks in Myanmar, and are often taken with equally sweet tea in the morning or afternoon.

Prime ingredients for Burmese sweets include grated coconut, coconut milk, rice flour (from white rice or sticky rice), cooked sticky rice, tapioca and various fruits. Some Burmese sweets have been influenced by Indian cooking and include more exotic ingredients such as semolina and poppy seeds. In general, Burmese sweets are slightly less syrupy-sweet than those of neighbouring Thailand, and often take a cake-like, seemingly Western form, such as *bein móun* and *móun pyit thalet,* Burmese-style 'pancakes' served sweet or savoury.

Drinks

Nonalcoholic Drinks

Black tea, brewed in the Indian style with lots of milk and sugar, is ubiquitous and cheap, costing around K200 per cup. Most restaurants and teashops also provide as much free Chinese tea as you can handle.

International and local-brand soft drinks are widely available. Real coffee can be found at a steadily increasing number of modern Western-style cafes in Yangon and other large cities. Elsewhere, coffee

Robert Carmack and Morrison Polkinghorne host food tours around Myanmar (http://globetrottinggourmet.com) and have also written the gorgeously illustrated *The Burma Cookbook: Recipes from the Land of a Million Pagodas.*

Rudyard Kipling famously referred to *ngapi,* the Burmese fermented fish condiment, as 'fish pickled when it ought to have been buried long ago'.

Myanmar's fruit offerings vary by region and season. Don't miss Pyin Oo Lwin's strawberries and Bago's pineapples. Mango is best from March to July; jackfruit from June to October.

drinkers might find themselves growing disturbingly attached to the 'three-in-one' packets of instant coffee (the 'three' being coffee, creamer and sugar), which you can have in teahouses for about K250.

Alcoholic Drinks

Across Myanmar there's little in the way of an alcohol-drinking culture; this is partly down to a lack of disposable income and also because the consumption of alcohol is looked down upon by the many Burmese Buddhists who interpret the fifth lay precept against intoxication very strictly.

However, with the advent of 'beer stations' – places that serve cheap draught beer – the number of urban locals who can afford a few glasses of beer after work is on the rise. In Yangon, you'll also find some sophisticated cocktail bars.

Meemalee (www. meemalee.com), a blog written by an English-Burmese cookbook author, covers Burmese food-related stories and recipes.

Beer

While a craft beer scene is a long way off, the opening up of Myanmar's economy is leading to a broadening of what's available to beer drinkers. Japanese beverage giant Kirin has taken a 55% stake in Myanmar Brewery Limited (MBL; http://myanmarbeer.com), producer of the top-selling Myanmar Beer. Its standard (green label) product is slightly lighter in flavour and alcohol (5%) than other Southeast Asian beers and costs around K800 a draught pint. Its new Premium brand is more wheaty and uses imported malt. The company also has a couple of other brands, including Black Shield stout. Carlsberg and Heineken have also come into the market with their own brands and local variations, such as Yoma and Regal 7. At fancier, urban bars you'll also find imported beers.

Liquors & Wines

The website www.hsaba.com, written by cookbook author Tin Cho Chaw, includes a blog that regularly features Burmese recipes.

Very popular in Shan State is an orange brandy called *shwe leinmaw*. Much of it is distilled in the mountains between Kalaw and Taunggyi. It's a pleasant-tasting liqueur and packs quite a punch. Near Taunggyi there's a couple of vineyards making wine and in Pyin Oo Lwin there are several sweet strawberry-based wines.

There are also stronger liquors, including *ayeq hpyu* (white liquor), which varies in strength from brandylike to almost pure ethyl; and *taw ayeq* (jungle liquor), a cruder form of *ayeq hpyu*. Mandalay is well known for its rums, and there is also the fermented palm juice known as toddy.

Where to Eat & Drink

Myanmar has three general dining/drinking scenarios: what's in Yangon (including many expat-oriented, high-end choices); what's in other oft-visited places, including Mandalay, Bagan, Inle Lake and Ngapali Beach (many traveller-oriented menus); and everywhere else.

Food can be quite cheap (from K1200 or K2500 for a full stomach) if you stick to roadside restaurants with their curry-filled pots or pick-and-point rice dishes. It's worth mentioning that these restaurants, though cheap,

---

DOS & DON'TS

→ A fork is held in the left hand and used as a probe to push food onto the spoon; you eat from the spoon.

→ Locals tend to focus on the flavours, not table talk, during meals.

→ If you're asked to join someone at a restaurant, they will expect to pay for the meal. Expect to do likewise if you invite a local out for a meal.

TEAHOUSE TREATS

When visiting a teahouse in Myanmar, abandon any preconceived notions of a fragrant cuppa served in a dainty China cup; the tea here is strong, often a bitter shot of black brew served in a minuscule glass mug with a dollop of sweetened condensed milk and a splash of tinned milk. To help you place your order, here is a short language lesson:

lăp'eq·ye – black tea served sweet with a dollop of condensed milk – the standard

cho bawq – a less sweet version of *lăp'eq·ye*

kyauq padaung – very sweet; the phrase comes from a famous sugar-palm-growing region near Bagan

cho kya – strongest tea, also served with condensed milk

Teahouses are also your best bet for breakfast, a light snack or sweet. Ethnic Burmese-run teahouses often emphasise noodles. *Móun·hìn·gà* is usually available as a matter of course, but other more obscure noodle dishes include *óun·nó k'auq·swèh* (thin wheat noodles in a mild coconut-milk-based broth), *myì shay* (thick rice noodles served with chicken or pork and a dollop of sticky rice 'glue') and *nàngyì dhouq* (a salad of wide rice noodles seasoned with chickpea flour). Teahouses that serve these dishes are also likely to serve fried rice and *t'ămìn dhouq* (rice salad), also great for breakfast.

Indian-owned teahouses often specialise in deep-fried dishes such as the ubiquitous samosas and *poori* (deep-fried bread served with a light potato curry), as well as oil-free breads such as *dosai* (southern Indian-style crepes) and *nanbyá* (naan bread), the latter often served with a delicious pigeon pea–based dip. And Chinese-style teahouses often feature lots of baked sweets as well as meaty steamed buns and yum cha–like nibbles.

don't always meet international hygiene standards. That said, you're usually looking at K3000 to K5000 for a meal. In many midsized towns there are basic stands and maybe a Chinese restaurant or two – and that's it.

Restaurants

The bulk of Myanmar eateries are basic, with concrete floors, assertive fluorescent lighting and occasionally a menu in barely comprehensible English. Burmese curry-based eateries are busiest (and many say freshest) at lunch. No menus are necessary at these; just go to the line of curries and point to what you want. A meal comes with a tableful of condiments, all of which are automatically refilled once you finish them. An all-you-can-eat meal can cost as little as K1500.

Chinese restaurants are found in most towns and many have sprawling menus, with as much as 50 rice or noodle and chicken, pork, lamb, fish, beef or vegetable dishes, almost always without prices. Veggie dishes start at around K800 or K1000; meat dishes at about K1200 or K1500.

More upmarket restaurants – some serving a mix of Asian foods, others specialising in one food type, such as pizza or Thai – can be found in Bagan, Mandalay, Inle Lake and especially Yangon. Also, most top-end hotels offer plusher eating places, sometimes set around the pool. Such comfort is rarer to come by off the beaten track.

Most restaurants keep long hours daily, usually from 7am to 9pm or until the last diner wants to stumble out, their belly full of curry or beer.

Quick Eats

Like most Southeast Asians, the people of Myanmar are great grab-and-go snackers. Stands at night markets, selling a host of sweets and barbecued meals and noodles, get going around 5pm to 8pm or later. Generally you can get some fried noodles, a few pieces of pork, or sticky rice wrapped in banana leaf for a few hundred kyat.

Juan Gallardo's Delicious Myanmar (www.myanmartravelessentials.com) combines local recipes with photographs and cultural notes on the Spaniard's travels around the country.

Drinking Venues

Outside the big cities, you'll be hard-pressed to find anything resembling the Western concept of a bar or pub. Most drinking is done at open-air barbecue restaurants, often called 'beer stations' in Burmese English. Opening hours are therefore the same as for restaurants. All but Muslim Indian restaurants keep cold bottles of beer handy (charging from K1700 in basic restaurants and up to K3000 or so in swankier ones). It's perfectly fine to linger for hours and down a few beers.

Teahouses

A convenient place to grab a cuppa or a quick snack, teahouses are also an important social institution in Myanmar, a key meeting place for family, friends or business associates. 'Morning teahouses' typically open from 6am to 4pm, while evening ones open from 4pm or 5pm and stay open till 11pm or later. Note, it's common to see children working in teahouses (p376).

Vegetarians & Vegans

If you're having issues with onion breath in Myanmar, it's because the Burmese allegedly consume the most onions per capita of any country in the world.

Vegetarians will find at least a couple of meat-free options at most restaurants in Myanmar. Many Burmese Buddhists abstain from eating the flesh of any four-legged animal and, during the Buddhist rain retreat around the Waso full moon, may take up a 'fire-free' diet that includes only raw vegetables and fruit. Some Indian or Nepali restaurants are vegan, and even meaty barbecues have a few skewered vegetables for grilling. The easiest way to convey your needs is saying '*ăthà măsà nain bù*' (I can't eat meat).

Habits & Customs

According to local beliefs, a baby will be born overweight if the mother indulges in bananas while pregnant.

At home, most families take their meals sitting on mats around a low, round table. In restaurants, chairs and tables are more common. The entire meal is served at once, rather than in courses. In Burmese restaurants each individual diner in a group typically orders a small plate of curry for himself or herself, while side dishes are shared among the whole party. This contrasts with China and Thailand, for example, where every dish is usually shared. If you eat at a private home, it's not unusual for the hostess and children to not join you at the table.

Traditionally, Burmese food is eaten with the fingers, much like in India, usually with the right hand. Nowadays, it's also common for urban Myanmar people to eat with a *k'ăyìn* (or *hkayìn;* fork) and *zùn* (spoon). These are always available at Burmese restaurants and are almost always given to foreign diners.

Food Glossary

Typical Burmese Dishes

ămèh·hnaq	အမဲနပ်	beef in gravy
ceq·thà·ăc'o·jeq	ကြက်သားအချိုချက်	sweet chicken
ceq·thà·gin	ကြက်သားကင်	grilled chicken (satay)
ceq·thà·jaw jeq	ကြက်သားကြော်ချက်	fried chicken
hìn	ဟင်း	curry
ămèh·dhà·hìn	အမဲသားဟင်း	beef curry
ceq·thà·hìn	ကြက်သားဟင်း	chicken curry
ăthì·ăyweq·hìn/thì·zoun·hìn·jo	အသီးအရွက်ဟင်း၊ သီးစုံဟင်းချို	vegetable curry
hìn·jo	ဟင်းချို	soup (clear or mild)
s'an·hlaw·hìn·jo	ဆန်လှော်ဟင်းချို	sizzling rice soup

s'éh·hnămyò·hìn·jo	ဆယ့်နှစ်မျိုးဟင်းချို	'12-taste' soup
móun·di	မုန့်တီ	*mount-ti* (Mandalay noodles and chicken/fish)
móun·hìn·gà	မုန့်ဟင်းခါး	*mohinga* (noodles and chicken/fish)
móun·s'i·jaw	မုန့်ဆီကြော်	sweet fried-rice pancakes
móun·zàn	မုန့်ဆန်း	sticky rice cake with jaggery (palm sugar)
myì shay	မြီးရှည်	Shan-style noodle soup
ngà·dhouq	ငါးသုပ်	fish salad
ngà·baùn·(douq)	ငါးပေါင်း(ထုပ်)	steamed fish (in banana leaves)
t'ămìn	ထမင်း	rice
kauq·hnyìn·baùn	ကောက်ညှင်းပေါင်း	steamed sticky rice
oùn·t'ămìn	အုန်းထမင်း	coconut rice
t'ămìn·gyaw	ထမင်းကြော်	fried rice
t'ădhì·móun	ထန်းသီးမုန့်	toddy-palm sugar cake
weq·thăni	ဝက်သနီ	red pork

Meat & Seafood

ămèh·dhà	အမဲသား	beef
ceq·thà	ကြက်သား	chicken
k'ăyú	ခရု	shellfish
ngă	ငါး	fish
ngăk'u	ငါးခူ	catfish
ngăshín	ငါးရှဉ့်	eel
ngăthălauq·paùn	ငါးသလောက်ပေါင်း	carp
pin·leh·za/ye·thaq·tăwa	ပင်လယ်စာ ၊ ရေသတ္တဝါ	seafood
pyi·jì·ngà	ပြည်ကြီးငါး	squid
weq·thà	ဝက်သား	pork

Vegetables

bù·dhì	ဘူးသီး	zucchini/gourd
ceq·thun·ni	ကြက်သွန်နီ	onion
gaw·bi·douq	ဂေါ်ဇီထုပ်	cabbage
hìn·dhì·hìn·yweq	ဟင်းသီးဟင်းရွက်	vegetables
hmo	မှို	mushrooms
ngăpyàw·bù	ငှက်ပျောဖူး	banana flower
kălăbèh	ကုလားပဲ	chick peas
k'ăyàn·dhì	ခရမ်းသီး	eggplant/aubergine
k'ăyàn·jin·dhì	ခရမ်းချဉ်သီး	tomato

moun·la·ú·wa	မုန်လာဥဝါ	carrot
pàn·gaw·p'i	ပန်းဂေါ်ဖီ	cauliflower
p'ăyoun·dhì	ဖရုံသီး	pumpkin
pèh·dhì	ပဲသီး	beans
pyaùn·bù	ပြောင်းဖူး	corn (cob)

Fruit

àw·za·thì	သြဇာသီး	custard apple ('influence fruit')
ceq·mauq·thì	ကြက်မောက်သီး	rambutan ('cockscomb fruit')
cwèh·gàw·dhì	ကျွဲကောသီး	pomelo
dù·yìn·dhì	ဒူးရင်းသီး	durian
lain·c'ì·dhì	လိုင်ချီးသီး	lychee
lein·maw·dhì	လိမ္မော်သီး	orange
meq·màn·dhì	မက်မန်းသီး	plum (damson)
măjì·dhì	မန်ကျည်းသီး	tamarind
nănaq·thì	နာနတ်သီး	pineapple
ngăpyàw·dhì	ငှက်ပျောသီး	banana
oùn·dhì	အုန်းသီး	coconut
pàn·dhì	ပန်းသီး	apple ('flower fruit')
shauq·thì	ရှောက်သီး	lemon
t'àw·baq·thì	ထောပတ်သီး	avocado ('butter fruit')
than·băya·dhì	သံပုရာသီး	lime
thiq·thì/ăthì	သစ်သီး ၊ အသီး	fruit
thăyeq·dhì	သရက်သီး	mango
thìn·bàw·dhì	သင်္ဘောသီး	papaya ('boat-shaped fruit')

Spices & Condiments

ceq·thun·byu	ကြက်သွန်ဖြူ	garlic
gyìn	ဂျင်း	ginger
hnàn	နှမ်း	sesame
hnìn·ye	နှင်းရည်	rose syrup
kălà·t'àw·baq	ကုလားထောပတ်	ghee
kùn·ya	ကွမ်းယာ	betel quid
meiq·thălin	မိတ်သလင်	galangal (white ginger-like root)
mye·bèh·(jaw)	မြေပဲ(ကြော်)	peanuts (fried)
nan·nan·bin	နံနံပင်	coriander
ngan·pya·ye	ငံပြာရည်	fish sauce
ngăyouq·thì	ငရုတ်သီး	chilli

ngăyouq·ye	ရေတ်ရည်	chilli sauce
oùn·nó	အုန်းနို့	coconut cream
p'a·la·zé	ဖါလာစေ့	cardamom
paun·móun	ပေါင်မုန့်	bread
pèh·ngan·pya·ye	ပဲငံပြာရည်	soy sauce
t'àw·baq	ထောပတ်	butter
tha·gu	သာကူ	sago/tapioca
t'oùn	ထုံး	lime (for betel)
s'à	ဆား	salt
s'ănwin	ဆနွင်း	turmeric
sha·lăka·ye	ရှာလကာရည်	vinegar
thăjà	သကြား	sugar
to·hù/to·p'ù	တိုဟူး၊တိုဖူး	tofu (beancurd)

Cold Drinks

ăyeq	အရက်	alcohol
bi·ya/tăbălin	ဘီယာ ၊ တစ်ပုလင်း	beer
can·ye	ကြံရည်	sugar-cane juice
lein·maw·ye	လိမ္မော်ရည်	orange juice
nwà·nó	နွားနို့	milk
oùn·ye	အုန်းရည်	coconut juice
p'yaw·ye/ă·è	ဖျော်ရည် ၊ အအေး	soft drink
s'o·da	ဆိုဒါ	soda water
t'àn·ye	ထန်းရည်	toddy
than·băya·ye	သံပုရာရည်	lime juice
ye-	ရေ	water
ye·thán	ရေသန့်	bottled water ('clean water')
ye·è	ရေအေး	cold water
ye·jeq·è	ရေကျက်အေး	boiled cold water
ye·nwè	ရေနွေး	hot water

Hot Drinks

kaw·fi	ကော်ဖီ	coffee
dhăjà·néh	သကြားနဲ့	with sugar
nó·s'i·néh	နို့ဆီနဲ့	with condensed milk
nwà·nó·néh	နွားနို့နဲ့	with milk
lăp'eq·ye·jàn/ye·nwè·jàn	လက်ဖက်ရည်ကြမ်း ၊ ရေနွေးကြမ်း	green tea (plain)
leq·p'eq·ye	လက်ဖက်ရည်	tea (Indian)

Architecture & Arts

For centuries the arts in Myanmar were sponsored by the royal courts, mainly through the construction of major religious buildings that required the skills of architects, sculptors, painters and a variety of artisans. Such patronage was cut short during British colonial rule and has never been a priority since independence. Even so, traditional art and architecture endures in Myanmar, mainly in the temples that are an ever-present feature of the landscape. There's also a growing contemporary art scene.

Architecture

Traditional Myanmar architecture is accomplished and artistic. Myanmar is a country of *zedi* (stupa), often called 'pagodas' in English. Wherever you are – boating down the river, driving through the hills, even flying above the plains – there always seems to be a hilltop *zedi* in view. Bagan (Pagan) is the most dramatic result of this fervour for religious monuments – an enthusiasm that continues today, as the mass rebuilding of temples at the site attests.

In the past, only places of worship were made of permanent materials. Until quite recently, all secular buildings – and most monasteries – were constructed of wood, so there are few original ones left to be seen. Even the great royal palaces, such as the last one at Mandalay, were made of wood. All the palaces you see today are reconstructions – often far from faithful – such as the Bagan Golden Palace made of concrete and reinforced steel.

Even so, there are still many excellent wooden buildings to be seen. Builders continue to use teak with great skill, and a fine country home can be a very pleasing structure indeed.

Zedi Styles

Early *zedi* were usually hemispherical (the Kaunghmudaw at Sagaing near Mandalay) or bulbous (the Bupaya in Bagan). The so-called Mon-style *pahto* is a large cube with small windows and ground-level passageways; this type is also known as a *gu* or *ku* (from the Pali-Sanskrit *guha*, meaning 'cave'). The more modern style is much more graceful – a curvaceous lower bell merging into a soaring spire, such as the Shwedagon Paya in Yangon (Rangoon) or the Uppatasanti Paya in Nay Pyi Taw.

The overall Bamar concept is similar to that of the Mayan and Aztec pyramids of Mesoamerica: worshippers climb a symbolic mountain lined with religious reliefs and frescoes.

Style is not always a good indicator of the original age of a *zedi*, as Myanmar is earthquake-prone and many (including the Shwedagon) have been rebuilt again and again. In places, such as Bagan and Inthein, near Inle Lake, ruined temples have been rebuilt from the base up with little or no respect for what the original would have looked like. In Bagan, for example, all *zedi* would have been traditionally covered with white or painted stucco, not left as the bare brick structures they are today.

Yangon Architecture Books

30 Heritage Buildings of Yangon by Sarah Rooney

Relics of Rangoon (www.relicsof rangoon.com) by Philip Heijmans

Yangon Echoes: Inside Heritage Homes by Virginia Henderson and Tim Webster

Best Buddhist Buildings

Shwedagon Paya (Yangon)

Ananda Pahto (Bagan)

Shwenandaw Kyaung (Mandalay)

Shwesandaw Paya (Pyay)

Shittaung Paya (Mrauk U)

Colonial & Modern Architecture

While many buildings erected during the British colonial period have been demolished or are facing the wrecking ball, those that survive are often well worth seeking out. They range from the rustic wood-and-plaster Tudor villas of Pyin Oo Lwin to the thick-walled, brick-and-plaster, colonnaded mansions and shophouses of Yangon, Mawlamyine (Mawlamyaing) and Myeik.

Yangon in particular is stocked with spectacular, if often crumbling, colonial gems, such as the Ministers Office, seat of British colonial power, and Sofaer's Building. Some such as the Strand Hotel and the Moseah Yeshua Synagogue have been spruced up either by commercial investment or private donations and overseas grants.

It wasn't just under British rule that Myanmar's architects thought on a grand scale. Post-independence Yangon in the 1950s saw the construction of some still stylish, modern buildings, such as the Nay Pyi Taw cinema and the Technical High School designed by British architect Raglan Squire. This latter building has recently been renovated and reopened as Singapore-Myanmar Vocational Training Institute (SMVTI), with the colourful and beautifully designed mosaic murals of traditional Myanmar life, applied to its courtyard walls, a particular highlight.

Contemporary Architecture

In the early 21st century, the military junta turned its back on Yangon to construct a new capital at Nay Pyi Taw. Starting from a clean slate, the government built on a grandiose, but unimaginative scale. Some buildings are copies of those in Yangon, such as Nay Pyi Taw's City Hall and Uppatasanti Paya, a replica of Shwedagon Paya. Practically empty 10-lane highways make for a surreal sight, while key buildings such as the mammoth National Assembly remain off-limits to mere mortals.

It has been left to more sophisticated architects and builders to take Myanmar's architectural legacy forward. These include the husband-and-wife team of Stephen Zawmoe Shwe and Amelie Chai, partners in SPINE Architects (http://spinearchitects.com). Most of their work, which includes residential and commercial projects, is in Yangon; Union Bar & Grill and Gekko are good examples of their style. They also designed the Amata Resort & Spa in Ngapali and the Bay of Bengal Resort at Ngwe Saung Beach.

Potentially exciting projects going forward include Yoma Strategic's Landmark Development in downtown Yangon, which will incorporate the old Burma Railways building by turning it into a heritage hotel.

Sculpture & Painting

Early Myanmar art was always a part of the religious architecture – paints were for the walls of temples, sculpture to be placed inside them. Many pieces, formerly in paya or *kyaung* (Burmese Buddhist monasteries), have been sold or stolen and, unfortunately, you'll easily find more Myanmar religious sculpture for sale or on display overseas than in Myanmar.

In the aftermath of the 1988 demonstrations, the government forbade 'selfish' or 'mad art' that didn't have clear pro-government themes. One artist, Sitt Nyein Aye, spent two months in custody for sketching the ruins of the former student union, which Ne Win had blown up in 1962. Subsequently many artists chose to play safe with predictable tourist-oriented works.

Censorship of art exhibitions is now in the past, allowing artists more freedom of expression and a mini-boom of galleries in Yangon. Among Myanmar artists attracting international are the couple Wah Nu and Tun

Amazing Wood Structures

Shwenandaw Kyaung (Mandalay)

U Bein's Bridge (Amarapura)

Bagaya Kyaung (Inwa)

Youqson Kyaung (Salay)

Pakhanngeh Kyaung (Pakokku)

Architectural Guide Yangon, by Ben Bansai, Elliot Fox and Manuel Oka, covers 110 buildings and has insightful essays that provide the full historical scope of the former capital's built legacy and potential.

The bronze Mahamuni Buddha, in Mandalay's Mahamuni Paya, may date back to the 1st century AD and is Myanmar's most famous Buddhist sculpture.

Win Aung, who create paintings, video art and installations based on their memories of growing up under the socialist-military regime. They have been written about in the *New York Times* and had their work purchased by the Guggenheim Museum. Nge Lay and Po Po represented Myanmar at the 2014 Singapore Biennale with pieces about education and spirituality.

A student activist in the late 1980s, Htein Lin (www.hteinlin.com) is a pioneer of performance art in Myanmar and had his work shown at the Singapore Biennale in 2016. Since moving back to Myanmar in 2013 he has worked on a project entitled *A Show of Hands,* capturing in plaster the arms of hundreds of former political prisoners, and acted as a co-curator of the first Yangon Art and Heritage Festival (www.yangon artandheritage.com) in 2015.

> Yangon-based art researcher Nathalie Johnson has created the website Myanmar Evolution (http://myanmart evolution.com) to support the growth of contemporary arts in the country.

Traditional Crafts

Apart from the following, other Myanmar crafts you may come across are paper parasols, silver- and metalware, and wood carvings.

Kammawa & Parabaik

Kammawa (from the Pali *kammavacha*) are narrow, rectangular slats painted with extracts from the Pali Vinaya (the Pitaka concerned with monastic discipline); specifically, these are extracts to do with clerical affairs. The core of a *kammawa* page may be a thin slat of wood, lacquered cloth, thatched cane or thin brass, which is then layered with red, black and gold lacquer to form the script and decorations.

The *parabaik* (Buddhist palm-leaf manuscript) is a similarly horizontal 'book', this time folded accordion-style, like a road map. The pages are made of heavy paper covered with black ink on which the letters are engraved.

> A US embassy cable released by WikiLeaks revealed that Senior General Than Shwe had thought it would be politically more popular to instruct crony businesses to create the Myanmar National League rather than spend US$1 billion on buying Manchester United, as his grandson had advised.

Lacquerware

The earliest lacquerware found in Myanmar can be dated to the 11th century and sports a very Chinese style. The techniques used today are known as *yun*, the old Bamar word for the people of Chiang Mai, from where the techniques were imported in the 16th century (along with some captured artisans) by King Bayinnaung. An older style of applying gold or silver to a black background dates back to, perhaps, the Pyay era (5th to 9th centuries) and is kept alive by artisans in Kyaukka, near Monywa.

Many lacquerware shops include workshops, where you can see the lengthy process involved in making the bowls, trays and other objects. The craftsperson first weaves a frame (the best-quality wares have a bamboo frame tied together with horse or donkey hairs; lesser pieces are made wholly from bamboo). The lacquer is then coated over the framework and allowed to dry. After several days it is sanded down with ash from rice husks and another coating of lacquer is applied. A high-quality item may have seven to 15 layers altogether.

The lacquerware is engraved and painted, then polished to remove the paint from everywhere except from within the engravings. Multicoloured lacquerware is produced by repeated engraving, painting and polishing. From start to finish it can take up to five or six months to produce a high-quality piece of lacquerware, which may have as many as five colours. A top-quality bowl can have its rim squeezed together until the sides meet without suffering any damage or permanent distortion.

> **Lacquerware Centres**
>
> *Kyaukka (near Monywa)*
>
> *Myinkaba (Bagan)*
>
> *New Bagan (Bagan Myothit; Bagan)*
>
> *Kyaingtong (Shan State)*

Tapestries & Textiles

Kalaga (tapestries) consist of pieces of coloured cloth of various sizes heavily embroidered with silver- or gold-coloured thread, metal sequins and glass beads, and feature mythological Myanmar figures in padded relief. The greatest variety is found in Mandalay, where most tapestries are produced.

Good-quality *kalaga* are tightly woven and don't skimp on sequins, which may be sewn in overlapping lines, rather than spaced side by side, as a sign of embroidery skill. The metals used should shine, even in older pieces; tarnishing means lower-quality materials.

Tribal textiles and weavings produced by the Chin, Naga, Kachin and Kayin can also be very beautiful, especially antique pieces. Among traditional hand-woven silk *longyis, laun-taya acheik,* woven on a hundred spools, are the most prized.

Old Myanmar Paintings in the Collection of U Win is one of the illustrated publications of the Thavibu Gallery (www.thavibu. com) specialising in Burmese art.

MYANMAR'S SPORTING LIFE

Martial arts are perhaps the longest-running sports that the people of Myanmar have patronised: the oldest written references to kickboxing in the country are found in the chronicles of warfare between Burma and Thailand during the 15th and 16th centuries. The British introduced football (soccer) in the 19th century and it remains Myanmar's most popular spectator sport.

Football

The Myanmar National League (MNL; www.themnl.com) was launched in 2009 and currently consists of 12 teams in the premier league and 10 in MNL-2. In MNL-1, Yangon United were the 2015 champions. Local TV broadcasts European games and teashops are invariably packed when a big match is screened.

Martial Arts

Myanma let-hwei (Myanmar kickboxing) is very similar in style to *muay thai* (Thai kickboxing), although not nearly as well developed as a national sport.

The most common and traditional kickboxing venues are temporary rings set up in a dirt circle (usually at *paya pwe* rather than sports arenas). All fighters are bare-fisted. All surfaces of the body are considered fair targets and any part of the body except the head may be used to strike an opponent. Common blows include high kicks to the neck, elbow thrusts to the face and head, knee hooks to the ribs and low crescent kicks to the calf. Punching is considered the weakest of all blows and kicking merely a way to soften up one's opponent; knee and elbow strikes are decisive in most matches.

Before the match begins, each boxer performs a dance-like ritual in the ring to pay homage to Buddha and to Khun Cho and Khun Tha, the *nat* whose domain includes Myanmar kickboxing. The winner repeats the ritual at the end of the match.

Chinlon

Also known as 'cane ball', *chinlone* is a game in which a woven rattan ball about 5in in diameter is kicked around. It also refers to the ball itself. Informally, any number of players can form a circle and keep the *chinlone* airborne by kicking or heading it soccer-style from player to player; a lack of scoring makes it a favourite pastime with locals of all ages.

In formal play, six players stand in a circle of 22ft circumference. Each player must keep the ball aloft using a succession of 30 techniques and six surfaces on the foot and leg, allotting five minutes for each part. Each successful kick scores a point, while points are subtracted for using the wrong body part or dropping the ball. The sport was included in the South East Asian Games held in Myanmar in December 2013.

A popular variation – and the one used in intramural or international competitions – is played with a volleyball net, using all the same rules as in volleyball except that only the feet and head are permitted to touch the ball.

Dance & Theatre

Myanmar's truly indigenous dance forms are those that pay homage to the *nat* (spirit beings). Most classical dance styles, meanwhile, arrived from Thailand. Today the dances most obviously taken from Thailand are known as *yodaya zat* (Ayuthaya theatre), as taught to the people of Myanmar by Thai theatrical artists taken captive in the 18th century.

The most Myanmar of dances feature solo performances by female dancers who wear strikingly colourful dresses with long white trains, which they kick into the air with their heels – quite a feat, given the restrictive length of the train.

Pwe is the generic word in Myanmar for theatre or performance and it embraces all kinds of plays and musical operas as well as dancing. An all-night *zat pwe* involves a recreation of an ancient legend or Buddhist Jataka (story of the Buddha's past lives), while the *yamazat pwe* pick a tale from the Indian epic Ramayana. In Mandalay, *yamazat* performers even have their own shrine.

Myanmar classical dancing emphasises pose rather than movement and solo rather than ensemble performances. In contrast the less common, but livelier, *yein pwe* features singing and dancing performed by a chorus or ensemble.

Most popular of all is the *a-nyeint,* a traditional *pwe* somewhat akin to early American vaudeville, the most famous exponents of which are Mandalay's Moustache Brothers and the satirist and film actor and director Zarganar.

Marionette Theatre

Youq-the pwe (Myanmar marionette theatre) presents colourful puppets up to 3.5ft high in a spectacle that some consider the most expressive of all the Myanmar arts. Developed during the Konbaung period, it was so influential that it became the forerunner to *zat pwe* as later performed by actors rather than marionettes. As with dance-drama, the genre's 'golden age' began with the Mandalay kingdoms of the late 18th century and ran through to the advent of cinema in the 1930s.

The people of Myanmar have great respect for an expert puppeteer. Some marionettes may be manipulated by a dozen or more strings. The marionette master's standard repertoire requires a troupe of 28 puppets including Thagyamin (king of the gods); a Myanmar king, queen, prince and princess; a regent; two court pages; an old man and an old woman; a villain; a hermit; four ministers; two clowns; one good and one evil *nat;* a Brahmin astrologer; two ogres; a *zawgyi* (alchemist); a horse; a monkey; a *makara* (mythical sea serpent); and an elephant.

It's rare to see marionette theatre outside tourist venues in Yangon, Mandalay or Bagan.

Music

Traditional Myanmar music, played loud the way the *nat* like it, features strongly in any *pwe*. Its repetitive, even harsh, harmonies can be hard on Western ears at first; Myanmar scales are not 'tempered', as Western scales have been since Bach. The music is primarily two-dimensional, in the sense that rhythm and melody provide much of the musical structure, while repetition is a key element. Subtle shifts in rhythm and tonality provide the modulation usually supplied by the harmonic dimension in Western music.

Classical Music

Classical-music traditions were largely borrowed from Siam musicians in the late 1800s, who borrowed the traditions from Cambodian conquests

Burmese Crafts: Past and Present by Sylvia Fraser-Lu details the foundations of Myanmar's artistic traditions and catalogues the major crafts from metalwork to umbrella making.

The beautifully painted little parasols you see around Myanmar are often made in Pathein – in fact, they're known as *Pathein hti* (Pathein umbrellas).

The Illusion of Life: Burmese Marionettes by Ma Thanegi gives readers a glimpse of the 'wit, spirit and style' of this traditional Burmese performance art.

centuries earlier. Myanmar classical music, as played today, was codified by Po Sein, a colonial-era musician, composer and drummer who also designed the *hsaing waing* (the circle of tuned drums, also known as *paq waing*) and formalised classical dancing styles. Such music is meant to be played as an accompaniment to classical dance-dramas that enact scenes from the Jataka or from the Ramayana.

Musical instruments are predominantly percussive, but even the *hsaing waing* may carry the melody. These drums are tuned by placing a wad of *paq-sa* (drum food) – made from a kneaded paste of rice and wood ash – onto the centre of the drum head, then adding or subtracting a pinch at a time till the desired drum tone is attained.

In addition to the *hsaing waing*, the traditional *hsaing* (Myanmar ensemble) of seven to 10 musicians will usually play: the *kye waing* (a circle of tuned brass gongs); the *saung gauq* (a boat-shaped harp with 13 strings); the *pattala* (a sort of xylophone); the *hneh* (an oboe-type instrument related to the Indian *shanai*); the *pa-lwe* (a bamboo flute); the *mi-gyaung* (crocodile lute); the *paq-ma* (a bass drum); and the *yagwin* (small cymbals) and *wa leq-hkouq* (bamboo clappers), which are purely rhythmic and are often played by Myanmar vocalists.

Folk

Older than Myanmar classical music is an enchanting vocal folk-music tradition still heard in rural areas where locals may sing without instrumental accompaniment while working. Such folk songs set the work cadence and provide a distraction from the physical strain and monotony of pounding rice, clearing fields, weaving and so on. This type of music is most readily heard in the Ayeyarwady Delta between Twante and Pathein.

An interesting developing project documenting Myanmar arts, culture and individual life stories is The Kite Tales (www.facebook.com/kitetalesmyanmar), which also has feeds on Twitter and Instagram.

Pop, Rock & Rap

Western pop music's influence first came in the 1970s, when singers such as Min Min Latt and Takatho Tun Naung sang shocking things such as Beatles cover versions or 'Tie a Yellow Ribbon Round the Old Oak Tree'. This led to long-haired, distorted-guitar rock bands such as Empire and Iron Cross (aka IC) in the 1980s. Over 25 years later, Iron Cross are still rocking, the Myanmar equivalent of the Rolling Stones.

Bands can have a stable of several singers who split stage time with the same backing band. Iron Cross, for example, features one of Myanmar's 'wilder' singers, Lay Phyu, but it can also tone it down as a backing band for the poppier stuff of other singers.

Female singers like Sone Thin Par and actor Htu Aeindra Bo win fans for their melodies – and looks – but the most interesting is the Celine Dion-esque Phyu Phyu Kyaw Thein (www.phyuphyukyawtheinonline.com). She sang with Jason Mraz at a concert in Yangon in December 2012, and serves as general secretary of the Myanmar Musician Association.

TRADITIONAL BURMESE MUSIC CDS

Mahagitá *Harp & Vocal Music from Burma* (2003; Smithsonian Folkways)

Various artists *Music of Nat Pwe: Folk & Pop Music of Myanmar* (2007; Sublime Frequencies)

Pat Waing *The Magic Drum Circle of Burma* (1998; Shanachie)

Various artists *Burma: Traditional Music* (2009; Air Mail Music)

White Elephants & Golden Ducks *Enchanting Musical Treasures from Burma* (1997; Shanachie)

Rap and hip-hop are huge with stars such as J-Me, Barbu, Myo Kyawt Myaung and heart-throb Sai Sai Kham Leng. Also look out for the female rap duo Y.A.K. Thxa Soe is a popular hip-hop singer whose 2007 hit 'I Like Drums' merged *nat* music with trance. Breaking out internationally are Me N Ma Girls, a toned-down Spice Girls–style troupe. Although dismissed initially as prepackaged pop, the Girls have gone on to somewhat distinguish themselves by being signed up by a US independent record label and playing a show at New York's Lincoln Center in 2013.

Also making a name for themselves overseas is the indie rock band Side Effect, who are based in Yangon. It's in this city that you're most likely to catch a live music gig. Check out the ones organised by Jam It! (p78).

Literature

Religious texts inscribed onto Myanmar's famous *kammawa* (lacquered scriptures) and *parabaik* (folding manuscripts) were the first pieces of literature as such, and began appearing in the 12th century. Until the 1800s, the only other works of 'literature' available were royal genealogies, classical poetry and law texts. A Burmese version of the Indian epic Ramayana was first written in 1775 by poet U Aung Pyo.

The first Myanmar novel, *Maung Yin Maung Ma Me Ma,* an adaptation of *The Count of Monte Cristo*, by James Hla Kyaw, was published in 1904. It's popularity spurred on other copycat works, such as the Burmese detective Maung San Sha, based on Sherlock Holmes.

More recently, Myanmar-born Nu Nu Yi Inwa, one of the country's leading writers with at least 15 novels and more than 100 short stories to her name, made the shortlist for the 2007 Man Asian Literary Prize with *Smile as They Bow*. The story, set at the Taungbyon Festival held near Mandalay, follows an elderly gay transvestite medium who fears losing his much younger partner to a woman in the heat of the weeklong festivities.

Eric Blair (aka George Orwell) worked in Myanmar from 1922 to 1927 as a policeman, an experience that informed his novel *Burmese Days*. First published in 1934, the book is sharply critical of colonial life in the country.

To catch up on the latest in local literature, visit the website of the Irrawaddy Literature Festival (www.irrawaddy litfest.com).

ZARGANA

Myanmar's most popular comedian is Maung Thura, better known by his stage name Zarganar (also spelled Zargana) meaning tweezers. Born into an intellectual and politically active family, he trained as a dentist in Yangon in the 1980s, a period during which he also worked as a volunteer literary teacher in Chin State, and formed part of a comedy troupe of students performing *a-nyeint* skit routines. Such was his success in the last role that he ended up on television, where he took astonishing risks for the time with his satirical material lampooning the military rulers.

His first stint in jail followed the 1988 street protests in Yangon. There were several other prison terms leading up to his last incarceration in 2008 when he criticised the government for its poor response to the tragedy of Cyclone Nargis. For this he was sentenced to 35 years in jail. *This Prison Where I Live* (http://thisprisonwhereilive.co.uk), a documentary by Rex Bloomstein, includes interviews with Zarganar filmed in 2007 before he was imprisoned. During his time in jail, Zarganar was awarded the inaugural PEN Pinter Prize for his writing.

After November 2011, when Zarganar was released, *This Prison Where I Live* was updated to include footage of him meeting with German comedian Michael Mittermeier, who also features in the documentary.

More recently, Zarganar is one of the founders of House of Media and Entertainment (HOME), a Yangon-based centre to train and support young filmmakers as well as encourage a new generation of fearless comedians. He also wrote a screenplay for a so-far ill-fated biopic of Aung San.

Also check out the poetry of Ko Ko Thett (www.kokothett.webs.com) and the novels of Myanmar-born, US-based Wendy Yone-Law, including *The Road to Wanting.*

Cinema

Myanmar has had a modest film industry since the early 20th century and it continues today producing low-budget action pics, romances and comedies that are a staple of cinemas, village video-screening halls and DVD sellers across the country. There's even an annual Academy Awards ceremony, which is one of the country's biggest social events, and a growing independent film and documentary scene with several film-related festivals in Yangon.

Among recent documentaries available on video or doing the festival rounds are Nic Dunlop's *Burma Soldier,* the moving story of a military recruit who loses two limbs to landmines and switches sides to become a democracy activist; the Oscar-nominated *Burma VJ*; *Youth of Yangon* (https://vimeo.com/58578845) about the city's skateboard scene; and *Nargis – When Time Stopped Breathing* (http://nargis-film.com), released in 2009 and the country's first feature-length documentary.

Going back to 1954, Myanmar actor Win Min Than was cast opposite Gregory Peck in *The Purple Plain,* the most credible of several WWII dramas set in Myanmar. *Beyond Rangoon* (1995; director John Boorman), a political tract/action flick set during the 1988 uprisings, had Georgetown, Penang, do a credible turn as the nation's then-turbulent capital. It starred several Myanmar actors, including Aung Ko, who plays an elderly guide to Patricia Arquette's American tourist galvanised into political activist.

Luc Besson's *The Lady* (2011) is a biopic about Aung San Suu Kyi, staring Michelle Yeo in the title role. Screened at film festivals around the world is the 2013 thriller *Kayan Beauties* (www.kayanbeauties.com), which paints a generally realistic portrait of Kayan life in Myanmar. All of the characters in the film are played by Kayan actors. Also look out for the delicate character study *The Monk* (2014), directed by poet and artist The Maw Naing.

There was controversy in June 2016 when *Twilight over Burma: My Life as a Shan Princess* was pulled from the Human Rights Human Dignity Film Festival, following government censorship. The Austrian-produced film is based on the life of Inge Eberhard (now Sargent), who married the Shan prince Sao Kya Seng and lived happily with him in Shan State until the military coup of 1962. Detained by the army, Sao Kya Seng died in mysterious circumstances.

Bones Will Crow: 15 Contemporary Burmese Poets, co-edited by James Byrne and Ko Ko Thett, is the first anthology of Burmese poetry ever to be published in the West.

The 2015 documentary *This Kind of Love* (www.thiskindoflovefilm.org), directed by Jeanne Hallacy and produced in association with Equality Myanmar, follows Burmese human rights educator and activist Aung Myo Min as he returns home after 24 years in exile.

Environment & Wildlife

Snow-capped mountains, steamy jungles, coral reefs, and open grasslands – you name it, Myanmar's environment has it. Scientists continue to discover new species amid the abundant biodiversity, but at the same time, the country's poor record on environmental laws and enforcement is killing off many others. Armed insurgencies, rampant resource extraction and unchecked infrastructure development are among the many dire threats to Myanmar's natural heritage.

Geography

A bit bigger than France and slightly smaller than Texas, Myanmar covers 261,228 sq miles and borders (clockwise from the west) Bangladesh, India, Tibet, China, Laos and Thailand, with 1199 miles of coastline facing the Bay of Bengal and the Andaman Sea. The country's south is similar to Malaysia and its north to northern India. The centre is an overlap of the two, producing 'zones' whose uniqueness is manifest in the scenery and creatures that hop around in it.

The area southwest of Yangon (Rangoon) is a vast delta region notable for its production of rice. Paddy fields are also an ever-present feature of Myanmar's central broad, flat heartland, known as the 'dry zone' for its lack of rain. This area is surrounded by protective mountain and hill ranges (*yoma* in Burmese). Most notable are the rugged Kachin Hills, which serve as the first steps into the Himalaya to the north; Hkakabo Razi, on the Tibetan border, which at 19,295ft is Southeast Asia's highest mountain; and Mt Victoria (Nat Ma Taung), west of Bagan in Chin State, which rises to 10,016ft.

Three major rivers – fed by monsoon downpours and melted Himalayan snows – cut north to south through the country. The Ayeyarwady (Irrawaddy) River, a 1240-mile-long waterway, is one of Asia's most navigable big rivers, feeding much of the country's rice fields. It connects lower Myanmar (based around Yangon) with upper Myanmar (around Mandalay). The 850-mile-long Chindwin River, originating in the Hukawng Valley of Kachin State, connects the northern hills with Myanmar's central zone, joining the Ayeyarwady between Mandalay and Bagan (Pagan). Rising on the Tibetan Plateau, the Thanlwin (Salween) River flows into Myanmar in its northeastern corner at China and empties into the Gulf of Mottama, near Mawlamyine (Mawlamyaing). Also, the Mekong River passes by on the short border with Laos.

Flora & Fauna

Myanmar, which sits on a transition zone between the plants and creatures of the Indian subcontinent, Southeast Asia and the Himalayan highlands, is a biodiversity hotspot. However, the troubled politics of the country over the last century have made it difficult for researchers to gain an accurate picture of the current state of the country's wildlife.

One end of the 1860-mile-long Himalaya mountain chain, formed when the Indian and Eurasian tectonic plates collided 140 million years ago, extends to Myanmar's Kachin State.

In February 2013 the Mandalay Region Legislative Assembly Committee set up the Irrawaddy River Conservation Commission, prompting environmentalists to call for the creation of a similar commission covering all of Myanmar's rivers.

Animals

When Marco Polo wrote about the lands now known as Myanmar in the 13th century, he described 'vast jungles teeming with elephants, unicorns and other wild beasts'. The unicorns, if they ever existed, have gone but it's difficult to know what else has been lost as well as the current state of the country's biodiversity.

The Wild Animals of Burma, published in 1967, is the most 'recent' work available and even this volume simply contains extracts from various surveys carried out by the British between 1912 and 1941, with a few observations dating to 1961. The US-based Wildlife Conservation Society (www.wcs.org) has engaged in a number of localised surveys, primarily in the far north, over the past few years, but currently nobody is attempting a full nationwide stocktake of plants and animals.

As with Myanmar's flora, the variation in Myanmar's wildlife is closely associated with the country's geographic and climatic differences. Hence the indigenous fauna of the country's northern half is mostly of Indo-Chinese origin, while that of the south is generally Sundaic (ie typical of Malaysia, Sumatra, Borneo and Java). In the Himalayan region north of the Tropic of Cancer (just north of Lashio), the fauna is similar to that found in northeastern India. In the area extending from Myitkyina in the north to the Bago Mountains in the central region, there is overlap between geographical and vegetative zones – which means that much of Myanmar is a potential habitat for plants and animals from all three zones.

Distinctive mammals found in dwindling numbers within the more heavily forested areas of Myanmar include leopards, fishing cats, civets, Indian mongooses, crab-eating mongooses, Himalayan bears, Asiatic black bears, Malayan sun bears, gaur (Indian bison), banteng (wild cattle), serow (Asiatic mountain goat), wild boars, sambar, barking deer, mouse deer, tapirs, pangolin, gibbons and macaques. Sea mammals include dolphins and dugongs.

According to the Asean Centre for Biodiversity (www.asean biodiversity.org), Myanmar is home to 300 species of mammal, 400 species of reptile and around 1000 bird species.

WWF Myanmar (www.wwf.org.mm/en) has partnered with the Wildlife Conservation Society to work on a national elephant conservation strategy.

MYANMAR'S WORKING ELEPHANTS

Myanmar is home to between 6000 and 10,000 Asian elephants, the second-largest population of this endangered species after India. This figure includes a captive population of approximately 5000, most of whom work in camps run by the government's Myanma Timber Enterprise (MTE; www.myanmatimber.com.mm).

Elephants have long been employed in Myanmar's logging industry. Some may find this an abuse of wild animals, but there is an argument that using elephant power to extract timber is more sustainable since roads don't need to be built into forests thus minimising damage of the environment. Also these working elephants are protected from poaching (unlike their wild cousins).

According to the Myanmar Timber Elephant Project (http://elephant-project.science), based at the University of Sheffield in the UK, the elephants typically work shifts of five hours after which they are free to forage, socialise and mate with wild elephants overnight in the forest. Low reproduction rates and deaths of calf elephants, however, have meant that wild elephants are still caught to maintain the working population.

The Myanmar Timber Elephant Project is working with the authorities to improve elephant management and healthcare so that the ideal balance can be found between the animals' working ability, survival and fertility, and to minimise calf deaths. The aim is for a self-sustaining working population, so no more wild elephants need to be captured.

Near to Kalaw in Shan State is Green Hill Valley (p219), a retirement home for elephants no longer fit for work in the timber camps. Founded by a family with a history of working with MTE, the project also embraces reforestation; as well as interacting with the elephants, helping to feed and bathe them, visitors can plant a tree in their nursery.

MYANMAR'S ECO TREASURE CHEST

Myanmar has long intrigued scientists, who believe that many critically endangered species, or even species that are new to science, might be living in closed-off parts of the country. As remote areas have opened up, the scientists' hopes have been proven correct.

Myanmar snub-nosed monkey In 2010 this new species of colobine monkey was discovered. It's estimated there's a population of between 260 and 330 of these primates living by the Mekong and Thanlwin Rivers in Kachin State.

Arakan forest turtles In 2009 a team of World Conservation Society scientists discovered five of these critically endangered species, less than a foot long and with a light brown shell, amid thick stands of bamboo in a sanctuary set up originally to protect elephants. In modern times, researchers had only previously seen a handful of captive examples.

Kitti's hog-nosed bat Prior to 2001, when it was located in Myanmar, the species that is also known as the bumblebee bat was thought to live only in a tiny part of western Thailand. At a length of 1.25in to 1.5in and weighing in at just 0.07oz, this is the world's smallest bat.

Gurney's pitta This stunningly bright, small bird underwent a dramatic decline during the 20th century, until only a single population in Thailand was known. However, it was also discovered in Myanmar in 2003, and is now thought to have a population there of as many as 26,000.

Leaf deer Also known as the 'leaf muntjac', this 25lb, 20in-tall mammal was confirmed in northern Myanmar in 1999. Its name was given because it can be wrapped up in a large leaf.

Since 2009 the Korea International Cooperation Agency (KOICA) has been supporting a reforestation project across Myanmar's dry zone (www.dryzonegreening.gov.mm/eng).

Reptiles and amphibians include 28 turtle species (of which seven are exclusive to Myanmar), along with numerous snake varieties, of which at least 39 are venomous, including the common cobra, king cobra (hamadryad), banded krait, Malayan pit viper, green viper and Russell's viper.

Myanmar is rich in birdlife, with an estimated 1067 recorded bird species, including five endemic species: the white-browed nuthutch (Sitta victoriae), hooded treepie (Crypsirina cucullata), Jerdon's minivet (Pericrocotus albifrons), white-throated babbler (Tudoides gularis) and Burmese bushlark (Mirafra micoptera). Coastal and inland waterways of the delta and southern peninsula are important habitats for Southeast Asian waterfowl.

Plants

In 2014 the New York Botanical Garden launched a conservation and training program to document and conserve plant diversity in Myanmar. Such a wide-ranging survey of the county's biodiversity hasn't been carried out since the 1920s.

As in the rest of tropical Asia, most indigenous vegetation in Myanmar is associated with two basic types of tropical forest: monsoon forest (with a distinctive dry season of three months or more) and rainforest (where rain falls more than nine months per year). It's said there are more than 1000 plant species endemic to the country.

Monsoon forests are marked by deciduous tree varieties, which shed their leaves in the dry season. Rainforests, by contrast, are typically evergreen. The area stretching from Yangon to Myitkyina contains mainly monsoon forests, while peninsular Myanmar to the south of Mawlamyine is predominantly a rainforest zone. There's much overlapping of the two – some forest zones support a mix of monsoon forest and rainforest vegetation.

In the mountainous Himalayan region, Myanmar's flora is characterised by subtropical broadleaf evergreen forest up to 6500ft; temperate semi-deciduous broadleaf rainforest from 6500ft to 9800ft; and, above this, evergreen coniferous, subalpine snow forest and alpine scrub. Along the Rakhine and Tanintharyi coasts are tidal forests in river estuaries, lagoons, tidal creeks and low islands. Such woodlands are characterised by mangroves and other coastal trees that grow in mud and are resistant to sea water. Beach and dune forests, which grow along these same coasts above the high-tide line, consist of palms, hibiscus, casuarinas and other tree varieties that can withstand high winds and occasional storm-sent waves.

The country's most famous flora includes an incredible array of fruit trees, more than 25,000 flowering species, a variety of tropical hardwoods, and bamboo. Cane and rattan are also plentiful.

Endangered Species

Of some 8233 known breeding species (of which 7000 are plants) in Myanmar, at least 103 of these (animals, birds and plants) are endangered, including the flying squirrel, tiger, Irrawaddy dolphin and three-striped box turtle. Both the one-horned (Javan) rhinoceros and the Asiatic two-horned (Sumatran) rhinoceros are believed to survive in very small numbers near the Thai border in Kayin State. The rare red panda (or cat bear) was last sighted in northern Myanmar in the early 1960s but is thought to still live in Kachin State forests above 6500ft.

Deforestation poses the greatest threat to Myanmar's biodiversity, but even in areas where habitat loss isn't a problem, hunting threatens to wipe out the rarer animal species. Wildlife laws are seldom enforced and poaching remains a huge problem. In June 2016, WWF Myanmar (http://www.wwf.org.mm/en) welcomed the National League for Democracy (NLD) government's plan to close down Mong La's notorious wildlife market, a well-known hub for open buying and selling of endangered species.

National Parks

By an optimistic account, about 7% of Myanmar's land area is covered by national parks and national forests, wildlife sanctuaries and parks, and other protected areas.

Sadly, such protection on paper is rarely translated into reality due to lack of adequate funding and effective policing. According to a report in the August 2012 edition of *Science Magazine,* 14 of Myanmar's 36 protected areas lack staff altogether, while the rest have too few rangers for effective patrolling and management.

Find out more about Myanmar's rivers and the environmental problems they face, including dams, at Burma Rivers Network (www.burmariver snetwork.org), an umbrella group of organisations.

The documentary *Of Oozies and Elephants* and an episode of BBC's *Wild Burma: Nature's Lost Kingdom* feature the vet Khyne U Mar, known as 'the elephant lady of Burma' for her studies of captive working elephants in Myanmar. Her research is supported by the Rufford Foundation (www. rufford.org).

ENVIRONMENT & WILDLIFE NATIONAL PARKS

TOP PARKS & RESERVES

PARK	SIZE	FEATURES	BEST TIME TO VISIT
Hkakabo Razi National Park	1472 sq miles	highest mountain in Myanmar; forests; rare species such as takin, musk and black barking deer, and blue sheep	Oct-Apr
Indawgyi Wetland Wildlife Sanctuary	299 sq miles	one of Southeast Asia's largest lakes; 120 species of birds	Jan-Apr
Inle Wetland Bird Sanctuary	642 sq miles	floating agriculture; birdlife, otters, turtles	year-round
Moeyungyi Wetlands	40 sq miles	125 species of birds	Nov-Apr
Mt Victoria (Nat Ma Taung) National Park	279 sq miles	second-highest mountain in Myanmar; rare birds and orchids	Nov-Mar
Popa Mountain Park	50 sq miles	extinct volcano; unique dry-zone ecosystem; monkeys	Nov-Mar

Rufous-necked hornbill found in Myanmar

Environmental Issues

Recycling and making use of every little thing is part of most people's daily life in Myanmar, disposability being a luxury of the rich. This said, the country is facing many challenges with regard to treatment of its precious environment.

Essentially no environmental legislation was passed from the time of independence in 1948 until after 1988. Government dictums, such as 'green the dry zone' and 'protect wildlife', were mostly words rather than action. Slowly, things are changing. Previously off-limit topics related to Myanmar's environment are now covered in the media, leading, occasionally, to reviews of government policy. The decision to suspend construction of the Myitsone Dam in September 2011 is one example of this.

The 2012 foreign investment law requires environmental impact statements for all major investment projects. Also during 2012, the Environmental Conservation Law was passed, and in 2014, Environmental Conservation Rules were issued. An Environmental Conservation Department has been established but, as with many areas of government in Myanmar, its officers need training and overall it lacks adequate funding and technical knowledge.

In January 2016 Myanmar's Ministry of Environmental Conservation and Forestry announced new requirements for environmental impact assessments (EIAs), with fines of up to US$5000 for companies failing to provide the necessary information.

Deforestation

Myanmar supposedly contains more standing forest, with fewer inhabitants, than any other country in Indochina. That said, it's also disappearing faster than almost anywhere else in Asia. Under military rule the forests were plundered. Illegal logging continues and is particularly difficult to combat in the areas where civil insurrections are ongoing. At a conference in Yangon in June 2016, U Nyi Nyi Kyaw, director general of the Ministry of Natural Resources and Environmental Conservation, admitted that his department was powerless to stop illegal logging.

Exports of raw timber have been banned from Myanmar since 2014, and at the time of research the ministry was proposing a one-year moratorium on timber extraction by logging operations run by the government's Myanma Timber Enterprise (MTE), which has a monopoly on the formal timber sector.

According to a 2015 report by UK-based watchdog the Environmental Investigation Agency (EIA), Myanmar lost a total of 1.7 million hectares of forest cover from 2001 to 2013. If nothing is done, the prediction is that 30 million hectares could be lost by 2030. One of the most troubled areas is the so-called 'dry zone', made up of heavily populated Mandalay, lower Sagaing and Magwe divisions. Little of the original vegetation remains in this pocket (which is about 10% of Myanmar's land, but home to a quarter of the population), due to growth in the area's population and deforestation.

Deforestation is also blamed for exacerbating damage from Cyclone Komen, a natural disaster in 2015 that forced 384,900 families to relocate and destroyed 972,000 acres of farmland.

Air & Water Pollution

Uncontrolled gold and other mining means that the release of pollutants into rivers and the sea is steadily increasing. The most noticeable aspect of pollution to travellers will be the piles of non-biodegradable waste, such as plastic bags, dumped at the edge of towns and villages and seen fluttering across the fields. Bans on the production and sale of polythene bags and cord exist in both Yangon and Mandalay but they are not strictly enforced.

Environmental experts are also concerned about the excessive use of chemical fertilisers and pesticides in agriculture and the run-off of these pollutants into the water supply. This has become an acute problem over recent years at Inle Lake, where there's been exponential growth in the number of commercial floating farms producing vegetables. Combined with pollution from chemical dyes used in textile processing and garbage related to increased tourism, the effect has been to turn placid Inle into a toxic pool in which fish die or struggle to survive.

On top of this, the expansion of rice cultivation near the lake and the building of more hotels is draining its water supply, causing it to shrink. In November 2012 a report entitled *Inlay Lake Conservation Project:*

Life in the Valley of Death (2008) by Dr Alan Rabinowitz is about his efforts to save Myanmar's rapidly dwindling tiger population by setting up the Hukuang Valley Tiger Reserve.

Organised Chaos, a report published in 2015 by the London-based Environmental Investigation Agencey (EIA; https://eia -international. org), documents surging illegal timber trade between Myanmar's Kachin State and China's Yunnan Province, worth almost half a billion dollars.

ENVIRONMENT & WILDLIFE ENVIRONMENTAL ISSUES

SAVING THE BIG CATS

In 2003, when the National Tiger Action Plan for Myanmar was published, it was reckoned there were as few as 150 of the big cats living in the country. The vast majority of them were concentrated in the Hukuang Valley Wildlife Sanctuary, the Htamanthi Wildlife Sanctuary and the Tenasserim Range in Southern Myanmar.

By 2010 this number was believed to have dropped to 85; more recent survey data is unavailable and the situation is believed to very grim.

There are a few flicker of hopes, however. A 2013 expedition to Myanmar sponsored by the Smithsonian Institute and filmed by the BBC in its *Wild Burma* program found evidence of tigers in two separate parts of the country. The Tiger Corridor, a joint initiative between Panthera (www.panthera.org) and the Wildlife Conservation Society (www.wcs.org), also aims to create a 4660-mile-long 'genetic corridor' for tigers stretching from Bhutan to Malaysia, with a large part of the corridor passing through Myanmar.

A Plan for the Future was released by the Institute for International Development-Myanmar (www.iid.org/myanmar.html). It outlines proposals to rehabilitate the lake by 2025, but also notes that an unchecked rise in tourism in the area is likely to put further strain on Inle's fragile environment.

Dams & Pipelines

In the last decade the authorities have embarked on a series of hydroelectric dam projects along the country's major rivers, creating a crescendo of economic, social and environmental problems. In a nod to public opinion in September 2011, a halt was called on the controversial Myitsone Dam on the headwaters of the Ayeyarwady River in Kachin State, a project that was being developed in conjunction with China.

Pressure is now on the NLD government to restart construction of the 6000-megawatt-generating dam. If the project is cancelled, Myanmar is liable to pay US$800 million to China in compensation. If work is resumed and the dam is completed, Myanmar is looking at earning either the much-needed annual revenue of US$500 million from China for the power generated, or having access to that power for the country's electrification.

In September 2013, the Indian government also cancelled its deal with Myanmar over the building of the Thamanthi Dam on the Chindwin River; if it had gone ahead, the construction of this dam would have flooded parts of Tamanthi Wildlife Sanctuary and Hukaung Tiger Reserve, the habitats of several endangered species, including tigers, elephants and the very rare Burmese roofed turtle.

Mining, Oil & Gas

In November 2012, locals protesting about the environmental and social impact of the Letpadaung copper mine in Sagaing Region, a joint venture between a Chinese company and a Myanmar military enterprise, were subjected to a brutal police crackdown. The mine's construction was subsequently suspended pending the investigation and conclusion of a parliamentary commission, chaired by Aung San Suu Kyi. The commission's recommendation was that the mining company resume operations, but only if certain conditions were met, such as better transparency and an environmental impact plan.

In 2014 Suu Kyi accused Thein Sein's government of ignoring the commission's recommendations. That same year clashes between police and farmers at the site left one farmer dead and dozens injured. Protestors were out in force again in May 2016, as the mining company reattempted to restart production at the site. The NLD's position is that operations can resume once the recommendations of the inquiry commission are met, but many locals want nothing less than the mine's cancellation.

Such democratic levels of transparency are something new for Myanmar's extractive industries. Also facing criticism for its adverse environmental impact is the Shwe Gas Project, a joint venture between the government's Myanmar Oil and Gas Enterprise (MOGE) and Indian and South Korean companies for the underwater extraction of natural gas and oil from the Bay of Bengal and its piping across Myanmar to China. The natural gas pipeline became operational in 2013, the oil pipeline in 2014.

For in-depth coverage of the major environmental issues facing Myanmar, download the report published by the Burma Environment Working Group (www.bewg.org), a coalition of environmental organisations and activists working in the country.

Earthrights International's Burma Project (www.earthrights.org) collects information about the human rights and environmental situation in the country, focusing on large-scale dams, oil and gas development, and mining.

Survival Guide

Responsible Travel

In the past few years, visitors have been flocking to Myanmar in the millions. This has put a strain on the country's already poorly functioning infrastructure as well as its fragile environment. Read on to discover how best to travel responsibly, engage respectfully with locals and make a positive impact.

Package Tours

Travelling independently rather than on a package tour will give you more control over where your money goes. If you pay for tours with overseas agents before arriving in Myanmar, it's possible that less of your money finds its way into the pockets of local citizens.

However, for travel to certain areas of Myanmar (ie those where you require a travel permit and/or would be advised to have a guide for trekking) travel agents are a convenient way to go and joining a tour might be the most economical route. To get an idea of how closely such a tour might adhere to responsible tourism principles, you could ask the following questions:

➡ Has your company vetted the work policies and practices of the tourism business providers used on the tour (ie level of wages paid, whether resources are used responsibly)?

➡ Does your company have any charitable programs in place to assist local communities and/or individuals?

➡ How much interaction might I have with locals on the tour?

➡ Can I hire different guides at each destination rather than travel with one guide for the whole trip?

Be wary of tours that treat minority groups as 'attractions'.

Goods & Services

For all its recent positive changes, Myanmar continues to be plagued by human rights abuses, distressing levels of poverty, and corruption.

Critics of independent travel argue that travellers' spending usually bottlenecks at select places. The more places at which you spend money, the greater the number of locals likely to benefit.

A few things to consider:

➡ Don't buy all of your needs (bed, taxi, guide, meals) from one source.

➡ Be conscious that behind-the-scenes commissions are

TOP TIPS

➡ Travel independently or in small groups rather than in a big tour group.

➡ Support small independent businesses and those that have charitable and sustainable tourism programs in place.

➡ Spread your money around: buy souvenirs across the country and hire different guides at each destination.

➡ Contribute to local charitable causes.

➡ Refuse to pay bribes.

➡ Be environmentally conscious in your travel choices: opt for buses, trains and river cruises over flights; avoid using air-conditioning.

➡ Be sensitive to, and respectful of, local customs and behaviour: dress and act appropriately when visiting religious sites and rural villages.

➡ Read up about Myanmar's history, culture and current situation.

➡ Check out Dos & Don'ts For Tourists (www.dosanddontsfortourists.com).

THE PERILS OF MASS TOURISM

Myanmar's National League for Democracy (NLD)-led government supports community-based tourism and welcomes visitors who are sensitive to the welfare of the people and environmental conservation, and who are keen to acquire an insight into cultural, political and social topics. In March 2016 the Ministry of Hotels and Tourism predicted six million inbound tourists for 2016, up 25% on the 4.68 million arrivals of 2015 and over seven times the 2010 total of 800,000. However, as tourism to Myanmar has exploded, the most established destinations – Bagan (Pagan), Inle and Kyaiktiyo – have struggled to cope.

The situation has prompted much discussion within Myanmar about the dangers as well as the benefits of mass tourism, and how lessons can be learnt from the experience of nearby countries. A Tourism Master Plan was set out by the former government in 2013 that includes developing an ecotourism management strategy; this is supported by the current government. The management of protected areas will be strengthened, biodiversity conserved and community-based income generation encouraged.

However, as the Myanmar Centre for Responsible Business noted in a report on the issue in 2015, a lack of capacity and resources means that implementation of such policies remains doubtful in the short run. The report also found that local communities are still not sufficiently engaged in decisions on tourism development. The role of NGOs such as Tourism Transpency (www.tourismtransparency.org) is key.

being paid on most things you pay for when in the company of a driver or guide.

➜ Plan en-route stops, or take in at least one off-the-beaten-track destination, where locals are less used to seeing foreigners.

➜ Mix up the locations from where you catch taxis and trishaws – and try to take trips with drivers who aren't lingering outside tourist areas.

➜ Try to eat at different family restaurants, and if you're staying at a hotel, eat out often. In Ngapali Beach, for example, local restaurants are just across the road from the beach and hotels.

➜ Buy handicrafts directly from the artisans as you travel around the country, or if you're spending most of your time in the same location, don't get all your souvenirs from one shop.

➜ Refuse to pay bribes.

➜ Check informed sources such as Tourism Transparency (www.tourismtransparency.org) and EcoBurma (www.ecoburma.com) about the situation in Myanmar so you can make informed choices when buying goods and services.

Social Interactions

Myanmar people are extremely friendly and happy to chat. Many locals, particularly in the more off-the-beaten path parts of Myanmar, cherish outside contact because they have so little.

Some things to keep in mind:

➜ Be respectful of local etiquette (p409) and culture.

➜ It's fine to raise political questions and issues but be sensitive in doing so; allow the local to direct the conversation.

➜ Be very careful around religious topics, ie showing disrespect – however unintentional – towards Buddha could land you in trouble.

➜ Always ask before photographing someone – most people will happily oblige but don't assume that they will. Show them the image you've created and if possible, have a print made that you can give to them. If they have a smartphone (increasingly they will), you might share the image digitally.

➜ Think carefully before accusing anyone of cheating you or of theft. Innocent people can suffer greatly by implication. For example, a bus driver can end up in very hot water if you report your camera stolen during a bus ride.

Charity & Donations

Tourism isn't going to fix all of Myanmar's problems, of course, but there are some small things you can do to help during your visit.

➜ Ask guesthouse owners, agents, teachers and monks about where you can best donate money for local projects.

➜ Patronise socially responsible businesses that support charitable causes. Travellers handing out sweets, pens or money to kids on hiking trails or outside attractions have had a negative impact (as you'll certainly see when begging kids follow you around a pagoda). It's not the best way to contribute to those in need, and many locals will advise you not to give to children anyway. If you want to hand out useful items, keep the following in mind:

DOS & DON'TS

Do

➡ Remove shoes on entering a Buddhist site or home.

➡ Dress respectfully: no shorts, short skirts or exposed shoulders.

➡ Ask before you photograph anyone.

Don't

➡ Touch anybody on the head (including a child).

➡ Pose with or sit on Buddha images.

➡ Point your feet at anyone or anything – apologise if you accidentally brush someone with your foot.

➡ Buy locally. This puts money into the local economy, and locals are more likely to use the gift!

➡ Give only to those with whom you've made some sort of personal bond, not to random supplicants. Otherwise you'll encourage a culture of begging.

➡ If you want to help a begging family, ask what they need. Often you can accompany them to the market and pick up food (a bag of rice, some vegetables, some fish).

➡ Some items from outside the country, such as books and magazines, are greatly appreciated, though.

Volunteerism

Life for many people in Myanmar can be quite desperate and its natural to feel the urge to help out in some way. There are opportunities to usefully volunteer (p416) and provide charity, but there are difficult issues to negotiate around this, too.

Whether it's working with children in orphanages, helping to build houses, or teaching English, so-called voluntourism is a fast-growing sector of the travel industry that you'll encounter in Myanmar. However, orphanage tourism, in particular, is a highly controversial development and one that Friends

International and Unicef have joined forces to educate the public about in their 'Think Before Visiting' (www.think childsafe.org/thinkbefore visiting) campaign.

According to Unicef, 73% of children in Myanmar's orphanages are not orphans. They will have one, if not both, parents alive and they will be in institutions for a variety of reasons, including poverty and domestic violence. Many children are in danger of abuse and neglect from carers, as well as exploitation and international trafficking, with those aged under three most at risk.

Things to keep in mind:

➡ Myanmar's best orphanages receive funding and support from wealthy benefactors, and don't need visitors.

➡ Other respectable, but less well endowed, orphanages do not ask for foreign volunteers, but for people to contribute much-needed items including vitamins, pencils and pens, and toys.

➡ If a place is promoting orphan tourism, then proceed with caution, as the adults may not always have the best interests of the children at heart.

➡ Child-welfare experts also recommend that any volunteering concerning children should involve a minimum three-month

commitment – having strangers drop in and out of their lives on short visits can be detrimental to a child's emotional well-being and development. Note that some organisations, for example, Friends International and Unicef, recommend that travellers never volunteer in an orphanage.

➡ If you do volunteer, think hard about what skills you have that will make a real difference to the children – working with the local staff, for example, to teach them English is likely to have a more sustainable impact.

➡ Don't volunteer at any orphanage without thoroughly researching it. Is it regulated? Does it require background checks on volunteers?

Environmental Concerns

Ecotourism is being trumpeted as a way forward for Myanmar's tourism industry, but it's an area that is plagued with problems. One of the most difficult issues is how best to balance the demands for economic and commercial development in some of Myanmar's poorest areas, with environmental protection. Travellers can assist in the following ways:

➡ Tread lightly and buy locally.

➡ Avoid (and report) instances where you see products or parts of products made from endangered species.

➡ Support ecotourism ventures and hire local guides when you go trekking.

➡ Visit the country's national parks and protected areas.

➡ Avoid adding to Myanmar's growing problem of what to do with litter by minimising its creation, ie refrain from the use of plastic bags and disposable plastic water bottles.

Directory A–Z

Accommodation

At the budget end of the scale are hostels and family-run guesthouses. In more rural destinations these might amount to very little: a spartan room with just a mosquito net, a fan that turns off at midnight (when the generator does) and a cold-water shower down the hall.

In the midrange are privately run hotels and guest-houses licensed to accept foreigners. To gain a hotel licence they supposedly must keep eight rooms and reach a certain standard. However, the vast majority of places, while modern, follow a standard, uncreative template: tiled rooms with air-con, a refrigerator and a private hot-water bathroom.

In key destinations (eg Yangon, Bagan, Inle Lake, Mandalay, Ngapali Beach) you'll find high-end hotels and resorts.

Airbnb has listings across Myanmar (with most in Yangon), but technically it is illegal for people to op-erate homestays. Officially sanctioned B&Bs are in their infancy (some exist in Kayin State) but more are likely to open up once new tourism laws are in place.

Nearly all accommodation choices include a simple breakfast in their rates. Staff at most can also change money, arrange laundry service (starting at K1000 per load at budget guesthouses), rent bikes, arrange taxis, sell transport tickets and find you local English-speaking guides.

All accommodation options are required to fill in forms that include a guest's passport and visa details.

Prices

Most hotels and guesthouses quote prices in either US dollars or kyat; you can usually pay in either currency.

Prices quoted at budget and midrange hotels include all taxes; top-end hotel prices often don't include up to 20% in taxes and service charges. Only a few hotels currently accept credit cards.

There are lower rates or it's possible to bargain a little at most hotels during the low season (May to October).

Customs Regulations

For the vast majority of visitors, clearing customs is a breeze, but it's important to be aware of the restrictions; for further details see www.myanmarcustoms.gov.mm.

Any foreign currency in excess of US$2000 is supposed to be declared upon entry. Besides personal effects, visitors are permitted to bring duty-free:

➡ 400 cigarettes
➡ 50 cigars
➡ 250g of tobacco
➡ 2L of alcoholic liquor
➡ 150ml of perfume.

BOOK YOUR STAY ONLINE

For more accommodation reviews by Lonely Planet authors, check out http://lonelyplanet.com/myanmar-burma/hotels. You'll find independent reviews, as well as recommendations on the best places to stay. Best of all, you can book online.

SLEEPING PRICE RANGES

The following price ranges refer to a double room or dorm bed.

$ less than US$50

$$ US$50–150; in Yangon US$50–200

$$$ more than US$150; in Yangon more than US$200

It's not a problem to bring a camera, video camera, laptop or mobile phone. You cannot bring in antiques, pornographic materials or narcotic drugs.

Export Restrictions

A wide variety of antiques cannot legally be taken out of the country, including the following:

➺ prehistoric implements and artefacts

➺ fossils

➺ old coins

➺ bronze or brass weights (including opium weights)

➺ bronze or clay pipes

➺ inscribed stones

➺ inscribed gold or silver

➺ historical documents

➺ religious images

➺ sculptures or carvings in bronze, stone, stucco or wood

➺ frescoes (even fragments)

➺ pottery

➺ national regalia and paraphernalia.

Electricity

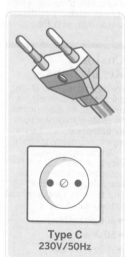

Type C
230V/50Hz

Type G
230V/50Hz

Connect (when it's working) to the electricity supply (230V, 50Hz AC). Power outages occur everywhere, Yangon and Mandalay included. Many smaller towns have short scheduled periods for electricity, usually a few hours in the afternoon and evening (power always seems to be available if Myanmar TV is airing a premiership soccer game!). Many hotels and shops run generators 24 hours, others keep them on only a few hours (eg 6pm to midnight, and a few hours in the morning).

Embassies & Consulates

Most foreign embassies and consulates are based in Yangon. Check the government's Ministry of Foreign Affairs (www.mofa.gov.mm) for more information.

Australian Embassy (Map p38; ☎01-251 810; www.burma. embassy.gov.au; 88 Strand Rd, Kyauktada)

Bangladeshi Embassy (Map p48; ☎01-515 275; www.bdem bassyyangon.org; 11B Than Lwin Rd, Kamayut)

Cambodian Embassy (Map p52; ☎01-549 609; 34 Kaba Aye Pagoda Rd, Bahan)

Canadian Embassy (Map p42; ☎01-384 805; www.canadaint-ernational.gc.ca; 9th fl, Centre-point Towers, 65 Sule Paya Rd, Kyauktada)

Chinese Embassy (Map p48; ☎01-221 281; http://mm.china-embassy.org/eng; 1 Pyidaungsu Yeiktha Rd, Dagon)

French Embassy (Map p42; ☎01-212 520; www.amba france-mm.org; 102 Pyidaungsu Yeiktha Rd, Dagon)

German Embassy (Map p48; ☎01-548 952; www.rangun. diplo.de; 9 Bogyoke Aung San Museum Rd, Bahan)

Indian Embassy (Map p38; ☎01-391 219; www.india embassyyangon.net; 545-547 Merchant St, Kyauktada)

Indonesian Embassy (Map p42; ☎01-254 465; http://kbri-yangon.org; 100 Pyidaungsu Yeiktha Rd, Dagon)

Israeli Embassy (Map p52; ☎01-515 155; http://embassies. gov.il/yangon; 15 Kabaung Rd, Hlaing)

Italian Embassy (Map p48; ☎01-527 100; www.ambyangon .esteri.it/ambasciata_yangon; 3 Inya Myaing Rd, Bahan)

Japanese Embassy (Map p48; ☎01-549 644; www. mm.emb-japan.go.jp; 100 Nat Mauk Rd, Bahan)

Korean Embassy (Map p52; ☎01-527 142; http://mmr.mofa. go.kr/english/as/mmr/main/ index.jsp; 97 University Ave Rd, Bahan)

Lao Embassy (Map p42; ☎01-222 482; A1 Diplomatic Quarters, Taw Win St, Dagon)

Malaysian Embassy (Map p42; ☎01-220 249; www.kln.gov. my/web/mmr_yangon; 82 Pyidaungsu Yeiktha Rd, Dagon)

Netherlands Embassy (Map p48; ☎01-230 6046; http:// myanmar.nlembassy.org; 43C Inya Myaing Rd, Bahan)

New Zealand Embassy (Map p48; ☎01-230 5805; yangon

office@mft.net.nz; 43 Inya Myiang Rd, Bahan)

Philippine Embassy (Map p38; ☑01-558 149; 7 Gandamar St, Yankin)

Singapore Embassy (Map p48; ☑01-559 001; www.mfa.gov.sg/content/mfa/overseas mission/yangon.html; 238 Dhama Zedi Rd, Bahan)

Sri Lankan Embassy (Map p42; ☑01-222 812; www.slembyan-gon.org; 34 Taw Win St, Dagon)

Thai Embassy (Map p48; ☑01-226 721; www.thai embassy.org/yangon/en; 94 Pyay Rd, Dagon)

UK Embassy (Map p38; ☑01-370 867, 01-370 865; www.gov.uk/government/world/burma; 80 Strand Rd, Kyauktada)

US Embassy (Map p52; ☑01-536 509; http://burma.usem-bassy.gov; 110 University Ave, Kamayut)

Vietnamese Embassy (Map p48; ☑01-511 305; www.viet-namembassy-myanmar.org/vi; 70-72 Than Lwin Rd, Bahan)

Etiquette

Myanmar etiquette is based on respect for others.

Greetings Both hands may be used to shake hands, and Myanmar women prefer to simply smile and make a slight nod. Don't kiss in public.

Eating The right hand is used for eating, the left for personal hygiene.

Temples, shrines & mosques Dress conservatively at all religious sites, ie no revealing clothes, and legs and shoulders covered. Shoes and shocks should be removed before entering the religious site. Also refrain from taking photos of Buddha statues.

Heads and feet Don't touch people on the head and avoid pointing your feet at people or religious objects when sitting.

Bargaining Gentle hagglling in markets and taxis is OK, but generally not in shops.

GLBTI Travellers

➜ Homosexuality is seen as a bit of a cultural taboo, though most locals are known to be tolerant of it, both for men and women.

➜ 'Carnal intercourse against nature' is legally punishable with imprisonment of up to 10 years. The law is rarely enforced, but it renders gays and lesbians vulnerable to police harassment.

➜ Gay and transgendered people in Myanmar are rarely 'out', except for 'third sex' spirit mediums who channel the energies of *nat* spirits.

➜ Some Buddhists believe that those who committed sexual misconduct (such as adultery) in a previous life become gay or lesbian in this one.

➜ Public displays of affection, whether heterosexual or homosexual, are frowned upon; a local woman walking with a foreign man will raise more eyebrows than two same-sex travellers sharing a room.

➜ For more information on GLBTI issues in Myanmar see Colours Rainbow (www.colorsrainbow.com). Also check Utopia-Asia (www.utopia-asia.com), which publishes a gay guide to Southeast Asia, including Myanmar.

➜ Agencies offering gay-friendly trips to Myanmar include **Purple Dragon** (☑in Thailand +66-2-236 1776; www.purpledrag.com) and **Gay Tours Myanmar** (☑in India +91-11-4100 3982; http://www.gaytourmyanmar.com).

Insurance

A travel-insurance policy is a very wise idea. There is a wide variety of policies and your travel agent will have recommendations.

Worldwide travel insurance is available at www.lonelyplanet.com/travel-insurance. You can buy, extend and claim online anytime – even if you're already on the road.

Internet Access

Wi-fi is the norm in big cities; most hotels, guesthouses, restaurants and cafes will have this and it's usually free. There are also plenty of internet cafes (usually used for online gaming). We've even found internet access in relatively remote locations, such as Mrauk U.

However, with low bandwidth and power outages it can often be a frustrating exercise to send and receive large files over the internet, particularly in rural areas.

Legal Matters

You have absolutely no legal recourse in case of arrest or detainment by the authorities, regardless of the charge. If you are arrested, you would most likely be permitted to contact your consular agent in Myanmar for possible assistance.

If you purchase gems or jewellery from persons or shops that are not licensed by the government, you run the risk of having them confiscated if customs officials find them in your baggage when you're exiting the country.

Drug trafficking crimes are punishable by death.

Maps

The best available is the 1:2,000,000 Periplus Editions *Myanmar Travel Map*, a folded map with plans for Mandalay, Yangon and the Bagan area, or the ITMB 1:1,350,000 *Myanmar (Burma)*. Another choice is the 1:1,500,000 Nelles *Myanmar*, a folded map on coated stock. Good places to buy maps online include International Travel Maps and

Books (www.itmb.com) and East View Map Link (www.maplink.com).

Myanmar-based Design Printing Services (www.dpsmap.com) prints useful tourist maps of Myanmar, Yangon, Mandalay and Bagan; sometimes these maps are sold locally for about K1000 or given away by tour agencies, at hotels and international gateway airports. For more detailed country-wide maps, contact Myanmar Information Management Unit (MIMU; www.themimu.info).

Meditation Courses

Several monasteries around the country (in particular in Yangon and Mandalay) run courses on *satipatthana vipassana* (insight-awareness meditation), where foreigners are welcome. Beginners are typically expected to sign up for a 10-day residential course to learn the basics. Longer stays (and special visas covering them) are also available. Expect the following:

➡ The courses are open to all and free; voluntary donations according to your means are accepted at the end of retreats.

➡ Meditators must follow eight precepts, including abstaining from food after noon and leading an austere lifestyle (no smoking or drinking; sleeping on basic beds often in shared accommodation).

➡ You will be expected to keep a 'noble silence' for

most of the 10 days, save for interviews with meditation teachers.

➡ Daily practice begins at 3am; breakfast is at 5.30am and lunch at 10am.

Myanmar's most famous monastery for meditation courses is **Mahasi Meditation Centre** (Map p48; ☑01-541 971; www.mahasi.org.mm; 16 Thathana Yeiktha Rd, Bahan) in Yangon. There is also **Dhamma Mandala** (☑09 204 4348, 02-39694; www.mandala.dhamma.org; Yaytagon Hill) near Mandalay.

Money

ATMs

There are now hundreds of ATMs across the country, with most clustered in tourist centres, such as Yangon, Bagan, Mandalay and Inle Lake. There is a withdrawal fee of K5000 and a withdrawal limit of K300,000 per transaction.

Don't rely on ATMs, though. The machines don't always work. Also make sure you keep records of ATMs transactions in case of any problems.

Banks

The most useful of the local banks (open 9am to 5pm Monday to Friday) are CB and KBZ, both of which now issue and accept MasterCard and Visa cards and have ATMs in which you can use overseas-issued cards for a K5000 charge per transaction.

Black Market

Do not change money with people on the street.

Credit Cards & Travellers Cheques

Travellers cheques are useless. However, in Yangon and other major tourist spots you'll increasingly find credit cards accepted by top-end hotels, restaurants and some shops.

Currency

Myanmar remains a predominantly cash economy. The national currency, the kyat (pronounced 'chat'), is divided into the following banknotes: K50, K100, K200, K500, K1000, K5000 and K10,000; you'll rarely come across the smaller denominations and if you do they're often in tatters.

The US dollar acts as an alternative currency with most guesthouses and hotels quoting prices and accepting payment in the greenback. Prices in our reviews alternate between kyat (K) and US dollars ($), depending on the currency in which prices are quoted at the place itself.

Items such as meals, bus tickets, trishaw or taxi rides, bottles of water or beer, and market items are usually quoted in kyat.

These days most places will accept either currency. When paying in US dollars, check the exchange rate being used and your change carefully. Locals tend to unload slightly torn bills that work fine in New York, but are likely to be worthless for the rest of your trip in Myanmar.

Donations & Bribes

Have some small notes (K50, K100, K200) ready when visiting a religious temple or monastery, as donations may be requested and you may wish to leave one even if it's not.

The government has vowed to fight corruption, but it's a fact that bribes remain an ingrained feature of large sections of Myanmar's economy. You may find that a small amount of 'tea money' is need to expedite certain services – use sense and discretion if you find yourself in such a situation.

Money Changers

You'll find official bank and private licensed exchange booths at places such as Yangon and Mandalay airports, Bogyoke Aung San Market and Shwedagon Paya in Yangon.

Never hand over your money until you've received the kyat and counted them. Honest money changers will expect you to do this. Considering that K10,000 is the highest denomination, you'll get a lot of notes. Money changers give ready-made, rubber-banded stacks of a hundred K1000 bills. It's a good idea to check each note individually. Often you'll find one or two (or more) with a cut corner or taped tears, neither of which anyone will accept.

Many travellers do the bulk of their exchanging in Yangon, then carry the stacks of kyat around the country. Considering the relative safety from theft, it's not a bad idea, but you *can* exchange money elsewhere and the spreading of ATMs is making such a strategy increasingly unnecessary.

Tipping

Tipping is not customary in Myanmar, though little extra 'presents' are sometimes expected (even if they're not asked for) in exchange for a service.

Airport If someone helps you with your bags, a small tip is welcomed.

Restaurants As wages are low, it's a good idea to leave change for waiters in restaurants.

Temples A small donation is appreciated if a caretaker is required to unlock a temple.

Taxes & Refunds

At many shops, hotels, restaurants, cafes and bars you will pay 5% government commercial tax (the local equivalent of VAT). At some places you will also pay a 10% private service tax.

There are no refunds to travellers on the commercial tax paid on goods exported from Myanmar.

Opening Hours

Banks 9am to 5pm Monday to Friday

Cafes and teashops 6am to 6pm

Government offices and post offices 9.30am to 4.30pm Monday to Friday

Restaurants 11am to 9pm

Shops 9am to 6pm

Photography

Photo-processing shops and internet cafes can burn digital photos onto a CD, but you should have your own adapter. Colour film – Fuji and Kodak – is available in Yangon and Mandalay.

Avoid taking photographs of military facilities, uniformed individuals, road blocks and strategic locations, such as bridges.

Most locals are very happy to be photographed, but

BRING NEW BILLS

In July 2016 the Central Bank of Myanmar urged banks and moneylenders to accept crumpled and old US dollar bills. That said, we would still recommend bringing pristine 'new' bills to Myanmar – that means 2006 or later bills that have colour and are in perfect condition: no folds, stamps, stains, writing marks or tears.

Bills damaged in any way will attract lower rates of exchange or may still be rejected. You will get the best exchange rates from US$100 bills, but it's also a good idea to bring some small dollar bills – ones, fives and 10s – and use them to pay for items directly.

always ask first. If you have a digital camera with a display screen, some locals (kids, monks, anyone) will be overjoyed to see their image. It's also very easy and cheap to get digital photos turned into prints that can then be given to people as presents.

Some sights, including some paya and other religious sites, charge a camera fee of K100 or so. Usually a video camera fee is a little more.

For tips on how to shoot photos, pick up Lonely Planet's *Travel Photography*.

Post

Most mail out of Myanmar gets to its destination quite efficiently. International-postage rates are a bargain: a postcard is K500, a 1kg package to Australia/UK/USA K16,200/18,900/20,700.

Post offices are supposed to be open from 9.30am to 4.30pm Monday to Friday but you may find some keep shorter hours.

DHL (Map p42; ☎01-215 516; www.dhl.com; 58 Wadan St, Lanmadaw; ☺8am-6pm Mon-Fri, to 2pm Sat) is a more reliable but expensive way of sending out bigger packages.

Local Delivery

If you don't want to be overburdened with your souvenir purchases as you travel around Myanmar, enquire whether the shop can package your gifts and arrange to have them delivered to a final destination hotel by bus – the extra fee is often minimal.

Public Holidays

Major fixed public holidays:

Independence Day 4 January

Union Day 12 February

Peasants' Day 2 March

Armed Forces Day 27 March

Workers' Day 1 May

Martyrs' Day 19 July

Christmas 25 December

The following public holiday dates vary according to the lunar calendar:

Thingyan three days in April

National Day mid-November to late December

Safe Travel

For the vast majority of visitors, travel in Myanmar is safe and should pose no serious problems.

➡ Some areas of the country remain off-limits due to ongoing civil war and/or landmines.

➡ In off-the-beaten-track places, where authorities are less used to seeing foreigners, the chances are high that you'll be kept an eye on.

➡ If you have any tattoos of buddha on your body, keep them covered up.

Bugs, Snakes, Rats & Monkeys

Mosquitoes, if allowed, can have a field day with you.

Bring repellent from home, as the good stuff (other than mosquito coils) is hard to come by. Some guesthouses and hotels don't provide mosquito nets.

Myanmar has a high incidence of deaths from snakebite. Watch your step in brush, forest and grasses.

Family-run guesthouses, particularly in rural areas, might have a rodent or two. Wash your hands before sleeping and try to keep food out of your room.

In a few sites, such as Hpo Win Daung Caves, near Monywa, or Mt Popa near Bagan (Pagan), you'll have monkeys begging for snacks. Take care as bites are possible.

Crime

While not unheard of, crimes such as mugging are rare in Myanmar. Locals know that the penalties for stealing, particularly from foreigners, can be severe. Most travellers' memories of locals grabbing their money are of someone chasing them down to return a K500 note they dropped. If someone grabs your bag at a bus station, it's almost certainly just a trishaw driver hoping for a fare.

Insurgents & Bombs

Ceasefire agreements between the government and many insurgent groups are making it easier to travel to previously off-limits parts of the country. However, the situation can and does change rapidly, so check current travel advisories. Landmines on the Myanmar side of the Thai border are another threat.

The presence of Shan and Wa armies along the Thailand–Myanmar border in northern Mae Hong Son makes this area dangerous. The Wa have reportedly sworn off drug production, but there's still plenty of amphetamines and opium crossing some border areas.

Scams & Hassle

Myanmar touts are pretty minor league in comparison with others in the region. Most hassle is due to commissions. These small behind-the-scenes payments are made, like it or not, for a taxi, trishaw driver or guide who takes you to a hotel, to buy a puppet or even to eat some rice.

When arriving at a bus station, you're likely to be quickly surrounded by touts, some of whom will try to steer you to a particular hotel that offers them a commission. Be wary of claims that your chosen place is 'no good', though in some cases we found that trishaw drivers who had warned us that 'foreigners can't stay there' ended up being correct. If you know where you want to go, persist and they'll take you.

This said, a few travel-related businesses and touts do go to creative lengths or use hard-sell techniques to rustle up customers, so try to keep your wits about you.

Be wary of fanciful offers of jade or other gems as some are filled with worthless rock or concrete mixture. And never buy gems on the street.

Many people may approach to say 'Hello' on the street. In some cases, they're just curious or want to practise some English. In other cases the conversation switches from 'What country you from?' to 'Where you need to go?' It's all pretty harmless.

Do not change money on the street.

Transport & Road Hazards

The poor state of road and rail infrastructure plus lax safety standards and procedures for flights and boats means that travelling can sometimes be dangerous.

Safety often seems to be the last consideration of both drivers and pedestrians.

Proceed with caution when crossing any road, particularly in cities where drivers are unlikely to stop if they are involved in an accident with a pedestrian. Traffic drives on the right in Myanmar, but the majority of cars are right-hand-drive imports, which add to the chance of accidents occurring.

Tattoos & Buddha Images

Depictions of images of Buddha deemed inappropriate or offensive by Buddhists have caused serious problems for visitors to Myanmar recently. In 2015 a New Zealand bar manager in Yangon (Rangoon) spent 10 months in jail for posting an image of Buddha wearing headphones on Facebook to promote a cheap drinks night. In 2016 a Spanish tourist was deported when monks in Bagan saw he had a tattoo of Buddha on his leg. Pay heed to such local religious sensitivities and moderate your behaviour accordingly.

Telephone

Mobile Phones

There are three mobile networks: government-owned MPT (www.mpt.com.mm) and the private operators Telenor Myanmar (www.telenor.com.mm) and Ooredoo (www.ooredoo.com.mm). All offer pay-as-you go SIM cards (around K12,000), which can be used with unlocked smartphones.

For call and text fees and internet plans, top-up cards of between K1000 and K10,000 are widely available.

Local Calls

Most business cards in Myanmar list a couple of phone numbers, as landlines frequently go dead and calls just don't go through.

Local call stands – as part of a shop, or sometimes just a table with a phone or two on a sidewalk – are fast disappearing following the introduction of affordable mobile phone services. If you do find one, a local call should be K100 per minute.

To dial long distance within Myanmar, dial the area code (including the '0') and the number.

A useful resource is the Myanmar Yellow Pages (www.myanmaryellowpages.biz).

International Calls

Internet cafes using Skype and other VOI protocols, official telephone (call) centres and top-end hotels are among the ways to call

LIVING ON MYANMAR TIME

Chances are that your bus or train will roll in late, but much of Myanmar actually does work on a different time system. Burmese Buddhists use an eight-day week in which Thursday to Tuesday conform to the Western calendar but Wednesday is divided into two 12-hour days. Midnight to noon is 'Bohdahu' (the day Buddha was born), while noon to midnight is 'Yahu' (Rahu, a Hindu god/planet). However, it's rare that the week's unique structure causes any communication problems.

The traditional Myanmar calendar features 12 28-day lunar months that run out of sync with the months of the solar Gregorian calendar. To stay in sync with the solar year, Myanmar inserts a second Waso lunar month every few years – somewhat like the leap-year day added to the Gregorian February. The lunar months of Myanmar are Tagu, March/April; Kason, April/May; Nayon, May/June; Waso, June/July; Wagaung, July/August; Tawthalin, August/September; Thadingyut, September/October; Tazaungmon, October/November; Nadaw, November/December; Pyatho, December/January; Tabodwe, January/February; and Tabaung, February/March.

Traditionally, Burmese kings subscribed to various year counts. The main one in current use, the *thekkayit*, begins in April and is 638 years behind the Christian year count. Therefore, the Christian year of 2017 is equivalent to the *thekkayit* of 1379. If an ancient temple you see sounds way too old, it may be because locals are using the *thekkayit*.

Another calendar in use follows the Buddhist era (BE), as used in Thailand, which counts from 543 BC, the date that Buddha achieved *nibbana*. Hence AD 2017 is 2560 BE.

---

overseas, though sometimes this can be done on the street through vendors offering use of their mobile phones.

Via a landline, it costs about US$5 per minute to call Australia or Europe and US$6 per minute to phone North America.

To call Myanmar from abroad, dial your country's international access code, then ☑95 (Myanmar's country code), the area code (minus the '0'), and the five- or six-digit number.

Time

The local Myanmar Standard Time (MST) is 6½ hours ahead of Greenwich Mean Time (GMT/UTC). When coming in from Thailand, turn your watch back half an hour; coming from India, put your watch forward an hour. The 24-hour clock is often used for train times.

Toilets

➡ Apart from most guesthouses, hotels and upmarket restaurants, squat toilets are the norm. Most of these are located down a dirt path behind a house.

➡ Usually next to the toilet is a cement reservoir filled with water, and a plastic bowl lying nearby. This has two functions: as a flush and for people to clean their nether regions while still squatting over the toilet.

➡ Toilet paper is available at shops all over the country, but not often at toilets. Some places charge a nominal fee to use the toilet.

➡ Sit-down toilets are not equipped to flush paper. Usually there's a small waste basket nearby to deposit used toilet paper.

➡ It's acceptable for men (less so for women) to go behind a tree or bush (or at the roadside) when nature calls.

➡ Buses and smaller boats usually don't have toilets.

Tourist Information

Ministry of Hotels & Tourism Tourist Information (MTT; Map p38; ☑01-252 859; www.myanmartourism.org; 118 Mahabandoola Garden St, Kyauktada; ⊙9am-4.30pm) Located in Yangon. This office is quiet, and often the staff have sketchy knowledge on restricted areas of the country.

Myanmar Travels & Tours (MTT; Map p169; ☑061-65040; ⊙8.30am-4.30pm) Located in New Bagan.

MTT (Myanmar Travel & Tours; Map p238; ☑02-60356; 68th St, 26/27; ⊙9.30am-6pm) Located in Mandalay. Efficient and generally helpful staff.

Travellers who want to arrange a driver, or have hotel reservations awaiting them, would do well to arrange a trip with the help of private travel agents in Yangon and other major cities. Many Myanmar 'travel agents' outside Yangon only sell air tickets.

Travel Agencies

For anything other than straightforward visits, you might want to call on the services of one of the following recommended domestic travel agencies.

Asian Trails (Map p42; 01-211 212; www.asiantrails. travel; 73 Pyay Rd, Dagon) This experienced outfit can arrange specific-interest tours of Myanmar, including cycling and mountaineering, as well as visits to remote areas.

Ayarwaddy Legend Travels & Tours (Map p38; 01-252 007; www.ayarwaddylegend.com; 104 37th St, Kyauttada) Can provide advice on visiting off-the-beaten-track areas, such as mountain climbing in Chin State.

Columbus Travels & Tours (Map p42; 01-229 245; www.travelmyanmar.com; 586 Strand Rd, Lanmawdaw) Established in 1993, Columbus also has branches in Mandalay, Bagan and Inle.

Diethelm Travel (Map p38; 01-203 751; www.diethelm travel.com/myanmar; 412 Merchant St, Botataung) Among other things, this five-decades-old Swiss-owned operation can arrange walking tours of Yangon, visits to an elephant camp near Kalaw or a beach safari from Ngapali.

Discovery DMC (Map p42; 01-388 330; http://discovery dmc.com; 42B Pantra Rd, Dagon) This experienced European-owned agency is well versed in arranging trips to areas that are off the beaten track and need permits.

Flymya (Map p42; 09 79797 8881; https://flymya.com; Lanmadaw Plaza, Latha) Online booking agency for hotels, domestic flights, express buses, car hire, tours and events.

Good News Travels (Map p52; 09 863 5066, 09 511 6256; www.myanmargoodnewstravel. com; Rm 18, 204 Yanshin Rd, East Yankin) The owner, William Myatwunna, is extremely personable and knowledgeable, and can help arrange visits across the country.

Journeys Myanmar (01-664 275; www.journeysmyanmar. com; 53 Nagayone Pagoda Rd, off Pyay Rd, Mayangone) Can arrange river trips on a wide range of luxury craft and other options. Also biking tours and sailing holidays in the Myeik Archipelago.

Khiri Travel (Map p38; 01-375 577; http://khiri.com; 1st fl, 5/9 Bo Galay Zay St, Botataung) The friendly, professional team offers biking and kayak trips in Shan and Kayin states, walking tours of markets and meetings with fortune-tellers, as well as many other options.

Myanmar Trekking (Map p52; 01-667 948; www.myanmar trekking.com; Rm 7, 4A Parami Rd, Mayangone) Worth consulting if you're interested in off-the-beaten-track trekking adventures across Myanmar.

Oway (Map p48; 09 45045 0601; www.oway.com.mm; 9th fl, Grand Myay Nu Tower, 6/38 Myay Nu St, Sanchaung) Online booking agency for a wide range of hotels, domestic flights, express buses, car hire and tours.

SST Tours (Map p38; 01-255 536; www.sstmyanmar.com; Rm 5-6, 2nd fl, Aung San Stadium, Mingalar Taung Nyunt) This ecotours specialist has excellent contacts in the country's national parks and reserves, and can arrange trips that will delight nature lovers.

Travel with Children

Travelling with children in Myanmar can be very rewarding as long as you come well prepared with the right attitude, the physical requirements and the usual parental patience.

➡ Lonely Planet's *Travel with Children* contains useful advice on travelling with kids on the road.

➡ People in Myanmar love children and in many instances will shower attention on your offspring, who will find ready playmates among their local counterparts.

➡ It may be confusing for some children (and distressing to adults) seeing children working at restaurants and teahouses. Sadly, this is an unavoidable fact in a country with high poverty levels.

Practicalities

➡ Myanmar has a low level of public sanitation, so parents would be wise to lay down a few ground rules with regard to maintaining their children's good health, such as regular hand washing.

➡ Children should especially be warned not to play with animals they encounter, as a precaution against rabies.

➡ Nappies (diapers) are hard to come by outside the major cities; come prepared if your travels will take you off the beaten track.

➡ Most high-end hotels and restaurants will have highchairs available.

➡ When travelling with children, it may be more comfortable getting about by private car.

Sights & Activities

➡ Rides on trishaws and in horse carts.

➡ Boat trips on Inle Lake in dugout canoes.

➡ Big Buddhist sights and ancient ruins can make for good learning experiences, including Yangon's Shwedagon Paya, the reclining Buddhas in Bago, or the 10-storey Buddha in Pyay. You can climb into the back of the lacquered Buddha image at Nan Paya in Salay.

➡ Some kids might dig ruins of old palace walls and moats, which you can see at places like Bagan and Mrauk U.

➡ Indulge in some face painting by trying on *thanakha* (yellow sandalwood-like paste), which is sold and applied from sidewalk stands around the country.

➡ There's excellent birdwatching at the Moeyungyi Wetlands near Bago.

➡ Traditional puppet shows are performed in Yangon, Bagan and Mandalay, as well as other places.

➡ Beaches at Ngapali, Chaung Tha and Ngwe Saung and Southern Myanmar.

➡ Myanmar's festivals, such as Thingyan in mid-April with its throwing of water, and Taunggyi's fire-balloon festival in October or November, can be a lot of fun.

Travellers with Disabilities

With its lack of paved roads or footpaths (even when present, the latter are often uneven), Myanmar presents many physical obstacles for the mobility-impaired. Rarely do public buildings (or transport) feature ramps or other access points for wheelchairs, and hotels make inconsistent efforts to provide access for the disabled.

For wheelchair travellers, any trip to Myanmar will require a good deal of planning. Before setting off, get in touch with your national support organisation (preferably with the travel officer, if there is one) and download Lonely Planet's free *Accessible Travel* guide from http://lptravel.to/AccessibleTravel.

Also try the following:

Accessible Journeys (www.disabilitytravel.com)

Mobility International USA (www.miusa.org) Advises disabled travellers on mobility issues and runs educational international exchange programs.

Nican (www.nican.com.au) In Australia.

Tourism for All (www.tourismforall.org.uk) In the UK.

Visas

E-Visas

Citizens of 100 countries can apply online for tourist visas via Myanmar's Ministry of Immigration and Population website: http://evisa.moip.gov.mm.

The cost is US$50. After your application is processed, you'll be emailed an approval letter. Print it out and give it to the passport official on arrival at the airport or designated land borders with Thailand and you'll be stamped into the country.

E-visas can be used at Yangon, Mandalay and Nay Pyi Taw international airports; and at three Thailand–Myanmar land border crossings, Tachileik, Myawadi (Myawaddy) and Kawthoung (Kawthaung). You can exit the country at any overland border crossing (although you will need a permit and permission to exit to China and India).

Citizens of 50 countries can also apply online for business visas (US$70, valid 70 days), but you'll need a letter of invitation from a sponsoring company and proof of your company's registration or business.

Applications

Tourist visas (28 days) are valid for up to three months from the date of issue. Starting the process a month in advance is the safe bet; these days the processing can take anything between a day and a week.

There are slight differences between the application procedures at Myanmar embassies in different countries. Some require two passport photos, others only one. Postal applications are usually OK, but it's best to check first with your nearest embassy about its specific application rules.

If you're already travelling, it's possible to get a tourist visa at short notice from the **Myanmar Embassy** (☏02 233 7250; www.myanmarembassybkk.com; 132 Th Sathon Neua/North, Bangkok; ⊘9am-noon & 1-3pm Mon-Fri; ⑤Surasak exit 3) in Bangkok; the cost is 1260B for same-day processing (application 9am to noon, collection 3.30pm to 4.30pm), 1035B for the next day.

Visa Extensions & Overstaying

Some travellers extend their trips by overstaying their visa. This is not normally a problem, as long as you don't overstay for more than 14 days. You will be charged US$3 a day, plus a US$3 registration fee, at the airport or land border as you exit the country. The fine can be paid in kyat as well but it's important to have the correct amount as receiving change is unlikely.

However, some hotels won't take guests who have overstayed their visas and domestic airlines may be unwilling to let you on planes. If you are overstaying, it's wise to stick with land routes and places within easy access of Yangon. There have been cases in the past of tourists being instructed to leave the country immediately if their visa has expired.

Volunteering

Volunteering opportunities in Myanmar include teaching, medicine, and assisting entrepreneurs and fledgling social businesses with skills and administration. There are plenty of NGOs but they usually employ skilled personnel and require a long-term commitment.

Organisations in Myanmar that often look for volunteers include the following:

KT Care Foundation Myanmar (www.ktcare.org)

Myanmore (www.myanmore.com) Publishes the free *Know It Myanmore* guide twice yearly, which has further details about volunteering opportunities; a PDF is available online.

UN Volunteers (http://unv.org/how-to-volunteer)

VIA (Volunteers in Asia; http://viaprograms.org)

Be very wary about visiting or volunteering to teach at orphanages – see www.think childsafe.org/think beforevisiting for more details.

Women Travellers

As in most Buddhist countries, foreign women travelling in Myanmar are rarely hassled on the road as they might be in India, Malaysia or Indonesia. However, we have heard a few reports of sexual harassment. Dressing modestly should help reduce this risk: wear a local *longyi* (sarong-style lower garment) instead of a skirt above the knee, and a T-shirt instead of a spaghetti-strap singlet.

Few Myanmar women would consider travelling without at least one female companion, so women travelling alone are regarded as slightly peculiar by the locals. Lone women being seen off on boats and trains by local friends may find the latter trying to find a suitably responsible older woman to keep them company on the trip.

If you didn't bring tampons, one good place to find them is Yangon's City Mart Supermarket.

'Ladies' (per the posted signs in certain areas) cannot go up to some altars or onto decks around stupas, including the one affording a close-up look at the famous Golden Rock at Kyaiktiyo, or apply gold leaf on the Buddha image at Mandalay's Mahamuni Paya. Also, women should never touch a monk; if you're handing something to a monk, place the object within reach of him, not directly into his hands.

Most locals tend to visit teahouses, restaurants or shops with members of the same sex. Asian women, even from other countries, travelling with a Western man may encounter rude comments.

Work

Citizens of 50 countries can apply for a single-entry business visa online.

Multiple-entry business visas, valid for up to a year, are not available online and require a foreigner to have visited Myanmar on three prior occasions. Whatever visa you have, it's important to make sure you don't overstay its validity – multiple-entry business visas require the holder to leave and return to Myanmar every 70 days.

Note, although some expats do use such visas to work full- or part-time in Myanmar, strictly a business visa is meant for conducting meetings and business, *not* for seeking and gaining employment – for that you will need a Long Stay Permit and Foreign Registration Certificate (FRC). To obtain such documents it is best to engage the services of a local visa and immigration specialist.

Among the work possibilities in Myanmar are teaching, journalism, medicine and a whole raft of NGOs. Online sources for jobs include www.work.com.mm and www.jobnet.com.mm.

Transport

GETTING THERE & AWAY

Flights, tours and rail tickets can be booked online at lonelyplanet.com/bookings.

Entering the Country

If you have your visa ready and a valid passport with at least six months of validity from the time of entry in hand, you should have no trouble entering Myanmar either by air or land.

There is no requirement for you to show an onward ticket out of the country in order to enter Myanmar.

Air

Airports & Airlines

Most international flights arrive at **Yangon International Airport** (✆01-533 031; Mingaladon; ✆). You can also fly directly into **Mandalay International Airport** (MDL; ✆02-27048, 02-27027) from China, Hong Kong, India, Singapore and Thailand, and **Nay Pyi Taw International Airport** (NYT; ✆09 79900 0196) from China and Thailand.

Airlines offer discounted tickets online depending on how far in advance you book. Good deals are often available from Bangkok, Kuala Lumpur and Singapore on budget airlines such as AirAsia and Silk Air.

In Myanmar you can buy international tickets from travel agents or online.

Land

Arriving and departing by land from China, India and Thailand is possible, although for China and India crossings you will need a permit.

Crossings from Bangladesh and Laos are currently not available but this could change at some point in the future. Also check the situation at your journey-planning stage as border crossings do close from time to time.

Sea

There are no international ferries or cruises to mainland Myanmar by sea. Visitors to the Myeik Archipelago often get to the islands from Thailand on live-aboard diving tours.

GETTING AROUND

Air

Airlines in Myanmar

Myanmar's domestic air service features a handful of overworked planes that have busy days, sometimes landing at an airport, leaving the engine on, unloading and

---

CLIMATE CHANGE & TRAVEL

Every form of transport that relies on carbon-based fuel generates CO_2, the main cause of human-induced climate change. Modern travel is dependent on aeroplanes, which might use less fuel per kilometre per person than most cars but travel much greater distances. The altitude at which aircraft emit gases (including CO_2) and particles also contributes to their climate change impact. Many websites offer 'carbon calculators' that allow people to estimate the carbon emissions generated by their journey and, for those who wish to do so, to offset the impact of the greenhouse gases emitted with contributions to portfolios of climate-friendly initiatives throughout the world. Lonely Planet offsets the carbon footprint of all staff and author travel.

BORDER CROSSINGS

There are currently entry and exit points from Myanmar's land borders at the six points detailed here. No bus or train service connects Myanmar with another country, nor can you travel by car or motorcycle across the border – you must walk across. E-visas (p416) are currently only available at the following Myanmar–Thailand borders: Tachileik, Myawaddy and Kawthaung. For other crossings have your visa ready in your passport before you get to the border.

➡ Mae Sai in northern Thailand to/from Tachileik in Shan State (p232)

➡ Mae Sot in Thailand to/from Myawaddy in Kayin State (p126)

➡ Ranong in Thailand to/from Kawthoung at far southern end of Tanintharyi Region (p139)

➡ Phu Nam Ron in Thailand to/from Htee Khee in Tanintharyi Region (p129)

➡ Ruili in Yunnan Province, China, to/from Mu-se in Shan State (p289)

➡ Moreh in India's Manipur state to/from Tamu in Sagaing Region

loading, and taking off in 20 minutes! This doesn't yield a spot-free safety record.

Between the main destinations of Yangon (Rangoon), Mandalay, Heho (for Inle Lake), Nyaung U (for Bagan) and Thandwe (for Ngapali Beach), you'll find daily connections. In many other places, there are spotless, largely unused airports serving, well, no flights other than visiting dignitaries on occasion.

Following is the contact information for airline offices in Yangon. These airlines all serve the same major destinations (ie from Yangon to/from Nay Pyi Daw, Mandalay, Bagan, Inle, Sittwe). Myanmar National Airlines serves the most extensive range of destinations.

Air Bagan (☏01-504 888; www.airbagan.com)

Air KBZ (☏01-372 977; www.airkbz.com)

Air Mandalay (☏01-525 488; www.airmandalay.com)

Asian Wings (☏01-516 654; www.asianwingsairways.com)

Golden Myanmar Airlines (☏09 97799 3000; www.gmairlines.com)

Mann Yadanarpon Airlines (☏01-656 969; www.airmyp.com)

Myanmar National Airlines (☏01-378 603; www.flymna.com)

Yangon Airways (☏01-383 100; www.yangonair.com)

Airport Codes

Many posted flight schedules around the country only use domestic airport codes, shown in the following table.

AIRPORT	CODE
Bhamo	BMO
Dawei	TVY
Heho (Inle Lake)	HEH
Homalin	HOX
Kalaymyo	KMV
Kawthoung	KAW
Kengtung	KET
Lashio	LSH
Mandalay	MDL
Mawlamyine	MNU
Myeik	MGZ
Myitkyina	MYT
Nay Pyi Taw	NPT
Nyaung U (Bagan)	NYU
Pathein	BSX
Putao	PBU
Sittwe	AKY
Tachileik	THL
Thandwe (Ngapali Beach)	SNW
Yangon	RGN

Schedules

Schedules are most reliable between main destinations, such as Yangon, Mandalay, Nyaung U and Heho, during the high season – but it's essential to always double-check departure times at least 24 hours before departure and again on the day itself. To smaller destinations, flights can be cancelled and reappear depending on demand.

Tickets

➡ Online booking and e-ticketing is available with all domestic airlines.

➡ One-way fares are half a return fare, and can be bought between six months and a day in advance. It's sometimes difficult to buy a ticket that departs from a town other than the one you are in.

➡ There is no domestic departure tax.

Bicycle

Outside the major cities, bicycles are a popular means for locals to get around and can be hired around the country by visitors.

Around Town

At popular tourist spots in Mandalay, Bagan and Inle Lake you'll see 'bike rental' signs; rates start at K2000 per day; top-end hotels and occasionally more far-flung places charge up to K4000. Most guesthouses in such places keep a few bikes on

Major Transport Routes

CHINA (TIBET)

BHUTAN

INDIA

BANGLA-DESH

CHINA

Pangsaw Pass

Putao

Myitkyina

Bhamo
Ruili
Katha
Mu-se

Kalaymyo

Nanhsan
Lashio

Homalin
Kyauk-myaung
Hsipaw

Chindwin River

Shwebo

Kyaukme

Monywa
Mingun

Pyin Oo Lwin

Sagaing
Mandalay

Myingyan

Pakokku
Nyaung U
Mt Popa

Meiktila
Pindaya

Mt Victoria
Bagan
Heho
Taunggyi

Mrauk U
Kyaukpadaung
Thazi
Kalaw
Shwenyaung

Kakku

Kyaingtong

Tachileik

Minbu
Magwe
Mae Sai

LAOS

Sittwe

Ayeyarwady River

NAY PYI TAW

Pyinmana

Chiang Rai

Taunggok

Pyay
Taungoo

Thandwe
Shwedaung

Bay of Bengal

Ngapali Beach

Kyaiktiyo

Chaung Tha
Bago
Hpa-an

Ngwe Saung
Thaton
Myawaddy

Pathein
Yangon
Mae Sot

Twante
Mawlamyine

Kyaikkami
Thanbyuzayat

ANDAMAN SEA

Mouths of the Ayeyarwady

Gulf of Mottama

Ye

THAILAND

Dawei

Htee Khee
Phu Nam Ron

Myeik

Gulf of Thailand

Kawthoung
Ranong

This map outlines major land and water routes you can use in Myanmar. Some require a government permit.

⊗ Border Crossing
○ Cities With Air Links (Some Require Permit)
● Towns With No Air Links
⊢⊣ Rail Route
--- Boat Route
≡ Yangon–Mandalay Hwy
— Government Permission Routes

0 — 200 km
0 — 120 miles

hand; if not, staff can track one down. Note the condition of the bike before hiring; check the brakes and pedals in particular. Many rental bikes have baskets or bells, but don't expect a crash helmet!

Sturdier Indian, Chinese or Thai imports are available (from K100,000) if you'd rather buy one. Some tours provide bikes, so you may be able to rent better quality ones from agents (eg EXO Travel in New Bagan).

Apart from in Yangon and Mandalay, vehicular traffic is quite light.

Long Distance

A few visitors bring their own touring bikes into Myanmar. There shouldn't be any problem with customs as long as you make the proper declarations upon entering the country.

Gradients are moderate in most parts of Myanmar that are open to tourism. Frontier regions, on the other hand, tend to be mountainous, particularly Shan, Kayin, Kayah and Chin states. You'll find plenty of opportunity everywhere for dirt-road and off-road pedalling. A sturdy mountain bike would make a good alternative to a touring rig, especially in the north, where main roads can resemble secondary roads elsewhere.

Some of the key routes around Myanmar:

➡ Thazi to Inle Lake via Kalaw

➡ Pyin Oo Lwin (Maymyo) to Lashio via Hsipaw

➡ Mandalay to Bagan via Myingyan

➡ Mandalay to either Monywa, Pyin Oo Lwin, Sagaing, Inwa (Ava) or Amarapura

November to February is the best time to cycle in terms of the weather.

There are basic bicycle shops in most towns, but they usually have only locally or Chinese-made parts to equip single-speed bikes. You can also buy lower

quality motorcycle helmets here; many are disturbingly adorned with swastikas – a fad, not a political alliance. Bring reflective clothing and plenty of insurance. Don't ride at night.

Travellers on a bike may end up needing to sleep in towns few travellers make it to, and a lack of licensed accommodation may be an issue. Technically, you will need permission from local immigration to stay at such places. Be patient. Most cyclists get permission from local authorities to stay one night, but the paperwork (coming with some frowns) may take an hour or so to arrange.

It's possible to store your bicycle in the undercarriage storage on buses, though you may have to pay a little extra. On smaller buses it's possible you'll be asked to buy a 'seat' for your bike.

Some bike tours connect the dots of Myanmar's greatest hits – going, for example, up the Pyay highway to Bagan then Mandalay, and back to Yangon via Meiktila and Taungoo. It's rougher going, but nicer riding, to reach some mountainous areas, like Inle Lake.

Some recommended tour companies:

Bike World Explores Myanmar (Map p52; ☑01-527 636; www. cyclingmyanmar.com; 10F Khapaung Rd, Hlaing; bike rental & guide from K15,000) Yangon-based company that also sells and rents bikes and can offer touring advice. It has several itineraries from three days of biking around Yangon (from US$450 minimum two people) to longer adventures heading out of Bagan into Chin State.

EXO Travel (Map p48; ☑in Yangon 01-860 4933; www. exotravel.com; 147 Shwegone-dine Rd, Bahan) Runs high-end cycle tours covering Mandalay to Bagan, the Shan Hills and sights in Mon State.

Spice Roads (☑in Thailand +66-2-381 7490; www. spiceroads.com) Bangkok-based

operation, offering five different itineraries, including an opportunity to cycle from Bangkok to Yangon over 14 days (from US$3595 per person). Another tour follows part of the old Burma Road from Pyin Oo Lwin to Mandalay.

Think Asia Travel & Tours (☑01-230 1293; www.think asia-tours.com; 3rd fl, 14 Mar Ga Rd, Ahlone) Yangon-based agency offering bike tours at Inle Lake, Kalaw and Mandalay.

Unchartered Horizons (Map p38; ☑09 97117 6085; www. uncharted-horizons-myanmar. com; 109 49th St, Botataung; half-/full-day tour from K42,000/65,000) As well as its great half- and full-day cycling tours around Yangon, this Yangon-based company runs adventurous biking and trekking tours in Chin, Rakhine and Shan states.

Boat

A great variety of boats – from creaky old government-run ferries to luxurious private cruise ships – ply Myanmar's waterways.

In addition to the rivers, it's possible to travel along the Bay of Bengal between Sittwe and Taunggok (north of Ngapali Beach).

Cargo Ships

Myanma Five Star Line (Map p38; ☑09 5129 5279; www.fasa. org.sg; 132-136 Thein Byu Rd, Botataung), the government-owned ocean transport enterprise, is only cargo now, but you can try to see about jumping on a boat to Thandwe, Taunggok or Sittwe, or south to Dawei, Myeik or Kawthoung, at some point in the future.

Ferries & Private Boats

Inland Water Transport (IWT; www.iwt.gov.mm) boats tend to be rather rundown and ramshackle, but provide remarkable glimpses into local river life. Many of the passengers on the long-distance ferries are traders

SURVIVING LONG-DISTANCE BUS TRIPS

Heed the following points and your long-distance bus trip will, possibly, be a bit more comfortable:

➡ Bring snacks and drinks by all means but don't worry too much about this. A bottle of water is often handed out on better-quality buses. There are usually no bathrooms on the bus, but frequent toilet-and-refreshment stops (when everyone must get off the bus to prevent anything being stolen) punctuate journeys.

➡ Often the TV blares for much of the trip – usually sticking with Myanmar-made concerts or movies detailing things such as, oh, protagonists dying bloody deaths in car crashes, but the occasional *Raiders of the Lost Ark* slips in.

➡ Take a jacket or blanket (preferably both) as temperatures can drop substantially at night; air-con can also make it chilly. And consider earplugs and an eye mask as well if you plan to grab a little shut-eye between toilet stops.

➡ Myanmar superstition says that when you're on a journey you shouldn't ask anyone 'How much longer?', or 'Brother, when will we arrive?', as this is only tempting fate.

➡ Try not to become alarmed when you see how some local passengers hold their breath whenever a bus approaches a particularly dodgy-looking bridge.

who make stops along the way to pick up or deliver goods.

Along the heavily travelled 262-mile-long Yangon–Pyay–Mandalay route, there are 28 ferry landings, where merchants can ply their trade. IWT offices are usually near the jetty. They can offer information, schedules and fare details, and usually tickets. IWT offices, officially, accept US dollars only.

Some short trips are handled with small covered wooden ferries that fit about 25 people. Often there are smaller, private boats you can negotiate to use with the driver. We include private boat services whenever possible. However, because of their size it's not always as safe riding with private boats compared with bigger government ferries.

Luxury Boats

Several luxury boats travel the upper and lower reaches of the Ayeyarwady (Irrawaddy) River as well as the Chindwin River. Rates usually include all meals and excursions from the boats. The starting point for most trips is either Bagan or Mandalay, but occasionally itineraries originate in Yangon.

Amara Cruise (www.amara group.net) Owned by a German and his Myanmar wife, this company runs cruises between Mandalay and Bagan (four days, three nights single/double from €2045/2614). There's also the option of a six-night Mandalay–Bhamo cruise. Its two medium-sized teak boats each have seven comfy cabins and are traditionally styled but recently built.

Avalon Waterways (⏺in USA +1-877-797-8791; www.avalon waterways.com) You'll spend 10 nights sailing between Bagan and Bhamo aboard the 18–state room *Avalon Myanmar*, built in 2015. The basic itinerary (from US$4349 per person) starts and finishes in Yangon – note airfares for getting to and from the cruise portion of the trip are extra.

Pandaw Cruises (www.pandaw. com) Offers various high-end cruises aboard a replica of the teak-and-brass IFC fleet, such as a 10-night trip between Yangon and Mandalay (single/double from US$2859/5718) and a 20-day itinerary that charts the Chindwin and upper reaches of the Ayeyarwady River (single/double US$7055/14,110). New since 2016 is its cruise from Ranong in southern Myanmar via the Myeik (Mergui) Archipelago to Yangon.

Paukan Cruises (www.ayra vatacruises.com) Beautifully restored river steamers are used for this company's trips, which range from one night between Mandalay and Bagan (single/twin from US$380/870) to 10-day itineraries including sights along the Chindwin River (single/twin US$4175/9600).

Road to Mandalay (www. belmond.com/road-to-man dalay-myanmar) These luxury cruises are run by the operators of the *Orient Express* and range between two and 12 nights on two boats. *The Road to Mandalay*, a 43-berth liner that is huge by Ayeyarwady standards, includes an on-board swimming pool and wellness centre. In high season it does mostly Bagan–Mandalay, but there are occasional trips to Bhamo, too. The newer, four-deck *Orcaella* has 25 cabins and also has a small top-deck pool, a fitness and wellness centre, and boutique. Three-day/two-night cruises start at US$660 per person.

Sanctuary Ananda (www. sanctuaryretreats.com) Launched in 2014, this sleek Myanmar-built craft offers 20 suites spread over three decks. There's a small plunge pool on the top deck and a spa/gym inside. Itineraries range from the three-day Bagan–Mandalay route (from UK£714 per person) to the

11 nights sailing between Mandalay and Yangon or Mandalay and Bhamo (both from UK£2989 per person).

The Strand Cruise (☑ in Thailand +66-9-4979 1324; www.thestrandcruise.com) Named after its sister property in Yangon, this new luxury boat has 27 en-suite cabins with floor-to-ceiling windows and tiny balconies for full river views. There's a small pool surrounded by sun loungers and complimentary spa treatments during the three- or four-night cruises between Mandalay and Bagan (or vice versa).

Viking River Cruises (www.vikingrivercruises.co.uk) This British operator runs the *Viking Mandalay*, refurbished in 2013, on its two-week Myanmar Explorer itinerary originating in Bangkok, with flights to Yangon and then onto Inle Lake and Mandalay where you board the boat for a trip downriver as far as Sale. Rates start around UK£5569 per person.

Bus

Almost always faster and cheaper than trains, Myanmar buses range from luxury air-conditioned express buses, less luxurious but nice buses (without air-con), local buses to mini 32-seaters.

Seat Classes & Conditions

Many long-haul trips allow the greatest comfort, with new(ish) air-conditioned express buses – some of which are quite nice. For several long-distance routes, many services leave between 4pm and 10pm or later, and arrive at the final destination in the wee hours (often 5am or 6am). There are a couple of reasons for this: local people can't afford to waste a working day on a bus so prefer to travel overnight; and the buses don't overheat as much by avoiding the punishing midday sun.

If you want extra air-con comfort but don't want to go the whole way on one of these routes, you usually have to pay the full fare (eg going from Mandalay to Taungoo you pay the full fare to Yangon) and will have to deal with the middle-of-the-night arrival time. Similarly, by paying the full fare for the route, you can jump on a bus at a stop along the way; for example, catch the Mandalay–Yangon bus at Meiktila. Staff at your guesthouse or hotel should be able to help with this.

Similar-sized but older buses, with no air-conditioning, make shorter-haul trips, such as direct links from Yangon to Pyay or Taungoo to Yangon.

Local 32-seat minibuses bounce along the highways too. These tend to use the aisles, if not for people, for bags of rice, veggies or (worst) dried fish. Sometimes the floor in front of you is filled too, so you'll find your knees to your chin for some bouncy hours. Getting up to stretch your legs while moving just isn't an option. (Try to sit in the front couple of rows, which sometimes have fewer bags stored, and better visibility.)

Travelling times for all forms of public road transport are very elastic and buses of all types do break down sometimes. Older buses often stop to hose down a hot engine. Some roads – one-lane, mangled deals (read: *very* rough) – don't help matters, and tyre punctures occur too.

Costs

Bus fares are in kyat. In some locations, foreigners may pay more than locals.

Reservations

From November to February it's wise to prebook buses a couple of days in advance for

BUS ROUTES

ROUTE	FARE (K)	DURATION (HR)
Bagan–Taunggyi	11,000	10
Mandalay–Bagan	8000-11,000	6
Mandalay–Hsipaw	5000	8
Mandalay–Taunggyi	10,000-13,000	7-8
Pyay–Bagan	14,000	12
Yangon–Bagan	14,200-15,500	9-10
Yangon–Bago	4000	2
Yangon–Chaung Tha Beach	8000-10,000	6-7
Yangon–Kyaiktiyo	8000	5
Yangon–Mandalay	11,000	9-10
Yangon–Pyay	5500	6
Yangon–Taunggyi (for Inle Lake)	15,000	11-12
Yangon–Thandwe (for Ngapali)	15,000	14

TRANSPORT CAR & MOTORCYCLE

ROAD DISTANCES (miles)

	Yangon	Mawlamyine	Nay Pyi Taw	Nyaungshwe	Mandalay	Myitkyina	Sittwe	Ngapali Beach	Hpa-an	Pyay	Pathein	Nyaung U
Mawlamyine	185											
Nay Pyi Taw	265	335										
Nyaungshwe	420	430	200									
Mandalay	420	500	185	175								
Myitkyina	795	900	515	465	350							
Sittwe	430	590	620	610	605	915						
Ngapali Beach	200	380	460	450	450	760	205					
Hpa-an	155	70	310	480	470	785	565	355				
Pyay	170	355	365	350	335	655	255	120	330			
Pathein	140	315	390	565	615	925	380	165	295	280		
Nyaung U	390	505	195	175	170	495	485	330	470	215	490	
Taunggyi	415	485	200	15	175	495	605	450	445	340	545	175

Approximate distances only

key routes, such as Bagan–Inle Lake. Seat reservations are made for all buses – you should be able to check the seating plan with the reservation agent.

Car & Motorcycle

Hiring a car and driver for part or all of a trip is a good way to go, though not cheap. To drive yourself, permission must be arranged via the government-run MTT and Road Transport Administration Department (RTAD; www.myanmarrtad.com).

Driving conditions can be poor but are often better than on many roads in Vietnam, Cambodia and Laos – and outside the major cities, traffic is comparatively light compared to Thai or Vietnamese roads. Of the 15,000 miles of roads in Myanmar, about half are paved; the remainder are graded gravel, unimproved dirt or simple vehicle tracks.

Hiring a Car & Driver

The best place to arrange a driver, perhaps for a full trip, is in Yangon, but it's possible to track down a 'taxi' or 'private car' from most travel agencies and guesthouses around the country, particu-larly in popular destinations, such as Bagan, Mandalay and Inle Lake.

When trying to find a car with driver, consider there are three unofficial types of cars:

Tourist cars These are reasonably new, air-conditioned cars run by a company that provides back-up or repairs in the event they break down. These are the most comfortable – and that air-con is handy when it's dusty and hot out – but the most expensive option, running to about US$150 to US$200 a day, depending on the length of the trip. This price includes petrol for up to 12 hours' driving per day and all of the driver's expenses.

Taxis A midrange option; these days there are plenty of taxis with working air-con on Yangon's roads and hiring one costs about K5000 per hour.

Private cars These vary in condition (eg there might be no air-con) and price dramatically, and there's less chance that you'll have any sort of replacement if the engine goes out mid-journey. Rates for these cost from US$60 or US$80 per day.

There are no car-rental agencies per se; **Europcar Myanmar** (www.europcar-myanmar.com) is a new set-up but currently rents cars with drivers. Most travel agencies in Yangon, Mandalay and Bagan – as well as guesthouses and hotels elsewhere – can arrange cars and drivers. They can also be booked online economically at **Oway** (Map p48; ☏ 09 45045 0601; www.oway.com.mm; 9th fl, Grand Myay Nu Tower, 6/38 Myay Nu St, Sanchaung) and **Flymya** (Map p42; ☏ 09 79797 8881; https://flymya.com; Lanmadaw Plaza, Latha).

Petrol & Tolls

Petrol costs K650 per litre. In rural parts of the country you'll find roadside stalls selling bottles of petrol.

Another cost to consider when travelling by car is the customary K100 to K200 'toll' collected upon entering many towns and villages throughout Myanmar. Many drivers are adept at handing these to the toll collectors while barely slowing down.

The toll for private cars using the expressway from Yangon to Mandalay is K5000, while to Nay Pyi Taw it's K2500.

Motorcycle & Mopeds

It's occasionally possible to rent a motorbike or moped, though few locals advertise this – and the authorities frown on it since they don't want to deal with the complications of visitors involved in accidents. In Mandalay and Myitkyina, for example, it's K10,000 per day to rent a motorbike. Unlike cyclists, you're required to wear a helmet in most towns.

Note that motorbikes and mopeds are banned in most of Yangon (they are common in the far north of the city near the airport and across the river in Dalah).

Hitching & Ride-Sharing

Hitching is never entirely safe in any country in the world, and we don't recommend it. Travellers who decide to hitch should understand that they are taking a small but potentially serious risk. People who do choose to hitch will be safer if they travel in pairs and let someone know where they are planning to go.

One extra reason to avoid hitching in Myanmar is that local drivers may not know which areas are off-limits to foreigners and may unwittingly transport them into such areas. In such cases the driver will probably be punished.

Local Transport

Larger towns in Myanmar offer a variety of city buses (*ka*), bicycle rickshaws or trishaws (*saiq-ka*, for sidecar), horse carts (*myint hlei*), ox carts, vintage taxis (*taxi*), more modern little three-wheelers somewhat akin to Thai *tuk-tuks* (*thoun bein*, meaning 'three wheels'), tiny four-wheeled 'blue taxi' Mazdas (*lei bein*, meaning 'four wheels') and modern Japanese pick-up trucks (*lain ka*, meaning 'line car').

Small towns rely heavily on horse carts and trishaws as the main mode of local transport. However, in big cities (Yangon, Mandalay, Pathein, Mawlamyine and Taunggyi) public buses take regular routes along the main avenues for a fixed per-person rate, usually K50 to K100.

Standard rates for taxis, trishaws and horse carts are sometimes 'boosted' for foreigners. Generally a ride from the bus station to a central hotel – often a distance of 1.25 miles or more – is between K1000 and K1500. Short rides around the city centre can be arranged for between K500 and K1000. You may need to bargain a bit.

Pick-up Trucks

Japanese-made pick-up trucks feature three rows of bench seats in the covered back. Most pick-ups connect short-distance destinations, making many stops along the way to pick up people or cargo. They are often packed (yet somehow never 'full' according to the driver). Pick-ups trace some useful or necessary routes, such as from Mandalay to Amarapura, from Myingyan to Meiktila, from Bagan to Mt Popa, and up to the Golden Rock at Kyaiktiyo. Unlike buses, they go regularly during the day.

Fares are not necessarily cheaper than those charged for local bus trips of the same length, and prices often go up more after dark. You can, however, pay 25% to 50% extra for a seat up the front. It's often worth the extra expense, if you don't want to do scrunch duty. Sometimes you may share your spot with a monk riding for free; usually you get exactly what you pay for ('the whole front'), unlike in some other parts of Southeast Asia.

Pick-ups often start from the bus station (in some towns they linger under a big banyan tree in the centre) and then, unlike many buses, make rounds through the central streets to snare more passengers.

Train

A train ride on Myanmar's narrow-gauge tracks is like going by horse, with the mostly antique carriages rocking back and forth and bouncing everyone lucky enough to have a seat on the hard chairs – sleep is practically impossible. Compared to bus trips on the same routes, taking the train means extra travel time, on top of which likely delays (of several hours, if you're unlucky) have to be factored in.

However, train travel is cheap now that foreigners pay the same as locals. Routes sometimes get to areas not reached by road and the services provide a chance to interact with locals. 'It's not as bad as some people say, not as good as you hope,' one wise local told us. The good news is that, in coming years, it will improve as the network receives much-needed upgrades.

The Network

First introduced by the British in 1877 with the opening of the 163-mile line between Yangon and Pyay, Myanmar's rail network now has over 3357 miles of 3.3ft-gauge track and 858 train stations.

Extensions to the network, adding another 2264 miles of track, are slowly under construction from Sittwe in the west to Myeik in the south. Japanese investment and train know-how is also helping to upgrade the main Yangon–Mandalay line and Yangon's Circle Line.

The 386-mile trip from Yangon to Mandalay, via Bago, Nay Pyi Taw and Thazi, is the most popular train ride visitors take. Since 2016, train 5/6, which leaves both Yangon and Mandalay at 3pm, uses new diesel electric locomotives and carriages bought from China. The

---

ROAD RULES: TO THE RIGHT!

All Myanmar traffic goes on the right-hand side of the road. This wasn't always so. In an effort to distance itself from the British colonial period, the military government instigated an overnight switch from the left to the right in 1970. Many cars either date from before 1970, or are low-cost Japanese models, so steering wheels are perilously found on the right-hand side – this becomes particularly dicey when a driver blindly zooms to the left to pass a car!

train's air-cushion suspension system provides for a smoother (but not faster) ride. There is no sleeper carriage on this service; if you wish to book a sleeper for this route, those are only available on train 3/4, which departs both cities at 5pm.

Other routes worth considering:

➡ Bagan to Yangon via Taungoo and Kyaukpadaung

➡ Mandalay (or Pyin Oo Lwin) to Lashio (or Hsipaw), which takes in hilly terrain missed by road (Paul Theroux managed to do this back when foreigners weren't supposed to, as described in his book *The Great Railway Bazaar*)

➡ Yangon to Mawlamyine via Bago, Kyaiktiyo and Mottawa

➡ Pyinmana to Kyaukpadaung (31 miles south of Bagan)

➡ Thazi to Shwenyaung (7 miles north of Inle Lake)

➡ Yangon to Pyay.

An express line connects Bagan (Nyaung U) with Mandalay, from where there are three other branch lines: one running slightly northwest across the Ava Bridge and up to Ye-U; one directly north to Myitkyina in Kachin State; and one northeast through Pyin Oo Lwin to Lashio in the northern part of Shan State.

Note, trains are classified by a number and the suffix 'Up' for northbound trains or 'Down' for southbound trains. Train numbers are not always used when purchasing tickets.

For more information on all routes and services, a good online source is www.seat61.com.

Classes & Facilities

Express trains offer two classes of passage – upper class and ordinary class; long-distance trains may also offer sleepers. The main difference between ordinary and upper class is that the seats recline and can be reserved in the latter, while ordinary class features hard upright seats that can't be reserved. Some trains also offer another class of service called 1st class, which is a step down from upper in comfort.

There are two types of sleeper carriage:

➡ standard sleeper – four-berth and two-berth compartments with doors onto a corridor and connections to the rest of the train

➡ special sleeper – a separate full-width compartment with four berths, a toilet and entrance door, but no access through the train. If you'd prefer to move around the train and meet fellow passengers, an upper-class seat will be better.

In both types of sleeper carriage, linens and blankets are provided. There's a ceiling fan and the windows open for ventilation.

Long-distance trains have dining cars accessible to passengers in 1st, upper and sleeper class. The food isn't bad – fried rice and noodles. Attendants can also take your order and bring food to your seat or pass it through the window.

Trains stop fairly often, too, with vendors on platforms offering all sorts of snacks. Bathrooms are basic;

there are also sinks to wash hands and brush teeth. Attendants sometimes hire out bamboo mats to spread on the floor in aisles or under seats if you can't sleep upright. It can get cold at night, so bring a jacket and/or a blanket.

The express trains are far superior to the general run of Myanmar trains. Other trains are late, almost by rule. It's not unheard of for the Mandalay–Myitkyina route, scheduled to take around 24 hours, to end up taking 40 hours. Even on the Yangon–Mandalay route delays are common, particularly in the rainy season when the tracks are prone to flooding.

Reservations

Tickets can be bought directly at the train stations. Smaller stations sometimes require some perseverance to get a ticket, as agents aren't used to foreigners climbing on.

A day or two's notice is usually enough to book a seat, but if you desire a coveted sleeper, you'll need at least a couple of days' notice – longer during the high season (November to March). If you hold a seat on a train pulling a sleeper car, you can try to upgrade to a berth after you board by paying the additional fare directly to the conductor.

If you're having trouble buying a ticket or making yourself understood at a train station, try seeking out the stationmaster (*yonepain* in Burmese) – the person at the station who is most likely to speak English and most inclined to help you get a seat.

Health

The following advice is a general guide only and does not replace the advice of a doctor trained in travel medicine.

Before You Go

Insurance

Make sure your travel insurance or separate private health insurance covers all possible health eventualities in Myanmar – the country's health system is far from ideal and although Yangon has international-standard hospitals for major incidents, an air evacuation to neighbouring countries may be required.

Recommended Vaccinations

Proof of yellow-fever vaccination will be required if you have visited a country in the yellow-fever zone (ie Africa or South America) within the six days prior to entering Myanmar. Otherwise, the World Health Organization (WHO) recommends the following vaccinations for travellers to Myanmar:

Adult diphtheria and tetanus Single booster recommended if none in the previous 10 years.

Hepatitis A Provides almost 100% protection for up to a year. A booster after 12 months provides at least another 20 years' protection.

Hepatitis B Now considered routine for most travellers. Given as three shots over six months. A rapid schedule is also available, as is a combined vaccination with hepatitis A.

Measles, mumps and rubella (MMR) Two doses of MMR are required unless you have had the diseases. Many young adults require a booster.

Polio There have been no reported cases of polio in Myanmar in recent years. Adults require only one booster for lifetime protection.

Typhoid Recommended unless your trip is less than a week and only to developed cities. The vaccine offers about 70% protection, lasts for two to three years and comes as a single shot. Tablets are also available but the injection is usually recommended as it has fewer side effects.

Varicella (chickenpox) If you haven't had chickenpox, discuss this vaccination with your doctor.

Medical Checklist

➡ Pack medications in their original, clearly labelled containers.

➡ Carry a signed and dated letter from your physician describing your medical conditions and medications, including their generic names.

➡ If you have a heart condition, bring a copy of your ECG taken just prior to travelling.

➡ Bring a double supply of any regular medication in case of loss or theft.

➡ Take out travel insurance.

Websites

Lonely Planet's *Healthy Travel – Asia & India* is packed with useful information. Other recommended references include *Travellers' Health* by Dr Richard Dawood and *Travelling Well* by Dr Deborah Mills. Online resources:

Centres for Disease Control and Prevention (CDC; www.cdc.gov)

MD Travel Health (www.mdtravelhealth.com)

World Health Organization (www.who.int/ith/)

HEALTH ADVISORIES

Consult your government's website on health and travel before departure:

Australia (http://smartraveller.gov.au)

Canada (www.phac-aspc.gc.ca)

New Zealand (www.safetravel.govt.nz)

UK (www.gov.uk/foreign-travel-advice)

USA (wwwnc.cdc.gov/travel)

In Myanmar

Availability & Cost of Health Care

Outside of Yangon, Myanmar medical care is generally dismal, and local hospitals should be used only out of desperation. Contact your embassy for advice, as staff will usually direct you to the best options.

Be aware that getting Western-style health care may not come cheap. An initial consultation with an international doctor in Yangon will cost at least US$50.

If you think you may have a serious disease, especially malaria, do not waste time – travel to the nearest quality facility to receive attention. It is always better to be assessed by a doctor than to rely on self-treatment.

Buying medication over the counter is not recommended in Myanmar, as fake medications and poorly stored or out-of-date drugs are common.

Infectious Diseases

The following are the most common infectious diseases for travellers:

Dengue fever Increasingly problematic throughout Myanmar. The mosquito that carries dengue bites day and night, so use insect avoidance measures at all times. Symptoms can include high fever, severe headache, body ache, a rash and diarrhoea. There is no specific treatment, just rest and paracetamol – do not take aspirin as it increases the likelihood of haemorrhaging.

Hepatitis A This food- and water-borne virus infects the liver, causing jaundice (yellow skin and eyes), nausea and lethargy. All travellers to Myanmar should be vaccinated against it.

Hepatitis B The only sexually transmitted infection (STI) that can be prevented by vaccination, hepatitis B is spread by body fluids, including sexual contact.

Hepatitis E Transmitted through contaminated food and water

and has similar symptoms to hepatitis A, but is far less common. It is a severe problem in pregnant women and can result in the death of both mother and baby. There is currently no vaccine, and prevention is by following safe eating and drinking guidelines.

HIV Unprotected sex is the main method of transmission.

Influenza Can be very severe in people over the age of 65 or in those with underlying medical conditions, such as heart disease or diabetes; vaccination is recommended for these individuals. There is no specific treatment, just rest and paracetamol.

Malaria While not noted in Yangon or Mandalay, malaria (which can be fatal if untreated) is very much present throughout the rest of rural Myanmar in altitudes below 1000m. Before you travel, seek medical advice on the right medication and dosage for you; note that some areas of the country have strains of the disease resistant to Mefloquine-based drugs. Wherever you are, wear long pants and sleeves and spray insect repellent to prevent bites. Also sleep in air-conditioned or screened rooms with mosquito nets over beds.

Rabies A potential risk, and invariably fatal if untreated, rabies is spread by the bite or lick of an infected animal (most commonly a dog or monkey). Pretravel vaccination means the postbite treatment is greatly simplified. If an animal bites you, gently wash the wound with soap and water, and apply iodine-based antiseptic. If you are not prevaccinated, you will need to receive rabies immunoglobulin as soon as possible.

Typhoid This serious bacterial infection is spread via food and water. Symptoms include high and slowly progressive fever, headache, a dry cough and stomach pain. Vaccination, recommended for all travellers spending more than a week in Myanmar and other parts of Southeast Asia, is not 100% effective so you must still be careful with what you eat and drink.

Traveller's Diarrhoea

By far the most common problem affecting travellers is usually caused by a bacteria. Treatment consists of staying well hydrated; use a solution such as Gastrolyte. Antibiotics such as Norfloxacin, Ciprofloxacin or Azithromycin will kill the bacteria quickly.

Loperamide is just a 'stopper', but it can be helpful in certain situations, such as if you have to go on a long bus ride. Seek medical attention quickly if you do not respond to an appropriate antibiotic.

Amoebic dysentery is very rare in travellers; one sign is if you have blood in your diarrhoea. Treatment involves two drugs: Tinidazole or Metronidazole to kill the parasite in your gut, and then a second drug to kill the cysts.

Giardiasis is relatively common. Symptoms include nausea, bloating, excess gas, fatigue and intermittent diarrhoea. The treatment of choice is Tinidazole, with Metronidazole being a second option.

Environmental Hazards

AIR POLLUTION

Air pollution, particularly vehicle pollution, is an increasing problem, particularly in Yangon. If you have severe respiratory problems, speak with your doctor before travelling to any heavily polluted urban centres. This pollution also causes minor respiratory problems, such as sinusitis, dry throat and irritated eyes. If troubled by the pollution, leave the city for a few days and get some fresh air.

DIVING

Divers and surfers should seek specialised advice before they travel to ensure their medical kit contains treatment for coral cuts and tropical ear infections, as well as the standard problems. Divers should ensure their travel insurance covers them for decompression illness.

Have a dive medical examination before you leave your home country – there are certain medical conditions that are incompatible with diving, and economic considerations may override health considerations for some dive operators in Myanmar.

FOOD

Rather than being overly concerned at street stalls, where food is freshly cooked to order, note that eating in restaurants is the biggest risk factor for contracting traveller's diarrhoea. Avoid shellfish, and food that has been sitting around in buffets. Peel all fruit, cook vegetables and soak salads in iodine water for at least 20 minutes. Eat in busy restaurants with a high turnover of customers.

HEAT

Many parts of Myanmar are hot and humid throughout the year. It can take up to two weeks to adapt to the hot climate. Swelling of the feet and ankles is common, as are muscle cramps caused by excessive sweating. Prevent these by avoiding dehydration and excessive activity in the heat.

Dehydration is the main contributor to heat exhaustion. Symptoms include feeling weak; headache; irritability; nausea or vomiting; sweaty skin; a fast, weak pulse; and a normal or slightly elevated body temperature. Treat by getting out of the heat, applying cool wet cloths to the skin, lying flat with legs raised and rehydrating with water containing a quarter of a teaspoon of salt per litre.

Heatstroke is a serious medical emergency. Symptoms come on suddenly and include weakness, nausea, a hot dry body with a body temperature of over 41°C, dizziness, confusion, loss of coordination, fits and eventual collapse and loss of consciousness. Seek medical help and commence cooling by getting the person out of the

heat, removing their clothes, and applying cool wet cloths or ice to their body, especially to the groin and armpits.

Prickly heat – an itchy rash of tiny lumps – is caused by sweat being trapped under the skin. Treat by moving out of the heat and into an air-conditioned area for a few hours and by having cool showers. Creams and ointments clog the skin so they should be avoided.

INSECT BITES & STINGS

Bedbugs Don't carry disease but their bites are very itchy. They live in the cracks of furniture and walls and then migrate to the bed at night to feed on you. You can treat the itch with an antihistamine.

Bees or wasps If allergic to their stings, carry an injection of adrenaline (eg an EpiPen®) for emergency treatment.

Jellyfish In Myanmar waters, most are not dangerous. If stung, pour vinegar onto the affected area to neutralise the poison. Take painkillers and seek medical advice if your condition worsens.

Leeches Found in humid rainforest areas. Don't transmit any disease but their bites can be itchy for weeks afterwards and can easily become infected. Apply an iodine-based antiseptic to any leech bite to help prevent infection.

Lice Most commonly inhabit your head and pubic area. Transmission is via close contact with an infected person. Treat with numerous applications of

an antilice shampoo, such as Permethrin.

Ticks Contracted after walking in rural areas. If you are bitten and experience symptoms such as a rash at the site of the bite or elsewhere, fever, or muscle aches, see a doctor. Doxycycline prevents tick-borne diseases.

SKIN PROBLEMS

Fungal rashes are common in humid climates; there are two that affect travellers. The first occurs in moist areas that receive less air, such as the groin, the armpits and between the toes. It starts as a red patch that slowly spreads and is usually itchy. Treatment involves keeping the skin dry, avoiding chafing and using an antifungal cream, such as Clotrimazole or Lamisil. *Tinea versicolor* is also common – this fungus causes small, light-coloured patches, most commonly on the back, chest and shoulders. Consult a doctor.

Cuts and scratches easily become infected in humid climates. Take meticulous care of any cuts and scratches to prevent complications, such as abscesses. Immediately wash all wounds in clean water and apply antiseptic. If you develop signs of infection (increasing pain and redness), see a doctor. Divers and surfers should be particularly careful with coral cuts as they easily become infected.

TAP WATER

➡ Never drink tap water.

➡ Check bottled water seals are intact at purchase.

➡ Avoid ice.

➡ Avoid fresh juices – they may have been watered down.

➡ Boiling water is the most efficient method of purifying.

➡ Iodine, the best chemical purifier, should not be used by pregnant women or those who suffer with thyroid problems.

➡ Ensure your water filter has a chemical barrier, such as iodine, and a pore size of less than four microns.

SNAKES

Myanmar is home to many species of both poisonous and harmless snakes. Assume all snakes are poisonous and never try to catch one. Always wear boots and long pants if walking in an area that may have snakes. First aid in the event of a snakebite involves pressure immobilisation with an elastic bandage firmly wrapped around the affected limb, starting at the bite site and working up towards the chest. The bandage should not be so tight that the circulation is cut off, and the fingers or toes should be kept free so the circulation can be checked. Immobilise the limb with a splint and carry the victim to medical attention. Do not use tourniquets or try to suck the venom out. Antivenom is available for most species.

Women's Health

Pregnant women should receive specialised advice before travelling. The ideal time to travel is between 16 and 28 weeks, when the risk of pregnancy-related problems is at its lowest and pregnant women generally feel their best. During the first trimester there is a risk of miscarriage and in the third trimester complications – such as premature labour and high blood pressure – are possible. It's wise to travel with a companion. Always carry a list of quality medical facilities available at your destination and ensure that you continue your standard antenatal care at these facilities. Avoid rural travel in areas with poor transport and medical facilities. Most of all, ensure that your travel insurance covers all pregnancy-related possibilities, including premature labour.

Malaria is a high-risk disease in pregnancy. WHO recommends that pregnant women do *not* travel to areas with Chloroquine-resistant malaria. None of the more effective antimalarial drugs are completely safe in pregnancy.

Traveller's diarrhoea can quickly lead to dehydration and result in inadequate blood flow to the placenta. Many of the drugs used to treat various diarrhoea bugs are not recommended in pregnancy. Azithromycin is considered safe.

Birth-control options may be limited, so bring adequate supplies of your own form of contraception. Heat, humidity and antibiotics can all contribute to thrush. Treatment is with antifungal creams and pessaries such as Clotrimazole. A practical alternative is a single tablet of Fluconazole (Diflucan). Urinary tract infections can be precipitated by dehydration or long bus journeys without toilet stops; bring suitable antibiotics.

Traditional Medicine

Throughout Myanmar traditional medical systems are widely practised. Folk remedies should be avoided, as they often involve rather dubious procedures with potential complications. In comparison, traditional healing systems such as Chinese medicine are well respected, and aspects of them are being increasingly used by Western medical practitioners.

All traditional Asian medical systems identify a vital life force, and see blockage or imbalance as causing disease. Techniques such as herbal medicines, massage and acupuncture are used to bring this vital force back into balance or to maintain balance. These therapies are best used for treating chronic fatigue, arthritis, irritable bowel syndrome, skin conditions and other chronic ailments. Don't use traditional medicines to treat serious acute infections, such as malaria.

Be aware that 'natural' doesn't always mean 'safe', and there can be drug interactions between herbal medicines and Western medicines. If you are using both systems, ensure that you inform both practitioners what the other has prescribed.

Language

Burmese is part of the Tibeto-Burman language family. As the national language of Myanmar (Burma), it has more than 40 million speakers, of whom more than 30 million use it as their first language. The variety of Burmese of Mandalay and Yangon, spoken throughout the central area of Myanmar, is considered the standard language. Many other languages are spoken in Myanmar, but with Burmese you'll be understood in the whole country.

There are two varieties of Burmese – one used in writing and formal situations, the other in speaking and informal context. The main differences are in vocabulary, especially the most common words (eg 'this' is di in spoken Burmese, but i in the written language). The phrases in this chapter are in the informal spoken variety, which is appropriate for all situations you're likely to encounter. Note that many Burmese nouns are borrowed from English, though the meaning and sound may be somewhat different.

In Burmese, there's a difference between aspirated consonants (pronounced with a puff of air after the sound) and unaspirated ones – you'll get the idea if you hold your hand in front of your mouth to feel your breath, and say 'pit' (where the 'p' is aspirated) and 'spit' (where it's unaspirated). These aspirated consonants in our pronunciation guides are said with a puff of air after the sound: ch (as in 'church'), k (as in 'kite'), ş (as in 'sick'), t (as in 'talk'); the following ones are pronounced with a puff of air before the

sound: hl (as in 'life'), hm (as in 'me'), hn (as in 'not'), hng (as in 'sing'), hny (as in 'canyon'). Note also that the apostrophe (') represents the sound heard between 'uh-oh', th is pronounced as in 'thin' and ţh as in 'their'.

There are three distinct tones in Burmese (the raising and lowering of pitch on certain syllables). They are indicated in our pronunciation guides by the accent mark above the vowel: high creaky tone, as in 'heart' (á), plain high tone, as in 'car' (à), and the low tone (a – no accent). Note also that ai is pronounced as in 'aisle', aw as in 'law', and au as in 'brown'.

BASICS

Burmese equivalents of the personal pronouns 'I' and 'you' have masculine and feminine forms, depending on the gender of the person indicated by the pronoun. These forms are marked as 'm/f' in phrases throughout this chapter. Depending on the pronoun (ie 'I' or 'you'), these abbreviations refer to the speaker or the person addressed.

Hello.	မင်္ဂလာပါ။	ming·guh·la·ba
Goodbye.	သွားမယ်နော်။	thwà·me·naw
Yes.	ဟုတ်ကဲ့။	hoh'·gé
No.	ဟင့်အင်း။	híng·ìn
Excuse me.	ဆောရီးနော်။	sàw·rì·naw
Sorry.	ဆောရီးနော်။	sàw·rì·naw
Please.	တဆိတ်လောက်။	duh·şay'·lau'
Thank you.	ကျေးဇူး	jày·zù
	တင်ပါတယ်။	ding·ba·de
You're welcome.	ရပါတယ်။	yá·ba·de
How are you?	နေကောင်းလား။	nay·gàung·là
Fine. And you?	ကောင်းပါတယ်။	gàung·ba·de
	ခင်ဗျား/ရှင်ရော။	king·myà/ shing·yàw (m/f)

WANT MORE?

For in-depth language information and handy phrases, check out Lonely Planet's *Burmese Phrasebook*. You'll find it at **shop.lonelyplanet.com**, or you can buy Lonely Planet's iPhone phrasebooks at the Apple App Store.

What's your name?

နာမည် ဘယ်လို ခေါ်သလဲ။	nang·me be·loh kaw·ţhuh·lè

My name is ...

ကျနော့်/ကျမ နာမည်က- - - ပါ။	juh·náw/juh·má nang·me·gá ... ba (m/f)

Do you speak English?

အင်္ဂလိပ်လို ပြောတတ်သလား။	ìng·guh·lay'·loh byàw·da'·thuh·là

I don't understand.

နားမလည်ဘူး။	nà·muh·le·bòo

ACCOMMODATION

Where's a ...?	- - - ဘယ်မှာလဲ။	... be·hma·lè
bungalow	ဘန်ဂလို	buhng·guh·loh
guesthouse	တည်းခိုခန်း	dè·koh·gàn
hotel	ဟိုတယ်	hoh·te

Do you have a ... room?	- - - ရှိသလား။	... shí·ţhuh·là
single	တစ်ယောက်ခန်း	duh·yau'·kàng
double	နှစ်ယောက်ခန်း	hnuh·yau'·kàng
twin	ခုတင်နှစ်လုံး ပါတဲ့အခန်း	guh·ding· hnuh·lòhng· ba·dé·uh·kàng

How much is it per night/person?

တစ်ည/တစ်ယောက် ဘယ်လောက်လဲ၊	duh·nyá/duh·yau' be·lau'·lè

Is there a campsite nearby?

ဒီနားမှာ စခန်းချရာနေရာ ရှိသလား။	di·nà·hma suh·kàng·chá·zuh·ya·nay·ya shí·ţhuh·là

DIRECTIONS

Where is ...?

- - - ဘယ်မှာလဲ။	... be·hma·lè

What's the address?

လိပ်စာက ဘာလဲ။	lay'·sa·gá ba·lè

Could you please write it down?

-ရေးမှတ်ထားပါ။	yày·hmuh'·tà ba

Can you show me (on the map)?

(မြေပုံပေါ်မှာ) ညွှန်ပြပေးပါ။	(myay·bohng·baw·hma) hnyoong·byá·bày·ba

Turn ...	- - - ကွေ့ပါ။	... gwáy·ba
at the corner	လမ်းထောင့်မှာ	làng·dáung·hma
at the traffic lights	မီးပွိုင့်မှာ	mì·pwáing·hma

It's ...

behind ...	- - - အနောက်မှာ။	... uh·nau'·hma
far away	အရမ်းဝေးတယ်။	uh·yàng wày·de
in front of ...	- - - ရှေ့မှာ။	... sháy·hma
left	ဘယ်ဘက်မှာ။	be·be'·hma
near ...	- - - နားမှာ။	... nà·hma
next to ...	- - - ဘေးမှာ။	... bày·hma
right	ညာဘက်မှာ။	nya·be'·hma
straight ahead	ရှေ့တည့်တည့်မှာ။	sháy·dé·dé·hma

EATING & DRINKING

Can you recommend a ...?	- - - တစ်ခု အကြံပေးနိုင်မလား။	... duh·kú uh·jang·bày· naing·muh·là
bar	အရက်ဆိုင်	uh·ye'·şaing
cafe	ကော်ဖီဆိုင်	gaw·pi·şaing
restaurant	စားသောက်ဆိုင်	sà·thau'·şaing

I'd like a/the ..., please.	- - - လိုချင်ပါတယ်။	... loh·jing·ba·de
table for (four)	(၄)ယောက်စာ စားပွဲ	(lày)·yau'·sa zuh·bwè
nonsmoking section	ဆေးလိပ် မသောက်ရတဲ့နေရာ	şày·lay' muh·thau'·yá· dé·nay·ya

I'd like (the) ..., please.	- - - ပေးပါ။	... bày·ba
bill	ဘောက်ချာ	bau'·cha
menu	မီနူး	mi·nù
that dish	အဲဒီဟင်းခွက်	è·di hìng·gwe'
wine list	ဝိုင်စာရင်း	waing·suh·yìng

Could you prepare a meal without ...?	- - - မပါဘဲ ပြင်ပေးနိုင်မလား။	... muh·ba·bè bying·bày· naing·muh·là
butter	ထောပတ်	tàw·ba'
eggs	ကြက်ဥ	je'·ú
fish sauce	ငံပြာရည်	ngang·bya·yay
meat	အသား	uh·thà
meat stock	အသားပြုတ်ရည်	uh·thà· byoh'·yay

Do you have vegetarian food?

သက်သတ်လွတ် စားစရာ ရှိသလား။	the'·tha'·lu' sà·zuh·ya shí·ţhuh·là

What would you recommend?

ဘာအကြံပေးမလဲ။	ba uh·jang·pày·muh·lè

What's the local speciality?
ဒီမြို့ကစပယ်ရှယ် di·myóh·gá suh·be·she
အစားအစာက ဘာလဲ။ uh·sà·uh·sa·gá ba·lè

Cheers!
ချီးယား။ chì·ya

Key Words

breakfast	မနက်စာ	muh·ne'·sa
lunch	နေ့လည်စာ	náy·le·za
dinner	ညစာ	nyá·za
snack	အဆာပြေ စားစရာ	uh·şa·byay sà·zuh·ya
fruit	အသီးအနှံ	uh·thì·uh·hnang
meat	အသား	uh·thà
vegetable	ဟင်းသီးဟင်းရွက်	hìng·ţhì·hìng·ywe'
bottle	တစ်ပုလင်း	duh·buh·ling
bowl	ပန်းကန်လုံး	buh·gang·lòhng
chopsticks	တူ	doo
cup	ခွက်	kwe'
fork	ခက်ရင်း	kuh·yìng
glass	ဖန်ခွက်	pang·gwe'
knife	ဓား	dà
napkin	လက်သုတ်ပုဝါ	le'·thoh'·buh·wa
plate	ပန်းကန်	buh·gang
spoon	ဇွန်း	zòong
teaspoon	လက်ဖက်ရည်ဇွန်း	luh·pe'·yay·zòong

Drinks

(cup of) coffee ...	ကော်ဖီ (၁)ခွက် - - -	gaw·pi (duh·)kwe' ...
(cup of) tea ...	လက်ဖက်ရည် (၁)ခွက် - - -	luh·pe'·yay (duh·)kwe' ...
with milk	နို့နဲ့	nóh·né
without sugar	သကြား မပါဘဲ	ţhuh·jà muh·ba·bè
wine	ဝိုင်	waing
red	အနီ	uh·ni
white	အဖြူ	uh·pyu
beer	ဘီယာ	bi·ya
drinking water	သောက်ရေ	thau'·yay
hot water	ရေနွေး	yay·nwày
milk	နို့	nóh
mineral water	ရေသန့်ဗူး	yay·ţháng·bòo
orange juice	လိမ္မော်ရည်	layng·maw·yay
soft drink	ဖျော်ရည်	pyaw·yay
sugarcane juice	ကြံရည်	jang·yay

SIGNS

အဝင်	Entrance
အထွက်	Exit
ဖွင့်	Open
ပိတ်ထားသည်	Closed
အခန်းအားရှိသည်	Vacancies
အခန်းအားမရှိပါ	No Vacancies
စုံစမ်းရန်	Information
ရဲစခန်း	Police Station
တားမြစ်နယ်မြေ	Prohibited
အိမ်သာ	Toilets
ကျား	Men
မ	Women
ပူ	Hot
အေး	Cold

EMERGENCIES

Help!	ကယ်ပါ။	ge·ba
Go away!	သွား။	thwà
Call ...	- - - ခေါ်ပေးပါ။	... kaw·bày·ba
a doctor	ဆရာဝန်	şuh·ya·wung
the police	ရဲ	yèh

I'm lost.
လမ်းပျောက်နေတယ်။ làng·byau'·nay·de

Where are the toilets?
အိမ်သာ ဘယ်မှာလဲ။ ayng·ţha be·hma·lè

I'm sick.
နေမကောင်းဘူး။ nay·muh·gàung·bòo

It hurts here.
ဒီမှာနာတယ်။ di·hma na·de

I'm allergic to (antibiotics).
(အင်တီဘားရောတစ်) (ing·di·bà·yàw·di')
နဲ့မတည့်ဘူး။ né muh·dé·bòo

SHOPPING & SERVICES

Where can I buy (a padlock)?
(သော့ခလောက်) ဘယ်မှာ (tháw·guh·lau') be·hma
ဝယ်လို့ရမလဲ။ we·lóh·yá·muh·lè

NUMBERS

1	တစ်	di'
2	နှစ်	hni'
3	သုံး	thòhng
4	လေး	làng
5	ငါး	ngà
6	ခြောက်	chau'
7	ခုနစ်	kung·ni'
8	ရှစ်	shi'
9	ကိုး	gòh
10	တစ်ဆယ်	duh·ṣe
20	နှစ်ဆယ်	hnuh·ṣe
30	သုံးဆယ်	thòhng·ze
40	လေးဆယ်	làng·ze
50	ငါးဆယ်	ngà·ze
60	ခြောက်ဆယ်	chau'·ṣe
70	ခုနစ်ဆယ်	kung·nuh·ṣe
80	ရှစ်ဆယ်	shi'·ṣe
90	ကိုးဆယ်	gòh·ze
100	တစ်ရာ	duh·ya
1000	တစ်ထောင်	duh·towng

Can I look at it?
ကြည့်လို့ရမလား။   jí·lóh yá·muh·là

Do you have any other?
တခြားရှိသေးလား။   duh·chà shí·ṭhày·là

How much is it?
ဒါဘယ်လောက်လဲ။   da be·lau'·lè

Can you write down the price?
ဈေးရေးပေးပါ။   zày yày·bày·ba

That's too expensive.
ဈေးကြီးလွန်းတယ်။   zày·jì·lùng·de

What's your lowest price?
အနည်းဆုံးဈေးက   uh·nè·zòhng·zày·gá
ဘယ်လောက်လဲ။   be·lau'·lè

There's a mistake in the bill.
ဒီပြေစာမှာ အမှား   di·byay·za·hma uh·hmà
ပါနေတယ်။   ba·nay·de

Where's a ...?	- - - ဘယ်မှာလဲ။	... be·hma·lè
bank	ဘဏ်တိုက်	bang·dai'
internet cafe	အင်တာနက် ကဖေး	ing·ta·ne' gá·pày
market	ဈေး	zày
post office	စာတိုက်	sa·dai'
tourist office	တိုးရစ်ရုံး	dòh·yi'·yòhng

TIME & DATES

What time is it?
အခု ဘယ်အချိန်လဲ။   uh·gòo be·uh·chayng·lè

It's (two) o'clock.
နှစ်နာရီ(ရှိပြီ)   (hnuh·na·yi) shí·bi

Half past (one).
(တစ်နာရီ) ခွဲ။   (duh·na·yi) gwè

morning	မနက် - - - နာရီ	muh·ne' ... na·yi
afternoon	နေ့လည် - - - နာရီ	náy·le ... na·yi
evening	ညနေ - - - နာရီ	nyá·nay ...na·yi
yesterday	မနေ့က	muh·náy·gá
tomorrow	မနက်ဖန်	muh·ne'·puhng

Monday	တနင်္လာနေ့	duh·nìng·la·náy
Tuesday	အင်္ဂါနေ့	ing·ga·náy
Wednesday	ဗုဒ္ဓဟူးနေ့	boh'·duh·hòo·náy
Thursday	ကြာသပတေးနေ့	jà·thuh·buh·dày·náy
Friday	သောကြာနေ့	thau'·ja·náy
Saturday	စနေနေ့	suh·nay·náy
Sunday	တနင်္ဂနွေနေ့	duh·nìng·guh·nway·náy

January	ဇန်နဝါရီလ	zuhn·nuh·wa·yi·lá
February	ဖေဖော်ဝါရီလ	pay·paw·wa·yi·lá
March	မတ်လ	ma'·lá
April	ဧပြီလ	ay·byi·lá
May	မေလ	may·lá
June	ဂျွန်လ	joong·lá
July	ဂျူလိုင်လ	joo·laing·lá
August	သြဂုတ်လ	àw·goh'·lá
September	စက်တင်ဘာလ	se'·ding·ba·lá
October	အောက်တိုဘာလ	ow'·toh·ba·lá
November	နိုဝင်ဘာလ	noh·wing·ba·lá
December	ဒီဇင်ဘာလ	di·zing·ba·lá

TRANSPORT

Public Transport

Is this the ... to (Moulmein)?	ဒါ (မော်လမြိုင်) သွားတဲ့ - - - လား။	da (maw·luh·myaing) thwà·dé ... là
boat	သင်္ဘော	thìng·bàw
bus	ဘတ်စ်ကား	ba'·suh·gà
plane	လေယာဉ်	lay·ying
train	ရထား	yuh·tà

At what time's the ... bus?	- - - ဘတ်စ်ကား ဘယ်အချိန် ထွက်မလဲ။	... ba'·suh·gà be·uh·chayng twe'·muh·lè
first	ပထမ	buh·tuh·má
last	နောက်ဆုံး	nau'·ṣòhng
next	နောက်	nau'

One ... ticket to (Taunggyi), please.	(တောင်ကြီး) - - - လက်မှတ် တစ်စောင် ပေးပါ။	(daung·jì) ... le'·hma' duh·zaung bày·ba
one-way	အသွား	uh·thwà
return	အသွား အပြန်	uh·thwà uh·byang

At what time does it leave?
ဘယ်အချိန် ထွက်သလဲ။   be·uh·chayng twe'·thuh·lè

How long does the trip take?
ဒီခရီးက ဘယ်လောက် ကြာမလဲ။   di·kuh·yì·gá be·lau' ja·muh·lè

Does it stop at (Bago)?
(ပဲခူး)မှာ ရပ်သလား။   (buh·gòh)·hma ya'·thuh·là

What's the next station?
နောက်ဘူတာက ဘာဘူတာလဲ။   nau'·boo·da·gá ba·boo·da·lè

Please tell me when we get to (Myitkyina).
(မြစ်ကြီးနား) ရောက်ရင် ပြောပါ။   (myi'·jì·nà) yau'·ying byàw·ba

Is this ... available?	ဒီ - - - အားသလား။	di ... à·thuh·là
motorcycle-taxi	အငှား မော်တော်ဆိုင်ကယ်	uh·hngà maw·daw· ṣaing·ke
rickshaw	ဆိုက်ကား	ṣai'·kà
taxi	တက္ကစီ	de'·guh·si

Please take me to (this address).
(ဒီလိပ်စာ)ကို ပို့ပေးပါ။   (di·lay'·sa)·goh bóh·bày·ba

Please stop here.
ဒီမှာရပ်ပါ။   di·hma ya'·ba

Driving & Cycling

I'd like to hire a ...	- - - ငှားချင်ပါတယ်။	... hngà·jing· ba·de
bicycle	စက်ဘီး	se'·bàyng
car	ကား	gà
motorbike	မော်တော်ဆိုင်ကယ်	maw·taw· ṣaing·ge

Is this the road to (Moulmein)?
ဒါ (မော်လမြိုင်) သွားတဲ့လမ်းလား။   da (maw·luh·myaing) thwà·dé·làng·là

I need a mechanic.
မက္ကင်းနစ်လိုချင်ပါတယ်။   muh·gìng·ni' loh·jing·ba·de

I've run out of petrol.
ဓာတ်ဆီကုန်သွားပြီ။   da'·ṣi gohng·thwà·bi

I have a flat tyre.
ဘီးပေါက်နေတယ်။   bàyng·pau'·nay·de

GLOSSARY

See p384 for some useful words and phrases dealing with food and dining.

Bamar – Burman ethnic group

betel – the nut of the areca palm, which is chewed as a mild intoxicant throughout Asia

Bodhi tree – the sacred banyan tree under which the Buddha gained enlightenment; also 'bo tree'

chaung – (gyaung) stream or canal; often only seasonal

chinlon – extremely popular Myanmar sport in which a circle of up to six players attempts to keep a rattan ball in the air with any part of the body except the arms and hands

chinthe – half-lion, half-dragon guardian deity

deva – Pali-Sanskrit word for celestial beings

dhamma – Pali word for the Buddhist teachings; called dharma in Sanskrit

furlong – obsolete British unit of distance still used in Myanmar; one-eighth of a mile

gaung baung – formal, turban-like hat for men; made of silk over a wicker framework

gu – cave temple

haw – Shan word for 'palace', a reference to the large mansions used by the hereditary Shan *sao pha*

hintha – mythical, swanlike bird; *hamsa* in Pali-Sanskrit

hneh – a wind instrument like an oboe; part of the Myanmar orchestra

hpongyi – Buddhist monk

hpongyi-kyaung – monastery; see also *kyaung*

hsaing – traditional musical ensemble

hsaing waing – circle of drums used in a Myanmar orchestra

hti – umbrella-like decorated pinnacle of a stupa

in – lake; eg Inle means little lake

IWT – Inland Water Transport

Jataka – stories of the Buddha's past lives; a common theme for temple paintings and reliefs

ka – city bus

kalaga – embroidered tapestries

kamma – Pali word for the law of cause and effect; called karma in Sanskrit

kammahtan – meditation; a *kammahtan kyaung* is a meditation monastery

kammawa – lacquered scriptures

kan – (gan) beach; can also mean a tank or reservoir

karaweik – a mythical bird with a beautiful song; also the royal barge on Inle Lake; *karavika* in Pali

KNLA – Karen National Liberation Army

kutho – merit, what you acquire through doing good; from the Pali *kusala*

kyaik – Mon word for paya

kyauk – rock

kyaung – (*gyaung*) Myanmar Buddhist monastery; pronounced 'chown'

kyi – (gyi) big; eg Taunggyi means big mountain

kyun – (gyun) island

lain ka – 'line car' or pick-up truck

lei bein – 'four wheels' or blue taxi

Lokanat – Avalokitesvara, a Mahayana Bodhisattva (buddha-to-be) and guardian spirit of the world

longyi – the Myanmar unisex sarong-style lower garment; sensible wear in a tropical climate; unlike men in most other Southeast Asian countries, few Myanmar men have taken to Western trousers

MA – Myanma Airways

Mahayana – literally 'Great Vehicle'; the school of Buddhism that thrived in north Asian countries like Japan and China, and also enjoyed popularity for a time in ancient Southeast Asian countries; also called the Northern School of Buddhism

MTT – Myanmar Travels & Tours

mudra – hand position; used to describe the various hand positions used by buddha images, eg abhaya mudra (the gesture of fearlessness)

myint hlei – horse cart

myit – river

myo – town; hence Maymyo (after Colonel May), Allanmyo (Major Allan) or even Bernard-myo

myothit – 'new town', usually a planned new suburb built since the 1960s

naga – multiheaded dragon-serpent from mythology, often seen sheltering or protecting the Buddha; also the name of a collection of tribes in northwest Myanmar

nat – spirit being with the power to either protect or harm humans

nat-gadaw – spirit medium (literally 'spirit bride'); embraces a wide variety of *nat*

nat pwe – dance performance designed to entice a *nat* to possess a *nat-gadaw*

NDF – National Democratic Force

ngwe – silver

nibbana – nirvana or enlightenment, the cessation of suffering, the end of rebirth; the ultimate goal of Buddhist practice

NLD – National League for Democracy

pagoda – generic English term for *zedi* or stupa as well as temple; see also paya

pahto – Burmese word for temple, shrine or other religious structure with a hollow interior

Pali – language in which original Buddhist texts were recorded; the 'Latin' of Theravada Buddhism

parabaik – folding Buddhist palm-leaf manuscripts

paya – a generic Burmese term meaning holy one; applied to buddha figures, *zedi* and other religious monuments

pwe – generic Burmese word for festival, feast, celebration or ceremony; also refers to public performances of song and dance in Myanmar, often all-night (and all-day) affairs

pyatthat – wooden, multiroofed pavilion, usually turretlike on palace walls, as at Mandalay Palace

Sanskrit – ancient Indian language and source of many words in the Burmese vocabulary, particularly those having to do with religion, art and government

sao pha – 'sky lord', the hereditary chieftains of the Shan people

sawbwa – Burmese corruption of the Shan word *sao pha*

saya – a teacher or shaman

sayadaw – 'master teacher', usually the chief abbot of a Buddhist monastery

shinpyu – ceremonies conducted when young boys from seven to 20 years old enter a monastery for a short period of time, required of every young Buddhist male; girls have their ears pierced in a similar ceremony

shwe – golden

sikhara – Indian-style, corn-cob-like temple finial, found on many temples in the Bagan area

sima – see thein

Slorc – State Law & Order Restoration Council

SPDC – State Peace & Development Council

stupa – see zedi

Tatmadaw – Myanmar's armed forces

taung – (daung) mountain, eg Taunggyi means 'big mountain'; it can also mean a half-yard (measurement)

taw – (daw) a common suffix, meaning sacred, holy or royal; it can also mean forest or plantation

tazaung – shrine building, usually found around *zedi*

thanakha – yellow sandal-wood-like paste, worn by many Myanmar women on their faces as a combination of skin conditioner, sunblock and make-up

thein – ordination hall; called *sima* in Pali

Theravada – literally 'Word of the Elders'; the school of Buddhism that has thrived in Sri Lanka and Southeast Asian countries such as Myanmar and Thailand; also called Southern Buddhism and Hinayana

Thirty, the – the '30 comrades' of Bogyoke Aung San who joined the Japanese during WWII and eventually led Burma (Myanmar) to independence

thoun bein – motorised three-wheeled passenger vehicles

Tripitaka – the 'three baskets'; the classic Buddhist scriptures consisting of the Vinaya (monastic discipline), the Sutta (discourses of the Buddha) and Abhidhamma (Buddhist philosophy)

USDP – Union Solidarity & Development Party

UWSA – United Wa State Army

vihara – Pali-Sanskrit word for sanctuary or chapel for buddha images

viss – Myanmar unit of weight, equal to 3.5lb

wa – mouth or river or lake; Inwa means 'mouth of the lake'

ye – water, liquid

yoma – mountain range

ywa – village; a common suffix in place names such as Monywa

zat pwe – Classical dance-drama based on Jataka stories

zawgyi – an alchemist who has successfully achieved immortality through the ingestion of special compounds made from base metals

zayat – an open-sided shelter or resthouse associated with a *zedi*

zedi – stupa, a traditional Buddhist religious monument consisting of a solid hemispherical or gently tapering cylindrical cone and topped with a variety of metal and jewel finials; *zedi* are often said to contain Buddha relics

zei – (zay or zè) market

zeigyo – central market

Behind the Scenes

SEND US YOUR FEEDBACK

We love to hear from travellers – your comments keep us on our toes and help make our books better. Our well-travelled team reads every word on what you loved or loathed about this book. Although we cannot reply individually to your submissions, we always guarantee that your feedback goes straight to the appropriate authors, in time for the next edition. Each person who sends us information is thanked in the next edition – the most useful submissions are rewarded with a selection of digital PDF chapters.

Visit **lonelyplanet.com/contact** to submit your updates and suggestions or to ask for help. Our award-winning website also features inspirational travel stories, news and discussions.

Note: We may edit, reproduce and incorporate your comments in Lonely Planet products such as guidebooks, websites and digital products, so let us know if you don't want your comments reproduced or your name acknowledged. For a copy of our privacy policy visit lonelyplanet.com/privacy.

OUR READERS

Many thanks to the travellers who used the last edition and wrote to us with helpful hints, useful advice and interesting anecdotes:

Alex Wharton, Amy Nguyen, Andrew Selth, Angela Tucker, Anita Kuiper, Annabel Dunn, Annette Lüthi, Anthony Lee, Bernard Keller, Carina Hall, Christina Pefani, Christoph Knop, Christoph Mayer, Claudia van Harten, Claudio Strepparava, Dalibor Mahel, Damian Gruber, David Jacob, Don Stringman, Elisabeth Schwab, Elisabetta Bernardini, Erik Dreyer, Florian Boos, Gabriella Wortmann, Garth Riddell, Gerd Eichele, Gill Reeves, Gillian Kennedy, Gregory Kipling, Guillaume Murris, Hans-Martin Stech, Helle MØller Jensen, Ida Degani, Ilona van der lee, Izzie Robinson, Jan den Boer, Jeff Randall, Jim Loughran, Joanna Benefield, Johannes Gregoritsch, John Schilling, Joost Sneller, Julia Oppel, Justin Straub, Kathrin Zormeier, Kees Mol, Ken Riekie, Luaay Elamir, Madeline Oliver, Manuela Wehrle, Maria Aviles, Marjolaine & Hanael Sfez, Martijn den Boer, Maurice Michon, Mauro Mori, Melissa Goldstein, Merja Akerlind, Michael Darley, Michal Rudziecki, Mollot Brice, Nigel Holmes, Noah Impekoven, Oddgeir Havn, Pamela Walker, Peter Novak, Philip Green, Rebecca Rosz, Ruth Banks, Sebastian Lübbert, Silke Wimme, Simon Spillmann, Simona Demel, Simone Schneider, Sjoerd Gilin, Stefan Arestis, Tamara Decaluwe, Terence Boley, Thomas Van Loock, Tim Elliott, Ylwa Alwarsdotter

WRITER THANKS

Simon Richmond

Many thanks to my fellow authors and the following people in Yangon: William Myatwunna, Thant Myint-U, Edwin Briels, Jessica Mudditt, Jaiden Coonan, Tim Aye-Hardy, Ben White, Myo Aung, Marcus Allender, Jochen Meissner, Khin Maung Htwe, Vicky Bowman, Don Wright, James Hayton, Jeremiah Whyte and Jon Keesecker.

David Eimer

Special thanks to Jochen Meissner for his invaluable Chin State insights, John in Tiddim for his local guidance and Marcus Allender. Thanks also to Laura Crawford at Lonely Planet for her support. As ever, thanks to everyone who passed on tips along the way, whether knowingly or unwittingly.

Adam Karlin

Cè-zù ba: first and foremost, my family: Po Chan, Tin Tin, Po Zaw and of course, my *pwa nghe* and beloved great aunt, the strongest woman I know: Tin Tin Thein. Thanks as well to mom and dad for always making Myanmar a central part of my life, to Laura for bringing me on board, to co-authors for all their help, and to Rachel and Sanda for the love that keeps me going. This book is for Gizmo.

Nick Ray
A big thanks to the people of Myanmar, whose warmth and humour, stoicism and spirit make it a happy yet humbling place to be. Thanks to fellow travellers and residents, friends and contacts in Myanmar who have helped shaped my knowledge and experience in this country. Biggest thanks are reserved for my wife, Kulikar, and children, Julian and Belle, as without their support and encouragement the occasional adventure in unexplored corners of the region would not be possible.

Regis St Louis
I'm deeply grateful to many in Myanmar – drivers, guides, innkeepers, students and countless others – who provided tips and insight into this great country. I'd also like to thank Win Tun and his family, Dr Chan Aye, Naw May Say, San Moe Zar, Mya Mya, Cho Oo, Armelle, Naing Naing, Maythinzar Soe, Simone Herault, Rosta, Tina Rehm, Edwin Briels and fellow authors Nick Ray, Simon Richmond, David Eimer and Adam Karlin. Biggest thanks to Cassandra and our daughters, Magdalena and Genevieve, for their enduring support.

ACKNOWLEDGEMENTS
Climate map data adapted from Peel MC, Finlayson BL & McMahon TA (2007) 'Updated World Map of the Köppen-Geiger Climate Classification', Hydrology and Earth System Sciences, 11, 163344.

Cover photograph: Local fisher in Inle Lake, Marco Bottigelli/AWL©

Illustration p46–47 by Michael Weldon

BEHIND THE SCENES

THIS BOOK

This 13th edition of Lonely Planet's *Myanmar (Burma)* guidebook was researched and written by Simon Richmond, David Eimer, Adam Karlin, Nick Ray and Regis St Louis. The previous two editions were written by Austin Bush, David Eimer, Mark Elliott, Nick Ray and Simon Richmond. This guidebook was produced by the following:

Destination Editor Laura Crawford

Product Editor Grace Dobell

Senior Cartographers Alison Lyall, Diana Von Holdt

Book Designer Jessica Rose

Assisting Editors Imogen Bannister, Pete Cruttenden, Helen Koehne, Kellie Langdon, Rosie Nicholson, Kristin Odijk, Simon Williamson

Cartographer Mick Garrett

Cover Researcher Naomi Parker

Thanks to Ryan Evans, Kirsten Rawlings, Kathryn Rowan, Moe Pwint Phyu, Lyahna Spencer, Amanda Williamson

Index